Key Science 4
– in 2 volumes –
with Resource Bank
and Teacher's Guide

Titles of Related Interest

Basic Chemistry Questions for GCSE
(National Curriculum Edition)
Bernard Abrams

Basic Physics Questions for GCSE
(National Curriculum Edition)
Bernard Abrams

Basic Biology Questions for GCSE
(National Curriculum Edition)
Chris Rouan

KEY SCIENCE 4

BOOK 1

Eileen Ramsden BSc PhD DPhil
Formerly of Wolfreton School, Hull

Jim Breithaupt BSc MSc
Head of Science and Mathematics, Wigan Campus, Wigan and Leigh College

David Applin BSc MSc PhD FRES
Head of Science, Chigwell School

Stanley Thornes (Publishers) Limited

First published in 1991 by:
Stanley Thornes (Publishers) Ltd
Ellenborough House
Wellington Street
CHELTENHAM GL50 1YD
England

Reprinted 1993
Reprinted 1994

A catalogue record of this book is available from the British Library.

ISBN 0-7487-0492-2 Book 1
    (0-7487-0494-9 Book 2)
    (0-7487-1719-6 Resource Bank)
    (0-7487-1723-4 Teacher's Guide)

Design and artwork by Cauldron Design Studio, Auchencrow,
Berwickshire.
Typeset by Word Power, Auchencrow, Berwickshire.
Printed and bound in Hong Kong

Contents

Contents of Book 1	viii
Preface	ix
Acknowledgements	x
Introduction	xi

Theme A   The Earth Our Home   1

Topic 1 The Earth in space   2
1.1 The Sun	2
1.2 The Moon	3
1.3 The planets	6
1.4 Comets	9
1.5 Star watch	11
1.6 Journey into space	15
1.7 Beyond the solar system	17

Topic 2 Planet Earth   19
2.1 The structure of the Earth	19
2.2 Evidence for the layered structure of the Earth	20
2.3 Earthquakes and volcanoes	23
2.4 Plate tectonics	24
2.5 Types of rock	31
2.6 Deformation of rocks	35
2.7 The forces which shape landscapes	37
2.8 The geological time scale	40

Topic 3 Life on Earth   42
3.1 Earth as a place to live	42
3.2 Variety of life	43
3.3 What's in a name?	46
3.4 Classification	48
3.5 Five Kingdoms	50

Theme B   Matter and Energy   75

Topic 4 Matter   76
4.1 The states of matter	76
4.2 Pure substances	77
4.3 Density	77
4.4 Change of state	78
4.5 Finding melting points and boiling points	79
4.6 Properties and uses of materials	83

Topic 5 Particles   88
5.1 The atomic theory	88
5.2 Elements and compounds	88
5.3 How big are atoms?	89
5.4 The kinetic theory of matter	90

Topic 6 Energy   95
6.1 What is energy?	95
6.2 Conservation of energy	98
6.3 Measuring energy	101
6.4 Energy on the move	103

Topic 7 Heat   105
7.1 Temperature	105
7.2 Thermal expansion	108
7.3 Heating things up	114
7.4 Latent heat	117
7.5 Heat transfer	120
7.6 More about conduction	121
7.7 Radiation	123
7.8 Keeping warm	126

Topic 8 Energy resources   128
8.1 Our energy needs	128
8.2 Fuel	130
8.3 Renewable energy resources	134
8.4 Energy for the future	136

Theme C   The Atom   141

Topic 9 Elements and compounds   142
9.1 Silicon	142
9.2 Gold	145
9.3 Copper and bronze	146
9.4 Iron	147
9.5 Carbon	147
9.6 Chlorine	149
9.7 Elements	149
9.8 The structures of some elements	150
9.9 Compounds	152
9.10 Mixtures and compounds	154

Topic 10 Symbols: formulas: equations   155
10.1 Symbols	155
10.2 Formulas	155
10.3 Valency	157
10.4 Equations	158

Topic 11 Inside the atom 160
11.1 Becquerel's key 160
11.2 Protons, neutrons and electrons 161
11.3 The arrangement of particles in the atom 162
11.4 How are the electrons arranged? 163
11.5 The Periodic Table 165
11.6 Isotopes 168

Topic 12 Radioactivity 170
12.1 What is radioactivity? 170
12.2 Radioactive decay 173
12.3 Making use of radioactivity 175
12.4 The dangers of radioactivity 179
12.5 The nuclear bomb 180
12.6 Nuclear reactors 182
12.7 Nuclear fusion 184
12.8 Disposal of radioactive waste 185
12.9 Safety 187

Topic 13 Ions 190
13.1 Which substances conduct electricity? 190
13.2 Molten solids and electricity 190
13.3 What happens when solutions conduct electricity? 193
13.4 More examples of electrolysis 195
13.5 Which ions are discharged? 196
13.6 Applications of electrolysis 197

Topic 14 The chemical bond 200
14.1 The ionic bond 200
14.2 Other ionic compounds 201
14.3 Ions and the Periodic Table 202
14.4 Formulas of ionic compounds 203
14.5 The covalent bond 205
14.6 Forces between molecules 207
14.7 Ionic and covalent compounds 208

Theme D Making Materials 211

Topic 15 Methods of separation 212
15.1 Raw materials from the Earth's crust 212
15.2 Pure substances from a mixture of solids 212
15.3 Solute from solution by crystallisation 213
15.4 Filtration: separation of a solid from a liquid 213
15.5 Centrifuging 213
15.6 Distillation 214
15.7 Separating liquids 215
15.8 Fractional distillation 216
15.9 Chromatography 218

Topic 16 Acids and Bases 220
16.1 Acids 220
16.2 Bases 223
16.3 Summarising the reactions of acids and bases 226
16.4 Neutralisation 227
16.5 Indicators and pH 228

Topic 17 Salts 230
17.1 Sodium chloride 230
17.2 Salts of some common acids 231
17.3 Water of crystallisation 231
17.4 Useful salts 232
17.5 Methods of making salts 236

Topic 18 The chemicals of life 239
18.1 Elements and compounds 239
18.2 Carbohydrates 240
18.3 Lipids 242
18.4 Proteins 245
18.5 Nucleic acids 247

Topic 19 Cell biology 251
19.1 Seeing cells 251
19.2 Movement into and out of cells 254
19.3 The nucleus 256
19.4 The dividing cell 258
19.5 Cells, tissues and organs 262

Theme E Air and Water 267

Topic 20 Air 268
20.1 Oxygen the life-saver 268
20.2 How oxygen and nitrogen are obtained from air 268
20.3 Uses of oxygen 270
20.4 Nitrogen 271
20.5 The nitrogen cycle 271
20.6 Carbon dioxide and the carbon cycle 273
20.7 The greenhouse effect 274
20.8 Carbon dioxide 276
20.9 Testing for carbon dioxide and water vapour 277
20.10 The noble gases 277

Topic 21 Oxygen 279
21.1 Blast-off 279
21.2 Test for oxygen 279
21.3 The percentage by volume of oxygen in air 280
21.4 A method of preparing oxygen in the laboratory 280
21.5 The reactions of oxygen with some elements 281
21.6 Oxides 281
21.7 Combustion 282
21.8 Fire extinguishers 284
21.9 Rusting 286

Topic 22 Water 287
22.1 The water cycle 287
22.2 Dissolved oxygen 288
22.3 Water treatment 288
22.4 Sewage works 289
22.5 Uses of water 290
22.6 Water: the compound 290
22.7 Pure water 291
22.8 Underground caverns 292
22.9 Soaps 293
22.10 Soapless detergents 294
22.11 Bleaches and alkaline cleaners 295
22.12 Hard water and soft water 295
22.13 Methods of softening hard water 296
22.14 Advantages of hard water 297

Topic 23 Air pollution 298
23.1 Smog 298
23.2 The problem 298
23.3 Dispersing air pollutants 299
23.4 Sulphur dioxide 299
23.5 Acid rain 300
23.6 Carbon monoxide 303
23.7 Oxides of nitrogen 304
23.8 Hydrocarbons 305
23.9 Smoke, dust and grit 306
23.10 Metals 307
23.11 Chlorofluorohydrocarbons 308

Topic 24 Water pollution 310
24.1 Pollution by industry 310
24.2 Thermal pollution 312
24.3 Pollution by sewage 312
24.4 Pollution by agriculture 313
24.5 Pollution by lead 316
24.6 Pollution by oil 316

Theme F Life Processes (1) 321

Topic 25 Nutrition 322
25.1 Plants make food by photosynthesis 322
25.2 Why do we need food? 327
25.3 Diet and food 335
25.4 Teeth 347
25.5 Digestion and absorption 352

Topic 26 Respiration 359
26.1 What is respiration? 359
26.2 Surfaces for gaseous exchange 363

Topic 27 Excretion 372
27.1 Getting rid of wastes 372
27.2 Excretion in plants 375

Theme G The Physical Environment 379

Topic 28 The weather 380
28.1 The weather: a matter of life and death 380
28.2 How the Earth is heated by the Sun 382
28.3 Weather maps 384
28.4 How clouds form 386
28.5 Clouds 387
28.6 Winter weather 388
28.7 Fronts 389

Topic 29 Land 392
29.1 Soil 392
29.2 Farming 398
29.3 Irrigation 399
29.4 Mechanisation and its effect on wildlife 400
29.5 Monoculture 402
29.6 Natural fertilisers: manure and slurry 402
29.7 Synthetic fertilisers 403
29.8 Straw burning 406
29.9 Herbicides 407
29.10 Insecticides 409
29.11 Fungicides and molluscicides 412
29.12 Energy 413
29.13 Hunger 416

Teachers' Notes 419
Numerical Answers 423
Index 425

Contents of Book 2

Introduction

Theme H Using Waves
    Topic 30 Waves
    Topic 31 Sound
    Topic 32 Light
    Topic 33 Electromagnetic waves

Theme I Forces
    Topic 34 Forces in balance
    Topic 35 Pressure
    Topic 36 Force and motion
    Topic 37 Machines and engines

Theme J Life Processes (II)
    Topic 38 Transport in living things
    Topic 39 Reproduction
    Topic 40 Responses and co-ordination
    Topic 41 Support and movement

Theme K Electricity
    Topic 42 Electric charges
    Topic 43 Circuits
    Topic 44 Magnetism
    Topic 45 Electronics

Theme L Our Natural Resources
    Topic 46 The speed of chemical reactions
    Topic 47 Chemical calculations
    Topic 48 Fuels
    Topic 49 Energy changes in chemical reactions
    Topic 50 Metals
    Topic 51 The chemical industry

Theme M Ecology
    Topic 52 Ecosystems
    Topic 53 Populations

Theme N Genetics and Evolution
    Topic 54 Inheritance and genetics
    Topic 55 Evolution

Teachers' Notes
Numerical Answers
Cumulative Index

Preface

Key Science 4 has been written for the National Curriculum at Key Stage 4. Two books and a Resource Pack cover both Profile Components at Levels 6 to 10. The text meets the requirements of the Double Award GCSE Science syllabuses of the six examining groups and can be used for Model A and Model B. We believe that teachers will find these books ideal for co-ordinated science and integrated science courses. Students who are taking a modular science course will find the core of the material which they need here too.

Key Science 4 makes use of a range of devices, often located in the margin, to enhance the text and to improve the accessibility of the text to the average student.

- **Explorations** and other practical activities are included to stimulate an investigative approach to science. To encourage the reader to try these activities, we have labelled them *Try this*. In the Resource Pack, we provide further opportunities for students to explore science through tackling projects and solving problems. References alongside the text give some indication of the wealth of photocopiable activities for teachers. The Resource Pack also includes notes on the aims and objectives of each Theme and highlights common issues, i.e. control.
- **Information technology** 'IT' appears in the National Curriculum both as a cross-curricular skill (analogous to literacy and numeracy) and as an element of the separate subjects. The value of information technology, however, extends through all of the attainment targets in science. The 'IT' entries in the book reflect the wide applications of information technology. These 'IT' features show how computer-assisted learning (perhaps of a direct tutorial nature), simulations using 'IT', databases, videodisc, datalogging and other educational uses of information technology can be used throughout science at Key Stage 4.

  Our consultants in information technology, Dr Jerry Wellington and Mr John Scaife, both of the Educational Research Centre, University of Sheffield, have provided expert guidance for students (alongside the text) and for teachers (in a section at the end of each book).
- **The nature of science**, is conveyed in the text through our sketches of the development of scientific concepts and theories. We hope also that the investigations which are suggested to students in the text and in the Resource Pack will foster in them a scientific attitude.
- **The social, economic, environmental and technological aspects of science** are emphasised throughout the text and in the Resource Pack. GCSE Science examinations and module tests include questions on these matters, and we have developed them wherever they arise from the content.
- **Checkpoints** at regular intervals in the text help students to review their work and test their comprehension. More taxing questions appear at the end of each theme and in the Resource Pack: questions which will exercise students' ability to apply their knowledge to novel situations, to analyse and interpret data and to solve problems. These longer questions co-ordinate the topics in the preceding theme and link up with other themes, giving students assistance in co-ordinating the branches of science.
- **Look at links** cross-references form a network throughout the two books. Their role is to help students to integrate the different branches of science and to appreciate the structure of the subject. The links have also helped us to avoid duplicating material. For the teacher, they have another benefit in that they make it easy to depart from our order of topics. Our order is not the only way in which the topics in the curriculum can be taught, and the Look at links cross-references will help those who want to take a different route through the text.
- **It's a fact, Science at work** and **Who's behind the science?** are margin features which are not 'syllabus' material: they are included to stimulate interest and to focus attention on social, economic, environmental, technological and historical aspects of science.
- **Summaries** at the end of each section highlight key points and encourage students to check on their grasp of the section which they have read and to revise points which they have not mastered.

Student's Note

We hope that this book will provide all the information you need and enough practice to enable you to do well in the tests and examinations in your GCSE Science course. However, examinations are not the most important part of your course: we hope also that you will develop a real interest in science, which will continue after your course is over. Finally, we hope that you enjoy using our book. If you do, our efforts will have been worthwhile!

Eileen Ramsden
Jim Breithaupt
David Applin

Acknowledgements

We would like to express our thanks to Mr Gavin Cameron, Mr Steve Hewitt and Mrs Sheila Rogers for their constructive comments on the Earth Science topic and to Mr David Haslam for his advice on some of the chemical topics.

Mr Gareth Williams has offered invaluable guidance on biological topics. We thank him for his careful reading of the text and for the questions which he has contributed.

Dr Jerry Wellington and Mr Jon Scaife have provided some excellent material on information technology, and we thank them for their contributions to the text.

We thank the following organisations and people who have supplied photographs.

Action Plus Photographic: Figure 4.1A (Tony Henshaw), p. 162
Alfred McAlpine plc: Figures 4.6A, 6.2B(b)
Allsport: Figure 25.2D (Gary Mortimore), p. 70 (athlete; Gray Mortimore), p. 321 (Bob Martin).
Ardea: Figures 24.6C (Francois Gahier), 26.2A(a) (John Clegg), 26.2A(b) (John Mason), 26.2E (P Morris)
Ariel Plastics: Figure 4.6D
Barr-Brown: Figure 18.5H
Biophoto Associates: Figures 3.4A(b), (c), 17.4C, 17.4D, 18.2E, 18.2F, 18.2G, 18.3B, 19.1D, 19.1F, 19.1H, 19.3A(a), (b), 19.4F, 25.1D(a), 25.4G, 25.5E, 25.5G, 26.1C, 26.2C, 26.2K(a), (b), 26.2M(a), (b), 26.2P(a), (b), p. 52 (cocci, vibrios), p. 53 (spirilla, bacilli), p. 54 (amoeba), p. 55 (spirogyra, euglena), p. 56 (field mushroom), p. 58 (moss), p. 61 (scot's pine), p. 62 (hydra), p. 63 (coral, jellyfish), p. 64 (planaria, fluke, tapeworm), p. 66 (snail, chiton), p. 67 (common muscle), p. 69 (spider, centipede, crayfish), p. 70 (lizard)
Bodleian Library, Oxford, UK: Figure 1.5D
British Canoe Union: Figure 4.6C
British Coal Board: Figure 8.2B
British Coal Open Cast: Figure 8.2A
British Gas: Figure 6.4A
British Library: Figure 1.5E
British Steel: Figure 9.4A
Bruce Coleman Ltd: Figures 3.3A (Hans Reinbard), 3.3B(a) (Scott Nielson), 3.3B(b) (Joe Van Warmer), 18.2H (Jane Burton)
Camera Press: Figures 2.4A (Benoit Gysemburgh), 12.5C (L Smillie), 12.5B, p. 182.
Diamond Information Council: Figure 9.5A
Dr David Applin: Figure 25.1D(b), p. 59 (fern), p. 60 (beech, buttercup), p. 63 (sea anenome), p. 65 (earthworm), p. 71 (frog)
Dr Eileen Ramsden: Figures 5.1A, 5.2A, 9.6A, 10.2A, 10.3A, 14.5B, 16.1A, 16.1B, 17.4B, 18.1A, 18.2A, 18.3C, 18.4A, 19.2A(a), (b), 22.9A, 22.10A, 29.9C(a), (b), 29.10B
Electricity Association: Figure 6.4B
Fenwall Electronics: Figure 7.1G
Fissons plc: Figure 17.4A
Gavin Cameron: Figures 2.6A, 2.6C
Geological Museum: Figure 2.8B
G H Zeal Ltd: Figure 7.1D
ICI Chemicals and Polymers: Figures 4.2A, 4.5D, 13.6C, 15.2A, 15.8B, p. 68
Independent Television News Ltd: Figure 28.1A
International Centre for Conservation Education: Figures 2E, 8.3D, 23.4A, 29.1E, 29.1H, 29.2A, 29.4A, 29.5A, 29.8A (Mark Boulton), 24.4A (Andy Purcell), 24.6D (Mark Tasker), 24.6E, 29.1G (Don Hinrichsen), 25.1A (Chris Rose), 28.1B (Trebor Snook), 29.1E (Howard Morland)
International Weather Productions: Figure 7.1A
John Walmsley: Figure 9.1B
Leslie Garland Picture Library: Figure 7.2C
Mary Evans Picture Library: Figures 1C, 1.5C, 7.3B, 7.3C, 7.3D, p. 160, p. 161
Michael Holford: Figure 9.3A
Mountain Camera: Figures 4.5E, 7.8C (John Cleare), 6.1A (Colin Montreath)
NASA: Figures 1.1A, 1.3C, 1.3D, 1.6A, 3.1A, 6.2B(a), 20.3A, 21.1A, p. 1
National Medical Slide Bank: Figure 6.1G
National Power: Figure 8.3B
Natural History Museum: Figure 3.2A (Dr N E Stork)

Natural History Photographic Agency: Figure 18.3A (Peter Johnson)
New Zealand Tourist Board: Figure 8.3G
Northern Irish Tourist Board: Figure 2.5C
Novosti Press Agency (APN): Figures 12.9B, p. 184
Oxford Scientific Films Ltd: Figures 3.4A(a) (Edwin Sadd), 19.4A, 19.4D(a), 25.4E (London Scientific Films), 19.4G (Carolina Biological Supply Co.), 20.5A (G I Bernard), 20.10A (L D Zell), 20.10B (Jack Dermid), 28.5A (Stuart Bebb), 29.9B(a) (Stan Osolinski), 29.9B(b) (Deni Brown), p. 57 (bread mould; J A L Cooke), p. 65 (mason worm; G I Bernard) (medical leech; Mike Birkhead), p. 67 (cuttlefish; Rodger Jackman), p. 71 (carp, pigeon; G I Bernard), p. 75 (Peter Gould), p. 141 (Sinclair Stammers), p. 267 (Stephen Dalton), p. 379 (Okapia)
Panos Pictures: Figures 24.3A(a) (J Hartley), 24.3(b) (Neil Cooper)
Peter Newark's Western Americana: Figure 9.2A
Popperfoto: Figures 7.2A (Colin Ingham), 2.5A, 6.2B(c), 18.5G, 18.5J, 24.6A, 24.6B Erik Hill), 24.6C (David Aka)
Quadrant Picture Library: Figure 13.6A
Reed Farmers Publishing Group: Figure 16.2A
Royal Observatory, Edinburgh: 1B, 1.4A
Science Photo Library: Figures 1D, 1.2A, 1.2D(c), 28.1D (Dr Fred Espenak), 1.2B(a), (b), (c), (d) (John Sanford), 1.2D(b) (John Bova), 1.7A, 7.7A, 23.11B, 25.1F (NASA), 1.7A(c) (Kim Gordon), 2.5E (Prof Stewart Lowther), 2.7D (Sinclair Stammers), 5.4B (Ben Johnson), 5.4C (Dr Mitsuo Ohtsuki), 5.4D (Dr M B Hursthouse), 7.1H (Chris Priest), 8.1A (Malcolm Fielding), 8.2F (Mere Words), 8.3C, 8.3E (Martin Bond), 9.1C (Dr G M Rackham), 9.5C (Harry Nor-Hansen), 12.1B (Hank Morgan), 12.1G (Lawrence Berkeley Laboratory), 12.3C (Philippe Plailly), 12.4A(a) (Alexander Tsiaras), 15.3B, 20.4B (Alex Bartel), 18.4B (David Scharf), 18.4C, 18.4D, 18.5I (Dr Arthur Lesk, Laboratory of Molecular Biology, MRC), 18.5E (Oxford Molecular Biophysics Laboratory), 19.1C (Larry Mulvehill), 20.1A (Susan Leavines), 20.4C, 21.8E (Adam Hart-Davies), 25.1C (Simon Fraser), 25.2G (Biophoto Associates), 25.2H (St Mary's Hospital Medical School), 25.3U(a) (Shelia Terry), 25.3U(b) (Andrew McClenaghan), 27.1A (Simon Fraser, Royal Victoria Infirmary, Newcastle Upon Tyne), 28.5B (John Heseltine), 28.5C (Angela Murphy), 28.6A (Claud Nuridsany, Marie Perennou), 29.2B (Peter Menzel), 29.3A (Peter Ryan), 25.5K, 25.5I
Scottish Hydroelectric plc: Figure 8.3A
Shell Photographic Library: Figures 8.2D, p. 211
Sotherbys: Figure 9.2B
Swiss National Tourist Board: Figure 2.7C
The Environmental Picture Library: Figures 23.3B (Philip Carr), 23.10A (David Townend), 24.1A (Alan Greig)
United Kingdom Atomic Energy Authority: Figure 8.2E, 12.1D, 12.3D, 12.4A(b), (c)
Weidenfield (Publishers) Ltd: Figure 18.5F
Woodmansterne Ltd: Figures 1.5B (Jeremy Marks), 2.5D, 2.6F
Wookey Hole Caves: Figure 22.8A

Portrait of Michael Faraday (p. 193) reproduced by courtesy of the National Portrait Gallery

We thank the following examining groups for permission to reproduce questions from examination papers:
London East Anglian Examining Group, Midland Examining Group, Northern Examining Association, Northern Ireland Schools Examination Council, Southern Examining Group, Welsh Joint Education Committee

The production of a science text book from manuscripts involves considerable effort, energy and expertise from many people, and we wish to acknowledge the work of all the members of the publishing team. We are particularly grateful to Penelope Barber (Senior Publisher), Adrian Wheaton (Science Publisher) and Lorna Godson (Editor), for their advice and support.

Finally we thank our families for the tolerance which they have shown and the encouragement which they have given during the preparation of this book.

Eileen Ramsden
Jim Breithaupt
David Applin

Introduction: THE WORLD OF SCIENCE

Part 1: adventures in science

The Mirror of Galadriel

In the book *Lord of the Rings*, amazing things happen to Gandalf and the hobbits. They risk their lives on a perilous journey to save their world. They journey through secret tunnels and unknown lands and they witness astonishing events. In the early part of their travels, they are invited to look into a magic mirror – a silver bowl filled with water. It shows 'things that were, and things that are, the things that yet may be.' But the viewer can't tell which it is showing!

Imagine you have travelled in time from two centuries ago to the present day. What would you make of television – a silver bowl showing events from the past and the present? Television is a product of the scientific age in which we live.

Science has many more amazing things to reveal. Imagine food 'grown' in a factory or round-the-world flight in a few hours or 'intelligent' computers that need no programming. These and many more projects are the subject of intense scientific research now. Fact is stranger than fiction.

Figure 1A ● What can you see?

Can you believe what you see?

Look at the picture in Figure 1A. *What can you see?* Some people see an old lady; others see a young woman. Different people looking at the same picture see different images.

Witnesses of an event often report totally different versions of the event. Invent a harmless incident and try it out in front of unsuspecting witnesses without warning them. Then ask them to say what happened. Each person will probably have a different story to tell.

In science, there are countless events to observe. The story or 'account' of an event in science should not differ from one observer to another. Otherwise, who could you believe?

Figure 1B ● The Pleiades

Star gazing

Look at the sky on a dark, clear night and you can see countless stars. *What can you tell just by looking at them?* Now imagine you're in a forest of trees in every direction. You're surrounded by different types and sizes of trees. *What do the trees have in common and how do they differ?*

Surveying the sky and surveying the forest both call for careful observations and measurements. Then you have to think about what your observations mean. But before you can make any measurements, you need to decide what to measure. *What could you measure when you look at the stars?*

Finding answers to questions is an important part of science. However, finding the questions to ask is even more important. Once you decide on the questions, you can begin to find the answers. If you don't ask the right questions, the answers will not be of much use.

How science works

Science involves finding out how and why things happen. Natural curiosity sometimes provides the starting point for a scientific investigation. Another investigation might set out to solve a certain problem and therefore have a definite aim. Even then, unexpected results may emerge to stimulate our natural curiosity.

The history of science has many examples where an important discovery or invention came about unexpectedly. The electric motor was invented when an electric generator was wired up wrongly at the Vienna Exhibition of 1873. X-rays, radioactivity and penicillin are further examples of unexpected scientific discoveries.

X-rays

In 1895, a German scientist called Wilhelm Röntgen was doing research work on the discharge of electricity through gases at very low pressure. He was fascinated by the subject of his research even though it seemed to be of little practical use. However, during the course of his experiments he discovered a new type of radiation which he called **X-rays**. You know how important X-rays are in medicine nowadays. Yet if Röntgen had told people that his work would lead to a means of making human flesh transparent, they would have laughed. No-one could have predicted that this life-saving discovery would come as a result of studying gases at low pressure.

Penicillin

Penicillin is an antibiotic which has saved countless lives. It was discovered accidentally. Alexander Fleming was working in a London hospital in 1929. One day he noticed a mould in a dish in which he was growing bacteria. He observed that no bacteria were growing near the mould. Fleming identified the mould as *Penicillium* and he deduced that it contained a substance that would kill bacteria. He called the substance penicillin and was able to extract it from the mould. He then tested it on animals and found that it would kill bacteria without harming the animals. During the Second World War, penicillin saved the lives of thousands of wounded soldiers. Fleming and his co-workers Ernst Chain and Howard Florey were awarded the Nobel Prize in 1945.

Figure 1C ● Wilhelm Röntgen and his X-ray apparatus

LOOK AT LINKS
for **X-rays**
See Theme H, Topic 33.2.

LOOK AT LINKS
Another unexpected scientific discovery was that of radioactivity. To find out more about it See Theme C, Topic 11.1.

The chance arrival of a mould in Fleming's lab was an accident. It needed a trained scientist to take advantage of this lucky accident. X-rays and radioactivity were discovered by accident too; however, all these important discoveries were made by highly-skilled scientists with the curiosity and imagination to recognise unusual events. 'Chance favours the prepared mind', as Louis Pasteur (the inventor of pasteurisation) said.

Figure 1D ● A penicillin pellet on a culture of bacteria – note the bacteria-free area surrounding it

Discoveries in science are unpredictable. No-one can predict which research projects will lead to exciting new developments because no-one knows what new areas of science lie waiting to be discovered beyond the frontiers of knowledge.

A scientific race

On 18 March 1987, more than two thousand scientists crammed into a conference room in New York to listen to progress reports on research into superconductivity. The conference had to be relayed to hundreds of scientists in adjacent rooms. Many of the scientists present had been working day and night for months to unlock the secrets of superconductors.

Superconducting materials have no electrical resistance. Electric cables and electric motors made from superconductors would be far more efficient than those made from ordinary conductors. Superconducting computers and magnets would be much more powerful. However, before 1987, most scientists thought that superconductors would work only at very low temperatures. Materials that are superconducting at room temperature would be a technological breakthrough.

The first superconductors were discovered in 1911 when certain metals were cooled to below –270 °C. In 1986, two European scientists, Georg Bednorz and Alex Müller, reported they had made a superconductor at 30 °C higher (–240 °C). Scientists round the world turned their attention to superconductors. Teams of scientists in different countries raced against each other to find superconductors which would work at higher temperatures. By March 1987, the temperature limit had been raised to –179 °C. By then the political leaders of the major industrial nations realised how important superconductors could become. The race continues because the benefits would be immense. The importance of Bednorz and Müller's work in starting the race was recognised when they received the 1987 Nobel Prize for physics.

Models and theories

In 1987, scientists in laboratories throughout the world worked round the clock to try to make new superconductors. Other scientists were busy with computers trying to work out why the new materials were superconducting. They made models of how the atoms of the new materials might be fixed together. They tested and changed the models using their computers until they found a model that explained what was observed in the laboratories. Understanding how and why new superconductors work is important since it can give vital clues to better superconductors.

LOOK AT LINKS
The story of **DNA** is told in Theme D, Topic 18.5.

The discovery of the structure of DNA is another example of the way scientific models can be invaluable. In the 1950s, scientists were eager to find the structure of genetic material. The most important substance in the genes was known to be **DNA (deoxyribonucleic acid)** - but what was DNA made off, and what did it look like? In Britain, Rosalind Franklin was using X-rays to probe the structure of DNA. Her results were explained by Francis Crick and James Watson. They suggested that DNA consists of two long spiral chains coiled round each other. The structure is known as a 'double helix'. Constructing a model of the structure was an enormous help to Crick and Watson in sorting out their ideas and in explaining the structure to other people. Nowadays, scientists use computer graphics to draw models of molecules from every angle.

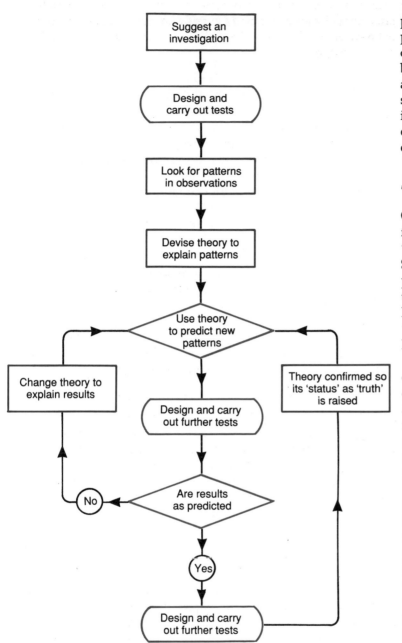

Figure 1E ● A good theory

A good theory or model is one which gives predictions that turn out to be correct. The predictions are tested in the laboratory. If they do not pass the test, the theory or model must be altered or even thrown out. The more tests a model or theory passes, the more 'faith' scientists have in it. However, complete faith is never possible. Someone, somewhere might one day make a discovery which can't be explained by the theory.

Scientists can be wrong

Over fifty years ago, people who suffered from arthritis in the legs could buy a 'radioactive' blanket to relieve the pain. Scientists thought that **radioactivity** penetrating deep into the tissues would warm the tissues and cure the disease. Now we know differently - if you have any radioactive 'leg warmers' in your attic, call the police for help!

Sometimes, scientific mistakes become evident more quickly. In 1988, two scientists, one from Britain and one from America, announced they had discovered how to create **nuclear fusion** 'in a test tube'. On a large scale, this would release vast quantities of energy using hydrogen atoms from water as the fuel.

Fusion happens continuously inside the Sun; hydrogen atoms at exceedingly high temperatures in the Sun's core fuse together to release solar energy. For more than thirty years, scientists working in large teams with huge powerful machines have tried to make 'fusion reactors'. The two scientists reckoned they had made this happen in a test tube at room temperature. Their announcement became headline news as other scientists tried to repeat their experiment. Gradually, it was realised that the original results were unreliable. However, scientists learn from their mistakes and research into 'cold fusion' continues. The only people who never make mistakes are those who never try.

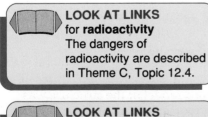

LOOK AT LINKS
for **radioactivity**
The dangers of radioactivity are described in Theme C, Topic 12.4.

LOOK AT LINKS
for **nuclear fusion**
See Theme C, Topic 12.7.

Beyond the frontiers

Who knows where a new discovery can lead? When Michael Faraday discovered how to generate electricity, he was asked 'What use is electricity, Mr Faraday?' He is reported to have replied 'What use is a new baby?' No one knows what might become of a new invention or a new discovery. More than 150 years later, life without electricity for most of us is unthinkable. Michael Faraday would have been truly astonished.

Part 2: activities in science

Do you like sport? Are you a keen disco dancer or do you prefer climbing? If you want to keep up with your hobbies and interests, read this section very carefully. You won't find any information about your favourite pastime but you will find lots of advice to help you study effectively - and still have time over for leisure!

Studying science is fun – if you approach it in the right spirit. However, your science course will not be your only subject and this is where the problem of fitting everything in arises. No doubt, you have coursework assignments and homework in a range of subjects and you will doubtless have tests and exams to prepare for. How can you fit everything in? Be positive and organise yourself! Here are some tips to help.

Your science course

GCSE balanced science courses cover a wide range of topics in biology, chemistry and physics. Astronomy and earth science also form part of a balanced science course. By studying all the main branches of science, you are keeping all your options open for post-GCSE studies.

The grades you are awarded at the end of your science course depend on your performance in practical assessments and end-of-course exams. Throughout your science course, you will carry out practical investigations to develop your knowledge and understanding of science and to sharpen your practical skills ready for practical assessments. Science is essentially a practical subject – that's why practical work is used to develop each topic.

Skills in science

A plumber carries a toolkit enabling most plumbing jobs to be carried out. Sometimes, a job needs a specialist tool so the plumber has to return to the workshop. There's no point in carrying round specialist tools if they're used only now and then. They would make the toolkit too heavy to carry.

To explore science, you need a scientific 'toolkit' which isn't too weighty. However, the toolkit you carry round isn't made up of equipment like microscopes and meters. Those are the specialist tools kept in the laboratory. Your toolkit consists of skills.

● *Practical skills*
Practical skills can be used whenever you are exploring or investigating science. Some of the skills involved are:
- deciding on suitable questions to form an investigation,
- planning the investigation,
- using equipment accurately to make observations and measurements,
- recording and using your observations and measurements,
- thinking about what your observations and measurements mean,
- using your conclusions to plan further investigations.

You will have used these skills in your previous science classes. Now you are going to use them to explore science at a higher level.

● *Mathematical skills*

Mathematical skills are essential to make full use of measurements from practical work. For example, you need to be able to use a calculator, to plot graphs and to use symbols, formulas and keys.

● *Communication skills*

Communication skills are important to tell other people what you are doing or intend to do. This might happen during an investigation when you want some advice or if you are working with other students. On completing an investigation, you may be asked to write a report to tell other people what you did and how successful your work has been.

● *Information technology skills*

Information technology skills such as using a computer or a wordprocessor are very important now. You may have already become very skilful at using a computer keyboard but the real skills are in knowing how computers can help you. In your science class, you could use a computer spread sheet to process and display information or you could delve into a data base to extract information. If you need to collect measurements from an experiment, you could use a data recorder. When this is connected to a computer, the results are worked out and displayed in graph or chart form for you. Also, when you need to write and present a report, you could use a word processor and a 'desk top publisher'. This would give your report a professional look - and even check your spelling for you!

● *Research skills*

Researching a topic may be necessary as part of a scientific survey or before you start practical investigations. This means reading up on the topic and, if possible, extracting information from sources which can range from advertising leaflets to computer data bases. For example, if you are asked to investigate the cleaning action of different washing powders, you could start by finding out what the maker of each powder claims.

Using these skills and your present knowledge of science, you're going to journey towards the frontiers of science. You might even cross into the unknown!

Studying science

How you use this book depends on the course you are following and on each topic being studied.

Designing and planning a practical investigation requires careful thought about the aim of the investigation. If necessary, carry out some initial investigations and read around the topic before setting your ideas on paper. Use the index at the back of the book to find the topic in the book.

Figure 2A ● Using this book

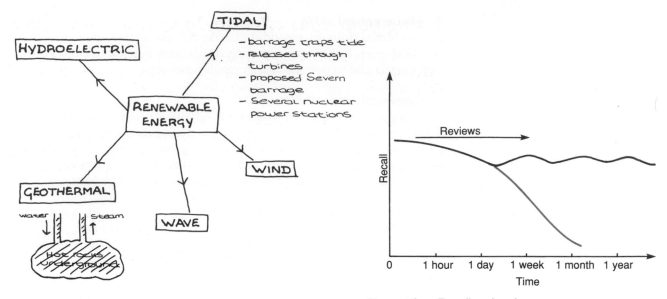

Figure 2B ● Making notes

Figure 2C ● Recall and review

Making notes is a skill to practise. You may need to make notes to help plan an investigation or you may be asked to make notes as a follow-up to practical work. As you read through the chosen topic, jot down the key points in rough then re-read to make sure you understand the key points and how they are linked. Use these key points as the framework for your notes.

Learning basic facts is important if you are to develop your understanding of science. You will have a data sheet or booklet to help you in exams and tests but you won't develop your grasp of the ideas in your course if you keep having to refer to a data booklet. The facts need to be inside your head to let your brain work on them! For example, to understand conservation of energy, you need to remember the main forms of energy and some examples of energy transformations.

Good notes are vital to help you remember basic facts. Make your notes attractive and easy to read; use sketches, colour, underlining, ticks, capitals and symbols to personalise your notes.

Understanding ideas and theories is a key part of learning science. Don't let your grasp of the concepts and ideas you meet in your science classes slip. Get to grips with each idea as you meet it; use this book to develop your understanding of topics discussed in class. Follow up class discussion and any notes given by your teacher by reading the appropriate part of the book.

To test your grasp of an idea or theory, try explaining it to a friend. If you can explain an idea or a theory successfully to someone, that means you must have understood it.

Use the checkpoints and questions in the book to test your recall of basic facts and how well you understand each topic. Checkpoints at intervals through each topic enable you to check your progress in grasping the basic facts and key ideas of each part of the topic. Longer questions at the end of each major theme enable you to test your grasp of how different topics link together.

Revising a topic at intervals is the best way to make sure you don't forget the key ideas and facts from the topic. Also, each practical investigation outlined in the book is written to remind you about a practical exercise carried out in the laboratory.

Figure 2C shows how recall drops with time; regular revision keeps topics fresh in your mind. Also, returning to a topic at intervals helps to improve your understanding of the topic.

Using your time effectively

Are you a person who is always putting things off? If your motto is 'never do today what you can do tomorrow', then you'll soon go under with your GCSE studies. Here's how to keep up with your work.

❶ **Be organised** – make a timetable for homework and private study. At GCSE, you are kept busy throughout the course with assignments, class tests, assessments and revision. Trying to keep up-to-date in half-a-dozen or more subjects is impossible without a timetable. You'll still find time for your favourite TV programmes, discos, charity walks, etc. without neglecting your studies – but only if you stick to your timetable.

Try to find a corner of your home where you can work undisturbed. A small table in a warm corner of your bedroom will do. Your work area should be well lit and comfortable. Make your study area attractive with one or two posters and make sure you have essential study aids (pen, pencil, eraser, paper, note book, textbook, calculator) at hand.

Figure 2D ● How not to study

❷ **Be active** – work in periods of about 30–40 minutes at a time. Most people can concentrate effectively up to about 30–40 minutes but not much more. Have a break between study periods and do something different altogether.

Set yourself a definite goal for each study session (e.g. revise a certain topic, answer a set homework question). If your goal is to revise a certain topic, read about it in your notes and this book. Then close your books and write down on a blank piece of paper what you remember about it. Then check what you have written against your notes and the book. Only reading is a sure way to lose concentration. Use questions from this and other books to test your recall and understanding of the topic.

❸ **Be optimistic** – when something goes wrong or you can't quite grasp something, take a break and return to it later. If you still can't crack it, work on something different and ask advice from your teacher as soon as you can. Often, some very minor point is all that prevents the penny dropping and it could be so obvious that you can't see it for looking!

Enjoy the challenge of your studies in science. There is enormous satisfaction in mastering a difficult idea or skill, and you may even make a new discovery or invention. Science is the product of the enquiring mind, asking questions and seeking answers about the world around us.

In your GCSE science course, you'll be studying topics that once racked the brains of famous scientists – and perhaps still do. When you're studying force and motion, remember that Galileo Galilei took years to understand what you're expected to grasp in weeks. However, Galileo didn't have basic scientific equipment such as stopclocks and forcemeters.

❹ **Be aware** – we live in the Scientific Age with new discoveries and inventions being announced almost every day. Wherever you go, watch out for science in use. Even a supermarket trip is a scientific experience – health foods, microwave meals, washing powders that are biodegradable, vacuum packed foods, etc., etc.

Your science course could be the gateway to an interesting and rewarding career. Who will be working in our science research and development laboratories when you're as old as your parents? Who will be operating in our hospital theatres? Who will be controlling our power stations and railways in the future? The short answer is YOU!

Figure 2E ● Science to help us preserve our environment: recycled paper and ozone friendly aerosols

THEME A
The Earth Our Home

Why has life evolved on a minor planet called Earth that orbits a middle-aged star called the Sun?

This star is part of one of many galaxies that make up the universe. Earth and the other planets in orbit round the Sun formed from molten rock billions of years ago. As Earth cooled, its outer layers solidified. Continents and oceans developed and a huge variety of life forms evolved. One particular life form is capable of making a scientific study of its environment!

TOPIC 1

THE EARTH IN SPACE

FIRST THOUGHTS

1.1 The Sun

The Sun and the Moon are the two most prominent objects in the sky. Why does the Moon's appearance change? What causes an eclipse? Read on to find out why.

IT

The Earth in Space
(program)

Use this program to try a *Teletype* simulation. This gives you 'news' on the computer screen as if it had just happened. Find out about:

- Ancient Chinese beliefs about the Sky Dragon,
- Egyptian explanations of why the Moon waxes and wanes,
- Copernicus' book of 1543.

Use the *Teletype* messages on the screen to read about Galileo's disagreement with the Vatican.

When did Newton publish his famous book? What was it called? Which side did it support: Galileo or the Vatican?

LOOK AT LINKS
for **gravity**
see Theme I, Topic 34.

We live near the edge of a fiery ball of gas we call the Sun. If the Sun died out, we would soon perish. All our energy comes, directly or indirectly, from the Sun. All forms of life need energy. So life on Earth depends on the Sun.

The Sun is a star. Stars are huge balls of hot gas that emit light. The Sun appears much bigger and brighter than any other star because we are so close to it.

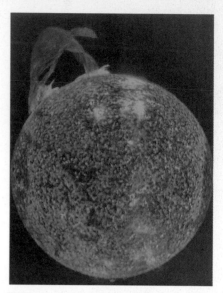

Figure 1.1A ● Solar activity

How far away is the Sun? Light from the Sun takes about eight minutes to reach Earth compared with about 4.2 years from the next nearest star, Proxima Centauri. The distance to the Sun's nearest neighbour is truly astronomical.

How big is the Sun? Its diameter is 110 times greater than Earth's. The distance from Earth to the surface of the Sun is about 100 solar diameters. Earth is one of the nine planets in orbit round the Sun. We can see the other planets because they reflect sunlight.

What keeps Earth in orbit round the Sun? The Sun's **gravity** stretches out into space and keeps the planets moving along their orbits. If the Sun's gravity was suddenly removed, Earth would shoot off into the cold depths of space.

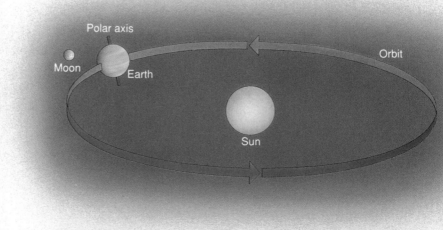

Polar axis

Moon   Earth   Orbit

Sun

Figure 1.1B ● The Earth's orbit

SUMMARY

Stars are huge balls of hot gas that emit light. Earth is a small planet in orbit round a star that we call the Sun. Planets do not emit light but they reflect sunlight.

Phases of the Moon

Our nearest neighbour in space, the Moon, orbits the Earth as Earth orbits the Sun. Even without a telescope, you can see that the Moon's surface has bright and dark areas and that it is covered with craters. We can see the Moon because it reflects sunlight. It orbits Earth once every 27¼ days, always keeping the same face towards Earth.

To Earth-bound observers, the Moon passes through a cycle of phases each month. This is because the amount of its sunlit face visible from Earth changes as it moves round Earth.

Figure 1.2A ● The Moon

IT'S A FACT

Ocean tides are caused by the Moon's gravity. Even though the Moon is so far from Earth, its pull is enough to raise the ocean by a few metres at opposite sides of Earth. Earth spins once each day so the two tidal bulges on opposite sides of Earth sweep round Earth giving two tides per day.

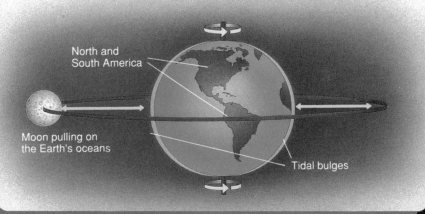

North and South America

Moon pulling on the Earth's oceans

Tidal bulges

IT

The Earth in Space
(program)

Well, is the Earth unique? Use the database (DIY base) in this program to find out:
- some of the main points about the Earth,
- how it differs from other planets,
- whether it has anything in common with another planet. Make notes under each heading.

1 **Full Moon** The Moon is in the opposite direction to the Sun from Earth so we see its sunlit face full-on. Although the Moon is at its brightest when full, features such as its craters are not so easy to make out because their shadows are short with the Sun directly above them.

3 **New Moon** Seen when the Moon is between the Earth and the Sun. The sunlit face of the Moon is then turned away from the Earth so that we only see a thin crescent of its sunlight surface. New Moon is about 14 days after Full Moon.

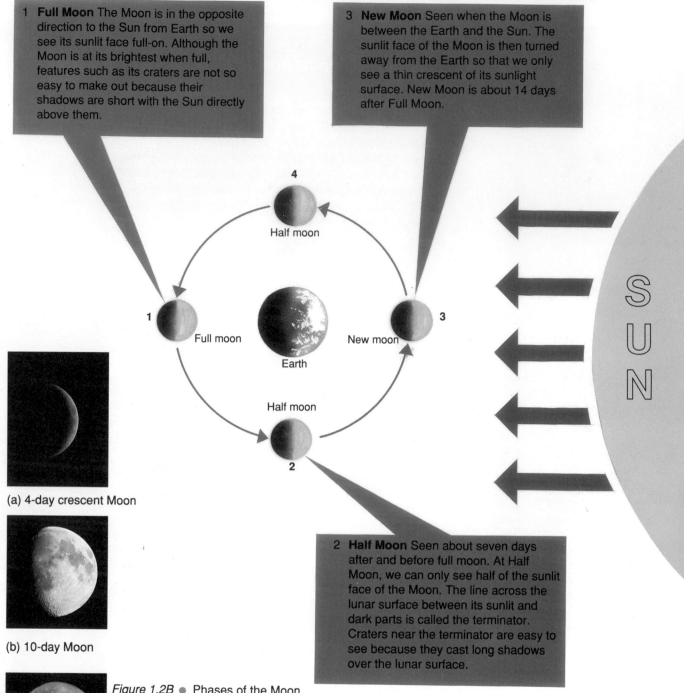

(a) 4-day crescent Moon

(b) 10-day Moon

2 **Half Moon** Seen about seven days after and before full moon. At Half Moon, we can only see half of the sunlit face of the Moon. The line across the lunar surface between its sunlit and dark parts is called the terminator. Craters near the terminator are easy to see because they cast long shadows over the lunar surface.

Figure 1.2B ● Phases of the Moon

(c) Full Moon

(d) 21-day Moon

Eclipses

Eclipses of the Sun and the Moon are predictable events. In ancient times, they were thought to foretell catastrophies and disasters! Eclipses happen when either Earth or the Moon passes into the other's shadow.

● Lunar eclipses
Lunar eclipses occur when the Moon passes through Earth's shadow. Figure 1.2C shows the idea. The shadow of Earth reaches far out into space, well beyond the Moon. Lunar eclipses take several hours and can be seen from any point on the night-time half of Earth.

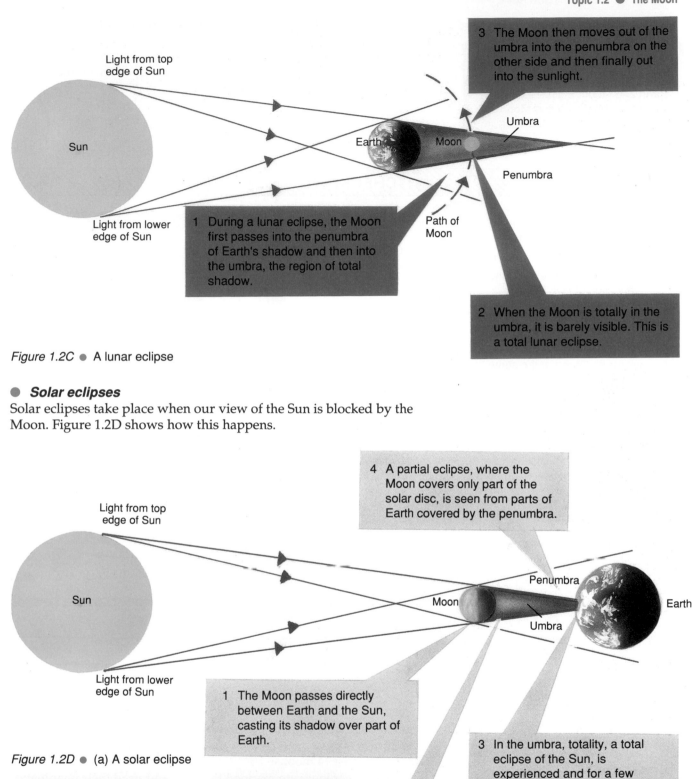

Light from top edge of Sun

3 The Moon then moves out of the umbra into the penumbra on the other side and then finally out into the sunlight.

Sun

Earth

Moon

Umbra

Penumbra

Path of Moon

Light from lower edge of Sun

1 During a lunar eclipse, the Moon first passes into the penumbra of Earth's shadow and then into the umbra, the region of total shadow.

2 When the Moon is totally in the umbra, it is barely visible. This is a total lunar eclipse.

Figure 1.2C ● A lunar eclipse

● *Solar eclipses*

Solar eclipses take place when our view of the Sun is blocked by the Moon. Figure 1.2D shows how this happens.

4 A partial eclipse, where the Moon covers only part of the solar disc, is seen from parts of Earth covered by the penumbra.

Light from top edge of Sun

Sun

Penumbra

Moon

Earth

Umbra

Light from lower edge of Sun

1 The Moon passes directly between Earth and the Sun, casting its shadow over part of Earth.

Figure 1.2D ● (a) A solar eclipse

3 In the umbra, totality, a total eclipse of the Sun, is experienced and for a few minutes the sky becomes completely dark.

2 Because the Moon is smaller than Earth, the umbra of its shadow does not cover the entire Earth.

(b) A partial solar eclipse

(c) A annular eclipse

SUMMARY

Phases and eclipses are caused by the relative positions of the Sun, Earth and Moon. Eclipses happen when the Sun, Earth and Moon are exactly in line with one another.

Sometimes the umbra does not reach Earth and then an **annular eclipse** is seen from Earth. This is where the solar disc forms a ring or annulus round the Moon. Total solar eclipses occur just as often as lunar eclipses but because totality covers only a small area of Earth, they are not seen as often.

CHECKPOINT

❶ In the picture opposite, the crescent moon is drawn incorrectly. Explain why the drawing is incorrect.

❷ (a) Sketch the phases of the Moon.
(b) Show the relative positions of the Moon, Earth and Sun at Half Moon.

❸ The Moon goes 360° round Earth once every 27.25 days. How far does it go round in (a) 1 day, (b) 1 week?

❹ Look for the Moon at the same time of night over successive nights. Does the Moon go round Earth from east to west or the other way?

❺ (a) Make a sketch to show the relative positions of the Moon, Earth and Sun during a solar eclipse.
(b) The Moon's orbit is tilted slightly relative to Earth's orbit as shown in the figure opposite. Use this to explain why solar eclipses do not occur every New Moon when the Moon is between Earth and the Sun.

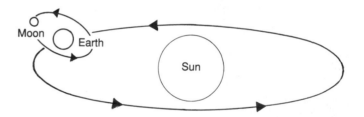

1.3 🌍 The Planets

FIRST THOUGHTS

How can you find a planet in the night sky? In this section, you can find out where to look and what to look for.

IT *The Earth in Space* (database)

Use the database in this package to explore the different planets. Start from the menu called *Look at Planets* and make your own explorations.

The Sun and the nine planets and their moons make up most of the solar system. It may surprise you to learn that other planets have moons. Jupiter has at least 14 moons!

Astronomers of long-ago mapped the stars and used their imagination to link groups of stars together. These groups are called **constellations**. We see them now much as they appeared thousands of years ago. One of the best known constellations is Orion, which was thought to resemble a warrior.

Seen from Earth, the other planets change their positions among the constellations from night to night. This is because they orbit the Sun and so the direction to each planet, from Earth, changes continuously. The word planet is the Greek word for wanderer. The astronomers of Ancient Greece named the planets after their gods who lived in the heavens.

How do the other planets compare with Earth? Figure 1.3A shows how they compare in terms of appearance, size and distance from the Sun. Here are one or two tips to help planet hunters!

Mercury is hard to find in the sky because it is so near the Sun. It can only be seen for an hour or so before sunrise and after sunset.

Venus is sometimes so bright in the night sky that it casts shadows. It moves further from the Sun than Mercury so we sometimes see it for several hours before sunrise and after sunset. Its brilliance after sunset is the reason why it is sometimes called the evening star.

Mars is closest to Earth when it is seen in the opposite direction to the Sun, as in Figure 1.3B. This is called opposition and it happens about once every two years. The progress of Mars through the constellations appears to reverse as Earth catches up with it near opposition.

Comparison of the planets

All measurements in terms of the Earth

	Diameter of planet (in Earth diameters)	Distance from Sun (in Sun–Earth distances)	Length of year (in Earth years)	Length of day (in Earth days)	Atmosphere	Composition	Appearance
Mercury	0.39	0.39	0.24	59	None	Rock	Cratered
Venus	0.97	0.72	0.61	243	Mostly carbon dioxide	Rock	Cloud covered
Earth	1	1	1	1	Mostly nitrogen and oxygen	Rock	Blue/green Some cloud
Mars	0.53	1.52	1.88	1.03	Mostly carbon dioxide	Rock	Red with white caps at poles
Jupiter	11.2	5.20	11.9	0.41	Mostly hydrogen	Fluid	Red/orange with bright and dark zones
Saturn	9.5	9.53	29.5	0.44	Mostly hydrogen	Fluid	Yellow/orange with bright and dark zones and rings
Uranus	3.7	19.2	84	0.67	Not known	Fluid	Greenish disc with bright and dark zones
Neptune	3.5	30	165	Not known	Not known	Fluid	Pale blue disc
Pluto	0.4	39	250	Not known	Not known	Probably rock	Too far to see

Earth's diameter = 12 735 km
Sun's diameter =1.39 million kilometres = 1.39×10^6 km
1 Astronomical Unit (AU) = Sun–Earth separation = 150 million kilometres = 150×10^6 km

SUN

0 —
3.2 —
6.0 —
8.3 —
12.6 —
43 —
79 —
159 —
249 —
324 —

Time for light to travel from Sun (in minutes)

Figure 1.3A ● The solar system

IT'S A FACT

You can find some of the planets for yourself in the night sky. Newspapers often feature a regular *Guide to the Night Sky* telling readers when and where to look for the planets.

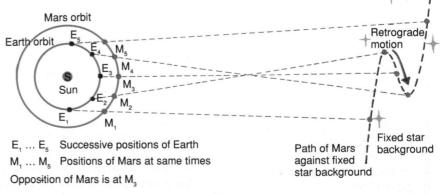

Mars orbit
Earth orbit
Retrograde motion
Sun
S
$E_1 \dots E_5$ Successive positions of Earth
$M_1 \dots M_5$ Positions of Mars at same times
Opposition of Mars is at M_3

Path of Mars against fixed star background

Fixed star background

Figure 1.3B ● The retrograde motion of Mars

Figure 1.3C ● Jupiter

Figure 1.3D ● (a) The rings of Saturn

Jupiter was first observed through a telescope by Galileo who discovered four moons in orbit round Jupiter. Another surprise from Jupiter is the presence of the Great Red Spot on its surface. This is thought to be a whirlwind. It was first observed by Galileo and is still active.

Saturn is an amazing sight seen through a telescope as it is circled by huge, thin rings which stretch out far above its equator. The rings are made of lots of micro moons, each orbiting Saturn while their own gravity keeps them in a thin disc. Saturn's axis is tilted at 29° to its orbit. This means that its rings are tilted and we see them at their best once every 14.5 years. Saturn has a number of moons too; the largest, Titan, is bigger than our Moon.

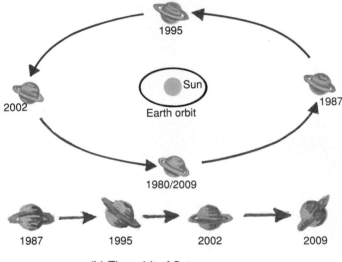

(b) The orbit of Saturn

The three planets beyond Saturn are too dim to see without the aid of a telescope.

Uranus was discovered in the eighteenth century. In 1977, astronomers discovered that Uranus has a ring system. The rings are too faint to be seen directly but they were first detected when Uranus passed in front of a star. Just before and after Uranus blocked the star out, the star blinked several times as each ring covered the star.

Neptune was discovered in 1846, as a result of detailed calculations on the orbit of Uranus. Astronomers found that Uranus did not move quite as predicted and they reasoned that an outer planet was responsible. They worked out where this outer planet ought to be and, sure enough, there it was!

Pluto, the outermost planet, was discovered from its effect on Neptune's orbit, although this was not until 1930. Its orbit is not circular so at times it is closer to the Sun than Neptune is.

Are there any more planets out there? Astronomers have known since 1801 about the minor planets, called asteroids, between Mars and Jupiter. The largest of these, Ceres, is about 1000 km in diameter although the others are much smaller. Some astronomers think there is a tenth planet beyond Pluto.

SUMMARY

The four inner planets, Mercury, Venus, Earth and Mars, are solid and much smaller than Jupiter, Saturn, Uranus and Neptune. These outer planets are giant balls of fluid. The outermost planet, Pluto, is thought to be small and solid.

CHECKPOINT

❶ Copy and complete the table below to compare the following planets.

	Mercury	Venus	Earth	Mars
Diameter				
Atmosphere				
Appearance				
Days per year				

❷ Make a scale diagram showing the orbits of the above planets (see Figure 1.3A).

❸ Work out the least distance and greatest distance, in terms of the distance from Sun to Earth, between
(a) Earth and Mars,
(b) Earth and Venus.

❹ As seen from Earth, the angle between Venus and the Sun changes as Venus moves along its orbit. Use your sketch to find the maximum angle between Venus and the Sun.

❺ (a) What is the least possible distance between Jupiter and Earth?
(b) Why does the brightness of Saturn change as it moves along its orbit?

1.4   Comets

FIRST THOUGHTS

In primitive civilisations, comets and meteors were regarded as signs of events to come. After working through this section, you will see that comets and meteors are entirely natural.

The appearance of a comet in the sky causes great excitement. In 1986, space probes were sent up from Earth to meet Halley's Comet and scientists learned a great deal about comets as a result. Before this, comets were thought to be huge chunks of frozen rock, but the space probes revealed a pitch black surface with jets of gas bursting through.

Comets orbit the Sun in non-circular orbits called ellipses. Their orbits usually stretch far beyond Pluto, taking many years to complete. As a comet approaches the inner part of the solar system, the Sun heats it up and turns some of its solid matter into a long tail of gases. The tail always points away from the Sun, driven away by the force of solar radiation. Comets far from the Sun are dark and impossible to see. But as a comet moves nearer the Sun, it gets hot and a glowing tail of gas forms which makes the comet visible.

Figure 1.4A ● Halley's comet

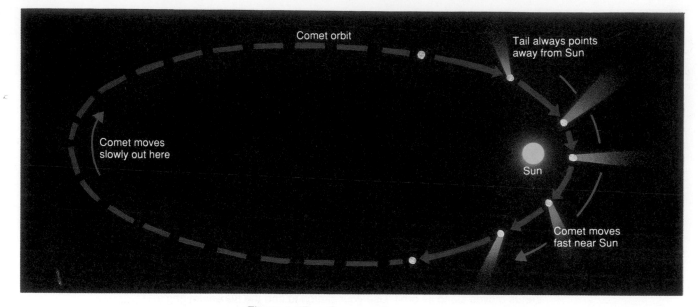

Figure 1.4B ● Comet paths

Halley's Comet can be seen from Earth every 76 years as it passes through the inner solar system. In 1910, its return was visible in daylight but in 1986, its return was less easy to see because it was in the same direction as the Sun when at its brightest. In 1682, Edmund Halley studied a bright comet and was the first person to realise that it had been seen several times before at intervals of about 76 years. He correctly predicted it would return in 1758 and so the comet was named after him.

● *Meteors*

Meteors, sometimes called shooting stars, can be breathtaking to see. They look like tiny balls of fire shooting across the sky. This happens when a particle of matter from space enters our atmosphere at high speed. Air resistance makes the particle so hot that it burns up. Sometimes, if the meteor is large enough, it does not burn up completely and falls to Earth as a meteorite. The largest known meteorite, thought to have fallen in prehistoric times, has a mass of more than 60 000 kg!

SUMMARY

Comets orbit the Sun in elliptical orbits, taking many years to complete each orbit. Meteors are particles of matter from space that burn up because they enter Earth's atmosphere at high speeds.

CHECKPOINT

❶ Why are comets visible only when they are near the Sun?

❷ When is Halley's Comet next expected to return?

❸ Use two drawing pins and some thread to draw an ellipse as shown in the figure opposite. This gives you an accurate sketch of a comet orbit with the Sun at one of the pinpoints. Mark the Sun on your sketch and show a comet with its tail near the Sun.

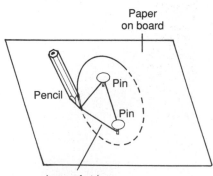

❹ (a) How does Earth's atmosphere help to protect us from meteorites?
   (b) The Moon and Mercury are both heavily cratered. Why?

❺ A bright comet is shown on the Bayeux Tapestry which depicts the Norman Conquest of England in 1066. Could this comet have been Halley's Comet? Explain your answer.

1.5 ● Star watch

The stars and the Sun have been used for timekeeping and navigation for centuries. Why do we have leap years? How can we use the stars to navigate? Astronomy has always been a very practical subject.

Earth spins round as it orbits the Sun. Its axis points in a fixed direction in space so that the **Pole Star** is always directly above Earth's North Pole. Anyone who is north of the equator can find due north by looking for the Pole Star.

In the northern hemisphere, if you watch the stars for a few hours, you will see that they move round the Pole Star. The stars appear to move round the sky once every 24 hours because Earth is spinning at a steady rate of one revolution every 24 hours. In Ancient Greece, astronomers imagined the stars were attached to an invisible spinning globe, the **celestial sphere**. Earth's equator projected onto this sphere is called the **celestial equator**.

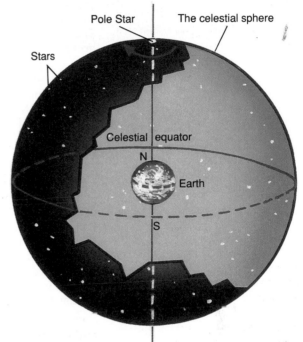

Figure 1.5A ● The celestial sphere

Science, religion and the solar system

● Ancient Greece

Astronomy is the oldest branch of science. In ancient civilisations, it was studied for practical reasons such as keeping a calendar. In Ancient Greece in about 500 BC Pythagoras devised a model to explain the motions of the stars across the sky. In this model, Earth is at the centre of an invisible spinning sphere on which the stars are fixed. The sphere carries the stars across the sky as it turns.

The Pythagorean model is a **geocentric** model which means that Earth is at the centre. This was very agreeable to the prophets and priests of Ancient Greece because their gods lived in the heavens above Earth.

An alternative model was put forward by Aristarchus in about 300 BC. He placed the Sun at the centre and relegated Earth into orbit around the Sun as no more than a spinning planet. *Why was this imaginative model rejected in favour of Pythagoras' model?*

Figure 1.5B ● Astronomical clock

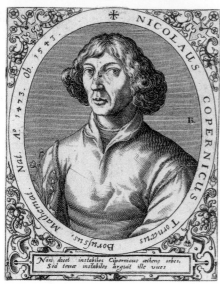

Figure 1.5C ● Nicolaus Copernicus

- If Earth spins, objects on its surface should be thrown off.
- If Earth moves round the Sun, the stars should change position in the constellations according to Earth's positions.
- In the Pythagorean model Earth is the most important body in the universe. Aristarchus' model would remove Earth from its special place.

In fact, the first two effects are very small but they can be detected using modern measuring equipment. An object weighs about 0.3% less at the equator than at the poles because of Earth's rotation. Also, nearby stars do change position very slightly in the constellations as Earth moves round the Sun. For example, Proxima Centauri, the nearest star, shifts its position in the constellation of the Centaur by 0.0004° as Earth moves from one side of the Sun to the other.

Aristarchus didn't have our modern methods for making such small measurements so he had no experimental support for his model. Keeping the geocentric model suited the rulers of Ancient Greece because it helped to maintain their privileged position over their subjects.

A more sophisticated geocentric model was developed by Ptolemy in 120 AD. He imagined that the Sun circled Earth and the other planets circled the Sun. This explained the retrograde motion of Jupiter and Mars and it remained the accepted model of the Universe for almost 2000 years.

● *The modern view*

Ptolemy's model dominated astronomy until the sixteenth century when a Polish monk called Nicolaus Copernicus decided to improve it. He wanted to simplify Ptolemy's model and his research led him to rediscover the ideas of Aristarchus. He published his ideas in a book, *De Revolutionibus*. His work is often credited with starting modern science!

In fact, Copernicus did not publish his book until 1543, the last year of his life. He must have realised that his ideas would challenge the authorities. This was a time of bitter conflict in Europe as Protestant reformers challenged the authority of the Church. Those who challenged the Church's teaching publicly were harshly treated. The Inquisition was set up by the Church to curb dissent. In Spain, more than 2000 people were burned to death by the Inquisition.

Faced with such hostility, those who supported the new ideas were in great personal danger. In 1591, Giordano Bruno, a Dominican friar, was imprisoned for his theory that the universe was infinite, made up of stars with their own planets. He was tried and burned at the stake in 1600.

NICOLAI COPERNICI

net, in quo terram cum orbe lunari tanquam epicyclo contineri diximus. Quinto loco Venus nono mense reducitur. Sextum denique locum Mercurius tenet, octuaginta dierum spacio circu currens. In medio uero omnium residet Sol. Quis enim in hoc pulcherrimo templo lampadem hanc in alio uel meliori loco poneret, quàm unde totum simul possit illuminare? Siquidem non inepte quidam lucernam mundi, alij mentem, alij rectorem uocant. Trimegistus uisibilem Deum, Sophoclis Electra intuente omnia. Ita profecto tanquam in solio regali Sol residens circum agentem gubernat Astrorum familiam. Tellus quoque minime fraudatur lunari ministerio, sed ut Aristoteles de animalibus ait, maximam Luna cum terra cognationem habet. Concipit interea à Sole terra, & impregnatur annuo partu. Inuenimus igitur sub hac

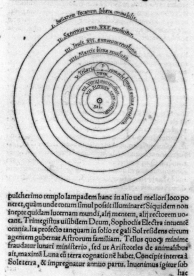

Figure 1.5D ● A page from *De Revolutionibus* showing Copernicus' model of the solar system

About this time, an Italian professor of mathematics, Galileo Galilei, began to take a scientific interest in the Copernican model. In 1609, he used a new invention called the telescope to study the sky. He discovered mountains and craters on the Moon and sunspots on the face of the Sun. His most important discovery was the moons of Jupiter. The four moons in orbit round Jupiter form a system like the planets in orbit round the Sun. Galileo made many important discoveries in other branches of science and mathematics. Although he was the most important scientist of his generation, the Church instructed him in 1616 to stop teaching the Copernican model.

For several years, he concentrated on other work but the appearance of three comets in 1618–1619 re-awakened his interest. In 1632, he published his case for the Copernican model in a book *Dialogue on the Two Chief Systems of the World*. His book provoked immediate hostility and in 1633 he was condemned by the Inquisition and was sentenced to life imprisonment in his country house in Italy where he died in 1642.

Galileo's discoveries in astronomy had shown the power of observation in understanding the natural world. He showed how to apply mathematics to understand motion. Isaac Newton, born in Protestant England in 1642, used Galileo's ideas to develop the mathematical principles of physics. Newton's theory of gravity left no doubt that Copernicus was right: Earth does move round the Sun.

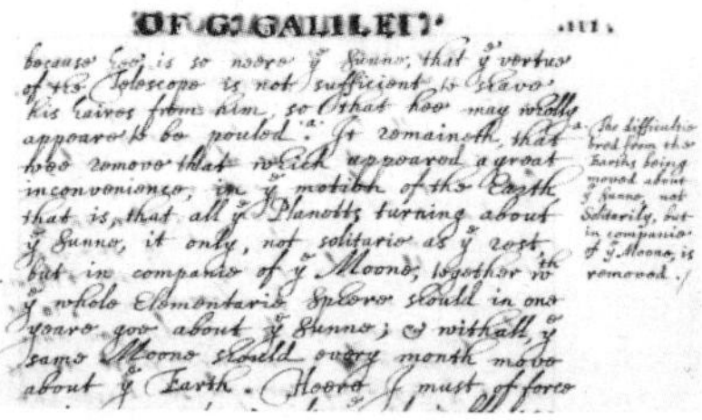

Figure 1.5E ● A page from Galileo's notebook describing the discovery of Jupiter's moons

Keeping time

One day is the time taken for Earth to turn on its axis once. Once every 24 hours, we see the Sun rise in the east and set in the west as Earth spins round.

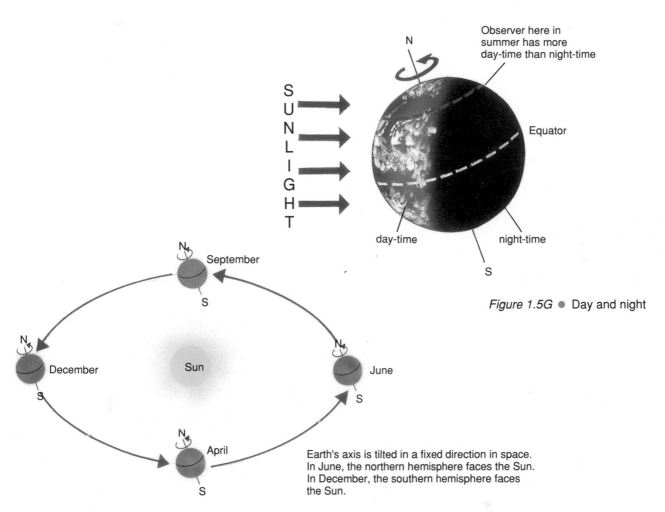

Figure 1.5G ● Day and night

Earth's axis is tilted in a fixed direction in space. In June, the northern hemisphere faces the Sun. In December, the southern hemisphere faces the Sun.

Figure 1.5F ● The seasons

TRY THIS

Over a few weeks, watch from home how the position of the setting sun changes on the horizon. If you're an early riser, watch the changing sunrise too! In Britain, at mid-summer, the Sun rises north of due east and climbs high in the sky before setting north of due west. At mid-winter, the Sun rises south of due east and sets south of due west.

One year is the time taken for Earth to orbit the Sun once. The year is divided up into **seasons** because Earth's axis is tilted in a fixed direction in space. On 21 June, the northern hemisphere faces the Sun directly so 21 June is the northern mid-summer. This is called the **summer solstice**.

Why do we get more daylight in the summer than in winter? This is because our hemisphere is tilted towards the Sun in summer. So each summer's day, we spend more time on the daylight side of Earth than on the night side.

Why do we have leap years? The reason is that the Earth turns 365¼ times each year as it orbits the Sun. By including an extra day every fourth year, we can ensure that the year changes on average at a fixed point on the Earth's orbit. *What do you think would happen if we didn't bother with the extra day?* Nothing too dramatic at first but mid-summer and mid-winter would happen 1 day earlier every 4 years. *What date would mid-summer become 100 years from now?*

Our calendar was established by Julius Caesar but even with leap years every fourth year it proved inaccurate by the Middle Ages. This is because there are not quite 365.25 days in a year. By the Middle Ages, the seasons had changed by ten days. So in 1582, Pope Gregory XIII issued a papal bull making 5 October into 15 October. He also decreed that the first year of a century would not be a leap year if it was divisible by 400. Protestant England ignored the new calendar until 1752, catching up by making 2 September into 14 September. However, the late conversion was made up for by changing the start of the year from 25 March to 1 January!

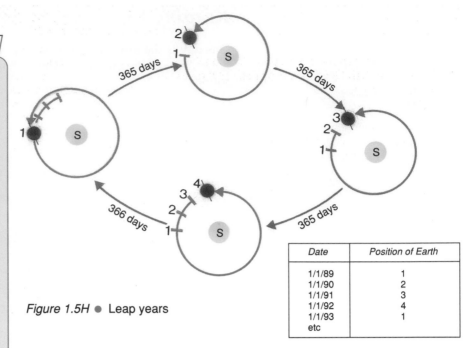

Figure 1.5H ● Leap years

Date	Position of Earth
1/1/89	1
1/1/90	2
1/1/91	3
1/1/92	4
1/1/93	1
etc	

The best place on Earth

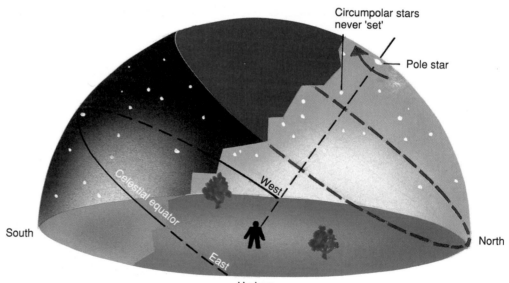

Figure 1.5I ● Circumpolar stars

Where is the best place to be on Earth to see all the stars? Anyone on the equator sees every star at some time. That's why observatories with huge telescopes are based near the equator.

Circumpolar stars are stars that never set. They are always above the horizon. The latitude of the observer determines which stars are circumpolar. From the UK, latitude 55° north of the equator, any star more than 35° north of the equator is circumpolar and so never sets. However, stars more than 35° south of the equator can never be seen from the UK. Stars between these latitudes rise and set each day. Whether you can see them at night depends on the time of night, the time of year and the latitude of the observer.

SUMMARY

Earth turns on its axis once per day and orbits the Sun once per year. The stars move across the sky due to Earth's rotation.

❶ The Pole Star can be found by first locating the Plough and then following the pointers of the Plough to the Pole Star.

(a) On a clear night, find the Plough and use it to locate the Pole Star. Sketch their positions,
(b) Repeat your sketch a few hours later. Explain the differences.

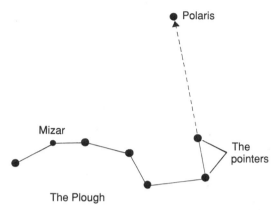

❷ Design an instrument to measure the angle of elevation (altitude) of a star above the horizon. If possible, construct and test your instrument by measuring the altitude of the Pole Star.

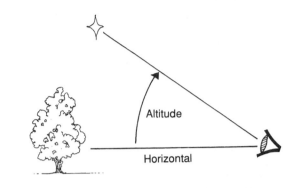

❸ (a) Earth moves the 360° around the Sun in 1 year. How far does it move in (i) 1 day, (ii) 1 week?
(b) Why does the Sun rise earlier in London than it does in New York?

1.6 Journey into Space

FIRST THOUGHTS

Some of the astonishing discoveries made by spaceflights to the planets are outlined here. Perhaps the most important discovery is that life on Earth is unique in the solar system.

Space probes have been sent to most of the planets. The information they have sent back has increased our knowledge of the planets enormously and will be useful when space colonies are eventually established. Even more important is the realisation that life does not seem to exist anywhere in the solar system except on Earth.

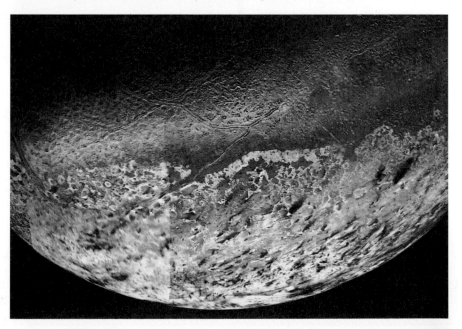

Figure 1.6A ● Triton

IT

Motion in Space
(program)

Use this program to try your own space walking and space mission. Move the astronaut around by firing the four gas jets. What do you notice about the astronaut's movement?

You will see that motion in space is very different to motion on Earth. What are the reasons?

SUMMARY

Earth is the only planet that supports life. Mars is likely to be the first planet on which space colonies are established. Space missions need to be planned very carefully and space probes take many months to reach their targets.

A trip round the Solar System

Space missions to the planets take years to plan and carry out. The flight paths of the Voyager and Pioneer probes were carefully worked out in advance so that each probe reached its target in the shortest possible time.

Voyager 2 was launched in 1977 on a path that took it in 12 years to the four giant planets, Jupiter, Saturn, Uranus and Neptune. The path of *Voyager 2* is shown in Figure 1.6B. As it approached each planet, the gravitational pull of the planet swung it round onto a flight path for the next planet. *Voyager 2* sent back amazing pictures of these planets, their moons and the ring systems of Saturn and Uranus. Astonishing discoveries were made from its pictures, including volcanoes on Jupiter's moon, Io, rings round Neptune, and most incredible of all, Triton. This is the largest of Neptune's moons, a freezing, volcanic and colourful world.

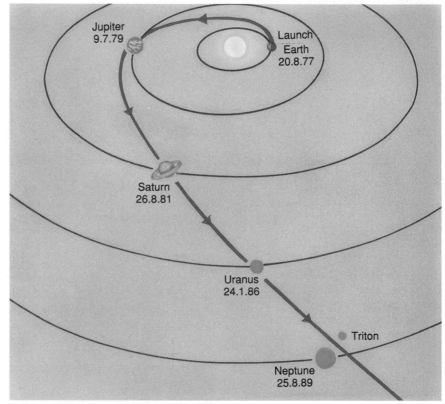

Figure 1.6B ● The flight path of the *Voyager 2* probe

CHECKPOINT

❶ Find out the year in which the following space events happened.
(a) The first artificial satellite was launched.
(b) The first person set foot on the Moon.

❷ Why is Mars the most Earth-like of the planets?

❸ Why would life on Venus be very harsh for visitors from Earth?

❹ Make a sketch of a possible flight path from Earth to Mars, showing their orbits to scale.

❺ Why would it be impossible to land on any of the giant planets?

1.7 Beyond the solar system

After working through this section, you will see that the Sun is just one of the countless stars in one of countless galaxies that make up the universe.

The Sun is one of millions of stars that form the Milky Way galaxy. The universe is made up of many galaxies, each one containing millions of stars. Light takes more than 10 000 million years to reach us from the most distant galaxies.

Radio telescopes like that at Jodrell Bank, England have been used to show that our galaxy is disc-shaped with spiral arms. Light takes about 100 000 years to cross the Milky Way galaxy and the Sun is about 30 000 light years from the galactic centre. On a clear night, the Milky Way can be seen stretching across the sky.

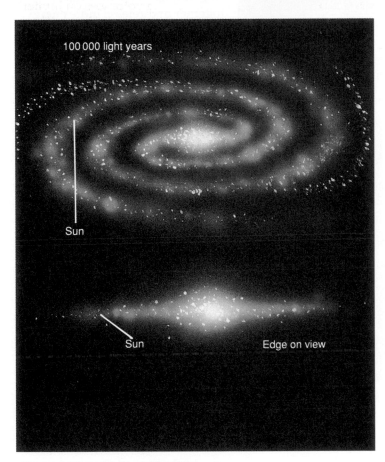

100 000 light years

Sun

Sun   Edge on view

Figure 1.7A ● (a) The Milky Way

(b) The Andromeda galaxy

(c) The Sombrero Hat galaxy

In 1987, a star in the southern hemisphere exploded and became the biggest supernova to be seen for four centuries. The Crab Nebula is thought to be the remnants of a supernova explosion that happened in about the eleventh century.

What differences can you see when you look from one star to another? Are the stars all the same? Even though they appear only as points of light astronomers can work out their size and temperature, how far away they are and how much energy they emit each second. All this information and much more is obtained by studying their light in detail and by using the laws of physics. For example, we know that if a glowing object is made hotter and hotter, its colour changes from red to orange to blue. So a blue star must be much hotter than a red star.

The birth and death of a star

Stars are thought to form out of clouds of gas and dust. The particles gather together under their own gravity which makes them more and more concentrated. As the 'protostar' becomes more and more dense it gets hotter and hotter. The temperature becomes so great that the atoms **fuse** together and release more energy. So it gets hotter and brighter. A star is born!

The planets formed from the same cloud of gas and dust as the Sun. Most of the cloud formed the Sun but relatively small amounts condensed outside the Sun to form the planets. The Sun's gravity prevents the planets from escaping into space.

Stars like the Sun will radiate energy for billions of years before they run out of atoms to fuse together. The Sun is about half way through its lifecycle. When the Sun does start to run short of fuel, it will swell up into a huge red ball, known as a **red giant**, stretching beyond Mercury. The star Betelgeuse in the constellation of Orion is a red giant. After the red giant stage, a star collapses in on itself and becomes a hot, dense white star, known as a **white dwarf**, until it gradually fades away. Big stars explode near the end of their lifecycle. Such an event is known as **supernova** and can outshine an entire galaxy while it lasts.

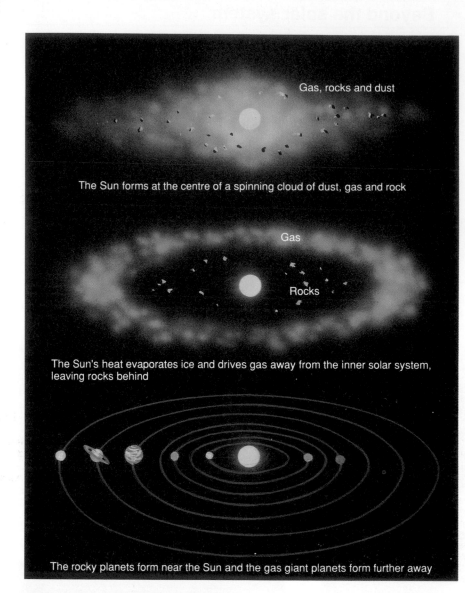

The Sun forms at the centre of a spinning cloud of dust, gas and rock

Gas, rocks and dust

Gas

Rocks

The Sun's heat evaporates ice and drives gas away from the inner solar system, leaving rocks behind

The rocky planets form near the Sun and the gas giant planets form further away

Figure 1.7B ● How the planets formed

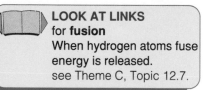
LOOK AT LINKS
for **fusion**
When hydrogen atoms fuse energy is released.
see Theme C, Topic 12.7.

SUMMARY

The universe is made up of many galaxies. Each galaxy contains millions of stars. The Sun is one of many stars in the Milky Way galaxy. Earth is a planet in orbit round the Sun. Life on Earth has existed for a tiny fraction of the age of the universe. Does life exist elsewhere?

The Big Bang

Scientists think the Universe is expanding. The most distant galaxies are known to be over 10 billion light years away and rushing away from Earth almost as fast as light. Looking at them is looking back in time because the light from them takes billions of years to reach Earth.

All the distant galaxies are moving away from each other as the universe expands. Billions of years ago, they must have been very close together. In fact, astronomers think that the universe originated in a massive explosion, **the Big Bang**. The rate of expansion is thought to be getting gradually slower. Maybe the universe will stop expanding and collapse in a few billion years time!

PLANET EARTH

2.1   The structure of the Earth

FIRST THOUGHTS

What is Earth like deep down, many kilometres below the surface? It sounds an impossible question to answer, but scientists have found methods of investigating the deep structure of the Earth.

The study of the Earth is called **geology**, and a person who works in this branch of science is called a **geologist**. The research work of geologists has enabled them to construct a model of Earth's structure (see Figure 2.1A).

How was Earth formed? A molten mass cooled down over millions of years. Dense materials sank deeper into the centre to form a core of dense molten rock. Less dense material remained on the surface to form a **crust** of solid rock (50 km thick). Gaseous matter outside the crust is the **atmosphere**. Earth's atmosphere is chiefly oxygen and nitrogen.

As Earth cooled, water vapour condensed to form rivers, lakes and oceans on the surface of Earth. No other planet has oceans and lakes, though Mars has some water vapour and polar ice caps.

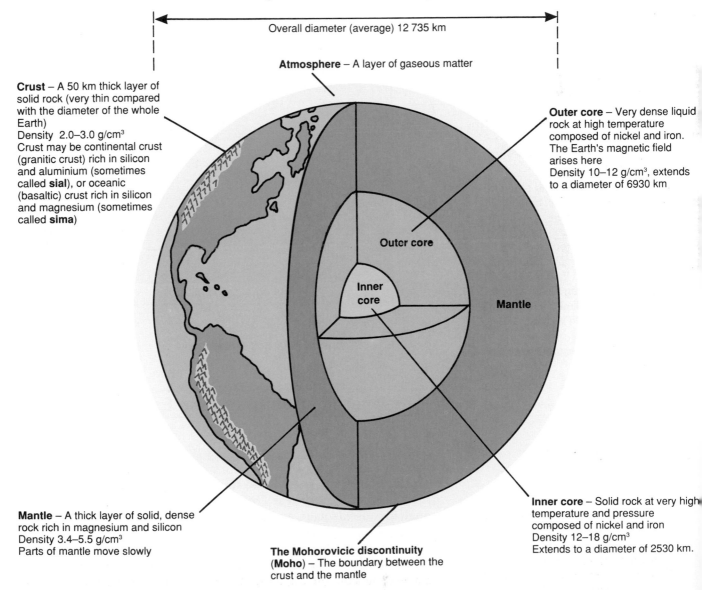

Overall diameter (average) 12 735 km

Atmosphere – A layer of gaseous matter

Crust – A 50 km thick layer of solid rock (very thin compared with the diameter of the whole Earth)
Density 2.0–3.0 g/cm³
Crust may be continental crust (granitic crust) rich in silicon and aluminium (sometimes called **sial**), or oceanic (basaltic) crust rich in silicon and magnesium (sometimes called **sima**)

Outer core – Very dense liquid rock at high temperature composed of nickel and iron. The Earth's magnetic field arises here
Density 10–12 g/cm³, extends to a diameter of 6930 km

Outer core

Inner core

Mantle

Mantle – A thick layer of solid, dense rock rich in magnesium and silicon
Density 3.4–5.5 g/cm³
Parts of mantle move slowly

The Mohorovicic discontinuity (Moho) – The boundary between the crust and the mantle

Inner core – Solid rock at very high temperature and pressure composed of nickel and iron
Density 12–18 g/cm³
Extends to a diameter of 2530 km.

Figure 2.1A ● The structure of the Earth

LOOK AT LINKS
for **soil**
The layer of soil is very thin compared with the thickness of the Earth's crust. The importance of this thin layer of soil is covered in
Theme G, Topic 29.0.

SUMMARY

The Earth has a layered structure: inner core, outer core, mantle, crust and atmosphere. The crust is composed of oceanic (basaltic) crust beneath the ocean floors and continental (granitic) crust, which forms the Earth's land masses. The boundary between the crust and the mantle is called the Moho. The study of the Earth is called geology.

Earth's crust

Earth's crust is composed of rocks and **soils**. Soils have been formed by the breakdown of rocks and vegetation. The crust is divided into continental and oceanic crust. Earth's overall diameter is 12 735 km.

Continental crust
- Forms continents and their shelves
- Up to 70 km thick in mountain ranges
- Density ~ 2.7 g/cm³
- Age: up to 3700 million years
- Same composition as granite rock
- Often called granitic crust
- Rich in silicon and aluminium
- The deeper parts of continental crust are of a denser material similar to oceanic crust.

Oceanic crust
- Beneath deep sea floors
- Average thickness 6 km
- Density ~ 3.0 g/cm³
- Age: up to 220 million years
- Same composition as basalt rock
- Often called basaltic crust
- Rich in silicon and magnesium
- Material similar to oceanic crust is thought to lie beneath the continents.

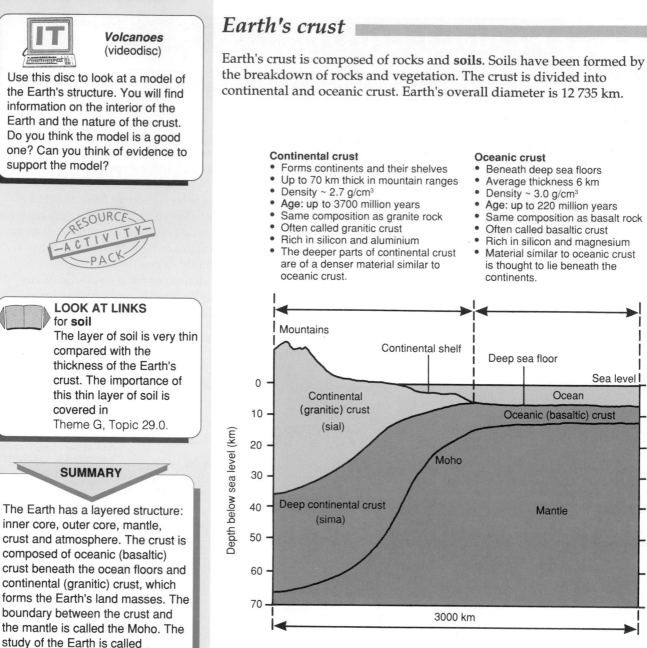

Figure 2.1B ● Continental crust and oceanic crust

2.2 ● The layered structure of the Earth

FIRST THOUGHTS

We cannot obtain information about the deep structure of Earth by mining or by drilling. The world's deepest mine is 3.5 km in depth, and the radius of Earth is over 6000 km. Evidence about the interior of Earth comes from the study of earthquakes and volcanoes.

Earthquakes

The study of earthquakes is called **seismology**. About 500 000 earthquakes occur every year. Only about 1000 of these are strong enough to cause damage, and only a few are serious. An earthquake occurs when forces inside Earth become strong enough to fracture large masses of rock and make them move. The energy which is released travels through the Earth as a series of shock waves. Earthquakes are limited to the rigid part of the crust. They cannot occur in the molten part of the mantle. Most earthquakes are generated within 600 km of Earth's surface. The point where an earthquake originates is called the

focus. The nearest point on Earth's surface directly above it is the **epicentre**. Shock waves are felt most strongly at the epicentre and then spread out from it. Earthquake shocks are recorded by an instrument called a **seismometer** (see Figure 2.2A).

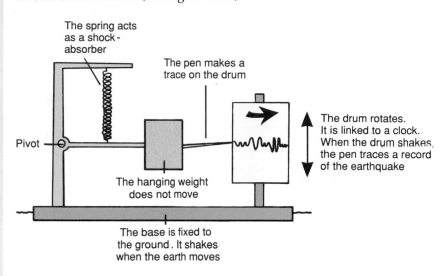

Figure 2.2A ● A seismometer

The recording is called a **seismogram**. The energy of the earthquake is measured on the **Richter scale**. Each point on the scale means an increase by a factor of ten: a scale of 5 is ten times as powerful as a scale of 4.

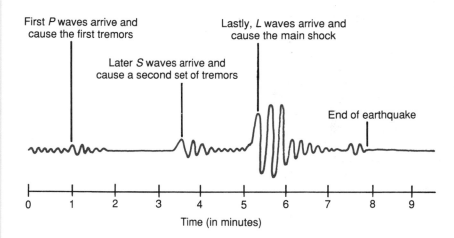

Figure 2.2B ● A seismogram

The seismogram in Figure 2.2B records three types of shock waves. *P* waves – **primary waves**, *S* waves – **secondary waves** and *L* waves – **long waves**. Figure 2.2C shows the difference between them.

The pattern of waves received by a seismometer depends on what the waves have passed through inside the Earth. Waves are either reflected (bounced back) or refracted (bent) when they travel from one type of material into another.

The positions of boundaries, e.g. the Moho, and the thicknesses and densities of the zones have all been worked out from the way that earthquake shock waves have been affected by passing through them. *S* waves do not pass through the outer core at all. Since it is known that *S* waves do not travel through liquids, this is evidence that the outer core is in the liquid state. This shows that its temperature must be very high.

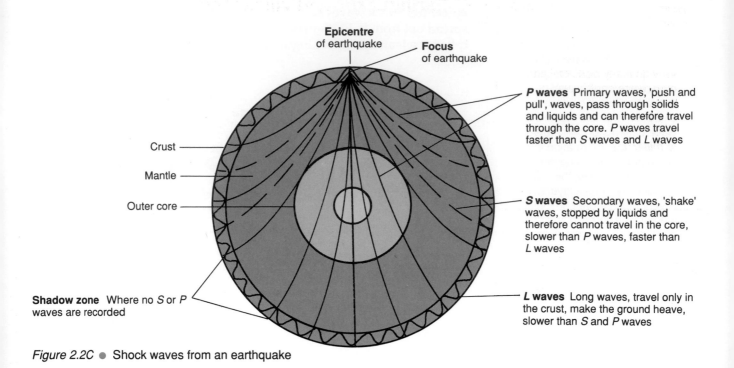

Epicentre of earthquake

Focus of earthquake

Crust

Mantle

Outer core

P waves Primary waves, 'push and pull', waves, pass through solids and liquids and can therefore travel through the core. P waves travel faster than S waves and L waves

S waves Secondary waves, 'shake' waves, stopped by liquids and therefore cannot travel in the core, slower than P waves, faster than L waves

Shadow zone Where no S or P waves are recorded

L waves Long waves, travel only in the crust, make the ground heave, slower than S and P waves

Figure 2.2C ● Shock waves from an earthquake

Volcanoes

The lava erupted by volcanoes gives information about the crust and upper mantle, where lava is produced, but not about deeper layers. Plotting on a map the places where volcanoes have occurred gives information about the regions of Earth where heat is being generated and causing volcanic activity.

Meteorites

Meteorites reach Earth from space. They are pieces of rock and dust which have been attracted towards Earth by Earth's gravity. Most meteorites burn up when they reach Earth's atmosphere, but some fall to Earth's surface. Geologists believe that meteorites may be samples of planetary material dating from the time of formation of the solar system.

Magnetism

Earth's magnetic field is evidence for the presence of iron in the core.

SUMMARY

Evidence for the structure of the Earth comes from:
• the patterns of shock waves produced by earthquakes
• material erupted by volcanoes
• the positions of earthquakes and volcanoes on the map
• meteorites
• the Earth's magnetic field.

CHECKPOINT

❶ The overall density of Earth is 5.5 g/cm³. The rocks in the Earth's crust have densities of 2.5 to 3.0 g/cm³. How can you explain the difference between these values and the much higher density of the whole Earth?

❷ Take a piece of string 3 m long. Imagine that this length represents the 3000 million years that have passed since the first living things appeared on Earth. Mark on the string the length that represents the 2 million years since the human race appeared.

2.3 ● Earthquakes and volcanoes

Why do many parts of Earth experience earthquakes and volcanoes? Why do some parts of Earth have neither? Geologists have found answers to this puzzle.

Earthquakes and volcanoes occur in certain parts of Earth's crust but not in others. Geologists speculated for many years on reasons for the difference. Some patterns emerge from Figure 2.3A.

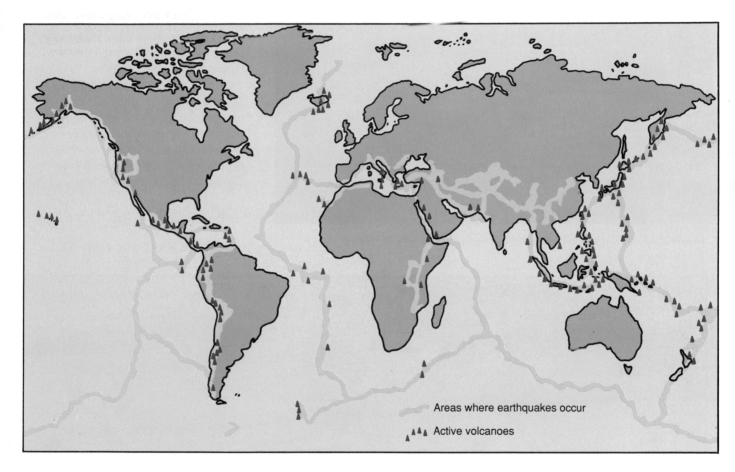

Areas where earthquakes occur

▲▲▲ Active volcanoes

Figure 2.3A ● Areas of earthquake and volcanic activity

- Earthquakes and volcanoes occur in belts of activity. The belts are hundreds of kilometres wide and thousands of kilometres long. In places, belts join up.
- On land, belts occur along chains of high mountains like the Alps.
- Beneath the sea, belts pass through the centres of oceans and through chains of volcanic islands like the Philippines.
- Surveys of the mid-ocean belts show that the sea floor rises to form chains of huge mountains beneath the sea. These mountain chains are called **oceanic ridges**. The mid-Atlantic ridge rises above sea-level to form Iceland.
- Surveys show that belts which pass through chains of islands are close to deep **oceanic trenches** on the sea floor. The same is true of mountain ranges near the edges of continents. A trench in the Pacific called the Peru–Chile trench runs parallel to the Andes.

SUMMARY

Earthquakes and volcanoes occur in belts of activity. These belts run:
- along mountain ranges
- along oceanic ridges (mountains on the sea floor)
- along oceanic trenches (deep channels in the sea floor)

2.4 ● Plate tectonics

Is Earth's crust really composed of separate moving pieces? It sounds amazing, but this is one of the newest scientific theories.

Geologists believe that the outer layer of Earth is made up of separate pieces called **plates**. Each plate is a piece of **lithosphere** (crust and uppermost layer of mantle) of 80–120 km in thickness. Movements in the mantle beneath make the plates move very slowly, a few centimetres per year. As a result, plates sometimes rub against each other. If stress builds up to a large extent, the plates may bend. When they spring back into shape, the ground shakes violently: there is an **earthquake**. There has to be a source of energy to produce the movement of plates. Many geologists believe that it is the heat given out when radioactive elements decay (see Figure 2.4L).

Figure 2.4A ● The result of an earthquake in Mexico City in 1986

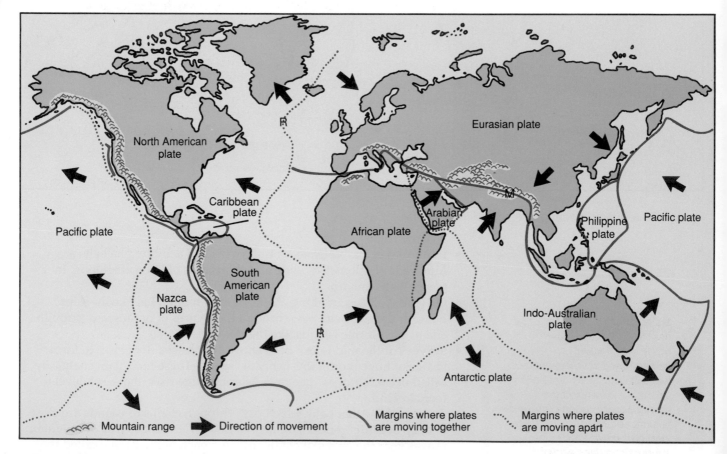

Mountain range ● Direction of movement ● Margins where plates are moving together ● Margins where plates are moving apart

Figure 2.4B ● The plates which make up Earth's crust

Boundaries

Boundaries between plates may be **constructive**, **destructive** or **conservative**.

Constructive boundaries occur where the plates are moving apart (see Figure 2.4C). Evidence for plate movement was found in the 1960s when the volcanoes along oceanic ridges were studied. Lava erupts from these volcanoes and cools to form new oceanic crust along the edges of the plates on either side. The plates move away from the ridge and the width of the ocean floor is increased. The process is called **sea-floor spreading**. An example is the mid-Atlantic trench.

IT'S A FACT

In April 1990 the second largest earthquake in Britain this century hit Clun in Shropshire. It registered 5.2 on the Richter scale.

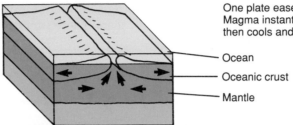

One plate eases away from another. Magma instantly rises to fill the gap, then cools and solidifies to form a ridge

— Ocean
— Oceanic crust
— Mantle

Figure 2.4C ● A constructive plate boundary. Material is added at the plate boundary and the plates move apart

Destructive boundaries occur where the plates are in collision (see Figure 2.4D). Oceanic trenches are regions where plates meet as they move together. When they meet, the edge of one plate is forced to slide beneath the other and move down into the mantle. This process is called **subduction**. The descending plate edge melts to become part of the mantle. Some oceans are shrinking in size as subduction occurs.

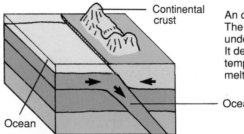

Continental crust

An ocean and a continent meet. The edge of the oceanic plate sinks under the less dense continental plate. It descends to a depth where the temperature is so high that the crust melts and becomes part of the mantle

— Oceanic crust

Ocean

Figure 2.4D ● A destructive plate boundary. Material descends from the plate boundary

Conservative boundaries occur where two plates slide past one another. The San Andreas fault in California is an example of a conservative boundary.

TRY THIS

Make a pan of porridge and heat it. Watch the patterns set up by convection currents. Can you see the subduction zones (where the skin sinks) and the spreading ridges (where the porridge boils up – the volcanoes!)? If you ever make jam, next time investigate subduction zones again!

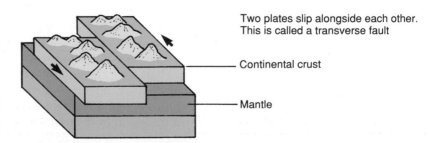

Two plates slip alongside each other. This is called a transverse fault

— Continental crust

— Mantle

Figure 2.4E ● A conservative plate boundary. No material is gained or lost

IT

Volcanoes
(videodisc)

Use this disc to compare world maps of volcanic activity with the pattern of 'plates' in the Earth's crust. Look at the films showing activity at the plate margins. Do you think that plate movement could affect the landscape?

The conveyor belt

As material is subducted at an oceanic trench and added at an oceanic ridge, the net effect is to convey material from one edge of a plate to another. Since the mass of material taken away at oceanic trenches is equal to the mass of material added at oceanic ridges, the plate remains the same size.

This movement of plates has been called a **conveyor belt**. Continents ride the conveyor belt beneath them: as the plates move, the continents on them move. This has been happening for thousands of millions of years. Although the rate is slow, only a few centimetres a year, the continents have already travelled thousands of kilometres. About 300 million years ago, northern Europe was near the equator, and tropical forests grew there. These later decayed to form coal deposits.

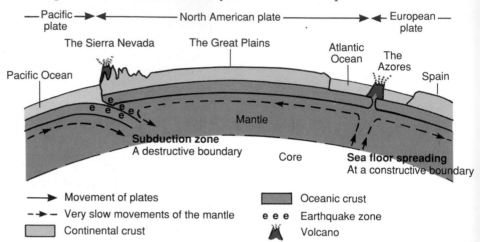

Figure 2.4F ● Movement of plates on the 'conveyor belt'

Figure 2.4G shows what happens when oceanic crust meets continental crust at a destructive plate boundary.

The oceanic plate sinks below the less dense continental plate. Some of the sediment on the surface of the oceanic plate is scraped off. It piles up on the landward side

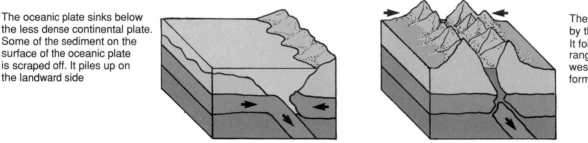

The sediment is compressed by the continental plate. It folds to form a mountain range. The Andes, on the west coast of South America, formed in this way

Figure 2.4G ● Collision between an oceanic plate and a continental plate: formation of a mountain range. (When two continents collide the sediments from both are squeezed up to form mountains.)

The theory of plate tectonics

You will remember the theory that Earth originated from a cloud of hot gas which condensed to form a ball of hot liquid. The densest materials sank into the **core** of the liquid while the less dense materials rose to the surface. There they cooled and solidified to form a **crust**. Until the twentieth century, scientists considered that Earth went on cooling until the present day. They thought that as the interior cooled and contracted, the crust folded to fit it and as a result mountain ranges were formed. Scientists compared the folding crust with the wrinkling of the skin of an apple as the inner part of the fruit dries out and shrinks.

SUMMARY

Earth's crust and the upper part of the mantle are together called the lithosphere. Geologists believe that the lithosphere consists of separate plates and that these plates are moving slowly. At oceanic ridges, the plates are moving apart. At oceanic trenches, the plates are moving together. When plates meet, continental crust is pushed up to form mountain ranges. Plate movement gives rise to earthquakes and volcanoes.

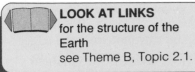

LOOK AT LINKS
for the structure of the Earth
see Theme B, Topic 2.1.

There were some mysteries which this view of Earth could not explain. For example, it is possible in the UK to find rocks and fossils which can only be formed in desert conditions. Mountains occur in ranges, not as isolated peaks. Earthquakes and volcanoes are collected in belts of activity and not scattered over Earth's surface.

Geologists noticed the similarity between the east coastline of South America and the west coastline of Africa (see Figure 2.4H). The coastlines look as though the continents could have been joined together in a previous era.

Figure 2.4H ● The 'jigsaw' fit of South America and Africa

If Africa and South America were once joined, how did the Atlantic come to be formed? In the eighteenth and nineteenth centuries, it was widely believed that a vast flood, such as Noah's flood in the Old Testament, had forced the continents apart. *And how did the Pacific ocean originate?* The nineteenth century belief was that a huge section of continental land mass was gouged out to form the moon and the hole that was left became the Pacific.

It was a German meteorologist (weather scientist) called Alfred Wegener who, in 1915, promoted the theory that the continents bordering the Atlantic were at one time joined together and had subsequently drifted apart. Wegener's ideas were not new, but he amassed more evidence in support of the theory of **continental drift** than previous workers had done.

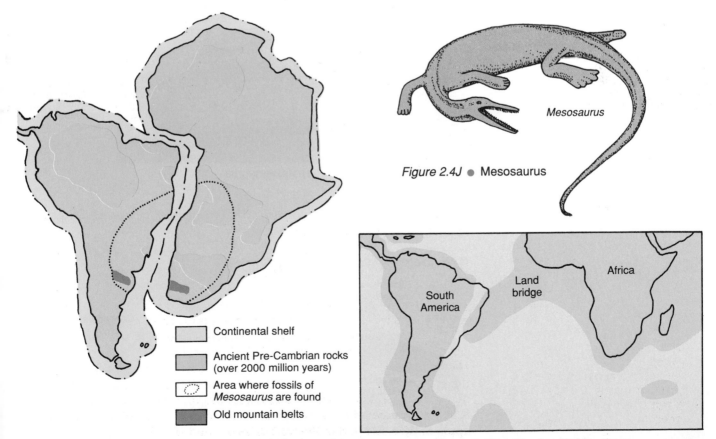

Continental shelf

Ancient Pre-Cambrian rocks (over 2000 million years)

Area where fossils of *Mesosaurus* are found

Old mountain belts

Figure 2.4I ● Evidence that South America and Africa were joined

Figure 2.4J ● Mesosaurus

Figure 2.4K ● The land bridge theory

Wegener described the matching up of geology, fossils and plant and animal populations on both sides of the Atlantic. He said, 'It is just as if we were to refit the torn pieces of a newspaper by matching the edges and check whether the lines of print run smoothly across. If they do, there is nothing left but to conclude that the pieces were in fact joined in this way.'

How can continents drift? Wegener put forward the theory that continental land masses float on a fluid, denser crust beneath them. According to his theory, continents can move horizontally, provided that there are forces acting on them, forces which last for geological eras. Wegener was unable to come up with a convincing idea to explain the force which must have driven continents apart.

The theory of continental drift is not restricted to South America and Africa. It is believed that long ago all the southern continents were joined together as one land mass, called **Gondwanaland** and the northern continents were joined to form a supercontinent called **Laurasia**. It is believed that at a still earlier time all the present-day continents were part of a single land mass, known as **Pangaea**, which began to break up and spread about 200 million years ago (see Figure 2.4O).

Wegener's theory was derided in 1915, but is accepted today. *Why did it take so long?* People's ideas were dominated by the belief that Earth was cooling, shrinking and folding. Some physicists considered that Earth's crust was too rigid for sideways movements of the kind Wegener was describing. A turning point came when geologists came to realise the magnitude of the heat produced by Earth's **radioactive materials**. It provides for all volcanic activity with plenty of heat to spare. *What happens to the excess heat?* In 1931, Arthur Holmes, a British geologist, put forward a suggestion that the excess heat was discharged by convection currents and that continental drift was powered by such currents. It took 30 years for Holmes' ideas to be widely accepted by earth scientists.

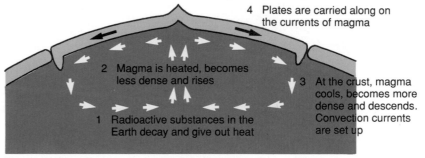

4 Plates are carried along on the currents of magma

2 Magma is heated, becomes less dense and rises

3 At the crust, magma cools, becomes more dense and descends. Convection currents are set up

1 Radioactive substances in the Earth decay and give out heat

Figure 2.4L ● Convection currents of magma

Why did the theory of continental drift eventually meet with success? Some of the evidence is summarised below.

● *Evidence of sea-floor spreading*

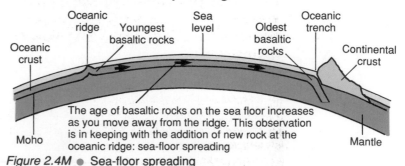

Oceanic ridge   Youngest basaltic rocks   Sea level   Oldest basaltic rocks   Oceanic trench

Oceanic crust   Continental crust

The age of basaltic rocks on the sea floor increases as you move away from the ridge. This observation is in keeping with the addition of new rock at the oceanic ridge: sea-floor spreading

Moho   Mantle

Figure 2.4M ● Sea-floor spreading

LOOK AT LINKS
for **radioactive materials**
see Theme C, Topic 12

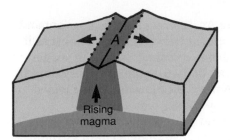

Band A The basalt which solidifies as the magma cools is magnetised normally with the North Pole as we know it

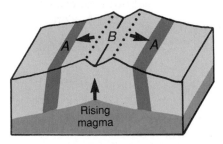

Band B The sea-floor has spread. The Earth's magnetic field has reversed. The basalt which now solidifies shows reversed magnetism. As band *B* solidifies, it pushes the two sides of band *A* apart

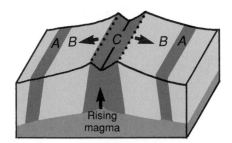

Band C The polarity of the Earth's magnetic field has changed again. Normally magnetised basalt solidifies at the centre of the ridge

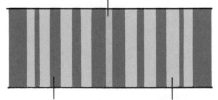

Ridge crest

Normal magnetism of basalt   Reverse magnetism of basalt

Note the symmetrical pattern of bands of normally magnetised basalt and reversely magnetised basalt on either side of the crest of the oceanic ridge. How could this symmetrical pattern have arisen without sea-floor spreading?

Figure 2.4N ● Pattern of magnetic stripes at an oceanic ridge

The youngest basalts on the ocean floor are at the oceanic ridges. As you move away from the ridges, the basalts get progressively older. The oldest parts of the oceanic crust are in the oceanic trenches and at the borders of the continents. No oceanic basalt more than 220 million years old has been found. Continental crust, in contrast, is over 1000 million years old.

Every few thousand years Earth's magnetism reverses its polarity. That is to say that over certain periods of time in the past the compass needle would have pointed to the South Pole instead of the North Pole. Oceanic floor basalts include minerals which contain iron and are therefore magnetic. As they crystallise, particles of iron line up with the magnetic field which is operating at the time.

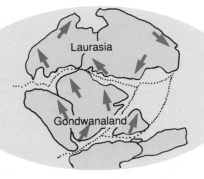

180 million years ago
The original land mass, Pangaea, had split into two major parts. Gondwanaland had started to break up

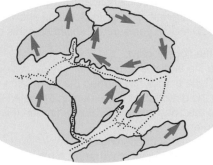

135 million years ago
Gondwanaland and Laurasia drifted northwards. The North Atlantic and Indian Oceans widened. The South Atlantic rift lengthened

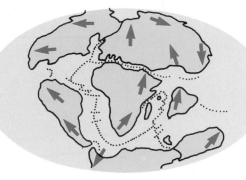

65 million years ago
South America had separated from Africa. Australia and Antarctica were still combined. The Mediterranean Sea had appeared. India was moving towards Asia

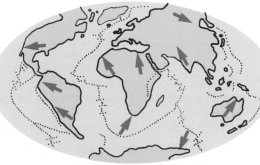

Today
South America has connected with North America. Australia has separated from Antarctica. India has collided with Asia

Figure 2.4O ● The formation of the continents

SUMMARY

According to the theory of sea-floor spreading, new oceanic crust is being formed along oceanic ridges. The new crust pushes older crust away from the ridges in mid-ocean towards the continents. In this way the sea floor is constantly spreading.

Sea-floor spreading is very uneven. As different lengths of a ridge spread by different amounts, cracks appear between them. These cracks are called transform faults. It is possible to calculate the rate of sea-floor spreading from magnetic data. It comes to 2–10 cm per year for different parts of ridges in different oceans. Figure 2.4O summarises the way continents have drifted apart due to sea-floor spreading.

This model of the Earth, in which rigid slabs of the crust jostle with one another on the surface of a sphere, is called **plate tectonics** (tectonics = construction). From the theory, it has been possible to predict accurately where earthquakes will occur. Unfortunately, earth scientists cannot yet predict the time when a future earthquake will occur.

CHECKPOINT

❶ Refer to Figure 2.4B on p 24.
(a) Name a plate that is surrounded on all sides by subduction zones.
(b) Name the mountain range, M.
(c) The line R—R is the mid-Atlantic ridge. Lava erupts along this ridge. What type of lava is it? Explain how eruptions arise from the movement of plates.
(d) The San Andreas fault passes through California. What is happening to the plates along this fault?
(e) Why does the UK experience few earthquakes and no serious quakes?
(f) Rocks on the Isle of Skye in Scotland show that volcanoes erupted there about 50 million years ago. Explain how this could have happened.

❷ Refer to the figure below.
(a) Name the features A, B and C.
(b) What type of rock has formed the mountain range, A?
(c) State the direction of movement in (i) Plate P, (ii) Plate Q and (iii) Plate R.
(d) Name the zone labelled E. Say what part this zone plays in plate movement.
(e) Explain what is happening at D.
(f) Explain how the mountain range A has been formed.

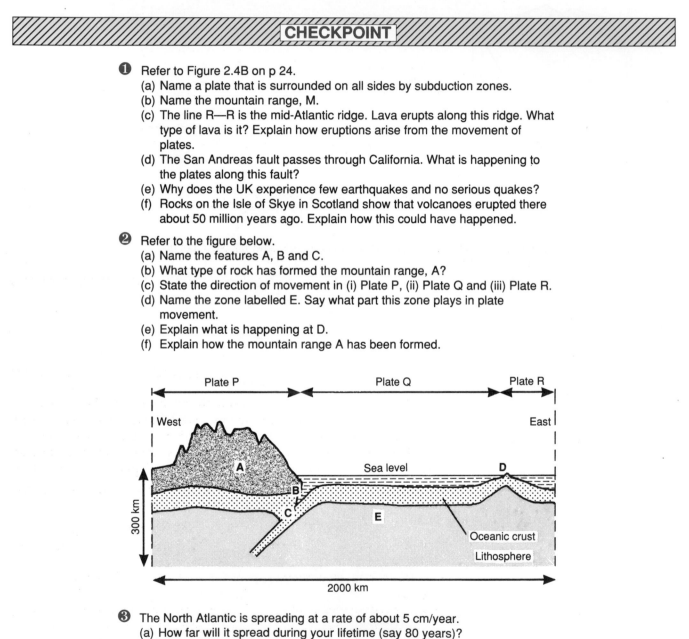

❸ The North Atlantic is spreading at a rate of about 5 cm/year.
(a) How far will it spread during your lifetime (say 80 years)?
(b) How tall are you?
(c) How does your answer to (a) compare with your answer to (b)?

❹ Outline two theories which explain how the Pacific Ocean was formed: the plate tectonic theory and a historical theory.

❺ What are the three different types of boundary between plates?

⑥ Refer to the figure below.
(a) How old is the ocean floor basalt at (i) the western edge of the ocean, (ii) 500 km east of the centre of the ocean and (iii) at the centre of the ocean?
(b) How do the measurements shown in the graph agree with the theory of sea-floor spreading?

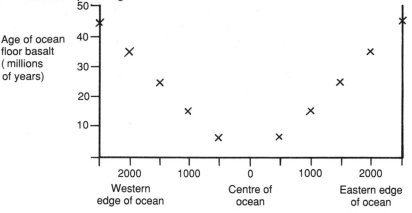

Distance from centre of ocean (km)

⑦ Imagine that you are a journalist who has just attended the 1926 conference at which Wegener put forward his theory of plate tectonics. Write an account for your magazine, *Science Weekly*, describing how other scientists reacted to Wegener's theory.

⑧ Briefly describe how the theory of plate tectonics explains:
(a) sea-floor spreading,
(b) continental drift.

⑨ Is it any use being able to predict where an earthquake will occur but not when? Explain your answer.

2.5 Types of rock

FIRST THOUGHTS

There are three main types of rock: igneous, sedimentary and metamorphic. In this section, you can find out which is which.

Igneous rocks

Sometimes enough heat is generated in the crust and upper mantle to melt rocks. The molten rock is called **magma**. Once formed, magma tends to rise. If it reaches Earth's surface, it is called **lava**. When cracks appear in Earth's crust, magma is forced out from the mantle on to the surface of Earth. It erupts as a **volcano**, a shower of burning liquid, smoke and dust.

Igneous rocks formed when the lava erupted from a volcano cools are:

- **basalt**, from free-flowing mobile lava,
- **rhyolite**, from slow-moving lava,
- **pumice**, from a foam of lava and volcanic gases.

Types of rock erupted by a volcano are:

- **agglomerate**, the largest rock fragments which settle close to the vent,
- **volcanic ash**, finer fragments of rock,
- **tuff**, compacted volcanic ash,
- **dust**, which may be carried over great distances by the wind. Sometimes, dust rises high into the atmosphere and affects the weather. This is what happened at Mount St Helens in the USA in 1980.

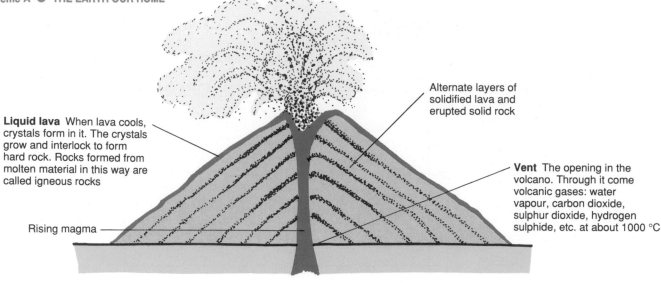

Liquid lava When lava cools, crystals form in it. The crystals grow and interlock to form hard rock. Rocks formed from molten material in this way are called igneous rocks

Alternate layers of solidified lava and erupted solid rock

Vent The opening in the volcano. Through it come volcanic gases: water vapour, carbon dioxide, sulphur dioxide, hydrogen sulphide, etc. at about 1000 °C

Rising magma

If lava solidifies in the vent, gas pressure builds up and there is likely to be a violent eruption. If this happens, lava and rock are forced out of the vent in a jet of volcanic gas. The mixture can travel rapidly down the side of a volcano causing death and destruction in its path.

Figure 2.5A ● A volcano

Figure 2.5B ● Lava rolling down the slopes of Mount Etna, one of the most active volcanoes.

Figure 2.5C ● Mount St. Helens during its second eruption. Dust and ash was spread for many miles around and stayed in the atmosphere for months

Figure 2.5D ● In 79AD, the city of Pompei was destroyed when a mixture of lava, rock and ash travelled quickly down the side of the volcano Vesuvias

Figure 2.5E ● The Giant's causeway in Northern Ireland is made from basalt, solidified lava

Sedimentary rocks

The formation of sedimentary rocks begins when solid particles settle out of a liquid or an air stream to form a **sediment**. The solid material comes from older rocks or from living organisms. All rocks exposed on Earth's surface are worn away by **weathering** and by **erosion**. The material that is worn away is transported by gravity, wind, ice, rivers and seas. The transported material may be fragments of rock, pebbles and grains of sand, or it may be dissolved in water. Eventually the transported material is deposited as a **bed** (layer) of sediment. It may be deposited on a sea bed, on a sea shore or in a desert. The beds of sediment are slowly compacted (pressed together) as other material is deposited above. Eventually, after millions of years, the pieces of sediment become joined together into a sedimentary rock. This process is called **lithification**. Examples of sedimentary rocks are:

- **limestone**, formed from the shells of dead animals,
- **coal**, formed from the remains of dead plants,
- **sandstone**, compacted grains of sand.

Metamorphic rocks

Igneous and sedimentary rocks can be changed by high temperature or high pressure into harder rocks. The new rocks are called **metamorphic rocks** (from the Greek for 'change of shape'). Examples of metamorphic rocks are:

- **marble**, formed when limestone is close to hot igneous rocks,
- **slate**, formed from clay, mud and shale at high pressure,
- **metaquartzite**, from metamorphism of sandstone.

The composition of the Earth's crust is: igneous rocks 65%, sedimentary rocks 8% and metamorphic rocks 27%. The differences are summarised in Table 2.1.

Table 2.1 ● Types of rock

	Igneous	Sedimentary	Metamorphic
Type of grain	Crystalline	Fragmental: grains do not usually interlock (They do in some limestones)	Crystalline
Direction of grain	Grains usually not lined up	Grains usually not lined up	Grains usually lined up
Mode of formation	Crystallisation of magma	Deposition of particles	Recrystallisation of other rocks
Fossil remains	Absent	May be present	Absent
Appearance when broken	Shiny	Usually dull	Shiny
Ease of breaking	Hard, not easily split, may crumble if weathered	May be soft and crumble, but some are hard to break	Hard, but may split in layers, may crumble if weathered
Examples	Basalt, granite, rhyolite, pumice	Limestone, clay, sandstone, mudstone	Marble, hornfels, slate, schist

The rock cycle

Only igneous rocks are formed from new material brought into the crust. The original crust of Earth must have been made entirely from igneous rocks. The slow processes by which metamorphic and sedimentary rocks are formed from igneous rock and also converted back into igneous rock is called the rock cycle (see Figure 2.5G).

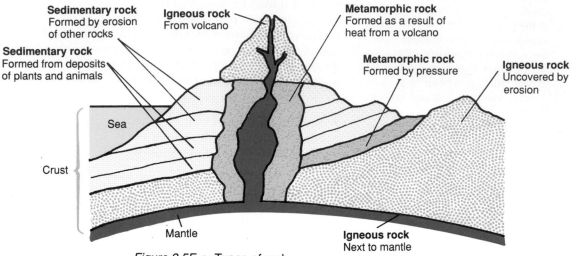

Sedimentary rock
Formed by erosion of other rocks

Sedimentary rock
Formed from deposits of plants and animals

Igneous rock
From volcano

Metamorphic rock
Formed as a result of heat from a volcano

Metamorphic rock
Formed by pressure

Igneous rock
Uncovered by erosion

Sea

Crust

Mantle

Igneous rock
Next to mantle

Figure 2.5F ● Types of rock

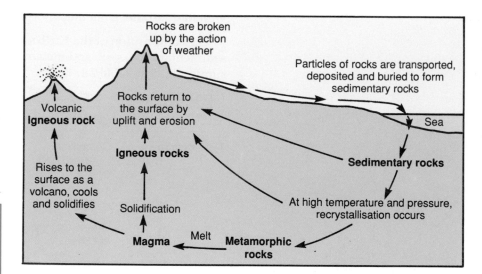

Rocks are broken up by the action of weather

Particles of rocks are transported, deposited and buried to form sedimentary rocks

Volcanic
Igneous rock

Rocks return to the surface by uplift and erosion

Igneous rocks

Sea

Sedimentary rocks

Rises to the surface as a volcano, cools and solidifies

Solidification

At high temperature and pressure, recrystallisation occurs

Magma   Melt   **Metamorphic rocks**

Figure 2.5G ● The rock cycle

SUMMARY

When volcanoes erupt, they emit volcanic gases, lava, ash and pieces of solid rock. Lava cools and solidifies to form igneous rock. The solid rock settles as agglomerate. Ash is compacted to form tuff. Rocks are weathered into smaller particles. These particles are deposited as a sediment, which becomes compacted to form sedimentary rock.
Igneous and sedimentary rocks may be changed by high temperature and pressure into metamorphic rock. The slow processes by which rock material is recycled are called the rock cycle.

CHECKPOINT

❶ Copy and complete this passage.
When volcanoes erupt, molten rock called _____ streams out of the Earth. It solidifies to form _____ rocks, e.g. _____ . When deposits of solid materials are compressed to form rocks, _____ rocks are formed, e.g. _____ . The action of heat and pressure can turn _____ rocks and _____ rocks into _____ rocks.

2.6 🌐 Deformation of rocks

The deformation of rocks is caused by forces acting within the crust. It results in the formation of **folds**, **faults**, **cleavage** and **joints**. The extent of deformation produced by a force depends on the type of rock: brittle rocks may fracture to produce a fault, while soft rocks may crumple to produce a fold.

Folding

When rocks are compressed (squeezed) they may become folded. Sedimentary rocks are often folded. The beds of rock which have been laid down are no longer horizontal; they are folded to bulge upwards (an **anticline**) or downwards (a **syncline**).

(a) A fold in limestone rock

Figure 2.6A ● Folding in sedimentary rock

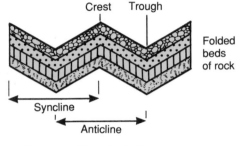

The formation of a fold

Cleavage

Cleavage is the splitting into thin sheets of rock under pressure. Slate is easily broken along **cleavage planes**. Slate is formed by the metamorphism of shales. Clay minerals and flaky minerals, such as mica, are recrystallised to lie perpendicular to the direction of maximum stress. The slate which results has a weakness in one plane along which it can be easily broken.

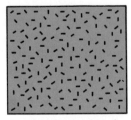

A mass of clay minerals, non-aligned

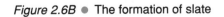

Figure 2.6B ● The formation of slate

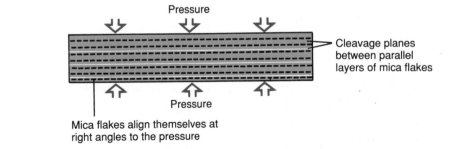

Faults

A powerful force can break rocks and cause faults (breaks) in the rock. A break allows rocks on one side of a fault to move against rocks on the other side of the fault. As long as forces keep acting, rocks will continue to keep moving against each other along the line of the fault. Since there is friction between the edges of rocks, the movement takes place in jerks. Each of these jerks may cause an earthquake.

Figure 2.6C ● (a) A vertical fault

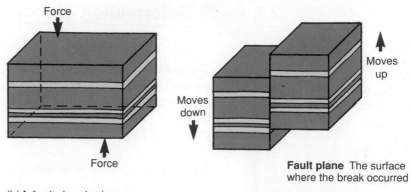

(b)A fault developing

Fault plane The surface where the break occurred

In Figure 2.6C the faults are vertical displacements. Horizontal displacements occur at faults where two of the Earth's plates slide past each other. The San Andreas fault which lies beneath California in the USA is of this type. There were severe earthquakes in California in 1838, 1906 and 1989.

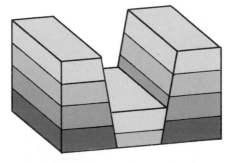
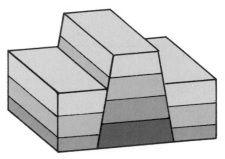

A rift valley. The subsidence of rock between faults creates a valley

A horst. A block of rock is left upstanding after rocks on both sides subside

Figure 2.6D ● (a) A rift valley. The valley has subsided between faults. It may become the course of a river or the site of a lake.
(b) A horst left standing when rocks on both sides subside

Joints

A fracture may occur without the rocks on either side moving relative to one another. Such a break cannot be called a fault because there is no displacement so it is called a **joint**. Joints in igneous rock may be caused by cooling and shrinking. Figure 2.6F shows joints in the limestone pavement at Malham Cove. Joints in sedimentary rocks may be caused by loss of water. Joints make a rock permeable to water. They provide weaknesses which may be affected by weathering.

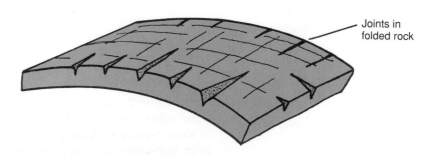

Joints in folded rock

Figure 2.6E ● Joints in folded rock

SUMMARY

Sedimentary rock is laid down in horizontal layers. These may be deformed by:
- folding, with the formation of synclines and anticlines
- cleavage, splitting into thin sheets
- faulting, developing breaks which allow slabs of rock to slide against one another
- jointing, developing breaks without any movement of rock.

Figure 2.6F ● Limestone pavement at Malham Cove

CHECKPOINT

❶ The figure shows a section through some layers of rock.
  (a) Explain the statement: *Limestone, shale and sandstone are* **sedimentary** *rocks*.
  (b) What type of rock is granite?
  (c) Explain how the granite could have pushed through the layers of sedimentary rock.
  (d) Explain the statement: *The layers of sedimentary rock in regions B and C have been* **metamorphosed**.
  (e) Why have the sedimentary rocks at *A* and *D* not been metamorphosed?

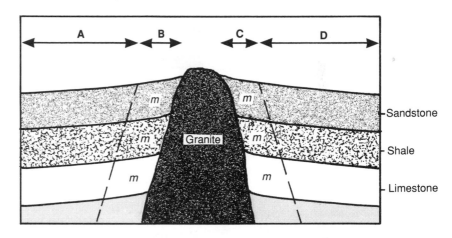

2.7 The forces which shape landscapes

What forces shaped the varied landscape that we see around us? What forces pushed up the mountain ranges, smoothed the plains and carved out the valleys?

Rocks are continually being broken down into smaller particles by forces in the environment. These processes are called **weathering**. Weathering may be brought about by:
- **physical forces**, especially in deserts and high mountains,
- **chemical reactions**, especially in warm, wet climates.

Rain

Water is an important weathering agent. Water expands when it freezes. If water enters a crack in a rock and then freezes, it will force the crack to open wider. When the ice thaws, water will penetrate further into the rock. After cycles of freeze and thaw, pieces of rock will break off.

Water reacts with some minerals, like mica. The reaction produces tiny particles which are easily transported away and deposited as a sediment of mud or clay.

LOOK AT LINKS
for the **water cycle**
see Theme E, Topic 22.1.

Rivers and streams

Rivers and streams carry water back to the oceans as part of the **water cycle**. A fast-flowing stream can carry a lot of particles in suspension (see Figure 2.7A). A very fast stream can push sand and pebbles along with it.

Running water causes erosion. The bed load and the suspension load rub against the bed and sides of the river channel. In addition, there are chemical reactions between water and rocks.

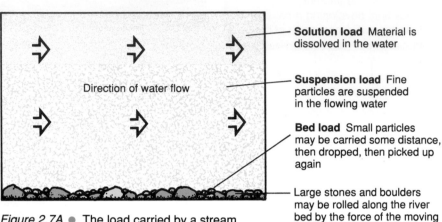

Solution load Material is dissolved in the water

Suspension load Fine particles are suspended in the flowing water

Bed load Small particles may be carried some distance, then dropped, then picked up again

Large stones and boulders may be rolled along the river bed by the force of the moving water

Figure 2.7A ● The load carried by a stream

SUMMARY

Some of the weathering processes are:
- expanding ice breaks up rock
- water breaks up some minerals, e.g. mica, and dissolves others
- running water brings about erosion.

Sediments are deposited when rivers lose speed: on the inside curve of river bends and where rivers flow into lakes and seas.

● *Deposition*

Rivers deposit the sand and gravel which they carry. The deposits form when rivers lose speed:
- on the inside curves of river beds,
- when a river flows into the sea or a lake.

TRY THIS

Accelerated weathering

1 Find a small screw-top bottle. Fill it completely with water, and screw on the cap. Place the bottle inside a plastic bag, and tie the bag. Place the bottle in a freezer, and leave it overnight.
   What happens? What has this to do with weathering?
2 Take 4 pieces of sandstone. Soak two pieces in water, and leave the other two dry. Place all four pieces in a freezer, and treat them as shown in the table.

Piece	Wet or dry	Treatment
1	Dry	Leave in the freezer for two weeks.
2	Dry	Take out every day for two hours; then replace.
3	Wet	Leave in the freezer for two weeks.
4	Wet	Take out every day, allow to thaw and replace.

What do you observe? What conclusions about weathering can you draw from your observation?

Underground water

LOOK AT LINKS
for **underground caverns**
see Theme E, Topic 22.

SUMMARY

Underground water reacts with limestone and other rocks to form soluble compounds. In time, underground caverns are formed.

Water can pass through certain kinds of rocks. It can seep through joints in beds of sedimentary rock. Such rocks, like limestone, are described as **permeable**. Other rocks, like sandstone, have tiny spaces between their mineral grains which allow water to enter. These rocks are **porous**.

Water held in rocks below the surface is called **ground water**. Some of it finds a way back to the surface to become a **spring**. Some of it remains as an underground reserve. About one third of the UK water supply is drawn from ground water.

Rain water causes weathering of rocks. This happens also below ground. Rain water permeates the ground and dissolves some minerals; gypsum is dissolved by rain. The acid in rain water reacts with limestone to form soluble compounds. Small openings in the rock become wider and in time form large underground passages which carry underground rivers and streams. When you visit **underground caves** you walk along dried-up river beds.

The sea

Erosion by the sea is illustrated in Figure 2.7B. The cave has been gouged out by waves at a weak point in the cliff, e.g. a joint. The arch has been formed by two caves meeting back to back. The sea stack has been left where the top of an arch has fallen away.

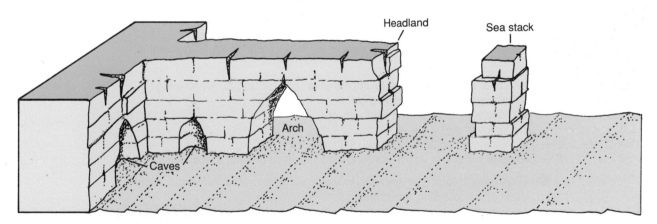

Headland   Sea stack

Arch

Caves

Figure 2.7B ● Landscaping by the sea

Glaciers

In some regions the temperature is low enough for snow to exist all the year round. As layers of snow build up, the lower levels become compressed into a mass of solid ice. When the ice begins to move under the influence of gravity, a **glacier** develops. Glaciers move slowly downhill, usually at less than 1 m/day. As glacial ice moves over a land surface, it wears down rocks by:

- **plucking**, freezing round pieces of rock and carrying them along,
- **grinding**, wearing down the rocks over which it is moving by means of the sharp rocks which become attached to the bottom of the glacier.

When a glacier melts, all the material which it carries is deposited.

Figure 2.7C ● Glacier

Wind

In dry desert regions, wind is a landscaping agent, for example in shaping sand dunes. Moisture holds particles of sand and soil together and makes it much more difficult for the wind to remove them. In moist regions, plants grow, and their roots bind the soil, making it much more difficult to erode.

SUMMARY

Forces which mould the landscape are:
• Rain, causing the formation of cracks in rock when it freezes
• Rivers and streams, transporting and depositing rock fragments
• Underground water, dissolving soluble minerals, e.g. gypsum, and reacting with limestone and other rocks to form soluble substances
• The sea, eroding rocks
• Glaciers, plucking rocks from the landscape and grinding land surfaces
• Wind, eroding sand and soil, especially in dry regions.

Figure 2.7D ● Sand dunes

CHECKPOINT

❶ Which of the following are needed for the formation of a glacier?
(a) mountains (b) steep-sided valleys (c) heavy snowfall (d) heavy rainfall
(e) low temperatures

❷ Which of the following are examples of (a) erosion and (b) weathering?
(i) Waves breaking against a cliff.
(ii) Rocks splitting after a cold winter.
(iii) Soil carried by the wind.
(iv) Sand carried along the bed of a river.
(v) The surface of a rock cracking after repeated heating and cooling.

❸ What kind of rock (sedimentary, igneous or metamorphic) is formed under each of the following conditions?
(a) Fragments of rock are formed by the action of frost and fall to the foot of a mountain.
(b) Particles of clay come out of suspension in still water.
(c) Dead plants sink to the bottom of a swamp.
(d) Shells and shell fragments are rolled along a sea floor.

FIRST THOUGHTS

2.8 The geological time scale

Geologists can date the different layers of rocks which they unearth. Inspecting the fossils which they find helps, and the radioactivity of the rock tells a story.

Figure 2.8A shows the **geological column**. It divides Earth's history (4600 million years) into **eras**. Each era is divided into **periods**. Human life evolved in the Quaternary period. When geologists describe a rock as being of the Silurian age, they mean that the rock was formed between 435 and 395 million years ago. It was during the Pre-Cambrian period that the Earth's crust solidified, oceans and atmospheres developed, and the first living organisms appeared.

Fossils

Geologists are able to say what period a rock dates from by examining the fossils that the rock contains. Fossils are the preserved remains of or marks made by dead plants and animals (see Figure 2.8B). If a rock contains the imprints of the shells of creatures known to have been living 300 million years ago, the rock may be Carboniferous.

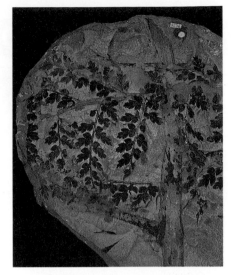

Figure 2.8B ● Carboniferous fossils

Relative dating

Relative dating does not give the age of rocks but enables you to classify them (arrange them) in order of age. If one sedimentary rock lies above another, it is very likely that the upper rock is younger than the lower one (although folding of the rocks can reverse the order). Fragments of rock included in another rock must be older than the rock that surrounds them.

Dating from radioactivity

Some elements are **radioactive**. They have unstable atoms which split up (decay) to form atoms of stable elements. Imagine that a rock contains the radioactive element A, which decays very slowly to form element B. Then the ratio of B to A in the rock increases as the years go by. A measurement of the ratio of B to A will give the length of time for which A has been decaying, that is, the age of the rock. It is by radioactive dating that the age of Earth has been established as 4600 million years.

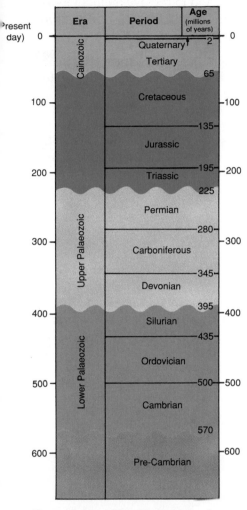

Figure 2.8A ● The geological column

CHECKPOINT

1 A geologist made a sketch of the beds of rock in a quarry (see the figure below). He tabulated the fossils which he found in the four layers of rock.

Layer	A	B	C	D	E	F
1	✓		✓	✓		
2	✓			✓	✓	✓
3	✓	✓		✓	✓	
4		✓		✓	✓	

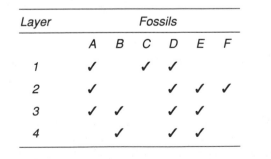

(a) Which fossil is found in all 4 layers?
(b) Which fossil is found only in the youngest limestone?
(c) Which fossil can be used to give the age of layer 2? Explain your answer.

LIFE ON EARTH

3.1 Earth as a place to live

FIRST THOUGHTS

Earth is home to millions of different kinds of living things. It seems likely that none of the other planets in the solar system support life.

What is it about Earth that enables it to support life? One factor is the distance between Earth and the Sun. Earth is close enough to the Sun for its surface temperature to be in the range in which life can exist. The energy of sunlight is converted by living things into the energy which they need for their life processes.

The size of Earth is a factor. It is massive enough to have a sufficiently large gravity to hold down an atmosphere. The gases oxygen, nitrogen, carbon dioxide and water vapour are essential for living organisms and are present in the air on Earth's surface.

Several factors combine to keep the temperature at the surface of Earth at an average of 30 °C.

- The distance of Earth from the Sun.
- The layer of ozone which surrounds Earth prevents too much ultraviolet light from the Sun reaching Earth. (Too much ultraviolet light destroys living organisms.)
- The layer of carbon dioxide and water vapour which blankets Earth prevents too much heat radiating from Earth into space. Without it, the temperature at the surface of Earth would be –30 °C.

There are at least 35 million different kinds of living organism on Earth. Their variety of appearance is enormous, as you will see in later sections of this topic. All living things, however, share certain characteristics, which non-living things do not. These are the **characteristics of life**.

IT'S A FACT

The first living things on Earth were probably simple bacteria like organisms. They originated about 4000 million years ago. The human race appeared about 3 million years ago.

LOOK AT LINKS
The characteristics of living organisms are:
1. They **move**; for **movement** see Topic 41.
2. They **feed**; for **nutrition** see Topic 25.
3. They **respire**; for **respiration** see Topic 26.
4. They **grow**; for **growth** see Topics 25 and 39.
5. They **excrete** waste products; for **excretion** see Topic 27.
6. They **reproduce**; for **reproduction** see Topic 39.
7. They are **sensitive to stimuli**; for **sensitivity** see Topic 40.

Figure 3.1A ● The Earth from space – 71% of the planet's surface is covered by water!

////////// **CHECKPOINT** //////////

❶ What would happen to the Earth's water if Earth were (a) nearer to and (b) further from the Sun?

❷ The Moon is about the same distance from the Sun as Earth is. The Moon is not massive enough to hold down an atmosphere. How does this affect the possibility of finding life on the Moon?

❸ **Mrs Gren** will help you remember the characteristics of living organisms. Complete the names of these processes which occur in living things.
M _____   R _____   S _____
G _____   R _____   E _____   N _____

❹ An aeroplane moves, it has to be 'fed' with fuel, and it gives out waste products. Do these characteristics prove that an aeroplane is alive? Explain your answer.

3.2 Variety of life

FIRST THOUGHTS

Have you ever thought about how many different living things there are in a garden? As you read about the variety of life think about:
- the large number of species of living things that we have named,
- the even greater estimate of the number of species awaiting discovery,
- using biological keys to identify living things.

Will we ever know all the species (a species is a particular type of living thing) of life on Earth? So far we know of about 5 million species but this figure is only a fraction of the millions of species that biologists estimate are awaiting discovery.

For example, techniques of collecting insects from the tops of trees in tropical rain forests lead us to believe that over 30 million new insect species are living in the leaves, branches, flowers and fruit.

IT'S A FACT

Over 600 new species of beetle have been discovered living in just one type of tree that grows in the rainforests of Costa Rica.

Figure 3.2A ● Machines make a fog of insecticide that knocks down insects living in the trees. They fall down the funnels into the collecting jars beneath. The catch is examined later on in the laboratory. After careful work new discoveries are given names and added to the list of species already known.

Figure 3.2B ● A deciduous wood

Using keys

How many kinds of living thing can you see in Figure 3.2B? You can see from the picture that leaves from trees litter the ground with a thick carpet of dead organic material. Leaf litter is a rich source of food and home for many small animals. Specimens collected from leaf litter can be grouped according to their appearance and structure. Each description is a clue that helps to identify a particular group of animals found in leaf litter. We call a set of clues a **key**.

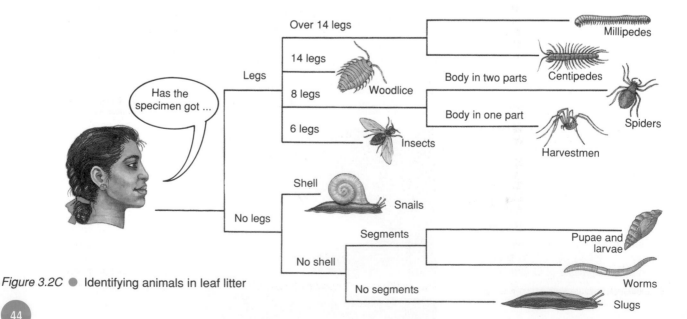

Figure 3.2C ● Identifying animals in leaf litter

IT'S A FACT

False scorpions are common in leaf litter but they are well hidden and very small (about 1–2.5 mm long) and little is known about them. False scorpions are relatives of true scorpions (together with spiders, harvestmen and mites) but they do not have a sting in the tail.

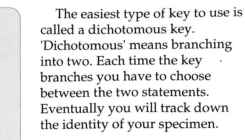

The easiest type of key to use is called a dichotomous key. 'Dichotomous' means branching into two. Each time the key branches you have to choose between the two statements. Eventually you will track down the identity of your specimen.

TRY THIS

Naming names

Amphibians are **vertebrates** (animals with backbones) that spend part of their lives on land and the rest of the time in water. Identify each of the illustrated specimens using the key on the next page, then draw a table by putting the correct letter against each name for all of the specimens.

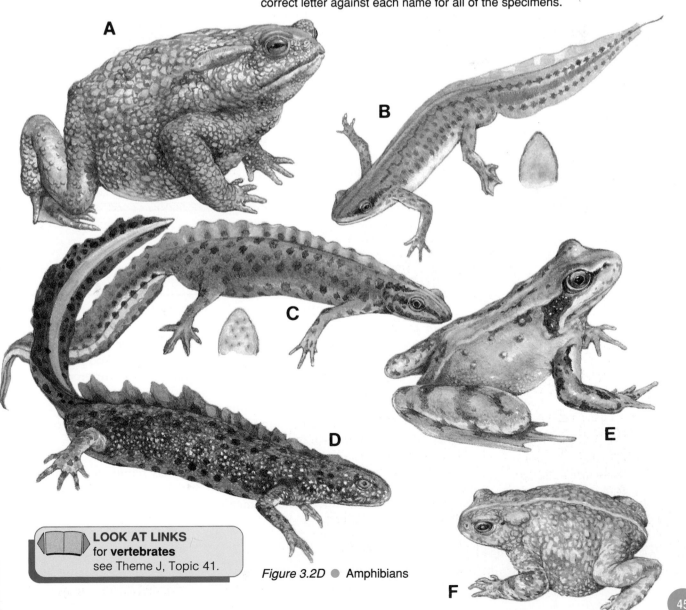

LOOK AT LINKS
for **vertebrates**
see Theme J, Topic 41.

Figure 3.2D ● Amphibians

● *Key to Amphibians*

1	The animal has a tail	**Newts**	go to 2
	The animal has no tail	**Frogs and toads**	go to 3
2	The newt has a rough warty skin, is dark brown with dark spots on top and has a yellow or orange belly blotched with black markings	**Great crested (warty) newt**	
	The newt has a smooth skin, is green or brownish in colour with or without dark spots; belly is yellow or orange and may be spotted; 10 cm or less in length	**Smooth or palmate newt**	go to 4
3	The animal has a smooth, moist skin and a dark flash behind the eye	**Common frog**	
	The animal has a warty skin and no dark flash behind the eye	**Toads**	go to 5
4	The throat is whitish and spotted	**Smooth newt**	
	The throat is pinkish and unspotted	**Palmate newt**	
5	The toad has a yellow stripe running down the middle of the back	**Natterjack toad**	
	There is no yellow stripe running down the middle of the back	**Common toad**	

A key in biology, therefore, is a guide to a name. Different keys are used to name different living things.

SUMMARY

Although about 5 million species of living thing have been described, millions more are estimated to await discovery, especially in tropical rain forests. Making a collection of living things in the environment will give an idea of life's variety. Biological keys help us to identify them.

CHECKPOINT

❶ Look at Figure 3.2A. Briefly describe the method being used to investigate the wildlife living in tropical treetops.

❷ What is leaf litter?

❸ (a) What is a biological key used for?
   (b) Suggest why certain characteristics like size, exact colour and mass are not suitable for keys.

3.3 What's in a name?

FIRST THOUGHTS

What's in a name?
This section emphasises the importance of biological names. As you read it think about:
• the confusion caused by having the same name for different living things and different names for the same living thing,
• Carolus Linnaeus who cleared up the confusion by defining each type of living thing with a species name,
• the meaning of 'species'.

Sometimes a living thing has several different names which describe it. For example, the plant shown in Figure 3.3A is called 'cuckoo pint', 'lords and ladies', 'parson-in-the-pulpit' and 'wake-robin' in different parts of the country.

On the other hand different living things are sometimes given the same name. For example, the robin in the USA is different from the robin in the UK. They are shown in Figure 3.3B. *List some of the differences between the two birds.*

If living things were known only by their everyday names, you can imagine the confusion there would be when British and American ornithologists (an ornithologist is someone who studies birds) spoke to each other about 'robins'.

Figure 3.3A ● Cuckoo pint

Figure 3.3B ●
a) The North American robin

b) The British robin

IT'S A FACT

A mule is the hybrid offspring from a mating between a horse and a donkey.

SUMMARY

The Swedish naturalist Carolus Linnaeus introduced the idea of the species. Each type of living thing is given a species name which distinguishes it from all other types of organism.

How can people describe living things to each other and know that they are talking about the same organism?

The Swedish scientist Linnaeus tackled this question in 1735. Linnaeus' system was to give each living organism a name consisting of two parts. The first part of the name is the name of the **genus** to which the organism belongs. The second part of the name is the name of the **species** to which the organism belongs. Since each name has two parts, the Linnaeus method of naming is called the **binomial system** (from the Latin: *bis* – twice, *nomen* – a name). The genus name begins with a capital letter; the species name begins with a small letter.

To illustrate how the binomial system works look at the biological name for human beings – *Homo sapiens*. Our species name is *sapiens* (Latin for 'wise'). Our genus name is *Homo*. The other species of our genus are now extinct.

So the binomial system clears up confusion over names. For example, ornithologists can easily distinguish between the robins mentioned earlier when the birds are called by their binomial names which are *Turdus migratorius* (common name North American robin) and *Erithacus rubecula* (common name British robin).

What, then, is a species? Most biologists agree that if individuals can sexually reproduce offspring which are themselves able to reproduce, then they belong to the same species. Sometimes members of closely related species mate and produce offspring called hybrids. However, animal hybrids are usually sterile, that is they cannot reproduce.

Different species of plant also form hybrids between themselves. Unlike most animal hybrids, hybrid plants are often fertile and able to produce offspring. This throws open the question 'What is a species?', to which there is no entirely satisfactory answer.

 **CHECKPOINT**

❶ Who was Linnaeus? Explain how his binomial system of biological names works.

❷ What is a hybrid? Use a named example in your explanation.

3.4 Classification

Why is it important to classify living things? Here are some points to think about:
- classification as a way of organising living things into groups,
- groups within groups,
- classification making sense of the variety of life.

Linnaeus' system is more than just a list of names cataloguing the variety of life on Earth. Linnaeus believed that as many characteristics as possible should be used to describe species, rather like the way we use characteristics to describe a type of car. Some characteristics are unique to the species but others are shared with other species. This means that species which have characteristics in common can be put together into groups.

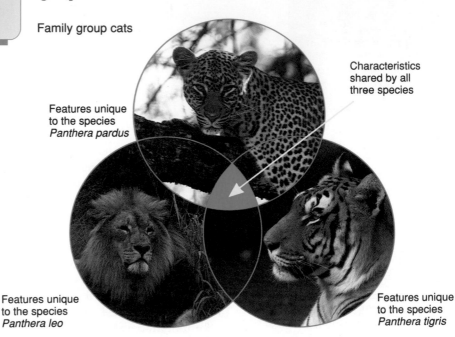

Family group cats

Characteristics shared by all three species

Features unique to the species *Panthera pardus*

Features unique to the species *Panthera leo*

Features unique to the species *Panthera tigris*

Figure 3.4A ● Unique features describe each species: shared features unite cats into a larger family group

Organising living things into groups means that we don't need to know everything about every species to be able to identify them. For example, we do not have to know about every insect species to know what an insect looks like!

Groups within groups

Groups can be combined to form larger groups. The cats (Figure 3.4A) are a **family** which belong to the **order** called carnivores. Also included in the order carnivores are dog, bear, seal and sealion. The carnivores and other orders are members of the **subclass** placentals, which is one of the **class** mammals.

Organising things into groups is called **classification**. Figure 3.4B. shows the classification of cats. It also shows that cats are part of a still larger group called a **phylum**. In this phylum mammals are grouped with fish, amphibians, reptiles and birds. All these animals have a feature in common – a backbone. Animals with backbones are called **vertebrates**.

Phyla (plural of phylum) come together in the largest group used in classification of all – the **kingdom**. For example, phylum 'vertebrates' along with 32 other phyla are grouped in the animal kingdom.

SUMMARY

Living things which have features in common are grouped together. The groups are named according to Linnaeus' system of classification, which creates groups within groups. This helps us to make sense of life's variety without having to know all about every living thing.

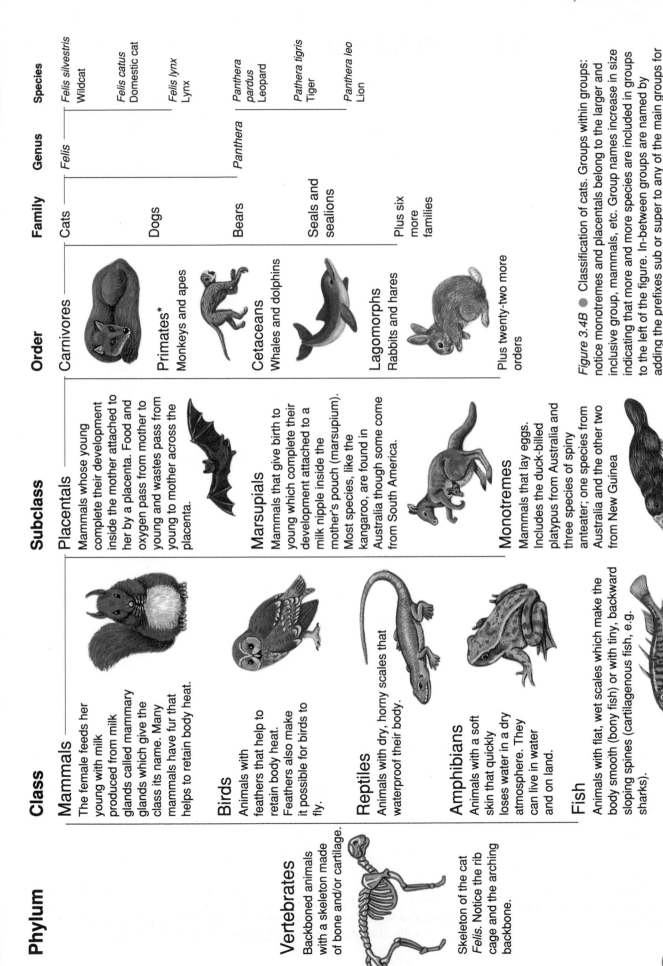

Phylum

Vertebrates
Backboned animals with a skeleton made of bone and/or cartilage.

Skeleton of the cat *Felis*. Notice the rib cage and the arching backbone.

Class

Mammals
The female feeds her young with milk produced from milk glands called mammary glands which give the class its name. Many mammals have fur that helps to retain body heat.

Birds
Animals with feathers that help to retain body heat. Feathers also make it possible for birds to fly.

Reptiles
Animals with dry, horny scales that waterproof their body.

Amphibians
Animals with a soft skin that quickly loses water in a dry atmosphere. They can live in water and on land.

Fish
Animals with flat, wet scales which make the body smooth (bony fish) or with tiny, backward sloping spines (cartilagenous fish, e.g. sharks).

Subclass

Placentals
Mammals whose young complete their development inside the mother attached to her by a placenta. Food and oxygen pass from mother to young and wastes pass from young to mother across the placenta.

Marsupials
Mammals that give birth to young which complete their development attached to a milk nipple inside the mother's pouch (marsupium). Most species, like the kangaroo, are found in Australia though some come from South America.

Monotremes
Mammals that lay eggs. Includes the duck-billed platypus from Australia and three species of spiny anteater; one species from Australia and the other two from New Guinea

Order

Carnivores

Primates*
Monkeys and apes

Cetaceans
Whales and dolphins

Lagomorphs
Rabbits and hares

Plus twenty-two more orders

Family

Cats

Dogs

Bears

Seals and sealions

Plus six more families

Genus

Felis

Panthera

Species

Felis silvestris
Wildcat

Felis catus
Domestic cat

Felis lynx
Lynx

Panthera pardus
Leopard

Pathera tigris
Tiger

Panthera leo
Lion

Figure 3.4B ● Classification of cats. Groups within groups: notice monotremes and placentals belong to the larger and inclusive group, mammals, etc. Group names increase in size indicating that more and more species are included in groups to the left of the figure. In-between groups are named by adding the prefixes sub or super to any of the main groups for a more detailed classification.

* Our order – humans are primates and close relatives of apes.

49

CHECKPOINT

❶ With the help of Figure 3.4A explain why organising living things into groups helps us to understand them.

❷ What does the word 'arthropods' mean literally?

❸ The diagram shows a plan for organising living things into groups. Copy the diagram and use the words provided to fill in the blank spaces. Kingdom and Family have been filled in to show the idea.

species   class   order   genus   phylum

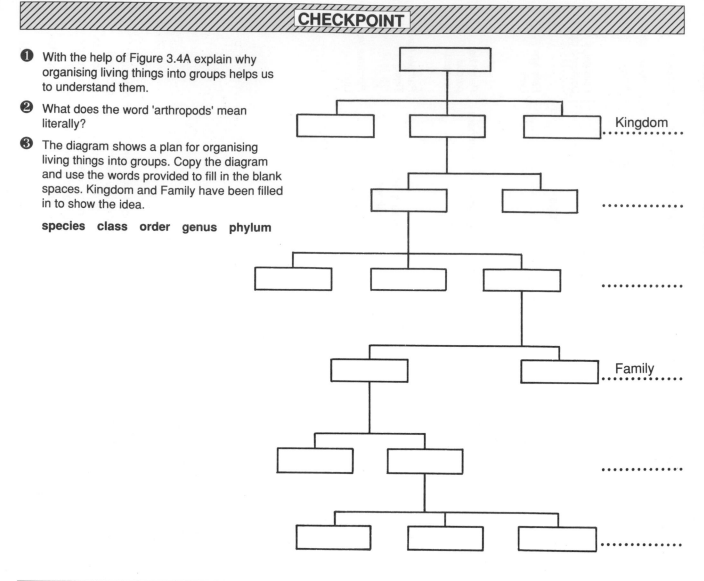

3.5   Five Kingdoms

FIRST THOUGHTS

The largest grouping of animals is the kingdom. Here we review the five kingdoms. As you read, think about:
- each kingdom, representing a way of life shared by all its members,
- the size of living things, ranging from the very small to the very large,
- how living things are adapted for their way of life.

There are five kingdoms. Living things in each kingdom obtain food in different ways. Their structure and body chemistry are different. Each kingdom, therefore, represents a way of life which all of its members share. This helps us to learn about the wide variety of living things. (See Figure 3.5A)

The organisms pictured in Figure 3.5B are not drawn to scale. They vary in size from single-celled bacteria only just visible under a light microscope to the giant redwoods (*Sequoiadendron giganteum*) which tower into the sky. The wide range of size of living things, from the very small to the very large is shown.

The Five Kingdoms

		Bacteria	Protists	Fungi	Plants	Animals
Cell Structures	Nucleus	Absent.	Present.	Present.	Present.	Present.
	Cell wall	Made of different polysaccharides (not cellulose).	Of different types in different species.	Made of polysaccharide (mainly chitin).	Made of polysaccharide (mainly cellulose).	Absent.
	Chloroplasts	Absent (although chlorophyll is found in some species).	Present in some species.	Absent.	Present.	Absent.
Bodies		Single-celled (unicellular) although clusters or chains of identical cells may form.	Most species are single-celled though some are made of many cells of different types (multicellular).	Nearly all species are multicellular although a few are unicellular.	All species are multicellular.	All species are multicellular.
Food		Some species make their own food by photosynthesis. Some species are parasites; they live off other living things. Some species are saprophytes. They secrete enzymes which digest plant and animal material and then absorb the digested food. Saprophytes cause decay and decomposition.	Some species make food by photosynthesis. Some species take in food from their environment in different ways and digest it in the body. A few species make food by photosynthesis and take it in from their surroundings.	Most species are saprophytes. Hyphae secrete enzymes onto organic material which once digested is absorbed. This causes decay and decomposition. Some species are parasites.	All species make their own food by photosynthesis.	All species take in food from the environment and digest it inside the body. Exceptions are parasites like the tapeworm which absorbs the semi-digested food of its host.

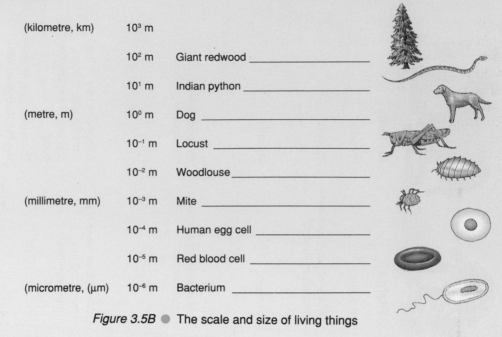

(kilometre, km)	10^3 m		
	10^2 m	Giant redwood _____	
	10^1 m	Indian python _____	
(metre, m)	10^0 m	Dog _____	
	10^{-1} m	Locust _____	
	10^{-2} m	Woodlouse _____	
(millimetre, mm)	10^{-3} m	Mite _____	
	10^{-4} m	Human egg cell _____	
	10^{-5} m	Red blood cell _____	
(micrometre, (μm)	10^{-6} m	Bacterium _____	

Figure 3.5B ● The scale and size of living things

Kingdom Bacteria

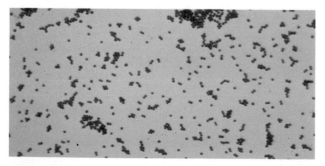

Vibrios are comma-shaped bacteria. The photograph shows *Desulfovibrio desulfuricans* which releases sulphur into the environment. If the bacteria are living in water rich in iron compounds, the sulphur they release reacts to form iron sulphide which glitters like gold (iron sulphide is called 'fool's gold').

Cocci bacteria are spherical in shape and may stick together in pairs, chains or clusters as illustrated opposite. The photograph illustrates *Staphylococcus aureus* which causes boils and food poisoning.

FACT FILE

- Bacteria are single celled organisms or organisms made up of chains or clusters of similar cells.
- They are called micro-organisms because they are only visible under the microscope.
- Their cell body has no distinct nucleus.
- Bacteria are found everywhere: in water, in the air and in the soil. They also live on and in other organisms.
- The cell shape helps to identify different types of bacteria.

BODY FACTS

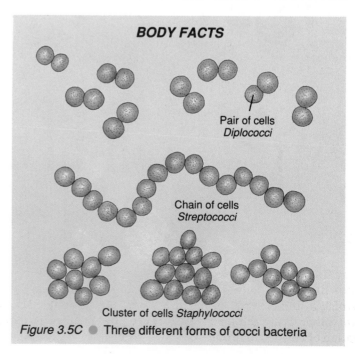

Pair of cells
Diplococci

Chain of cells
Streptococci

Cluster of cells *Staphylococci*

Figure 3.5C ● Three different forms of cocci bacteria

Careful study of pages 52 to 71 will help you to understand the way of life of different organisms from each kingdom. Some of the organisms will be familiar to you; others will not. Many have been selected because they are easy to obtain and study. Each of the sections on particular kingdoms and phyla contains a fact file, body file and food file on representative organisms of that group. The files list important characteristics of the organisms shown, give details of their appearance and describe how they feed.

Kingdom Bacteria

FOOD FACTS

Most bacteria are **saprophytes** and are responsible for decay and decomposition. Bacterial cells secrete enzymes which convert dead organic matter and dead organisms into food which the cells absorb. Some bacteria are parasites, that is they live by feeding on the tissues of other organisms. Bacteria which cause disease belong to this group. Other bacteria can obtain their food through photosynthesis or by making use of chemicals like sulphur and hydrogen sulphide which they extract from the environment.

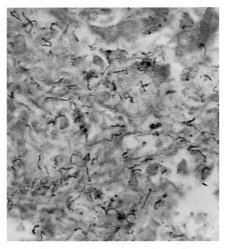

Spirilla bacteria look like tightly coiled springs. The photograph shows *Treponema pallidum* which causes the **sexually transmitted disease**, syphilis.

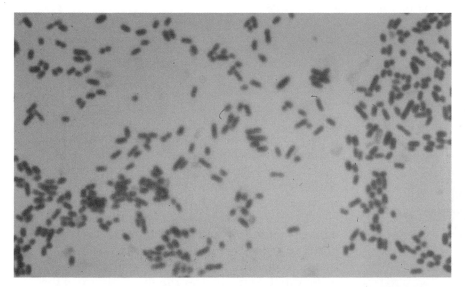

Bacilli bacteria are rod-shaped and can form into filaments of cells that look like the hyphae of fungi. The photograph shows *Escherichia coli* which is found in the human intestine. More is known about *E.coli* than any other living thing because it is used by scientists to investigate a wide range of biological problems.

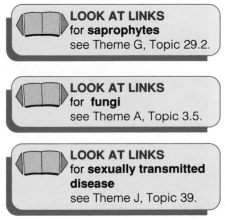

LOOK AT LINKS
for **saprophytes**
see Theme G, Topic 29.2.

LOOK AT LINKS
for **fungi**
see Theme A, Topic 3.5.

LOOK AT LINKS
for **sexually transmitted disease**
see Theme J, Topic 39.

Kingdom Protists

TRY
THIS

Place some filaments of *Spirogyra* on a microscope slide and cover them with a few drops of water. Put a cover slip in place and examine the filaments under the low-power objective of a microscope. Draw what you see and label the cell wall and chloroplast.

LOOK AT LINKS
for **calcium carbonate**
The importance of the delicate shells of these amoebas is described in the carbon cycle.
See Theme E, Topic 20.6.

FACT FILE

- Protists include both single celled organisms and also organisms made of filaments of cells.
- Their cell bodies have distinct nuclei.
- Protists are neither animals, plants, fungi nor bacteria.

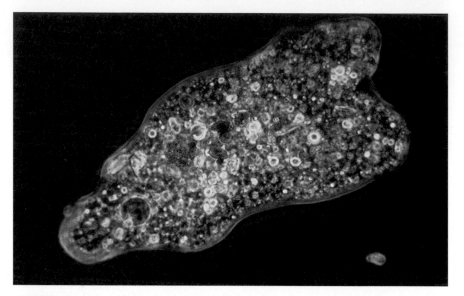

Amoeba lives in ponds and ditches. Flowing extensions (called pseudopodia: literally meaning 'false feet') of its single-celled body change its shape. Movement occurs when they flow in a particular direction. The name *Amoeba* describes all single-celled organisms that have pseudopodia. The bodies of some are surrounded by delicate shells of **calcium carbonate**. Some types of amoeba are parasites and can cause dysentery in their animal hosts.

RESOURCE
ACTIVITY
PACK

Bladder wrack is a brown seaweed, common along the sea shore. Its body is made of branched, flat fronds. The holdfast at the end of the short stalk holds the seaweed in place on exposed rocks. Pairs of air-filled sacs (called bladders, hence the common name) help the plant to float when it is covered in water. The whole plant is limp and slimy to touch. These features protect it against the action of waves. The limp seaweed can bend and sway in the moving water and water can flow freely over the slimy surface of the fronds.

Kingdom Protists

BODY FACTS

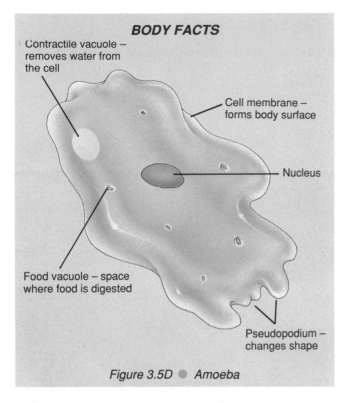

Contractile vacuole – removes water from the cell

Cell membrane – forms body surface

Nucleus

Food vacuole – space where food is digested

Pseudopodium – changes shape

Figure 3.5D ● Amoeba

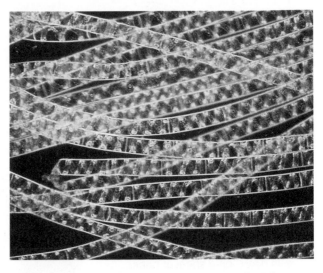

Spirogyra forms filaments of cells joined end to end. The filaments make a green tangled mat on the surface of ponds. Each cell is surrounded by a wall made of cellulose which in turn is surrounded by a layer of slimy substance called mucilage. A chloroplast winds in a spiral against the inner wall of each cell, giving *Spirogyra* its name.

FOOD FACTS

The diagram shows how *Amoeba* captures its food. Pseudopodia flow around the food particle which *Amoeba* detects by sensing the chemicals released into the water by the food. The pseudopodia join around the food particle and a food vacuole forms in the cell body. Digestion takes place in the food vacuole. The method of feeding by capturing food in this way is called phagocytosis.

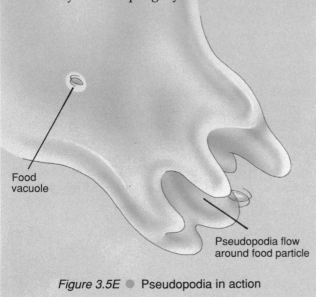

Food vacuole

Pseudopodia flow around food particle

Figure 3.5E ● Pseudopodia in action

Euglena is a single celled organism that lives in ponds and puddles, especially where there is a high level of nitrogen compounds. It has chloroplasts and therefore can photosynthesise its food. However, like *Amoeba*, it can gather food from the environment. Single cells closely related to *Euglena* do not have chloroplasts and obtain food only by feeding. Other close relatives develop chloroplasts in bright light but lose them when they are kept in the dark. *Euglena* and closely related organisms display both plant and animal characteristics. This makes it difficult to put them into either the animal or plant kingdom and they are therefore included within the protists.

Kingdom Fungi

Cut a mushroom in half longitudinally (down through the middle). Describe what you see in a few sentences. Draw the mushroom and label the cap, stalk and gills.

Make a spore print. Cut the cap off an open mushroom. Place it, gills down, on a sheet of paper, fix it there with a pin and leave it for several days. When you remove the mushroom cap there will be a pattern on the paper of spores which have fallen from the gills. A spore-print is easily spoiled if touched, but they can be sealed with a spray of clear varnish and then mounted. Look at it through a hand lens and you will see the spores more clearly. Draw what you see.

FACT FILE

- Fungi are made up of slender tubes called hyphae (singular, hypha).
- The mass of hyphae which form an individual is called the mycelium (plural, mycelia).
- Fruiting bodies produce spores. Each spore can grow and develop into a new mycelium.

Field mushroom: the fruiting body is all that we see above ground. The word 'mushroom' refers to the field mushroom which can be eaten. However, many types of so-called 'toadstool' make a good meal while others are very poisonous. So, 'mushroom' and 'toadstool' have little meaning. Mushrooms and some toadstools are edible; other toadstools are not. A few species are fatal if eaten! NEVER collect fungi for the table unless you are certain of their identification - BE SAFE NOT SORRY.

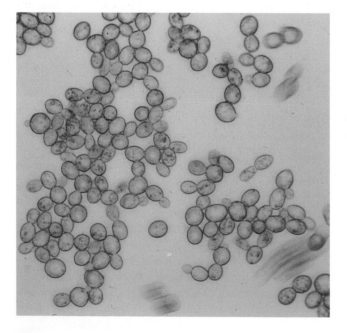

Yeasts do not grow hyphae but live as single cells. Their name *Saccharomyces* means 'sugar fungi' and they are commonly found where ever sugar occurs. For thousands of years yeast has been used to ferment the sugars in rice and barley to produce beer, and the sugar in grapes to make wine. Yeast added to dough ferments the sugar in the dough to produce carbon dioxide. This makes the dough rise.

Kingdom Fungi

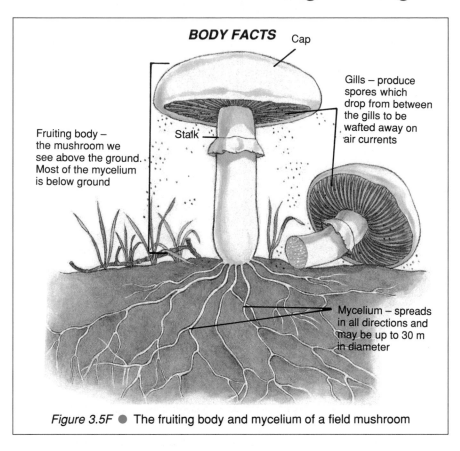

BODY FACTS

Cap

Gills – produce spores which drop from between the gills to be wafted away on air currents

Stalk

Fruiting body – the mushroom we see above the ground. Most of the mycelium is below ground

Mycelium – spreads in all directions and may be up to 30 m in diameter

Figure 3.5F ● The fruiting body and mycelium of a field mushroom

FOOD FACTS

The hyphae secrete enzymes which convert dead organic material in the soil into food which the hyphae absorb. Obtaining food in this way is called saprophytism. Most fungi are saprophytes but some are parasites, feeding on the living tissue of plants and animals.

IT'S A FACT

A lichen is a close partnership between an alga and a fungus. The algal cells grow in the fungal mycelium. They make food by photosynthesis and some of it is passed to the fungus. The fungus cannot survive without the alga. However, the alga does quite well on its own and grows even faster when free of the fungus.

Bread mould hyphae spread over and into uncovered food, spoiling it. They form a mat-like mycelium. Hyphae (called aerial hyphae) poke up into the air, each carrying a capsule-shaped fruiting body. In the picture you can see that some are black, a sign that they contain ripe spores. Soon they will burst open, releasing a cloud of spores which are carried away on the air currents. If the spores land in a suitable place they will grow into new mycelia.

Other types of mould also spoil food but some add flavour. For example, blue cheeses such as Gorgonzola, Stilton and Roquefort owe their taste to the moulds which create the blue veins in them.

The mould *Penicillium notatum* produces a substance which can destroy bacteria. The substance, called **penicillin**, is an antibiotic used to fight diseases caused by bacteria.

RESOURCE ACTIVITY PACK

Plant Kingdom 1: Spore-producing plants

FACT FILE

- The plants reproduce by means of spores.
- Water is needed for the sperm to swim to the eggs.
- Spore-producing plants live on land in damp habitats.

Mosses quickly lose water in a dry atmosphere, so the plants live in damp places such as the banks of streams and the woodland floor where the air is moist. They cannot draw water from the ground as ferns and seed-producing plants do. They rely on capillary action to soak up water like a sponge. Closely fitting leaves help the capillary movement of water. This mechanism for water collection limits the plant's size. The tallest species of moss is only about 40 cm high and most are much shorter.

In summer, stalks grow from the moss plants, each carrying a capsule which contains spores. When ripe the capsule opens and the spores are shaken out to be carried away on air currents. If spores land on damp soil, they develop into new moss plants.

Plant Kingdom 1: Spore-producing plants

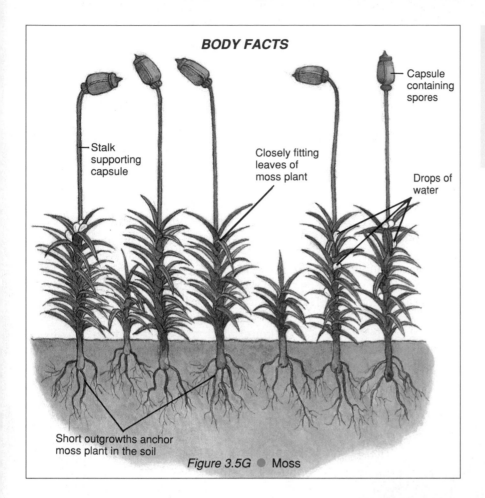

BODY FACTS

Stalk supporting capsule

Closely fitting leaves of moss plant

Capsule containing spores

Drops of water

Short outgrowths anchor moss plant in the soil

Figure 3.5G ● Moss

FOOD FACTS

Moss leaves are thin and delicate, each made up of only a few layers of cells. Chloroplasts in the cells of the leaves make food by photosynthesis.

Ferns have clumps of leaves called fronds which grow near the top of a thick stem. Roots sprout from the base of each clump, anchoring the plant firmly into the soil. Each leaf is built up of leaflets called pinnae which stand out on either side of a sturdy rib that runs through the centre of the leaf. Each leaflet is further subdivided into lobe-shaped pinnules.

A double row of greenish-white patches develops on the underside of the pinnae. Each patch consists of a group of spore-producing capsules which darken as the spores mature. When ripe, the capsules break open and the spores shoot out to be carried away on air currents.

A waxy layer waterproofs the plant's surfaces, reducing water loss. Ferns can live in a drier environment than moss, although it grows best in damp, shady places. Tissues in the roots, stem and leaves draw water from the soil and carry it to all parts of the plant. They also strengthen and support the plant which is much bigger than the moss plant, growing to a height of a metre or more.

Plant Kingdom 2: Seed-producing plants

FACT FILE

- Plants reproduce by means of seed which protects the embryo plant from drying out on land.
- The sperm of seed-producing plants is transported to the eggs by pollen grains.
- Very successful land plants are able to live in dry, hot places where there is little water.

Beech trees are widespread on gentle slopes and low lying land. They are woody plants with massive trunks covered with smooth bark and bearing a crown of thick branches which carry leaves. New wood grows every year, increasing the girth of the tree. A cross-section of a tree trunk shows rings for each year's growth. Counting the annual rings will tell you the age of the tree. The beech tree's growth is greatest in the spring. Every autumn its broad leaves are shed. Plants that lose their leaves in this way are described as **deciduous**. Beech trees are **perennial**; that is they keep on growing and producing seeds for many years. A beech tree can live for 200 years or more.

Buttercup grows in meadows and unimproved grassland. It is a non-woody **annual**; that is it grows from seed to maturity and produces new seeds all within one growing season. It then dies with the onset of the first frosts, leaving the seed to lie dormant through the winter ready to grow when conditions improve the following spring. Non-woody plants are called **herbaceous** plants.

Plant Kingdom 2: Seed-producing plants

Scots Pine trees grow naturally in cool climates. They cover hill slopes and valleys with thick forests. The Scots Pine is a large tree with a crown of branches covered with rough scaly bark. Short shoots growing from the branches carry clusters of needle-like leaves which are lost and replaced throughout the year. This is why the Scots pine and trees like it are called **evergreens**: they are covered with leaves all year round. Cones form on young branches that grow in spring. If the tree is damaged a sticky resin oozes out from the wound and plugs it, preventing infection by disease-carrying organisms.

BODY FACTS

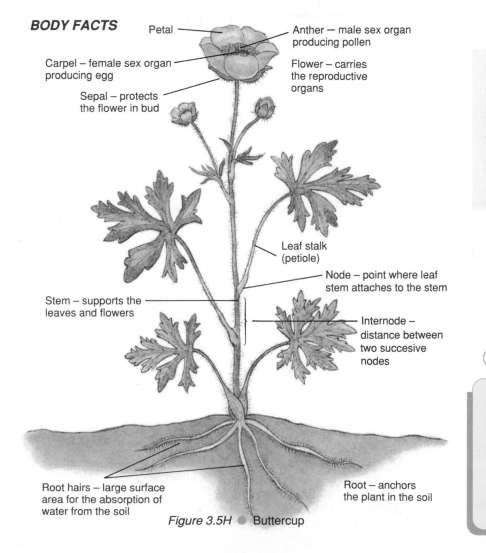

Petal

Anther — male sex organ producing pollen

Carpel – female sex organ producing egg

Flower – carries the reproductive organs

Sepal – protects the flower in bud

Leaf stalk (petiole)

Node – point where leaf stem attaches to the stem

Stem – supports the leaves and flowers

Internode – distance between two succesive nodes

Root hairs – large surface area for the absorption of water from the soil

Root – anchors the plant in the soil

Figure 3.5H ● Buttercup

FOOD FACTS

Buttercup leaves are complex structures. Each leaf is made up of different types of cell. The cells nearest the upper surface receive most light and have the most chloroplasts for photosynthesis.

IT'S A FACT

Some trees live for a very long time. For example the Cedar of Lebanon lives for up to 1000 years. However, Bristlecone pines may be much older. They grow high in the mountains of eastern California and some are believed to be over 4000 years old.

Animal Kingdom 1: Hydra and its relatives

FACT FILE

- The body shape shows radial symmetry: that is it has no front or rear and its parts are arranged evenly 'in the round'.
- Tentacles surround an opening which is both mouth and anus.
- Stinging cells are used to capture prey.

Hydra lives in ponds and water-filled ditches. It hangs from water plants and other firm surfaces and trails its tentacles in the water. The tentacles carry sting cells which can paralyse small organisms which touch them. *Hydra* can then feed on its defenceless prey.

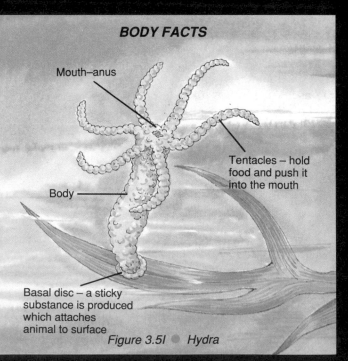

BODY FACTS

Mouth–anus

Tentacles – hold food and push it into the mouth

Body

Basal disc – a sticky substance is produced which attaches animal to surface

Figure 3.5l ● *Hydra*

FOOD FACTS

Food enters and undigested remains leave by the same opening - the mouth–anus.

Animal Kingdom 1: Hydra and its relatives

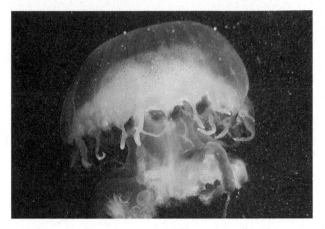

Sea anemone. The specimen in the picture is called beadlet. It lives attached to rocks in pools that are left as the tide moves down the sea-shore.

Jellyfish usually hang, bell-like, in water with the tentacles floating around the mouth. When the bell pulses in and out the water jet which is produced propels the animal through the water. Most types of jellyfish live in the sea, but a few live in ponds and streams.

Coral is made from limestone which hydra-like animals secrete around themselves. It builds up into reefs in warm sunlit seas. The Great Barrier Reef off the northeast coast of Australia is 2000 kilometres long and the world's largest reef.

IT'S A FACT

The sea blubber *Cyanea* is the largest jellyfish in the world. Its tentacles are more than 30 metres long and the bell measures over 3 metres in diameter.

IT'S A FACT

Hydra takes its name from a mythical water-snake with nine heads. An ancient Greek legend tells that the hero Hercules was sent to kill the monster. Hercules cut off each of Hydra's heads but the ninth was immortal so he rolled a huge rock over it, trapping it for ever.

TRY THIS

Looking for Hydra

Hydra lives in ponds and ditches where there are floating water lily leaves. The best time to find *Hydra* is between the months of May and October. Look at the undersides of the leaves. *Hydra* is only just visible to the naked eye, so you have to look carefully! Dab off specimens with a fine paint brush and place them in a jar filled with water from the pond.

Another way of finding *Hydra* is to scoop duckweed into a jar of pond water and leave it overnight. Look at the jar next day and specimens will probably be seen attached to the sides of the jar or hanging down from the tiny roots of the floating duckweed.

Animal Kingdom 2: Flatworms

FACT FILE

- Flatworms have flattened bodies with upper (dorsal) and lower (ventral) surfaces.
- Their body shape shows bilateral symmetry.
- Flatworm bodies have a front end (anterior) and a rear end (posterior).
- Many of the different types of flatworm are parasites.

Planaria is a flatworm which is common in ponds and streams where it lives under stones and plants. Notice the eyespots at the front end. They do not form images like our eyes but are sensitive to changes in light and shade. Other sense organs help the animal to test new environments as it moves forward.

FOOD FACTS

In Planaria the digestive cavity branches to all parts of the animal and its outline is just visible through the body wall. A part called the pharynx pokes out from the mouth–anus and captures small animals or breaks off fragments of dead larger ones. Most non-parasitic flatworms obtain their food in this way. Most parasitic flatworms feed either like the tapeworm or fluke shown here.

Fluke is a common flatworm parasite. The specimen illustrated lives in the livers of sheep and cattle. It feeds on the tissue and blood of the liver causing great damage and even death. Notice the branching digestive cavity.

Tapeworm is a common flatworm parasite that lives in the intestines of vertebrates surrounded by the host's semi-digested food. The body is long and flat and, unlike *Planaria*, made up of sections called proglottides. The front end is called the scolex and has hooks and suckers which fasten the tapeworm to the inner lining of the host's intestine. The tapeworm does not have a digestive cavity. It absorbs some of the host's semi-digested food through its body wall. Tapeworms are particular about where they live. For example, a dog tapeworm is not usually found in humans or other animals; we say that tapeworms are 'host specific'.

BODY FACTS

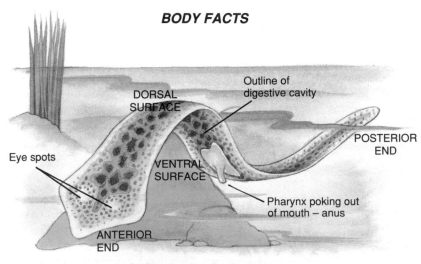

DORSAL SURFACE

Outline of digestive cavity

POSTERIOR END

Eye spots

VENTRAL SURFACE

Pharynx poking out of mouth – anus

ANTERIOR END

Figure 3.5J ● Planaria

Animal Kingdom 3: Larger worms

FACT FILE

- The body of the worm is long and thin with a distinct head end.
- The body is made up of many rings, called segments.
- The body is bilaterally symmetrical.

FOOD FACTS

The worm has a mouth at the head end and an anus at the rear end. The digestive cavity is an open tube that runs the length of the body. The means of taking in food and the means of passing out the undigested remains of a meal are separated. Food can therefore be digested and processed more efficiently than in flatworms which have only one opening to the digestive cavity.

BODY FACTS

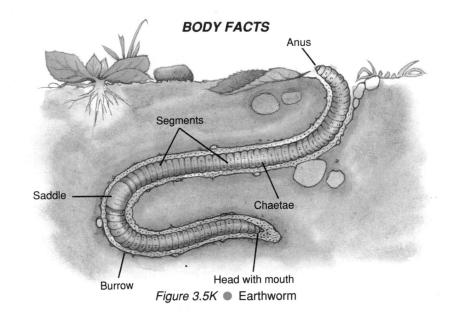

Figure 3.5K ● Earthworm

Earthworms are so-called because they live in soil. One hectare of fertile grassland may support more than seven million earthworms! A worm makes its burrow by taking in soil through its mouth. The soil is finely ground up in the intestine where any organic material is extracted for food. The remains are passed out through the anus to form a cast above ground. Notice the saddle which is formed from thickened segments. It produces envelopes of mucus. Each of these makes a protective cocoon around a fertilised egg.

Medical leeches live in ponds and streams and feed on the blood of different vertebrate hosts. The leech has suckers which fix it to the host's body. It makes a small cut in the host's skin. Blood flows freely with the help of an anti-coagulant which the leech produces. The anticoagulant stops the host's blood from clotting. A leech may take in up to five times its own weight of blood in a single meal and may not need another one for several months. When full, it drops from the host and digests the blood. Even until the nineteenth century doctors used to think that taking blood from a person who was ill would help them to recover. They used leeches to 'let blood' from the patient. This is why doctors were given the nick-name 'leeches'.

IT'S A FACT

Flatworms, probably imported in food from New Zealand, are attacking earthworms in Northern Ireland. The flatworms grow up to 15 cm long and feed on the earthworms. Scientists are trying to find ways of controlling them before the damage to earthworm populations becomes too serious.

Animal Kingdom 4: Molluscs

Although surrounded by a shell, snails are food for a variety of animals. For example, the picture shows a thrush hitting a snail against a stone to smash open the shell to get at the juicy flesh inside. The stones they use are called 'thrushes' anvils'.

FACT FILE

- The body of a mollusc is made up of a head, a foot, a mantle and a visceral mass which contains the digestive cavity and other organs.
- The mantle of a mollusc produces the shell. This is outside the body of some molluscs but is inside the body of others.
- The body shape shows bilateral symmetry.
- There is no segmentation in the body of a mollusc.

Garden snails live under stones, rotting plants and in other damp, cool places. The foot of the snail moves the animal along on a trail of slimy mucus. If disturbed, it withdraws into its protective shell. This also helps to reduce the loss of water from the body. In dry weather the snail may retreat into its shell and secrete a film of mucus (called the epiphragm) across the opening. By sealing the animal inside further water loss is avoided. When it rains the epiphragm is cast off and the snail becomes active again.

Chiton lives on the sea shore attached to rocks and stones. The shell is made of eight overlapping plates and fits over the animal. When large waves threaten a chiton's grip on its rocky platform, the animal draws the shell down around itself, sealing itself away from danger.

Animal Kingdom 4: Molluscs

BODY FACTS

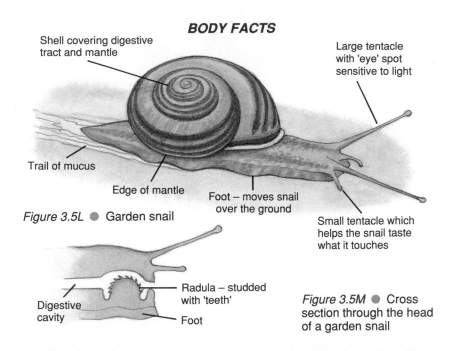

Shell covering digestive tract and mantle

Large tentacle with 'eye' spot sensitive to light

Trail of mucus

Edge of mantle

Foot – moves snail over the ground

Small tentacle which helps the snail taste what it touches

Figure 3.5L ● Garden snail

Digestive cavity

Radula – studded with 'teeth'

Foot

Figure 3.5M ● Cross section through the head of a garden snail

FOOD FACTS

Figure 3.5M is a cross-section through the head of a garden snail. It shows the radula which is a file-like tongue that the snail uses to rasp fragments of food into its mouth. All molluscs have a radula except for the molluscs that have two shells, such as mussels.

The cuttlefish is a close relative of the squid and the octopus. Its shell, which is inside the body, is called the cuttlebone. It lives in shallow water near the sea-shore, half buried in sand during the day. At night, it swims over the sea-bed in search of the crabs, fish and prawns which are its food. The siphon, or funnel, is able to produce a water jet that can propel the animal through the water in any direction at high speed. When threatened, a cuttlefish can squirt an inky liquid into the water. Under the black cloud it creates, the cuttlefish can escape unseen by predators.

Common mussels live in shallow water near the sea-shore. The mussel attaches itself by the foot to rocks and stones. Two shells close round the animal. Water is drawn through the crack where the shells meet and filtered for food. Mussels and their close relatives, oysters, are fished to provide delicacies for the dinner table.

Animal Kingdom 5: Insects and their relatives

FACT FILE

- The body of an insect is covered by a hard outer layer called the exoskeleton.
- Jointed limbs are adapted variously as legs for walking, paddles for swimming and for many other uses.
- The head and other regions of the body are formed from segments of the exoskeleton fused together.
- The insect head is well developed and has compound eyes.

The Locust shows the body features typical of most insects. It has two pairs of wings and is a strong flier. Its exoskeleton has a waxy, waterproof layer which helps to reduce the loss of water from the locust's body. This feature is so successful that locusts live in hot dry places where few other types of animal survive. All insects are waterproofed in this way, which is why there are so many of them living on land.

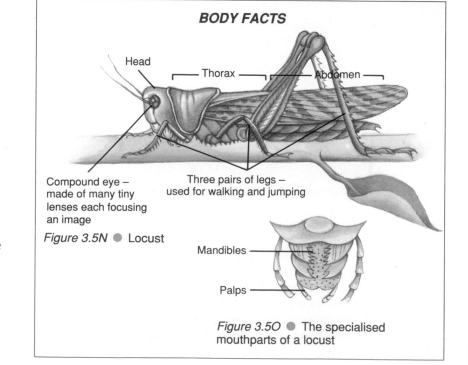

BODY FACTS

Head

Thorax

Abdomen

Compound eye – made of many tiny lenses each focusing an image

Three pairs of legs – used for walking and jumping

Figure 3.5N ● Locust

Mandibles

Palps

Figure 3.5O ● The specialised mouthparts of a locust

Animal Kingdom 5: Insects and their relatives

FOOD FACTS

Figure 3.5O shows the specialised mouthparts of a locust. The mandibles have saw-like edges which work like scissors. They cut up and chew plant food which the other mouthparts guide into the mouth. The palps help the locust to taste what it touches. Other species of insects, e.g. house fly, butterfly, have mouthparts which are specialised in different ways to utilise different food sources.

The Garden spider spins sticky webs in which it catches its prey. Not all spiders spin webs; some chase their prey, others lie hidden in wait to ambush their victims. Like that of insects, the exoskeleton of the spider is waterproofed. They can live, therefore, in hot dry places. There are two regions to the body of a spider, a fused head and thorax with four pairs of legs and no wings and an abdomen.

Crayfish live in clean, clear streams. Their body is divided into two regions, an abdomen and a fused head and thorax, with pairs of limbs adapted for swimming, catching food and other uses. Crabs, shrimps and prawns are close relatives of crayfish that live in the sea. The woodlouse is another close relative that lives on land. The woodlouse does not have the waterproof layer present in the exoskeleton of insects and spiders and is therefore restricted to living under stones, rotting wood and in other damp places.

The Centipede is carnivorous and lives on land. Like the woodlouse, it does not have a waterproof exoskeleton and is also restricted to living in damp places. The millipede, a close relative of the centipede feeds on dead leaves and other plant remains. The body is divided into a head and a trunk which carries many pairs of legs.

Animal Kingdom 6: Vertebrates

FACT FILE

- All vertebrates have a vertebral column (backbone) which runs along the dorsal (top) surface of the body.
- The backbone extends to form a tail.
- Vertebrates have internal skeletons, called endoskeletons which are most often made of bone.
- Limbs are variously adapted for swimming, walking and flying.

Lizards are reptiles and are fully adapted for life on land. Their skin is dry and covered with horny scales which restrict water loss from the body. All reptiles are waterproofed like this and so can live in hot, dry places. They lay eggs in which the young develop, protected by a hard shell. Water, therefore, is not necessary for breeding.

BODY FACTS

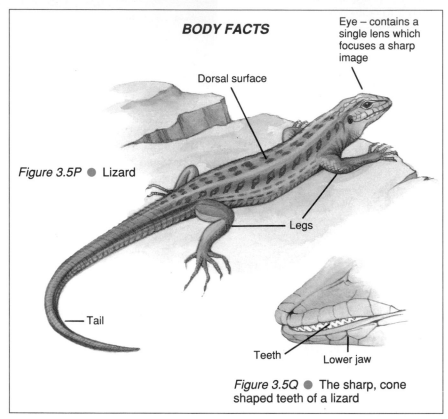

Eye – contains a single lens which focuses a sharp image

Dorsal surface

Figure 3.5P ● Lizard

Legs

Tail

Teeth

Lower jaw

Figure 3.5Q ● The sharp, cone shaped teeth of a lizard

FOOD FACTS

The cone-shaped teeth of a lizard grip and chew food. In different mammals teeth are different shapes adapted for cutting, piercing or grinding food.

Homo sapiens is a species of mammal. Us! Humans have mammalian features and characteristics. We care for our young, which the female feeds in early life with milk from her mammary glands (breasts). We have hair, which helps to conserve body heat, though we do not have as much as other mammals. We have a small tail bone called the coccyx at the base of our backbone. Most mammals move by using all four limbs, but we stand upright and our forelimbs are adapted as hands, able to carry out different tasks. Our large brains and our dexterous hands mean that we have more control over our environment than the members of any other species.

Animal Kingdom 6: Vertebrates

The Frog is an amphibian. The adult frog lives on land but breeds in water-filled ditches and ponds. Fertilised eggs hatch into swimming tadpoles which grow and develop into adults. The change from tadpole to adult is called metamorphosis. Toads and newts are also amphibians. Toads, like frogs, divide their time between water and land, but newts rarely leave the water even as adults. The frog's skin is soft and wet and in dry air the body quickly loses water. So frogs, toads and most amphibians live in wet environments.

The carp is a species of bony fish. Its skeleton is made of bone. It lives on the bottom of muddy rivers and lakes. Different species of sea-living bony fish, like cod, plaice and haddock, are important sources of food. Bony fish have a swim-bladder, a gas-filled sac that helps the fish to control its depth in the water.

Fish without a swim bladder, for example sharks and skates, use their fins to control their depth. In such fish the skeleton is made of cartilage: they are cartilaginous fish. Stroking the body of a cartilaginous fish from tail to head feels like stroking sand paper, but scales covering the body of a bony fish feel smooth. The gill flap is another feature which distinguishes the two types of fish, bony fish have them but cartilaginous fish do not.

The Pigeon is a domestic bird which is descended from the rock dove which makes its home on cliffs and craggy hills. In towns and cities, tall buildings substitute for cliffs (as far as the pigeons are concerned). Birds are covered with feathers which make flying possible and keep in body heat. Feathers are covered in oil which keeps out water and prevents them from getting waterlogged in the rain. The oil is produced from a special gland commonly called the 'parson's nose'. Instead of teeth, birds have a beak which is adapted differently in different species to deal with various types of food. Birds lay eggs protected by a hard shell, usually in a nest.

SUMMARY

Living things are organised into five kingdoms which represent different ways of life. Some living things are very small and only visible under the microscope, others are very large. All are adapted for their way of life.

CHECKPOINT

❶ Look at Figure 3.5A. With the help of named examples, summarise the different way of life represented by the five kingdoms.

❷ Compare the appearance of yeast, bread mould and the field mushroom.

❸ Why can fern plants live in a drier environment than mosses?

❹ Using the buttercup and beech tree as examples, explain the meaning of the words annual and perennial. State an important function of wood.

❺ (a) What kind of symmetry is shown by the body of (i) a mussel and (ii) a jellyfish?
   (b) Explain how the type of symmetry suits the way each animal spends its life.

❻ Snails and frogs live in water and on land. What prevents the animals losing too much water when on land?

❼ List the features that make humans mammals. Which ones help us to have more control over our lives and the environment than any other kind of living thing?

? THEME QUESTIONS

● *Topic 1*

1 (a) Copy and complete the following sentences, using the words in italics below.
At midday, the Sun reaches its _____ point in the sky. At this point, its direction is due _____ . Each day, the Sun _____ in the east and _____ in the west. The daily motion of the Sun across the sky is caused by the Earth _____ at a steady rate about an axis through its _____ .
sets   south   poles   turning   rises   highest

(b) In the figure below, which position (A, B, C or D) shows the correct position of the Earth at (i) mid-winter in the northern hemisphere, (ii) mid-spring in the northern hemisphere?

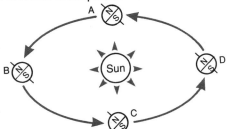

(c) Huge flocks of birds can often be seen in Britain in early winter, migrating from arctic countries. Why? What happens to these birds after each winter?

2 (a) Copy the figure below and use your sketch to show the position of the Moon when it appears as (i) a full moon, (ii) a new moon.

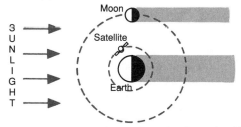

(b) A lunar eclipse takes place when the Sun, the Earth and the Moon lie in a straight line. Why do we not see a lunar eclipse every full moon?

(c) A satellite orbits the Earth once every two hours as shown above. Solar panels on board the satellite convert solar energy into electricity for the satellite's circuits.
(i) What happens to the electricity supply from these panels when the satellite passes into the Earth's shadow?
(ii) The panels are used to charge batteries on board the satellite. Why are the batteries needed?

3 The universe is about 15 000 million years old. The solar system was formed about 10 000 million years ago. The earliest traces of humans are 200 000 years old.
Suppose the age of the universe is scaled down to 24 hours. On this scale:
(a) how long ago was the solar system formed?
(b) how long ago did human life begin?

4 (a) Imagine you are planning to send a space probe to Venus.
(i) Why is it necessary to use a huge rocket to launch the probe into space?
(ii) The figure below shows the orbits of Earth and Venus. Copy the diagram and show a possible flight path from Earth to Venus.

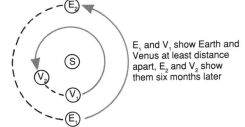

E_1 and V_1 show Earth and Venus at least distance apart, E_2 and V_2 show them six months later

(b) The atmosphere of Venus is much hotter than the Earth's atmosphere. Why?

5 (a) The Earth is an insignificant planet in orbit around a middle-aged star called the Sun. Five centuries ago, the Earth was believed to be at the centre of the universe. Outline one piece of evidence that the Earth goes round the Sun, not the Sun round the Earth.

(b) Galileo Galilei did not agree with the teaching of the Church that the Earth was at the centre of the universe. Galileo was forced to admit his 'error' in public. With your friends, write and act a short play about Galileo's show trial.

● *Topic 2*

6 A river carries material along with it, as large particles, as small particles and in solution.
(a) How does the river transport large particles, e.g. pebbles?
(b) How does the river transport fine particles, e.g. clay?
(c) When the river flows into a lake, what happens to (i) the large particles and (ii) the fine particles?
(d) Explain how (c) leads to the formation of sedimentary rocks.

7 The diagram shows part of the rock cycle.

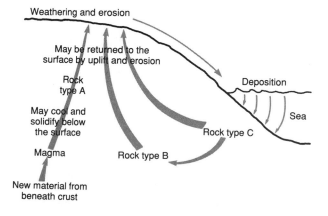

(a) What names are given to the **three types** of rock shown in the diagram?

(b) Suggest **two** features you would expect sedimentary rocks to have.

(c) Suggest **two** conditions necessary to convert sedimentary rocks to metamorphic rocks.

(d) Suggest **two** methods by which rocks at the surface might be weathered.

(e) The diagram below shows the type and structure of the rocks and the underground water level in a place where crude oil (petroleum) and natural gas (methane) are likely to be trapped. Copy the diagram and write the letter O on the diagram where you would expect crude oil to be and the letter G where you would expect natural gas to be. Show the oil level.

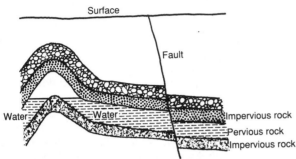

(f) The type and structure of the rocks underground can affect our lives in many ways. The following table shows two ways in which this can happen. Copy the table and add **three** more ways.

Cause	Effect
Local stone used as building material	Many local buildings have a similar appearance
Underground deposits of crude oil (petroleum)	Chemical industries have been set up in the area

(SEG)

8 Tackle this question after you have studied the water cycle (Theme E, Topic 22).

(a) Which type of rock is most likely to absorb water: igneous, sedimentary or metamorphic? Explain your answer.

(b) Describe how the types of rock in different areas can influence the water cycle.

● *Topic 3*

9 Read the descriptions of the following animal or plant groups and try to decide which group each refers to.

(a) Lays eggs with a shell on land. Have wings and feathers but no teeth.

(b) Body divided into three parts. Have antennae (feelers), six legs and wings.

(c) Have chlorophyll but only primitive roots, stems and leaves. Reproduce by means of spores.

(d) Not segmented. Body often surrounded by a shell. Move by means of a muscular 'foot'.

(e) No chlorophyll. Feed either by parasitic or saprophytic means. Reproduce by means of spores.

(f) Warm blooded. Have hair and produce milk from special glands.

10 Use the key to identify the seashore animals **A, B, C, D, E** and **F**.

❶	Animal divided into segments	Go to ❷
	Not divided into segments	Go to ❸
❷	Animal has large pincers	Lobster
	No large pincers	Centipede
❸	Animal has a shell	Go to ❹
	No shell	Go to ❺
❹	Shell with two pieces	Cockle
	Shell with one piece	Winkle
❺	Animal has five arms	Starfish
	Animal has many tentacles	Sea anemone

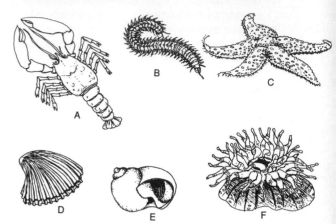

11 Decide, on the basis of their structure, which is the odd one out in each of the following lists.

(a) snail, locust, spider, centipede,

(b) mould, toadstool, seaweed, mushroom,

(c) frog, salamander, newt, lizard,

(d) carp, dolphin, shark, salmon,

(e) larch, daisy, sycamore, dandelion.

12 Use the key to identify the leaves of common trees in the diagrams below.

❶	Leaves simple (not divided into leaflets)	Go to ❷
	Leaves compound (divided into leaflets)	Go to ❺
❷	Leaves divided into five lobes	Sycamore
	Leaves not divided into five lobes	Go to ❸
❸	Edge of leaf smooth	Privet
	Edge of leaf not smooth	Go to ❹
❹	Edge of leaf toothed	Silver birch
	Edge of leaf with rounded lobes	Oak
❺	Leaflets arranged like fingers of a hand	Horse chestnut
	Leaflets paired on leaf axis	Mountain ash

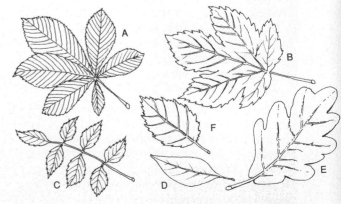

THEME B
Matter and Energy

Earth and all the other planets in the universe are made of matter. How many different kinds of matter are there? They are countless: far too many for one book to mention, but in Theme B we start to answer the question. What does matter do: how does it behave? The study of how matter behaves is called chemistry. Can one kind of matter change into a different kind of matter? The answer to the question is 'yes, it can': provided that it receives energy.

Energy enables changes to take place. The study of energy in its different forms is a major part of physics.

The ideas about matter and energy in this theme are used in later themes, such as the chemical reactions that take place inside plants and animals. The study of living things is biology. You will use your knowledge of matter and energy in your study of biological processes, such as photosynthesis and respiration

TOPIC 4 ● MATTER

4.1 ● The states of matter

What is a state of matter? How do states of matter differ? These are questions for you to explore in this topic.

Figure 4.1A ● Ice skaters

Everything you see around you is made of matter. The skaters, the skates, the ice and all the other things in Figure 4.1A are different kinds of matter.

The skaters are overcoming friction as they glide across the frozen pond. *How do they manage this?* They change one kind of matter, ice, into another kind of matter, water. A thin layer of water forms between a skate and the ice, and this reduces friction and enables the skater to glide across the pond. The water beneath the skate refreezes as the skater moves on. *How are skaters able to melt ice? Why does it refreeze behind them?* Read on to find out.

The different kinds of matter are **solid** and **liquid** and **gaseous** matter. These are called the **states of matter**. Table 4.1 summarises the differences between the three chief states of matter. The symbols (s) for solid, (l) for liquid and (g) for gas are called **state symbols**. Later you will use another state symbol, (aq), which means 'in aqueous (water) solution'.

Table 4.1 ● States of matter

State	Description
Solid (s)	Has a fixed volume and a definite shape. The shape is usually difficult to change.
Liquid (l)	Has a fixed volume. Flows easily; changes its shape to fit the shape of its container.
Gas (g)	Has neither a fixed volume nor a fixed shape; changes its volume and shape to fit the size and shape of its container. Flows easily; liquids and gases are called **fluids**. Gases are much less dense than solids and liquids.

SUMMARY

The three chief states of matter are:
- solid (s): fixed volume and shape,
- liquid (l): fixed volume; shape changes,
- gas (g): neither volume nor shape is fixed.

Liquids and gases are fluids.

4.2 Pure substances

Most of the solids, liquids and gases which you see around you are mixtures of substances.

* Rock salt, the impure salt which is spread on roads in winter, is a mixture of salt and sand and other substances.
* Crude oil is a mixture of petrol, paraffin, diesel fuel, lubricating oil and other liquids.
* Air is a mixture of gases.

Some substances, however, consist of one substance only. Such substances are **pure substances**. For example, from the mixture of substances in rock salt chemists can obtain pure salt which is 100% salt.

Figure 4.2A ● Rock salt and pure salt

4.3 Density

Table 4.1 tells you that gases are much less **dense** than solids and liquids. What does **dense** mean? What is **density**? The two lengths of car bumper shown in Figure 4.3A have the same volume. You can see that they do not have the same mass. The steel bumper is heavier than the plastic bumper. This is because steel is a more **dense** material than the plastic; steel has a higher **density** than the plastic has.

$$\text{Density} = \frac{\text{Mass}}{\text{Volume}}$$

The unit of density is kg/m³ or g/cm³. The density values of some common substances are shown in Table 4.2.

Table 4.2 ● Density

Substance	Density (g/cm³)
Air	1.2×10^{-3}
Aluminium	2.7
Copper	8.92
Ethanol	0.789
Gold	19.3
Hydrogen	8.33×10^{-5}
Iron	7.86
Lead	11.3
Methane	6.67×10^{-4}
Oxygen	1.33×10^{-3}
Silver	10.5
Water	1.00

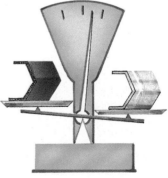

Figure 4.3A ● Two objects with the same volume

You can see that the gases are much less dense than any of the solid or liquid substances.

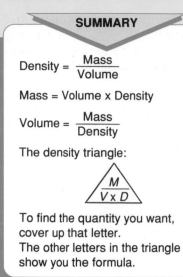
CHECKPOINT

❶ A worker in an aluminium plant taps off 300 cm³ of the molten metal. It weighs 810 g. What is the density of aluminium?

❷ An object has a volume of 2500 cm³ and a density of 3.00 g/cm³. What is its mass?

❸ Mercury is a liquid metal with a density of 13.6 g/cm³. What is the mass of 200 cm³ of mercury?

❹ 50.0 cm³ of metal A weigh 43.0 g
52.0 cm³ of metal B weigh 225 g
Calculate the density of each metal. Say whether they will float or sink in water.

4.4 Change of state

Matter can change from one state into another. Some changes of state are summarised in Figure 4.4A.

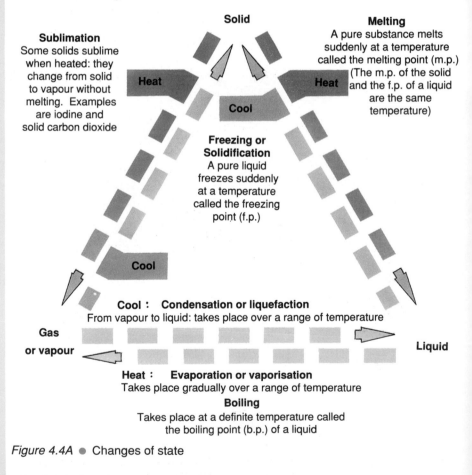

Figure 4.4A ● Changes of state

Sometimes gases are described as **vapours**. A liquid evaporates to form a vapour. A gas is called a vapour when it is cool enough to be liquefied.

Vapour $\xrightarrow{\text{Either cool or compress without cooling}}$ Liquid

LOOK AT LINKS
The energy change during a change of state can be measured.
See Theme B, Topic 7.4.

SUMMARY

Matter can change from one state into another.
The changes of state are:
- melting
- freezing or solidification
- evaporation or vaporisation
- condensation or liquefaction
- sublimation

The hotter a liquid is, the faster it evaporates. At a certain temperature, it becomes hot enough for vapour to form in the body of the liquid and not just at the surface. Bubbles of vapour appear inside the liquid. When this happens, the liquid is boiling, and the temperature is the boiling point of the liquid.

CHECKPOINT

❶ Copy the diagram below. Fill in the names of the changes of state. (Some of them have two names.)

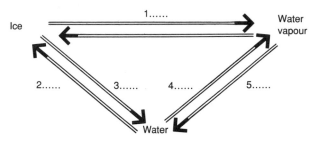

Ice → 1...... → Water vapour

2...... 3...... 4...... 5......

Water

❷ Give the scientific name for each of these changes.
(a) A puddle of water gradually disappears.
(b) A mist appears on your glasses.
(c) A mothball gradually disappears from your wardrobe.
(d) The change that happens when margarine is heated.

4.5 Finding melting points and boiling points

You can identify substances by finding their melting points and boiling points. Accuracy is essential, as you will see in this section

● Finding the melting point of a solid

Figure 4.5A shows an apparatus which can be used to find the melting point of a solid. To get an accurate result:
- first note the temperature at which the solid melts,
- allow the liquid which has been formed to cool and note the temperature at which it freezes.

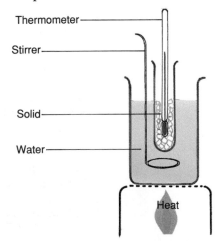

Thermometer

Stirrer

Solid

Water

Heat

First, find the m.p. of the solid. Heat the water in the beaker. Stir. Watch the thermometer. When the solid melts, note the temperature. Stop heating

Now find the f.p. of the liquid. Let the liquid cool. watch the thermometer. When the liquid begins to freeze, the temperature stops falling. It stays the same until all the liquid has solidified

Figure 4.5A ● Finding the melting point of a solid (for solids which melt above 100 °C, a liquid other than water must be used)

The apparatus shown in Figure 4.5A will work between 20 °C and 100 °C. For solids with melting points above 100 °C, a liquid with a higher boiling point than water must be used. For liquids which freeze below room temperature, a liquid with a lower freezing point than water must be used. A mixture of ice and salt can be used down to –18 °C (see Figure 4.5B).

Stir. Watch the thermometer. The temperature falls and then remains constant at freezing point of the liquid while the liquid freezes

— Thermometer

— Stirrer

— Water

— Ice-salt mixture (freezes below 0 °C)

Figure 4.5B ● Finding the freezing point of water

1. The temperature of the solid rises.
2. The solid starts to melt. The temperature remains steady at T_m (the m.p. of the solid) as long as there is any solid left

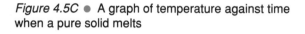

Temperature

T_m

1

2

3

4

Time

3. All the solid has melted

4. The temperature of the liquid rises

Figure 4.5C ● A graph of temperature against time when a pure solid melts

SUMMARY

The apparatus shown in Figure 4.5A or 4.5B can be used to find the melting point of a solid and the freezing point of a liquid.
- The temperature of a pure solid stays constant while it is melting.
- The temperature of a pure liquid stays constant while it is freezing.

If the solid is a pure substance, a graph of temperature against time as the solid melts will look like Figure 4.5C.

If you have a pure solid and you do not know what it is, you can use its melting point to find out. Chemists have drawn up lists of pure substances with their melting points. You find the melting point of the unknown solid and compare it with the listed melting points. *Which of the solids could be X?*

Solid	Melting point (°C)
Unknown solid X	116
Benzamide	132
Butanamide	116
Ethanamide	82

Figure 4.5D ● A truck spreading salt on an icy road in winter

SUMMARY

The melting point can be used to identify an unknown pure solid. The presence of an impurity lowers the melting point

If a solid is not pure, the melting point will be low, and the impure solid will melt gradually over a range of temperatures. Look at Figure 4.5D and explain why the ice on the road melts.

● *Finding the boiling point of a liquid*

Figure 4.5E shows an apparatus which can be used to find the boiling point of a non-flammable liquid. For a flammable liquid a distillation apparatus, e.g. Figure 15.6A must be used.

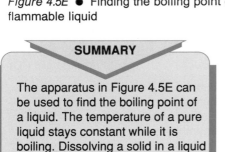

When the liquid boils, note the temperature shown by the thermometer. This is the boiling point of the liquid

— Test tube

— Liquid

Heat

Figure 4.5E ● Finding the boiling point of a non-flammable liquid

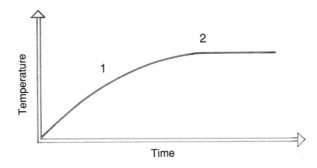

1. The temperature of the liquid rises
2. The liquid starts to boil. The temperature stays constant at the boiling point until all the liquid has vaporised

Figure 4.5F ● A graph of temperature against time when a pure liquid is heated

---

SUMMARY

The apparatus in Figure 4.5E can be used to find the boiling point of a liquid. The temperature of a pure liquid stays constant while it is boiling. Dissolving a solid in a liquid raises the boiling point.

While a pure liquid is boiling, the temperature remains steady at its boiling point. All the heat going into the liquid is used to vaporise the liquid and not to raise its temperature. Figure 4.5F shows a graph of temperature against time when a pure liquid is heated.

A mixture of liquids, such as crude oil, boils over a range of temperature. If a solid is dissolved in a pure liquid, it raises the boiling point.

Figure 4.5G ● Why will he have difficulty in brewing a strong cup of tea?

The boiling point of a liquid depends on the surrounding pressure. If the surrounding pressure falls, the boiling point falls. The boiling point of water on a high mountain is lower than 100 °C. An increase in the surrounding pressure raises the boiling point (see Figure 4.5H).

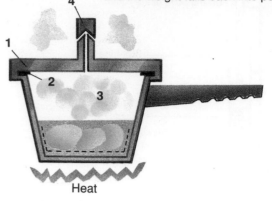

1. The lid is tightly fastened to the pan

2. A rubber sealing ring prevents steam escaping

3. The pressure of the steam builds up. The b.p. of water rises to about 120 °C. Food cooks more quickly than at 100 °C

4. The control valve. If the pressure of steam becomes too high, it lifts the weight. Some steam escapes, and the weight falls back into position

Heat

Figure 4.5H ● How a pressure cooker works

Boiling points are stated at standard pressure (atmospheric pressure at sea level). Boiling points can be used to identify pure liquids. You take the boiling point of the liquid you want to identify; then you look through a list of boiling points of known liquids and find one which matches. *Which of the liquids could be the unknown substance X?*

No two substances have both the same boiling point and the same melting point.

Liquid	Boiling point (°C)
Substance X	111
Benzene	80
Methylbenzene	111
Naphthalene	218

SUMMARY

The boiling point of a liquid is stated at standard pressure.
- At lower pressures, the boiling point is lower.
- At higher pressure, the boiling point is higher.

CHECKPOINT

❶ A pupil heated a beaker full of ice (and a little cold water) with a Bunsen burner. She recorded the temperature of the ice at intervals until the contents of the beaker had turned into boiling water. The table shows the results which the pupil recorded.

Time (*minutes*)	0	2	4	6	8	10	12	14	16
Temperature (°C)	0	0	0	26	51	76	100	100	100

(a) On graph paper, plot the temperature (on the vertical axis) against time (on the horizontal axis).
(b) On your graph, mark the m.p. of ice and the b.p of water.
(c) What happens to the temperature while the ice is melting?
(d) What happens to the temperature while the water is boiling?
(e) The Bunsen burner gives out heat at a steady rate. Explain what happens to the heat energy (i) when the beaker contains a mixture of ice and water at 0 °C, (ii) when the beaker contains water at 100 °C and (iii) when the beaker contains water at 50 °C.

❷ Bacteria are killed by a temperature of 120 °C. One way of sterilising medical instruments is to heat them in an autoclave (a sort of pressure cooker: see the figure opposite). The table shows the effect of pressure on the boiling point of water.

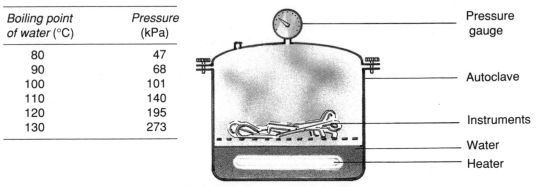

Boiling point of water (°C)	Pressure (kPa)
80	47
90	68
100	101
110	140
120	195
130	273

Pressure gauge

Autoclave

Instruments

Water

Heater

(a) Why are the instruments not simply boiled in a covered pan?

(b) What pressure must the autoclave reach to sterilise the instruments?

(o) What is the value of standard pressure in kPa (kilopascals)?

4.6 Properties and uses of materials

FIRST THOUGHTS

Properties of materials
- Hardness
- Toughness
- Strength
- Flexibility
- Elasticity
- Solubility
- Density (Topic 4.3)
- Melting point (Topic 4.5)
- Boiling point (Topic 4.5)
- Conduction of heat (Topics 7.5 and 7.6)
- Conduction of electricity (Topic 13)

Types of matter from which things are made are called **materials**. Different materials are used for different jobs. The reason is that their different **properties** (characteristics) make them useful for different purposes. You will see a list of properties in the margin. Some of them have been mentioned earlier in this topic. Conduction of heat and electricity will be covered in later topics. Now let us look at the rest.

Hardness

It is difficult to change the shape of a hard material. A hard material will dent or scratch a softer material. A hard material will withstand impact without changing. Table 4.3 shows the relative hardness of some materials on a 1–10 scale.

Table 4.3 ● Relative hardness of materials

Material	Relative hardness	Uses
Diamond	10.0	Jewellery, cutting tools
Silicon carbide	9.7	Abrasives
Tungsten carbide	8.5	Drills
Steel	7–5	Machinery, vehicles, buildings
Sand	7.0	Abrasives, e.g. sandpaper
Glass	5.5	Cut glass can be made by cutting glass with harder materials.
Nickel	5.5	Used in coins; hard-wearing
Concrete	5–4	Building material
Wood	3–1	Construction furniture
Tin	1.5	Plating steel food cans

LOOK AT LINKS
for **diamond**
To find out what makes diamond so hard, see Theme C, Topic 9.9; for metals see Theme L.

Toughness and brittleness

Construction workers on building sites wear 'hard hats' to protect themselves from falling objects. A hard hat is designed to absorb the energy of an impact. The hat material is **tough**, that is, it is difficult to break, although it may be dented by the impact. In comparison, a brick is

Figure 4.6A ● Hardness

difficult to dent and will shatter if dropped onto a concrete floor. The brick is **brittle**. Glass is another brittle material. These materials cannot absorb the energy of a large force without cracking. If a still larger force is applied the cracks get bigger and the materials shatter.

Composite materials

To make brittle materials tougher you have to try to stop them cracking. Mixing a brittle material with a material made of fibres, e.g. glass fibre or paper, will often do this. The fibres are able to absorb the energy of a force and the brittle material does not crack. Plaster is a brittle material. Plasterboard is much tougher. It is made by coating a sheet of plaster with paper fibres. It is a **composite material**. Glass-reinforced plastic (GRP) is a mixture of glass fibre and a plastic resin.

Figure 4.6C ● A GRP canoe

Paper
/ Made of fibres

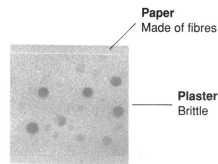

Plaster
Brittle

Figure 4.6B ● Plasterboard

Figure 4.6D ● Corrugated plastic roof

SUMMARY

Materials may be:
• hard – resistant to impact, difficult to scratch,
• tough – difficult to break, will 'give' before breaking,
• brittle – will break without 'giving',
• composite – made of more than one substance.

Concrete has great compressive strength, but it can crack if it is stretched. For construction purposes, **reinforced concrete** is used. Running through this composite material are steel rods which act like the glass fibres in GRP.

The shape of a piece of material alters its strength. Corrugated cardboard is used for packaging. Corrugated iron sheet and corrugated plastic sheet are used for roofing.

Strength

A strong material is difficult to break by applying force. The force may be a stretching force (e.g. a pull on a rope), or a squeeze (e.g. a vice tightening round a piece of wood), or a blow (e.g. a hammer blow on a lump of stone). A material which is hard to break by stretching has good **tensile strength**; a material which is hard to break by crushing has good **compressive strength**. The tensile strength of a material depends on its cross-sectional area.

Flexibility

While a material is pulled it is being stretched: it is under **tension**. While a material is squashed it is being compressed: it is under **compression**. When a material is bent, one side of the material is being stretched while the opposite side is being compressed. A material which is easy to bend without breaking has both tensile strength and compressive strength. It is **flexible**.

Figure 4.6E ● It's flexible

Elasticity

You can change the shape of a material by applying enough force. When you stop applying the force, some materials retain their new shapes; these are **plastic** materials. Other materials return to their old shape when you stop applying the force; these are **elastic materials**.

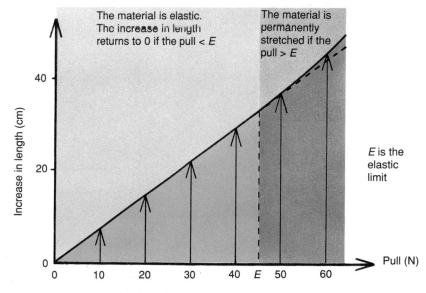

Figure 4.6F ● Increasing length

SUMMARY

Materials may have tensile strength (resistance to stretching), compressive strength (resistance to pressure), flexibility (both tensile and compressive strength) or elasticity (the ability to return to their original shape after being stretched).

When you pull an elastic material, it stretches – increases in length. At first, when you double the pull, you double the increase in length. As the pull increases, however, you reach a point where the material no longer returns to its original shape. This pull is the **elastic limit** of the material. Increasing the pull still more eventually makes the material break (see Figure 4.6F).

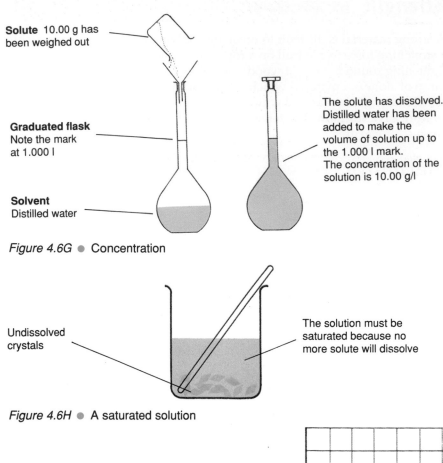

Solute 10.00 g has been weighed out

Graduated flask Note the mark at 1.000 l

Solvent Distilled water

The solute has dissolved. Distilled water has been added to make the volume of solution up to the 1.000 l mark. The concentration of the solution is 10.00 g/l

Figure 4.6G ● Concentration

Undissolved crystals

The solution must be saturated because no more solute will dissolve

Figure 4.6H ● A saturated solution

Solubility

A solution consists of a **solvent** and a **solute**. The solute, which may be a solid or a liquid or a gas, dissolves in the solvent. Water is the most common solvent, but there are many others such as ethanol (alcohol) and trichloroethane (trichlor). A **concentrated** solution contains a high proportion of solute; a **dilute** solution contains a small proportion of solute. The **concentration** of a solution is the mass of solute dissolved in a certain volume, say one litre, of the solution (see Figure 4.7G).

A solution that contains as much solute as it is possible to dissolve at that temperature is a **saturated** solution (Figure 4.7H).

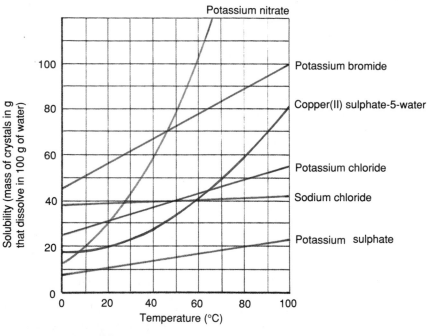

Figure 4.6I ● Some solubility curves

The concentration of solute in a saturated solution is the **solubility** of the solute at that temperature. Solubility is stated as the mass in grams of the solute that will saturate 100 grams of solvent at a certain temperature. A graph of solubility against temperature is called a **solubility curve**.

As you can see from the Figure 4.6I the solubilities of most solutes increase with temperature. When a saturated solution is cooled, it can hold less solute at the lower temperature and some solute comes out of solution: it crystallises. Gases, on the other hand, are less soluble at higher temperatures.

SUMMARY

Solubility = the mass of solute that will saturate 100 g of solvent at a stated temperature.

CHECKPOINT

❶ (a) Name two materials than can be used to drill through steel.
   (b) Why can a steel blade slice through tin?
   (c) Name a material that is used to make wood smooth.
   (d) Why are diamond-tipped saws used to slice through concrete?
   (e) Name two materials which can be used to cut glass.
   (f) Why is nickel a better coinage material than tin?

❷ (a) Name two tough materials. Say what they are used for.
   (b) Name two brittle materials. Say what can be done to make them tougher.

❸ Use the information in the table below to answer this question.

Cross-sectional area (mm²)	1	2	4	6	8	10
Breaking force (N)	0.5	1	2	3	4	5

   (a) On a piece of graph paper, plot the breaking force (on the vertical axis) against the cross-sectional area (on the horizontal axis).
   (b) From the shape of the graph, say how the breaking force alters when the cross-sectional area (i) doubles, (ii) increases by a factor of 10.
   (c) Write a sentence saying how the tensile strength of the material depends on the cross-sectional area.

❹ Name a material to fit each of the following descriptions:
   hard, soft, strong, flexible, tough, brittle, composite.

❺ Do the following materials need good tensile strength or good compressive strength?
   a tent rope, a tow bar, a stone wall, an anchor chain, a concrete paving stone, a building brick, a rope ladder.

❻ Classify the following materials as either plastic or elastic:
   plasticine, pottery clay, a rubber band, a balloon, 'potty putty'.

❼ Taran needs to make a solution of some large crystals. Which of the following suggestions would help her?
   (a) Crush the crystals before adding them to water.
   (b) Add the crystals to water one at a time.
   (c) Warm the water.
   (d) Stir the mixture of water and crystals.
   (e) Add the water dropwise to the crystals.

❽ Refer to Figure 4.6I.
   (a) What mass of potassium bromide will dissolve in 100 g of water at
       (i) 20 °C and (ii) 100 °C?
   (b) What will happen when the solution in (a) is cooled from 100 °C to 20 °C?
   (c) What mass of water is needed to dissolve 40 g of potassium sulphate at 80 °C?
   (d) When 1.00 kg of water saturated with copper(II) sulphate-5-water is cooled from 70 °C to 20 °C, what mass of solid crystallises?
   (e) A 100 g mass of water is saturated with sodium chloride and potassium chloride at 100 °C. When the solution is cooled to 20 °C, what mass of (i) sodium chloride and (ii) potassium chloride crystallises?

❾ On graph paper, plot a solubility curve for potassium chlorate(V) from the data given below.

Solubility (g/100 g water)	8	11	14	18	24	31	39	50
Temperature (°C)	20	30	40	50	60	70	80	90

One kilogram of water is saturated with potassium chlorate(V) at 90 °C and then cooled to 40 °C. What mass of crystals will separate from solution?

PARTICLES

5.1 The atomic theory

FIRST
THOUGHTS

What exactly is an atom, and why did the atomic theory take nearly 2000 years to catch on? Combine your imagination and your experimental skills in this section to find out why.

The idea that matter consists of tiny particles is very, very old. It was first put forward by the Greek thinker Democritus in 500 BC. For centuries the theory met with little success. People were not prepared to believe in particles which they could not see. The theory was revived by a British chemist called John Dalton in 1808. Dalton called the particles **atoms** from the Greek word for 'cannot be split'. According to Dalton's **atomic theory**, all forms of matter consist of atoms.

The atomic theory explained many observations which had puzzled scientists. Why are some substances solid, some liquid and others gaseous? When you heat them, why do solids melt and liquids change into gases? Why are gases so easy to compress? How can gases diffuse so easily? In this topic, you will see how the atomic theory provides answers to these questions and many others.

5.2 Elements and compounds

LOOK AT LINKS
for **elements** and **compounds**
This account of elements and compounds continues in Theme C, Topic 9.

There are two kinds of pure substances: **elements** and **compounds**. An element is a simple substance which cannot be split up into simpler substances. Iron is an element. Whatever you do with iron, you cannot split it up and obtain simpler substances from it. All you can do is to build up more complex substances from it. You can make it combine with other elements. You can make iron combine with the element sulphur to form iron sulphide. Iron sulphide is made of two elements chemically combined: it is a compound.

The smallest particle of an element is an **atom**. In some elements, atoms do not exist on their own: they join up to form groups of atoms called **molecules**. Figure 5.2A shows models of the molecules of some elements.

SUMMARY

Matter is made up of particles. Pure substances can be classified as elements and compounds. Elements are substances which cannot be split up into simpler substances. The smallest particle of an element is an atom. In many elements, groups of atoms join to form molecules.

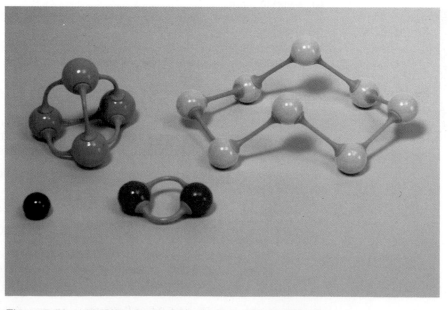

Figure 5.2A ● Models of molecules (helium, He; oxygen, O_2; phosphorus, P_4; sulphur, S_8)

SUMMARY

Compounds are pure substances
that contain two or more elements
chemically combined. Many
compounds are made up of
molecules; others are made up of
ions. All gases consist of
molecules.

A compound is a pure substance that contains two or more elements. The elements are not just mixed together: they are chemically combined. Many compounds consist of molecules, groups of atoms which are joined together by **chemical bonds**. All gases, whether they are elements or compounds, consist of molecules. Figure 5.2B shows models of molecules of some compounds.

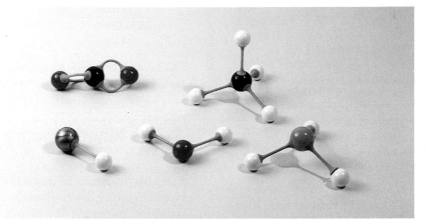

Figure 5.2B ● Models of molecules of some compounds (carbon dioxide, CO_2; methane, CH_4; ammonia, NH_3; water, H_2O; hydrogen chloride, HCl)

Some compounds do not consist of molecules; they are made up of electrically charged particles called **ions**. The word particle can be used for an atom, a molecule and an ion. Gaseous compounds and compounds which are liquid at room temperature consist of molecules.

5.3 How big are atoms?

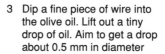

IT

Molecules
(program)

Use this program to study the way
that particles behave in a container
according to the kinetic theory of
matter.
• Change the temperature. What
  happens to the particles?
• Change another of the variables.
  What happens?
Remember: this is a model of the
way particles behave – it is a
computer simulation.

Hydrogen atoms are the smallest. One million hydrogen atoms in a row would stretch across one gain of sand. Five million million hydrogen atoms would fit on a pinhead. A hydrogen atom weighs 1.7×10^{-24} g; the heaviest atoms weigh 5×10^{-22} g.

How big is a molecule?

You can get an idea of the size of a molecule by trying the experiment shown in Figure 5.3A. This experiment uses olive oil, but a drop of detergent will also work. You can try this experiment at home.

1 Fill a clean tea tray
   with clean water

2 Sprinkle fine talcum
   powder on the surface

3 Dip a fine piece of wire into
   the olive oil. Lift out a tiny
   drop of oil. Aim to get a drop
   about 0.5 mm in diameter

4 Dip the wire into the water.
   The droplet of oil spreads
   out and pushes back the
   talcum powder. Measure
   as well as you can the area
   of the patch of olive oil

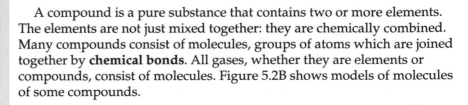

Figure 5.3A ● Estimating the size of a molecule

Sample results

Diameter of drop = 0.5 mm
Volume of drop = $(0.5 \text{ mm})^3$ = 0.125 mm³
Area of patch = $(25 \text{ cm})^2$ = $(250 \text{ mm})^2$ = 6.25 x 10⁴ mm²
Volume of patch = area x depth (d)
    0.125 mm³ = 6.25 x 10⁴ mm² x d

$$d = \frac{0.125 \text{ mm}^3}{6.25 \times 10^4 \text{ mm}^2}$$

d = 2 x 10⁻⁶ mm

The layer is only 2 x 10⁻⁶ mm deep (two millonths of a millimetre). We assume that it is one molecule thick.

SUMMARY

Atoms are tiny! A pinhead would hold 5 x 10¹² hydrogen atoms. Olive oil molecules are 2 x 10⁻⁶ mm in diameter.

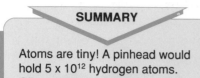

FIRST THOUGHTS

Particles in motion: what does this idea explain? The difference between solids, liquids and gases for a start, and the beauty of crystalline solids.

5.4 ● The kinetic theory of matter

The **kinetic theory of matter** states that matter is made up of small particles which are constantly in motion. (Kinetic comes from the Greek word for 'moving'.) The higher the temperature, the faster they move. In a solid, the particles are close together and attract one another strongly. In a liquid the particles are further apart and the forces of attraction are weaker than in a solid. Most of a gas is space, and the particles shoot through the space at high speed. There are almost no forces of attraction between the particles in a gas.

Scientists have been able to explain many things with the aid of the kinetic theory.

Solid, liquid and gaseous states

The differences between the solid, liquid and gaseous states of matter can be explained on the basis of the kinetic theory.

A solid is made up of particles arranged in a regular 3-dimensional structure. There are strong forces of attraction between the particles. Although the particles can vibrate, they cannot move out of their positions in the structure.

When a solid is heated, the particles gain energy and vibrate more and more vigorously. Eventually they may break away from the solid structure and become free to move around. When this happens, the solid has turned into a liquid: it has melted.

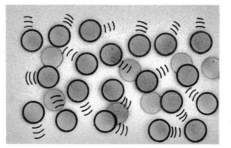

In a liquid the particles are free to move around. A liquid therefore flows easily and has no fixed shape. There are still forces of attraction between the particles.

When a liquid is heated, some of the particles gain enough energy to break away from the other particles. The particles which escape from the body of the liquid become a gas.

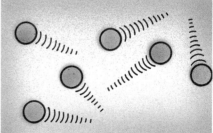

In a gas, the particles are far apart. There are almost no forces of attraction between them. The particles move about at high speed. Because the particles are so far apart, a gas occupies a very much larger volume than the same mass of liquid.

The molecules collide with the container. These collisions are responsible for the pressure which a gas exerts on its container.

Figure 5.4A ● The arrangement of particles in a solid, a liquid and a gas

Growing crystals
Prepare a saturated solution of alum (aluminium potassium sulphate). Put a few drops on to a microscope slide. Watch through the microscope while crystals form. Draw the shape of the crystals. Other solutions you can try are copper(II) sulphate, sodium chloride, lead(II) iodide, sodium ethanoate, potassium manganate(VII), chrome alum (chromium potassium sulphate).

Crystals

Crystals are a very beautiful form of solid matter. A crystal is a piece of solid which has a regular shape and smooth faces (surfaces) which reflect light (see Figure 5.4B). Different salts have differently shaped crystals. *Why are many solids crystalline?* Viewing a crystal with an electron microscope, scientists can actually see individual particles arranged in a regular pattern (see Figure 5.4C). It is this regular pattern of particles which gives the crystal a regular shape.

Figure 5.4B ● Crystals of copper(II) sulphate

LOOK AT LINKS
for **X-rays**
X-ray photographs played a big part in working out the structure of DNA.
see Theme D, Topic 18.5.

X-rays can be used to work out the way in which the particles in a crystal are arranged. Figure 5.4D shows the effect of passing a beam of X-rays through a crystal on to a photographic film. X-rays blacken photographic film. The pattern of dots on the film shows that the particles in the crystal must be arranged in a regular way. From the pattern of dots, scientists can work out the arrangement of particles in the crystals.

SUMMARY

The kinetic theory of matter can explain the differences between the solid, liquid and gaseous states, and also how matter can change state. X-ray photographs show that crystals consist of a regular arrangement of particles.

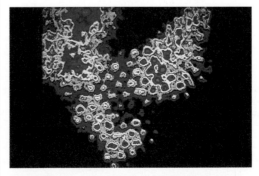

Figure 5.4C ● An electron microscope picture of uranyl acetate: each spot represents a single uranium atom

Figure 5.4D ● X-ray pattern from crystals of the metal palladium

FIRST THOUGHTS

How do solids dissolve, how do liquids vaporise and how do gases diffuse? Imagine particles in motion, and you will be able to explain all these changes.

Dissolving

Crystals of many substances dissolve in water. You can explain how this happens if you imagine particles splitting off from the crystal and spreading out through the water. See Figure 5.4E.

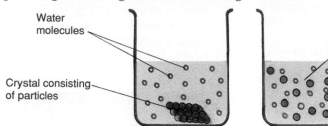

Water molecules

Crystal consisting of particles

Particles of crystal mixed up with water molecules

Figure 5.4E ● A coloured crystal dissolving

Diffusion

What evidence have we that the particles of a gas are moving? The diffusion of gases can be explained. **Diffusion** is the way gases spread out to occupy all the space available to them. Figure 5.4F shows what happens when a jar of the dense green gas, chlorine, is put underneath a jar of air.

On the theory that gases consist of fast-moving particles, it is easy to explain how diffusion happens. Moving molecules of air and chlorine spread themselves between the two gas jars.

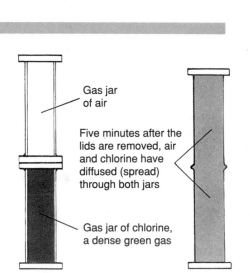

Gas jar of air

Five minutes after the lids are removed, air and chlorine have diffused (spread) through both jars

Gas jar of chlorine, a dense green gas

Figure 5.4F ● Gaseous diffusion

SUMMARY

Gases diffuse: they spread out to occupy all the space available to them. The kinetic theory of matter explains gaseous diffusion.

FIRST THOUGHTS

This section describes Brownian motion. You will see how neatly the kinetic theory can explain it.

Brownian motion

Figure 5.4G shows a smoke cell and the erratic path followed by a particle of smoke.

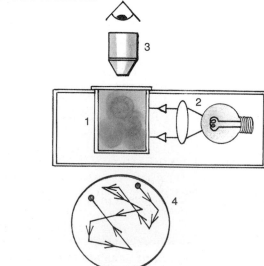

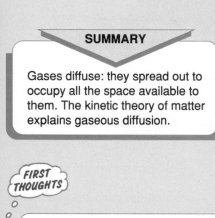
IT

Molecules (program)

Use this program to study the way that particles behave in a container according to the kinetic theory of matter.
- Change the temperature. What happens to the particles?
- Change another of the variables. What happens?

1 A small glass cell is filled with smoke

2 Light is shone through the cell

3 The smoke is viewed through a microscope

4 You see the smoke particles constantly moving and changing direction. The path taken by one smoke particle will look something like this

Figure 5.4G ● A smoke cell

We call this kind of motion **Brownian motion** after the botanist, Robert Brown, who first observed it. Figure 5.4H shows the explanation of Brownian motion.

Brownian motion in a liquid
In 1785, Robert Brown was using a microscope to observe pollen grains floating on water. He was amazed to see that the pollen grains were constantly moving about and changing direction. It was as if they had a life of their own.

Brown could not explain what he saw. You have the kinetic theory of matter to help you. Can you explain, with the aid of a diagram, what was making the pollen grains move?

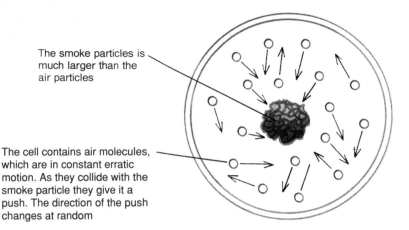

The smoke particles is much larger than the air particles

The cell contains air molecules, which are in constant erratic motion. As they collide with the smoke particle they give it a push. The direction of the push changes at random

Figure 5.4H ● Brownian motion

SUMMARY

Brownian motion puzzled scientists until the kinetic theory of matter offered an explanation.

Evaporation

When a liquid evaporates, it becomes cooler (see Figure 5.4I).

FIRST THOUGHTS

Why can you cool a hot cup of tea by blowing on it? Read this section to see if your idea is correct.

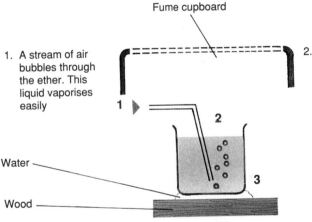

Fume cupboard

1. A stream of air bubbles through the ether. This liquid vaporises easily

2. The stream of air carries ether vapour out of the beaker. For safety the experiment is done in a fume cupboard as ether is very flammable

Water

Wood

3. As ether evaporates, it takes heat from its surroundings. The water between the beaker and the wood freezes

Figure 5.4I ● The cooling effect produced when a liquid evaporates

LOOK AT LINKS
The kinetic theory explains the gas laws.
See Theme B, Topic 7.2.

The kinetic theory can explain this cooling effect. Attractive forces exist between the molecules in a liquid (see Figure 5.4J). Molecules with more energy than average can break away from the attraction of other molecules and escape from the liquid. After the high energy molecules have escaped, the average energy of the molecules which remain is lower than before: the liquid has become cooler.

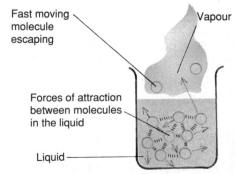

Fast moving molecule escaping

Vapour

Forces of attraction between molecules in the liquid

Liquid

Figure 5.4J ● Evaporation

SUMMARY

When a liquid evaporates, it takes heat from its surroundings. You can speed up evaporation by heating the liquid and by blowing air over it.

What happens when you raise the temperature? More molecules have enough energy to break away from the other molecules in the liquid. The rate of evaporation increases.

What happens if you pass a stream of dry air across the surface of the liquid? The dry air carries vapour away. The particles in the vapour are prevented from re-entering the liquid, that is, condensing. The liquid therefore evaporates more quickly.

CHECKPOINT

❶ Explain the following statements in terms of the kinetic theory.

(a) Water freezes when it is cooled sufficiently.
(b) Heating a liquid makes it evaporate more quickly.
(c) Heating a solid makes it melt.

❷ The solid X does not melt until it is heated to a very high temperature. What can you deduce about the forces which exist between particles of X?

❸ Of the five substances listed in the table below which is/are (a) solid (b) liquid (c) gaseous (d) unlikely to exist?

Substance	Distance between particles	Arrangement of particles	Movement of particles
A	Close together	Regular	Move in straight lines
B	Far apart	Regular	Random
C	Close together	Random	Random
D	Far apart	Random	Move in straight lines
E	Close together	Regular	Vibrate a little

❹ Supply words to fill in the blanks in this passage.

A solid has a fixed _____ and a fixed _____. A liquid has a fixed _____, but a liquid can change its _____ to fit its container. A gas has neither a fixed _____ nor a fixed _____. Liquids and gases flow easily; they are called _____. There are forces of attraction between particles. In a solid, these forces are _____, in a liquid they are _____ and in a gas they are _____.

❺ Imagine that you are one of the millions of particles in a crystal. Describe from your point of view as a particle what happens when your crystal is heated until it melts.

❻ Which of the two beakers in the figure opposite represents (a) evaporation, (b) boiling? Explain your answers.

❼ When a stink bomb is left off in one corner of a room, it can soon be smelt everywhere. Why?

❽ Beaker A and dish B contain the same volume of the same liquid. Will the liquid evaporate faster in A or B? Explain your answer.

❾ Why can you cool a cup of hot tea by blowing on it?

❿ A doctor dabs some ethanol (alcohol) on your arm before giving you an injection. The ethanol makes your arm feel cold. How does it do this?

Vapour leaving the surface of the liquid

Bubbles of vapour

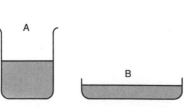

A

B

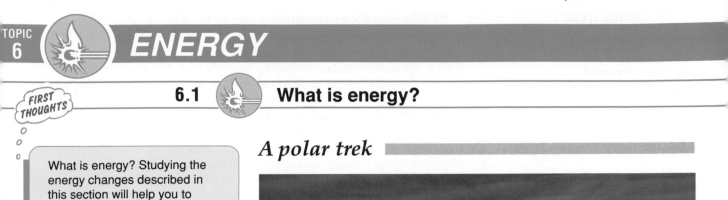

TOPIC 6 ENERGY

6.1 What is energy?

What is energy? Studying the energy changes described in this section will help you to understand.

A polar trek

Figure 6.1A ● A polar expedition

Imagine you are a polar explorer about to set off for a few days on an expedition from base camp. *What sort of preparations would you make for your expedition?* You would obviously need suitable weatherproof clothing, a supply of food and a suitable means of transport. The clothing must keep you warm and dry; food is essential so you can keep working and transport saves you getting tired trudging across ice and snow. If your clothing was not very effective or your food ran out or your transport broke down, your survival would be at stake. Clearly, polar explorers must make very careful preparations for their expeditions! They must plan to make the most of their resources to keep warm and to keep working.

Using energy

Energy is what makes things work (i.e. makes things move or makes changes happen). Without energy, nothing could be made to work. The petrol in the fuel tank of a car is used to make the car move. A car that runs out of petrol stops moving because no more energy is left – until the tank is refilled.

Energy is needed to warm things up. Rub your hands together vigorously and they become warmer. Your muscles have supplied the energy that warmed your hands up. Another example is when you switch an electrical room heater on. The heater warms you up because it gives out energy from the electricity supply.

Here are a list of five sorts of work. *Which ones need energy?*

Figure 6.1B ● Using energy

- Running an errand to the shops
- Making a cup of coffee
- Reading this book
- Lifting a book off the floor
- Holding a shelf up while it is fixed in position

Space invaders
Hornets that raid beehives are cooked to death by the bees. Scientists have discovered that an invading hornet is quickly engulfed by hundreds of bees that generate heat through shivering their wings. The temperature in the ball of bees rises and the hornet dies. The bees survive because they are able to withstand higher temperatures than the hornet.

You have probably realised that energy is needed to run and to lift things. The energy to do these jobs comes from the muscles of the body. Also, unless you prefer cold coffee, energy is needed to provide hot water. *What about reading or holding the shelf steady?* These are jobs that do not involve making the book or the shelf move. However, reading a page involves using the eye muscles and, hopefully, brain power too!

Holding a shelf is a task that needs energy to keep the muscles contracted. Blood pumped through the muscles delivers energy to the muscles to keep them taut. Since the shelf does not move, all the energy supplied to the muscles makes the muscles warm. This is a bit like an electric motor that tries unsuccessfully to lift a weight. The electrical energy supplied to the motor makes the motor hot.

Forms of energy

Objects can have energy in different forms. For example, winding up the mainspring of a clockwork toy car stores energy in the spring. When the spring unwinds, it drives the wheels and the car moves. The wound-up spring is said to contain **potential energy**. Any moving object is said to have **kinetic energy**. When the car is moving, potential energy in the spring is being changed into kinetic energy of the car. In other words, energy is changing from one form into another when the car is moving.

Figure 6.1C ● Clockwork motors

Potential energy is energy stored due to position. A weight raised above the ground has potential energy due to its position. A spring in tension has potential energy because its position differs from when there is no tension in it.

Figure 6.1D ● Gaining potential energy

Another example of energy changing from one form into another is when you use a torchbulb. The torch battery pushes electric current through the torchbulb when the torch is switched on. As a result, the torchbulb emits light energy. The battery converts **chemical energy** into **electrical energy** and the torchbulb converts the electrical energy into **light energy**.

LOOK AT LINKS
for **chemical energy**
Energy changes in chemical reactions are discussed in Theme L, Topic 49.

LOOK AT LINKS
for **photosynthesis**
Plants convert energy from
sunlight into chemical
energy in their leaves. How
is this achieved?
see Theme F, Topic 25.1.

Can you think of an example where light energy is changed into the energy of chemical bonds? This is what happens when a plant makes food. Light is needed for a plant to make sugars from carbon dioxide and water. This process is called **photosynthesis**. The light energy is converted into the chemical energy of the sugar molecules. The energy in the food made by the plants is passed on to animals that eat the plants.

Water + Carbon dioxide $\xrightarrow{\text{sunlight + chlorophyll}}$ Food + Oxygen

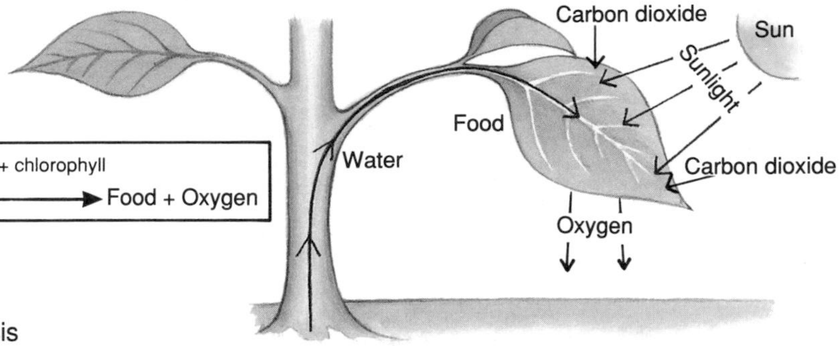

Figure 6.1E ● Photosynthesis

We obtain our food from plants or from animals fed on plants. We all need food to keep going, so the next time you charge round the sports field, remember you got your energy from sunlight. Not all the energy from the food is used to keep you going. Your muscles produce **heat** when they are at work and if you are a very noisy sportsperson, some is used to create **sound energy**.

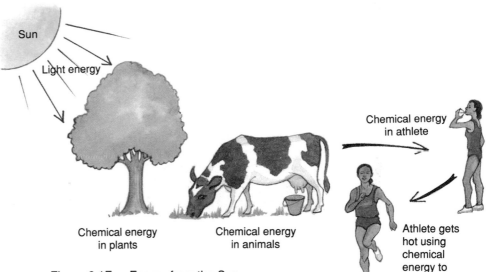

Figure 6.1F ● Energy from the Sun

Nuclear energy is used to keep heart pacemakers going. Ordinary batteries are unsuitable, even though they can be made small enough. This is because they don't last long enough and the user would need to be 'opened up' every time the battery needed changing. Using a small radioactive source gives enough energy to operate a pacemaker for years. The pacemaker converts nuclear energy into electrical energy in the form of pulses to keep the heart beating steadily.

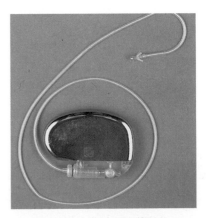

Figure 6.1G ● A heart pacemaker

SUMMARY

Energy is needed to make things work or to warm things up. Objects can possess energy in different forms. Energy can be changed from any form into any other form.

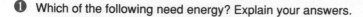

CHECKPOINT

❶ Which of the following need energy? Explain your answers.

(a) Running up a flight of steps.
(b) Holding a book out in front of you.
(c) Balancing on a tightrope.
(d) Floating in the sea.

❷ Each of the following devices is designed to convert energy from one form into another form. For each device, write down what form of energy it uses and what this is changed into.

(a) A hair dryer   (e) A candle
(b) A door bell   (f) An electric kettle
(c) A jet engine   (g) A bicycle
(d) A radio   (h) A windmill

❸ Write down the name of a device that is designed to change:
(a) electrical energy into light energy,
(b) electrical energy into potential energy,
(c) electrical energy into heat.

FIRST THOUGHTS

○
 ○
  ○

> Why do we believe that energy can neither be created nor destroyed? Read on to find out why.

6.2   Conservation of energy

Strike a match and you will cause chemical energy to be released as the match burns. The substance on the match head ignites and reacts with oxygen from the air to release chemical energy. *What happens to the chemical energy?* The burning match produces heat and light which are different forms of energy. This is an example where one form of energy is changed into two or more different forms of energy.

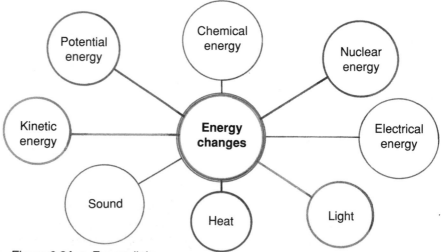

Figure 6.2A ● Energy links

Most energy changes involve energy changing from one form into two or more different forms. Devices designed to change energy into a particular form often produce other forms of energy as well. For example, an electric torch is designed to change chemical energy (in a battery) into light energy. However the torch bulb releases heat which warms the bulb holder up. In fact, powerful lamps like stage lights get really hot when in use.

Figure 6.2B ● Some energy changes

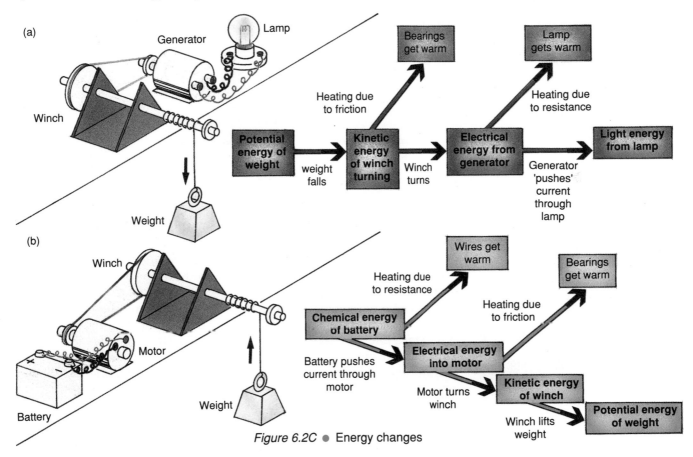

Figure 6.2C ● Energy changes

Some more energy changes are shown in Figures 6.2B and 6.2C. Each one involves changing energy from one form into different forms. *What do these changes have in common with each other?*

1. **Energy must be present in one form or another to start with**.

In other words, energy can't be produced from nowhere. Fuels such as coal and oil contain chemical energy produced millions of years ago by the growing plants absorbing sunlight.

2. **Energy changing from one form into another involves either heating or working**.

In other words, energy changes occur when something is forced to happen (i.e. making something work) or when there is a temperature difference. Heat is energy 'on the move' due to temperature difference. Look again at Figure 6.2C and check that all the arrows for energy changes show 'working' or 'heating'.

TRY THIS

Design and test a motor driven by an elastic band. Use an elastic band, a cotton bobbin and a matchstick to make a 'motor' in which energy stored in the elastic band is changed into kinetic energy. How would you test your motor to see how it compares with a similar motor made by a friend?

When energy changes from one form into other forms, how much energy is there at the end of the change compared with the start? Can you think of a situation where the energy changes back to the form it started in?

Squash players use very bouncy balls which rebound very effectively. Try releasing such a ball from a fixed height above a flat surface and see how high it rebounds. You ought to find out that a really bouncy ball almost regains its initial height. Figure 6.2D shows the energy changes after an ideal ball is released. The potential energy of the ball is recovered fully after the bounce. This example shows quite clearly that no energy is lost.

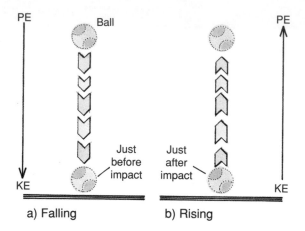

a) Falling   b) Rising

Figure 6.2D ● A bouncy ball

How would dropping a cricket ball or a hockey ball onto a flat surface compare with dropping a squash ball? This time there would be little bounce and the ball would not return to its initial height. Only part of the initial potential energy is recovered after the bounce. *What happens to the potential energy that is lost?* The impact of the ball on the floor heats the ball and floor slightly and sound energy is also produced.

When energy changes from one form into other forms, the total amount of energy after the change is equal to the total amount of energy at the start. **Energy is always conserved**. This means that when it is changed from any one form into any other, the total amount of energy after the change is always equal to the amount at the start. Scientists have tested the conservation of energy principle many times. But their experiments have always led to the same conclusion:

Energy is always conserved.

SUMMARY

- Energy can change from any one form into other forms.
- In any energy change, energy is conserved even though it may be changed into many different forms.

///////// **CHECKPOINT** /////////

❶ Which of the following energy changes are due to something being forced to move and which are due to heating?
   (a) Changing chemical energy into potential energy when a book is lifted.
   (b) Using electrical energy to warm water in a kettle.
   (c) Using chemical energy to warm your hands by rubbing them together.
   (d) Drying damp clothes by hanging them outside on a washing line.

❷ Each of the following situations involves energy changing from one form into several other forms. Describe the energy changes in each situation.
   (a) Clapping your hands together loudly.
   (b) Using an electric motor to raise a weight.
   (c) Throwing a ball into the air.
   (d) Using a gas cooker to boil an egg.

6.3 Measuring energy

FIRST THOUGHTS

Energy and power as measurable quantities are introduced here. They are used extensively in later topics so read on carefully.

IT'S A FACT

James Joule was a nineteenth century scientist who investigated lots of energy changes. On honeymoon in Switzerland he and his wife visited waterfalls to find out if the water at the bottom was warmer than at the top. He reasoned that the loss of potential energy due to the fall ought to produce heat which would warm the water. In fact, using an accurate thermometer he discovered the water at the bottom was cooler than at the top. He realised that this was because of the cooling effect of the water spray.

When energy changes into different forms, how much energy goes into each form? To answer this question, we need to measure how much energy is needed to heat things or to force them to move.

Imagine you have the job of carrying lots of bricks up a ladder. A certain amount of energy is needed to lift one brick up by one metre. To lift two bricks by one metre or one brick by two metres requires twice as much energy. To lift ten bricks up by five metres requires 50 times as much energy as lifting one brick up by one metre. We could measure energy in units of the amount needed to lift one brick by one metre. But the brick would need to be a 'standard' brick with a known weight.

The **joule** (J) is the scientific unit of energy. One joule is the energy needed to lift an object of weight one newton by one metre. So if each brick in the above example has a weight of 20 N, the energy needed to lift one brick by 1 m would be 20 J. *How much energy would be needed to lift 100 bricks by 5 m?*

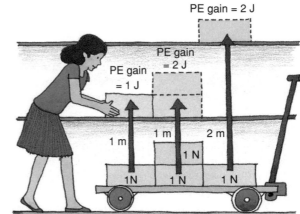

Figure 6.3A ● Using joules

Energy is always measured in joules, no matter what form the energy is in. Energy in any given form can be used to lift a known weight by a measured height. In this way, energy in any given form can be measured in joules. For example, you could measure the energy stored in a catapult by measuring how high the catapult can throw a known weight.

TRY THIS

An energetic challenge

In games lessons, Simon and Kevin are always trying to outdo each other. Simon has challenged Kevin to a rope-climbing competition to see who can shin up the rope the fastest. Their friends time them and use a metre rule to measure how high they climb.

Here are the results:

	Kevin	Simon
Time taken (s)	6.2	5.5
Height gain (m)	3.5	3.5

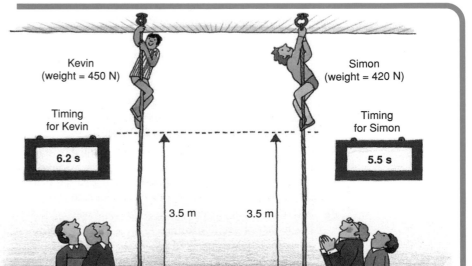

Figure 6.3B ● Who is more powerful?

Simon claims victory but Kevin insists that they must take account of body weight. Off they go to the science laboratory where there is a set of bathroom scales marked in newtons.

Kevin's weight = 450 N

Simon's weight = 420 N

Who gains more potential energy climbing the rope?

Kevin gained 450 J for every metre gain of height (= 450 N x 1 m). So he gained 1575 J in total (= 450 N x 3.5 m) to climb the rope.

How much potential energy does Simon gain in total?

Who is the more energetic of the two?

Simon claims his muscles are more powerful since he climbed faster.

How much potential energy did Simon gain per second? How much did Kevin gain per second? Is Simon's claim correct?

Power is the rate at which energy is used.

The unit of power is the **watt** (W) which is equal to one joule per second (J/s).

Machines designed to do jobs are rated in terms of how much power they use. For example, a 3000 W electric winch uses 3000 J of electrical energy each second when it is switched on. Heaters and lamps are also rated in watts. A 1.5 kW heater uses 1500 J of electrical energy each second. *How long would it take a 100 W lamp to use 1500 J of electrical energy?*

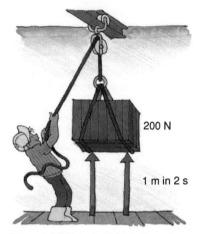

Figure 6.3C ● A 100 watt worker

| Energy used | = | Power supplied | x | Time taken |
| (in joules) | | (in watts) | | (in seconds) |

SUMMARY

Energy is always measured in joules. Power is the rate at which energy is used. The unit of power is the watt which equals 1 joule per second. The energy used by a device can be worked out if its power and time of use are known.

CHECKPOINT

❶ How much energy is used in each of the following situations?
(a) A 60 W hairdrier is used for 60 seconds.
(b) A 150 W lamp is used for 2 hours.
(c) A 3 kW electric kettle is used for 5 minutes.
(d) Two 60 W lamps are used together for 30 minutes.

❷ In an investigation to estimate the power of a gas cooker ring, a student finds that 1 litre of water in a pan heated by gas reaches boiling point in 250 seconds. The student then times how long a 2.0 kW electric kettle takes to heat 1 litre of water to boiling point from the same initial temperature. She finds the kettle takes 200 seconds to do this.
(a) Do you think the gas cooker ring is more powerful than the electric kettle?
(b) How much energy was supplied to the kettle to heat the water?
(c) What was the power of the gas cooker ring?

❸ You could estimate your leg power by running upstairs or stepping up and down repeatedly. What would you measure to make this estimate and how would you work out your leg power from your measurements? Would you expect your leg power to be more or less than your arm power?

❹ Your heart never stops pumping blood round your body throughout your life. The power of a typical human heart is about 1 W. How much energy is used by a typical heart in one day?

6.4 Energy on the move

Electricity is a very convenient means of moving energy from where it is generated to where it is needed. How does it compare with other means of transporting energy?

How is energy supplied to your home? Most homes are connected to mains electricity cables that supply electricity produced in power stations. Natural gas is supplied to homes through a network of underground pipes called the gas mains. The gas is pumped through the pipes to your home from a gas terminal. This is where the gas is fed into the system from tankers or from undersea pipe lines joined to gas rigs.

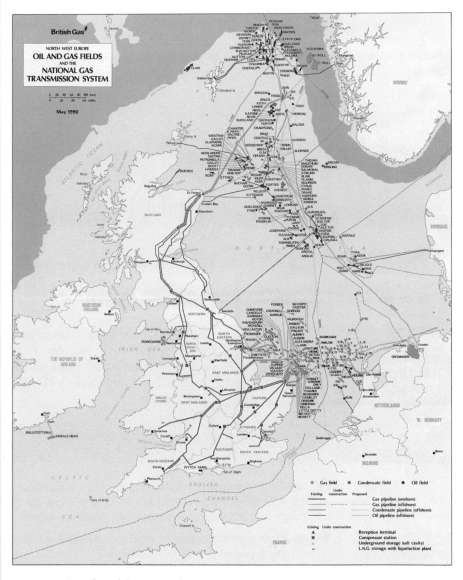

Figure 6.4A ● Supplying natural gas

Pressure is needed to force gas through a pipe. The pressure in a gas pipe is applied at a pumping station. Valves are needed to make sure the gas does not flow back towards the terminal. The pressure inside a mains gas pipe must not be too high, otherwise gas would leak from the pipe.

When natural gas is burned, carbon dioxide and carbon monoxide gases are produced and released into the atmosphere. This also happens when coal or oil is burned. Electricity is 'clean' in this respect since electrical appliances do not give **greenhouse gases** such as carbon dioxide. However, power stations that burn fossil fuels (i.e. coal, oil or gas) release these gases to produce electricity.

IT'S A FACT

Gas supplied to homes and offices is used for heating and cooking. More than fifty years ago, gas was also used for lighting. Gas lamps in streets were lit by a lamplighter who was employed to turn the lamps on and off every day.

LOOK AT LINKS
for **greenhouse gases**
see Theme E, Topic 20.7.

Figure 6.4B ● A domestic electricity meter

Measuring electrical energy

Every home using mains electricity is connected via an electricity meter. The meter registers the electrical energy used in **kilowatt hours**. One kilowatt hour is the amount of electrical energy used by a 1 kW electric heater in 1 hour. For example, a 3 kW electric heater used for 5 hours would use 15 kilowatt hours of electrical energy. This would increase the meter reading by 15 'units'.

For low voltage circuits, a **joulemeter** may be used to measure electrical energy. Fig 6.4C shows a joulemeter connected into a circuit to measure the electrical energy used by a torchbulb. The joulemeter must be read before the switch is closed and then again when the switch is re-opened. The difference between the two readings gives the number of joules supplied.

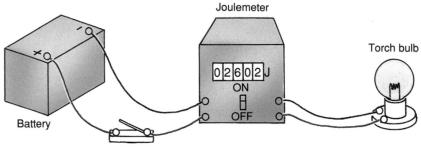

Figure 6.4C ● Using a joulemeter

Human energy

Our bodies need food to obtain energy. We need energy to enable our muscles to do work. The blood system carries glucose from the digestive system to the muscles. Here glucose reacts to supply energy to the muscles. The heart forces blood through the arteries and veins of the blood system.

SUMMARY

Electricity and gas are used to supply energy to most homes. A complete circuit is needed to supply electricity. The blood system is like a complete circuit, used to supply energy to the muscles.

CHECKPOINT

❶ Jasmin and Imram are discussing the relative merits of gas and electricity for home heating. Jasmin thinks that electricity is best because it is 'clean'. Imram isn't sure about this argument. What do you think?

❷ (a) A gas leak can cause an explosion. Natural gas is odourless so another gas is added to make it smell. Why?
   (b) Why is it important not to light a match or switch a light on if you suspect a gas leak at home?

❸ Alan is using a joulemeter to measure the energy used by an electric heater. The joulemeter reads 2602 J initially. He closes the battery switch for exactly 5 minutes, then opens the switch. The meter now reads 17 587 J.
   (a) How much energy was used?
   (b) Work out the power of the heater in watts.

❹ The electricity mains and the gas mains both move energy from one place to another.
   (a) What carries the energy in each case?
   (b) What happens to the energy carriers in each case after releasing the energy?

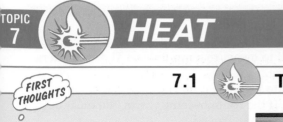

HEAT

TOPIC 7

7.1 ● Temperature

FIRST THOUGHTS

What do the butcher, the baker and the candlestick maker have in common? Read on to find out.

Figure 7.1A ● The weather forecast

Our everyday lives are affected by temperature in lots of ways. The clothes you choose to wear each day, the food you eat, how well you feel; all these depend in some way on temperature. When you read the weather forecast and learn that tomorrow's outdoor temperature is expected to be as high as 30 °C, you can look forward to a hot and sunny day!

Temperature scales

Temperature is a measure of hotness. **Fixed points** are used to define a scale of temperature. These points are 'degrees of hotness' that can be set up precisely. They are usually melting points or boiling points of pure substances.

● *The Celsius scale*

The Celsius scale, denoted by °C, is defined by two fixed points, which are;

1 **Ice Point** at 0 °C; this is the temperature at which pure ice melts.
2 **Steam point** at 100 °C; this is the temperature at which pure water boils at standard atmospheric pressure.

IT'S A FACT

Body temperature for a healthy person is about 37 °C. Someone in a fever might get as hot as 40 °C but if their temperature gets as high as 45 °C, there's not much hope! The human body has a remarkable control system, keeping each of us at about 37 °C, no matter where we are.

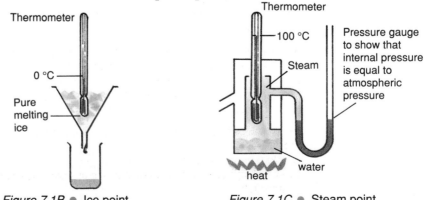

Figure 7.1B ● Ice point   *Figure 7.1C* ● Steam point

Thermometers

What is it that the butcher, the baker and the candlestick maker have in common? The answer is that they all need to measure temperature. Thermometers are used to measure temperature.

The butcher has a cold room to keep meat in. A thermometer is used to make sure the room stays cold. If the room became warm, the meat in it would go off and would have to be destroyed.

The baker has an oven to bake bread. If the oven gets too hot, the bread is burnt. A thermometer probe inside the oven is used to give a temperature reading on a meter outside.

The candlestick maker melts wax and pours it into moulds to make the candles. He uses a thermometer to make sure the molten wax is not too hot.

Thermometers are made in all shapes and sizes but they all must be calibrated (i.e. marked with a scale). This is usually done in °C, marking the ice point reading as 0° and the steam point reading as 100°. The scale between these two marks is then divided into 100 degrees. Fig 7.1D shows the result.

● *Liquid-in-glass thermometers*

These are based on the principle that liquids expand much more than solids when heated. Mercury and coloured ethanol (alcohol) are the usual thermometer liquids. When the thermometer bulb is warmed up, the liquid in it expands but the glass bulb expands very little. As a result, the liquid is forced out of the bulb and along the capillary tube in the stem. The temperature is measured from the position of the end of the liquid thread in the stem.

● *Clinical thermometers*

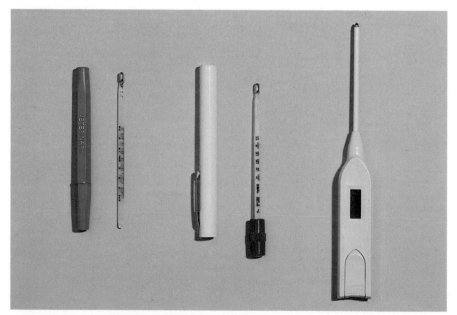

Figure 7.1D ● A range of clinical thermometers

Clinical thermometers are designed to measure body temperature accurately. They are liquid-in-glass thermometers with a scale from about 35 °C to 45 °C in graduations of 0.1 °C. The capillary tube is constricted near the bulb, as shown in Figure 7.1E. This is to prevent the liquid returning to the bulb after the thermometer is removed from the patient. In this way, the user doesn't have to take the reading while the

LOOK AT LINKS
Electrical thermometers linked to microcomputers can be used to record changing temperatures automatically. The measurements can be displayed as a graph of temperature against time. See Theme K, Topic 45.7.

Figure 7.1E ● A clinical thermometer

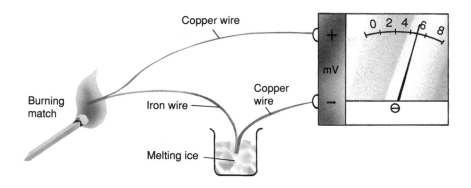

Figure 7.1F ● A thermocouple thermometer

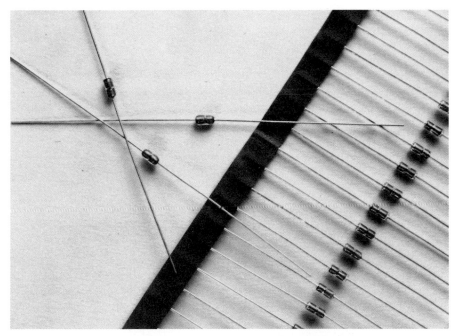

Figure 7.1G ● Thermistors

thermometer is actually in the patient. After the thermometer has been removed from the patient and read, it is given a quick flick to make the liquid return to the bulb.

● *Thermocouple thermometers*

These are electrical thermometers that use the fact that when two different metals are placed in contact, a voltage develops between them. This voltage varies with temperature. An iron wire and a copper wire can be used to make a thermocouple thermometer. One of the junctions is kept in melting ice at 0 °C while the other one is used as the temperature probe. The voltmeter can be calibrated directly in °C.

● *Thermistor thermometers*

Thermistor thermometers use electrical resistors called thermistors. The resistance of a thermistor changes with temperature. This is why it can be used to measure temperature. The thermistor is usually plugged into an electronic circuit designed to give a read-out in °C on a digital display. The circuit usually has two variable resistors to set the ice point read-out at 0 °C and the steam point read-out at 100 °C.

● *Temperature strips*

Temperature strips change colour when warmed. Each strip is designed so that its colour alters from blue to red as it is warmed.

SUMMARY

The Celsius scale is defined in terms of ice point (0 °C) and steam point (100 °C). All thermometers must be calibrated. Different types of thermometers are used for different purposes.

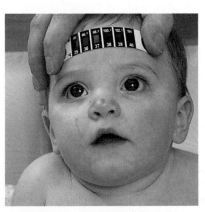

Figure 7.1H ● A forehead temperature strip

///// **CHECKPOINT** /////

❶ Say what type of thermometer you would choose;
   (a) to measure the body temperature of an adult,
   (b) to measure the body temperature of a baby,
   (c) to measure the temperature in a greenhouse,
   (d) to monitor the water temperature at the outflow of a solar heating panel,
   (e) to monitor the soil temperature in a plant experiment.

❷ The following measurements were made when a thermocouple thermometer was being compared with a mercury-in-glass thermometer;

Voltmeter reading (mV)	0	1.5	3.0	4.5	6.0	7.5
M-in-G reading (°C)	0	20	40	60	80	100

   (a) Plot a graph of the voltmeter reading (on the vertical axis) against the mercury-in-glass thermometer reading.
   (b) Use your graph to work out the voltmeter reading for 50 °C on the mercury-in-glass thermometer.

❸ Weather stations often use specially-designed thermometers to record the highest and the lowest temperature each day. The figure shows the construction of one of each type.
   (a) Why is mercury used in the maximum thermometer and alcohol used in the minimum thermometer?
   (b) What was the highest temperature reached by the maximum thermometer?
   (c) What was the lowest temperature reached by the minimum thermometer?
   (d) How could you reset each thermometer?

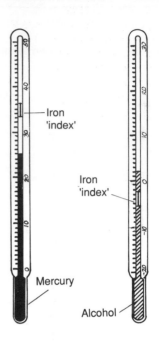

Iron 'index'

Iron 'index'

Mercury

Alcohol

7.2 Thermal expansion

> Thermal expansion can be a nuisance. It can also be put to good use. This section will tell you how.

(a) Filling a balloon with hot air

Materials expand, if allowed, when heated. Gases are capable of expanding much more than solids or liquids. Figure 7.2A shows how the expansion of gas may be demonstrated; warming the test tube by hand is enough to make the air in it expand and push the thread of water up the tube. Hot-air balloonists use this principle to go up in the air. A burner under the balloon causes the balloon to fill with hot air which then lifts the balloon.

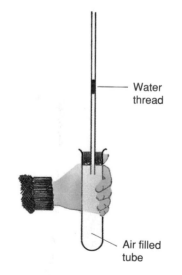

Water thread

Air filled tube

(b) Demonstrating expansion

Liquid-in-glass thermometers make use of the thermal expansion of mercury or alcohol. Water is a very unusual liquid because it contracts when heated from 0 to 4 °C; above 4 °C, it expands like most other liquids. Water pipes can split if they freeze up in winter. This is due to the water trying to expand as it cools from 4 °C to freezing point. If the ends of the pipe are already frozen up, tremendous pressure can build up in the middle as the water freezes and this may split the pipe.

Figure 7.2A ● Expansion of a gas

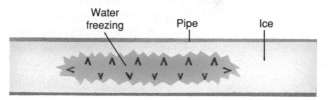

Figure 7.2B ● Water freezing

Expansion gaps are necessary in buildings to allow for thermal expansion. Outdoor temperatures can change by as much as 50 °C from winter to summer. Building materials expand due to rise of temperature. *What do you think would happen if there were no expansion gaps?* Motorway bridges are made in concrete sections with expansion gaps between the sections. The expansion gaps are filled with soft material like rubber to stop chunks of rock falling in. Railway tracks too are designed to allow for thermal expansion. Gaps between rails are essential or else the tracks would buckle in hot weather.

Figure 7.2C ● Expansion gaps in a motorway bridge

Expansion can be very useful. For example, train wheels are fitted with steel tyres by heating the tyre. This makes it expand slightly so it can then be fitted on to the wheel. Then, as the tyre cools, it contracts to make a very tight fit on the wheel.

● **The bimetallic strip**
Different materials expand by different amounts. A brass bar would give more expansion than an iron bar of the same length for the same temperature rise. Brass expands more than iron.

The bimetallic strip consists of a strip of brass bonded to a strip of steel. When the temperature rises, the brass expands more than steel so the bimetallic strip bends. This is used in **thermostats** designed to control heaters or operate fire alarms.

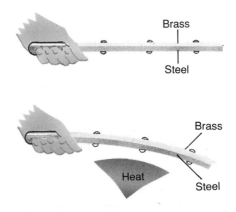

Figure 7.2D ● The bimetallic strip
(a) Cold (b) Hot

- In the alarm circuit shown in Figure 7.2E, the strip bends towards the contact screw when the temperature increases. The strip bends until it touches the contact screw which sets the alarm off.
- In a heater control, the strip bends away from the contact when it gets too hot: So the heater is switched off when the temperature reaches a certain point.

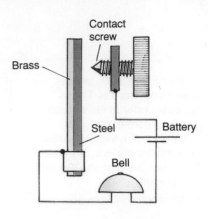

Figure 7.2E ● An alarm

Expansion of gases

Figure 7.2F shows how to measure the volume of a gas at different temperatures. As the water bath is warmed, the gas trapped in the glass tube becomes hotter and expands, pushing the liquid thread up the tube. The length of the gas column increases. This is a measure of the gas volume.

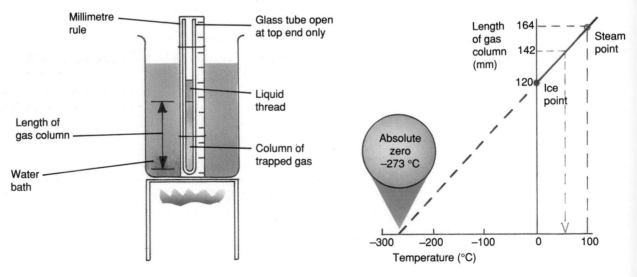

Figure 7.2F ● Measuring the expansion of a gas (a) Using a water bath (b) Typical results

Suppose the gas volume is measured at ice point and at steam point. Typical measurements are plotted on the graph in Figure 7.2F. The straight line drawn between the two points cuts the temperature axis at −273 °C no matter which gas or how much gas is in the tube. This is the **absolute zero of temperature**, the lowest possible temperature.

The absolute scale of temperature is based on absolute zero. The scale is used by scientists because it is a measure of the average kinetic energy of a molecule. The unit of temperature on this scale, the kelvin (denoted by K) is named after Lord Kelvin who first developed the idea of the absolute temperature scale. The scale is defined so that temperature values in °C can be converted to kelvins by adding 273.

> Temperature in kelvins = Temperature in °C + 273

The gas laws

● *Charles' law*

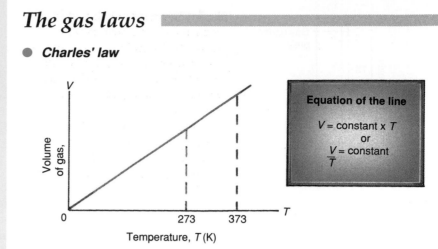

Figure 7.2G ● Charles' Law

The tube of gas in Figure 7.2F may be used as a thermometer. By measuring the length of the gas column, the temperature can be read off the graph. For example, if the length is midway between ice point and steam point, the temperature must be 323 K (= 50 °C).

In more general terms, the straight line drawn through absolute zero may be represented by an equation.

> Volume = constant x Absolute temperature
> or V = constant x T
> (provided the pressure and mass of gas are constant)

This equation, known as **Charles' Law,** can be used to work out the absolute temperature for any given volume if the constant in the equation is known.

Worked example   The volume of a fixed mass of gas at constant pressure in a tube at ice point (273 K) is 80 mm³. Work out the absolute temperature when the volume is 87 mm³.

Solution
Since V = constant x T

then $\dfrac{V}{T}$ = constant

for any values of V and T provided the mass of gas and the pressure are the same.

so $\dfrac{V}{T} = \dfrac{V_0}{T_0}$

where V_0 = 80 mm³, T_0 = 273 K, V = 87 mm³ and T is to be worked out

hence $\dfrac{87}{T} = \dfrac{80}{273}$

therefore $T = \dfrac{87 \times 273}{80} = 297$ K

● Boyle's Law

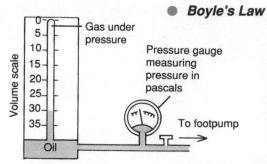

Pressure (Pa)	100	120	150	180
Volume (cm³)	36	30	24	20
Pressure x Volume (Pa cm³)	3600	3600	3600	3600

Figure 7.2H ● Testing Boyles Law

The volume of a gas depends on its pressure as well as its temperature. Figure 7.2H shows how to measure the volume of gas at different pressures while the temperature is maintained constant. The measurements show that the product (pressure x volume) is constant. This is known as Boyle's law, named after Robert Boyle who first discovered the law in 1662.

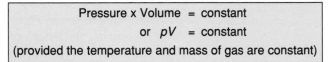

> Pressure x Volume = constant
> or *pV* = constant
> (provided the temperature and mass of gas are constant)

● The pressure law

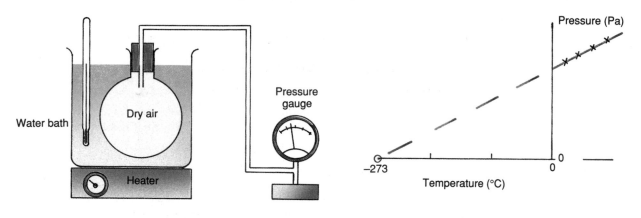

Figure 7.2I ● Measuring pressure against temperature

The pressure of a fixed volume of gas increases as the temperature increases. Figure 7.2I shows how to measure gas pressure at different temperatures. The results show that the gas pressure is proportional to the absolute temperature of the gas. This may be written as an equation.

> Pressure = constant x Absolute temperature
> or *p* = constant x *T*
> (provided the volume and mass remain constant)

● The combined gas law

The three separate gas laws may be written in a single equation which can be used for any change of pressure, volume or temperature.

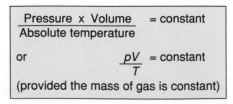

> $$\frac{\text{Pressure x Volume}}{\text{Absolute temperature}} = \text{constant}$$
>
> or $\frac{pV}{T} = \text{constant}$
>
> (provided the mass of gas is constant)

Worked example In a chemical reaction, 5.00 cm³ of gas are collected in a test tube at 110 kPa pressure and a temperature of 290 K. Work out the volume of this gas at a pressure of 100 kPa and a temperature of 273 K.

Solution The combined gas law may be written as

$$\frac{p_1 V_1}{T_1} = \frac{p_2 V_2}{T_2}$$

where p_1 = 110 kPa   and p_2 = 100 kPa
V_1 = 5.00 cm³ V_2 = to be worked out
T_1 = 290 K T_2 = 273 K

Substituting these values into the equation above gives

$$\frac{110 \times 5.00}{290} = \frac{100 \times V_2}{273}$$

Rearranging $V_2 = \dfrac{110 \times 5.00 \times 273}{100 \times 290} = 5.18$ cm³

SUMMARY

Gases, solids and most liquids expand, if allowed, when heated. The expansion of a solid is greater the higher the temperature rise. Different solids expand by different amounts. Bimetallic strips are used in thermostats to switch appliances on or off. The combined gas law may be used to work out changes of pressure, volume and temperature of a gas.

CHECKPOINT

1 Explain;
(a) why expansion gaps are necessary between concrete sections in buildings,
(b) why these gaps are usually filled with soft material.

2 The figure below shows a gas thermostat. If the oven gets too hot, the valve closes a little to lessen the flow of gas. Explain why this happens.

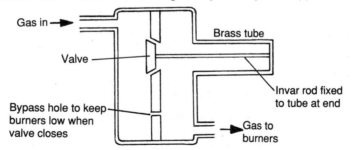

Gas in →
Valve
Brass tube
Invar rod fixed to tube at end
Bypass hole to keep burners low when valve closes
Gas to burners

3 In an experiment to measure thermal expansion of iron, a 50 cm iron bar was heated from 20 °C to 320 °C and its length increased by 1.5 mm. How much expansion would you expect for;
(a) a 50 m rail heated from 20 °C to 320 °C
(b) a 50 m rail heated from 20 °C to 40 °C?

4 Work out the unknown quantity in each of the following changes involving a fixed mass of gas.

	Initial conditions			Final conditions		
	Pressure (kPa)	Volume (m³)	Temperature (K)	Pressure (kPa)	Volume (m³)	Temperature (K)
(a)	100	3.0	300	100	?	400
(b)	100	3.0	300	150	2.0	?
(c)	100	3.0	300	?	1.5	400
(d)	100	3.0	?	150	3.0	400
(e)	100	?	300	200	2.0	400

7.3 Heating things up

How easily can different materials be heated or cooled? Investigations outlined in this section show you how to test different materials to answer this question.

Have you ever noticed how hot a piece of metal can get in sunlight? A stone of similar size gets a little warmer in the sun, but the metal can get quite hot. The metal panels of a parked car can get very hot in the sun. Some things heat up more easily than others. Hammering a piece of lead repeatedly makes it hot; do the same to a piece of steel of the same mass and it will warm up much less.

Investigating heating

To make something hotter, it must be given energy. Suppose two different objects of the same material are heated by giving them the same amount of energy. *Will they have the same temperature rise?*

For example, suppose an electric heater connected to a joulemeter is used to heat water in a plastic cup. The mass of water could be measured and the rise of temperature could be measured. The joulemeter could be used to measure the energy supplied. The test could then be repeated using twice as much water with the same amount of energy being supplied. Some results from the test are shown in the table.

Investigations show that when energy is supplied to a given material to warm it up, the temperature rise depends on the following three factors:

1. **The amount of energy supplied**
   For any given object, the temperature rise is proportional to the energy supplied. In this test, if 0.1 kg of water had been supplied with 10 000 J of energy, its rise of temperature would have been 24 °C
2. **The mass of the material**
   For a given amount of energy supplied, the temperature rise is inversely proportional to the mass. In other words, doubling the mass halves the temperature rise, etc.
3. **The type of material being heated**
   Some materials heat up more easily than others

Mass of water (kg)	0.10	0.20
Energy supplied (J)	5000	5000
Temperature rise (°C)	12	6

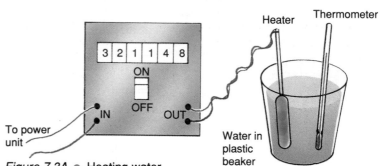

Figure 7.3A ● Heating water

The results show that the larger the mass, the smaller the temperature rise for the same amount of energy supplied. *Can you work out what temperature rise to expect for a mass of water of 0.30 kg supplied with 5000 J of energy?*

● Specific heat capacity

The **specific heat capacity, *c*,** of a material is defined as the energy needed to raise the temperature of 1 kg of material by 1 °C. The unit of specific heat capacity is J/kg/°C.

Consider the results from the test using water.
- 5000 J of energy raises the temperature of 0.10 kg of water by 12 °C.
- For ten times the mass, ten times as much energy is needed. 50 000 J of energy raises the temperature of 1.0 kg of water by 12 °C.
- For a 1 °C rise, only $\frac{1}{12}$ as much energy is needed

$$\frac{50\ 000\ J}{12} \simeq 4200\ J$$

4200 J of energy raises the temperature of 1.0 kg of water by 1 °C. Hence the specific heat capacity for water is approximately 4200 J/kg /°C.

The steps in this calculation can be summarised by the following equation

$$\text{Specific heat capacity} = \frac{\text{Energy supplied}}{\text{Mass} \times \text{Temperature rise}}$$

To work out the energy needed to raise the temperature of a given mass, the above equation can be rearranged to give

Energy supplied = Mass × Specific heat capacity × Temperature rise
  (in joules)   (in kg)   (in J/kg/°C)   (in °C)

Table 7.1 ● Some specific heat capacities

Material	Water	Oil	Aluminium	Iron	Copper	Lead	Concrete
Specific heat capacity (J/kg/°C)	4200	2100	900	390	490	130	850

The **heat capacity**, *C*, of an object is the energy needed to raise its temperature by 1 °C. The unit of *C* is J/°C.

If the object is made of a single material.

Heat capacity = Mass × Specific heat capacity

For example, an aluminium kettle of mass 2.00 kg, the specific heat capacity of aluminium is 900 J/kg/°C. Therefore the heat capacity of the kettle is 1800 J/°C (= 2.00 × 900).

If the object is made of several materials, its heat capacity can be worked out by adding together the heat capacities of the individual materials. For example, the heat capacity of a 2.00 kg aluminium kettle containing 1 kg of water is 1800 + 4200 = 6000 J/°C. This means that 6000 J of energy must be supplied for each °C temperature rise.

Caloric and the Count

About 200 years ago, there were two conflicting theories about the nature of heat. One school of thought considered heat as a form of motion of atoms, essentially as a form of energy although ideas about energy were not well-understood then. The fact that objects became hot through friction when rubbed was the basis of the theory.

Figure 7.3B ● Sir Humphry Davy

Figure 7.3C ● Count Rumford

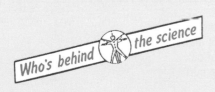

Who's behind the science

Figure 7.3D ● James Prescott Joule

The other group, the Calorists, supposed that heat was a fluid which they called 'caloric'. When a hot object was placed in contact with a cold object, caloric transferred from the hot object to the cold object to make the hot object cooler and the cold object warmer. Experiments involving transfer of heat between hot and cold bodies supported the caloric theory. They explained heating due to friction by supposing that tiny particles created by the rubbing action released caloric. The **calorie** as a unit of heat (equal to the energy needed to heat 1 g of water by 1 °C) dates from this time.

The caloric theory was the accepted view about the nature of heat until it was challenged by Count Rumford in Munich in 1798. He was born Benjamin Thompson in North America and had to flee to Europe during the American Revolution because he remained loyal to Britain. He was a restless, energetic person who developed great enthusiasm and interest in science and founded the Royal Institution in Britain. He settled in Bavaria where he was made Minister of War and was given the title Count Rumford in recognition of his work there.

Rumford measured the temperature rise of a 50 kg brass cannon when a blunt steel drill was applied to it. After 30 minutes, the temperature had risen by 40 °C and just 54 g of metal dust had been produced. The idea that heat from 54 g of metal dust could raise the temperature of a 50 kg brass cannon by 40 °C seemed unlikely to Rumford. More importantly, he realised that the supply of heat was inexhaustible – provided the drill kept turning.

The calorists insisted that the results could be explained if solid metal was much easier to heat than metal dust. The dispute was settled in 1799 by Sir Humphry Davy. He showed that two pieces of ice below freezing point melted when rubbed together. The fact that water at 2 °C was produced could only be explained in terms of work done.

In Manchester in1840, James Joule took the investigations further. He measured the specific heat capacity of water by different methods, all involving doing work to heat the water. All the methods gave the result as 4.2 J/g/°C. This proved conclusively that heat is a form of energy. The scientific unit of energy is named after Joule in recognition of his work.

CHECKPOINT

❶ Use the information in Table 7.1 to explain the following statements.
(a) A mass of lead heats up more easily than an equal mass of aluminium.
(b) A mass of water heats up less easily than an equal mass of oil.
(c) A metal seat gets much hotter than a bucket of water in the sun.

❷ How much energy is needed for each of the following?
(a) To raise the temperature of 2.0 kg of aluminium by 30 °C.
(b) To raise the temperature of 0.05 m³ of water in a water tank from 20 °C to 60 °C. (Assume the density of water is 1000 kg/m³).
(c) To heat a 20 kg concrete block in a storage heater from 10 °C to 40 °C.
(d) To heat 1.50 kg of water in a copper kettle of mass 0.050 kg from 20 °C to boiling point.

❸ Water can be heated using electricity, coal, or even peanuts. Design an experiment to measure the energy from a peanut when it burns and heats water.

❹ (a) A 3.0 kW electric kettle is capable of heating 2.0 kg of water from 20 °C to 100 °C in 300 seconds. How much electrical energy is supplied and how much of the energy is used to heat the water? Explain why more energy is supplied than is used to heat the water.
(b) Water in a plastic jug was put in a fridge where it cooled from 15 °C to 5 °C in 600 seconds. If the mass of water in the jug was 0.8 kg, how much energy was removed from it to reduce its temperature? How much energy was removed each second?

7.4 Latent heat

In a busy kitchen, water is boiled in a kettle and frozen in a freezer. What energy changes are involved in these processes? What is the cost of each of these processes?

In the kitchen

Heat some water in a saucepan. As the water warms up, water vapour comes off its surface. This is because water in the liquid state is changing into water vapour. This is the process of **vaporisation**. As the water becomes hotter, it reaches a temperature at which vaporisation takes place throughout the water. Bubbles of vapour rise to the surface – the water boils.

Suppose you put an egg into some water which is being heated. The temperature of the water rises until it reaches boiling point. No further increase in temperature occurs while the water boils, even though heat is still being supplied. On 'full heat', the water boils vigorously but doesn't cook the egg any faster. Turn the 'heat' down on the cooker so the water is just 'on the boil'. This stops the kitchen steaming up and saves fuel.

The energy supplied to vaporise water is called **latent heat**. It is needed to break the attractive forces between the molecules.

Condensation is the reverse of vaporisation. For example, when a lot of steam is produced in a kitchen, water may be seen running down window panes or wall tiles. This happens because the steam condenses on the cold surfaces. Latent heat is given out in condensation.

Investigating boiling

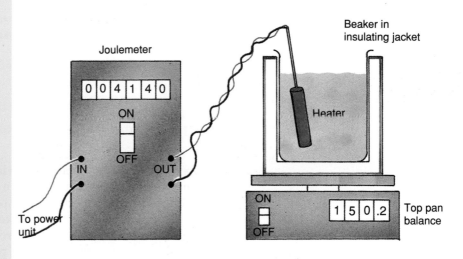

Figure 7.4A ● Measuring the specific latent heat of vaporisation of water

How much energy is needed to vaporise water? Figure 7.4A shows how this can be measured. Here are some measurements from this apparatus;

Joulemeter reading (J)	0	4600	9200	13 800	18 400
Top pan balance reading (kg)	0.152	0.150	0.148	0.146	0.144

As the water boiled away, the total mass on the balance went down. *Can you work out how much energy was needed to boil away 0.001 kg of water?* The results in the table above should give 2300 J for this calculation. To vaporise 1.00 kg of water, 2 300 000 J (= 2300 J x 1000) would be needed.

The **specific latent heat of vaporisation, *l*,** of a pure liquid is the energy needed to vaporise 1 kg of pure liquid without change of temperature. The unit of *l* is J/kg (or MJ/kg).

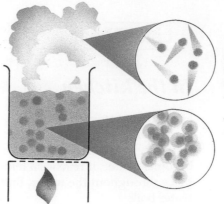

Molecules in the vapour state move about much faster than molecules in the liquid state and are much further apart

water molecules moving about

Figure 7.4B ● From water to steam

Therefore, the energy needed to vaporise a certain mass m of pure liquid is equal to mass $m \times$ specific latent heat of vaporisation l.

Solution Work out the energy needed to raise the temperature of the water to 100 °C and then the energy needed to boil the water away.

To raise the temperature of 0.50 kg of water from 20 °C to 100 °C

Energy needed = Mass x Specific heat capacity x Temperature rise
               = 0.50 kg x 4200 J/kg/°C x 80°C = 168 000 J = 0.168 MJ

To boil away 0.50 kg of water

Energy needed = Mass x Specific latent heat
               = 0.50 kg x 2 300 000 J/kg = 1 150 000 J = 1.15 MJ

The total energy needed = 0.168 + 1.15 = 1.32 MJ

Using a freezer

Ice cubes from a freezer melt quickly in a kitchen. During melting, there is no change in the temperature of the substance. The energy needed to melt a substance is called **latent heat of melting**. It is used to enable the molecules of the substance to break free from each other.

Put a plastic beaker of water in a freezer and the reverse process happens. The water cools to freezing point then it turns to ice. The freezer takes energy from the water.

Food in a freezer is preserved because micro-organisms need water for growth. The water content of the food is frozen and micro-organisms can not multiply. However, freezing does not kill the micro-organisms and they revive when the food thaws out. Food from a freezer must be cooked thoroughly to kill any micro-organisms in it before being eaten.

● Specific latent heat

When any liquid solidifies, latent heat is given out by the substance as the molecules bond more closely together. For example, a test tube of wax gives out heat when the liquid solidifies. The word latent means 'hidden'; when a liquid turns into a solid, energy 'hidden' in the bonds between the molecules is released. When food is put into a freezer, its water content turns into ice and latent heat is given out. This is taken away by the refrigeration unit of the freezer.

The energy removed from food put in a freezer depends on the mass of food and the type of food. Doubling the mass means that twice as much energy must be removed.

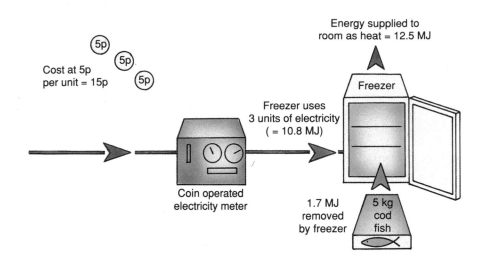

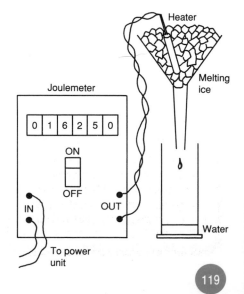

Figure 7.4C ● The cost of freezing

The **specific latent heat of fusion, *l*,** of a substance is the energy needed to melt 1 kg of solid (or given out when 1 kg of solid freezes) without change of temperature. The unit of *l* is J/kg.

To work out the energy removed when freezing a substance, its mass must be known and its specific latent heat. For example, to freeze 5.00 kg of water at 0 °C, the energy to be taken away is 5.00 x 340 000 J (= 1.7 MJ). This is because the latent heat of fusion of ice is 340 000 J/kg so to freeze each kg of ice, 340 000 J of energy must be removed. To melt 5.00 kg of water at 0 °C, 5.00 x 340 000 J of energy must be supplied.

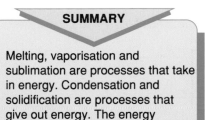

SUMMARY

Melting, vaporisation and sublimation are processes that take in energy. Condensation and solidification are processes that give out energy. The energy involved in these changes is called latent heat.

Energy needed (or given out)	= Mass x	Specific latent heat
(in joules)	(in kg)	(in J/kg)

CHECKPOINT

❶ Describe the energy changes in each of the following situations.

(a) Clearing a misted car window using an electric demister heater.
(b) Freezing home-baked fruit pies in a deep freeze.
(c) Distilling ethanol (alcohol).

❷ The figure opposite shows an experiment to measure the specific latent heat of ice.

With the heater switched off, 0.024 kg of water was collected in the beaker in 5.00 minutes. The beaker was then emptied and replaced as shown. With the heater switched on for 5.00 minutes, the joulemeter reading increased from 3500 J to 18 500 J. During this time, 0.068 kg of water was collected in the beaker.

(a) Some of the ice in the funnel melted when the heater was off. Why?
(b) How much ice was melted in 5 minutes due to the heater being on?
(c) How much energy was supplied by the heater in this time?
(d) Work out the specific latent heat of ice from the above results.

3. Carlos has just completed a half-marathon and is hot, tired and sweaty. He wants to use an anti-perspirant to stop sweating but Louise tells him it's not such a good idea while he is still hot. Why?
4. Design an experiment to test whether a cup of hot water placed in a freezer freezes faster than cold water. If possible, try out your ideas. You may be surprised by the result.
5. A 3.0 kW electric kettle is fitted with a thermal cut-out designed to switch it off as soon as the water boils. Unfortunately, the cut-out does not operate correctly and allows the water to boil for 30 seconds longer than it is supposed to.
   (a) How much electrical energy is used in this time?
   (b) The specific latent heat of vaporisation of water is 2.3 MJ/kg. Use this value and your answer to (a) to work out the mass of water boiled away in this time.
   (c) If you used this kettle in your kitchen, what would happen to the steam it produced?

7.5 Heat transfer

FIRST THOUGHTS

Different methods of heat transfer are compared here with a brief look at some applications.

Look around your home and make a list of the types of heaters you find. Include central heating radiators in your list. Heaters keep your home warm by using energy in a particular form to supply heat.

Heat convectors

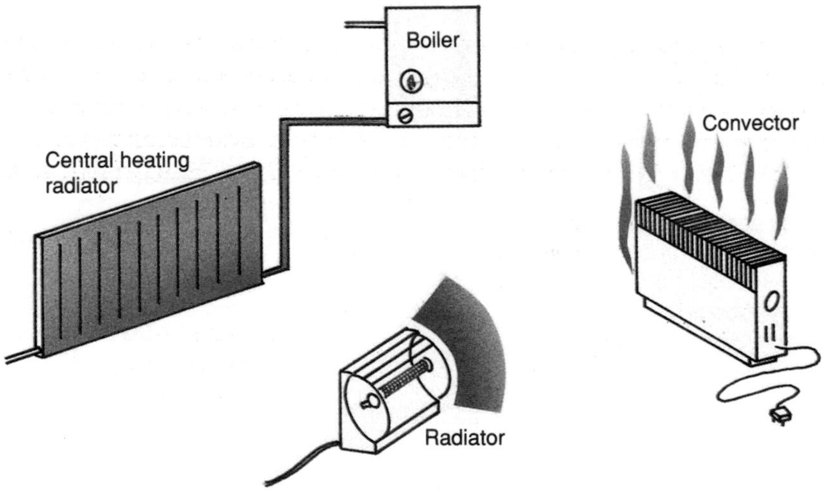

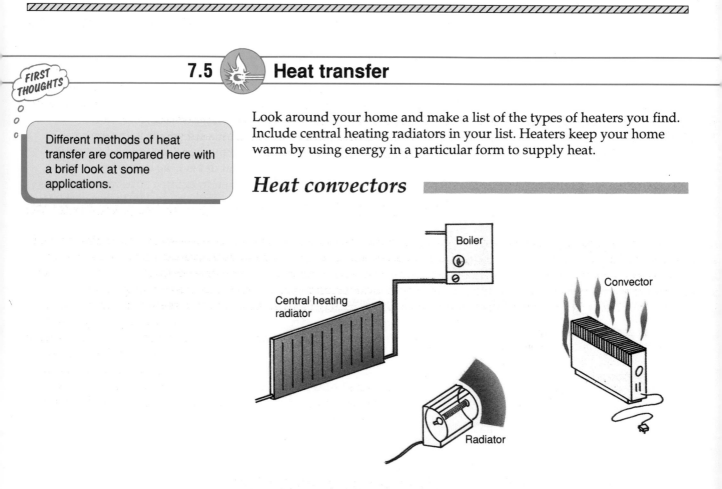

Figure 7.5A ● Heaters at home

Convectors are designed to heat the air in a room. They rely on the fact that hot air, being less dense than cold air, rises. In a convector, a heating element warms the air which rises. The warm air is replaced by cold air which in turn is heated. In this way the warm air circulates and the room heats up.

A simple demonstration of convection is shown in Figure 7.5B. The hot gases from the burning candle go straight up the chimney above the candle. Cold air is drawn down the other chimney to replace the air leaving the room.

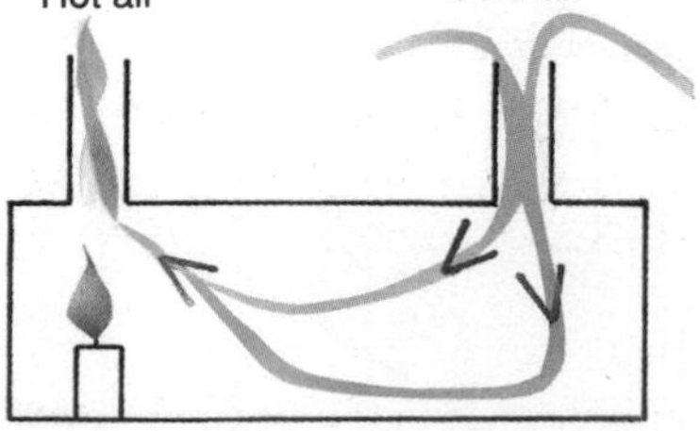

Figure 7.5B ● Convection

Housewarming
(program)

Work in a small group. This program allows you to explore the way that energy can be conserved at home. Load the program and try using different fuels. Which heating system is most efficient?

Try running the simulation through a whole year – how successful were you in saving money?

Convection happens whenever a liquid or a gas is heated. Water from a hot water tank is usually drawn off near the top of the tank. This is because the hot water in the tank rises to the top. If the feed pipe for the hot water tap was connected near the bottom of the tank, it would draw cold water.

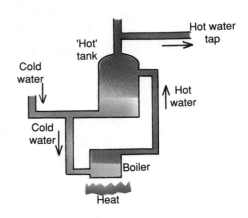

Figure 7.5C ● The hot water system

Heat radiators

Radiators like the one in Figure 7.5A are designed to 'throw' heat from the heating element into the room. The curved shiny metal panel behind the heating element is important because it reflects heat from the element into the room. Heat **radiation** is carried by **infra-red** waves emitted from the heating element. No substance is needed for transfer by heat radiation because infra-red waves can travel through a vacuum. Heat from the Sun is carried by this type of radiation.

Heat conductors

Central heating radiators transfer heat to the room by convection as well as by radiation. Each hot radiator panel warms the nearby layers of air which carry heat to other parts of the room by convection of air currents. *How does the panel get hot?* Water from the central heating boiler is pumped through the panel via pipes. The water is cooler when it leaves the panel than when it enters. This is because it gives up energy to heat the room. This energy passes through the metal walls of the radiator from the inside to the outside of the radiator. The process where heat passes through a solid is called **conduction**. Radiator panels made from plastic would be little use because plastic is a much poorer conductor of heat than metal is. Heat can pass through liquids and gases by conduction as well as by convection.

SUMMARY

Heat transfer can be by conduction, convection or radiation.
- Radiation: no substance is needed to transfer heat.
- Convection: when a liquid or a gas is heated, the hot fluid rises, taking heat with it.
- Conduction: heat passes through a solid, liquid or gas.

FIRST THOUGHTS

7.6  ## More about conduction

Thermal conductors and insulators are compared in this section and their uses outlined.

Conductors

Why do saucepans have plastic or wooden handles? If the handle was made from metal, what would happen when you took hold of a hot saucepan? Why must the handle be made from material that is a poor conductor of heat?

● *Testing thermal conductors*
To test how well different materials conduct heat, rods coated with wax could be heated as shown in Figure 7.6A. The rods need to be the same

size. As heat passes along each rod, the wax along the rod melts. The best conductor is the rod which 'de-waxes' fastest. Look carefully at Figure 7.6A to decide which material is the best and which is the poorest conductor of heat. Metals are much better **thermal conductors** (conductors of heat) than non-metals. Copper is one of the best thermal conductors.

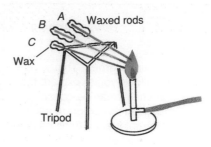

Figure 7.6A ● Comparing conductors

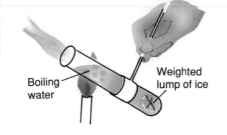

Figure 7.6B ● Testing water

How well does water conduct heat? Heat a test-tube of water near the top with a 'weighted' ice cube near the bottom. Even when the water at the top starts boiling, the ice cube does not melt. Water is a poor conductor of heat.

Insulators

Insulators are used to lag pipes, lofts, hot water tanks and many other objects. Insulators are very poor conductors. Wrapped round hot objects, they act as a barrier, reducing the heat loss. Fibre glass insulation is a popular choice for insulating the lofts of homes. This material is manufactured in thick layers and sold in rolls. Trapped air is an effective insulator too. Fibre glass layers contain lots of tiny pockets of trapped air. Thermal clothing, designed to wear outdoors in winter, contains materials with lots of tiny air pockets.

Tests show that the heat flow per second passing through each square metre of a material depends on the following factors.

- The thickness of the material: using more layers cuts down the heat flow.
- The temperature difference across the material: the greater the difference from the hot side to the cool side, the greater the heat flow.
- The type of material chosen: some materials are better insulators than others.

Figure 7.6C ● Loft insulation

SUMMARY

Metals are the best conductors of heat. Materials used for thermal insulation are very poor conductors of heat. The heat flow per square metre through a material increases as the temperature difference across the material increases. Making the material thicker reduces the heat flow.

CHECKPOINT

❶ Explain why;
   (a) an electric iron has a plastic handle and a metal base,
   (b) fitting an insulation jacket to a domestic hot water tank saves money,
   (c) wrapping a block of ice cream in paper helps to stop it melting.

❷ In the ice cube experiment shown in Figure 7.6B, suppose the ice cube was at the top of the tube and the tube was heated at the bottom. Would the ice cube melt more easily this time? Explain your answer.

❸ Keith's parents are planning to put insulation down in their loft. His mother works out that the insulation ought to cut the heat loss by 80 J/s for each °C of temperature difference.
   (a) How much energy will be 'saved' in 1 day when the temperature difference is 10 °C?
   (b) Keith's father works out that their heating costs 1.5p per million joules. How much money will be saved in (a)?
   (c) The insulation material costs them £80. How many days like (a) will it take to pay for it?

❹ In an experiment to test the effectiveness of insulation material, hot water was poured into a test-tube and the water temperature was measured at intervals while it cooled. The test was then repeated with the same volume of water, with the tube wrapped in the insulating material. The results are shown below.

Time (min)	Temperature (°C)	
	Unwrapped tube	Wrapped tube
0	70	70
1	64	67
2	60	64.5
3	57	62
4	55	60
5	53.5	58.5

   (a) Plot graphs of temperature (on the vertical axis) against time for both the wrapped and the unwrapped tube on the same axis.
   (b) How long did each tube take to cool from 70 °C to 65 °C?
   (c) How effective was the insulating material?

FIRST THOUGHTS

7.7 ☀ Radiation

The nature and properties of radiant heat are outlined here through investigation and applications.

In winter at night, a clear starry sky usually means it's going to be very cold by the next morning. This happens because of heat radiation going from the ground out into space. During the daytime, heat radiation from the Sun reaches the Earth and warms the ground. At night, when the sky is clear, the ground temperature falls as the ground radiates energy into space.

Satellites fitted with special cameras sensitive to heat radiation give very interesting pictures. Towns and cities show up because they emit much more radiation than rural areas.

All objects emit heat radiation. Heating an object up makes it radiate more energy. Cooling it makes it radiate less. Have you ever walked into a refrigerated cold storage room? Don't get locked in because you radiate your energy away very quickly and you would soon freeze! Go into a hot

7.8 ● Keeping warm

In this section you will find out which are the most effective methods for keeping warm in winter. You could help to reduce your home heating costs by studying this section carefully.

Keeping warm at home

Home heating costs money, not just to buy heaters but to pay for the fuel used. The amount of fuel we use as a nation each year to keep warm is equivalent to 30 million tonnes of coal! Better insulation in our homes cuts down on fuel bills and could reduce the need for more power stations.

Double glazing
Cuts down on outdoor noise as well as reducing heat losses. Sealed double-glazed units consist of two panes of glass with a layer of dry air between. Another effective way of cutting out heat losses through a window is to draw the curtains!

Aluminium foil
Placed between a radiator panel and the wall, the foil reflects heat radiation away from the wall. Radiator panels are often fixed on walls under windows, otherwise the air near the window would be cold

Draught excluders
Fitted around doors they help to keep us warm in winter. Cutting out the airflow can be very dangerous where gas and coal fires and paraffin heaters are used. There all use up the oxygen from the air and usually produce the harmless products, carbon dioxide and water. If there is insufficient air flow these fuels burn to form the poisonous gas, carbon monoxide. So never use draught excluders to block air vents

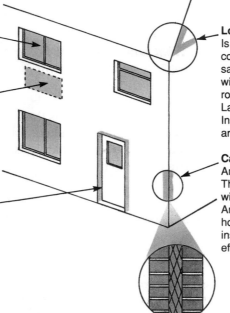

Loft insulation
Is very cost effective. This means the initial costs for the material are soon repaid by the savings from reduced fuel bills. A home without loft insulation loses heat through the roof almost as quickly as if there were no roof. Lagging the hot water tank saves money too. Insulation jackets are manufactured to fit around hot water tanks

Cavity wall insulation
Another popular method of reducing fuel bills. The outer walls of a house are double-brick with a cavity between the two layers of bricks. An air filled cavity cuts down heat losses: however, by filing the cavity with suitable insulation foam, it becomes an even more effective barrier against heat losses

Figure 7.8A ● Keeping warm at home

Domestic heating
(program)

Use this program to study the way that a house or flat can be constructed to conserve heat. How does the living temperature inside the flat or house affect their heating bills? What are the best ways of saving money?

Find out what the *U*-value of a material is by using the program. Which materials have high *U*-values?

● U-*values*
Materials used to insulate homes are rated in terms of their **U-value**. This is the rate of heat flow passing through one square metre of material when the temperature difference across the material is 1 °C. For example, a wall with a *U*-value of 1.6 W/m²/°C lets 1.6 J pass through each square metre each second when the temperature inside is 1 °C higher than outside.

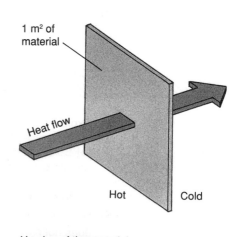

1 m² of material

Heat flow

Hot   Cold

U-value of the material
= heat/s passing per m²
for 1°C temperature difference

Figure 7.8B ● U-value

IT'S A
FACT

The chill factor is the decrease in skin temperature due to adverse weather. Rain may cause a chill factor of 5–10 °C but strong winds as well as rain may increase it to 20 °C.

SUMMARY

There are a variety of measures that can be taken to reduce heat losses from homes. These measures reduce fuel bills. Suitable clothing is needed to keep warm outdoors in winter.

Keeping warm outdoors

What about when you go outdoors in winter? Outdoor clothing for winter use must let your body 'breathe' otherwise sweating can make you uncomfortable. Another problem is that your clothing must not absorb rain. If it did, you would become chilled and if there was any wind, you might even freeze. This is because the rain evaporates, a process that needs energy. The effect of the wind is to increase the rate of evaporation which means that energy is lost even faster. So there are a number of factors to be considered in the choice of materials for outdoor clothes.

Figure 7.8C ● The chill factor

CHECKPOINT

❶ Hot drinks can be kept warm in a vacuum flask. The figure opposite shows a cross-section of this type of flask.
  (a) Why does the inner flask have silvery walls?
  (b) Why is there a vacuum between the silvery walls of the inner flask?
  (c) Polythene is used to hold the inner flask in position in the can. Why is polythene chosen?
  (d) Why is it important to keep the lid on the flask when it is filled with hot liquid?

❷ Keeping warm in winter is a major problem for elderly people. They can suffer from hypothermia, a condition which happens when the body gets too cold and the victim becomes unconscious. What advice would you give to help an elderly person at home to keep warm without running up big fuel bills?

❸ Design an experiment to investigate the chill factor. Use a test-tube containing hot water as a 'body'. State what additional equipment you would use, what measurements you would make and how you would use your measurements.

❹ (a) Work out the energy loss per second through the windows and wall of the house in the figure opposite. Use the information in the picture.
  (b) How much energy per second is needed to keep the inside of this house at 20 °C when the outdoor temperature is 0 °C?
  (c) The house in the figure has gas-fired central heating. The cost of gas is 36p per therm and one therm gives 106 MJ of energy. Work out the cost per hour of keeping the house at 20 °C when it is freezing outside.

Stopper
Polythene
Can
Silvery walls
Hot liquid
Vacuum
Polythene

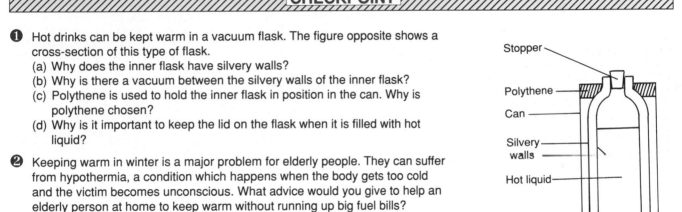

Total wall area of house = 70 m²

Total window area of house = 8 m²

	U-value (W/m²/°C)
Windows	3.2
Walls	0.6

TOPIC 8 ● ENERGY RESOURCES

8.1 ● Our energy needs

FIRST THOUGHTS

Find out in this section how much energy we as a nation use in a year and where it comes from.

If energy cannot be created or destroyed, why do we need to keep searching for new sources of energy? Jobs need energy: what happens to the energy used after the job is done? The problem with energy is that it spreads out when it is used.

Figure 8.1A ● Energy for fun

How much energy do you use in a day? To keep warm in winter, you could switch an electric heater on. Suppose your heater uses 1000 joules of electrical energy each second. If used for a whole day, it would use

$$1000 \times 24 \times 60 \times 60 = 86.4 \text{ MJ}$$

More energy would be needed to feed you, entertain you, carry you about and so on. In fact, on average, each person in the United Kingdom needs about 500 MJ each day. *Where does it all come from and where does it all go?*

- **Useful energy** is the energy that is used to do a particular task.
- **Primary energy** is the total energy needed to supply useful energy.

Energy is used to heat water in a kettle to make a hot drink. But much more energy is 'needed' than is used. This is because the energy used by the kettle is in a convenient form delivered to where we want to use it. The energy to heat the kettle may have come from an oil-fired power station. Energy is needed to change the energy in the oil to a convenient form and deliver it to the user. Suppose making a hot drink uses 1 MJ of electrical energy and 0.5 MJ of energy is used to produce and deliver the electrical energy to you. The total energy needed to make the drink (i.e. the primary energy) is therefore 1.5 MJ, just part of the 500 MJ of primary energy each of us needs per day on average.

IT ***BP Energy File*** (database)

Use this database to see how much energy is used in different places and to find out which fuels are used to supply it.

LOOK AT LINKS
for **fossil fuels**
see Theme L, Topics 48.4
and 48.5.

How much energy does the United Kingdom need in one year? Each person needs about 500 MJ in a day and there are about 50 million people in the UK. Reach for your calculator and work out the nation's primary energy need per year. More than 8 million, million, million joules!

Where do we get all this energy from? Life on Earth depends on the Sun because most forms of energy that we use come, directly or indirectly, from the Sun.

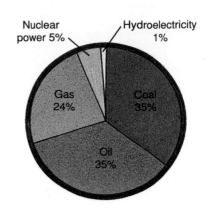

Figure 8.1B ● Britain's energy supplies

Fuels such as coal and oil were formed millions of years ago from prehistoric forests and marine organisms. Layer upon layer of decaying vegetation became compressed and eventually formed coal and other **fossil fuels**. Energy from the Sun made these forests grow so when we burn coal or oil we are releasing energy that arrived on Earth long ago. Uranium, the fuel used in nuclear reactors, has always been part of the Earth's crust. Coal and oil are examples of primary fuels because they can be used to produce secondary fuels such as electricity or petrol which must be made.

Renewable energy resources such as hydroelectricity and solar power use processes that are part of our natural environment. Energy from these resources is 'tapped off' and used. Coal, oil and uranium are not renewable resources because they were formed long ago; once used as fuel, they cannot be replaced. The term 'renewable' is used for energy from sources that are constantly replenished. For example, energy from hydroelectricity comes from rainwater running down hill, and this is part of the natural **water cycle**.

Figure 8.1B shows how the United Kingdom energy needs were met in the mid-1980s. Fuel reserves are limited and, sooner or later, there will be no more oil or gas or coal or uranium. Some scientists think that gas reserves will be used up by the year 2025. *How old will you be then?*

LOOK AT LINKS
for **water cycle**
see Theme E, Topic 22.1.

SUMMARY

Energy always spreads out when it is used. Our present energy needs are met by using fuels such as gas, oil, coal and uranium. Little use is made of renewable energy resources at present.

CHECKPOINT

❶ Make a list of the secondary fuels you use between getting up in the morning and arriving at school. What do you use each type of fuel for?

❷ In Figure 8.1B, if oil was not available, how would this affect the usage of energy in terms of transport, heating, industry and so on?

❸ World energy reserves are shown in the figure opposite.
  (a) Which fuels will run out first at the present rate of usage?
  (b) How will the absence of this fuel affect people in general?
  (c) Which type of fuel would appear to offer the best long-term supply of energy?
  (d) What factors make predictions about the use of energy uncertain?

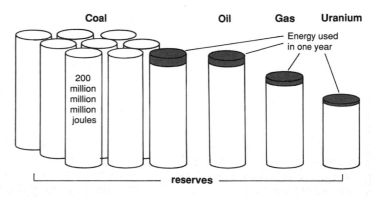

8.2 Fuel

FIRST
THOUGHTS

Why is it important to use our fuel reserves carefully? What are the benefits of each type of fuel? Which fuels are likely to be in short supply in the future?

Fossil fuels such as coal, oil and gas lie underground and are often difficult to extract. Some coalfields in coastal areas extend beneath the sea-bed. Recovery of coal from such mines is much more complicated than recovery from open-cast mines. Open-cast mines are mines where the coal seams can easily be reached by tunnels rather than vertical shafts. Oil and gas fields under the sea bed are much more difficult to reach than fields under dry land. As the demand for fossil fuels increases, so the search for new fields is being extended to remote regions of the world. However, reserves of fossil fuels are not unlimited.

Figure 8.2A ● Open cast mining

Agriculture depends on petroleum; the **petrochemicals industry** makes **pesticides** that farmers use to protect their crops from insects and weeds. Without the petrochemicals industry we should have fewer modern drugs and medicines. Most manufacturing industries depend on the oil industry. Without oil, our cars, trains, boats, planes would be useless. Without oil and gas, our present economy would collapse returning us to primitive living conditions. Unless scientists find substitutes for oil and gas, our future is going to be a low-technology future. This is what you hear described as the **world energy crisis**. It crops up constantly in newspaper articles and TV programmes.

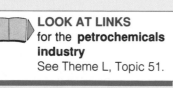
LOOK AT LINKS
for the **petrochemicals industry**
See Theme L, Topic 51.

LOOK AT LINKS
for the **pesticides**
See Theme G, Topic 29.

Coal

Coal will continue to be an important fuel for many years to come. Britain is literally built on coal and new coalfields like Selby in Yorkshire are being developed to meet future energy needs. Coal-fired power stations produce much of our electricity.

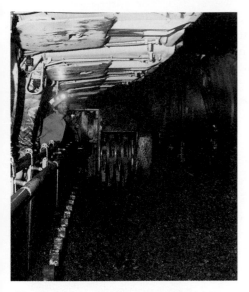

Figure 8.2B ● Inside a coal mine

Research scientists have found methods of making liquid fuels from coal.

$$\text{Coal} + \text{Hydrogen} \xrightarrow[\text{pressure with a catalyst}]{\text{At high temperature and}} \text{Liquid hydrocarbon fuel}$$

This fuel can be used to power diesel engines. South Africa has invested in enormous coal **liquefaction** plants for making transport fuel. These factories are unhealthy places to work in because contact with the products can cause skin cancer.

Coal can also be used as a source of fuel gas. The gasification of coal is less risky and less expensive than liquefaction. It is done by heating coal and then passing steam over the residue. A mixture of gaseous fuels is formed.

$$\text{Coal} \xrightarrow{\text{Heat then steam}} \text{Fuel gas (Carbon monoxide + Hydrogen + Methane)}$$

There are drawbacks, however, over increasing coal production. Open-cast mining ruins the landscape. underground mining creates spoil heaps, great mounds of soil and rock that have been dug out of the mine. A spoil heap collapsed on the Welsh village of Aberfan in 1968, killing dozens of people.

Oil and natural gas

Oil and natural gas reserves throughout the world are likely to be used up by the middle of the twenty-first century unless major new fields are discovered. Searching for new oilfields takes scientists to remote parts of the world like Alaska. Oil rigs in the North Sea are designed to withstand extremely hostile weather conditions. One of the most important products from oil is petrol. Scientists in several countries are trying to develop alternative fuels for cars.

Natural gas is mostly methane and is found trapped in pockets underground, often below the sea-bed. Gas is used in homes for heating and cooking.

Figure 8.2C ● Drilling for oil

Figure 8.2D ● Oil rig

Power Plan
(program)

This program shows you the names and locations of the nuclear power stations in Britain. Look at their locations. Why are they near the coast? Study the types of reactor. What are the two main types shown here?

Try the challenge game in which you have to keep Britain's electricity supply going.

Tar sands and oil shales are sources of oil which have not yet been exploited. This is because it is too costly to extract oil from them at present. Tar sands are deposits of tar in sand. Oil shales are deposits of oil in porous shale rocks.

Nuclear fuels

● *Fission*

Figure 8.2E ● Torness nuclear power station

LOOK AT LINKS
for **radioactive waste**
see Theme C, Topic 12.9.

Uranium is the fuel for nuclear power stations. Uranium ores were formed in the Earth's crust billions of years ago. Uranium ores must be refined before they are suitable for using as fuel. One tonne of uranium can give the same amount of energy as one million tonnes of coal. However, nuclear power stations have disadvantages. The waste products from nuclear fuel are highly radioactive and must be stored for thousands of years until they become harmless.

Nuclear reactors are designed to produce heat which drives steam turbines to generate electricity. Reactors must be continually monitored to ensure radioactive fuel does not escape. Inside a nuclear reactor, the temperature and pressure are very high and the materials used for the reactor must withstand these extreme conditions.

Figure 8.2F ● Storage of radioactive waste

LOOK AT LINKS
for **nuclear power**
The processes of fusion
and fission are described
in Theme C, Topics 12.1,
12.2 and 12.7 and the
operation of a fission
reactor is explained in
Theme C, Topic 12.6.

SUMMARY

Most of our present energy needs
are met by using fossil fuels and
uranium. Fossil fuels add to the
'greenhouse effect' and will result
in a warming of the atmosphere.
Uranium fuels produce radioactive
waste products that must be stored
for many years.

● *Fusion*

Fusion reactors are nuclear
reactors that do not use
uranium as the fuel. Instead,
the two isotopes of hydrogen
called **deuterium** and **tritium**
will be used. Deuterium can be
obtained from water and
tritium can be made within the
reactor from the light metal
lithium. Although the reactor
structure will become
radioactive, the waste
produced will be easier to deal
with. Waste from fusion
reactors needs to be stored for
much shorter periods than
waste from uranium reactors.
Fusion reactors themselves are
much safer than uranium
reactors. Fusion reactors are still
at the experimental stage, and
many more years of research
are needed to find out whether
they will be able to produce
electricity on a large scale.

Figure 8.2G ● JET – the Joint
European Torus – is the world's largest
and most powerful fusion experiment.
It aims to produce fusion reactions
similar to those which occur in the
Sun. JET is a collaborative venture
involving 14 European nations.

CHECKPOINT

❶ Many homes were heated by coal fires before 1960. Smoke and fog
together produce an unhealthy atmosphere called 'smog' which can last
for days. Converting homes to gas or electric heating has eliminated the
smog problem.
  (a) Why did the introduction of gas and electric heating in homes
      eliminate the smog problem?
  (b) Why is it important that waste gases from coal-fired power stations
      should be cleansed of smoke?
  (c) What sort of illnesses could be caused by breathing in smog?

❷ France has few reserves of coal. Why has the French government built
many more nuclear power stations than Britain has?

❸ In 1988, the Central Electricity Generating Board estimated that the
demand for electricity in the year 2000 would be 15 000 MW greater than
in 1988.
  (a) How many 1000 MW power stations need to be built to meet this
      demand?
  (b) What type of power stations should be built to meet this demand?
      Explain your answer.

❹ (a) Nuclear power stations are generally located far away from cities.
      Why?
  (b) Power stations need vast quantities of water in their cooling systems.
      How does this limit the number of possible locations?

❺ The demand for electricity varies during each day, as shown in the figure
opposite.
  (a) Why is demand highest in the evening?
  (b) Demand becomes very small after midnight. Why?
  (c) Why is demand in winter greater than in summer?

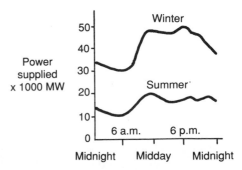

8.3 ● Renewable energy resources

FIRST THOUGHTS

The alternatives to present fuel supplies are outlined and compared in this section. Are these alternatives realistic? Read on to find out.

IT'S A FACT

At the end of popular TV programmes, electricity demand surges as people leave their TV sets and make hot drinks. Pumped storage schemes as at Dinorwic in North Wales are designed to help engineers cope with such surges of demand. When there is little demand for electricity, water from a low-level reservoir is pumped uphill to a reservoir up in the mountains. When demand suddenly rises, the flow is reversed and electricity is produced.

LOOK AT LINKS
for **biomass**
Sugar cane and maize are grown in some tropical countries to make ethanol which can be used to fuel cars. Brazil is one country that has reduced its dependence on imported oil by using ethanol from crops to run cars.
See Theme L, Topic 48.3.

SUMMARY

Renewable energy resources are natural processes that can be 'tapped' to supply useful energy. Materials used in these processes are replaced by natural means. Renewables could provide up to 33% of our energy needs.

The Sun's energy drives the earth's atmosphere like a huge engine, creating rain, wind and waves. Plants absorb energy from sunlight. Scientists reckon that the amount of the sun's energy reaching the Earth each second is about 1 million million million (= 10^{18}) joules. Just a tiny fraction of this vast amount of energy would be enough to meet our energy needs. No fuel would be needed. We would be using energy from the Sun as it arrives and the Sun has 5000 million years to go before it runs short of its fuel.

Renewable energy is a term used to describe energy supplied by processes that are part of our natural environment. For example, windmills are machines that produce useful energy from the energy of the wind. Windmills have been around for many centuries but now there is renewed interest in using wind energy to meet our energy needs. The oil reserves will run out, the use of coal may need to be limited, nuclear reactors may be considered too risky. Can renewable energy resources meet our needs in the future?

Hydroelectricity is produced from the potential energy given up by rainwater running off mountains. The water is channelled so it flows downhill through huge turbines which produce electricity. In the mid 1980s, hydroelectric power stations supplied less than 0.25% of the UK's primary energy needs. Large hydro schemes in Wales and the Scottish Highlands could supply more of our present energy needs. With no fuel needed, the cost of hydroelectricity is much less than electricity from coal or uranium powered stations.

Figure 8.3A ● Hydroelectricity

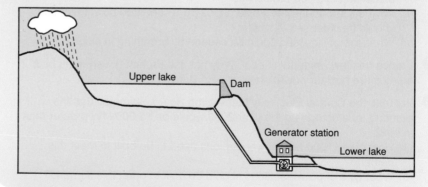

Upper lake

Dam

Generator station

Lower lake

Figure 8.3B ● Tidal power

Tidal power stations in suitable coastal areas are designed to trap each rising tide behind a barrage. The high tide is then released into the sea through turbines in the barrage to make electricity. One of the most promising sites in Britain is the Severn estuary where the incoming tide is reflected by the estuary banks making it even higher.

Wavepower is another promising energy resource. Scientists reckon that each metre of suitable coastline could give about 20 kW of power. Just 50 km of coastline would give the same power output as a 1000 MW nuclear power station. Some scientists think that wavepower could supply 10% of the UK's energy needs.

Wave-powered electricity generators would need to withstand extreme weather conditions. They would not produce a constant supply of electricity but they could be used to feed energy into pumped storage schemes.

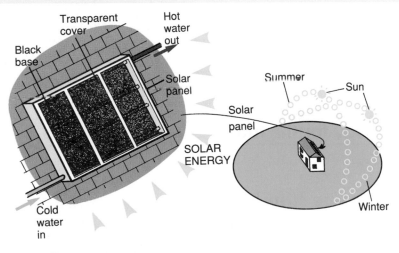

Figure 8.3C ● Wave power

Solar energy can be collected directly using solar heating panels or solar cells. Solar panels fitted to south-facing roofs can be very effective. Water trickling through the panels is heated directly by the Sun. Even on cloudy days in Britain, a solar panel of area 11 m² could collect 300 W of solar energy. A south-facing roof covered with solar panels could supply the hot-water needs of a house. Solar heating could produce the equivalent of ten 1000 MW power stations.

Figure 8.3E ● Solar energy

Biomass is material from living organisms. Wood, charcoal and ethanol are examples of biomass fuels. Methane gas from rotting plant and animal matter is called **biogas**. Many farms have a methane generator which produces methane for heating. Household rubbish tipped into landfill sites also generates biogas. In the UK, refuse from homes and factories could provide sufficient biogas for heating to supply 10% of national energy needs.

Figure 8.3D ● Using biomass

Aerogenerators are driven by wind. They can be much larger than old-style windmills and much more powerful. However, the output of an aerogenerator is not steady because it varies with windspeed.

Clusters of aerogenerators in remote areas could make a big contribution to our energy needs. Imagine a cluster of 100 aerogenerators over an area of 10 x 10 km, each generator producing 5 MW of electricity. Two such clusters would give the same output as a 1000 MW power station.

Figure 8.3F ● Wind power

Geothermal energy from the hot interior of the earth can raise the temperature of underground rocks in the earth's crust to more than 200 °C. Water pumped down to these rocks is converted into steam which can then be used to drive turbines that make electricity.

Some geothermal wells produce their own hot water from water that has gradually seeped into sedimentary layers in the Earth's crust. The energy from a single geothermal well could heat several large blocks of flats or offices. Geologists reckon that geothermal energy could supply up to 3% of the UK's primary energy needs.

Figure 8.3G ● Geothermal energy

135

//////// **CHECKPOINT** ////////

❶ (a) Why are tropical countries better able to produce biomass fuels than countries like Britain?

(b) Use the figure opposite to find out how much solar energy per square metre falls on Britain each year on average.

(c) What area of solar panels would each person in Britain need to obtain an annual energy supply of about 200 000 MJ from solar energy?

❷ (a) Tidal power is a much more reliable source of energy than wind power or wavepower. Why?

(b) How would people be affected by a tidal power station being built in their locality?

❸ Make a list of renewables that can supply energy for
(a) running vehicles,
(b) home heating,
(c) running electric trains.

❹ If you lived on a small isolated island with a population less than 100, which renewable resource would meet your community's needs best? Copy the map opposite and, on your copy, show how and where you would obtain renewable energy.

Annual average solar radiation

| 2 - 3,000 | 3 - 4,000 | 4 - 5,000 | 5 - 6,000 | 6 - 7,000 | 7 - 8,000 | over 8,000 |

Megajoules/sq metre/year

Lighthouse

Wooded area

Harbour

Sands

Hill

Radio mast

Cliffs

Sands

//

8.4 **Energy for the future**

What options are available for meeting future energy demands? What are the advantages and disadvantages of each option? Choices made now will affect you throughout your lifetime!

FIRST THOUGHTS

RESOURCE ACTIVITY PACK

Alternative supplies

The demand for energy has risen throughout the twentieth century as more and more labour-saving machines have come into use. As living standards have gone up, so too has the demand for energy. Fuels such as oil will soon be in short supply. *Can alternative supplies of energy be developed?*

Nuclear power could be developed to supply much of our electricity but many people are unhappy about the disposal of nuclear waste. Also, electric vehicles would need to be developed to take the place of petrol – powered vehicles – unless coal or biomass can be used to produce an alternative fuel to petrol.

Coal is in plentiful supply and known reserves would last several centuries at the present rate of usage. Coal could fill the gap left by dwindling oil and gas reserves. However, the greenhouse effect is partly due to burning fossil fuels so this may limit use of coal as a fuel.

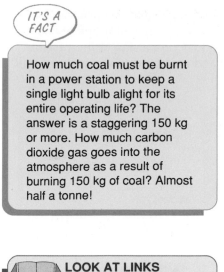

IT'S A FACT

How much coal must be burnt in a power station to keep a single light bulb alight for its entire operating life? The answer is a staggering 150 kg or more. How much carbon dioxide gas goes into the atmosphere as a result of burning 150 kg of coal? Almost half a tonne!

LOOK AT LINKS
What is the drawback of warming river water?
see Theme E, Topic 24.2.

Renewable energy resources could meet much more of Britain's energy needs than at present. This is attractive to many people but money and new skills are needed to develop and build 'renewable energy' power stations. Politicians need to be made more aware of the importance of renewable energy resources.

Save it!

What happens to all the energy we get from fuel and renewable resources? Industry, transport and homes use about 50% of the total and about 30% is exported. At present, the other 20% is wasted. Finding ways of doing jobs more efficiently would reduce this colossal wastage. So too would switching off unwanted lights! Better insulation in our homes is another big saver.

Combined heat and power (CHP) stations would save fuel by supplying 'waste' heat to local factories and offices. Any power station needs huge quantities of water to keep its turbines cool. In non-CHP stations, the hot water from the cooling system is discharged into a reservoir or river. A CHP station is designed to supply this hot water to local buildings. Figure 8.4A shows the overall savings made by replacing a 100 MW non-CHP station with a CHP station.

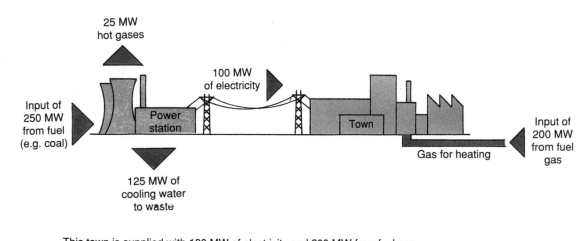

This town is supplied with 100 MW of electricity and 200 MW from fuel gas.
The total power input from fuel is 450 MW because the power station wastes 150 MW

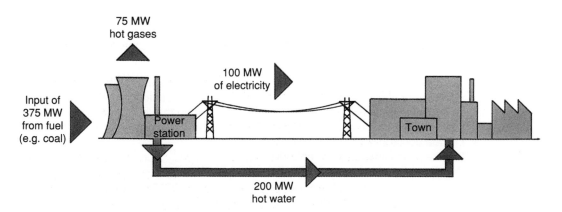

This town is supplied with 100 MW of electricity and 200 MW of hot water.
The total fuel input is 375 MW which is a saving of 75 MW compared with the non-CHP station

Figure 8.4A ● Saving fuel (a) A non-CHP power station (b) A CHP power station

Could the energy gap caused by dwindling oil and gas reserves be filled by renewable energy resources and more efficient usage of energy? The answer is yes – if people are willing to accept a slower increase in their standard of living. If not, nuclear and coal-fired power stations will continue to be needed.

SUMMARY

Energy for the future will depend on coal, nuclear power, renewable resources and more efficient energy usage. Planning is essential to ensure continued energy supplies. Otherwise, living standards will not continue to rise and may even fall.

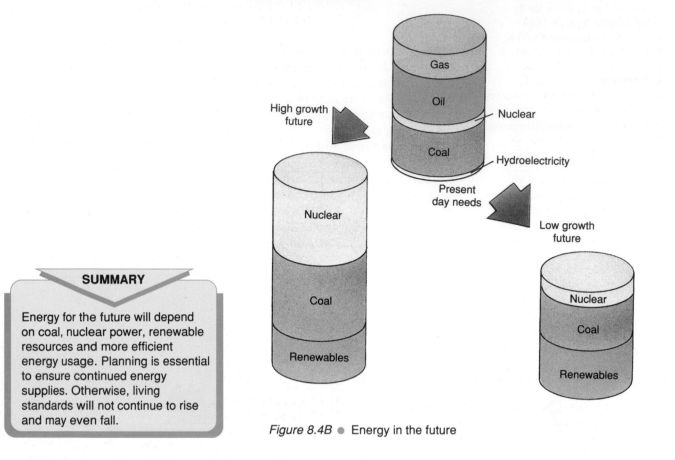

Figure 8.4B ● Energy in the future

CHECKPOINT

❶ (a) Supplies of energy from renewable sources such as windpower and wavepower are not as reliable as fuels such as coal. Why?
(b) Hydroelectric power stations are designed to use electricity to pump water uphill as well as being able to produce electricity. The water flow can be reversed within minutes. Why is this useful?

❷ The increasing use of computers in the future will allow many people to work from their homes. How will this affect the demand for energy?

❸ Suppose the Government proposed to build a cluster of aerogenerators a few miles from your home in place of a planned nuclear power station far away. Some residents in your area have formed an action group to oppose the windfarm. However, the local Green party welcome the proposals.
(a) List the points in favour of the windfarm.
(b) List the points against the windfarm.
(c) Which side would you support?
Perhaps you and your friends would like to form two opposing groups to discuss and debate the proposal.

❹ How should our future needs be met? Outline the choices you support, giving reasons for your choices. If possible, form a group to discuss the choices available.

? THEME QUESTIONS

● **Topic 4**

1 A solid X melts at 58 °C. Which of the following substances could be X?
 A Chloroethanoic acid, m.p. 63 °C
 B Diphenylamine, m.p. 53 °C
 C Ethanamide, m.p. 82 °C
 D Trichloroethanoic acid, m.p. 58 °C

2 An impure sample of a solid Y melts at 77 °C. Which of these solids could be Y?
 E Dibromobenzene, m.p. 87 °C
 F 1, 4-Dinitrobenzene, m.p. 72 °C
 G 3-Nitrophenol, m.p. 97 °C
 H Propanamide, m.p. 81 °C

3 An impure sample of liquid Z boils at 180 °C. Which of these liquids could be Z?
 I Benzoic acid, b.p. 249 °C
 J Butanoic acid, b.p. 164 °C
 K Hexanoic acid, b.p. 205 °C
 L Methanoic acid, b.p. 101 °C

4 Which of the substances listed below are (a) solid (b) liquid (c) gaseous at room temperature?

Pure substance	A	B	C	D	E	F
Melting point (°C)	8	−92	41	63	−111	−30
Boiling point (°C)	101	−21	182	189	11	172

5 The graph shows how the temperature of a substance rises as it is heated. At A, the substance is a solid.
 (a) Say what happens:
  (i) between A and B,   (iv) between D and E,
  (ii) between B and C,   (v) between E and F.
  (iii) between C and D,
 (b) Name the temperatures T_1 and T_2.

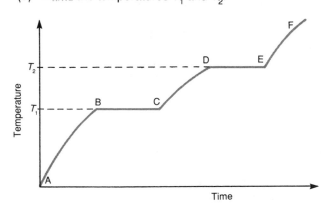

● **Topic 5**

6 (a) Sue is inflating a weather balloon, which will rise 10 km into the atmosphere. Pat advises Sue to fill the balloon only partially when it is on the ground. Why does Pat say the balloon should not be filled completely?
 (b) Michael pumps up his car tyres before driving from Britain to sunny Spain. When he arrives, his friend Jose advises him to let some of the air out of his tyres. Why does Jose advise doing this?

7 The table gives the solubility of potassium nitrate at various temperatures.

Temperature (°C)	0	10	20	40	60
Solubility (g per 100 g of water)	13	21	32	64	110

 (a) On graph paper, plot solubility (on the vertical axis) against temperature (on the horizontal axis). Draw a smooth curve through the points. Use your graph to answer (b) and (c).
 (b) What is the solubility of potassium nitrate at 30 °C?
 (c) At what temperature is the solubility of potassium nitrate 85 g/100 g?
 (d) A 100 g mass of water is saturated with potassium nitrate at 60 °C and cooled at 30 °C. What happens?

8 The diagram shows what happens when you breathe.

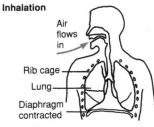

The diaphragm contracts and flattens, so increasing the volume of the chest cavity.
What does this do to the air pressure in the cavity? Why does it cause air to flow into the lungs?

The diaphragm relaxes and pushes up into the chest cavity.
What does this do to the air pressure in the cavity? Why does it cause air to flow out of the lungs?

● **Topic 6**

9 Sally and Jane decide to compare their work rates. They each lift as many 10 newton sandbags as they can on to a table in 1 metre high in 1 minute. Here are their results:

	Sally	Jane
Weight of sandbag (N)	10	10
Distance lifted (m)	1	1
Number of sandbags lifted	30	36
Time of exercise (min)	1	1

 (a) What total weight does Sally lift in 1 minute?
 (b)   Work done = Weight x Distance
 Jane lifts a total of 360 N. Calculate how much work she does.
 (c) Why do they both do the exercise for the same amount of time?

(NEA Dual Award)

10 A group of fifth year students planning an expedition to the Lake District decide to do some scientific research before they go. They decide to look at what activity they are fit for and how far they can walk in a day. Their findings are shown below.

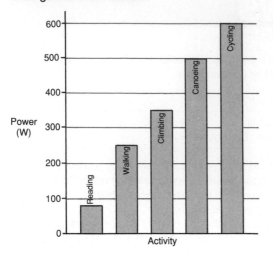

(a) (i) What power is required for canoeing?
(ii) What pattern connects the power and the type of activity in the bar chart?
(iii) The group decides on a walking expedition. One of the students is interested in how much energy he will use up in one minute. He reads the power rating at 250 W (joules/second). How much energy does he use in one minute?

(NEA Dual Award)

● *Topic 7*

11 (a) Explain why the smoke coming out of chimneys continues to rise up through the surrounding air. Why will the smoke eventually stop rising?
(b) An apparatus set up to investigate the effect of heating water is shown below.

Draw a sketch graph showing what readings you would expect to take from the two thermometers. How is heat transmitted to the thermometer labelled B, other than by conduction, convection and radiation?

(c) In an experiment with this apparatus it was found that the temperature of 500 cm³ of water was raised from room temperature to boiling point in 8 minutes exactly. The bunsen burner had a heat output of 875 J/s. What percentage of the heat from the bunsen passed into the water?
(It takes 4.2 J to heat 1 g of water through 1 °C. Water has a density of 1 g/cm³)

(MEG Combined Science)

12 1 kilogram of rock will lose or gain 800 joules of heat energy as its temperature changes by one degree Celsius.
1 kilogram of water will lose or gain 4200 joules of heat energy as its temperature changes by one degree Celsius.

(a) Which **one** of these two substances will need the most heat energy to increase the temperature of 1 kg by 10 °C?
(b) 1 kg rock and 1 kg of water, at the same temperature, lose energy at the same rate, until their temperatures fall by 10 °C.
Which substance will take longest for this to happen?
Explain your answer.

(SEG Integrated Science)

● *Topic 8*

13 (a) Electrical power could be obtained from the tides by building dams.
The table lists some of the places which are being considered and gives information about tidal power schemes in these places.

Location	Barrage length (m)	Power output (MW)	Cost of energy (p/kWh)
Loch Broom	500	29	13.9
Mersey	1750	620	3.6
Morecambe Bay	16 600	3040	4.3
Severn	17 000	7200	3.7
Thames	9000	1120	8.3
Wash	19 600	2760	7.2

(i) Electricity from coal-fired power stations costs about 4 pence per kilowatt hour. Which places in the table would produce cheaper electricity than this?
(ii) Many people think the Morecambe Bay scheme is worthwhile. Suggest a reason why.
(b) (i) A tidal scheme is more expensive to build than a coal-fired power station. But it is cheaper to run. Explain this.
(ii) Morecambe Bay would have a power output of 3040 MW but Loch Broom could produce only 29 MW.
What does the power output depend on?
(c) The map below shows Morecambe Bay.

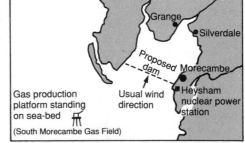

Explain how people living in Silverdale might feel about:
(i) natural gas from the South Morecambe Gas Field,
(ii) nuclear energy from Heysham power station,
(iii) the Morecambe Bay tidal scheme,
as alternative energy sources.
In your answer consider facts already given in this question and anything you already know about these types of energy source.

(LEAG Combined Science)

THEME C
The Atom

'Matter is composed of atoms.'
This is what John Dalton said in 1808. What a simple statement this appears to be! Yet the complex developments that followed from this statement fill the whole of physics and chemistry.

What are atoms?

How many different kinds are there?

How do atoms differ from even smaller particles?

You will find some of the answers to these questions in Theme C.

ELEMENTS AND COMPOUNDS

9.1 Silicon

FIRST THOUGHTS

Elements; they're *elementary*: they are simple substances, and there are 106 of them – all different. You have already met many useful elements, like silicon and gold.

LOOK AT LINKS
for **silicon chips**
See Theme K, Topic 45.

The tiny chip in the mighty micro

Before 1950, a computer was a massive combination of circuits and valves which took up a whole room. Nowadays, a microcomputer the size of a typewriter can do the same job as the old-style computer. Microcomputers can be fitted in aeroplanes and spacecraft. The size and weight of the old-style computers made this impossible. Many people own a personal computer, a PC, to streamline jobs such as budgeting their expenses. The change in computer size has been brought about by the use of **silicon chips**. Figure 9.1A shows an electronic circuit built on to the surface of a silicon chip. Such circuits are very reliable because they are less affected by age, moisture and vibration than the old-style circuits.

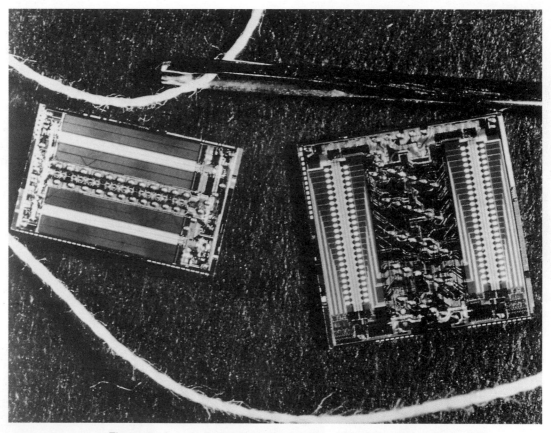

Figure 9.1A ● An integrated circuit built on the surface of a silicon chip

IT

Chemdata
(program)

Use this computer program to explore the properties of different elements. What patterns can you discover by using this program?

Silicon is an **element**. An element is a pure substance which cannot be split up into simpler substances. Elements are classified as metallic elements and non-metallic elements. Silicon is a non-metallic element. Most elements are either electrical conductors (substances which allow an electric current to flow through them) or electrical insulators (substances which do not allow an electric current to pass through them). Silicon is an unusual element in being a **semiconductor**: its behaviour is between that of a conductor and that of an insulator.

Figure 9.1B ● An electron diffraction micrograph of silicon

The first step in making a silicon chip is to slice large crystals of silicon into wafers. Then tiny areas of the wafer are treated with other elements which make silicon become an electrical conductor. The result is the creation of a thousand electronic circuits on each wafer. A chip 0.5 to 1.0 cm across contains thousands of tiny electrical switches called **transistors**. They allow on–off electric signals, which are the basis of computers, to occur at very high speeds.

● *Number crunching*
Very difficult and long calculations can be done on a computer. Computers operate so rapidly that they can solve in minutes problems that would take weeks to compute by hand. This is why computers are used to obtain fast and accurate weather forecasts. Earth scientists use computers to record the readings of their **seismometers** all over the world. The use of computers to process information is called **information technology**.

● *Tedious jobs*
Keeping track of records is a job for a computer. Debiting and crediting accounts, keeping a list of the stock in a shop or factory and such jobs are handled easily by a computer because a computer can repeat the same procedure over and over without error.

● *Planning ahead*
Using computers can help businesses to plan ahead. They can try out various plans and see how each will affect profits. In a similar way, computers can be used to try out various approaches to environmental problems to see how each approach will affect the animal and plant populations.

● *Data-logging*
Computers are used in science for recording and storing measurements. A sensor which measures pH, temperature, humidity, etc., can be connected to a microcomputer. The readings are recorded and displayed as a table or as a chart or as a graph. This can be useful for taking readings over a long period of time, e.g. monitoring water pollution, monitoring weather conditions, recording the temperature in the core of a nuclear reactor, recording the light emitted by a distant star.

LOOK AT LINKS
for **weather forecasting**
You will find more about forecasting the weather
See Theme E, Topic 28.

LOOK AT LINKS
for **seismometer**
Do you remember how a seismometer works?
See Theme A, Topic 2.3.

IT'S A FACT

Plans for the car of the future include a radar set and a computer to tell the driver how far ahead the next car is. It will make fast driving much safer.

═══ *SCIENCE AT WORK* ═══

Jobs which once used to be done laboriously by hand are now done in a fraction of the time by computer. Computers have taken the drudgery out of a lot of jobs. They have also contributed to safety in aeroplanes and in industrial plants. The use of microcomputers has created jobs in the manufacture of computers (hardware) and the writing of computer programs which tell the computer what to do (software). The new jobs are technical jobs. Skilled people are needed to fill them.

Figure 9.1C ● Using microcomputers

Computer programs are used as sources of information on a multitude of topics; such programs are called d**ata bases**. In forensic science, materials found at the scene of a crime are analysed. This information can be fed into a computer to become part of a data base which could help the police to solve a similar crime.

● *Word processing*

Computers with a word processor program are used in place of typewriters. Some programs enable the user to do 'desktop publishing'. This is used to present reports for business and scientific purposes in a neat, clear, easy-to-read format.

● *Your science lessons*

You can use microcomputers in your science lessons for various purposes:
- extracting information from data bases or making your own database,
- using a spreadsheet to display results from an experiment in a table or graph,
- using computer programs to test your ideas,
- recording readings from sensors and displaying and analysing the results.

SUMMARY

The element silicon is a semiconductor. Silicon is used to make transistors (devices which allow current to flow in one direction only). Circuits built on to silicon chips are the basis of the microcomputer industry.

CHECKPOINT

❶ Can you think of jobs which are done by microcomputers in;
(a) shops (b) the car industry (c) schools (d) homes?

How do you and your family benefit from the use of micros in shops and the car industry? Do you benefit from the use of micros in any other way?

❷ (a) What kinds of jobs are lost through the introduction of computers?
(b) What kinds of jobs are created by the spread of computers?
(c) Can the people who lose their jobs as a result of (a) take the jobs created in (b)? If your answer is *yes*, explain why. If your answer is *no*, explain what you think could be done to solve the problem.

❸ Would space travel have been possible before the age of the microcomputer? Explain your answer.

9.2  Gold

The prospector's dream element

Gold has always held a great fascination for the human race. Gold occurs **native**, that is, as the free element, not combined with other elements. For thousands of years, people have been able to collect gold dust from river beds and melt the dust particles together to form lumps of gold. We can still see some of the objects which the goldsmiths made thousands of years ago because gold never tarnishes. For centuries, people used gold coins.

Figure 9.2B ● Gold jewellery

Figure 9.2A ● Panning for gold

Gold is a metallic element. The shine and the ability to be worked into different shapes are characteristic of metals. Unlike gold, most metals tarnish in air. Gold is not attacked by air or water or any of the other chemicals in the environment. It is used in electrical circuits when it is essential that the circuits do not corrode. For example, in microcomputers gold wires connect silicon chips to external circuits. Spacecraft use gold connections in their electrical circuits.

SUMMARY

Gold is a metallic element. It conducts electricity and is easily worked. Unlike many other metals, gold never becomes tarnished. Gold is used for jewellery and in electrical circuits which must not corrode.

CHECKPOINT

❶ Why has gold always been a favourite metal for jewellers to work with?

❷ What use is made of gold in modern technology?

❸ Dentists use gold to fill teeth. Why is gold a suitable metal for this job?

9.3 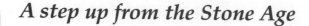 Copper

> More metallic elements and some alloys:
> * Copper, bronze and the Bronze Age
> * Iron, steel and the Industrial Revolution

IT'S A FACT

> What happened in 1886?
> Three thousand miles of copper cable were laid under the Atlantic.
> What for?
> This was the start of the transatlantic telegraph system.

A step up from the Stone Age

Thousands of years ago, Stone Age humans found lumps of copper embedded in rocks. Attracted by the colour and shine of copper, they hammered it into bracelets and necklaces. Then they started to use copper to make arrowheads, spears, knives and cooking pans. They found that copper tools did not break like the stone tools they were used to. Copper knives could be ground to a sharper edge than stone, and copper dishes did not crack as pottery bowls did. The shine, the ability to be worked into different shapes and the ability to conduct heat are typical of metals. Copper is a metallic element.

Stone Age people also discovered the alloy of copper and tin called **bronze** (a mixture of metals is called an alloy). Bronze is harder than copper or tin and can be ground to a sharper edge. Bronze weapons and tools made such a difference to the way people lived that they gave their name to the Bronze Age. Thanks to the new tools hunting and farming no longer occupied all the time of all the members of the community. Some people were able to spend time on painting, making pottery and building homes. The arrival of the Bronze Age was the beginning of civilisation.

Copper is still an important metal. Copper is a good electrical conductor – a typical metal. It is easily drawn into wire. Copper wire is used in electrical circuits. Wires, cables, overhead power lines, switches and windings in electrical motors are made of copper. Half the world's production of copper (total 8 million tonnes a year) is used by electrical industries.

Figure 9.3A ● Bronze in use

CHECKPOINT

❶ What advantages did copper tools have over tools made of (a) stone and (b) gold?

❷ Explain why the discovery of bronze was so important that it gave its name to the Bronze Age.

❸ What is the most important use of copper today?

9.4  Iron

Our most important metal

Our ancestors discovered how to extract iron from iron-bearing rocks over 3000 years ago. They used iron to make hammers, axes and knives, which did not break like stone tools and did not bend like bronze tools. Iron tools and weapons made such a difference to the way the human race lived that they gave their name to the Iron Age.

Many centuries later, iron and steel made the Industrial Revolution possible. The various types of **steel** are alloys of iron with carbon and other elements. Iron and steel are hard and strong: they can be hammered into flat blades and ground to a cutting edge. Our way of life in the twentieth century depends on machines made of iron and steel, buildings constructed on a framework of steel girders, and cars, lorries, trains, railways and ships made of steel.

Iron is a typical metallic element. An exceptional characteristic of iron is that it can be magnetised.

LOOK AT LINKS
for **iron** and **steel**
You can read about the chemistry of iron and steel in Theme L, Topic 50.9.

SUMMARY

Iron is a metallic element. Steel is an alloy. Being hard and strong, iron and steel are used for the manufacture of tools, machinery, motor vehicles, trains and ships.

Figure 9.4A ● A steel furnace

9.5 Carbon

Diamond and graphite

FIRST THOUGHTS

Some non-metallic elements:
- Can brilliant diamond and greasy graphite be the same element?
- Can the killer, chlorine, save lives?

Why are diamonds so often used in engagement rings? The sparkle of diamonds comes from their ability to reflect light. The 'fire' of diamonds arises from their ability to split light into flashes of colour. The hardness of diamonds means that they can be worn without becoming scratched. Diamonds are 'for ever'. Diamond is the hardest naturally occurring substance. The only thing that can scratch a diamond is another diamond.

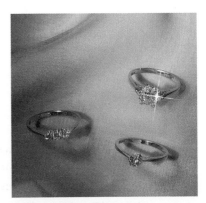

Figure 9.5A ● Diamonds

LOOK AT LINKS
Biologists who want to look at thin sections of plant and animal material with an electron microscope use diamond knives for cutting thin sections
See Theme D, Topic 19.

SUMMARY

Diamonds are beautiful jewels. Diamond is the hardest naturally occurring material. Small diamonds are used in industry for cutting, grinding and drilling.

Graphite is a slightly shiny grey solid, which conducts electricity. Graphite is used as a lubricant and as an electrical conductor. Diamond and graphite are allotropes (pure forms) of the element, carbon.

The hardness of diamond finds it many uses in industry. It is able to cut through metals, ceramics, glass, stone and concrete. Diamond-tipped saws slice silicon wafers from large crystals of silicon. As well as for cutting, diamonds are used for grinding, sharpening, etching and polishing. Oil prospectors would not be able to drill through hard rock without the help of drills studded with small diamonds (see Figure 9.5B). A 20 cm bit may be studded with 60 g of small diamonds.

Figure 9.5B ● Oil rig workers using a diamond studded drill

Diamond is a strange material, prized for its beauty and its usefulness. It is one form of the non-metallic element carbon.

Graphite is a shiny dark grey solid. It is so soft that it rubs off on your fingers and on paper. Pencil 'leads' contain graphite mixed with clay. Graphite is also used as a lubricant, in cars for example. Graphite is a second form of the element carbon. It is unusual in that it is the only non-metallic element which conducts electricity (see Topic 13.1).

Diamond and graphite are both pure forms of carbon. They are called **allotropes** of carbon. The existence of two or more crystalline forms of an element is called **allotropy**. Small diamonds (micron size, 10^{-6} m) can be made by heating graphite to a high temperature (1300 °C) under high pressure (60 000 atmospheres) for a few minutes. You can read more about the difference between the allotropes in Topic 9.8.

CHECKPOINT

❶ How are small industrial diamonds made?

❷ If the process for making industrial diamonds is carried on for a week, large gem-sized diamonds can be obtained. These large diamonds are dearer than natural diamonds. Why do you think this is so?

❸ What uses are made of diamonds? What characteristics of diamond make it suitable for the uses you mention?

❹ What is graphite used for? Why is graphite a suitable material for the uses you mention?

9.6 Chlorine

The life-saver

Chlorine is a killer. Its most infamous use was in the First World War when the German Army released cylinders of chlorine gas. The poisonous green cloud was driven by the wind into the trenches occupied by the British and French forces. Thousands of soldiers died, either choking on the gas or being shot as they retreated.

Chlorine is now used to kill germs. It is the bactericide which the water industry uses to make sure that our water supply is safe to drink. Chlorine has saved more lives than any other chemical. Before chlorine was used in the disinfection of the water supply, deaths from water-borne diseases, such as cholera and dysentery, were common. These diseases are still common in parts of the world which do not have safe water to drink.

Chlorine is a non-metallic element. Many household bleaches and disinfectants contain chlorine.

Figure 9.6A ● Bleach and disinfectant

IT'S A FACT

The man who thought up the plan of using chlorine in warfare was the German chemist, Fritz Haber. Before the war, Haber won the Nobel prize for his discovery of a method of manufacturing ammonia. Haber said, 'A man belongs to the world in time of peace but to his country in times of war'. Haber's wife was so distressed by his involvement in the war that in 1916 she committed suicide.

The British scientist, Michael Faraday, was asked to develop poison warfare during the Crimean War, but he refused.

IT'S A FACT

In 1831, an epidemic of cholera hit London, and 50 000 people died. The cholera germs had been carried in the drinking water. That can't happen now that the water supply is disinfected with chlorine.

LOOK AT LINKS
for chlorine and safe drinking water
See Theme E, Topic 22.3.

9.7 Elements

FIRST THOUGHTS

You will have noticed that in science there is a need to classify things: to sort them into groups of similar members. Elements can be classified as metallic and non-metallic elements, with some exceptions.

Gold, copper, and iron are typical **metallic elements**. Like all metallic elements, they conduct electricity. Many of the metallic substances we use are not elements; they are **alloys**. Steel, brass, bronze, gunmetal, solder and many others are alloys. An alloy is a combination of two or more metallic elements and sometimes non-metallic elements also. Silicon, carbon and chlorine are **non-metallic elements**. Some of their characteristics are **typical** of non-metallic elements, but some are **atypical** (not typical). Diamond is atypical in being shiny; most non-metallic elements are dull. Graphite is the only non-metallic element that conducts electricity. Silicon is one of the few semiconductors of electricity.

LOOK AT LINKS
You will remember classifying animals and plants in Theme A, Topic 3.

There are 92 elements found on Earth. A further 14 elements have been made by scientists. Table 9.1 summarises the characteristics of metallic elements and non-metallic elements. You will see that there are many differences. Metallic and non-metallic elements also differ in their **chemical reactions**.

Table 9.1 ● Characteristics of metallic and non-metallic elements

Metallic elements	Non-metallic elements
Solids, except for mercury which is a liquid.	Solids and gases, except for bromine which is a liquid.
Hard and dense.	Most of the solid elements are softer than metals, but diamond is very hard.
A smooth metallic surface is shiny, but many metals tarnish in air, e.g. iron rusts.	Most are dull, but diamond is brilliant.
The shape can be changed by hammering: they are **malleable**. They can be pulled out into wire form: they are **ductile**.	Many solid non-metallic elements break easily when you try to change their shape. Diamond is the exception in being hard and strong.
Conduct heat, although highly polished surfaces reflect heat.	Poor thermal conductors.
Good electrical conductors.	Poor electrical conductors, except for graphite. Some are semi-conductors, e.g. silicon.
Make a pleasing sound when struck: are **sonorous**.	Are not **sonorous**.

LOOK AT LINKS
for **chemical reactions**
For oxides of metals and non-metals, see Topic 16.2 and 21.3. For the reactions of metals, see Topic 50.3.

SUMMARY

Table 9.1 lists the differences between metallic and non-metallic elements. Alloys are combinations of metallic elements and sometimes non-metallic elements also.

9.8 The structures of some elements

FIRST THOUGHTS

The structure of an element means the arrangement of particles in the element. As you study this section, think about how the structure of an element affects the properties of that element.

LOOK AT LINKS
for **molecules**
See Theme B, Topic 5.1.

Can you name an element which fits each of these descriptions?
(a) a solid metallic element
(b) a liquid metallic element
(c) a solid non-metallic element
(d) a gaseous non-metallic element
(e) a hard solid element
(f) a soft solid element
(g) a shiny element
(h) a dull element

How do these differences arise? The reason lies in the different arrangements of atoms in the different elements. In many elements the atoms are bonded together in groups called **molecules**.

Oxygen, chlorine and many non-metallic elements consist of individual molecules. There are strong bonds between the atoms in the molecules, but between molecules there is only a very weak attraction. The molecules move about independently, and these elements are gaseous.

Sulphur is a yellow solid. There are two forms of sulphur, which form differently shaped crystals. The crystals of **rhombic sulphur** are octahedral; those of **monoclinic sulphur** are needle-shaped. Rhombic and monoclinic sulphur are **allotropes** of sulphur: the only difference between them is the shape of their crystals (see Figure 9.8A). The reason why the crystals are shaped differently is that the sulphur molecules are packed into different arrangements in the allotropes.

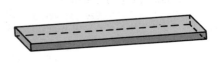

LOOK AT LINKS
for the **metallic bond**
Why are metals so strong?
See Theme L, Topic 50.2.

DID YOU KNOW?

In 1985, new allotropes of carbon were discovered. They consist of molecules containing 30–70 carbon atoms. The allotropes are known as **fullerenes**. The structure of a fullerene molecule is a closed cage of carbon atoms. The most symmetrical structure is buckminsterfullerene, C_{60}, which is a perfect sphere of carbon atoms. It is named after the geodesic domes designed by the architect Buckminster Fuller. The atoms are bonded together in 20 hexagons and 12 pentagons, which fit together like those on the surface of a football. Fullerenes have been nicknamed 'bucky balls'.

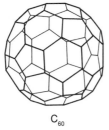

C_{60}

Scientists believe they will find important applications as semiconductors, superconductors, lubricants, catalysts and in batteries.

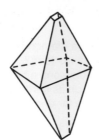

Figure 9.8A ● Allotropes of sulphur (x20)

Figure 9.8B shows a model of diamond. The structure is described as **macromolecular** or **giant molecular**. You can see that the carbon atoms form a regular arrangement. A crystal of diamond contains millions of carbon atoms arranged in this way. Every carbon atom is joined by chemical bonds to four other carbon atoms. It is very difficult to break this structure. The macromolecular structure is the source of diamond's hardness.

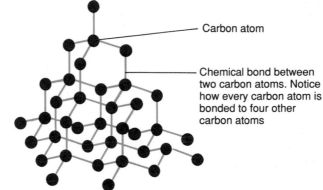

Carbon atom

Chemical bond between two carbon atoms. Notice how every carbon atom is bonded to four other carbon atoms

Figure 9.8B ● The arrangement of carbon atoms in diamonds

Figure 9.8C shows a model of graphite. Like diamond, graphite is a crystalline solid with a macromolecular structure. Graphite has a **layer structure**. Within each layer, the carbon atoms are joined by chemical bonds. Between layers, there are only weak forces of attraction. These weak forces allow one layer to slide over the next layer. This is why graphite is soft and rubs off on your fingers. The structure of graphite enables it to be used as a lubricant and in pencil 'leads' to mark paper.

SUMMARY

The carbon atoms in diamond are joined by chemical bonds to form a giant molecular structure.

Carbon atom

Bond between carbon atoms. Notice how the carbon atoms are bonded in a flat layer

There are weak chemical bonds between layers

A second layer of carbon atoms bonded together

Figure 9.8C ● The arrangement of carbon atoms in graphite

CHECKPOINT

❶ (a) What kind of atoms are there in a diamond?
   (b) What kind of structure do the atoms form?
   (c) Why does this structure make diamond a hard substance?
   (d) What uses of diamond depend on its hardness?
   (e) Why are diamonds often chosen for engagement rings?

❷ (a) Explain how its structure makes graphite less hard than diamond.
   (b) Why are diamond and graphite called allotropes?
   (c) What is graphite used for?

❸ Say how the allotropes differ and how they resemble one another.

FIRST THOUGHTS

9.9 **Compounds**

The Verey distress rocket contains the metallic element magnesium. When it is heated – when the fuse is lit – magnesium burns in the oxygen of the air. It burns with a brilliant white flame. A white powder is formed. This powder is the compound, magnesium oxide. A change which results in the formation of a new substance is called a **chemical reaction**. A chemical reaction has taken place between magnesium and oxygen. The elements have combined to form a compound.

> Magnesium + Oxygen → Magnesium oxide
> Element + Element → Compound

A compound is a pure substance which contains two or more elements chemically combined. A compound of oxygen and one other element is called an **oxide**. Making a compound from its elements is called **synthesis**.

Chemical reactions can synthesise compounds, and chemical reactions can also decompose (split up) compounds. Some compounds can be decomposed into their elements by heat. An example is silver oxide (see Figure 9.9B). The chemical reaction that takes place is

> Silver oxide   →(Heat)   Silver + Oxygen
> Compound   Elements

*Most of the substances you see around you are not elements: they are compounds.
Compounds can be made from elements by chemical reactions.*

LOOK AT LINKS
for **oxides**
Many oxides can be synthesised by burning elements in oxygen
See Theme E, Topic 21.3.

RESOURCE
–ACTIVITY–
PACK

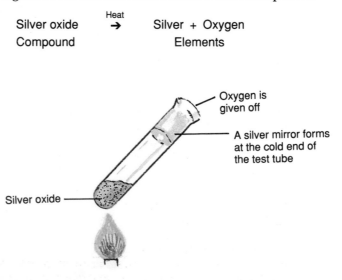

Figure 9.9A ● The thermal decomposition of silver oxide

Oxygen is given off

A silver mirror forms at the cold end of the test tube

Silver oxide

Splitting up a compound by heat is called **thermal decomposition**.

Some compounds can be decomposed into their elements by the passage of a direct electric current. An example is sodium chloride (common salt) which is a compound of sodium and chlorine. A compound of chlorine with one other element is called a **chloride**.

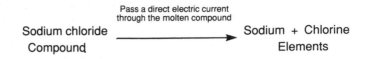

Pass a direct electric current
through the molten compound

Sodium chloride ————————————————→ Sodium + Chlorine
Compound   Elements

The chemical reaction that occurs when a compound is split up by means of electricity is called **electrolysis**.

Water is a compound. It can be electrolysed to give the elements hydrogen and oxygen (see Figure 9.9B).

Water is a compound of hydrogen and oxygen. You could call it hydrogen oxide. It is possible to make water by a chemical reaction between hydrogen and oxygen.

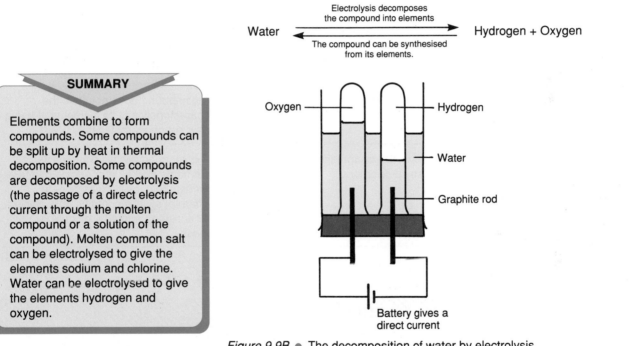

Electrolysis decomposes
the compound into elements

Water ⇄ Hydrogen + Oxygen

The compound can be synthesised
from its elements.

SUMMARY

Elements combine to form compounds. Some compounds can be split up by heat in thermal decomposition. Some compounds are decomposed by electrolysis (the passage of a direct electric current through the molten compound or a solution of the compound). Molten common salt can be electrolysed to give the elements sodium and chlorine. Water can be electrolysed to give the elements hydrogen and oxygen.

Figure 9.9B ● The decomposition of water by electrolysis

CHECKPOINT

❶ In a chemical change, a new substance is formed. In a physical change, no new substance is formed. Say which of the following changes are chemical changes.
(a) Evaporating water.   (d) Cracking an egg.
(b) Electrolysing water.   (e) Boiling an egg.
(c) Melting wax.

❷ Which of the following brings about a chemical change?
(a) Heating magnesium.
(b) Heating silver oxide.
(c) Heating sodium chloride.
(d) Passing a direct electric current through copper wire.
(e) Passing a direct electric current through molten salt.

9.10 Mixtures and compounds

Try to explain the difference between a mixture and a compound. Then read this section, and see whether you are right.

There are a number of differences between a compound and a mixture of elements. A mixture can contain its components in any proportions. A compound has a **fixed composition**. It always contains the same elements in the same percentages by mass. You can mix together iron filings and powdered sulphur in any proportions, from 1% iron and 99% sulphur to 99% iron and 1% sulphur. When a chemical reaction takes place between iron and sulphur, you get a compound called iron(II) sulphide. It always contains 64% iron and 36% sulphur by mass. Table 9.2 summarise the differences between mixtures and compounds.

Table 9.2 ● Differences between mixtures and compounds

Mixtures	Compounds
A mixture can be separated into its parts by methods such as distillation and dissolving.	A chemical reaction is needed to split a compound into simpler compounds or into its elements.
No chemical change takes place when a mixture is made.	When a compound is made, a chemical reaction takes place, and often heat is given out or taken in.
A mixture behaves in the same way as its components.	A compound does not have the characteristics of its elements. It has a new set of characteristics.
A mixture can contain its components in any proportions.	A compound always contains its elements in fixed proportions by mass; for example, calcium carbonate (marble) always contains 40% calcium, 12% carbon and 48% oxygen by mass.

SUMMARY

A compound is a pure substance which consists of two or more elements chemically combined. The components of a mixture are not chemically combined. Table 9.2 lists the differences between mixtures and compounds.

CHECKPOINT

❶ Group the following into mixtures, compounds and elements:
rain water, sea water, common salt, gold dust, aluminium oxide, ink, silicon, air.

❷ Name an element which can be used for each of the following uses:
surgical knife, pencil 'lead', wedding ring, saucepan, crowbar, thermometer, plumbing, electrical wiring, microcomputer circuit, disinfecting swimming pools, fireworks, artists' sketching material.

❸ What are the differences between a mixture of iron and sulphur and the compound iron sulphide?

❹ (a) What happens when you connect a piece of copper wire across the terminals of a battery? What happens when you disconnect the wire from the battery? Is the copper wire the same as before or has it changed?
(b) What happens when you hold a piece of copper in a Bunsen flame for a minute and then switch off the Bunsen? Is the copper wire the same or different?
(c) What type of change or changes occur in (a) and (b)?

SYMBOLS; FORMULAS; EQUATIONS

TOPIC 10

10.1 Symbols

FIRST THOUGHTS

Molly had a little dog
Her dog don't bark no more
'Cos what she thought was H_2O
Was really H_2SO_4
Anon
This rhyme shows the importance of getting your formulas right!

For every element there is a **symbol**. For example, the symbol for sulphur is S. The letter S stands for one atom of sulphur. Sometimes, two letters are needed. The letters Si stand for one atom of silicon: the symbol for silicon is Si. The symbol of an element is a letter or two letters which stand for one atom of the element. In some cases the letters are taken from the Latin name of the element, Ag from *argentum* (silver) and Pb from *plumbum* (lead) are examples. Table 10.1 gives a short list of symbols. There is a complete list at the end of the book.

SUMMARY

The symbol of an element is a letter or two letters which stand for one atom of the element.

Table 10.1 ● The symbols of some common elements

Element	Symbol	Element	Symbol	Element	Symbol
Aluminium	Al	Gold	Au	Oxygen	O
Barium	Ba	Hydrogen	H	Phosphorus	P
Bromine	Br	Iodine	I	Potassium	K
Calcium	Ca	Iron	Fe	Silver	Ag
Carbon	C	Lead	Pb	Sodium	Na
Chlorine	Cl	Magnesium	Mg	Sulphur	S
Copper	Cu	Mercury	Hg	Tin	Sn
Fluorine	F	Nitrogen	N	Zinc	Zn

10.2 Formulas

Figure 10.2A ● A model of one molecule of carbon dioxide

For every compound there is a formula. The formula of a compound contains the symbols of the elements present and some numbers. The numbers show the ratio in which atoms are present. The compound carbon dioxide consists of molecules. Each molecule contains one atom of carbon and two atoms of oxygen. The formula of the compound is CO_2. The 2 below the line multiplies the O in front of it. To show three molecules of carbon dioxide you write $3CO_2$.

Sand is impure silicon dioxide (also called silicon(IV) oxide). It consists of macromolecules, which contain millions of atoms. There are twice as many oxygen atoms as silicon atoms in the macromolecule. The formula of silicon dioxide is therefore SiO_2.

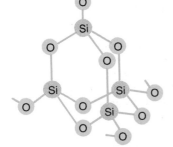

Figure 10.2B ● The structure of silicon(IV) oxide

The formulas of some of the compounds mentioned in this chapter are:
- Water, H_2O (two H atoms and one O atom; the 2 multiplies the H in front of it).
- Sodium chloride, NaCl (one Na; one Cl).
- Silver oxide, Ag_2O (two Ag: one O).
- Iron(II) sulphide, FeS (one Fe; one S).

The formula for aluminium oxide is Al_2O_3. This tells you that the compound contains two aluminium atoms for every three oxygen atoms. The numbers below the line multiply the symbols immediately in front of them.

The formula for calcium hydroxide is $Ca(OH)_2$. The 2 multiplies the symbols in the brackets. There are 2 oxygen atoms, 2 hydrogen atoms and 1 calcium atom. To write $4Ca(OH)_2$ means that the whole of the formula is multiplied by 4. It means 4Ca, 8O and 8H atoms. Table 10.2 lists the formulas of some common compounds.

Analysis
(program)

Use the program to practise identifying a range of unknown elements and compounds.

Table 10.2 ● The formulas of some common compounds

Compound	Formula
Water	H_2O
Carbon monoxide	CO
Carbon dioxide	CO_2
Sulphur dioxide	SO_2
Hydrogen chloride	HCl
Hydrochloric acid	HCl(aq)
Sulphuric acid	$H_2SO_4(aq)$
Nitric acid	$HNO_3(aq)$
Sodium hydroxide	NaOH
Sodium chloride	NaCl
Sodium sulphate	Na_2SO_4
Sodium nitrate	$NaNO_3$
Sodium carbonate	Na_2CO_3
Sodium hydrogencarbonate	$NaHCO_3$
Calcium oxide	CaO
Calcium hydroxide	$Ca(OH)_2$
Calcium chloride	$CaCl_2$
Calcium sulphate	$CaSO_4$
Calcium carbonate	$CaCO_3$
Calcium hydrogencarbonate	$Ca(HCO_3)_2$
Copper(II) oxide	CuO
Copper(II) sulphate	$CuSO_4$
Aluminium chloride	$AlCl_3$
Aluminium oxide	Al_2O_3
Ammonia	NH_3
Ammonium chloride	NH_4Cl
Ammonium sulphate	$(NH_4)_2SO_4$

SUMMARY

The formula of a compound is a set of symbols and numbers. The symbols show which elements are present in the compound. The numbers give the ratio in which the atoms of different elements are present.

10.3 Valency

Some atoms can form only one chemical bond. They can therefore combine with only one other atom. Elements with such atoms are said to have a **valency** of one. Hydrogen has a valency of one, and chlorine has a valency of one.

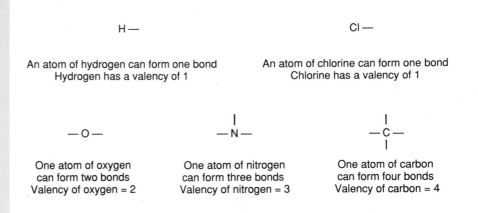

H —

Cl —

An atom of hydrogen can form one bond
Hydrogen has a valency of 1

An atom of chlorine can form one bond
Chlorine has a valency of 1

— O —

— N —

— C —

One atom of oxygen
can form two bonds
Valency of oxygen = 2

One atom of nitrogen
can form three bonds
Valency of nitrogen = 3

One atom of carbon
can form four bonds
Valency of carbon = 4

LOOK AT LINKS
Topic 14.4 deals with how to work out the formulas of ionic compounds.

The formula of a compound depends on the valencies of the elements in the compound. When hydrogen combines with chlorine, oxygen, nitrogen and carbon, the compounds formed have the formulas:

H — Cl   H — O — H   H — N — H   H — C — H

These are the compounds hydrogen chloride (HCl), water (H_2O), ammonia (NH_3), and methane (CH_4). They have different formulas because of the valencies of the elements Cl, O, N and C are different.

Figure 10.3A ● Models of HCl, H_2O, NH_3 and CH_4

SUMMARY

The formula of a compound depends on the valencies of the elements in the compound.

Some elements have more than one valency. Sulphur, for example, forms compounds in which it has a valency of 2, e.g. H_2S, compounds in which it has a valency of 4, e.g. SCl_4, and compounds in which it has a valency of 6, e.g. SF_6.

10.4 Equations

In a chemical reaction, the starting materials, the **reactants**, are changed into new substances, the **products**. The atoms present in the reactants are not changed in any way, but the bonds between the atoms change. Chemical bonds are broken, and new chemical bonds are made. The atoms enter into new arrangements as the products are formed. Symbols and formulas give us a nice way of showing what happens in a chemical reaction. We call this way of describing a chemical reaction a **chemical equation**.

Example 1 Copper and sulphur combine to form copper sulphide. Writing a **word equation** for the reaction

Copper + Sulphur → Copper sulphide

The arrow stands for **form**.

Writing the symbols for the elements and the formula for the compound gives the chemical equation

$Cu + S$ → CuS

Adding the state symbols

$Cu(s) + S(s)$ → $CuS(s)$

Why is this called an equation? The two sides are equal. On the left hand side, we have one atom of copper and one atom of sulphur; on the right hand side, we have one atom of copper and one atom of sulphur combined as copper sulphide. The atoms on the left hand side and the atoms on the right hand side are the same in kind and in number.

Balancing Equations (program)

Practise the art of balancing chemical equations by using this program. You will need to supply the correct formulas for some elements and compunds in the equation.

Example 2 Calcium carbonate decomposes when heated to give calcium oxide and carbon dioxide. The word equation is

Calcium carbonate → Calcium oxide + Carbon dioxide

The chemical equation is

$CaCO_3(s)$ → $CaO(s) + CO_2(g)$

Example 3 Carbon burns in oxygen to form the gas carbon dioxide. The word equation is

Carbon + Oxygen → Carbon dioxide

We must use the formula O_2 for oxygen because oxygen consists of molecules which contain two oxygen atoms. The chemical equation is

$C(s) + O_2(g)$ → $CO_2(g)$

Example 4 Magnesium burns in oxygen to form the solid magnesium oxide.

$$\text{Magnesium} + \text{Oxygen} \rightarrow \text{Magnesium oxide}$$

$$Mg(s) + O_2(g) \rightarrow MgO(s)$$

There is something wrong here! The two sides are not equal. The left hand side has two atoms of oxygen; the right hand side has only one. Multiplying MgO by 2 on the right hand side should fix it

$$Mg(s) + O_2(g) \rightarrow 2MgO(s)$$

Now there are two oxygen atoms on both sides, but there are two magnesium atoms on the right hand side and only one on the left hand side. Multiply Mg by 2

$$2Mg(s) + O_2(g) \rightarrow 2MgO(s)$$

The equation is now **a balanced chemical equation**. Check up.
On the left hand side, number of Mg atoms = 2; number of O atoms = 2.
On the right hand side, number of Mg atoms = 2; number of O atoms = 2.
The equation is balanced.

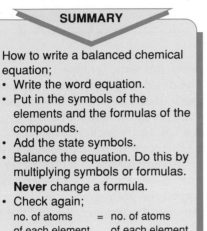

SUMMARY

How to write a balanced chemical equation;
• Write the word equation.
• Put in the symbols of the elements and the formulas of the compounds.
• Add the state symbols.
• Balance the equation. Do this by multiplying symbols or formulas. **Never** change a formula.
• Check again;

| no. of atoms of each element on LHS | = | no. of atoms of each element on RHS |

CHECKPOINT

❶ Refer to the table of elements at the end of the book, (i.e. the Periodic Table). Write down the names and symbols of the elements with atomic numbers 8, 10, 20, 24, 38, 47, 50, 80, 82. Say what each of these elements is used for. (The term 'atomic number' will be explained in Topic 11.)

❷ Give meanings of the state symbols (s), (l), (g), (aq). (See Topic 4.1 if you need to revise.)

❸ Try writing balanced chemical equations for the following reactions.
(a) Zinc and sulphur combine to form zinc sulphide.
(b) Copper reacts with oxygen to form copper(II) oxide.
(c) Sulphur and oxygen form sulphur dioxide.
(d) Magnesium carbonate decomposes to form magnesium oxide and carbon dioxide.
(e) Hydrogen and copper(II) oxide form copper and water.
(f) Carbon and carbon dioxide react to form carbon monoxide.
(g) Magnesium reacts with sulphuric acid to form hydrogen and magnesium sulphate.
(h) Calcium reacts with water to form hydrogen and a solution of calcium hydroxide.
(i) Zinc reacts with steam to form hydrogen and zinc oxide.
(j) Aluminium and chlorine react to form aluminium chloride.

❹ Write balanced chemical equations for the following reactions.
(a) Zinc and sulphur combine to form zinc sulphide, ZnS
(b) Copper and chlorine combine to form copper(II) chloride, $CuCl_2$
(c) Sulphur burns in oxygen to form sulphur dioxide, SO_2
(d) Magnesium carbonate decomposes to form magnesium oxide and carbon dioxide
(e) Calcium burns in oxygen to form calcium oxide.

❺ How many atoms are present in the following?
(a) $CaCl_2$ (b) $3CaCl_2$ (c) $Cu(OH)_2$ (d) $5Cu(OH)_2$ (e) H_2SO_4 (f) $3H_2SO_2$
(g) $2NaNO_3$ (h) $3Cu(NO_3)_2$

TOPIC 11 ● INSIDE THE ATOM

11.1 ● Becquerel's key

In 1896, a French physicist, Henri Becquerel, left some wrapped photographic plates in a drawer. When he developed the plates, he found the image of a key. The plates were 'fogged' (partly exposed). The areas of the plates which had not been exposed were in the shape of a key. Looking in the drawer, Becquerel found a key and a packet containing some uranium compounds. He did some further tests before coming to a strange conclusion. He argued that some unknown rays, of a type never met before, were coming from the uranium compounds. The mysterious rays passed through the wrapper and fogged the photographic plates. Where the key lay over the plates, the rays could not penetrate, and the image formed on the plates.

Photographic plate

Figure 11.1A ● Becquerel's key

A young research worker called Marie Curie took up the problem in 1898. She found that this strange effect happened with all uranium compounds. It depended only on the amount of uranium present in the compound and not on which compound she used. Madame Curie realised that this ability to give off rays must belong to the 'atoms' of uranium. It must be a completely new type of change, different from the chemical reactions of uranium salts. This was a revolutionary new idea. Marie Curie called the ability of uranium atoms to give off rays **radioactivity**.

Marie Curie's husband, Pierre, joined in her research into this brand new branch of science. Together, they discovered two new radioactive elements. They called one **polonium**, after Madame Curie's native country, Poland. They called the second **radium**, meaning 'giver of rays'. Its salts glowed in the dark.

Many scientists puzzled over the question of why the atoms of these elements, uranium, polonium and radium, give off the rays which Marie Curie named radioactivity. The person who came up with an explanation was the British physicist, Lord Rutherford. In 1902 he suggested that radioactivity is caused by atoms splitting up. This was another revolutionary idea. The word 'atom' comes from the Greek word for 'cannot be divided'. When the British chemist John Dalton put forward his Atomic Theory in 1808, he said that atoms cannot be created or destroyed or split. Lord Rutherford's idea was proved by experiment to be correct. We know now that many elements have atoms which are unstable and split up into smaller atoms.

Who's behind the science

The Curies worked for four years in a cold, ill-equipped shed at the University of Paris. From a tonne of ore from the uranium mine, Madame Curie extracted a tenth of a gram of uranium. The Curies published their work in research papers and exchanged information with leading scientists in Europe. A year later, they were awarded the Nobel prize, the highest prize for scientific achievement. Pierre Curie died in a road accident. Marie Curie went on with their work and won a second Nobel prize. She died in middle-age from leukaemia, a disease of the blood cells. This was caused by the radioactive materials she worked with.

11.2 ● Protons, neutrons and electrons

FIRST THOUGHTS

Atoms are made up of even smaller particles: protons, neutrons and electrons. As you read this section try to visualise how these particles are arranged inside the atom.

The work of Marie and Pierre Curie, Rutherford and other scientists showed that atoms are made up of smaller particles. These **subatomic particles** differ in mass and in electrical charge. They are called **protons**, **neutrons** and **electrons** (see Table 11.1).

Table 11.1 ● Sub-atomic particles

Particle	Mass (in atomic mass units)	Charge
Proton	1	$+e$
Neutron	1	0
Electron	0.0005	$-e$

Who's behind the science

Rutherford had an easier life in science than the Curies. He arrived in Britain from New Zealand in 1895. By the age of 28, he was a professor. He worked in the universities of Montreal in Canada, Manchester and Cambridge. He was knighted in 1914 and made Lord Rutherford of Nelson in 1931. His co-worker Otto Hahn (see p. 182) described him as 'a very jolly man'. Many stories were told about Rutherford. He would whistle 'Onward, Christian soldiers' when the research work was going well and 'Fight the good fight' when difficulties had to be overcome.

Protons and neutrons both have the same mass. We call this mass one **atomic mass unit**, one u (1.000 u $= 1.67 \times 10^{-27}$ kg). The mass of an atom depends on the number of protons and neutrons it contains. The electrons in an atom contribute very little to its mass. The number of protons and neutrons together is called the **mass number**.

Electrons carry a fixed quantity of negative electric charge. This quantity is usually written as $-e$. A proton carries a fixed charge equal and opposite to that of the electron. The charge on a proton can be written as $+e$. Neutrons are uncharged particles. Whole atoms are uncharged because the number of electrons in an atom is the same as the number of protons. The number of protons (which is also the number of electrons) is called either the **atomic number** or the **proton number**. You can see that

> Number of neutrons = Mass number − Atomic (proton) number

For example, an atom of potassium has a mass of 39 u and an atomic (proton) number of 19. The number of electrons is 19, the same as the number of protons. The number of neutrons in the atom is

$$39 - 19 = 20$$

Relative atomic mass

The lightest of atoms is an atom of hydrogen. It consists of one proton and one electron. Chemists compared the masses of other atoms with that of a hydrogen atom. They use **relative atomic mass**. The relative atomic mass, A_r, of calcium is 40. This means that one calcium atom is 40 times as heavy as one atom of hydrogen.

LOOK AT LINKS
for **relative atomic mass**
You will learn about relative atomic mass on the carbon-12 standard in Theme L, Topic 47.1.

> Relative atomic mass of an element $= \dfrac{\text{Mass of one atom of the element}}{\text{Mass of one atom of hydrogen}}$

CHECKPOINT

1 Some relative atomic masses are:

$A_r(H) = 1$, $A_r(He) = 4$, $A_r(C) = 12$, $A_r(O) = 16$, $A_r(Ca) = 40$.

Copy and complete the following sentences.

(a) A calcium atom is _____ times as heavy as an atom of hydrogen.
(b) A calcium atom is _____ times as heavy as an atom of helium.
(c) One carbon atom has the same mass as _____ helium atoms.
(d) _____ helium atoms have the same mass as two oxygen atoms.
(e) Two calcium atoms have the same mass as _____ oxygen atoms.

2 Element E has atomic number 9 and mass number 19. Say how many protons, neutrons and electrons are present in one atom of E.

3 State (i) the atomic number and (ii) the mass number of:
(a) an atom with 17 protons and 18 neutrons,
(b) an atom with 27 protons and 32 neutrons,
(c) an atom with 50 protons and 69 neutrons.

11.3 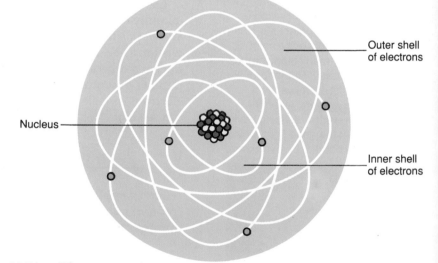 The arrangement of particles in the atom

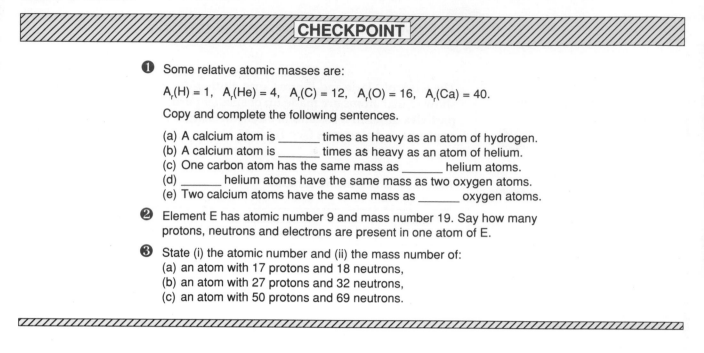

IT'S A FACT

If the nucleus of an atom was the size of a cricket ball, the nearest electron would be in the stands.

Nucleus

Outer shell of electrons

Inner shell of electrons

Figure 11.3A ● The structure of an atom

Lord Rutherford showed, in 1914, that most of the volume of an atom is space. Only protons and electrons were known in 1914; the neutron had not yet been discovered. Rutherford pictured the massive particles, the protons, occupying a tiny volume in the centre of the atom. Rutherford called this the **nucleus**. We now know that the nucleus contains neutrons as well as protons. The electrons occupy the space outside the nucleus. The nucleus is minute in volume compared with the volume of the atom.

The electrons of an atom are in constant motion. They move round and round the nucleus in paths called **orbits**. The electrons in orbits close to the nucleus have less energy than electrons in orbits distant from the nucleus.

11.4 How are the electrons arranged?

Figure 11.4A illustrates the electrons of an atom in their orbits. The orbits are grouped together in **shells**. A shell is a group of orbits with similar energy. The shells distant from the nucleus have more energy than those close to the nucleus. Each shell can hold up to a certain number of electrons. In any atom, the maximum number of electrons in the outermost group of orbits is eight.

Atomic Theory
(program)

Play the games in this package to investigate the nuclei and electron orbits of different atoms.

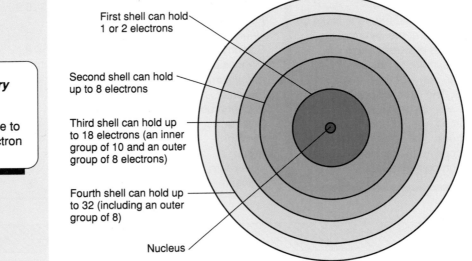

First shell can hold 1 or 2 electrons

Second shell can hold up to 8 electrons

Third shell can hold up to 18 electrons (an inner group of 10 and an outer group of 8 electrons)

Fourth shell can hold up to 32 (including an outer group of 8)

Nucleus

Figure 11.4A ● Shells of electron orbits in an atom

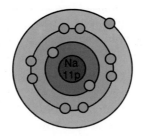

Figure 11.4B ● The arrangement of electrons in the oxygen atom

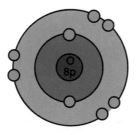

Figure 11.4C ● The electron configuration of sodium

The atomic number of an element tells you the number of electrons in an atom of the element. The electrons fill the innermost orbits in the atom first. An atom of oxygen has 8 electrons. Two electrons enter the first shell, which is then full. The other 6 electrons go into the second shell (see Figure 11.4B).

An atom of sodium has atomic number 11. The first shell is filled by 2 electrons, the second shell is filled by 8 electrons, and 1 electron occupies the third shell. The arrangement of electrons can be written as (2.8.1). It is called the **electron configuration** of sodium. Table 11.2 gives the electron configurations of the first 20 elements.

SUMMARY

The atoms of all elements are made up of three kinds of particles. These are:
- protons, of mass 1 u and electric charge $+e$
- neutrons, of mass 1 u, uncharged
- electrons, of mass 0.0005 u and electric charge $-e$.

The protons and neutrons make up the nucleus at the centre of the atom. The electrons circle the nucleus in orbits. Groups of orbits with the same energy are called shells. The 1st shell can hold 2 electrons; the 2nd shell can hold 8 electrons; the 3rd shell can hold 18 electrons. The arrangement of electrons in an atom is called the electron configuration.

Table 11.2 ● Electron configurations of the atoms of the first twenty elements

Element	Symbol	Atomic (proton) number	Number of electrons in ...				Electron configuration
			1st shell	2nd shell	3rd shell	4th shell	
Hydrogen	H	1	1				1
Helium	He	2	2				2
Lithium	Li	3	2	1			2.1
Beryllium	Be	4	2	2			2.2
Boron	B	5	2	3			2.3
Carbon	C	6	2	4			2.4
Nitrogen	N	7	2	5			2.5
Oxygen	O	8	2	6			2.6
Fluorine	F	9	2	7			2.7
Neon	Ne	10	2	8			2.8
Sodium	Na	11	2	8	1		2.8.1
Magnesium	Mg	12	2	8	2		2.8.2
Aluminium	Al	13	2	8	3		2.8.3
Silicon	Si	14	2	8	4		2.8.4
Phosphorus	P	15	2	8	5		2.8.5
Sulphur	S	16	2	8	6		2.8.6
Chlorine	Cl	17	2	8	7		2.8.7
Argon	Ar	18	2	8	8		2.8.8
Potassium	K	19	2	8	8	1	2.8.8.1
Calcium	Ca	20	2	8	8	2	2.8.8.2

CHECKPOINT

❶ Silicon has the electron configuration (2.8.4). What does this tell you about the arrangement of electrons in the atom? Sketch the arrangement. (See Figures 11.4B and 11.4C for help.)

❷ Sketch the arrangement of electrons in the atoms of (a) He (b) C (c) F (d) Al (e) Mg. (See Table 11.2 for atomic numbers.)

❸ Copy this table, and fill in the missing numbers.

Particle	Mass number	Atomic number	Number of ...		
			protons	neutrons	electrons
Nitrogen atom	14	7	-	-	-
Sodium atom	23	-	-	-	11
Potassium atom	39	-	19	-	-
Uranium atom	235	92	-	-	-

11.5 ● The Periodic Table

The physical and chemical properties of elements and the arrangement of electrons in atoms of the elements; they all fall into place in the Periodic Table.

Let us see how the electron configurations of the elements tie in with their chemical reactions. Some interesting patterns emerge when the elements are taken in the order of their atomic numbers and then arranged in rows. A new row is started after each noble gas (see Table 11.3). The arrangement is called the Periodic Table. You will have seen copies of the Periodic Table on the walls of chemistry laboratories. It simplifies the job of learning about the chemical elements.

Periodic Properties
(program)

This program allows you to explore the different properties of the elements in the Periodic Table. Load the program. Look for patterns in the properties of the elements. Try making predictions about some of the elements' properties and see if they are correct.

Table 11.3 ● A section of the Periodic Table

	Group 1	Group 2	Group 3	Group 4	Group 5	Group 6	Group 7	Group 0
Period 1	H (1)							He (2)
Period 2	Li (2.1)	Be (2.2)	B (2.3)	C (2.4)	N (2.5)	O (2.6)	F (2.7)	Ne (2.8)
Period 3	Na (2.8.1)	Mg (2.8.2)	Al (2.8.3)	Si (2.8.4)	P (2.8.5)	S (2.8.6)	Cl (2.8.7)	Ar (2.8.8)
Period 4	K (2.8.8.1)	Ca (2.8.8.2)						

Elements which have the same number of electrons in the outermost shell fall into vertical columns. The eight vertical columns of elements are called **groups**. The group number is the number of electrons in the outermost shell, except for Group 0, in which the elements have a full shell of 8 electrons. The horizontal rows of elements are called **periods**. The first period contains only hydrogen and helium. The second period contains the elements lithium to neon. The complete Periodic Table is shown on p. 452 of Book 2.

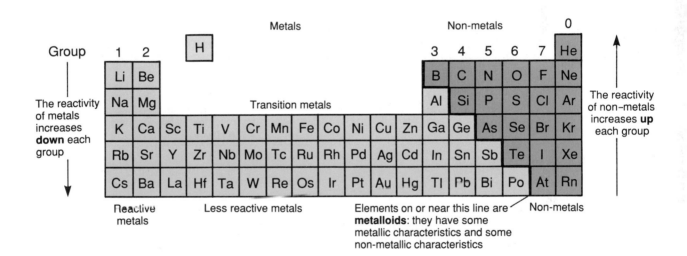

Figure 11.5A ● The Periodic Table

Patterns in the Periodic Table

1 Metallic elements appear at the left of the table.
2 Non-metallic elements appear at the right of the table.
3 There are borderline elements, such as silicon and germanium.
4 Group 1 is a set of very reactive metals called the **alkali metals**. The reactivity increases from top to bottom of the group.
5 Group 7 is a set of very reactive non-metals called the **halogens**. The reactivity decreases from top to bottom of the group.
6 Group 0 is a set of unreactive gases called the **noble gases**.
7 The metallic elements 21–30, 39–48 and 72–80 are known as **transition elements**.

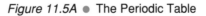

Key
(program)

Use the program to explore the different elements of the Periodic Table. Look out for as many patterns as you can find.

● The noble gases

The elements in group 0 are helium, neon, argon, krypton, xenon and radon. These elements are called the noble gases. They are present in air (see Topic 20). The noble gases exist as single atoms, e.g. He, Ne. Their atoms do not combine in pairs to form molecules as do the atoms of most gaseous elements, e.g. O_2, H_2. For a long time, no-one was able to make the noble gases take part in any chemical reactions. In 1960, however, two of them, krypton and xenon, were made to combine with the very reactive element, fluorine. *Why are the noble gases so exceptionally unreactive?* Chemists came to the conclusion that it is the full outer shell of electrons that makes the noble gases unreactive.

● The alkali metals

The elements in group 1 are lithium, sodium, potassium, rubidium and caesium. They are a set of very similar metallic elements (see Table 11.4). They are known as the **alkali metals** on account of the strongly alkaline nature of their hydroxides. They all have one electron in the outer shell.

Table 11.4 ● The alkali metals (with iron for comparison)

Element	Symbol	m.p. (°C)	b.p. (°C)	Density (g/cm³)	Hardness	Reaction with ... air	Reaction with ... water	Reaction with ... non-metallic elements
Lithium	Li	180	1336	0.53		All burn vigorously to form an oxide of formula M_2O (M = symbol for metal)	All are stored under oil. They react vigorously with cold water to give hydrogen and the hydroxide MOH. The hydroxides are all strong alkalis.	All combine with non-metals to form salts (and oxides). The salts are crystalline ionic solids. The alkali metals are the cations (positive ions) in the salts.
Sodium	Na	98	883	0.97	Softer than iron			
Potassium	K	64	759	0.86				
Rubidium	Rb	39	700	1.53				
Caesium	Cs	29	690	1.9				
Iron	Fe	1530	3000	7.86		Burns to form an oxide	Reacts slowly with water to form rust. Reacts quickly with steam to give hydrogen and an oxide	Combines when heated with most non-metals. Form salts in which iron is the cation (positive ion).

N.B. Reactivity increases down the group.

● The halogens

The elements in Group 7 are fluorine, chlorine, bromine and iodine. These elements are a set of very reactive non-metallic elements (see Table 11.5). They are called **the halogens** because they react with metals to form salts. (Greek: halogen = salt-former)

Table 11.5 ● The halogens

Element	Symbol	m.p. (°C)	b.p. (°C)	Colour	Reaction with metals to form salts	Reaction with hydrogen to form the compound HX	
Fluorine	F	−223	−188	Pale yellow	Dangerously reactive	Explodes	
Chlorine	Cl	−103	−35	Yellow-green	Readily combines to form chlorides.	Explodes in sunlight	Reactivity decreases down the group
Bromine	Br	−7	59	Red-brown	Combines when heated to form bromides	Reacts when heated	
Iodine	I	114	184	Purple-black	Combines when heated to form iodides. The halogens are the anions (negative ions) in their salts.	Reaction is not complete	

The history of the Periodic Table

The person who has the credit for drawing up the Periodic Table is a Russian scientist called Dimitri Mendeleev. He extended the work of a British chemist called John Newlands. In 1864, 63 elements were know to Newlands. He arranged them in order of relative atomic mass. When he started a new row with every eighth element, he saw that elements with similar properties fell into vertical groups. He spoke of 'the regular periodic repetition of elements with similar properties'. This gave rise to the name 'periodic table'. Sometimes, there were misfits in Newlands' table, for example, iron did not seem to belong where he put it with oxygen and sulphur. Newlands' ideas were not accepted.

Mendeleev had an idea about the troublesome misfits. He realised that many elements had yet to be discovered. Instead of slotting elements into positions where they did not fit he left gaps in the table. He expected that when further elements were discovered they would fit the gaps. He predicted that an element would be discovered to fit into the gap he had left in the table below silicon.

Table 11.6 ● The predictions which Mendeleev made for the undiscovered element which he called 'eka-silicon' (below silicon) compared with the properties of germanium

	Mendeleev's predicted properties for eka-silicon, Ek (1871)	The properties of germanium Ge (discovered in 1886)
Appearance	Grey metal	Grey-white metal
Density	~ 5.5 g/cm^3	5.47 g/cm^3
Relative atomic mass	73.4	72.6
Melting point	~ 800 °C	958 °C
Reaction with oxygen	Forms the oxide EkO$_2$. The oxide EkO may also exist.	Forms the oxide GeO$_2$ GeO also exists

By the time Mendeleev died in 1907, many of the gaps in the table had been filled by new elements. The noble gases were unknown to Mendeleev when he drew up his table. The first of them was discovered in 1894. As the noble gases were discovered, they all fell into place between the halogens and the alkali metals. They formed a new group, Group 0. This was a spectacular success for the Periodic Table.

SUMMARY

The chemical properties of elements depend on the electron configurations of their atoms. The unreactive noble gases all have a full outer shell of 8 electrons.

The reactive alkali metals have a single electron in the outer shell.

The halogens are reactive non-metallic elements which have 7 electrons in the outer shell: they are 1 electron short of a full shell.

In the Periodic Table, elements are arranged in order of increasing atomic (proton) number in 8 vertical groups. The horizontal rows are called the periods.

CHECKPOINT

❶ (a) Which of the alkali metals float on water?
(b) Which of the alkali metals can be cut with a knife made of iron?
(c) Which of the alkali metals melt at the temperature of boiling water?
(d) Why would it be very dangerous to put an alkali metal into boiling water?
(e) What is another name for sodium chloride?
(f) What would you expect rubidium chloride to look like?
(g) The alkali metals are kept under oil to protect them from the air. Which substances in the air would attack them?
(h) What pattern can you see in (i) the melting points (ii) the boiling points of the alkali metals?

❷ (a) Which of the halogens is (i) a liquid and (ii) a solid at room temperature (20 °C)?
(b) Why is fluorine not studied in school laboratories?
(c) Write the formulas for (i) sodium iodide (ii) potassium fluoride.

❸ (a) When was germanium discovered?
(b) How do the properties of germanium compare with Mendeleev's prediction?
(c) How long did Mendeleev have to wait to see if he was right?
(d) In which group of the Periodic Table does germanium come?
(e) What important articles are manufactured from germanium and silicon?

11.6 Isotopes

There are two sorts of chlorine atom and three sorts of hydrogen atom. You can find out the difference between them in this section.

Atoms of the same element all contain the same number of protons, but the number of neutrons may be different. Forms of an element which differ in the number of neutrons in the atom are called **isotopes**. For example, the element chlorine, with relative atomic mass 35.5, consists of two kinds of atom with different mass numbers.

17 electrons   17 electrons

17 protons   17 protons
18 neutrons   20 neutrons

Mass number 35   Mass number 37

Figure 11.6A ● The isotopes of chlorine

Since the chemical reactions of an atom depend on its electrons, all chlorine atoms react in the same way. The number of neutrons in the nucleus does not affect chemical reactions. The different forms of chlorine are isotopes. Their chemical reactions are the same. In any sample of chlorine, there are three chlorine atoms with mass 35 u for each chlorine atom with mass 37 u so the average atomic mass is

$$\frac{(3 \times 35) + 37}{4} = 35.5 \text{ u}$$

The isotopes of chlorine are written as $^{35}_{17}\text{Cl}$ and $^{37}_{17}\text{Cl}$. The isotopes of hydrogen are $^{1}_{1}\text{H}$, $^{2}_{1}\text{H}$ and $^{3}_{1}\text{H}$. They are often referred to as hydrogen-1, hydrogen-2 and hydrogen-3. Hydrogen-2 is also called deuterium, and hydrogen-3 is also called tritium.

Isotopes are atoms of the same element which differ in the number of neutrons. They contain the same number of protons (and therefore the same number of electrons).

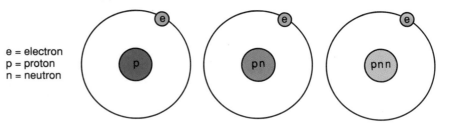

e = electron
p = proton
n = neutron

Figure 11.6B ● The isotopes of hydrogen

Isotopes are shown as $^{A}_{Z}X$, where X is the chemical symbol, A is the mass number (i.e. the number of neutrons and protons) and Z is the atomic number (i.e. the number of protons).

CHECKPOINT

❶ Hydrogen, deuterium and tritium are isotopes.
(a) Copy and complete this sentence.
Isotopes are _____ of an element which contain the same number of _____ and _____ but different numbers of _____ .
(b) Copy and complete the table.

	Hydrogen	Deuterium	Tritium
Atomic number			
Mass number			

(c) Write the formula of the compound formed when deuterium reacts with oxygen.
(d) Explain why isotopes have the same chemical reactions.

❷ Write the symbol with mass number and atomic number (as above) for each of the following isotopes.
(a) oxygen with 8 protons and 8 neutrons
(b) argon with 18 protons and 22 neutrons
(c) bromine with 35 protons and 45 neutrons
(d) chromium with 24 protons and 32 neutrons

❸ Two of the atoms described below have similar chemical properties. Which two are they?
Atom X contains 9 protons and 10 neutrons.
Atom Y contains 13 protons and 14 neutrons.
Atom Z contains 17 protons and 18 neutrons.
Explain your answer.

❹ Strontium-90 is a radioactive isotope formed in nuclear reactors. It can be accumulated in the human body because it follows the same chemical pathway through the body as another element X which is essential for health. After referring to the position of strontium in the Periodic Table, say which element you think is X.

❺ Sodium has the electron arrangement (2.8.1).
(a) Draw and label a diagram to show how the protons, neutrons and electrons are arranged in a sodium atom.
(b) Explain why sodium is electrically uncharged.
(c) Rubidium is in the same group of the Periodic Table as sodium. Would you expect rubidium to be a metal or a non-metal?
(d) How would you expect rubidium to be stored?
(e) What products would you expect to be formed when rubidium reacts with cold water? How could you test each of these products?

TOPIC 12 ● RADIOACTIVITY

12.1 ● What is radioactivity?

> Radioactivity: what is it?
> How was it discovered?
> What are α-, β-, γ-radiation?
> These are some of the things
> you will find out in this section

The changes which Marie Curie described as radioactivity are **nuclear changes**. A nuclear change is quite different from a chemical change. In a chemical change, bonds between atoms are broken, and new bonds are made, but the nuclei of the the atoms stay the same. In a nuclear change, new atoms of different elements are formed because the nuclei change. Marie Curie and her fellow scientists knew their work was revolutionary, but none of them could have imagined how it would change the world.

Isotopes which give off radioactivity are said to be **radioactive**. They are **radioisotopes**. The atoms of radioactive isotopes each have an unstable nucleus. The nucleus becomes stable by emitting small particles and energy. The particles and energy are called **radioactivity**; the breaking-up process is **radioactive decay**.

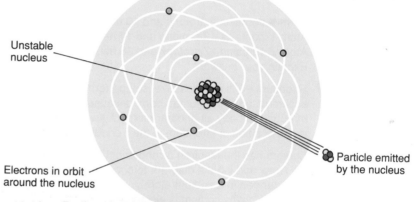

Unstable nucleus

Electrons in orbit around the nucleus

Particle emitted by the nucleus

Figure 12.1A ● Radioactive decay

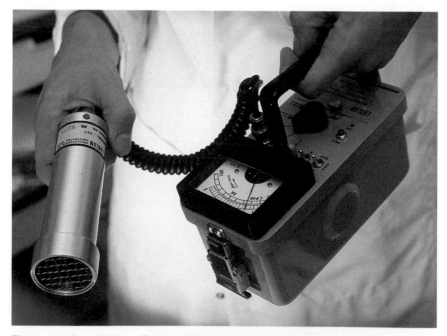

Figure 12.1B ● Using a Geiger–Müller tube.
(NOTE: experiments on radioactivity must only be done by a teacher.)

Investigating radioactivity

One way to detect radioactivity is to use a Geiger–Müller counter (named after its inventors). When radioactive particles enter it, a Geiger–Müller counter gives out a clicking sound. The number of clicks per minute is called the count rate. Even when there is no radioactive source nearby, the counter still clicks occasionally. This is due to **background radioactivity** from certain building materials and from cosmic radiation (from space). When you measure the count rate of a radioactive source, you have to subtract the background count.

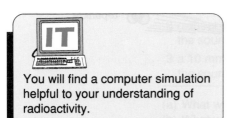

Figure 12.1C ● The penetrating power of radiation

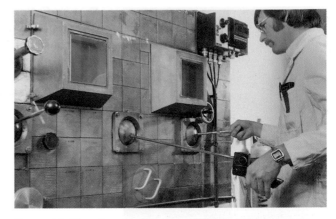

Figure 12.1D ● Lead bricks shield workers from radiation

You will find a computer simulation helpful to your understanding of radioactivity.

There are three types of radioactivity: **alpha-radiation** (α-radiation), **beta-radiation** (β-radiation) and **gamma-radiation** (γ-radiation). They differ in penetrating power (see Figure 12.1C). A thin metal foil will stop α-radiation, but a metal plate about 5 mm thick is needed to stop β-radiation, and γ-radiation will penetrate several centimetres of lead. γ-radiation passes through the skin and can penetrate bone. It can cause burns and cancer. People who work with sources of γ-radiation protect themselves by building a wall of lead bricks between themselves and the source (see Figure 12.1D).

The nature of α, β and γ-radiations

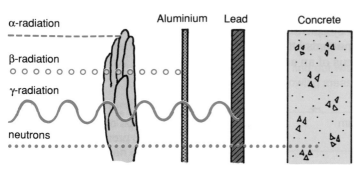

Figure 12.1E ● Radiations in a magnetic field

What are these mysterious radiations? This was the question that Lord Rutherford and other scientists tackled early in this century. Within ten years of Henri Becquerel's discovery of radioactivity, scientists had unravelled the mystery. They discovered three new types of radiation by using a magnetic field to separate them (see Figure 12.1E). Scientists invented new instruments, like the Geiger–Müller counter and the cloud chamber (see Figure 12.1F) to use in their study.

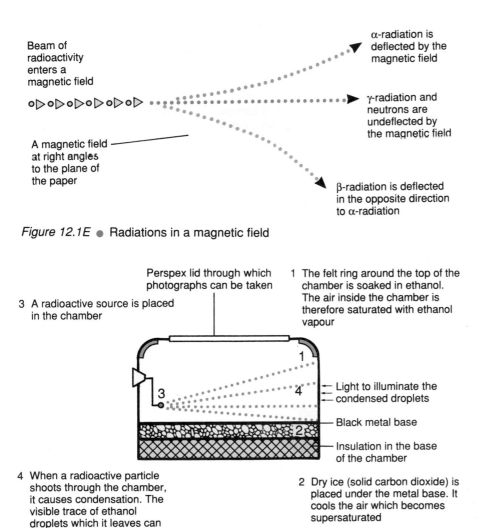

Perspex lid through which photographs can be taken

3 A radioactive source is placed in the chamber

1 The felt ring around the top of the chamber is soaked in ethanol. The air inside the chamber is therefore saturated with ethanol vapour

Light to illuminate the condensed droplets

Black metal base

Insulation in the base of the chamber

4 When a radioactive particle shoots through the chamber, it causes condensation. The visible trace of ethanol droplets which it leaves can then be photographed.

2 Dry ice (solid carbon dioxide) is placed under the metal base. It cools the air which becomes supersaturated

Figure 12.1F ● A cloud chamber

171

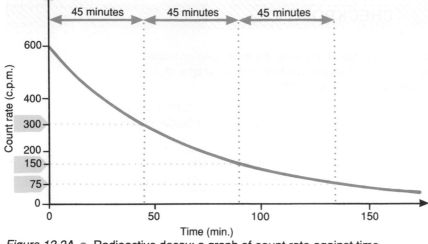

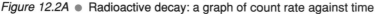

Figure 12.2A ● Radioactive decay: a graph of count rate against time

You can see from the graph that:
• the time taken for the count to fall from 600 to 300 c.p.m is 45 minutes,
• the time taken for the count to fall from 300 to 150 c.p.m is 45 minutes,
• the time taken for the count to fall from 150 to 75 c.p.m is 45 minutes.

The time for the activity to fall to half its value is the same, no matter what the original activity is. This time is called the **half-life**. The half-life of the isotope in this example is 45 minutes.

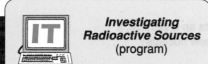

The disintegration of a radioactive nucleus is a **random** process. No-one can say when an individual nucleus will suddenly split up. However, for a large number of nuclei, you can predict how many nuclei will disintegrate in a certain time. This is a bit like throwing dice. You can't predict what number you will get with a single throw, but if you threw 1000 dice you would expect one-sixth of them to come up with the number 4 and so on.

Suppose you have a sample of material which contains 1000 radioactive nuclei and that 10 per cent disintegrate per hour. After one hour, 100 nuclei will have disintegrated, leaving 900. During the next hour, 90 (10% of 900) will disintegrate to leave 810. The table shows the number of radioactive nuclei remaining as each hour passes.

Investigating Radioactive Sources (program)

Use this program to check your knowledge of radioactivity and half-life. You will be asked to study three experiments with different radioactive sources.

Table 12.1 ● The number of radioactive nuclei that decay every hour

Time from the start (hours)	0	1	2	3	4	5	6	7
No. of radioactive nuclei present	1000	900	810	729	656	590	530	477
No. of nuclei that decay in the next hour	100	90	81	73	66	59	53	48

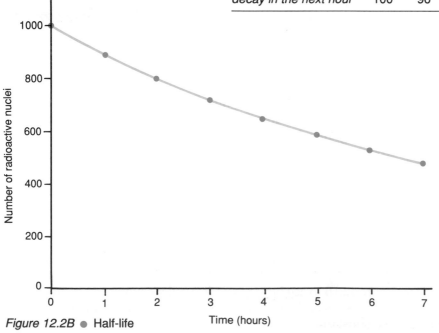

Figure 12.2B ● Half-life

Figure 12.2B shows how the number of radioactive nuclei changes with time. The rate of decay is proportional to the number of radioactive nuclei left. The half-life can be read from the graph. It is the time taken for the number of nuclei to fall from, say, 1000 to 500.

SUMMARY

The activity of a radioisotope is the number of its nuclei that disintegrate per second. The half-life of a radioisotope is the time taken for its activity to fall to half its original value.

CHECKPOINT

❶ Sodium-24 is a radioisotope used in medicine. Its half-life is 15 hours. A solution containing 8.0 mg of the isotope is prepared. What mass of isotope remains after (a) 15 hours (b) 30 hours (c) 5 days?

❷ Cobalt-60 is a radioisotope made by placing cobalt in a nuclear reactor. It has a half-life of 5 years. The activity of a piece of cobalt-60 is 32.0 kBq. How long would it take for its activity to fall to (a) 16.0 kBq (b) 1.0 kBq?

❸ In Figure 12.2B, how long would it take for the count rate to fall from 800 c.p.m to 100 c.p.m?

❹ The following measurements were made in an experiment using a Geiger–Müller tube near a radioactive source.

Time (hours)	0	0.5	1.0	1.5	2.0	2.5
Count (c.p.m.)	510	414	337	276	227	188

The background count was 30 c.p.m.
(a) The initial count rate from the source alone was 480 c.p.m (510–30). This is the corrected count rate. Work out the corrected count rates for the other readings.
(b) Plot a graph of the count rate (on the vertical axis) against time.
(c) Use your graph to find the half-life of the source.

FIRST THOUGHTS

12.3 ⚛ Making use of radioactivity

When a new discovery is made, scientists are keen to find ways of using the discovery both in research and in everyday life. Radioactivity is a good example of a fascinating discovery for which many useful applications have been found.

Carbon-14 dating

Carbon is made of the isotopes carbon-12, carbon-13 and carbon-14. The isotope carbon-14 is radioactive. It has a half-life of 5700 years. Carbon-14 is present in the carbon dioxide which living trees use in photosynthesis. After a tree dies, it can take in no more carbon-14. The carbon-14 already present decays slowly; carbon-12 does not change. The ratio of the

LOOK AT LINKS
for **radiocarbon dating**
You will now understand better what was said about radioactive dating of rocks in Theme A, Topic 2.9. You will meet the importance of dating fossils for the theory of evolution in Theme N, Topic 55.

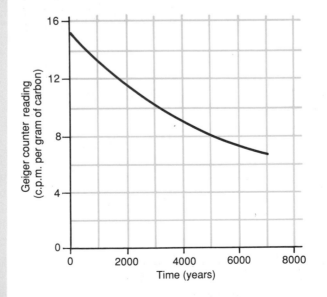

Figure 12.3A ● Carbon-14 dating

amount of carbon-14 left in the wood to the amount of carbon-14 in living trees can be used to tell the age of the wood. Animals take in carbon-14 in their food while they are alive. After their death, the proportion of carbon-14 in their bones tells how long it is since they died. A carbon-14 decay curve is shown in Figure 12.3A.

Other radio-isotopes

Radioactive isotopes differ enormously in their half-lives. Some are listed in Table 12.2.

Table 12.2 ● Some radioactive isotopes

Isotope	Radiation	Half-life	Isotope	Radiation	Half-life
Uranium-238	α	5000 million years	Iodine-131	β	8 days
Uranium-235	α	700 million years	Sodium-24	β	15 hours
Plutonium-239	α, γ	24 000 years	Uranium-239	β	24 minutes
Carbon-14	β	5700 years	Strontium-93	β, γ	8 minutes
Strontium-90	β	59 years	Barium-143	β	12 seconds
Caesium-137	β, γ	30 year	Polonium-213	α	4 millionths
Cobalt-60	γ	5 years			of a second

Scientists have found many uses for radioactive isotopes. Figures 12.3 B–E show some of them.

Figure 12.3B ● Separating radioactive isotopes for medical use

● **Medical uses**

Radioactivity can be used to penetrate the body and kill cancerous tissue. Cobalt-60 and caesium-137 are often used for this purpose. They emit γ-rays. The dose of radiation must be carefully calculated to destroy cancerous tissue and leave healthy tissue alone. *Why is a γ-emitter used, rather than an α- or a β-emitter for this job?*

Radiation is used to destroy germs on medical instruments. It is more convenient than boiling, and it is also more efficient. Cobalt-60 is often used. *Why is a γ-emitter better than an emitter of α- or β-radiation for this job?*

The thyroid gland in the throat takes iodine from food and stores it. To find out whether the thyroid is working correctly, a patient is given food containing iodine-131, a β-emitter. The radioactive iodine can be detected as it passes through the body. The half-life of iodine-131 is 8 days. After a few weeks, there will be little left in the patient's body. *Can you explain why a β-emitter is better than a γ-emitter for this purpose?*

Figure 12.3C ● Radioactivity in agriculture

● *Agricultural Research*
This research worker is studying the uptake of fertilisers by plants. He has used a fertiliser containing phosphorus-32. This isotope is a β-emitter with a half-life of 14 days. By measuring the radioactivity of the leaves, the scientist can find out how much fertiliser has reached them.

● *Industrial Uses*
This research worker is measuring engine wear. The pistons of this engine have been in a nuclear reactor. Some of the metal atoms have become radioactive. As the engine runs, the pistons wear away and radioactive atoms enter the lubricating oil. The more the engine wears, the more radioactive the oil becomes. You can tell how well a lubricating oil reduces engine wear by timing the uptake of radioactivity.

Figure 12.3E shows the production of metal foil (e.g. aluminium baking foil). The detector measures the amount of radiation passing through the foil. If the foil is too thick, the detector reading drops. The detector sends a message to the rollers, which move closer together to make the foil thinner. *Why must the source be a β-emitter, not an α- or a γ-emitter? Why does it need to have a long half-life? Can you suggest a suitable isotope (see Table 12.2)?*

Figure 12.3D ● Measuring engine wear

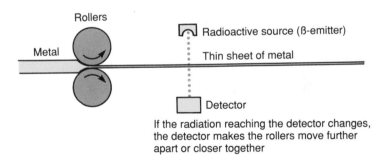

Figure 12.3E ● The manufacture of metal foil

Radioactivity and food

Food spoilage is a serious problem. About 20% of the world's food is lost through spoilage. The major cause is the bacteria, moulds and yeasts which grow on food. Some bacteria produce waste products which are toxic to people and cause the symptoms of food poisoning (sickness and diarrhoea). There are thousands of cases of food poisoning every year and some are fatal. Now there is an answer.

Irradiation of food with γ-rays kills 99% of disease-carrying organisms. These include *Salmonella*, which infects a lot of poultry, and *Clostridium*, the cause of botulism, which is often fatal. Spices, which are likely to contain micro-organisms as they are imported from tropical countries, can be irradiated with no loss of flavour. Irradiating potatoes is useful because it stops them sprouting without affecting the taste. The treatment is not suitable for all foods. Red meats turn brown and develop an

SCIENCE AT WORK

If you see this sign on food, it means that the food has been irradiated.

unpleasant taste, eggs develop a smell, shrimps turn black and tomatoes go soft.

Some people fear that irradiated food will be radioactive. In fact, foods contain a natural low level of radioactivity, and the treatment increases this level only slightly. The dose of radiation which the food receives is carefully calculated. By the time the food is eaten, the extra radioactivity has decayed. The best proof that irradiation is safe is that you can not detect it.

CHECKPOINT

❶ In 1985, a body was found in a peat bog in Norfolk. The reading which scientists obtained for the carbon-14 radioactivity of the body was 9 c.p.m. per gram of carbon.
  (a) Archaeologists called the body Pete Marsh. Where do you think they got the idea for the name?
  (b) Refer to Figure 12.3A, which shows a decay curve for carbon-14. How long ago did Pete Marsh die?

❷ Testing the filling of cans on a production line.
  Can A is full, but something has gone wrong on the production line, and Can B is only partly filled. Can you design a scheme for using a radioactive source and a detector to tell whether the cans coming off the production line are completely filled? Say whether you would use a source of α or β or γ radiation and say what kind of half-life would be suitable. Choose an isotope from Table 12.2 which could be used.

❸ Detecting leaks.
  Imagine that you are a scientist working for a water company. An underground pipe 2 km long is leaking. You want to find out where the leak is without digging up the pipe. You decide to add a radioactive isotope to the water at one end of the pipe and then drive slowly along the route which the pipe takes, testing the ground with a Geiger–Müller counter. If you detect radioactivity you will know where the underground leak is.

  Which radioisotope will you choose from Table 12.2? You will need:
  • an element which forms a water-soluble compound,
  • radiation which can penetrate the soil,
  • a half-life which will give you time to drive slowly along the route,
  • to avoid contaminating the water for long.

❹ A firm which manufactures plastic syringes gets an order from a hospital. The hospital wants the syringes to be sterile. The firm cannot sterilise the syringes by heating because this would soften the plastic. What can the firm do? (See Table 12.2 for details of radioactive isotopes.)

❺ An engineer is planning a method of checking the stability of an oil rig which is to be used in the North Sea. She decides to mix a radioactive isotope with the concrete which fixes the legs of the oil rig to the sea bed. Then she can install a detector to find out whether there is any movement in the concrete.

  Which isotope from Table 12.2 should she choose? Concrete contains calcium compounds so the isotope should be chemically similar to calcium. It should have a suitable half-life.

12.4 The dangers of radioactivity

FIRST THOUGHTS

As well as being useful, radioactivity can be dangerous. People who work with it must understand the science in what they are doing. This sign is the radioactivity hazard sign.

We make good use of radioactivity. However, large doses of radiation are dangerous. Exposure to a high dose of radiation burns the skin. Delayed effects are damage to the bones and the blood. People who are exposed to a lower level of radiation for a long time may develop leukaemia (a disease of the blood cells) and cancer. When radioactive elements get inside the body, they are very dangerous. They irradiate the body organs near them, and the risk of cancer is very great. Even an emitter of α-rays, the rays with least penetrating power, can do immense damage if it gets inside the body. Fairly low doses of radioactivity can damage human **genes**. This may result in the birth of deformed babies. People who work with radioactive sources take precautions to protect themselves.

SUMMARY

Radioactive isotopes are used in medicine, in research and in industry. Workers handling radioactive materials take precautions to shield themselves from radiation.

(a) This worker is wearing protective clothing so that radioactive material does not get onto his hands or clothes

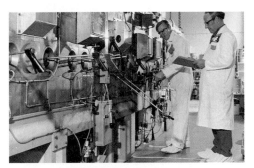

(b) These workers are using long handled tools to distance themselves from radioactive sources

(c) A film badge measures the dose of radiation its wearer receives

Figure 12.4A ● Precautions

● *They didn't know what the symbol meant*

In the city of Goiania in Brazil in 1987, two junk collectors broke into a disused medical clinic and stole a heavy cylindrical object, which they took to be lead. They sold the metal cylinder to a junk yard. It emitted an eerie blue light from narrow slits. The manager of the junk yard hammered the head off the cylinder. Inside lay a capsule containing a powdery blue substance which stuck to the skin and glowed. It was caesium-137 a radioactive isotope which is used in cancer therapy. Massive doses of the γ-radiation from caesium-137 cause leukaemia, bleeding, sterility and cataracts. The dealer did not know this: he thought the bluish powder was so pretty and shiny that he gave away bits of it to his neighbours. Almost immediately, those who touched it became sick and feverish. One man stored some under his bed because he wanted to see it glow in the dark. Several children rubbed it on their bodies, and their skin became blistered and burnt.

As a result of handling caesium-137, 20 people were taken to hospital, and 50 more people were put under medical observation, 25 homes were evacuated, and a large area of the city was cordonned off while the authorities cleared the area of radioactivity.

CHECKPOINT

❶ Why is it essential for people who handle radioactive material to wear gloves?

❷ Why do people build lead walls to protect them from γ-emitters but not from α-emitters?

❸ Why are α-emitters dangerous if they get on to your hands?

❹ The radioisotope iodine-131 is used for medical diagnosis. It has a half-life of 8 days. On 1 January, a doctor injects a patient with a solution containing 0.04 g of iodine-131. What is the maximum mass of iodine-131 that could be left in the patient's body on 2 January? Why is the actual mass less than this?

12.5 ⚛ The nuclear bomb

FIRST THOUGHTS

Splitting the atom was a marvellous achievement. Who could have foreseen the horrifying use that would be made of this discovery?

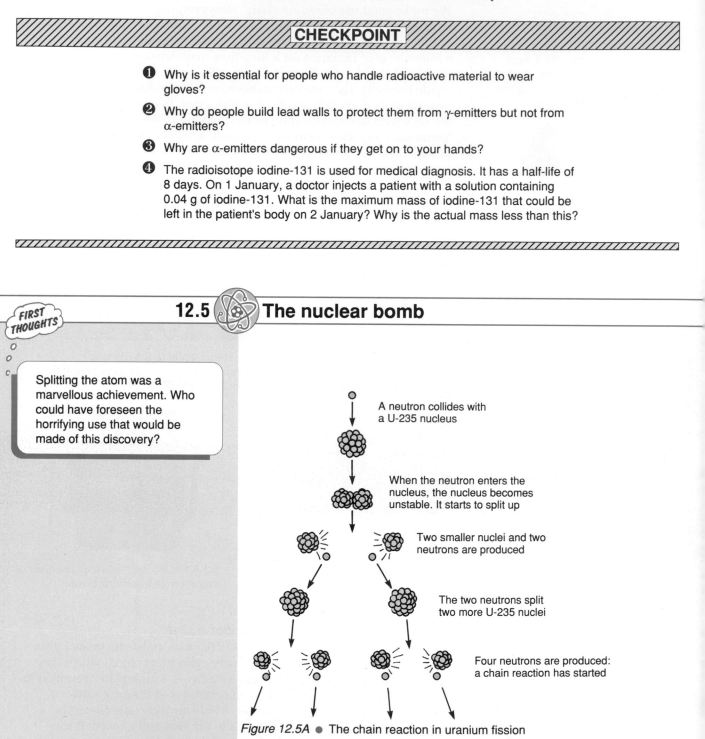

A neutron collides with a U-235 nucleus

When the neutron enters the nucleus, the nucleus becomes unstable. It starts to split up

Two smaller nuclei and two neutrons are produced

The two neutrons split two more U-235 nuclei

Four neutrons are produced: a chain reaction has started

Figure 12.5A ● The chain reaction in uranium fission

A German scientist called Otto Hahn made history in 1939. He split the atom! Hahn had been experimenting on firing neutrons at different types of nuclei. When neutrons struck uranium nuclei, some nuclei of uranium-235 split into two new nuclei and two neutrons. **Nuclear fission** (nucleus splitting) had occurred. The electrons of the original uranium-235 atom divided themselves between the two nuclei and two new atoms were formed. At the same time, an enormous amount of energy was released.

The energy given out was much greater than the energy given out in a chemical reaction. The energy which is released in nuclear fission is called **nuclear energy** (and also called **atomic energy**). The discovery that energy on a grand sale could be obtained from nuclear fission was made in 1939. Soon afterwards, the Second World War broke out. Scientists on both sides began trying to invent an 'atom bomb', a bomb which would release nuclear energy.

Figure 12.5A shows what happens in a block of uranium-235. The fission of one U-235 nucleus produces two neutrons. These two neutrons split two more uranium nuclei, producing four neutrons. A chain reaction is set off. In a large block of uranium-235, it results in an explosion. In a small block of uranium-235, an explosion does not occur because many neutrons escape from the surface before producing fission. A nuclear bomb consists of two blocks of uranium-235, each smaller than the critical mass. The bomb is detonated by firing one block into the other to make a single block which is larger than the critical mass. The detonation is followed by an atomic explosion.

Figure 12.5B   Hiroshima after the bomb

On 6 August, 1945, a uranium bomb was dropped on the Japanese city of Hiroshima. It destroyed 60 percent of the city, and killed 140 000 people.

A huge mushroom-shaped cloud rose to a height of 10 km. A plutonium bomb was dropped on the city of Nagasaki three days later. Half the city was destroyed and thousands of people were killed in the blast. There had been air raids before which had destroyed large parts of cities and killed thousands of people. This time, the damage had been done in seconds by a single bomb. One nuclear bomb had done as much damage as 20 000 tonnes of TNT. There was a new horror as the unknown danger of nuclear radiation and fall-out revealed itself.

Where was Otto Hahn, who first split the uranium atom, when the bomb fell on Hiroshima? He was one of a group of German scientists who were interned in Britain. He was distressed by the thought of the great misery which the bomb had caused. Hahn told the officer in charge of the internment camp that when he first saw that fission might lead to an atomic bomb he had thought of suicide.

Figure 12.5C ● A CND rally

Thousands of people received a large dose of radiation, from which they never recovered. The damage was so terrible that no nation has used nuclear weapons since. Many nations have huge stockpiles of nuclear weapons. The Campaign for Nuclear Disarmament (CND) wants nations to destroy their stockpiles in case an accident brings about another nuclear explosion.

Some of the scientists who worked on nuclear fission foresaw a new age, the 'atomic age', in which the energy of the atomic nucleus could be used for great benefit to mankind. They did not want to usher in the atomic age with a bomb. One group of scientists proposed that the USA should demonstrate the new bomb on a desert or on a barren island and then tell Japan to surrender or face atomic bombs. The military decision to drop the bombs was the result of the huge casualties suffered in the war against Japan. It was estimated that a million more lives would be lost in an invasion of Japan. Even after the first bomb was dropped, Japan refused to surrender. After the second bomb, the emperor himself ended the war, inspite of an attempt by a group of army officers to depose him and continue the fight.

12.6 Nuclear reactors

FIRST THOUGHTS

This section shows how nuclear power stations utilise the energy of fission (splitting atomic nuclei) and explores the hope of harnessing the energy of fusion (joining atomic nuclei) in the future.

Nuclear reactors obtain energy from the same reaction as the nuclear bomb: the fission of uranium-235. In reactors, fission is carried out in a controlled way. Reactors use naturally occurring uranium, which is a mixture of uranium-235 and uranium-238. Uranium-235 only undergoes fission with slow neutrons. Figure 12.6A shows a nuclear reactor. Neutrons from the fuel rods go into the graphite core, where they collide with graphite atoms and lose kinetic energy. The graphite is called a 'moderator' because it slows down the neutrons. The neutrons then pass into the fuel rods and cause fission. The boron rods control the rate of fission by absorbing some of the neutrons. The heat generated by nuclear fission warms a coolant fluid which circulates through the moderator.

Sensors in the core of a nuclear reactor register the temperature. The information is fed into a computer which logs the data. If the temperature rises too high, the computer sounds an alarm and activates safety procedures. Only computers can calculate with the speed needed to monitor a reactor safely.

LOOK AT LINKS
for **nuclear power**
How much electricity is generated by Britain's nuclear power stations? Would there be a shortage of electricity if nuclear power stations were closed?
See Theme B, Topic 8.1.

IT'S A FACT

The first nuclear reactor was built in an old squash court under a football stadium in Chicago in 1942. In charge was an Italian, Enrico Fermi, who had fled from Fascism in his native country to the USA in 1938. He assured the scientists present that the chain reaction would not get out of hand. It was held in check by a control rod. The control rod was pulled further and further out of the reactor. The neutron count rate rose and rose. Finally, Fermi ordered the reactor to be shut down. The scientists and engineers who saw the demonstration were impressed.

The coolant may be water (as in pressurised water reactors) or a gas, e.g. carbon dioxide (as in gas cooled reactors). The heat is used to turn water into steam. The steam drives a turbine and generates electricity.

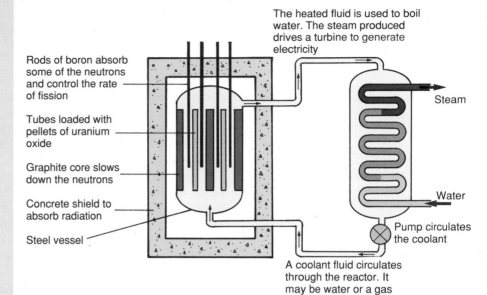

Figure 12.6A ● A nuclear reactor

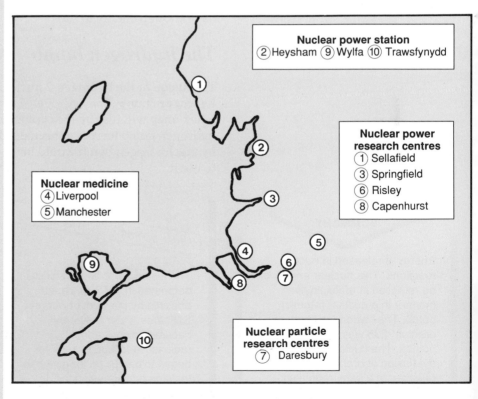

Figure 12.6B ● The nuclear industry in North-west England and North Wales

12.7 Nuclear fusion

One glass of water could provide the same amount of energy as 1 tonne of petrol! The source of this energy is nuclear fusion. When two atoms of hydrogen-2 (deuterium) collide at high speed, the nuclei fuse together.

$$^2_1H + {}^2_1H \longrightarrow {}^3_2He + {}^1_0n$$

An isotope of helium and a neutron are produced. A large amount of energy is released when two light nuclei fuse together. It gives more hydrogen-2 atoms the energy they need to fuse with other atoms. Thus a chain reaction starts. There is no shortage of hydrogen-2 because it occurs in water as ^2H_2O. Nuclear reactors of the future may use the fusion process as a source of nuclear energy.

There are enormous technical difficulties with fusion. The hydrogen-2 atoms must be heated to a very high temperature before they will fuse. Repulsion between the two positive charges sets in when the nuclei get close. If the atoms are moving fast enough, this repulsion can be overcome. The reactor must be made of materials which will withstand very high temperatures. Scientists are still working on the problems of obtaining energy from fusion.

The products of fusion are not radioactive. However, the metal structure in which fusion takes places does become radioactive by interaction with the neutrons produced in fusion. Fusion reactors of the future would, like fission reactors, involve the disposal of both high-level and low-level radioactive waste.

The Sun obtains its energy from the fusion of hydrogen-2 atoms. In the Sun, the temperature is about 10 million °C, and the hydrogen-2 atoms have enough energy to fuse.

The hydrogen bomb

The fusion of the hydrogen-2 nuclei is the source of energy in the **hydrogen bomb**. The hydrogen-2 atoms are raised to the temperature at which they will fuse by the explosion of the uranium-235 bomb. The hydrogen bomb has never been used in warfare. The destruction caused by one hydrogen bomb would be so widespread that no nation has dared to use it.

IT'S A FACT

The first successful controlled fusion experiment took place on 13 August 1978 in Princeton University, USA. A temperature of 60 million °C was reached for 0.10 seconds.

SUMMARY

Energy is released in nuclear reactions. This nuclear energy can be released in an explosive manner in a nuclear (atomic) bomb. The fission (splitting) of uranium-235 was used in nuclear bombs. The nuclear energy from the fission of uranium-235 is released in a safe, regulated manner in a nuclear power station. The fusion (joining together) of small nuclei also releases energy. The fusion of hydrogen-2 nuclei is the source of energy in the hydrogen bomb.

Who's behind the science

The fusion bomb which Russia detonated in 1953 was made possible by the work of Andrei Sakharov. Later Sakharov became anxious about radioactive fallout. In 1957 he began to campaign for a stop to tests on nuclear weapons. In 1968, he was sacked from his post in a research institute and later interned as a dissident. After his release in 1986, he continued to be active in politics until his death in 1989.

12.8 Disposal of radioactive waste

Everyone who uses radioactive materials has to find a solution to the problem of disposing safely of radioactive waste.

Radioactive waste comes from uranium mines, nuclear power stations, hospitals and research laboratories. It must be disposed of in some place where it is not a health hazard. The method used for waste disposal depends on whether the radioactivity is low-level, intermediate-level or high-level.

Low-level waste

Power stations produce a lot of slightly radioactive cooling water. This passes through long pipes out to sea. It is discharged 1–2 km from the shore.

Laboratory equipment and protective clothing are placed in metal containers. These are buried (see Figure 12.8A).

Soil cover replaced and replanted

Low level waste packed into containers and buried

Figure 12.8A ● Burial of low-level solid waste

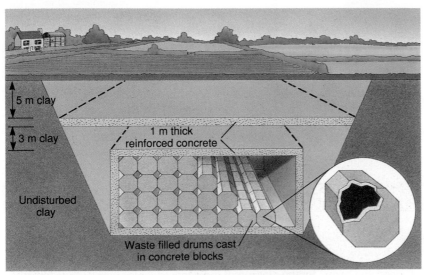

5 m clay

3 m clay

1 m thick reinforced concrete

Undisturbed clay

Waste filled drums cast in concrete blocks

Figure 12.8B ● Burial of intermediate-level solid waste

Intermediate-level waste

Nuclear power stations produce large quantities of intermediate waste. Figure 12.8B shows one method of disposal. Drums containing waste are cast in concrete and buried under 8 m of clay. Another method is to bury drums of waste deep underground in disused mines.

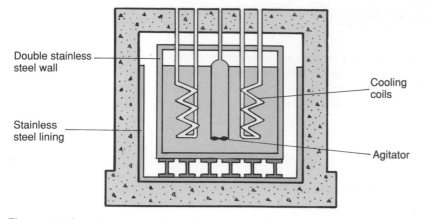

Double stainless
steel wall

Cooling
coils

Stainless
steel lining

Agitator

Figure 12.8C ● A storage tank for high-level liquid waste

High-level waste

Nuclear reactors contain fuel rods (see Figure 12.6A). After a time, the fuel rods must be replaced. The spent fuel rods are highly radioactive. They are stored in cooling ponds of water until they are less radioactive. Then they are removed to a special treatment plant where they are dissolved in acid. The solution must be stored and cooled until it becomes less radioactive (see Figure 12.8C).

Computers monitor the radioactivity and temperature of stores of high-level waste and keep a record of the measurements.

Liquid waste can be **vitrified** (turned into glass). France stores vitrified high-level waste, and Britain plans to start using this method. Figure 12.8D shows deep underground burial of steel canisters containing vitrified waste. There is a shortage of land sites for this purpose. British Nuclear Fuels Ltd is planning to store radioactive waste in tunnels under the sea (see Figure 12.8E).

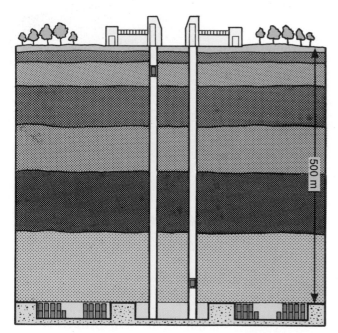

Figure 12.8D ● Deep underground burial of high level radioactive waste

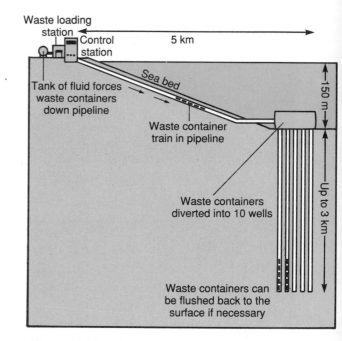

Waste loading station

Control station

5 km

Tank of fluid forces waste containers down pipeline

Sea bed

Waste container train in pipeline

150 m

Waste containers diverted into 10 wells

Up to 3 km

Waste containers can be flushed back to the surface if necessary

Figure 12.8E ● An undersea tunnel for the storage of radioactive waste

CHECKPOINT

① Why is a clay site chosen for the burial of intermediate-level waste (see Figure 12.8B) rather than a sandy soil?

② Some countries use disused salt mines for the storage of radioactive waste. Why do they feel sure that such sites will be dry? Why is it necessary to store the waste in dry conditions?

❸ When British Nuclear Fuels planned to build a site like that in Figure 12.8D in Humberside, people all over the county protested strongly. They said they did not want a 'nuclear dump in our back yard'. Posters read, 'Say no to a shallow grave'. The plan was dropped.

(a) Why do you think that people did not want a site of this kind in the county?

(b) Is it fair to describe the site as 'a shallow grave'?

(c) What will happen if every county refuses to store radioactive waste?

(d) Waste from nuclear power stations contains plutonium. How long does plutonium have to be stored before it has lost (i) half its radioactivity (ii) three quarters of its radioactivity? (See Table 12.3)

(e) Compose a letter to your local newspaper. Explain *either* why you think your county should accept a burial site for radioactive waste *or* why you think your county should resist such a plan.

12.9 ⚛ Safety

FIRST THOUGHTS

Background radioactivity

> As you read this section, try to weigh up the advantages of nuclear power against the dangers.

Radioactive materials occur naturally in rocks, in soil and in the air. The low level of radioactivity which they give out is called **background radioactivity**. Figure 12.9A shows the radiation we receive from natural sources and from artificial sources.

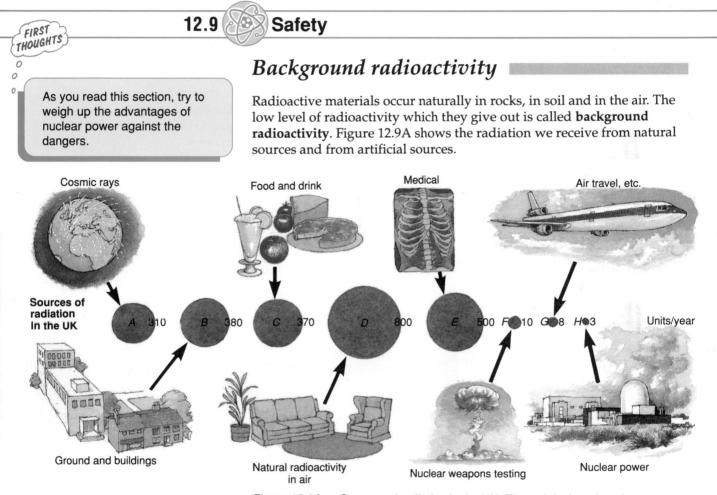

Figure 12.9A ● Sources of radiation in the UK. The unit is the microsievert, a measure of the effect of radioactivity on cells

Accidents

● *Windscale*

They call it 'the day the reactor caught fire'. It happened at Windscale in Cumbria on 11 October 1957. The power station is now called Sellafield. The reactor overheated and graphite rods caught fire. They managed to put out the fire by flooding the reactor with water. Radioactive isotopes were blown from the reactor over the Lake District. In fact, no-one was injured in the accident.

LOOK AT LINKS
for **genetic damage**
The effect of radiation on genetic material is discussed further in Theme N, Topic 54.

● Three Mile Island

A bigger accident happened in Three Mile Island in the USA in 1979. The reactor was a pressurised water reactor. The pumps which fed cold water into the reactor stopped and the temperature of the reactor shot up. After two hours, the operators rectified the fault. It took a week for the temperature to fall. The reactor was crippled. A cloud of radioactive substances fell over the island. Over three million litres of cooling water were radioactive. Luckily, no-one was injured in the accident. There may be long-term effects on health, however. In 1985, permission was given to reopen the plant. The public have staged such huge demonstrations against the reopening of the power station that work has not yet begun.

● Chernobyl

The worst nuclear accident happened in 1986 at the Chernobyl power station in the USSR. It was a pressurised water reactor with a graphite moderator, and a loss of cooling water caused the reactor to overheat. Steam reacted with graphite to produce hydrogen, which exploded. The explosion set the building on fire. Firemen battled heroically to put out the blaze. Many of those who fought the fire have since died of leukaemia. The reactor also caught fire. It burned for days while people tried to bring it under control. When the core of the reactor reached 5000 °C, they feared that it might melt the container and burn its way down into the earth. Helicopters managed to get near enough to drop sand and lead on the burning reactor to cool it.

Figure 12.9B ● The Chernobyl power station taken from a helicopter after the explosion

The roof of the reactor blew off in the explosion, and a cloud of radioactive material spread over the Ukraine in the USSR and drifted over other European countries. A week later, the cloud of radioactive material reached the UK.

From the area round Chernobyl, 135 000 people were evacuated. Thirty or more people died in the accident, and hundreds suffered from radiation sickness. People who received a smaller dose of radiation may develop leukaemia or cancer in the future. The final toll will not be known for many years.

Could Chernobyl happen here? The Chairman of the Central Electricity Generating Board answered this question in 1986. These are some of the points he made.

- The Chernobyl design is not used outside the USSR.
- The design is poor: the reactor is unstable when operated at low power.
- The operators at Chernobyl ignored some safety instructions.
- Chernobyl had no automatic fast-acting shutdown system to close the reactor if it became unsafe.
- The CEGB reactors all have computer-controlled safety systems which can shut down reactors if faults are detected.

CHECKPOINT

❶ Look at Figure 12.9A.
  (a) Background radiation is made up of sources A, B, C and D. What dose of radiation do these sources add up to?
  (b) Radiation from sources E, F, G and H is under our control. What dose of radiation do these sources add up to?
  (c) Which of the sources under our control adds the most to our total dose of radiation? What is the difficulty in reducing the dose from this source of radiation?
  (d) What is the total dose of radiation we receive in a year? What fraction of this comes from (i) nuclear power stations and (ii) nuclear weapons testing?

❷ Russia did not announce the accident at Chernobyl until after Sweden had detected an increase in atmospheric radioactivity. What do you think that a country which has a nuclear accident should do? If the neighbouring countries had known that a cloud of radioactive fallout was on the way, what precautions could they have taken?

❸ Strontium-90 is produced in nuclear reactors. It is radioactive. Why are babies especially at risk if an accident releases strontium-90 into the environment? (The clue is in the Periodic Table. Which elements resemble strontium? Which of these elements is present in milk?)

Further reading   You will find more about nuclear power stations and nuclear bombs and missiles in *Extending Science 9: Nuclear Power* by R E Lee (Stanley Thornes (Publishers) Ltd).

TOPIC 13 IONS

13.1 Which substances conduct electricity?

FIRST THOUGHTS

Some elements and compounds conduct electricity. You can find out how they do it in this topic.

LOOK AT LINKS
for **circuit diagrams**
You will learn another way of drawing circuit diagrams in Theme K, Topic 43.

SUMMARY

• **Solids.** Metallic elements, alloys and graphite (a form of carbon) conduct electricity.
• **Liquids.** Solutions of acids, alkalis and salts conduct electricity.

Electrical wires are often made of the metal copper. Copper is an **electrical conductor**: it allows electricity to pass through it. *Are all metals electrical conductors? Are there substances other than metals that conduct?* Figure 13.1A shows how you can test a solid to find out whether it conducts electricity.

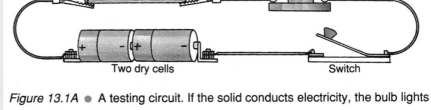

Figure 13.1A ● A testing circuit. If the solid conducts electricity, the bulb lights

Figure 13.1B shows a beaker of liquid. The two graphite rods in the liquid are **electrodes**: they can conduct a direct electric current into and out of the liquid. *Draw a circuit diagram like Figure 13.1A showing how you could test the liquid to see whether it conducts electricity.*

You should start your study of this topic by doing some experiments on conduction. *Are your results like those in Table 13.1?*

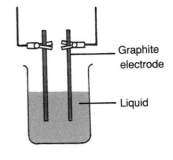

Figure 13.1B ● Test this liquid

Table 13.1 ● Electrical conductors

Solids	Liquids
Metallic elements	Mercury, the liquid metal
Alloys (mixtures of metals)	Solutions of acids, bases and salts
Graphite (a form of carbon)	Molten salts
(Solid compounds do not conduct.)	(Liquids such as ethanol and sugar solution do not conduct.)

13.2 Molten solids and electricity

LOOK AT LINKS
for **metals**
What enables metals to conduct? It is the metallic bond.
See Theme L, Topic 50.2.

When a solid, e.g. a **metal**, conducts electricity, the current is carried by electrons. The battery forces the electrons through the conductor. The metal may change, for example it may become hot, but when the current stops flowing, the metal is just the same as before. When a metal conducts electricity, no chemical reaction occurs. When a molten salt conducts electricity, chemical changes occur, and new substances are formed.

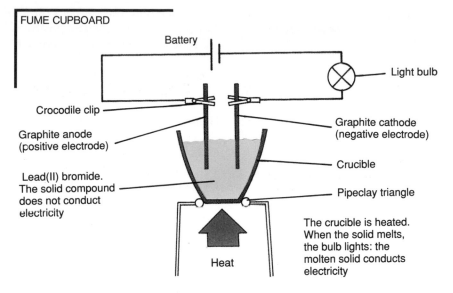

Figure 13.2A ● Passing a direct electric current through lead(II) bromide (TAKE CARE: do not inhale bromine vapour)

Which electrode is which?
AnoDe
AD → ADD → + → positive
The anode is positive...
and the cathode is negative.

Figure 13.2A shows an experiment to find out what happens when a direct electric current passes through a molten **salt**. A salt is a compound of a metallic element with a non-metallic element or elements. Lead(II) bromide is a salt with a fairly low melting point. The container through which the current passes is called a **cell**. The rods which conduct electricity into and out of the cell are called **electrodes**. The electrode connected to the positive terminal of the battery is called the **anode**. The electrode connected to the negative terminal is called the **cathode**. The electrodes are usually made of elements such as platinum and graphite, which do not react with electrolytes.

When the salt melts, the bulb lights, showing that the molten salt conducts electricity. At the positive electrode (anode), bromine can be detected. It is a non-metallic element, a reddish-brown vapour with a very penetrating smell. (TAKE CARE: do not inhale bromine vapour) At the negative electrode (cathode), lead is formed. After cooling, a layer of lead can be seen on the cathode.

The experiment shows that lead(II) bromide has been split up by the electric current. It has been **electrolysed**. Compounds which conduct electricity are called **electrolytes**. Remember that all substances consist of particles (see Theme B, Topic 5). Since bromine goes only to the positive electrode, it follows that bromine particles have a negative charge. Since lead appears at the negative electrode only, it follows that lead particles have a positive charge. These charged particles are called **ions**. Positive ions are called **cations** because they travel towards the cathode. Negative ions are called **anions** because they travel towards the anode.

How do ions differ from atoms? A bromide ion, Br^-, differs from a bromine atom, Br, in having one more electron. The extra electron gives it a negative charge.

Bromine atom + Electron → Bromide ion
$$Br \quad + \quad e^- \quad → \quad Br^-$$

A lead(II) ion differs from a lead ion by having two fewer electrons. It therefore has a double positive charge, Pb^{2+}.

Lead atom → Lead ion + 2 Electrons
$$Pb \quad → \quad Pb^{2+} \quad + \quad 2e^-$$

IT

Ionic and Molar Chemistry
(program)

This program will help you to work out chemical formulas and to balance chemical equations. Also use this program to learn more about the theory of electrolysis and ionic bonding.

What happens when the ions reach the electrodes? They are **discharged**: they lose their charge. The positive electrode takes electrons from bromide ions so that they become bromine atoms.

Bromide ion → Bromine atom + Electron (taken by positive electrode)
$$Br^-(l) \rightarrow Br(g) + e^-$$

Then bromine atoms pair up to form bromine molecules:

$$2Br(g) \rightarrow Br_2(g)$$

The negative electrode gives electrons to the positively charged lead ions so that they become lead atoms.

Lead ion + 2 Electrons (taken from the negative electrode) → Lead atom
$$Pb^{2+}(l) + 2e^- \rightarrow Pb(l)$$

The electrons which are supplied to the anode by the discharge of bromine ions travel round the external circuit to the cathode. At the cathode, they combine with lead(II) ions (see Figure 13.2B).

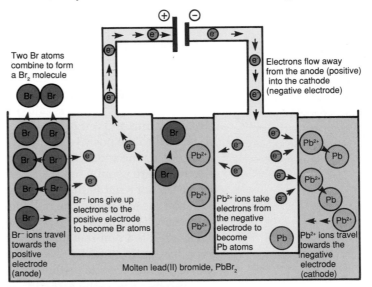

Figure 13.2B ● The flow of electrons

SUMMARY

Some compounds conduct electric current when they are molten. As they do they are electrolysed, that is, split up by the current. The explanation of electrolysis is that these compounds are composed of positive and negative ions.

Lead(II) bromide is an uncharged substance because there are two Br^- ions for each Pb^{2+} ions. The formula is $PbBr_2$. *Why does solid lead(II) bromide not conduct electricity?*

In the solid salt, the ions cannot move. They are fixed in a rigid three-dimensional structure. In the molten solid, the ions can move and make their way to the electrodes.

You will have noticed that lead(II) ions have two units of charge, whereas bromide ions have a single unit of charge. By experiment, it is possible to find out what charge an ion carries. Table 13.2 shows the results of such experiments.

Table 13.2 ● Some common ions

Positive ions			Negative ions	
+1	+2	+3	−1	−2
Hydrogen, H^+	Copper, Cu^{2+}	Aluminium, Al^{3+}	Bromide, Br^-	Oxide, O^{2-}
Sodium, Na^+	Iron(II), Fe^{2+}	Iron(III), Fe^{3+}	Chloride, Cl^-	Sulphide, S^{2-}
Potassium, K^+	Lead(II), Pb^{2+}		Iodide, I^-	Carbonate, CO_3^{2-}
	Magnesium, Mg^{2+}		Hydroxide, OH^-	Sulphate, SO_4^{2-}
	Zinc, Zn^{2+}		Nitrate, NO_3^-	

13.3 ● Solutions and conduction

FIRST THOUGHTS

The best way to begin this topic is by doing experiments to find out what types of solutions are electrolysed.

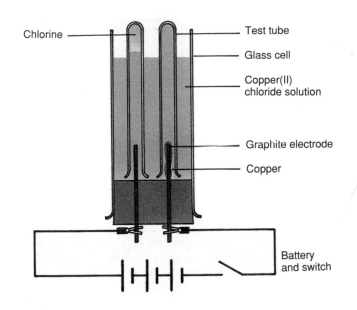

Figure 13.3A ● Electrolysis of copper(II) chloride

Who's behind the science

The scientist who did the first work on electrolysis was Michael Faraday. He was born in 1791, the son of a blacksmith. He received only a very basic education. When he was apprenticed to a London book binder, books on chemistry and physics came into his hands. He found them fascinating and led him to study science in his spare time. He attended a series of lectures given by Sir Humphry Davy, the director of the Royal Institution. Faraday wrote up the lectures and illustrated them with careful diagrams. He sent the notebook to Davy, asking for some kind of work in the laboratory. Davy agreed, and Faraday soon became a capable research assistant. On Davy's retirement, Faraday became director of the Royal Institution. Faraday is famous for his discovery of electromagnetic induction and for his work on the chemical effects of electric currents. In 1834, he put forward the theory that electrolysis could be explained by the existence of charged particles of matter. We now call them *ions*.

In Figure 13.3A a solution of the salt copper(II) chloride is being electrolysed. At the positive electrode (anode), bubbles of the gas chlorine can be seen. The negative electrode (cathode), becomes coated with a reddish brown film of copper.

Look at Figure 13.3A. At which electrode is copper deposited? Which kind of charge must copper ions carry? At which electrode is chlorine given off? Which kind of charge must chloride ions carry?

When they reach the electrodes, the ions are discharged.
At the negative electrode

Copper(II) ion + 2 Electrons (taken from the cathode) → Copper atom
$$Cu^{2+}(aq) + 2e^- → Cu(s)$$

At the positive electrode

Chloride ion → Chlorine atom + Electron (given up at the anode)
$$Cl^-(aq) → Cl(g) + e^-$$

Pairs of chlorine atoms then join to form molecules.

$$2Cl(g) → Cl_2(g)$$

The electrons given to the anode by the discharge of chloride ions travel round the external circuit to the cathode. At the cathode, they combine with copper(II) ions.

To make sure you understand it, draw a diagram showing what happens to the ions and electrons in the electrolysis of copper(II) chloride solution. You can refer to Figure 13.2B for help.

Solid copper(II) chloride does not conduct electricity, but a solution of the salt in water does conduct. It is not the water in the solution that makes it conduct: experiment shows that water is a very poor electrical conductor. *What is the reason for the difference in behaviour between the solid and the solution?* In a solid, the ions are fixed in position, held together by strong attractive forces between positive and negative ions. In a solution of a salt, the ions are free to move (see Figure 13.3B).

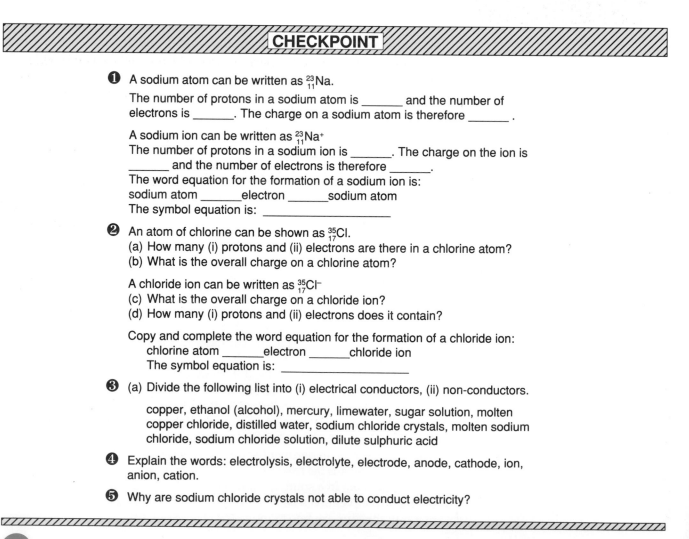

Water is a non-conductor because it is not ionic

The crystalline solid is a non-conductor because the ions are held in a rigid structure

The solution is a good conductor because the ions are now free to move

Figure 13.3C ● The ions must be free to move

SUMMARY

When a direct electric current is passed through solutions of some compounds, they are electrolysed, that is, split up by the current. Chemical changes occur in the electrolyte, and, as a result, new substances are formed.
Compounds which are electrolytes consist of positively and negatively charged particles called ions. In molten **ionic** solids and in solutions, the ions are free to move.

● *Safety matters*

Tap water conducts electricity. Never handle electrical equipment with wet hands. If the equipment is faulty, you run a much bigger risk of getting a lethal shock if you have wet hands.

Non-electrolytes and weak electrolytes

Some liquids and solutions do not conduct electricity. It follows that these **non-electrolytes** consist of molecules, not ions. Some substances conduct electricity to a very slight extent. They are **weak electrolytes**. These compounds consist mainly of molecules, which do not conduct. A small fraction of the molecules split up to form ions which do conduct. Such compounds are **partially ionised**.

CHECKPOINT

❶ A sodium atom can be written as $^{23}_{11}Na$.

The number of protons in a sodium atom is _____ and the number of electrons is _____. The charge on a sodium atom is therefore _____ .

A sodium ion can be written as $^{23}_{11}Na^+$
The number of protons in a sodium ion is _____. The charge on the ion is _____ and the number of electrons is therefore _____.
The word equation for the formation of a sodium ion is:
sodium atom _____ electron _____ sodium atom
The symbol equation is: _____

❷ An atom of chlorine can be shown as $^{35}_{17}Cl$.
   (a) How many (i) protons and (ii) electrons are there in a chlorine atom?
   (b) What is the overall charge on a chlorine atom?

A chloride ion can be written as $^{35}_{17}Cl^-$
   (c) What is the overall charge on a chloride ion?
   (d) How many (i) protons and (ii) electrons does it contain?

Copy and complete the word equation for the formation of a chloride ion:
   chlorine atom _____ electron _____ chloride ion
   The symbol equation is: _____

❸ (a) Divide the following list into (i) electrical conductors, (ii) non-conductors.

   copper, ethanol (alcohol), mercury, limewater, sugar solution, molten copper chloride, distilled water, sodium chloride crystals, molten sodium chloride, sodium chloride solution, dilute sulphuric acid

❹ Explain the words: electrolysis, electrolyte, electrode, anode, cathode, ion, anion, cation.

❺ Why are sodium chloride crystals not able to conduct electricity?

13.4 More examples of electrolysis

Sometimes the products formed when solutions are electrolysed are difficult to predict, but there are rules to help you.

IT

Electrolysis
(program)

Use this program to see a computer simulation of electrolysis in action. You can study the movement of ions and the jobs done by the anode and cathode.

Sodium chloride solution

When molten sodium chloride (common salt) is electrolysed, the products are sodium and chlorine. When the aqueous solution of sodium chloride is electrolysed, the products are hydrogen (at the negative electrode) and chlorine (at the positive electrode). To explain how this happens, we have to think about the water present in the solution. Water consists of molecules, but a very small fraction of the molecules ionise into hydrogen ions and hydroxide ions.

$$\text{Water} \rightarrow \text{Hydrogen ions} + \text{Hydroxide ions}$$
$$H_2O(l) \rightarrow H^+(aq) + OH^-(aq)$$

Hydrogen ions are attracted to the negative electrode as well as sodium ions. Sodium ions are more stable than hydrogen ions. It is easier for the negative electrode to give an electron to a hydrogen ion than it is for it to give an electron to a sodium ion. Sodium ions remain in solution while hydrogen ions are discharged to form hydrogen atoms. These atoms join in pairs to form hydrogen molecules.

$$H^+(aq) + e^- \rightarrow H(g)$$
$$2H(g) \rightarrow H_2(g)$$

Although the concentration of hydrogen ions in the solution is very low, it is kept topped up by the ionisation of more water molecules.

At the positive electrode, there are chloride ions and also hydroxide ions. The hydroxide ions have come, in very low concentration, from the ionisation of water molecules. Chloride ions are discharged while hydroxide ions remain in solution.

Copper(II) sulphate solution

When copper(II) sulphate is electrolysed, copper is deposited on the cathode, and oxygen is evolved at the anode. The oxygen comes from the water in the solution. At the positive electrode, there are hydroxide ions, OH^-, as well as sulphate ions, SO_4^{2-}. The hydroxide ions have come in low concentration from the ionisation of water molecules (see above). It is easier for the positive electrode to take electrons away from hydroxide ions than from sulphate ions, and hydroxide ions are discharged. The OH groups which are formed exist for only a fraction of a second before rearranging to give oxygen and water.

$$OH^-(aq) \rightarrow OH(aq) + e^-$$
$$4OH(aq) \rightarrow 2H_2O(l) + O_2(g)$$

Although only a tiny fraction of water molecules is ionised, once hydroxide ions have been discharged, more water molecules ionise to replace them with fresh hydroxide ions.

Dilute sulphuric acid

Figure 13.4A shows the electrolysis of dilute sulphuric acid.

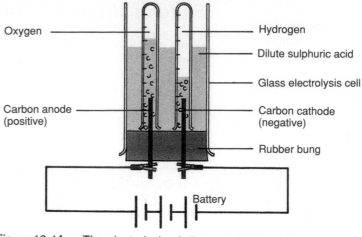

Figure 13.4A ● The electrolysis of dilute sulphuric acid

13.5 Which ions are discharged?

You will have seen that some ions are easier to discharge at an electrode than others.

Cations

Some metals are more **reactive** than others. The ions of very reactive metals are difficult to discharge. Sodium is a very reactive metal. When it reacts, sodium atoms form sodium ions. It is difficult to force a sodium ion to accept an electron and turn back into a sodium atom. Hydrogen ions are discharged in preference to sodium ions. The ions of less reactive metals, such as copper and lead, are easy to discharge.

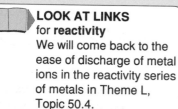

LOOK AT LINKS
for **reactivity**
We will come back to the ease of discharge of metal ions in the reactivity series of metals in Theme L, Topic 50.4.

Figure 13.5A ● Sodium ions do not want to accept electrons

Anions

Sulphate ions and nitrate ions are very difficult to discharge. When solutions of sulphates and nitrates are electrolysed, hydroxide ions are discharged instead, and oxygen is evolved.

SUMMARY

Water is ionised to a very small extent into $H^+(aq)$ ions and $OH^-(aq)$ ions. These ions are discharged when some aqueous solutions are electrolysed. The ions of very reactive metals, e.g. Na^+, are difficult to discharge. In aqueous solution, hydrogen ions are discharged instead. Hydrogen is evolved at the negative electrode. The anions SO_4^{2-} and NO_3^- are difficult to discharge. In aqueous solution, OH^- ions are discharged instead, and oxygen is evolved at the positive electrode.

CHECKPOINT

❶ Copy and complete this passage.

When molten sodium chloride is electrolysed, _____ is formed at the positive electrode and _____ is formed at the negative electrode.

When aqueous sodium chloride is electrolysed, _____ is formed at the positive electrode and _____ is formed at the negative electrode. The reaction that takes place at the positive electrode is

_____

and the reaction that takes place at the negative electrode is

_____

❷ A solution of potassium bromide is electrolysed. At one electrode a colourless gas is given off. At the other a brown vapour appears.
(a) At which electrode does the brown vapour appear? Which ions have been discharged?
(b) Which gas is produced at the other electrode? Which ions have been discharged?
(c) Write equations for the discharge of the ions at each electrode.

FIRST THOUGHTS

13.6 ⚛ **Applications of electrolysis**

Electrolysis is useful for:
• electroplating,
• extracting metals from their ores,
• manufacturing chemicals.

Electroplating

Some metals are prized for their strength and others for their beauty. Beautiful metals like silver and gold are costly. Often, objects made from less expensive metals are given a coating of silver or gold. The coating layer must stick well to the surface. It must be even and, to limit the cost, it should be thin. Depositing the metal by electrolysis is ideal. The technique is called **electroplating**.

Electroplating is used for protection as well as for decoration. You may have a bicycle with chromium-plated handlebars. The layer of chromium protects the steel underneath from rusting. Chromium does not stick well to steel. Steel is first electroplated with copper, which adheres well to steel, then it is nickel-plated and finally chromium-plated. The result is an attractive bright surface which does not corrode.

The rusting of iron is a serious problem. One solution to the problem is to coat iron with a metal which does not corrode. Food cans must not rust. They are made of iron coated with tin. Tin is an unreactive metal, and the juices in foods do not react with it.

═══ **SCIENCE AT WORK** ═══

Do you know what happens when a group makes a recording? Sound waves activate a machine which cuts a groove in a soft plastic disc. This disc is coated with graphite so that it will conduct. Then it is electroplated with a thick layer of metal. The metal plating is prised off the plastic disc and used to stamp out copies of the original.

LOOK AT LINKS
for **rust**
Rusting, the problem and its prevention, is covered in Theme E, Topic 21.9.

Figure 13.6A ● Chromium plate

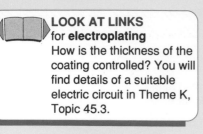
LOOK AT LINKS
for **electroplating**
How is the thickness of the coating controlled? You will find details of a suitable electric circuit in Theme K, Topic 45.3.

SUMMARY

Electroplating is used to coat a cheap metal with an expensive metal. It is used to coat a metal like iron, which rusts, with a metal which does not corrode, e.g. tin or zinc.

Electroplating is used to give a thin even layer of tin. A layer of zinc is applied to iron in the manufacture of 'galvanised' iron. Often, electroplating is employed.

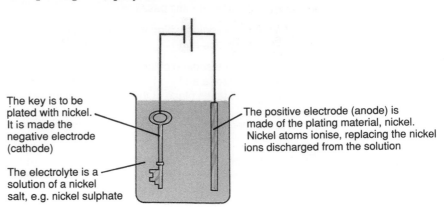

The key is to be plated with nickel. It is made the negative electrode (cathode)

The electrolyte is a solution of a nickel salt, e.g. nickel sulphate

The positive electrode (anode) is made of the plating material, nickel. Nickel atoms ionise, replacing the nickel ions discharged from the solution

Figure 13.6B ● Electroplating

Extraction of metals from their ores

Reactive metals are difficult to extract from their ores. For some of them, electrolysis is the only method which works. Sodium is obtained by the electrolysis of molten dry sodium chloride, and aluminium is obtained by the electrolysis of molten aluminium oxide.

Electrolysis can also be used as a method of purifying metals. Pure copper is obtained by an electrolytic method.

LOOK AT LINKS
for **extracting metals**.
See Theme L, Topic 50.8.

Manufacture of sodium hydroxide

The three important chemicals, sodium hydroxide, chlorine and hydrogen are all obtained from the plentiful starting material, common salt. The method of manufacture is to electrolyse a solution of sodium chloride (common salt) in a diaphragm cell.

SUMMARY

Electrolysis is used in the extraction of some metals from their ores, e.g. sodium, aluminium, copper.

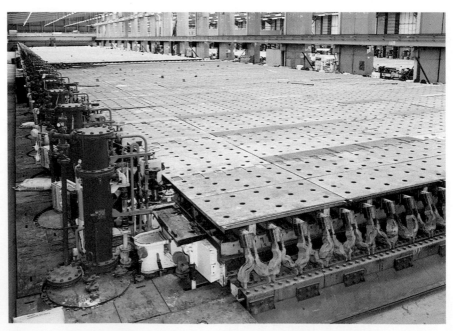

Figure 13.6C ● A room of diaphragm cells for the electrolysis of sodium chloride

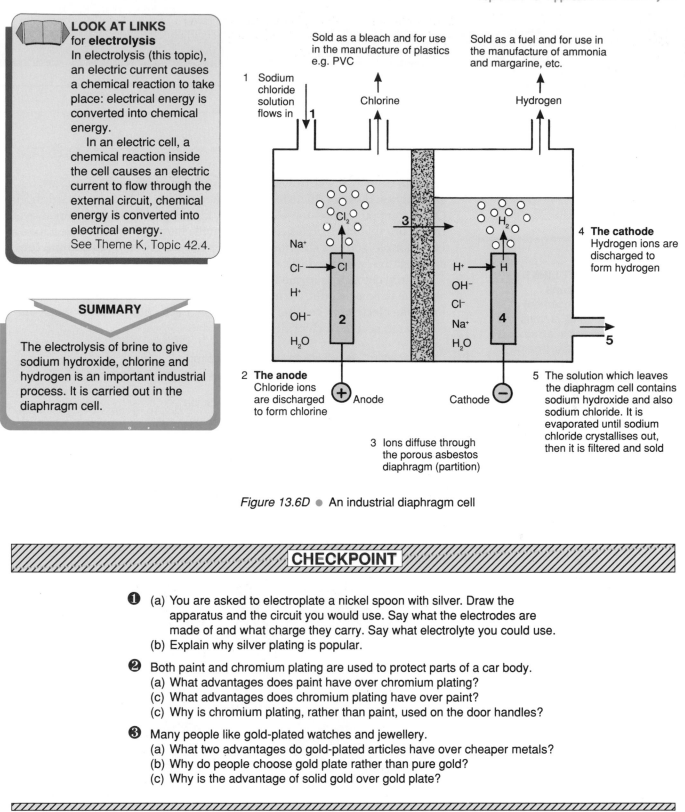

LOOK AT LINKS
for **electrolysis**

In electrolysis (this topic), an electric current causes a chemical reaction to take place: electrical energy is converted into chemical energy.

In an electric cell, a chemical reaction inside the cell causes an electric current to flow through the external circuit, chemical energy is converted into electrical energy.

See Theme K, Topic 42.4.

SUMMARY

The electrolysis of brine to give sodium hydroxide, chlorine and hydrogen is an important industrial process. It is carried out in the diaphragm cell.

Sold as a bleach and for use in the manufacture of plastics e.g. PVC

Sold as a fuel and for use in the manufacture of ammonia and margarine, etc.

1 Sodium chloride solution flows in

Chlorine

Hydrogen

4 **The cathode**
Hydrogen ions are discharged to form hydrogen

2 **The anode**
Chloride ions are discharged to form chlorine

5 The solution which leaves the diaphragm cell contains sodium hydroxide and also sodium chloride. It is evaporated until sodium chloride crystallises out, then it is filtered and sold

3 Ions diffuse through the porous asbestos diaphragm (partition)

Figure 13.6D ● An industrial diaphragm cell

CHECKPOINT

❶ (a) You are asked to electroplate a nickel spoon with silver. Draw the apparatus and the circuit you would use. Say what the electrodes are made of and what charge they carry. Say what electrolyte you could use.
(b) Explain why silver plating is popular.

❷ Both paint and chromium plating are used to protect parts of a car body.
(a) What advantages does paint have over chromium plating?
(c) What advantages does chromium plating have over paint?
(c) Why is chromium plating, rather than paint, used on the door handles?

❸ Many people like gold-plated watches and jewellery.
(a) What two advantages do gold-plated articles have over cheaper metals?
(b) Why do people choose gold plate rather than pure gold?
(c) Why is the advantage of solid gold over gold plate?

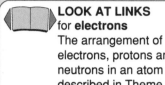

14.1 The ionic bond

What holds the atoms in a compound together? What holds the ions in a compound together? You can find out in this topic.

LOOK AT LINKS
for **electrons**
The arrangement of electrons, protons and neutrons in an atom is described in Theme C, Topic 11.1.

LOOK AT LINKS
for **electrostatic attraction**
See Theme K, Topic 42.2.

Sodium chloride

Topic 13 dealt with electrolysis. You found that some compounds are electrolytes: they conduct electricity when molten or in aqueous solution. Other compounds are non-electrolytes. Electrolysis can be explained by the theory that electrolytes consist of small charged particles called **ions**. For example, sodium chloride consists of positively charged sodium ions and negatively charged chloride ions, Na^+ Cl^-.

Sodium chloride is formed when sodium (a metallic element) burns in chlorine (a non-metallic element). During the reaction, each sodium atom loses one **electron** to become a sodium ion. Each chlorine atom gains one electron to become a chloride ion.

$$\text{Sodium atom} \rightarrow \text{Sodium ion} + \text{Electron}$$
$$Na \rightarrow Na^+ + e^-$$

$$\text{Chlorine atom} + \text{Electron} \rightarrow \text{Chloride ion}$$
$$Cl + e^- \rightarrow Cl^-$$

When particles have opposite electric charges, a force of attraction exists between them. It is called **electrostatic attraction**. In sodium chloride, the sodium ions and chloride ions are held together by electrostatic attraction. The electrostatic attraction is the **chemical bond** in the compound, sodium chloride. It is called an **ionic bond** or **electrovalent bond**. Sodium chloride is an ionic or electrovalent compound. The compounds which conduct electricity when they are melted or dissolved are electrovalent compounds.

Figure 14.1A ● There is an attraction between sodium ions and chloride ions

A pair of ions, Na^+ Cl^-, does not exist by itself. It attracts other ions. The sodium ion attracts chloride ions, and the chloride ion attracts sodium ions. The result is a three-dimensional structure of alternate Na^+ and Cl^- ions. (Figure 14.1B) This is a **crystal** of sodium chloride. The crystal is uncharged because the number of sodium ions is equal to the number of chloride ions. The forces of attraction between the ions hold them in position in the structure. Since they cannot move out of their positions, the ions cannot conduct electricity. When the salt melts, the three-dimensional structure breaks down, the ions can move towards the electrodes and the molten solid can be electrolysed. There are millions of ions in even the tiniest crystal. The structures of ionic solids, such as sodium chloride, are described as **giant ionic structures**.

SUMMARY

Sodium and chlorine react to form positive sodium ions and negative chloride ions. The electrostatic attraction between these oppositely charged ions is an ionic bond or electrovalent bond.

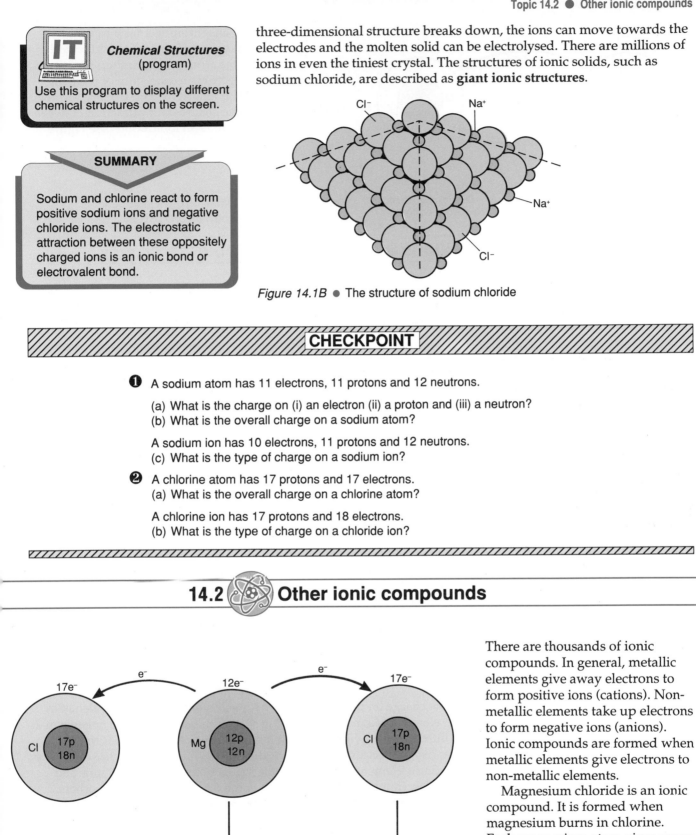

Figure 14.1B ● The structure of sodium chloride

CHECKPOINT

❶ A sodium atom has 11 electrons, 11 protons and 12 neutrons.

(a) What is the charge on (i) an electron (ii) a proton and (iii) a neutron?
(b) What is the overall charge on a sodium atom?

A sodium ion has 10 electrons, 11 protons and 12 neutrons.
(c) What is the type of charge on a sodium ion?

❷ A chlorine atom has 17 protons and 17 electrons.
(a) What is the overall charge on a chlorine atom?

A chlorine ion has 17 protons and 18 electrons.
(b) What is the type of charge on a chloride ion?

14.2 Other ionic compounds

$17e^-$

$12e^-$

$17e^-$

Cl 17p 18n

Mg 12p 12n

Cl 17p 18n

Mg gives away two electrons to become Mg^{2+} (12p, 12n, 10e$^-$)

Cl gains one electron to become Cl$^-$ (17p, 18n, 18e$^-$)

Figure 14.2A ● The formation of magnesium chloride

There are thousands of ionic compounds. In general, metallic elements give away electrons to form positive ions (cations). Non-metallic elements take up electrons to form negative ions (anions). Ionic compounds are formed when metallic elements give electrons to non-metallic elements.

Magnesium chloride is an ionic compound. It is formed when magnesium burns in chlorine. Each magnesium atom gives away two electrons. The cation formed therefore has two positive charges, Mg^{2+}. Since a chlorine atom wants only one electron, a magnesium atom has to combine with two chlorine atoms (see Figure 14.2A).

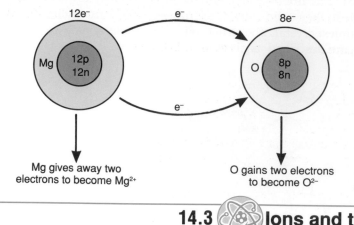

Mg gives away two
electrons to become Mg^{2+}

O gains two electrons
to become O^{2-}

Magnesium combines with
oxygen to form magnesium oxide.
One atom of magnesium gives two
electrons to one atom of oxygen.
The ions Mg^{2+} and O^{2-} are formed.
The electrostatic attraction between
them is an ionic bond (see Figure
14.2B).

Figure 14.2B ● The formation of an ionic bond
between atoms of magnesium and oxygen

14.3 Ions and the Periodic Table

Investigating ions

You learned about the Periodic Table in Topic 11. Now you can find out
how useful it is when it comes to remembering the charge on an ion.

Element	Symbol for ion	Group of Periodic Table
Sodium	Na^+	
Potassium	K^+	
Calcium	Ca^{2+}	
Magnesium	Mg^{2+}	
Aluminium	Al^{3+}	
Nitrogen	N^{3-}	
Oxygen	O^{2-}	
Sulphur	S^{2-}	
Chlorine	Cl^-	
Bromine	Br^-	

- Copy the table. Fill in the number of the Group in the Periodic Table to which
  each of the elements belongs.
- What is the connection between the charge on a cation and the number of the
  Group in the Periodic Table to which the element belongs?
- What is the connection between the charge on an anion and the number of the
  Group in the Periodic Table to which the element belongs?
- What would you expect to be the charge on (a) a barium ion (Group 2) and (b)
  a fluoride ion (Group 7)?

The charge on the ions formed by an element is called the valency of
that element. Magnesium form Mg^{2+} ions: magnesium has a valency of 2.
Sodium forms Na^+ ions: sodium has a valency of 1. Oxygen forms O^{2-}
ions: oxygen has a valency of 2. Iodine forms I^- ions: iodine has a valency
of 1. Some elements have a variable valency. Iron forms Fe^{2+} ions and
Fe^{3+} ions: iron has a valency of 2 in some compounds and 3 in others.

Non-metallic elements often combine with oxygen to form anions, e.g.
sulphate, SO_4^{2-} and nitrate, NO_3^-.

- **Metallic elements**
  Charge on cation = Number of the Group in the Periodic Table to
  which the element belongs = Valency of element
- **Non-metallic elements**
  Charge on anion = 8 – Number of Group in Periodic Table to which the
  element belongs = Valency of element

CHECKPOINT

❶ Copy and complete the following passage (lithium is an alkali metal in Group 1 and fluorine is a halogen in Group 7).

Lithium and fluorine combine to form _____ fluoride. When this happens, each lithium atom gives _____ to a fluorine atom. Lithium ions with a _____ charge and fluoride ions with a _____ charge are formed. The _____ ions and _____ ions are held together by a strong _____ attraction. This _____ attraction is a chemical bond. This type of chemical bond is called the _____ bond or _____ bond. A _____ dimensional structure of ions is built up.

❷ Sodium is a silvery-grey metal which reacts rapidly with water. Chlorine is a poisonous green gas. Sodium chloride is a white, crystalline solid, which is used as table salt. Explain how the sodium in sodium chloride differs from sodium metal. Explain how the chlorine in sodium chloride differs from chlorine gas.

❸ Say which of the following elements give (a) positive ions, (b) negative ions: calcium, potassium, sulphur, barium, zinc, oxygen, iron, iodine, lithium, fluorine, aluminium.
(The Periodic Table will help you.)

❹ There are two differences between
(a) a sodium ion, Na^+ (2.8), and a neon atom, Ne (2.8);
(b) a chloride ion, Cl^- (2.8.8), and an argon atom, Ar (2.8.8).
What are the differences?

14.4 Formulas of ionic compounds

FIRST THOUGHTS

How do you work out the formula of an ionic compound? You balance the charges on the ions, and suddenly formulas make sense!

Ionic and Molar Chemistry
(program)

This program will help you to work out chemical formulas and to balance chemical equations. Also, use the program to study ionic and covalent bonding.

Ions are charged, but ionic compounds are uncharged. A compound has no overall charge because the sum of positive charges is equal to the sum of negative charges. In magnesium chloride, $MgCl_2$, every magnesium ion, Mg^{2+}, is balanced in charge by two chloride ions, $2Cl^-$.

Figure 14.4A ● The charges balance

This is how you can work out the formulas of electrovalent compounds.

Compound: Magnesium chloride

The ions present:	Mg^{2+} $\quad$ Cl^-
The charges must balance:	One Mg^{2+} ion needs two Cl^- ions.
Ions in the formula:	Mg^{2+} and $2Cl^-$ ions
The formula is:	$MgCl_2$

Some atoms can form more than one covalent bond.

- A water molecule, H_2O, consists of an oxygen atom covalently bonded to two hydrogen atoms

$$H — O — H$$

- In a molecule of ammonia, NH_3, a nitrogen atom bonds to three hydrogen atoms

$$
\begin{array}{c}
H — N — H \\
| \\
H
\end{array}
$$

- In **methane** (North Sea gas), CH_4, a carbon atom forms covalent bonds with four hydrogen atoms

$$
\begin{array}{c}
H \\
| \\
H — C — H \\
| \\
H
\end{array}
$$

- In a molecule of oxygen, O_2, the atoms are joined by a **double bond**

$$O = O$$

- In carbon dioxide, CO_2, a carbon atom bonds to two oxygen atoms. Each of the bonds is a double bond

$$O = C = O$$

- In ethene, C_2H_4, there is a double bond between the carbon atoms

$$
\begin{array}{cc}
H & H \\
| & | \\
C & = C \\
| & | \\
H & H
\end{array}
$$

LOOK AT LINKS
for **methane**.
See Theme L, Topic 48.1.

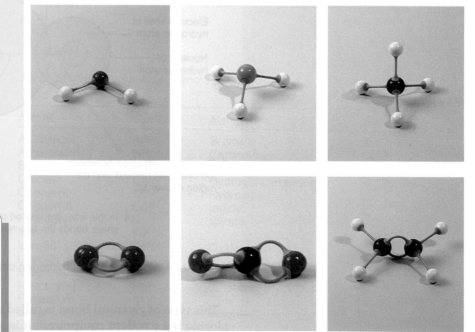

Figure 14.5B ● Covalent molecules
(a) water, H_2O (b) amonia, NH_3 (c) methane, CH_4 (d) oxygen, O_2
(e) carbon dioxide, CO_2 (f) ethene, C_2H_4

SUMMARY

Compounds which are non-electrolytes contain covalent bonds. In a covalent bond, the outer electron shells of two atoms overlap. The overlapping region is attracted to both atomic nuclei and therefore bonds the atoms.

❶ Two atoms of chlorine combine to form a molecule, Cl_2. Neither chlorine atom wants to give an electron: both want to gain an electron. The figure shows a pair of chlorine atoms. They have come close enough together for their outer electron shells to overlap.
Explain how this satisfies the need for both chlorine atoms to gain electrons. Explain how the overlapping electron shells bond the atoms together.

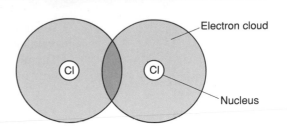

Electron cloud

Nucleus

14.6 Forces between molecules

Covalent substances can be solids, liquids or gases. Gases consist of separate molecules. The molecules are far apart, and there are almost no forces of attraction between them.

In liquids there are forces of attraction between the molecules. In some covalent substances, the attractive forces between molecules are strong enough to make the substances solids. Ice is a solid. There are strong covalent bonds inside the covalent water molecules and weaker attractive forces between molecules (see Figure 14.6A). The forces of attraction between molecules hold them in a three-dimensional structure. It is described as a **molecular structure**.

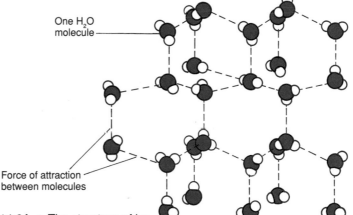

One H_2O molecule

Force of attraction between molecules

Figure 14.6A ● The structure of ice

Diamond is an **allotrope** of carbon. Diamond has a structure in which every carbon atom is joined by covalent bonds to four other carbon atoms (see Figure 9.8B). Millions of carbon atoms form a giant molecule. The structure is giant molecular or macromolecular.

Graphite, the other allotrope of carbon, has a layer structure (see Figure 9.8C). Strong covalent bonds join the carbon atoms within each layer. The layers are held together by weak forces of attraction.

❶ (a) Why does diamond have a high melting point?
(b) Why is it very difficult to scratch a diamond?
(c) why does graphite rub off on to your hands?

❷ Solid iodine consists of shiny black crystals. Iodine vapour is purple. What is the difference in chemical bonding between solid and gaseous iodine?

14.7 ⚛ Ionic and covalent compounds

What difference does the type of bond make to the properties of ionic and covalent compounds?
The physical and chemical characteristics of substances depend on the type of chemical bonds in the substances.

Table 14.2 ● Differences between ionic and covalent compounds

Ionic compounds	Covalent compounds
Ionic compounds consist of a giant structure of positive and negative ions.	Covalent compounds consist of separate uncharged molecules.
Ionic compounds are held together by strong ionic bonds – the attractive forces between positive ions and negative ions.	Strong covalent bonds join atoms inside the molecules. Weak bonds operate between molecules. Some covalent compounds form macromolecular structures, e.g. silica (sand) and ice.
Ionic compounds are electrolytes. They conduct electricity, when molten or in solution, and are split up in the process.	Covalent compounds are non-electrolytes. They do not conduct electricity
Ionic compounds have high melting points: they are solids at room temperature.	Covalent compounds are generally low melting point solids or liquids or gases. Substances with giant molecular structures have high melting and boiling points.

SUMMARY

The type of chemical bonds present, ionic or covalent, decides the properties of a compound, e.g. its physical state (s, l, g), boiling and melting points, electrolytic conductivity.

CHECKPOINT

❶ What kind of bonding would you expect between the following pairs of elements? (The Periodic Table on p 000 will help you.)

(a) K and Br   (c) Ca and S   (e) S and O
(b) Mg and I   (d) Ca and O   (f) F and O

❷

Solid	State	Melting point	Does it conduct electricity?
A	Solid	650 °C	Conducts when molten
B	Liquid	−20 °C	Does not conduct
C	Solid	700 °C	Does not conduct when molten
D	Solid	85 °C	Does not conduct when molten
E	Gas	−100 °C	Does not conduct

From the information in the table, say what you can about the chemical bonds in A, B, C, D and E.

❸ Below are five statements. Give a piece of evidence (e.g. a physical or chemical property of the substance) in support of each statement.
(a) An aqueous solution of sodium chloride contains ions.
(b) Copper exists as positive ions in copper(II) sulphate solution.
(c) Ethanol (alcohol) is a covalent compound.
(d) The forces between oxygen molecules are very weak.
(e) The forces between iodine molecules are stronger than the forces between oxygen molecules.

? THEME QUESTIONS

● **Topic 9**

Element	Agron	Bromine	Calcium	Carbon	Chlorine	Gold	Hydrogen	Mercury	Phosphorus	Sulphur
Metal or non-metal	N-M	N-M	M	N-M	N-M	M	N-M	M	N-M	N-M
Melting point (°C)	−189	−7	850	3730 (sublimes)	−101	1060	−259	−39	44 (white) 590 (red)	113 (rh) 119 (mono)
Boiling point (°C)	−186	59	1490	4830	35	2970	−252	357	280	445
Density (g/cm³)	0.0017	3.1	1.5	2.3 (gr) 3.5 (di)	0.003 017	19.3	0.000 083	13.6	1.8 (wh) 2.3 (red)	2.1 (rh) 2.0 (mono)

For questions 1–10 refer to the table of elements above.

1 Name the element with (a) the highest melting point (b) the lowest melting point.

2 Name the element with (a) the greatest density and (b) the lowest density.

3 Name the metal with (a) the lowest melting point and (b) the highest melting point.

4 Name the element which is liquid at room temperature and is (a) a metal (b) a non-metal.

5 Write down the names of all the elements which are (a) metals (b) non-metals.

6 Write down the names of all the elements which are (a) solids (b) liquids (c) gases.

7 Name the element which has the smallest temperature range over which it exists as a liquid.

8 Name the gaseous element which is (a) the most dense (b) the least dense.

9 Name the solid element which is (a) the most dense (b) the least dense.

10 Why are two sets of values given for (a) sulphur (b) phosphorus?

● **Topic 10**

11 Copy out these equations into your book, and then balance them.

(a) $H_2O_2(aq)$ → $H_2O(l) + O_2(g)$
(b) $Fe(s) + O_2(g)$ → $Fe_3O_4(s)$
(c) $Mg(s) + N_2(g)$ → $Mg_3N_2(s)$
(d) $P(s) + Cl_2(g)$ → $PCl_0(s)$
(e) $P(s) + Cl_2(g)$ → $PCl_5(s)$
(f) $SO_2(g) + O_2(g)$ → $SO_3(g)$
(g) $Na_2O(s) + H_2O(l)$ → $NaOH(aq)$
(h) $KClO_3(s)$ → $KCl(s) + O_2(g)$
(i) $NH_3(g) + O_2(g)$ → $N_2(g) + H_2O(g)$
(j) $Fe(s) + H_2O(g)$ → $Fe_3O_4(s) + H_2(g)$

12 (a) Use the Periodic Table to answer the following questions:
(i) Give the symbols for the elements carbon and sodium.
(ii) Give the symbol for any inert gas.
(iii) Give the symbol for any element in Group 7 (the Halogens)
(iv) Give **one** reason why the symbol for helium is He and not H.

(b) One molecule of carbon dioxide contains one atom of carbon and two atoms of oxygen. Its formula is written as CO_2.
Write the formula of:
(i) a molecule of sulphur dioxide, which has one atom of sulphur and two atoms of oxygen.
(ii) a molecule of sulphuric acid, which contains two atoms of hydrogen, one atom of sulphur and four atoms of oxygen.

● **Topic 11**

13 The element X has atomic number 11 and mass number 23. State how many protons and neutrons are present in the nucleus. Sketch the arrangement of electrons in an atom of X.

14 Atom A has atomic number 82 and mass number 204. Atom B has atomic number 80 and mass number 204. How many protons has atom A? How many neutrons has atom B? Are atoms A and B isotopes of the same element? Explain your answer.

15 Explain why Mendeleev fitted the elements into vertical groups in his Periodic Table. Why did he fit lithium, sodium, potassium, rubidium and caesium into the same group? Why did he leave some gaps in his table? The noble gases were discovered after Mendeleev had written his Periodic Table. What do they have in common (a) in their chemical reactions, (b) in their electronic configurations and (c) in their positions in the Periodic Table?

16 The structure of one molecule of an industrial solvent, dichloromethane, is shown below.

(a) How many atoms are there in one molecule of dichloromethane?

(b) How many bonds are there in one molecule of dichloromethane?

● *Topic 12*

17 Phosphorus-32 is radioactive, with a half life of 14 days. A solution of sodium phosphate, containing phosphorus-32, gives a count rate of 6000 c.p.m in a Geiger–Müller counter. What will be the count rate after (a) 56 days (b) 140 days?

18 An engineer needs to put a radioactive isotope into an oil pipeline to investigate a leak. The isotope chosen must have a suitable half-life and emit a suitable type of radiation. Which of the following list would be suitable?

Isotope	Emission	Half-life
Copper-29	β	13 hours
Iodine-131	β, γ	8 days
Nitrogen-16	β, γ	7 seconds
Phosphorus-32	β	14 days
Sulphur-35	β	87 days
Sodium-24	β, γ	15 hours
Thallium-208	β, γ	3 minutes

Give reasons for your choice.

19 Why are people more worried about the accident risk posed by nuclear power stations than the accident risk in using cars?
This is not an easy question, and perhaps you would like to form a group to discuss it.

20 Argon-44 is a radioactive isotope. The amount of argon-44 in a sample was measured every ten minutes over a period of one hour. The results are shown in the table.

Radioactive argon remaining in the sample (%)	100	58	33	19	10	6	4
Time (min)	0	10	20	30	40	50	60

(a) Explain the meaning of 'radioactive' when used to describe an atom.
(b) On graph paper, draw a graph to show how the percentage of argon-44 in the sample changed during the hour.
(c) Use your graph to find the time when only 50% of the argon-44 was left in the sample.
(d) Some of the waste from nuclear power stations contains radioactive isotopes with very long half-lives. These isotopes give out large amounts of radiation.
(i) Explain why getting rid of this waste is a problem.
(ii) How could this waste be stored safely?
(LEAG)

● *Topic 13*

21 Describe how you could use a battery and a torch bulb to test various materials to find out whether they are electrical conductors.
Divide the following list into conductors and non-conductors:
silver, steel, polythene, PVC, brass, candle wax, lubricating oil, dilute sulphuric acid, petrol, alcohol, sodium hydroxide solution, sugar solution, limewater

22 (a) Name three types of substance that conduct electricity.
(b) Why can molten salts conduct electricity while solid salts cannot?
(c) Why can solutions of salts conduct electricity while pure water cannot?
(d) Explain why metal articles can be electroplated but plastic articles cannot.

23 Name the substances A to H in the table. Write equations for the discharges of the ions which form these substances.

Electrolyte	Anode	Cathode
Copper(II) chloride solution	A	B
Sodium chloride solution	C	D
Dilute sulphuric acid	E	F
Sodium hydroxide solution	G	H

24 Your aunt runs a business making souvenirs. She asks your advice on how to electroplate a batch of small brass medallions with copper. Describe how this could be done. Draw a diagram of the apparatus and the circuit she could use.

25 In the electrolysis of potassium bromide solution, what element is formed (a) at the positive electrode (b) at the negative electrode? Why does the solution around the negative electrode become alkaline?

● *Topic 14*

26 (a) Explain why the ionic compound $PbBr_2$ melts at a higher temperature than the covalent compound CH_2Br_2.
(b) You can smell the compound $CHCl_3$, chloroform. You cannot smell the compound KCl. What difference in chemical bonding is responsible for the difference?

27 The diagram shows apparatus that could be used in a laboratory to find out the effect of an electric current on an aqueous solution of sodium chloride.

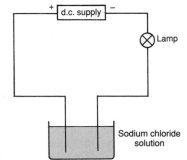

(a) On a copy of the diagram, (i) label the cathode, (ii) show the direction of flow of the electrons.
(b) What **two** observations would show that the solution conducts an electric current and that a chemical reaction is taking place?
(c) For the product formed at the positive electrode (i) give its name (ii) write the word equation for its formation.
(d) Give **one** reason why sodium is **not** a product when an electric current is passed through aqueous sodium chloride solution. (LEAG)

THEME D
Making Materials

The Earth's crust and atmosphere supply us with many different materials. The study of the way materials behave is the science of chemistry. One of the jobs which chemists do is to find methods of separating useful substances from the Earth's crust. Industry uses these substances, e.g. metals, limestone and salt, as raw materials for the manufacture of the machines, buildings, fuels, medicines and possessions which we need. Chemists also work out ways for changing the substances which are found in nature into new substances. These changes are called chemical reactions.

TOPIC 15 METHODS OF SEPARATION

15.1 Raw materials from the Earth's crust

The Earth provides all the raw materials we use. The problem is to separate the substances we want from the mixture of substances which makes up the Earth's crust.

The Earth's crust and atmosphere provide us with all the raw materials that we use: metals, oil, salt, sand, limestone, coal and many other resources. We use these substances as the raw materials for the manufacture of the houses, clothing, tools, machines, means of transport, medicines and all the other goods which we need. Few useful raw materials are found in a pure form in the Earth's crust. It is usual to find raw materials that we want mixed up with other materials. Chemists have worked out methods of separating substances from mixtures. Table 15.1 summarises some of them.

Table 15.1 ● Methods of separating substances from mixtures

Mixture	Type	Method
Solid + Solid		Make use of a difference in properties, e.g. solubility or magnetic properties
Solid + Liquid	Mixture	Filter
Solid + Liquid	Solution	Crystallise to obtain the solid Distil to obtain the liquid
Liquid + Liquid	Miscible (form one layer)	Use fractional distillation
Liquid + Liquid	Immiscible (form two layers)	Use a separating funnel
Solid + Solid	In solution	Use chromatography

IT

Make a Million
(program)

Try this game. You are invited to produce new materials using different chemical processes and the necessary raw materials. Your task is to make it a financial success.

15.2 Pure substances from a mixture of solids

Dissolving one of the substances

There are vast deposits of **rocksalt** in Cheshire. A salt mine is shown in Figure 15.2A. One method of mining salt is to insert charges of explosives in the rock face and then detonate them.

Rocksalt is crushed and used for spreading on the roads in winter to melt the ice. For many uses, pure salt (sodium chloride) is needed. It can be obtained by using water to dissolve the salt in rocksalt, leaving the rock and other impurities behind.

Figure 15.2A ●
Winsford salt mine

RESOURCE
ACTIVITY
PACK

SUMMARY

A soluble substance can be separated from a mixture by dissolving it to leave insoluble substances behind.

15.3 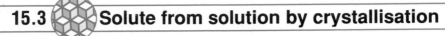 Solute from solution by crystallisation

While the solvent is evaporating, dip a cold glass rod into the solution from time to time. When small crystals form on the rod, take the solution off the water bath and leave it to cool

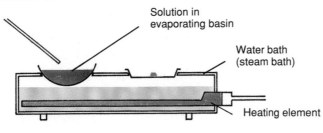

Solution in evaporating basin

Water bath (steam bath)

Heating element

Figure 15.3A ● Evaporating a solution to obtain crystals of solute

A laboratory method of evaporating a solution until it crystallises is shown in Figure 15.3A. The salt industry uses large scale evaporators which run non-stop. Figure 15.3B shows another method.

Figure 15.3B ● Salt pans in the Canary Islands. Sea water flows into the 'pans' and much of the water evaporates in the hot sun. When the brine has became a saturated solution, salt crystallises. The sea water is pumped through sluice gates where the salt crystals are filtered out.

15.4 Filtration: separating a solid from a liquid

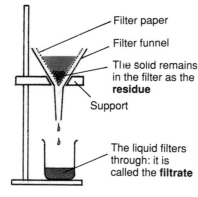

Filter paper

Filter funnel

The solid remains in the filter as the **residue**

Support

The liquid filters through: it is called the **filtrate**

Figure 15.4A ● Filtration

A Buchner funnel has a perforated plate, which is covered by a circle of filter paper

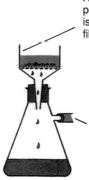

A pump is connected to the side-arm flask. It speeds up the flow of liquid through the funnel

Figure 15.4B ● Filtration under reduced pressure

Filtration can be used to separate a solid and a liquid. The filter must hold back solid particles but be fine enough to allow liquid to pass through. Figure 15.4A shows a laboratory apparatus for filtering through filter paper. Figure 15.4B shows a faster method: filtering under reduced pressure. In Topic 22.3, you will see how important filtration is in the purification of our drinking water.

15.5 Centrifuging

Biochemists have developed methods of growing bacteria as a source of **high-protein food**. When bacteria are allowed to grow in a warm solution of nutrients, they multiply so fast that they can double in mass every 20 minutes. From time to time, the harvest of bacteria is separated from the nutrient solution. Bacteria are too small to be separated by filtration. They are so small that they are **suspended** (spread out) in the liquid. They do not settle to the bottom as heavier particles

LOOK AT LINKS
for **high-protein food**
See Theme F, Topic 25.2.

would do, and they do not dissolve to form a solution. They can be separated by the method of **centrifuging** (centrifugation). The suspension of bacteria and liquid is placed inside a centrifuge and spun at high speed. The motion causes bacteria to separate from the suspension and sink to the bottom of the centrifuge tubes. Figure 15.5A shows a small laboratory centrifuge.

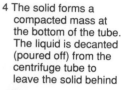

1 The suspension is poured into a glass tube inside the centrifuge

2 Another tube is used to balance the first

3 As the centrifuge spins, solid particles settle to the bottom of the tube

4 The solid forms a compacted mass at the bottom of the tube. The liquid is decanted (poured off) from the centrifuge tube to leave the solid behind

SUMMARY

* Filtration will separate a solid from a liquid.
* Centrifuging will separate a suspended solid from solution.

Figure 15.5A ● Centrifuging a suspension

CHECKPOINT

❶ Describe how you would obtain both the substances in the following mixtures of solids.
   (a) A and B: Both A and B are soluble in hot water, but only A is soluble in cold water.
   (b) C and D: Neither C nor D is soluble in water. C is soluble in ethanol, but D is not.

❷ In Trinidad and some other countries, tar trickles out of the ground. It is a valuable resource. The tar is mixed with sand and gravel. Suggest how tar may be separated from these substances.

❸ Blood consists of blood cells and a liquid called plasma. When a sample of blood is taken from a person, the blood cells slowly settle to the bottom. How can the separation of blood cells from plasma be speeded up?

❹ Suggest how you could obtain the following:
   (a) iron filings from a mixture of iron filings and sand,
   (b) wax from a mixture of wax and sand,
   (c) sand and gravel from a mixture of both,
   (d) rice and salt from a mixture of both.

15.6 Distillation

LOOK AT LINKS
for **drinking water**
Why is water more important than food?
See Theme F, Topic 25.2.

Sometimes you need to separate a solvent from a solution. In some parts of the world, drinking water is obtained from sea water. The method of **distillation** is employed. Figure 15.6A shows a laboratory scale distillation apparatus. The processes that take place are:
* in the distillation flask, **vaporisation**: liquid → vapour
* in the condenser, **condensation**: vapour → liquid.
Vaporisation followed by condensation is called **distillation**.

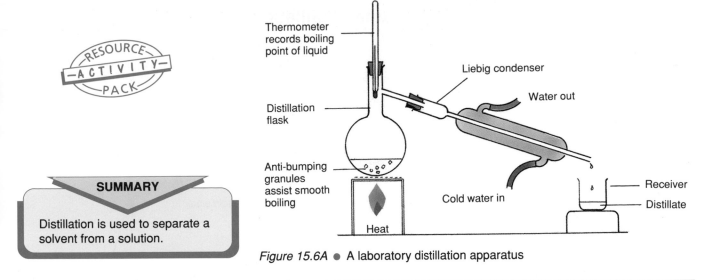

Thermometer records boiling point of liquid

Liebig condenser

Water out

Distillation flask

Anti-bumping granules assist smooth boiling

Cold water in

Receiver

Distillate

Heat

Figure 15.6A ● A laboratory distillation apparatus

RESOURCE -ACTIVITY- PACK

SUMMARY

Distillation is used to separate a solvent from a solution.

CHECKPOINT

❶ Why do some countries in the Persian Gulf obtain drinking water by distilling sea water? You will need to consider (a) the other sources of water and (b) the cost of fuel for heating the still.

❷ Imagine that you are cast away on a desert island. You have two ways of obtaining drinking water. One is by separating pure water from sea water. The other is by collecting dew.

(a) Think of a way of obtaining pure water from sea water. You do not have a proper distillation apparatus, but you have some matches and an empty petrol tin which were in the lifeboat. You find wood, bamboo canes, palm trees and coconuts on the island. Make a sketch of your design. With other members of your class, make a display of your sketches.

(b) Every night on the island there is a heavy dew. How can you collect some of this dew? You have a sheet of plastic from the lifeboat. Again, sketch your idea. Then you can make another class display.

(c) Write a letter to a 10 year-old, telling how you survived the shipwreck and how you obtained drinking water until you were rescued.

15.7 ⬡ Separating liquids

Using a separating funnel to separate immiscible liquids

When some liquids are added to each other, they do not mix: they form separate layers. They are said to be **immiscible**. They can be separated by using a separating funnel.

1 The mixture of immiscible liquids is poured in. It settles into two layers (or more) as the liquids do not mix

2 The tap is opened to let the bottom layer run into a receiver

3 The tap is closed and the receiver is changed. The tap is opened to let the top layer run out

SUMMARY

Immiscible liquids can be separated by means of a separating funnel.

Figure 15.7A ● A separating funnel

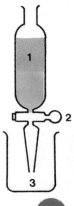

215

15.8 Fractional distillation

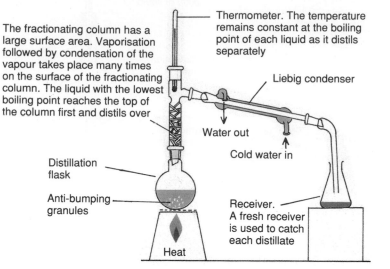

The fractionating column has a large surface area. Vaporisation followed by condensation of the vapour takes place many times on the surface of the fractionating column. The liquid with the lowest boiling point reaches the top of the column first and distils over

Thermometer. The temperature remains constant at the boiling point of each liquid as it distils separately

Liebig condenser

Water out

Cold water in

Distillation flask

Anti-bumping granules

Receiver. A fresh receiver is used to catch each distillate

Heat

Figure 15.8A ● Fractional distillation

An industrial fractional distillation plant uses a temperature sensor and a microcomputer to monitor the course of the distillation.

When liquids dissolve in one another to form a solution, instead of forming separate layers, they are described as **miscible**. Distillation can be used to separate a mixture of miscible liquids. Whisky manufacturers want to separate ethanol (alcohol) from water in a solution of these two liquids. They are able to do this because the two liquids have different boiling points: ethanol boils at 78 °C, and water boils at 100 °C. Figure 15.8A shows a laboratory apparatus which will separate a mixture of ethanol and water into its parts or **fractions**. The process is called **fractional distillation**. The temperature rises to 78 °C and then stays constant while all the ethanol distils over. When the temperature starts to rise again, the receiver is changed. At 100 °C, water starts to distil, and a fresh receiver is put into position to collect it.

Figure 15.8B ● An industrial distillation plant

Continuous fractional distillation

Crude petroleum oil is not a very useful substance. By fractional distillation, it can be separated into a number of very useful products (see Figure 15.8C). In the petroleum industry, fractional distillation is made to run continuously (non-stop). Crude oil is fed in continuously, and the separated fractions are run off from the still continuously. These fractions are not pure substances. Each is a mixture of substances with similar boiling points. The fractions with low boiling points are collected from the top of the fractionating column. Fractions with high boiling points are collected from the bottom of the column.

LOOK AT LINKS
for **fractional distillation**
The importance of
petroleum oil fractions as
fuels and as raw materials
is discussed in Theme L,
Topic 48.4.

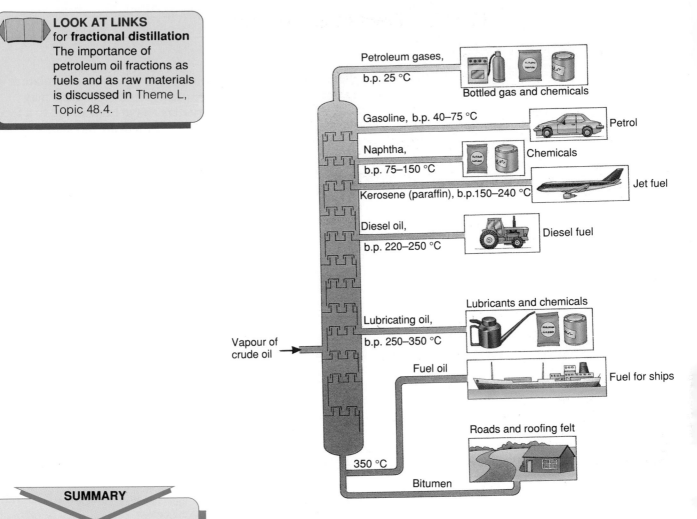

Figure 15.8C ● Continuous fractional distillation of crude oil

SUMMARY

Liquids are separated from a
solution by fractional distillation.
The process can be made to run
continuously, e.g., in the
fractionation of crude petroleum oil.

CHECKPOINT

❶ Your 12 year-old sister wants to know what you have been doing in your science lessons. Write a technical report, in words which she can understand, explaining *why* the petroleum industry distils crude oil and *how* fractional distillation works.

❷ Your sister pours vinegar into the bottle of cooking oil by mistake. She asks you to help her to put things right. How could you separate the two liquids?

❸ In Hammond Innes' novel, *Ice Station Zero*, a vehicle breaks down because the villains have put sugar in the petrol tank. Explain how you could separate the sugar from the petrol.

❹ After a collision at sea, thousands of litres of oil escape from a tanker. A salvage ship sucks up a layer of oil mixed with sea water from the surface of the sea.
(a) Describe how you could separate the oil from the sea water.
(b) Say why it is important to be able to do this.

15.9 Chromatography

Frequently, chemists want to **analyse** a mixture. (**Analysis** of a mixture means finding out which substances are present in it.) Chemists may want to find out which dyes and preservatives have been added to a food substance. They may want to find out whether there are any harmful substances present in drinking water. Chromatography is one method of separating the solutes in a solution. Figure 15.9A shows **paper chromatography**. When a drop of solution is applied to the chromatography paper, the paper absorbs the solutes, that is, binds them to its surface. As the solvent rises through the paper, the solvent competes with the paper for the solutes. Some solutes stay put; others dissolve in the solvent and travel in it up the paper. A solute which is very soluble in the solvent travels through the paper faster than a solute which is only slightly soluble. When the solvent reaches the top of the paper, the process is stopped. Different solutes have travelled different distances. The result is a **chromatogram**.

When analytical chemists use chromatography, they may compare their results with a computer data base to see which substances travel at the same rate as the substances they want to identify.

Computers help to solve crimes. Materials found at the scene of a crime can be analysed by chromatography. The results can be stored by the computer as a data base to help with the solution of similar crimes.

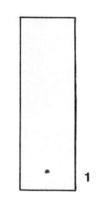

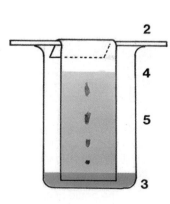

1 A drop of solution is touched on to the chromatography paper. The solvent evaporates. A spot of solute remains

2 The chromatography paper hangs from a glass rod. It must not touch the sides of the beaker

3 The spot of solute must be above the level of the solvent in the beaker

4 The solvent front. The solvent has travelled up the paper to this level

5 Spots of different substances present in the solute. As the substances travel through the paper at different speed, they become separated. The result is a chromatogram

Figure 15.9A ● Paper chromatography

Many solvents are used in chromatography. Ethanol (alcohol), ethanoic acid (vinegar) and propanone (a solvent often called acetone) are common. A chemist has to experiment to find out which solvent gives a good separation of the solutes. With a solvent other than water, a closed container should be used so that the chromatography paper is surrounded by the vapour of the solvent (see Figure 15.9B).

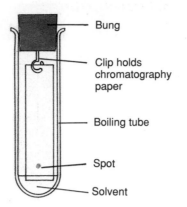

Bung

Clip holds chromatography paper

Boiling tube

Spot

Solvent

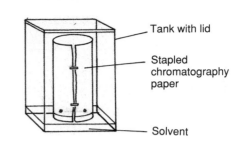

Tank with lid

Stapled chromatography paper

Solvent

SUMMARY

Chromatography can be used to separate the solutes in a solution. It is used in analysis, that is, in finding out what substances are present in a mixture.

Figure 15.9B ● Chromatography with a solvent other than water

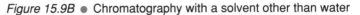

CHECKPOINT

❶ A chemist is asked to find out what substances are present in two mixtures, M_1 and M_2. He makes a chromatogram of the two mixtures and a chromatogram of some substances which he suspects may be present. The figure below shows his results.
Can you interpret his results? What substances are present in M_1 and M_2?

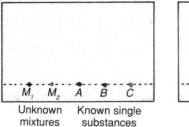

M_1 M_2 A B C

Unknown mixtures

Known single substances

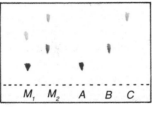

M_1 M_2 A B C

❷ Imagine that you are a detective investigating forged bank notes. Your investigations take you to a house where you find a printing press and some inks. Describe how you would find out whether these inks are the same as those used to make the bank notes.

❸ Dr Ecksplor discovers a strangely coloured orchid in Brazil. Professor Seeker finds an orchid of the same colour in Ecuador. The two scientists wonder whether the two flowers contain the same pigment. They feel sure that the pigment does not dissolve in water.
(a) Why do they feel sure that the pigment does not dissolve in water?
(b) Describe an experiment which they could do to find out whether the two orchids contain the same pigment.

❹ An analytical chemist has the task of finding out whether the red colouring in a new food product contains any dyes which are not permitted in foods. She runs a chromatogram on the food colouring and on some of the permitted red food dyes. The figure opposite shows her results. What conclusion can you draw from these chromatograms?

Note: Dye 1 = E122 Carmoisine, Dye 2 = E162 Beetroot red, Dye 3 = E128 Red 2G, Dye 4 = E120 Cochineal, Dye 5 = E124 Ponceau 4R, Dye 6 = E160 Capsorubin

Dyes which are allowed in foods are given **E numbers**.

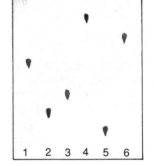

1 2 3 4 5 6

(a) Chromatogram of permitted dyes

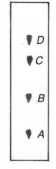

D

C

B

A

(b) Chromatogram of red food colouring

TOPIC 16  ACIDS AND BASES

16.1  Acids

FIRST THOUGHTS

Can you say what the elements in each of these sets of materials have in common?
List A: lime juice, vitamin C, stomach juice, vinegar
List B: toothpaste, household ammonia, Milk of Magnesia, lime

If you have remembered, well done! You will learn more about acids and bases in this topic.

LOOK AT LINKS
for **digestion**
See Theme F, Topic 25.2.

This symbol means **corrosive**. Concentrated acids always carry this symbol.

Industrial Chemistry Pack
(program)

Work in small groups. Using the first part of this program you can investigate the manufacture of sulphuric acid. What are the important factors involved?

Cells in the linings of our stomachs produce hydrochloric acid. This is a powerful acid. If a piece of zinc was dropped into hydrochloric acid of the concentration which the stomach contains, it would dissolve. In the stomach, hydrochloric acid works to kill bacteria which are present in foods and to soften foods. It also helps in **digestion** by providing the right conditions for the enzyme pepsin to begin the digestion of proteins.

Sometimes the stomach produces too much acid. Then the result is the pain of 'acid indigestion' and 'heartburn'. The many products which are sold as 'antacids' and indigestion remedies all contain compounds that can react with hydrochloric acid to neutralise (counteract) the excess of acid. In this chapter, we shall look at the properties (characteristics) of acids and the substances which react with them.

A sour taste usually shows that a substance contains an acid. The word 'acid' comes from the Latin word for 'sour'. Vinegar contains ethanoic acid, sour milk contains lactic acid, lemons contain citric acid and rancid butter contains butanoic acid. For centuries, chemists have been able to extract acids such as these from animal and plant material. They call these acids **organic acids**. As chemistry has advanced, chemists have found ways of making sulphuric acid, hydrochloric acid, nitric acid and other acids from minerals. They call these acids **mineral acids**. Mineral acids in general react much more rapidly than organic acids. We describe mineral acids as **strong acids** and organic acids as **weak acids**. Table 16.1 lists some common acids.

Solutions of acids (and other substances) can be **dilute solutions** or **concentrated solutions**. A dilute solution contains a small amount of acid per litre of solution. A concentrated solution contains a large amount of acid per litre of solution. Solutions of acids are always called, say, dilute hydrochloric acid or concentrated hydrochloric acid. Concentrated acids are very corrosive, and you need to know which type of solution you are dealing with.

Table 16.1 ● Some common acids

Acid	Strong or weak	Where you find it
Ascorbic acid	Weak	In fruits. Also called Vitamin C
Carbonic acid	Weak	In fizzy drinks: these contain the gas carbon dioxide which reacts with water to form carbonic acid.
Citric acid	Weak	In fruit juices, e.g. lemon juice
Ethanoic acid	Weak	In vinegar
Hydrochloric acid	Strong	In digestive juices in the stomach; also used for cleaning ('pickling') metals before they are coated
Lactic acid	Weak	In sour milk
Nitric acid	Strong	Used for making fertilisers and explosives
Phosphoric acid	Strong	In anti-rust paint; used for making fertilisers
Sulphuric acid	Strong	In car batteries; used for making fertilisers

Figure 16.1A ● Some common acids

Figure 16.1B ● The acid taste

LOOK AT LINKS
for the **reactions of metals**
See Theme L, Topic 50.3.

LOOK AT LINKS
for **bases**
See Theme D, Topic 16.2.

LOOK AT LINKS
for **electrolysis of solutions of acids**; for **neutralisation**
See Theme C, Topic 13.4;
Theme D, Topic 16.4.

What do acids do?

❶ **Acids have a sour taste.**
You will know the taste of lemon juice (which contains citric acid) and vinegar (which contains ethanoic acid). **Do not taste any of the strong acids.**

❷ **Acids change the colour of substances called indicators.**
For example, acids turn blue litmus red (see Table 16.4).

❸ **Acids react with many metals to produce hydrogen and a salt of the metal.**
Hydrogen is an element. It is a colourless, odourless (without smell) gas and is the least dense of all the elements. With air, hydrogen forms an explosive mixture, which is the basis of a test for hydrogen. If you put a lighted splint into hydrogen, you hear an explosive 'pop' (see Figure 16.1C).

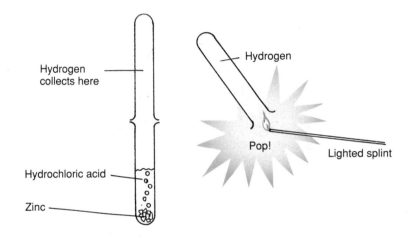

Figure 16.1C ● (a) Making hydrogen   (b) Testing for hydrogen

Some metals, e.g. copper, react very slowly with acids. Some metals, e.g. sodium, react dangerously fast. Much heat is given out, and the hydrogen which is formed may explode. Examples of metals which react at a safe speed are magnesium, zinc and iron.

$$
\begin{array}{ccccccc}
\text{Zinc} & + & \text{Sulphuric acid} & \rightarrow & \text{Hydrogen} & + & \text{Zinc sulphate} \\
Zn(s) & + & H_2SO_4(aq) & \rightarrow & H_2(g) & + & ZnSO_4(aq)
\end{array}
$$

❹ **Acids react with carbonates to give carbon dioxide, a salt and water.**
Acid indigestion is caused by an excess of hydrochloric acid in the stomach. Some indigestion tablets contain magnesium carbonate. The reaction that takes place when magnesium carbonate reaches the stomach is

$$
\begin{array}{ccccccccc}
\text{Magnesium} & + & \text{Hydrochloric} & \rightarrow & \text{Carbon} & + & \text{Magnesium} & + & \text{Water} \\
\text{carbonate} & & \text{acid} & & \text{dioxide} & & \text{chloride} & & \\
MgCO_3(s) & + & 2HCl(aq) & \rightarrow & CO_2(g) & + & MgCl_2(aq) & + & H_2O(l)
\end{array}
$$

Other anti-acid tablets contain sodium hydrogencarbonate. In this case, the reaction that happens in the stomach is

$$
\begin{array}{ccccccccc}
\text{Sodium} & + & \text{Hydrochloric} & \rightarrow & \text{Carbon} & + & \text{Sodium} & + & \text{Water} \\
\text{hydrogencarbonate} & & \text{acid} & & \text{dioxide} & & \text{chloride} & & \\
NaHCO_3(s) & + & HCl(aq) & \rightarrow & CO_2(g) & + & NaCl(aq) & + & H_2O(l)
\end{array}
$$

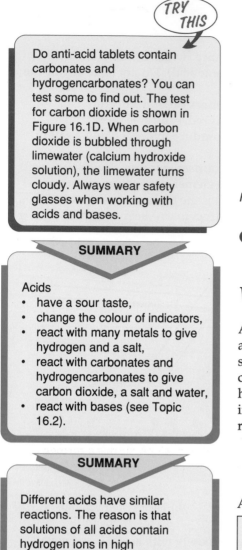

SUMMARY

Acids
* have a sour taste,
* change the colour of indicators,
* react with many metals to give hydrogen and a salt,
* react with carbonates and hydrogencarbonates to give carbon dioxide, a salt and water,
* react with bases (see Topic 16.2).

SUMMARY

Different acids have similar reactions. The reason is that solutions of all acids contain hydrogen ions in high concentration. The hydrogen ions are responsible for the typical reactions of acids.

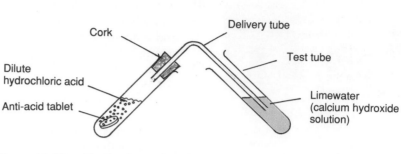

Figure 16.1D ● Testing for carbon dioxide

❺ **Acids neutralise bases**
(See Topic 16.4.)

What is an acid?

A Swedish chemist called Svante Arrhenius explained why different acids have so much in common. He put forward the theory that aqueous solutions of all acids contain hydrogen ions, $H^+(aq)$, in high concentration. By 'high' concentration, he meant a concentration much higher than that in water. This theory explains many reactions of acids, including **neutralisation**, **electrolysis of solutions** of acids and the reaction of metals with acids

Metal atoms	+	Hydrogen ions	→	Metal ions	+	Hydrogen molecules
M(s)	+	$2H^+(aq)$	→	$M^{2+}(aq)$	+	$H_2(g)$

Arrhenius gave this definition of an acid:

> **An acid is a substance that releases hydrogen ions when dissolved in water.**

A solution of a strong acid has a much higher concentration of hydrogen ions than a solution of a weak acid. A solution of a strong acid therefore reacts much more rapidly than a solution of a weak acid.

CHECKPOINT

❶ Where in the kitchen could you find
  (a) a weak acid with a pleasant taste?
  (b) a weak acid with an unpleasant taste?
  (c) a weak acid with a very sour taste?

❷ What is the difference between a concentrated solution of a weak acid and a dilute solution of a strong acid?

❸ What is the difference between a concentrated solution of sulphuric acid and a dilute solution of sulphuric acid? Why do road tankers of sulphuric acid carry the sign shown opposite?

❹ *Toffee Recipe 1*   Boil sugar and water with a little butter until the mixture thickens. Pour into a greased tray to set.
Toffee Recipe 2   Repeat Recipe 1. When the mixture thickens, add vinegar and 'bicarbonate of soda' (sodium hydrogencarbonate). Pour into a greased tray to set.
One of these recipes gives solid toffee. The other gives a honeycomb of toffee containing bubbles of gas. Which recipe gives the honeycomb? Why?

CORROSIVE

❺ Rosie and Luke visited the underground caves in the limestone rock at Wookey Hole in Somerset. A guide told them that the chemical name for limestone is calcium carbonate. The children took a small piece of limestone rock to school and did an experiment with it. They put a piece of rock in a beaker and added dilute hydrochloric acid. Immediately, bubbles of gas were given off. (See the figures opposite)

(a) Why must you always wear safety glasses when working with acids?
(b) What is the name of the gas in the bubbles?
(c) What chemical test could they do to 'prove' what the gas was?

Rosie lit a candle, and then tilted the beaker so that gas poured on to it (see lower figure). The candle went out.

(d) What *two* things about the gas did this experiment tell the children?
(e) What could the gas be used for?

Their teacher prepared a gas jar of the gas. Luke added distilled water and shook the gas jar. Then he added litmus solution.

(f) What colour did the indicator turn? (See Table 16.1 and *What do acids do?* for help.)

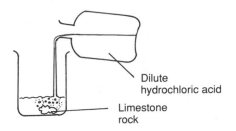

(a) Adding acid to limestone

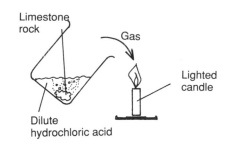

(b) Testing the gas on a lighted candle

16.2 Bases

Figure 16.2A ● Spreading lime

Bases are substances that neutralise (counteract) acids. Figure 16.2A shows a farmer spreading the base called 'lime' (calcium hydroxide) on a field. Some soils are too acidic to grow good crops. 'Liming' neutralises some of the acid and increases the **soil fertility**.

The product of the reaction between an acid and a base is a neutral substance, neither an acid nor a base, which is called a **salt**. Lime (calcium hydroxide) is a base. It reacts with nitric acid in the soil to form the salt calcium nitrate and water

Calcium hydroxide + Nitric acid ➔ Calcium nitrate + Water

A definition of a base is:

> **A base is a substance that reacts with an acid to form a salt and water only.**

Acid + Base ➔ Salt + Water

Soluble bases are called **alkalis**. Sodium hydroxide is an alkali; it reacts with an acid to form a salt and water.

Sodium hydroxide + Hydrochloric acid ➔ Sodium chloride + Water
$NaOH(aq)$ + $HCl(aq)$ ➔ $NaCl(aq)$ + $H_2O(l)$

LOOK AT LINKS
for **soil fertility**
See Theme G, Topic 29.1.

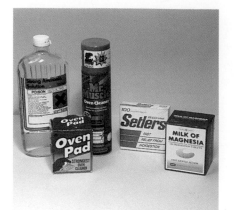

Figure 16.2B ● Some common bases

Limewater (calcium hydroxide solution) is an alkali. A test for carbon dioxide is that it turns limewater cloudy. The reaction is an acid–base reaction to form a salt and water.

Carbon dioxide + Calcium hydroxide → Calcium carbonate + Water
$$CO_2(g) + Ca(OH)_2(aq) → CaCO_3(s) + H_2O(l)$$

The salt, calcium carbonate, appears as a cloud of insoluble white powder.

Table 16.2 ● Some common bases

Base	Strong or weak	Where you find it
Ammonia	Weak	In cleaning fluids for use as a degreasing agent; also used in the manufacture of fertilisers
Calcium hydroxide	Strong	Used to treat soil which is too acidic
Calcium oxide	Strong	Used in the manufacture of cement, mortar and concrete
Magnesium hydroxide	Strong	In anti-acid indigestion tablets and Milk of Magnesia
Sodium hydroxide	Strong	In oven cleaners as a degreasing agent; also used in soap manufacture

Table 16.2 lists some common bases. Different bases have a number of reactions in common.

❶ Bases neutralise acids (see previous page).
❷ Soluble bases can change the colour of **indicators**, e.g. turn red litmus blue (see Table 16.4).
❸ Soluble bases feel soapy to your skin. The reason is that soluble bases convert some of the oil in your skin into **soap**. Some household cleaning solutions, e.g. ammonia solution, use soluble bases as degreasing agents. They convert oil and grease into soluble soaps which are easily washed away.
❹ A solution of an alkali in water contains hydroxide ions, $OH^-(aq)$. This solution will react with a solution of a metal salt. Most metal hydroxides are insoluble. When a solution of an alkali is added to a solution of a metal salt, an insoluble metal hydroxide is **precipitated** from solution. (A precipitate is a solid which forms when two liquids are mixed.) For example

LOOK AT LINKS
for **soap**
You will see how soap and detergents work in Theme E, Topic 22.9.

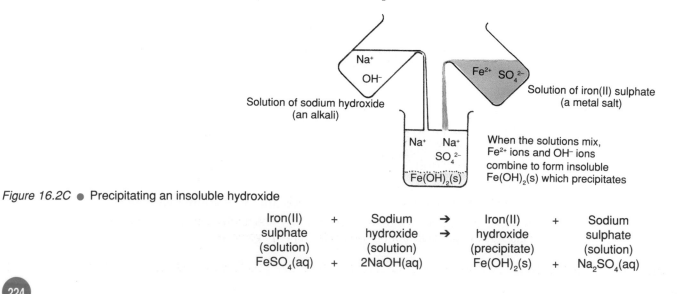

Figure 16.2C ● Precipitating an insoluble hydroxide

Iron(II) sulphate (solution)	+	Sodium hydroxide (solution)	→	Iron(II) hydroxide (precipitate)	+	Sodium sulphate (solution)
$FeSO_4(aq)$	+	$2NaOH(aq)$	→	$Fe(OH)_2(s)$	+	$Na_2SO_4(aq)$

A solution of a strong base contains a higher concentration of hydroxide ions than a solution of a weak base.

Table 16.3 ● Examples of bases

Metal oxides	Metal hydroxides	Alkalis (soluble bases)
Copper(II) oxide, CuO	Sodium hydroxide, NaOH	Sodium hydroxide, NaOH
Zinc oxide, ZnO	Magnesium hydroxide, $Mg(OH)_2$	Potassium hydroxide, KOH
		Calcium hydroxide, $Ca(OH)_2$
(Most metal oxides and hydroxides are insoluble)		Ammonia solution, $NH_3(aq)$

SUMMARY

Bases neutralise acids to form salts. Soluble bases are called alkalis. Metal oxides and hydroxides are bases. Alkalis change the colours of indicators. They are degreasing agents, and have a soapy 'feel'. Solutions of alkalis contain hydroxide ions, $OH^-(aq)$ in high concentration.

Ionic equations

There is another way of writing the equation of the reaction between iron(II) sulphate and sodium hydroxide. The reaction is the combination of iron(II) ions and hydroxide ions. The sodium ions and sulphate ions take no part in the reaction, and the equation can be written without them.

$$Fe^{2+}(aq) + 2OH^-(aq) \rightarrow Fe(OH)_2(s)$$

This is called an **ionic equation**.

CHECKPOINT

❶ (a) Write the names of the four common alkalis.
(b) Write the names of four insoluble bases.

❷ Four bottles of solution are standing on a shelf in the prep room. Their labels have come off and are lying on the floor. They read, Copper(II) sulphate, Iron(II) sulphate, Iron(III) sulphate and Zinc sulphate. The lab assistant knows that some insoluble metal hydroxides are coloured (see the table below).

Hydroxide	Formula	Colour
Copper(II) hydroxide	$Cu(OH)_2(s)$	Blue
Iron(II) hydroxide	$Fe(OH)_2(s)$	Green
Iron(III) hydroxide	$Fe(OH)_3(s)$	Rust
Magnesium hydroxide	$Mg(OH)_2(s)$	White
Zinc hydroxide	$Zn(OH)_2(s)$	White

She adds sodium hydroxide solution to a sample of each solution. Her results are:
Bottle 1 White precipitate
Bottle 2 Rust-coloured precipitate
Bottle 3 Blue precipitate
Bottle 4 Green precipitate
Say which label should be stuck on each bottle.

❸ Write the formulas for the bases: calcium oxide, copper(II) oxide, zinc oxide, magnesium hydroxide, iron(II) hydroxide, iron(III) hydroxide.

16.3 Summarising the reactions of acids and bases

Figure 16.3A summarises the reactions of hydrochloric acid, a typical strong acid.

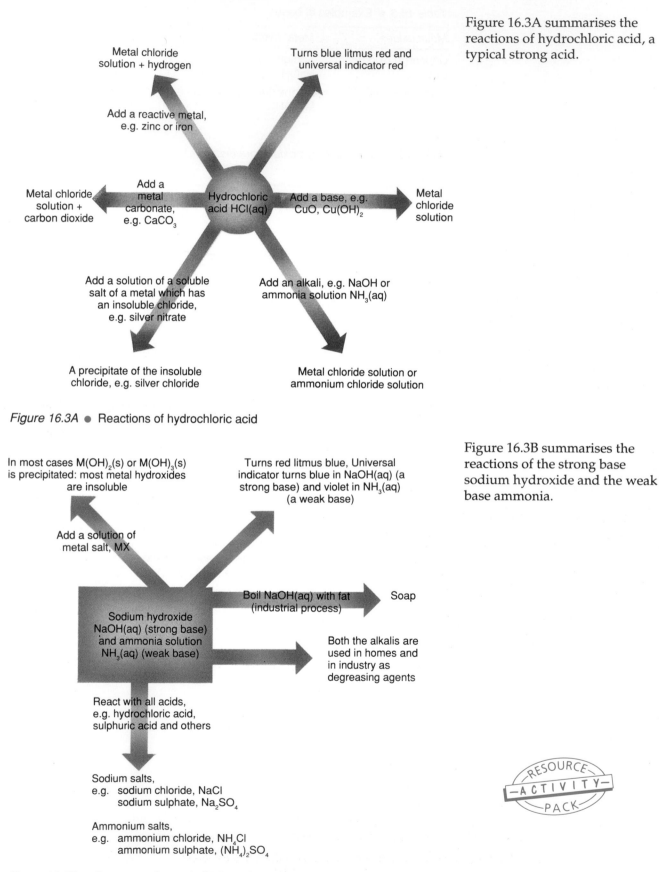

Figure 16.3A ● Reactions of hydrochloric acid

Metal chloride solution + hydrogen

Turns blue litmus red and universal indicator red

Add a reactive metal, e.g. zinc or iron

Metal chloride solution + carbon dioxide

Add a metal carbonate, e.g. CaCO₃

Hydrochloric acid HCl(aq)

Add a base, e.g. CuO, Cu(OH)₂

Metal chloride solution

Add a solution of a soluble salt of a metal which has an insoluble chloride, e.g. silver nitrate

Add an alkali, e.g. NaOH or ammonia solution NH₃(aq)

A precipitate of the insoluble chloride, e.g. silver chloride

Metal chloride solution or ammonium chloride solution

Figure 16.3B summarises the reactions of the strong base sodium hydroxide and the weak base ammonia.

In most cases M(OH)₂(s) or M(OH)₃(s) is precipitated: most metal hydroxides are insoluble

Turns red litmus blue, Universal indicator turns blue in NaOH(aq) (a strong base) and violet in NH₃(aq) (a weak base)

Add a solution of metal salt, MX

Boil NaOH(aq) with fat (industrial process)

Soap

Sodium hydroxide NaOH(aq) (strong base) and ammonia solution NH₃(aq) (weak base)

Both the alkalis are used in homes and in industry as degreasing agents

React with all acids, e.g. hydrochloric acid, sulphuric acid and others

Sodium salts,
e.g. sodium chloride, NaCl
sodium sulphate, Na₂SO₄

Ammonium salts,
e.g. ammonium chloride, NH₄Cl
ammonium sulphate, (NH₄)₂SO₄

Figure 16.3B ● Some reactions of alkalis (soluble bases)

RESOURCE –ACTIVITY– PACK

16.4 Neutralisation

What takes place when an acid neutralises a soluble base? An example is the reaction between hydrochloric acid and the alkali (soluble base) sodium hydroxide solution.

Hydrochloric acid	+	Sodium hydroxide	→	Sodium chloride	+	Water
HCl(aq)	+	NaOH(aq)	→	NaCl(aq)	+	$H_2O(l)$
acid	+	*alkali*	→	*salt*	+	*water*

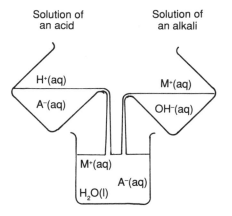

Solution of an acid — Solution of an alkali

$H^+(aq)$
$A^-(aq)$

$M^+(aq)$
$OH^-(aq)$

$M^+(aq)$
$A^-(aq)$
$H_2O(l)$

$H^+(aq)$ ions and $OH^-(aq)$ ions have combined to form water molecules, $H_2O(l)$

The solution is a solution of the salt MA

Figure 16.4A ●
Acid + alkali → salt + water

When the solutions of acid and alkali are mixed, hydrogen ions, $H^+(aq)$, and hydroxide ions, $OH^-(aq)$ combine to form water molecules.

$$H^+(aq) + OH^-(aq) → H_2O(l)$$

Sodium ions, $Na^+(aq)$, and chloride ions, $Cl^-(aq)$ remain in the solution, which becomes a solution of sodium chloride. If you evaporate the solution, you obtain solid sodium chloride.

> **Neutralisation is the combination of hydrogen ions from an acid and hydroxide ions from a base to form water molecules. In the process, a salt is formed.**

What happens when an acid neutralises an insoluble base? An example is the reaction between sulphuric acid and copper(II) oxide

Sulphuric acid	+	Copper(II) oxide	→	Copper(II) sulphate	+	Water
$H_2SO_4(aq)$	+	CuO(s)	→	$CuSO_4(aq)$	+	$H_2O(l)$
acid	+	*base*	→	*salt*	+	*water*

Hydrogen ions and oxide ions, O^{2-}, combine to form water

$$2H^+(aq) + O^{2-}(s) → H_2O(l)$$

The resulting solution contains copper(II) ions and sulphate ions: it is a solution of copper(II) sulphate. If you evaporate it, you will obtain copper(II) sulphate crystals.

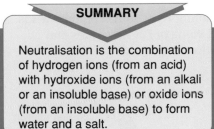

SUMMARY

Neutralisation is the combination of hydrogen ions (from an acid) with hydroxide ions (from an alkali or an insoluble base) or oxide ions (from an insoluble base) to form water and a salt.

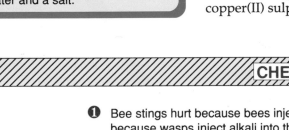

CHECKPOINT

❶ Bee stings hurt because bees inject acid into the skin. Wasp stings hurt because wasps inject alkali into the skin.

Your little brother is stung by a bee. You are in charge. What do you use to treat the sting: 'bicarbonate of soda' (sodium hydrogencarbonate), calamine lotion (zinc carbonate), vinegar (ethanoic acid) or Milk of Magnesia (magnesium carbonate)? Would you use the same treatment for a wasp sting? Give reasons for your answers.

❷ 'Acid drops' which you buy from a sweet shop contain citric acid.

• Put an acid drop in your mouth.
• Put some baking soda (sodium hydrogencarbonate) on your hand.
• Lick some of the baking soda into your mouth.

What happens to the taste of the acid drop? Why does this happen?

16.5  Indicators and pH

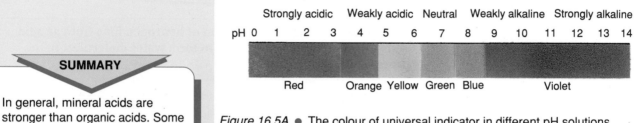

A pH sensor and a microcomputer can be used to record and display changes in pH. This technique is useful for showing how pH changes over a period of time. It is used for monitoring manufacturing processes, water pollution and the rate at which foodstuffs go sour.

Table 16.4 ● The colours of some common indicators

Indicator	Acidic colour	Neutral colour	Alkaline colour
Litmus	Red	Purple	Blue
Phenolphthalein	Colourless	Colourless	Pink
Methyl orange	Red	Orange	Yellow

Universal indicator turns different colours in strongly acidic and weakly acidic solutions. It can also distinguish between strongly basic and weakly basic solutions (see Figure 16.5A). Each universal indicator colour is given a **pH number**. The pH number measures the acidity or alkalinity of the solution. For a neutral solution, pH = 7; for an acid solution, pH < 7; for an alkaline solution, pH > 7.

Figure 16.5A ● The colour of universal indicator in different pH solutions

SUMMARY

In general, mineral acids are stronger than organic acids. Some bases are stronger than others. Ammonia is a weak base. The pH of a solution is a measure of its acidity or alkalinity. Universal indicator turns different colours in solutions of different pH.

Figure 16.5B shows the pH values of solutions of some common acids and alkalis. Some salts do not have a pH value of 7. Carbonates and hydrogencarbonates are alkaline in solution.

IT'S A FACT

Why must you never use both ammonia as a degreaser and chlorine as a bleach on the same cleaning job?
Don't do it! You could get a dangerous reaction between them.

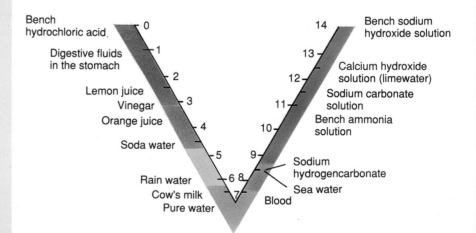

Figure 16.5B ● The pH values of some different solutions

SUMMARY

We use many acids and bases in everyday life. Tables 16.1 and 16.2 list some common acids and bases. The pH values of some solutions are given in Figure 16.5B.

CHECKPOINT

❶ Say whether these substances are strongly acidic, weakly acidic, neutral, weakly basic or strongly basic:
(a) cabbage juice, pH = 5.0 (b) pickled cabbage, pH = 3.0 (c) milk, pH = 6.5
(d) tonic water, pH = 8.2 (e) washing soda, pH = 11.5 (f) saliva, pH = 7.0
(g) blood, pH = 7.4

❷ You know what it feels like to be stung by a nettle. Is the substance which the nettle injects an acid or an alkali or neither? Think up a method of extracting some of the substance from a nettle and testing to see whether the extract is acidic or alkaline or neutral. If your teacher approves of your plan, try it out.

❸ Figure 16.5A shows the colours of universal indicator. What colour would you expect universal indicator to be when added to each of the following?
(a) distilled water (b) lemon juice (c) household ammonia (d) battery acid
(e) oven cleaner

❹

Liquid	pH value	Reaction with acid
A	1.0	None
B	8.5	Produces a salt, carbon dioxide and water
C	8.5	Produces a salt and water
D	13	Produces a salt and water

Uncle Harry is suffering from acid indigestion. Explain to him why it would not be a good idea to drink either Liquid A or Liquid D. Would you advise him to take Liquid B or Liquid C? Explain your choice.

❺ The oven sprays which are sold for cleaning greasy ovens contain a concentrated solution of sodium hydroxide.
Why does sodium hydroxide clean the greasy oven?
Why does sodium hydroxide work better than ammonia?
What two safety precautions should you take to protect yourself when using an oven spray?
Why do domestic cleaning fluids contain ammonia, rather than sodium hydroxide?
Why do soap manufacturers use sodium hydroxide, rather than ammonia?

❻

Crop	Wheat	Potatoes	Sugar beet
pH	6	9	7

The table shows the most suitable values of pH for growing some crops.
(a) Which crop grows best in (i) an acidic soil and (ii) an alkaline soil?
(b) A farmer wanted to grow sugar beet. On testing, he found that his soil had a pH of 5. Name a substance which could be added to the soil to make its pH more suitable for growing sugar beet.
(c) How does the substance you mention in (b) act on the soil to change its pH?

❼ Describe a test which you could do in the laboratory to show that citric acid is a weaker acid than sulphuric acid.

❽ Pair them up. Give the pH of each of the solutions listed.

Solution		pH	
1	Ethanoic acid	A	7.0
2	Sodium chloride	B	1.0
3	Sulphuric acid	C	5.0
4	Ammonia	D	13.0
5	Sodium hydroxide	E	9.0

TOPIC 17 ● SALTS

17.1 ● Sodium chloride

FIRST THOUGHTS

Sodium chloride, NaCl, is the salt which we call 'common salt' or simply 'salt'. The average human body contains about 250 g of sodium chloride.

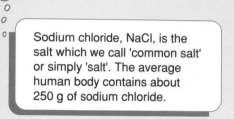

LOOK AT LINKS
for **excretion**
See Theme F, Topic 27.

IT'S A FACT

A French army under Napoleon I invaded Russia in 1812. The harsh Russian winter forced the French army to retreat. Salt starvation was one of the hardships which Napoleon's soldiers endured on their retreat from Moscow. Shortage of salt lowered their resistance to disease and epidemics spread; it prevented their wounds from healing and led to infection and death.

Sodium chloride is essential for life: it enables muscles to contract, it enables nerves to conduct nerve impulses, it regulates osmosis and it is converted into hydrochloric acid, which helps digestion to take place in the stomach. Deprived of sodium chloride, the body goes into convulsions; then paralysis and death may follow. When we sweat, we lose both water and sodium chloride. We also **excrete** sodium chloride in urine. Our kidneys control the quantity of sodium chloride which we excrete. If we eat too much salt, our kidneys excrete sodium chloride; if we eat too little salt, our kidneys excrete water but no sodium chloride.

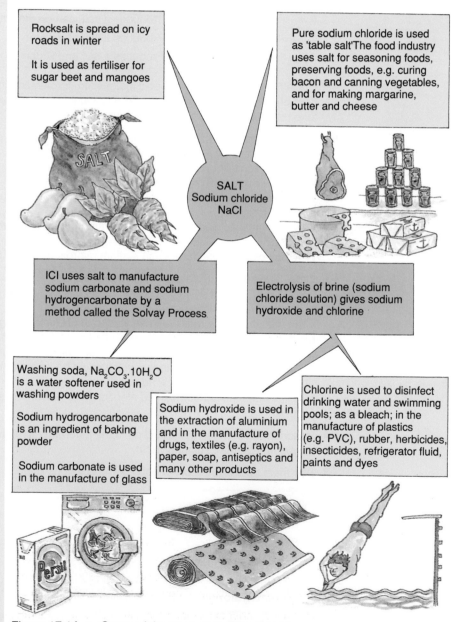

Rocksalt is spread on icy roads in winter

It is used as fertiliser for sugar beet and mangoes

Pure sodium chloride is used as 'table salt'. The food industry uses salt for seasoning foods, preserving foods, e.g. curing bacon and canning vegetables, and for making margarine, butter and cheese

SALT
Sodium chloride
NaCl

ICI uses salt to manufacture sodium carbonate and sodium hydrogencarbonate by a method called the Solvay Process

Electrolysis of brine (sodium chloride solution) gives sodium hydroxide and chlorine

Washing soda, $Na_2CO_3.10H_2O$ is a water softener used in washing powders

Sodium hydrogencarbonate is an ingredient of baking powder

Sodium carbonate is used in the manufacture of glass

Sodium hydroxide is used in the extraction of aluminium and in the manufacture of drugs, textiles (e.g. rayon), paper, soap, antiseptics and many other products

Chlorine is used to disinfect drinking water and swimming pools; as a bleach; in the manufacture of plastics (e.g. PVC), rubber, herbicides, insecticides, refrigerator fluid, paints and dyes

Figure 17.1A ● Some of the uses of sodium chloride

17.2 Salts of some common acids

While some of the salts which we use occur naturally in the Earth's crust, others must be made by chemists.

Many salts can be made by neutralising acids. In a salt, the hydrogen ions in the acid have been replaced by metal ions or by the ammonium ion. Salts of hydrochloric acid are called **chlorides**. Salts of sulphuric acid are called **sulphates**. Salts of nitric acid are called **nitrates**. See Table 17.1.

Table 17.1 ● Salts of some common acids

Acids	Salts
Hydrochloric acid $HCl(aq)$	Sodium chloride, $NaCl$ Calcium chloride, $CaCl_2$ Iron(II) chloride, $FeCl_2$ Ammonium chloride, NH_4Cl
Sulphuric acid $H_2SO_4(aq)$	Sodium sulphate, Na_2SO_4 Zinc sulphate, $ZnSO_4$ Iron(III) sulphate, $Fe_2(SO_4)_3$
Nitric acid HNO_3	Sodium nitrate, $NaNO_3$ Copper(II) nitrate, $Cu(NO_3)_2$

17.3 Water of crystallisation

The crystals of some salts contain water. Such salts are called **hydrates**. Examples are:

Copper(II) sulphate-5-water, $CuSO_4.5H_2O$, *blue*
Cobalt(II) chloride-6-water, $CoCl_2.6H_2O$, *pink*
Iron(II) sulphate-7-water, $FeSO_4.7H_2O$, *green*

The water present in the crystals of hydrated salts gives them their shape and their colour. It is called **water of crystallisation**. The formula of the hydrate shows the proportion of water in the crystal, e.g. five molecules of water to each pair of copper ions and sulphate ions: $CuSO_4.5H_2O$.

When blue crystals of copper(II) sulphate-5-water are heated gently, the water of crystallisation is driven off. The white powdery solid that remains is anhydrous (without water) copper(II) sulphate.

Copper(II) sulphate-5-water	→	Water	+	Copper(II) sulphate
(blue crystals)	→	(vapour)	+	(white powder, *anhydrous*)
$CuSO_4.5H_2O(s)$	→	$5H_2O(g)$	+	$CuSO_4(s)$

If copper(II) sulphate crystals are left in the air, they slowly lose some or all of their water of crystallisation.

SUMMARY

- Some salts occur naturally, but most of them must be made by the chemical industry.
- Some salts crystallise with water of crystallisation. This gives the crystals their shape and, in some cases, their colour.

CHECKPOINT

❶ Name the salts with the following formulas: NaI, NH_4NO_3, KBr, $BaCO_3$, Na_2SO_4, $ZnCl_2$, $CrCl_3$, $NiSO_4$, $CaCl_2$, $MgCl_2$.

❷ Write formulas for the salts: potassium nitrate, potassium bromide, iron(II) chloride, iron(II) sulphate, iron(III) bromide, ammonium chloride.

❸ State the number of oxygen atoms in each of these formulas:
(a) Pb_3O_4 (b) $3Al_2O_3$ (c) $Fe(OH)_3$ (d) $MgSO_4.7H_2O$ (e) $Co(NO_3)_3.9H_2O$

❹ The table shows how samples of four substances change in mass when they are left in the air.

Substance	Mass of sample fresh from bottle (g)	Mass of sample after 1 week in the air (g)
A	13.10	13.21
B	15.25	15.25
C	11.95	5.01

Which of the three substances in the table (a) loses water of crystallisation on standing (b) absorbs water from the air and (c) is unchanged by exposure to air?

❺ *Barbara: Bother! The holes in the salt cellar are blocked again. I wonder why that happens.*
Razwan: It happens because sodium chloride absorbs water from the air.
Gwynneth: My mum puts a few grains of rice in the salt cellar. That stops it getting clogged.

(a) Explain why the absorption of water by sodium chloride will block the salt cellar.
(b) Explain how rice grains stop the salt cellar clogging.
(c) Describe an experiment which you could do to show that what you say in (b) is correct.

❻ When a tin of biscuits is left open, do the biscuits absorb water vapour from the air or give out water vapour? Describe an experiment which you could do to find out.

17.4  Useful salts

LOOK AT LINKS
for **NPK fertilisers**
See Theme G, Topic 29.9.

Salts – who needs them? Farmers, doctors, dentists, industrial manufacturers, photographers: they all use salts in their work.

● *Agricultural uses*

NPK fertilisers are mixtures of salts. They contain ammonium nitrate and ammonium sulphate to supply nitrogen to the soil. They contain phosphates to supply phosphorus and potassium chloride as a source of potassium.

Potato blight used to be a serious problem. It destroyed the potato crop in Ireland in 1846. Thousands of people starved and many more were forced to leave the country in search of food. Now, the fungus which causes potato blight can be killed by spraying with a solution of a simple salt, copper(II) sulphate. This fungicide is also used on vines to protect the grape harvest.

Figure 17.4A ● NPK fertiliser

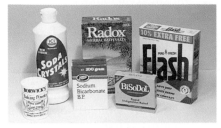

Figure 17.4B ● Washing soda, bath salts, baking powder

LOOK AT LINKS
for **water softners**
See Theme E, Topic 22.12.

● *Domestic uses*

Sodium carbonate-10-water is known as 'washing soda'. It is used as a **water softener**. It is an ingredient of washing powders and is also sold as bath salts.

Sodium hydrogencarbonate is known as 'baking soda'. It is added to self-raising flour. When heated at a moderate oven temperature, it decomposes.

Sodium hydrogencarbonate	→	Sodium carbonate	+	Carbon dioxide	+	Steam
$2NaHCO_3(s)$	→	$Na_2CO_3(s)$	+	$CO_2(g)$	+	$H_2O(g)$

The carbon dioxide and steam which are formed make bread and cakes 'rise'.

● *Medical uses*

Figure 17.4C shows someones leg being set in a plaster cast. Plaster of Paris is the salt calcium sulphate-$\frac{1}{2}$-water, $CaSO_4.\frac{1}{2}H_2O$. It is made by heating calcium sulphate-2-water, $CaSO_4.2H_2O$, which is mined. When plaster of Paris is mixed with water, it combines and sets to form a strong 'plaster cast'. It is also used for plastering walls.

People who are always tired and lacking in energy may be suffering from anaemia. This illness is caused by a shortage of haemoglobin (the red pigment which contains iron) in the blood. It can be cured by taking iron compounds in the diet. The 'iron tablets' which anaemic people may be given often contain iron(II) sulphate-7-water.

Patients who are suspected of having a stomach ulcer may be given a 'barium meal'. It contains the salt barium sulphate. After a barium meal, an X-ray photograph of the body shows the path taken by the salt. Being large, barium ions show up well in X-ray photographs.

═══ **SCIENCE AT WORK** ═══

Liquid crystals are a form of matter which has a regular structure like a solid and which flows like a liquid. Many liquid crystals change their colour with the temperature. A recent invention uses the behaviour of liquid crystals to diagnose appendicitis. A thin plastic film coated with a suitable liquid crystal is placed on the patient's abdomen. Since an inflamed appendix produces heat, it shows up immediately as a change in the colour of the film. Appendicitis can be difficult to diagnose by other methods because the pain is often felt some distance from the appendix. Can you think of some further uses of liquid crystal temperature strips?

LOOK AT LINKS
Temperature strips as thermometers are discussed in Theme B, Topic 7.1.

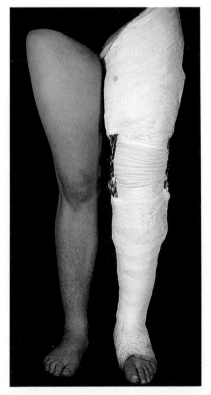

Figure 17.4C ● A patient having his leg set in a plaster cast

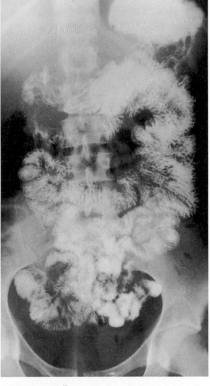

Figure 17.4D ● X-ray photograph of a patient after consuming a barium meal

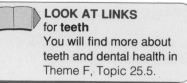

Fluoridation

The fluoride story started in 1901 when Fred McKay began work as a dentist in Colorado, USA. Many of his patients had mottled teeth or dark brown stains on their teeth. He could find no information about this condition and called it 'Colorado Brown Stain'. He became convinced that the stain was caused by something in the water. After Oakley in Idaho changed its source of drinking water, the children there no longer developed mottled or stained teeth. The drinking water in a number of towns was analysed and showed that teeth were affected when there were over 2 p.p.m (parts per million) of fluoride in the drinking water. It affected children's teeth more than adults' teeth. McKay also noticed that people with 'Colorado Brown Stain' had less dental decay than other patients!

You can use a microcomputer and a histogram program to display these results as a bar graph.

● Fluorides for healthy teeth

Why do dentists recommend that people use toothpastes containing the salt calcium fluoride? Tooth enamel reacts with calcium fluoride to form a harder enamel which is better at resisting attack by mouth acids. To make sure that everyone gets protection from tooth decay, many water companies add a small amount of calcium fluoride to drinking water. The concentration of fluoride ions must not rise above 1 p.p.m. Spending 7p per person each year on fluoridation saves the National Health Service £6 per person each year in dentistry. Some people are violently opposed to the fluoridation of water supplies. This is because they are worried about the effects of drinking too much fluoride. Worldwide, 230 million people drink fluoridated water.

In 1945, a British dentist called Weaver inspected the teeth of children from North Shields and South Shields. These two towns are on opposite banks of the River Tyne. Tables 17.2 and 17.3 show the results (rounded off) of Weaver's inspection of 1000 children aged 5 and 1000 children aged 12. The figures give the number of DMF (decayed, missing or filled) teeth per 1000 teeth. The numbers of teeth in each position in both upper and lower jaws and on both left and right sides have been added together. At the time, the water supplies contained:

North Shields 0.25 p.p.m fluoride, South Shields 1.40 p.p.m fluoride.

Table17.2 ● Survey of 1000 children aged 5 years

Position of tooth	Number of DMF teeth per 1000 teeth	
	North Shields	South Shields
1	265	155
2	200	100
3	135	55
4	675	440
5	725	485

Table17.3 ● Survey of 1000 children aged 12

Position of tooth	Number of DMF teeth per 1000 teeth	
	North Shields	South Shields
1	45	20
2	60	20
3	15	10
4	70	25
5	75	30
6	725	490
7	160	75

(a) On graph paper, draw a bar graph of the number of DMF teeth in each position for 5 year-olds in (i) North Shields and (ii) South Shields. Shade the bars for the two towns differently.
(b) Draw similar bar graphs for 12 year-olds in (i) North Shields and (ii) South Shields.
(c) What do you observe from your bar graphs about the teeth of children in North Shields compared with South Shields (i) at 5 years and (ii) at 12 years?
(d) What is the fundamental difference between the teeth of a 5 year-old and those of a 12 year-old?
(e) How did the fluoride content of the water in North Shields compare with that in South Shields?
(f) What can you deduce from these figures about the effect of fluoride in drinking water on the health of children's teeth?
(g) Remember 'Colorado Brown Stain'? What is the maximum safe fluoride level?

● Industrial uses
Sodium chloride has many uses in industry; see Figure 17.1A.

● Photography
Silver bromide, AgBr, is the salt which is used in black and white photography. Light affects silver bromide. A photographic film is a piece of celluloid covered with a thin layer of gelatin containing silver bromide. When you take a photograph, light falls on to some areas of the film. In exposed areas of film, light converts some silver ions, Ag^+, into silver atoms, which are black. These black atoms form a *latent image* of the object.

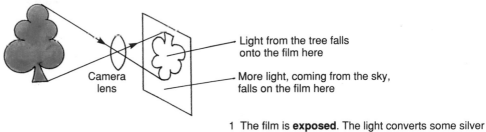

Light from the tree falls onto the film here

More light, coming from the sky, falls on the film here

Camera lens

1 The film is **exposed**. The light converts some silver ions, Ag^+, into silver atoms, which are black. The more light that falls on the film, the more silver ions are converted. These black atoms form a **latent image** of the tree ('latent' means hidden)

2 The film is **developed**. It is placed in a 'developer' solution which continues the process started by light, converting more silver ions in the areas affected by light into silver atoms

3 The film is placed in a solution of **fixer** which removes unchanged silver bromide

4 The result is a **negative**. The tree appears light against a dark background

5 To make a **print** the negative is placed on a piece of light-sensitive printing paper and exposed to light. The pattern of dark and light areas in the print is the reverse of that of the negative

Figure 17.4E ● Black and white photography

SUMMARY

Salts are used in agriculture, in the home, in medicine and in industry. Methods of making salts are therefore important.

Some of these useful salts are mined, e.g. sodium chloride, magnesium sulphate and calcium sulphate. Others must be made by the chemical industry, e.g. silver bromide and copper(II) sulphate.

17.5 Methods of making salts

> Since salts are so useful, chemists have found methods of making them. This topic describes the methods.

The method which you choose for making a salt depends on whether it is soluble or insoluble. Soluble salts are made by neutralising an acid. Insoluble salts are made by adding two solutions. Table 17.4 summarises the facts about the solubility of salts.

Table 17.4 ● Soluble and insoluble salts

Salts	Soluble	Insoluble
Chlorides	Most are soluble	Silver chloride Lead(II) chloride
Sulphates	Most are soluble	Barium sulphate Calcium sulphate Lead(II) sulphate
Nitrates	All are soluble	None
Carbonates	Sodium and potassium carbonates	Most are insoluble
Ethanoates	All are soluble	None
Sodium salts	All are soluble	None
Potassium salts	All are soluble	None
Ammonium salts	All are soluble	None

Methods for making soluble salts

An acid is neutralised by adding a metal, a solid base or a solid metal carbonate or a solution of an alkali.

Method 1: Acid + Metal → Salt + Hydrogen
Method 2: Acid + Metal oxide → Salt + Water
Method 3: Acid + Metal carbonate → Salt + Water + Carbon dioxide
Method 4: Acid + Alkali → Salt + Water

The practical details of Methods 1–3 are as follows.

Step one Add an excess (more than enough) of the solid to the acid (see Figure 17.5A).

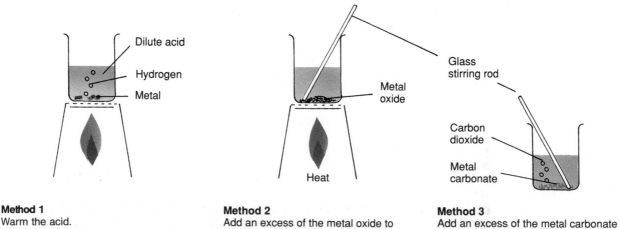

Method 1
Warm the acid.
Switch off the Bunsen.
Add an excess of the metal to the acid.
Wait until no more hydrogen is evolved.
The reaction is then complete.

Method 2
Add an excess of the metal oxide to the acid. Wait until the solution no longer turns blue litmus red. The reaction is then over

Method 3
Add an excess of the metal carbonate to the acid. Wait until no more carbon dioxide is evolved. The reaction is then over

Figure 17.5A ● Adding an excess of the solid reactant to the acid

Step two Filter to remove the excess of solid (Figure 17.5B).

Step three Gently evaporate the filtrate (Figure 17.5C).

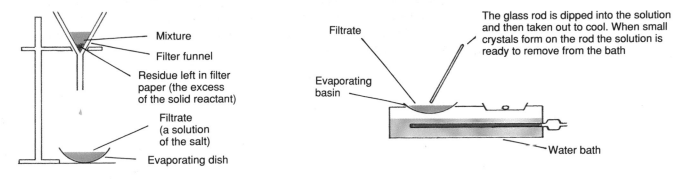

Mixture

Filter funnel

Residue left in filter paper (the excess of the solid reactant)

Filtrate (a solution of the salt)

Evaporating dish

Figure 17.5B ● Filtering to remove the excess of solid reactant

The glass rod is dipped into the solution and then taken out to cool. When small crystals form on the rod the solution is ready to remove from the bath

Filtrate

Evaporating basin

Water bath

Figure 17.5C ● Evaporating the filtrate

Step four As the solution cools, crystals of the salt form. Separate the crystals from the solution by filtration. Use a little distilled water to wash the crystals in the filter funnel. Then leave the crystals to dry.

● *Acid + alkali*

Method 4 Reaction between an acid and an alkali

Ammonia is an alkali. The preparation of ammonium salts is important because they are used as fertilisers. A laboratory method for making ammonium sulphate is shown in Figure 17.5D.

SUMMARY

Soluble salts are made by the reactions:
• Acid + Reactive → Salt + Hydrogen
  metal
• Acid + Metal → Salt + Water
  oxide
• Acid + Metal → Salt + Water + Carbon
  carbonate   dioxide
In these three methods, an excess of the solid reactant is used, and unreacted solid is removed by filtration.

1 Add the ammonia solution to the dilute sulphuric acid, stirring constantly

2 From time to time, remove a drop of acid on the end of the glass rod. Spot it on to a strip of indicator paper on a white tile. When the test shows that the solution has become alkaline, stop adding ammonia. You have now added an excess of ammonia

3 Evaporate the solution until it begins to crystallise. Leave it to stand. Filter to obtain crystals of ammonium sulphate

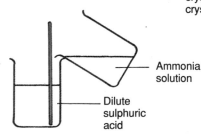

Ammonia solution

Dilute sulphuric acid

Figure 17.5D ● Making ammonium sulphate

SUMMARY

Soluble salts can be made by the reaction:
• Acid + Alkali → Salt + Water
  This method is used for ammonium salts. An excess of ammonia is added. The excess is removed when the solution is evaporated.

Method for insoluble salts

Insoluble salts are made by mixing two solutions. For example, you can make the insoluble salt barium sulphate by mixing a solution of the soluble salt barium chloride with a solution of the soluble salt sodium sulphate. When the two solutions are mixed, the insoluble salt barium sulphate is precipitated (thrown out of solution). What do you think remains in solution? The method is called **precipitation**.

● Precipitation

The equation for the reaction is

Barium chloride	+	Sodium sulphate	→	Barium sulphate	+	Sodium chloride
$BaCl_2(aq)$	+	$Na_2SO_4(aq)$	→	$BaSO_4(s)$	+	$2NaCl(aq)$

An ionic equation can be written for the reaction

Barium ions	+	Sulphate ions	→	Barium sulphate
$Ba^{2+}(aq)$	+	$SO_4^{2-}(aq)$	→	$BaSO_4(s)$

The ionic equation shows only the ions which take part in the precipitation reaction: the barium ions and sulphate ions.

SUMMARY

Insoluble salts are made by precipitation. A solution of a soluble salt of the metal is added to a solution of a soluble salt of the acid.
Remember
• All nitrates are soluble.
• All sodium, potassium and ammonium salts are soluble.

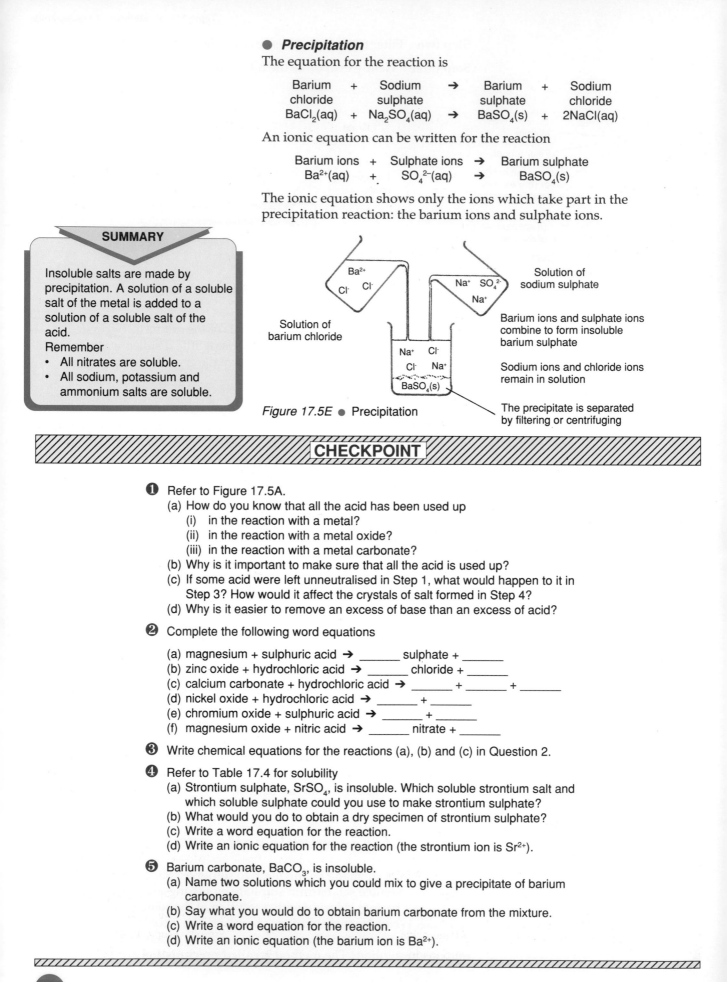

Solution of barium chloride

Solution of sodium sulphate

Barium ions and sulphate ions combine to form insoluble barium sulphate

Sodium ions and chloride ions remain in solution

The precipitate is separated by filtering or centrifuging

Figure 17.5E ● Precipitation

CHECKPOINT

❶ Refer to Figure 17.5A.
  (a) How do you know that all the acid has been used up
    (i) in the reaction with a metal?
    (ii) in the reaction with a metal oxide?
    (iii) in the reaction with a metal carbonate?
  (b) Why is it important to make sure that all the acid is used up?
  (c) If some acid were left unneutralised in Step 1, what would happen to it in Step 3? How would it affect the crystals of salt formed in Step 4?
  (d) Why is it easier to remove an excess of base than an excess of acid?

❷ Complete the following word equations

  (a) magnesium + sulphuric acid → _____ sulphate + _____
  (b) zinc oxide + hydrochloric acid → _____ chloride + _____
  (c) calcium carbonate + hydrochloric acid → _____ + _____ + _____
  (d) nickel oxide + hydrochloric acid → _____ + _____
  (e) chromium oxide + sulphuric acid → _____ + _____
  (f) magnesium oxide + nitric acid → _____ nitrate + _____

❸ Write chemical equations for the reactions (a), (b) and (c) in Question 2.

❹ Refer to Table 17.4 for solubility
  (a) Strontium sulphate, $SrSO_4$, is insoluble. Which soluble strontium salt and which soluble sulphate could you use to make strontium sulphate?
  (b) What would you do to obtain a dry specimen of strontium sulphate?
  (c) Write a word equation for the reaction.
  (d) Write an ionic equation for the reaction (the strontium ion is Sr^{2+}).

❺ Barium carbonate, $BaCO_3$, is insoluble.
  (a) Name two solutions which you could mix to give a precipitate of barium carbonate.
  (b) Say what you would do to obtain barium carbonate from the mixture.
  (c) Write a word equation for the reaction.
  (d) Write an ionic equation (the barium ion is Ba^{2+}).

TOPIC 18 — THE CHEMICALS OF LIFE

18.1 Elements and compounds

FIRST THOUGHTS

Life – what a mystery it is! Are the compounds in living things different from those in the rest of the Universe? Do they have some mysterious property of life?

All matter is made of chemical elements and their compounds. The compounds in living organisms are made up of the same elements as the rest of the universe. They obey the same laws of physics and chemistry. The elements that living organisms need come from the environment; from the Earth and its atmosphere. There are twenty of them. Six of them together make up 95% (by mass) of living matter. In order of abundance, they are carbon, hydrogen, nitrogen, oxygen, phosphorus and sulphur. A list of the symbols, CHNOPS, will help you to remember them.

What, then, makes something composed of ordinary chemicals live? That is a difficult question! Part of the answer lies in the chemistry of carbon compounds. Living things are made of water, salts and carbon compounds.

(a) Methane, CH_4, released by cattle

(b) Carbon dioxide, CO_2, in exhaled breath

(c) Urea, $CO(NH_2)_2$, excreted in urine

Figure 18.1A ● Models of the molecules of some simple carbon compounds

An atom of carbon can form four covalent bonds. Figure 18.1A shows some simple carbon compounds which occur in living things. Atoms of carbon are able to combine to form long chains. Many of the carbon compounds in living things have much larger molecules than those shown in Figure 18.1A. Often such compounds are formed by small molecules joining up to form large molecules. The carbon compounds in living things are called **organic compounds**. Some examples are listed in Table 18.1.

LOOK AT LINKS
for **organic compounds**
The formation of covalent bonds was described in Theme C, Topic 14.5. There is more about organic chemistry, the chemistry of carbon compounds, in Theme L, Topics 51.4, 51.5, 51.6, 51.7.

Table 18.1 ● Organic compunds

Substances with small molecules which can combine to form large molecules		Substances with large molecules which are formed as a result
Sugars	→	Starch, cellulose, chitin (Topic 18.2)
Fatty acids and glycerol	→	Lipids (Topic 18.3)
Amino acids	→	Proteins (Topic 18.4)
Nucleotides	→	Nucleic acids (Topic 18.5)

18.2 Carbohydrates

Sugars

Carbohydrates are compounds containing carbon, hydrogen and oxygen only. Carbohydrates do a vital job in all living organisms: they provide energy. When carbohydrates react with oxygen, carbon dioxide and water are formed and energy is released. This reaction takes place slowly inside cells. Energy is released in a controlled way and used by the cells for all their activities. The process by which living cells release energy is called **cellular respiration**. Most of our energy is obtained from the respiration of carbohydrates (usually glucose), although living organisms also respire fats, oils and proteins.

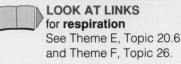

What do sugar and starch, the cell walls of plants and the exoskeletons of insects have in common? This section will tell you!

LOOK AT LINKS
for **respiration**
See Theme E, Topic 20.6
and Theme F, Topic 26.

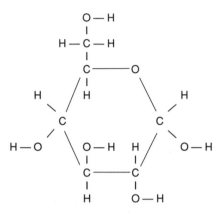

(b) The formula for glucose in full

Carbohydrates include sugars, starches and cellulose. Two of the simplest carbohydrates are the sweet-tasting sugars **glucose** and **fructose**. They both have the formula $C_6H_{12}O_6$, but the structures (the arrangement of atoms) of their molecules are different. The structure of a molecule of glucose is shown in Figure 18.2A. As you can see, six of the atoms are joined to form a ring. Sugars with one ring of atoms are called **monosaccharides** (mono = one). There are two kinds of monosaccharides: **hexoses**, which contain 6 carbon atoms, e.g. glucose and fructose, and **pentoses**, which contain 5 carbon atoms, e.g. ribose, $C_5H_{10}O_5$.

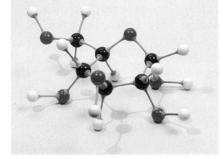

(a) Model of a glucose molecule

Figure 18.2A ● Glucose

(c) The formula in a shorthand form

Two molecules of glucose can combine to form one molecule of the sugar maltose, $C_{12}H_{22}O_{11}$.

Glucose → Maltose + Water
$2C_6H_{12}O_6(aq)$ → $C_{12}H_{22}O_{11}(aq)$ + $H_2O(l)$

Maltose is a **disaccharide**: its molecules contain two sugar rings. Sucrose (table sugar) is another disaccharide. It is formed from glucose and fructose.

Glucose + Fructose → Sucrose + Water

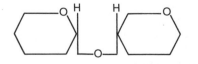

Figure 18.2B ● The formula for maltose in shorthand form

Starch, glycogen and cellulose

Starch (a stored food substance in plant cells), glycogen (a stored food substance in animal cells) and cellulose (of which plant cell walls are composed) are all carbohydrates, although they do not taste sweet. Starch and glycogen are slightly soluble in water; cellulose is insoluble. These compounds are **polysaccharides**. Polysaccharides are carbohydrates whose molecules contain a large number (hundreds) of sugar rings (see Figure 18.2C).

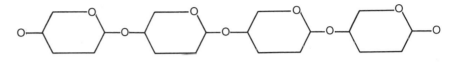

Figure 18.2C ● Part of a starch molecule

In starch, glycogen and cellulose, the molecules are long chains of glucose rings. Polysaccharides differ in the length and structure of their chains (see Figure 18.2D).

As starch and glycogen are only slightly soluble they can remain in the cells of an organism without being dissolved out and therefore make good food stores (see Figures 18.2E and F). Cells convert starch and glycogen into glucose, which is soluble. Glucose is oxidised in the cells to release energy.

Some polysaccharides are building materials. Cellulose fibres make the walls of plant cells (see Figure 18.2G). The tough framework of fibres makes the plant cell wall rigid. Another polysaccharide that provides a strong structure is chitin. It forms the exoskeleton round insects' bodies which protects their insides (see Figure 18.2H).

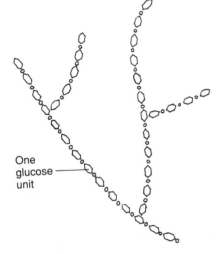

Figure 18.2D ● A model of part of a starch molecule

One glucose unit

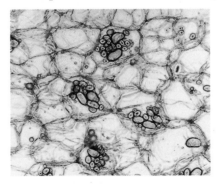

Figure 18.2E ● A thin section of potato stained with iodine. Note the grains of starch which have been stained black

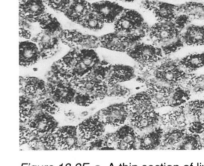

Figure 18.2F ● A thin section of liver. Note the glycogen stained pink

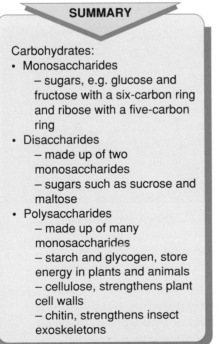

Figure 18.2G ● Plant cell wall. (x10 000) Note the frame work of cellulose fibres

Figure 18.2H ● A chitin-impregnated exoskeleton

SUMMARY

Carbohydrates:
- Monosaccharides
  - sugars, e.g. glucose and fructose with a six-carbon ring and ribose with a five-carbon ring
- Disaccharides
  - made up of two monosaccharides
  - sugars such as sucrose and maltose
- Polysaccharides
  - made up of many monosaccharides
  - starch and glycogen, store energy in plants and animals
  - cellulose, strengthens plant cell walls
  - chitin, strengthens insect exoskeletons

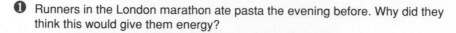

CHECKPOINT

❶ Runners in the London marathon ate pasta the evening before. Why did they think this would give them energy?

❷ Explain why rice, bread and potatoes are 'high-energy foods'.

❸ Give two examples of the importance of cellulose and chitin as building materials in living things.

❹ Glucose, maltose and starch are carbohydrates. Answer the following questions about them.
(a) Which one tastes sweet?
(b) Which two are very soluble in water?
(c) List the elements that make up all three.
(d) The formula of glucose is $C_6H_{12}O_6$. What is the ratio number of atoms of hydrogen: number of atoms of oxygen?
(e) The formula of maltose is $C_{12}H_{22}O_{11}$. What is the ratio number of atoms of hydrogen: number of atoms of oxygen?
(f) Using your answers to (d) and (e), try to explain where the name 'carbohydrate' comes from.
(g) The 'shorthand' formula for glucose is

Draw the shorthand formulas for maltose and starch.

18.3 Lipids

FIRST THOUGHTS

Have you seen brands of margarine and cooking oil described as 'high in polyunsaturates' and wondered what it means? This section will tell you.

What are lipids?

Lipids is a name for **fats** and **oils**. Lipids are made of carbon, hydrogen and oxygen. A difference between fats and oils is that most fats are solid at room temperature and most oils are liquid at room temperature. Fats and oils have a 'greasy' feel and are insoluble in water.

Fats and oils are important as:

- **Sources of energy**. Fats and oils are stores of energy. In cellular respiration, lipids provide about twice as much energy per gram as carbohydrates.
- **Insulation**. Mammals have a layer of fat under the skin. This layer helps to keep the animals warm. Whales and seals which live in Antarctic waters have an especially thick layer of fat, called blubber, to protect them from extreme cold.

Figure 18.3A ● Fur seals.

- **Protection**. Delicate organs, such as the kidneys, are protected by a layer of hard fat.
- **Food**. Vitamins A, D and E are soluble in fats and oils. Foods containing lipids provide animals with these essential vitamins.

Fats and oils are also used to build cells. Look at the magnified picture of a **cell membrane** in Figure 18.3B. You can see two 'tramlines', which scientists think are composed of molecules of a **phospholipid** – a fat containing phosphorus.

LOOK AT LINKS
for **cell membranes**
See Theme D, Topic 19.1.

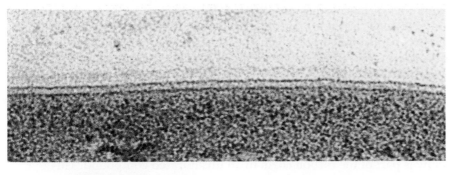

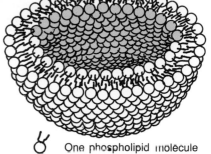

A magnified view of the 'tramlines' shows a double layer of phospholipid molecules

One phospholipid molecule

(a) A photograph of a cell membrane taken through an electron microscope. Part of the cell membrane shows as two 'tramlines'. (x250 000)

Figure 18.3B ● Cell membrane

(b) The diagram shows how scientists interpret the photograph

Saturated and unsaturated fats and oils

LOOK AT LINKS
The importance of fats and oils in the diet is discussed in Theme F, Topic 25.

Do you watch your diet? Many people are concerned about having too much fat in their diet, particularly **saturated fats**. Let us consider what the term saturated means here.

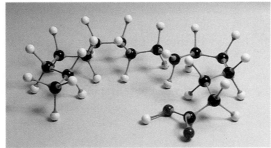

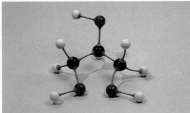

(a) Model of a molecule of glycerol

(c) Model of a molecule of fatty acid (hexadecanoic acid)

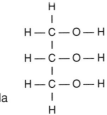

(b) The formula of glycerol

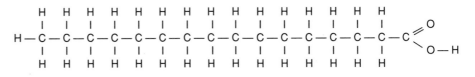

(d) The formula of hexadecanoic acid. Can you see how the acid gets its name? (hexa = six, deca = ten)

Figure 18.3C ● Glycerol and hexadecanoic acid

Fats and oils are compounds of fatty acids and glycerol (see Figure 18.3C). One molecule of glycerol can combine with three molecules of a fatty acid to form a molecule of a triglyceride and three molecules of water. **Lipids** are mixtures of triglycerides.

Glycerol + Fatty acid → Triglyceride + Water

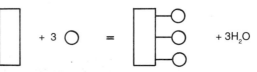

LOOK AT LINKS
for **saturated** and **unsaturated** compounds
See Theme L, Topic 51.4.

Like other organic compounds, fatty acids may be saturated or unsaturated. If there is one double bond between carbon atoms, the

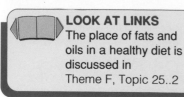
LOOK AT LINKS
The place of fats and oils in a healthy diet is discussed in Theme F, Topic 25..2

compound is described as **unsaturated**. If there is more than one double bond between carbon atoms, the acid is described as **polyunsaturated**. Below is part of the carbon chain in a saturated compound. This compound is described as saturated because it cannot combine with any more hydrogen atoms.

$$\begin{array}{c}
\text{H}\ \ \text{H}\ \ \text{H}\ \ \text{H}\ \ \text{H}\ \ \text{H}\ \ \text{H}\ \ \text{H}\ \ \text{H} \\
\mid\ \ \mid\ \ \mid\ \ \mid\ \ \mid\ \ \mid\ \ \mid\ \ \mid\ \ \mid \\
-\text{C}-\text{C}-\text{C}-\text{C}-\text{C}-\text{C}-\text{C}-\text{C}-\text{C}- \\
\mid\ \ \mid\ \ \mid\ \ \mid\ \ \mid\ \ \mid\ \ \mid\ \ \mid\ \ \mid \\
\text{H}\ \ \text{H}\ \ \text{H}\ \ \text{H}\ \ \text{H}\ \ \text{H}\ \ \text{H}\ \ \text{H}\ \ \text{H}
\end{array}$$

Below is part of the carbon chain in an unsaturated compound. This compound is described as unsaturated because it can add more hydrogen atoms across the double bond.

$$\begin{array}{c}
\text{H}\ \ \text{H}\ \ \text{H}\ \ \text{H}\ \ \text{H}\ \ \text{H}\ \ \text{H}\ \ \text{H}\ \ \text{H} \\
\mid\ \ \mid\ \ \mid\ \ \mid\ \ \mid\ \ \mid\ \ \mid\ \ \mid\ \ \mid \\
-\text{C}-\text{C}-\text{C}-\text{C}-\text{C}-\text{C}=\text{C}-\text{C}-\text{C}- \\
\mid\ \ \mid\ \ \mid\ \ \mid\ \ \mid\ \ \ \ \ \ \ \ \ \ \mid\ \ \mid \\
\text{H}\ \ \text{H}\ \ \text{H}\ \ \text{H}\ \ \text{H}\ \ \ \ \ \ \ \ \ \ \text{H}\ \ \text{H}
\end{array}$$

Below is part of the carbon chain in a polyunsaturated compound

$$\begin{array}{c}
\text{H}\ \ \text{H}\ \ \text{H}\ \ \text{H}\ \ \text{H}\ \ \text{H}\ \ \text{H}\ \ \text{H}\ \ \text{H} \\
\mid\ \ \mid\ \ \mid\ \ \mid\ \ \mid\ \ \mid\ \ \mid\ \ \mid\ \ \mid \\
-\text{C}-\text{C}-\text{C}-\text{C}=\text{C}-\text{C}-\text{C}=\text{C}-\text{C}- \\
\mid\ \ \mid\ \ \mid\ \ \ \ \ \ \ \ \ \ \mid\ \ \ \ \ \ \ \ \ \ \mid \\
\text{H}\ \ \text{H}\ \ \text{H}\ \ \ \ \ \ \ \ \ \ \text{H}\ \ \ \ \ \ \ \ \ \ \text{H}
\end{array}$$

The fats which contain glycerol combined with saturated fatty acids are called saturated fats. Fats which contain glycerol combined with unsaturated fatty acids are called unsaturated fats or polyunsaturated fats, depending on the number of double bonds in a molecule. Animal fats contain a large proportion of saturated compounds and are solid. Plant oils contain a large proportion of unsaturated compounds and have lower melting points. Many scientists believe that eating a lot of saturated fat increases the risk of heart disease.

SUMMARY

Lipids (fats and oils) are mixtures of compounds of glycerol with organic acids. These compounds can be saturated (with only single bonds between carbon atoms) or unsaturated (with a double bond between carbon atoms) or polyunsaturated (with more than one carbon–carbon double bond per molecule).

CHECKPOINT

❶ (a) Say which are the fats and which are the oils.
   soft margarine, butter, lard, hard margarine, cooking oil
   (b) What is the main physical difference between fats and oils?

❷ Refer to Figure 18.3A. What feature helps the seals to keep warm?

❸ Briefly explain why fats and oils are better stores of energy than carbohydrates are.

❹ Briefly explain the difference between saturated and unsaturated fats.

❺ The manufacturers of *Flower* margarine claim that their product encourages healthy eating because it is 'low in saturated fats'.
   (a) What do they mean by 'low in saturated fats'?
   (b) Name a product which contains much saturated fat.
   (c) What particular benefit to health is claimed for products such as *Flower*?

❻ The following equation represents the formation of a fat.

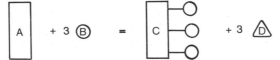

   (a) Name the substances A and D.
   (b) Name one substance which could be B.
   (c) Name one fat and one oil which could be C.

18.4 Proteins

FIRST THOUGHTS

Muscle, skin, hair and haemoglobin: what do they have in common? You can find out in this section.

Proteins are compounds which contain carbon, hydrogen, oxygen, nitrogen and sometimes sulphur. Proteins are vitally important because:

Proteins are the materials from which new tissues are made. If organisms are to grow and if they are to repair damaged tissues, they need proteins.

Enzymes are proteins. None of the reactions which take place in animals and plants would take place rapidly enough without enzymes. Hormones are proteins which control the activities of organisms. Proteins can be oxidised in respiration to provide energy.

Every protein molecule is made from a large number of molecules of **amino acids**. The simplest amino acid is **glycine**

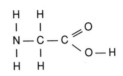

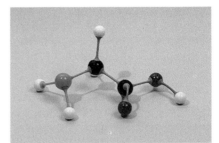

Figure 18.4A ● Model of a glycine molecule

There are about 20 amino acids. They have the general formula

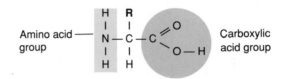

R is a different group of atoms in each amino acid; it can be —H, —CH$_3$, —CH$_2$OH and many other groups. In the following equations, each shape represents a different amino acid.

Two amino acids can combine to form a **peptide** and water

$$\square + \bigcirc \rightarrow \square\!-\!\bigcirc + H_2O$$

The peptide which is formed can combine with more amino acids. Many different amino acids can combine to form a long chain

$$\square + \bigcirc + \triangle + \bigcirc \rightarrow \square\!-\!\bigcirc\!-\!\triangle\!-\!\bigcirc + 3H_2O$$

Peptides are molecules with up to 15 amino acids.
Polypeptides are molecules with 15–100 amino acids.
Proteins have still larger molecules. Part of a protein molecule is shown below.

LOOK AT LINKS
for **protein**
Which foods provide protein in our diet?
See Theme F, Topic 25.

IT'S A FACT

Fifteen million children die each year of starvation and disease. You will have seen pictures of children with swollen abdomens. They are suffering from a disease called kwashiorkor. They are getting some food but are starved of protein.

LOOK AT LINKS
for **making protein**
See Theme D, Topic 19.

Dr Max Perutz began work on the structure of haemoglobin in 1936. It took over 20 years to find out that the molecule contains 574 amino acid groups, arranged in four chains. With a total of 10 000 atoms, the molecule has a mass 65 000 times that of a hydrogen atom.

LOOK AT LINKS
for **kwashiorkor**
See Theme F, Topic 25.2.

Essential and non-essential amino acids

Animals are able to make some amino acids in their bodies, but they cannot make all the amino acids they need. They must obtain the ones they cannot make from their diet. The amino acids that animals need to obtain from their diet are called **essential amino acids**. The amino acids which animals can make themselves are called **non-essential amino acids**.

A protein which contains all the essential amino acids is called a **first-class protein**. Such proteins are found in lean meat, fish, cheese and soya beans. A protein which lacks essential amino acids is called a **second-class protein**. Such proteins are found in flour, rice and oatmeal. In parts of the world where rice is the staple diet, kwashiorkor is common.

The chain of amino acid groups in a protein is folded and twisted into a certain three-dimensional shape. The part that a protein plays in a living organism depends on the shape of its molecules. The shape is decided by the order (sequence) of amino acid groups in the protein molecule.

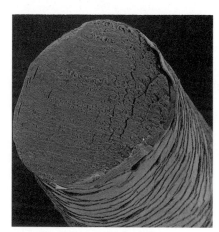

Figure 18.4B ● Cross section of a human hair. Hair, nails, claws and feathers consist chiefly of the protein keratin. (x800)

Figure 18.4C ● Insulin. In 1953, Dr Frederick Sanger of the UK reported the complete sequence of amino acids in the protein insulin. This was the first time that a protein structure had been worked out. Insulin controls blood sugar levels. Its molecule is one of the smallest protein molecules.

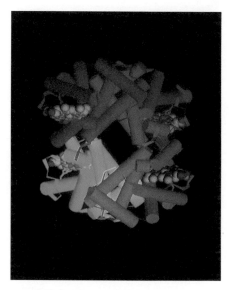

Figure 18.4D ● Haemoglobin. In 1959, Dr Max Perutz worked out the shape of the haemoglobin molecule. Haemoglobin is the red pigment in blood which transports oxygen round the body. The haemoglobin molecule is larger than the insulin molecule.

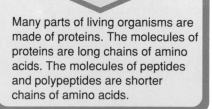

SUMMARY

Many parts of living organisms are made of proteins. The molecules of proteins are long chains of amino acids. The molecules of peptides and polypeptides are shorter chains of amino acids.

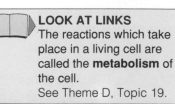

LOOK AT LINKS
The reactions which take place in a living cell are called the **metabolism** of the cell.
See Theme D, Topic 19.

Enzymes, an important group of proteins

Many chemical reactions take place inside a cell. The speeds at which the cell reactions take place are controlled by **catalysts** called **enzymes**. Enzymes are proteins. There are thousands of enzymes in living things. We say that enzymes are **specific**; this means that each enzyme catalyses a certain chemical reaction or a type of chemical reaction. The substance which the enzyme helps to react is called its **substrate**. The enzyme amylase increases the speed at which starch reacts with water to form sugars.

Starch + Water ➔ Sugars

LOOK AT LINKS
A substance which increases the speed of a chemical reaction without being used up in the reaction is called a **catalyst**.
See Theme L, Topic 51.1.

SUMMARY

Enzymes are an important group of proteins. They catalyse the reactions which take place in living cells.

The enzyme has a group of atoms called the **active site**. Part of the substrate molecule fits into the active site. This fit has been described as 'like a lock and key'.

The starch molecule is attacked by a water molecule. Weakened by its bonds to the enzyme, the starch molecule is hydrolysed to form two molecules of sugar.

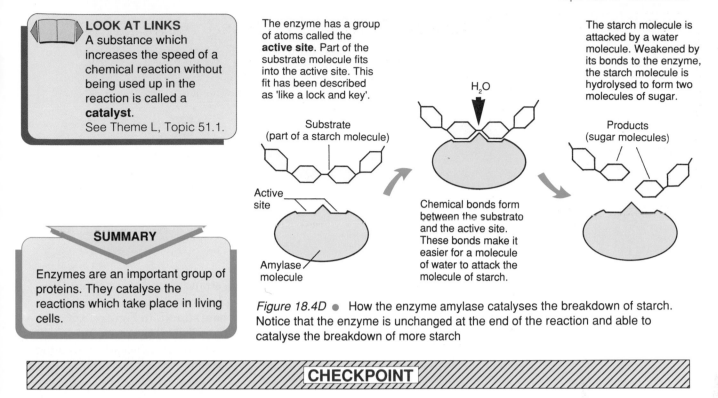

Chemical bonds form between the substrate and the active site. These bonds make it easier for a molecule of water to attack the molecule of starch.

Figure 18.4D ● How the enzyme amylase catalyses the breakdown of starch. Notice that the enzyme is unchanged at the end of the reaction and able to catalyse the breakdown of more starch

CHECKPOINT

❶ What is the difference between (a) a peptide and a polypeptide (b) a polypeptide and a protein?

❷ (a) To what group of chemical compounds do enzymes belong?
 (b) What vital job do enzymes do?
 (c) Give the names of three substrates on which enzymes work and the names of the products that are formed.

FIRST THOUGHTS

18.5 Nucleic acids

When two scientists found out the structure of DNA, there was great excitement in the scientific world, and they won Nobel prizes. Why is DNA so important? What is so special about the structure? You can find out in this section.

LOOK AT LINKS
for **RNA** and **DNA**
See Theme D, Topic 19.3.

RNA and DNA

The nucleic acids are ribonucleic acid (RNA) and deoxyribonucleic acid (DNA). DNA occurs in cell nuclei. The genes that living things inherit from their parents are lengths of DNA. The information that a cell needs to assemble molecules of amino acids in the correct order to make protein molecules is present in its DNA. RNA occurs in nuclei and cytoplasm. It transfers the information contained in DNA to the places in the cell where proteins are made.

RNA and DNA have large complex molecules made up from smaller molecules of compounds called **nucleotides** (see Figure 18.5A).

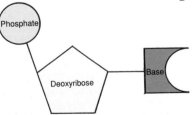

Figure 18.5A ● A nucleotide in DNA. The five-carbon sugar deoxyribose occurs in DNA. The base is one of four: adenine, cytosine, guanine or thymine. (In RNA the sugar ribose occurs, and the base uracil is present instead of thymine.)

Nucleotides combine to form nucleic acids. The phosphate group of one nucleotide molecule combines with the sugar group of another. A strand of alternate sugar groups and phosphate groups is formed. The bases attached to the sugar groups stick out from the strand (see Figure 18.5B).

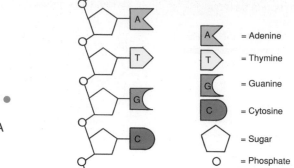

Figure 18.5B ●
Part of a
strand of DNA

A = Adenine
T = Thymine
G = Guanine
C = Cytosine
= Sugar
= Phosphate

A DNA molecule consists of two such strands bonded together. The bases sticking out from one sugar–phosphate strand bond to bases sticking out from a second sugar–phosphate strand. In Figure 18.5C you will notice that C bonds to G and A bonds to T. This is always the case in DNA. (Remember, in RNA, the base uracil is present instead of thymine.)

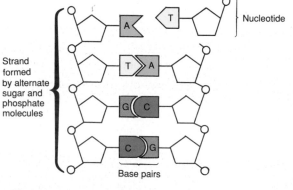

Nucleotide

Figure 18.5C ● Part of a molecule of DNA. Notice how two sugar–phosphate strands are joined along their lengths as their bases combine

Strand formed by alternate sugar and phosphate molecules

Base pairs

Who's behind the science

Erwin Chargaff, a biochemist, discovered that the amounts of adenine (A) and thymine (T) in DNA are equal and the amounts of guanine (G) and cytosine (C) are equal. This led to the idea of the one-to-one pairings of adenine–thymine and cytosine–guanine. Chargaff's rule, as it came to be known, helped Francis Crick and James Watson to construct their model of DNA.

As two strands of sugar–phosphate groups combine to form a molecule of DNA, the result resembles a ladder: the sugar–phosphate strands form the sides and base pairs form the rungs. The 'ladder' is in fact twisted into a spiral shape (see Figure 18.5D) so perhaps a spiral staircase is a better comparison. The shape is called a **double helix** – two intertwined spiral strands.

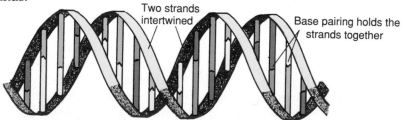

Two strands intertwined

Base pairing holds the strands together

Figure 18.5D ● The double helix: two connected spiral strands

CHECKPOINT

❶ (a) Name three types of group present in a nucleotide.
  (b) Which sugar gives DNA its name?
  (c) Briefly explain why DNA got the name 'the double helix'.
  (d) The letters ATCG stand for bases. Name the four bases.
  (e) Briefly explain the meaning of 'base pairs'.

The DNA story

The Nobel Prize awards were founded in 1901 in the will of Alfred Nobel, the Swedish chemist who invented dynamite. Nobel stated that the prizes should be awarded to those 'who have conferred the greatest benefit on mankind'.

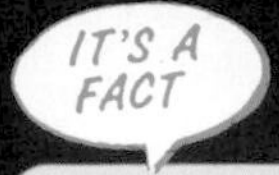

Scientists recognised the vital importance of DNA in cells, and were therefore keen to discover its structure. Many scientists worked on the problem, using different techniques. Success came in 1953 when James Watson and Francis Crick combined all the evidence from the different research workers. They succeeded in building a model of DNA which fitted all the facts. This model was the double helix (see Figure 18.5D). So excited were Watson and Crick that they dashed out of the Cavendish Laboratory of Cambridge University, England, and ran along the street, looking for people to tell about their discovery.

The technique of X-ray crystallography was of prime importance. It involves passing a beam of X-rays through a crystal onto a photographic plate. X-rays affect photographic plates, and a pattern can be seen when the plate is developed. The pattern depends on the arrangement of the atoms in the crystal.

Rosalind Franklin of King's College, London, together with Maurice Wilkins, obtained the X-ray crystallography pictures that gave Watson and Crick the vital clues they needed to build the DNA model. Her work was essential to the discovery. She died in 1958. Whether, if she had lived longer, she would have shared the Nobel Prize that Watson, Crick and Wilkins later won, we cannot say.

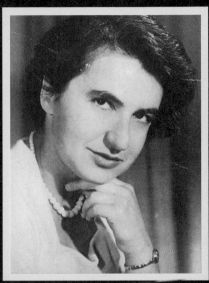

Figure 18.5F ● Rosalind Franklin

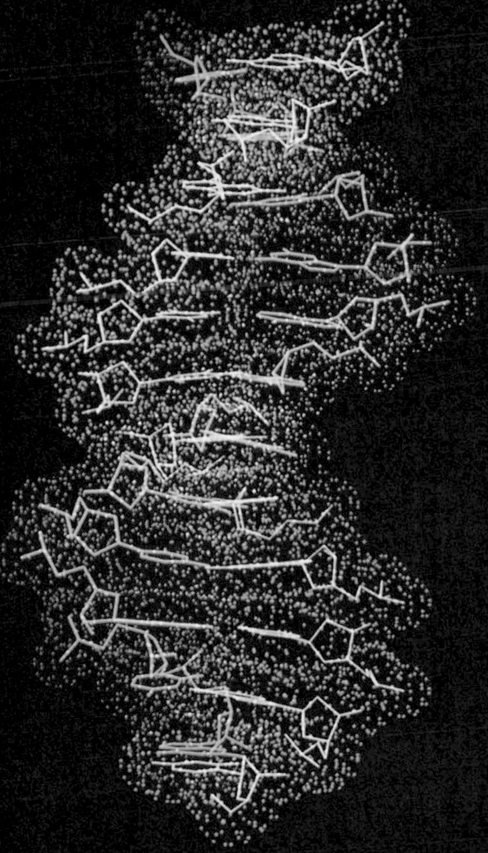

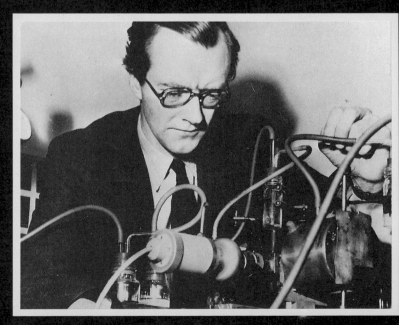

Figure 18.5E ● A computer graphics image of the DNA double helix looking from the side

Figure 18.5G ● Maurice Wilkins with X-ray equipment similar to that used by his co-worker, Rosalind Franklin

Figure 18.5H ● James Watson, an American biologist (left) and Francis Crick, a British physicist turned biologist (right) with their model of DNA at the Cavendish Laboratory, Cambridge. You can see the spiral pattern of the double helix. Notice the model sugar ring at Watson's left shoulder.

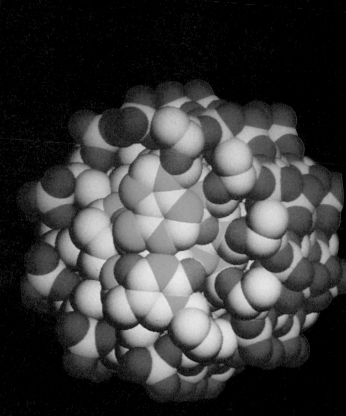

Figure 18.5H ● A space-filling computer graphics image of DNA showing an end-on view of its double helix structure

Figure 18.5J ● Six of the 1962 Nobel Prize winners on the eve of the award ceremony. From left to right: Maurice Wilkins, John Steinbeck (winner of the literature prize), John Kendrew, Max Perutz, Francis Crick and James Watson

Francis Crick, James Watson and Maurice Wilkins received the Nobel Prize from the King of Sweden for finding the structure of DNA in 1962. Also receiving prizes that year were Max Perutz for finding the structure of haemoglobin and John Kendrew for his work on the structure of myoglobin (the first protein to have its three dimensional structure worked out).

SUMMARY

The famous double helix, the structure of DNA, was worked out by James Watson and Francis Crick on the basis of the X-ray crystallography of DNA by Rosalind Franklin.

TOPIC 19 — CELL BIOLOGY

19.1 — Seeing cells

FIRST THOUGHTS

Cells were first seen in 1665 when the British scientist Robert Hooke looked at cork under his microscope. His discovery is one example of the way in which an advance in technology – in this case the microscope – leads to scientific discoveries. Modern microscopes reveal the structure of cells in great detail.

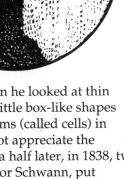

Figure 19.1A ● Robert Hooke's drawing of the outline of cork cells (from *Micrographia*, 1665)

Figure 19.1A shows what Robert Hooke saw when he looked at thin strips of cork with his microscope. He called the little box-like shapes **cells** because they reminded him of the small rooms (called cells) in which monks live. The scientists of the day did not appreciate the importance of Hooke's discovery. A century and a half later, in 1838, two German biologists, Mathias Schleiden and Theodor Schwann, put forward a **cell theory of life**. Their theory has been altered slightly in the light of later discoveries. Modern cell theory states:

- All living things are made of cells.
- New cells are formed when old cells divide into two.
- All cells are similar in structure and function (the way they work), but not identical.
- The structure of an organism depends on the way in which the cells are organised.
- The functions of an organism (the way it works) depend on the functions of its cells.

The more we know about the structure and function of cells, the better we shall be able to understand how a whole organism functions.

Microscopes

Most cells are too small to be seen with the naked eye. Without microscopes, we should know very little about them. Figure 19.1B shows a modern light microscope. A lamp lights the specimen, which the observer views through two **magnifying lenses**. The total magnification is given by

$$\text{Total magnification} = \text{Magnifying power of specimen} \times \text{Magnifying power of eyepiece} \times \text{Magnifying power of objective lens}$$

The best light microscopes can magnify structures up to 1500 times their original size (×1500). At this high magnification, the image becomes less clear because the lenses cannot distinguish between small structures lying close together. This limit of magnification is called the resolving power of the microscope. A microscope which uses a beam of electrons instead of a beam of light has a greater resolving power. Such a microscope is called a **transmission electron microscope** (see Figure

LOOK AT LINKS
for **magnifying lenses**
See Theme H, Topic 32.4.

LOOK AT LINKS
for **electron microscopes**
Learn more about the effect of magnetic fields on electron beams in Theme K, Topic 44.4.

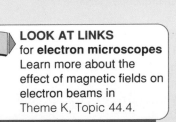

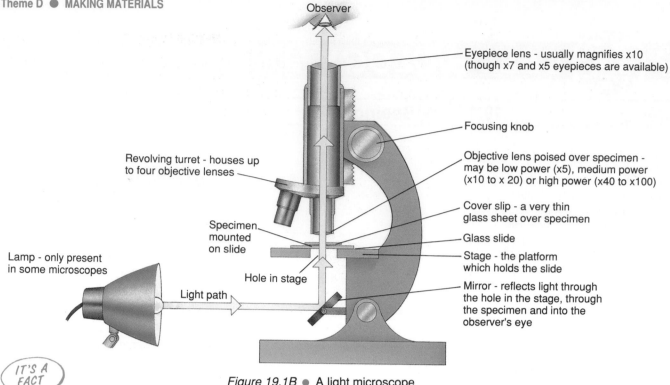

Figure 19.1B ● A light microscope

The transmission electron microscope was invented in 1930. The first commercial instrument was built in 1938. It was used to study metals. Later, biologists found to their surprise that the electron beam did not destroy biological specimens. The powerful new microscope opened up a new world. It revealed cell structures which no-one had ever seen before. The science of cell biology took off.

19.1C). It can magnify up to 500 000 times (x500 000) without loss of clarity. The transmission electron microscope enables you to see the structure of cells in great detail; that is, the **fine structure**. As we cannot see electrons, the electron beam is used to give a fluorescent image on a screen, which can be photographed.

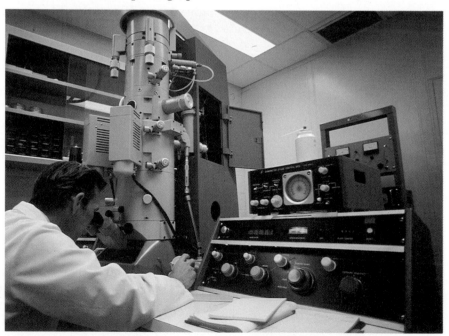

Figure 19.1C ● A transmission electron microscope (TEM)

SUMMARY

The invention of the light microscope led to the discovery of cells. The electron microscope has revealed the fascinating world inside the cell and opened up the study of cell biology.

Some of the photographs in this book give a three-dimensional view of living things, for example, Figure 19.1H on the opposite page. These photographs are taken with a **scanning electron microscope**. The beam of electrons inside a scanning electron microscope does not pass through the specimen: the beam is reflected by the surface of the specimen and therefore shows the surface in great detail.

LOOK AT LINKS
Look at Figure 3.5A. It summarises the differences between plant cells, animal cells and bacterial cells.

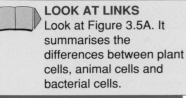

Cell structure

Plant cells, animal cells and bacterial cells are different from one another. However, they also have features in common. Figures 19.1D–I illustrate the differences and the similarities. The drawings have been made from views of cells under the transmission electron microscope.

Figure 19.1D ● A typical animal cell. Features of different cells viewed under the electron microscope have been combined to form this generalised picture.

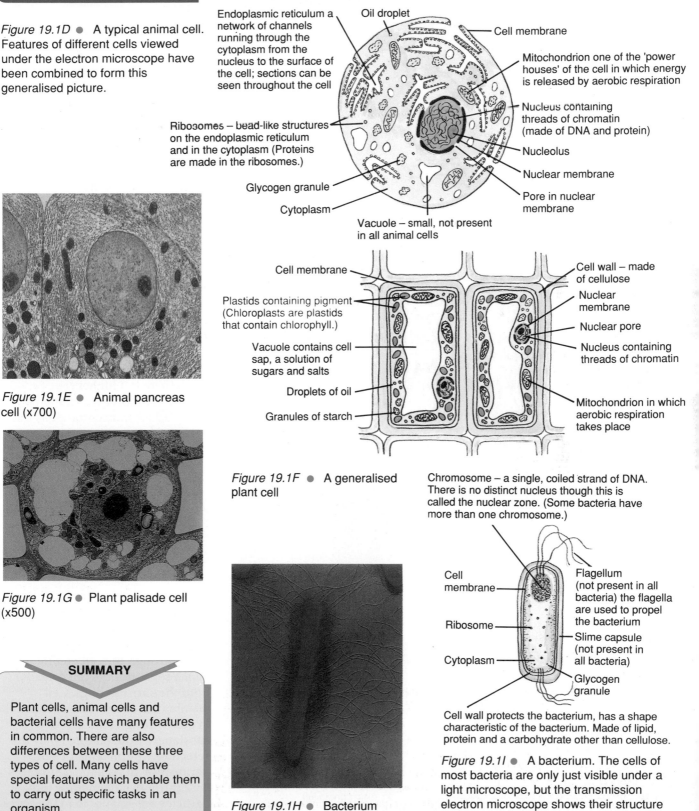

Endoplasmic reticulum a network of channels running through the cytoplasm from the nucleus to the surface of the cell; sections can be seen throughout the cell

Oil droplet

Cell membrane

Mitochondrion one of the 'power houses' of the cell in which energy is released by aerobic respiration

Ribosomes – bead-like structures on the endoplasmic reticulum and in the cytoplasm (Proteins are made in the ribosomes.)

Nucleus containing threads of chromatin (made of DNA and protein)

Nucleolus

Nuclear membrane

Pore in nuclear membrane

Glycogen granule

Cytoplasm

Vacuole – small, not present in all animal cells

Figure 19.1E ● Animal pancreas cell (x700)

Figure 19.1G ● Plant palisade cell (x500)

Cell membrane

Plastids containing pigment (Chloroplasts are plastids that contain chlorophyll.)

Vacuole contains cell sap, a solution of sugars and salts

Droplets of oil

Granules of starch

Cell wall – made of cellulose

Nuclear membrane

Nuclear pore

Nucleus containing threads of chromatin

Mitochondrion in which aerobic respiration takes place

Figure 19.1F ● A generalised plant cell

Chromosome – a single, coiled strand of DNA. There is no distinct nucleus though this is called the nuclear zone. (Some bacteria have more than one chromosome.)

Cell membrane

Ribosome

Cytoplasm

Flagellum (not present in all bacteria) the flagella are used to propel the bacterium

Slime capsule (not present in all bacteria)

Glycogen granule

Cell wall protects the bacterium, has a shape characteristic of the bacterium. Made of lipid, protein and a carbohydrate other than cellulose.

Figure 19.1I ● A bacterium. The cells of most bacteria are only just visible under a light microscope, but the transmission electron microscope shows their structure in detail.

Figure 19.1H ● Bacterium (x3000)

SUMMARY

Plant cells, animal cells and bacterial cells have many features in common. There are also differences between these three types of cell. Many cells have special features which enable them to carry out specific tasks in an organism.

❶ Compare the structures of the three types of cell in Figures 19.1E, G and I. Then copy and complete the table below. Put a tick in each space if the structure is present. Add any comments needed to distinguish between the structures. As an example chromatin has been filled in for you.

Structure in cell	Bacterium	Plant cell	Animal cell
Cell membrane			
Cell wall			
Cytoplasm			
Nucleus			
Nuclear membrane			
Chromatin	✓ one chromosome	✓ many chromosomes	✓ many chromosomes
Endoplasmic reticulum			
Mitochondria			
Ribosomes			
Chloroplast			
Vacuole			

19.2 Movement into and out of cells

Cells need a non-stop supply of water and the substances dissolved in it to stay alive. This is why there is constant movement of solutions inside cells and also into and out of cells. After reading this section you will be able to explain what is happening to the plant in Figure 19.2A.

Diffusion

Diffusion is the movement of a substance through a solution or through a gas. In a solution, diffusion happens when there is a higher concentration of a substance in one part of the solution than in another. Then the substance diffuses. It spreads out until the concentration is the same throughout the solution. Diffusion is very important in the solutions inside cells.

Figure 19.2A ● (a) A plant wilting through lack of water
(b) The same plant recovering after watering

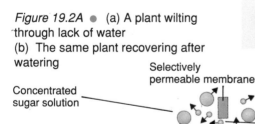

Concentrated sugar solution

Selectively permeable membrane

Dilute sugar solution

Pore in membrane

Sugar molecule

Water molecule

There are fewer water molecules on this side of the membrane and therefore fewer water molecules pass from left to right

There are more water molecules on this side of the membrane, therefore more water molecules pass from right to left

Figure 19.2B ● Osmosis

Osmosis

Movement of substances take place through the cell membrane which separates the cell contents from the surroundings. Cell membranes allow some substances to pass through and stop other substances from passing: they are **selectively permeable** or **semipermeable**. In general, substances pass through a membrane if their particles are smaller than the pores in the membrane.

When two solutions are separated by a selectively permeable membrane, water passes through the membrane in both directions. The net flow of water is from the more dilute solution to the more concentrated solution. The flow continues until the two concentrations are equal. The flow of water from a more dilute solution to a more concentrated solution is called **osmosis**.

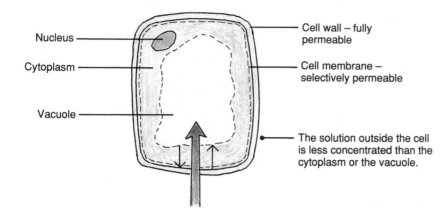

Nucleus

Cytoplasm

Vacuole

Cell wall – fully permeable

Cell membrane – selectively permeable

The solution outside the cell is less concentrated than the cytoplasm or the vacuole.

Water flows through the cell wall and cell membrane into the cytoplasm and into the vacuole. The increased pressure of water in the vacuole presses the cytoplasm against the cell wall. When the cell contains as much water as it can hold, the cell is fully **turgid**

Figure 19.2C ● A turgid cell

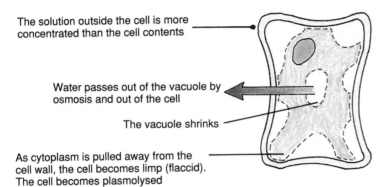

The solution outside the cell is more concentrated than the cell contents

Water passes out of the vacuole by osmosis and out of the cell

The vacuole shrinks

As cytoplasm is pulled away from the cell wall, the cell becomes limp (flaccid). The cell becomes plasmolysed

Figure 19.2D ● A plasmolysed cell

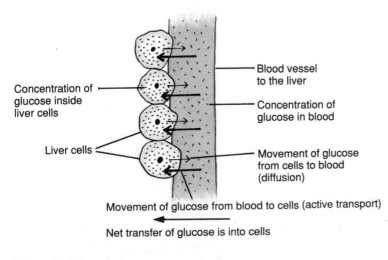

Concentration of glucose inside liver cells

Liver cells

Blood vessel to the liver

Concentration of glucose in blood

Movement of glucose from cells to blood (diffusion)

Movement of glucose from blood to cells (active transport)

Net transfer of glucose is into cells

Figure 19.2E ● Active transport

● Turgor and plasmolysis

Osmosis takes place between the cytoplasm and the solution outside the cell. The changes happening inside the cells due to osmosis bring about visible changes in the plant. When a plant cell is placed in a less concentrated solution, water passes through the cell wall and membrane, through the cytoplasm and into the vacuole. The cell becomes **turgid**. (see Figure 19.2C).

Sometimes plant cells may be placed in a more concentrated solution, although this does not often happen in nature. Then water passes out of the vacuole, out of the cytoplasm, out through the cell membrane and cell wall into the solution outside the cell. The pressure of the vacuole on the cytoplasm decreases until the cytoplasm pulls away from the cell wall. The cell becomes limp, rather like a partly blown-up balloon. Cells in this condition are described as **plasmolysed** (see Figure 19.2D).

Active transport

Sometimes substances move across the cell membrane from a region where they are present in low concentration to a region where they are present in high concentration. That is, they move in the reverse direction to normal diffusion. Such movement is called **active transport**. By this means, cells may build up stores of substances which would otherwise be spread out by diffusion (see Figure 19.2E). Active transport requires more energy than normal diffusion.

❶ Refer to Figure 19.2A. Explain fully, with the aid of a diagram, what has happened in the plant cells to produce the change from photograph (a) to photograph (b).

❷ The following three conversations take place in a kitchen. Give scientific explanations for all three observations.
  (a) *Michael*   Why are you putting that celery in a jug of water?
      Kate   It will keep crisper in water.
  (b) *Jonathan*   I've sprinkled sugar on my strawberries and it's gone all pink.
      Beth   That's because it makes the juice come out.
  (c) *Jasper*   I cut some chips earlier and put them in salt water to keep.
      Miranda   They seem to have shrunk!

❸ (a) Explain what is meant by a semi-permeable or selectively permeable membrane.
  (b) The figure opposite shows a bag made from visking tubing (a semi-permeable membrane) filled with a 15% salt solution (15 g of salt per 100 g of water). Draw sketches to show the changes that will happen if the beaker contains (i) distilled water (ii) 7% salt solution (iii) 15% salt solution (iv) 30% salt solution.

❹ Peas are sometimes preserved by drying them.
  (a) How much water do dried peas take up when they are soaked in water? Plan an experiment to find out. You should plan a quantitative experiment – that is to measure the exact quantity (e.g. mass) of water absorbed by a known mass of dried peas.
  (b) What makes the cells of a pea absorb water when the pea is placed in water? Describe what happens inside the cells. Use scientific words to describe the difference between the cells in the dried pea and the cells in the soaked pea.
  (c) Water does not flow into a dried pea indefinitely. What makes the flow of water stop?

❺ Explain the difference between osmosis and active transport. Give one example of the importance of active transport.

Glass tube

Level of salt solution

Visking tubing tied at the bottom to form a bag, filled with 15% salt solution, and tied tightly at the top around the glass tube

Beaker

IT'S A FACT

More than 30% of the energy released by cellular respiration is used in the active transport of substances into cells.

19.3 The nucleus

An imaginary journey

Figure 19.3A ● Journey into the nucleus

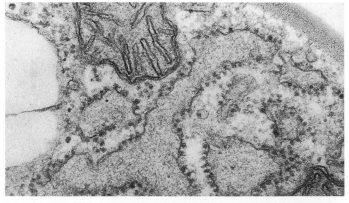

(a) The rope-like endoplasmic reticulum extends throughout the cell. Note the clusters of ribosomes (0.02 µm wide) and the mitochondrion at the top of the photo (10 µm long, 1 µm across).

(b) The nucleus lies ahead surrounded by the nuclear membrane. The pits are nuclear pores (0.005 µm across).

Imagine you are shrinking! You become smaller and smaller until you can pass through one of the pores in the cell membrane. Once inside the cytoplasm, you set off in search of the nucleus. You know that the endoplasmic reticulum connects the cell membrane to the nucleus so you follow it through the cytoplasm (see Figure 19.3A(a)). Your journey takes you past sausage-shaped mitochondria and globular ribosomes, until you come up against a wall. It is the nuclear membrane, pitted with holes (see Figure 19.3A (b)). Hoping that these are nuclear pores, you plunge through one of them. You are inside the nucleus! It looks like an explosion in a spaghetti factory. Everywhere you can see coiled strands of the nucleic acids, DNA and RNA. These are the molecules that control the activities of the whole cell.

Making proteins

LOOK AT LINKS
for **proteins**
See Theme D, Topic 18.4.

A vital activity which takes place in cells is the manufacture of **proteins**. To make one molecule of a certain protein, hundreds or thousands of amino acid molecules must combine in the right order. The substance responsible for getting the order right is **DNA**. Present in the nucleus, DNA carries instructions – called a **code** – for combining amino acids in the right order.

DNA contains the bases adenine, thymine, guanine and cytosine (A, T, G and C). The base uracil (U) is found in RNA instead of thymine. There are about twenty amino acids. The instructions needed to assemble one amino acid in its correct place in the protein molecule are contained in a row of three bases: a **codon** (see Figure 19.3B).

LOOK AT LINKS
for **genetic code**
Genetics is the science of how characteristics are passed from one generation to the next.
See Theme N, Topic 54.

This codon can be written as AAG
The codon, AAG, codes for lysine

Figure 19.3B ● A row of three bases forms a codon

Each amino acid has a different codon, GGC codes for (gives instructions for) the amino acid glycine, and AAG codes for lysine. A length of DNA which codes for the whole of one protein is called a **gene**. This is why the DNA code is called the **genetic code**.

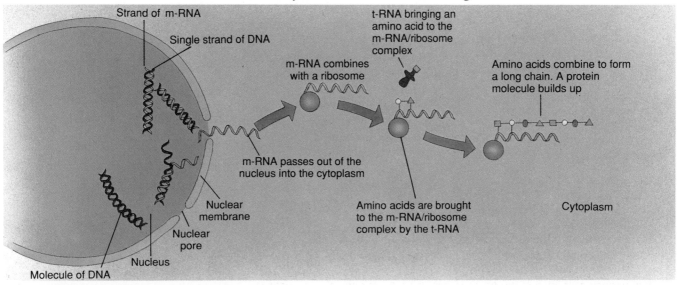

Figure 19.3C ● How DNA controls protein synthesis

DNA is present in the nucleus. Proteins are synthesised on the ribosomes in the cytoplasm. *How do the instructions for making proteins travel from DNA to the ribosomes?* DNA employs a messenger to take instructions to where they are needed. This messenger is a substance called messenger-RNA (m-RNA).

Messenger-RNA forms in the nucleus after a DNA double helix unwinds. Each single strand of DNA attracts bases, which combine to form a strand of m-RNA. Because of the way it is assembled, m-RNA is a complement of one strand of DNA. It can travel through the nuclear pores into the cytoplasm where it bonds to a ribosome. Another type of RNA is involved at this stage. Transfer-RNA (t-RNA) brings amino acids to the m-RNA–ribosome complex. The amino acids become attached to the m-RNA–ribosome complex and then combine with one another to form a long chain of amino acids: a protein molecule. The order in which amino acids combine is the result of the code on m-RNA, which is a copy of the code on one of the strands of DNA. See Figure 19.3C

The chemical reactions which take place in a cell are catalysed by enzymes, and enzymes are proteins. In controlling which proteins are made in a cell, DNA controls enzyme production and therefore the whole of the structure and all the functions of the cell.

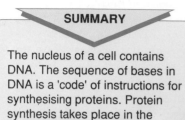

SUMMARY

The nucleus of a cell contains DNA. The sequence of bases in DNA is a 'code' of instructions for synthesising proteins. Protein synthesis takes place in the cytoplasm. DNA employs messenger-RNA to carry the code out of the nucleus to the ribosomes in the cytoplasm. Amino acids are sorted into the correct order by the messenger-RNA on the ribosomes. The amino acids combine to form a protein. By controlling protein synthesis, DNA controls the whole life of the cell.

CHECKPOINT

❶ Explain the difference between a codon and a gene.

❷ Copy the following sequence of bases.

A A T C C T G A C T A G

How many codons are contained in this section of DNA? Assume the first codon begins at the left hand end and that codons do not overlap. Mark off the codons on the sequence. Assuming that each codon codes for one amino acid, how many amino acids are represented in this section of DNA?

❸ (a) Where in the cell is protein made?
(b) Why is making new protein essential for the cell?

19.4 ◈ The dividing cell

FIRST THOUGHTS

The cells which make up living things die due to accidents and age. To survive, an organism must be able to make new cells as fast as its old cells die. To grow, an organism must be able to make new cells at an even faster rate.

LOOK AT LINKS
for **meiosis**
In meiosis each daughter cell receives only half a set of chromosomes Sex cells (eggs and sperm) are produced by meiosis. Why? See Theme J, Topic 39.

New cells are formed when old cells divide into two. The cells which divide are called **parent cells**, and the new cells are called **daughter cells**. Two overlapping processes take place:
● The nucleus divides into two. There are two ways of dividing: **mitosis** and **meiosis**. We shall deal only with mitosis in this section.
● The cytoplasm divides.

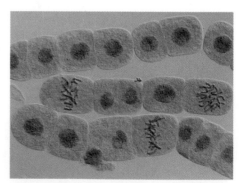

Figure 19.4A ● Cells dividing by mitosis

DNA replication

Before mitosis takes place, new DNA is made inside the nucleus. The process is called **replication** because each chromosome makes an exact copy – a replica – of itself.

Figure 19.4B ● DNA replication

(a) The double helix unwinds to form two single strands

(b) A new strand of DNA forms alongside each of the original strands of DNA. Each new strand combines with an old strand to form a new molecule of DNA. In this way, two new molecules of DNA are formed. Each is a replica of the original.

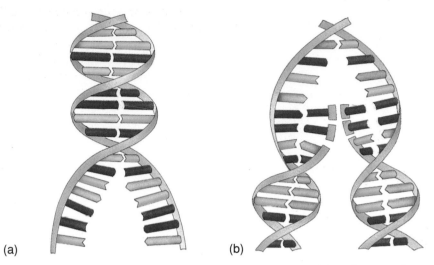

(a)   (b)

Hundreds of thousands of nucleotide bases may add each second to the growing strand of DNA. Occasionally the wrong base adds by mistake. Then the new DNA formed is slightly different from the original. This change is called a **mutation**.

IT'S A FACT

A chromosome contains about 10 000 times its own length of DNA. Two metres of DNA can coil up sufficiently tightly to cram into one cell nucleus.

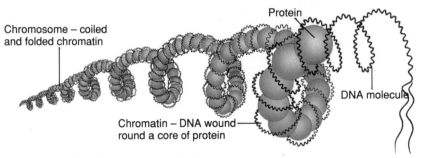

Figure 19.4C ● The structure of a chromosome

SUMMARY

The nucleus contains chromosomes. A chromosome consists of DNA wound round a core of protein and folded tightly into a compact structure. Genes are lengths of DNA molecules which code for proteins.

Chromosomes consist of folded strands of DNA coiled round a protein core (see Figure 19.4C). The DNA part of the structure controls the **inheritance** of characteristics.

The stages in mitosis

Before mitosis takes place, new DNA is made in the nucleus. Each chromosome then divides into a pair of identical **chromatids** (see Figure 19.4D). The first sign of cell division by mitosis is when the chromosomes can be seen more easily under the microscope. This happens because chromatin coils up to form shorter and thicker chromosomes.

Figure 19.4D ● Chromosomes

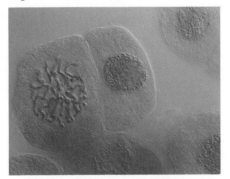

(a) Chromosomes become visible in the nucleus as chromatin coils up

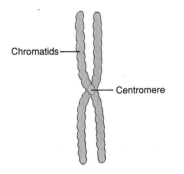

(b) A chromosome: a pair of chromatids joined at a point called the centromere

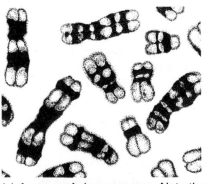

(c) A group of chromosomes. Note the differing positions of the centromeres

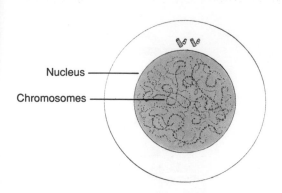

Nucleus

Chromosomes

Parent cell

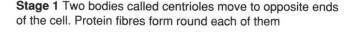

Protein fibres

Centrioles

Stage 1 Two bodies called centrioles move to opposite ends of the cell. Protein fibres form round each of them

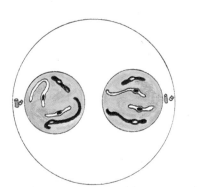

Stage 2 The protein fibres arrange themselves between the centrioles into a structure called the spindle. The nuclear membrane has disappeared. Pairs of chromatids arrange themselves on the equator of the spindle.
NOTE: the spindle of a plant cell forms without the help of centrioles.

Stage 3 The centromeres divide into two. The new centromeres separate and move along the spindle, one to each end of the cell. They carry their chromatids with them.

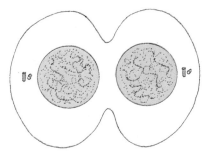

Stage 4 The chromatids are now the new chromosomes. They gather into two bunches. A nuclear membrane forms around each bunch.

Stage 5 Two daughter cells have been formed. Each has the same number of chromosomes as the parent cell.

Figure 19.4E ● The stages of mitosis. (Only four chromosomes are shown in detail.)

● *Division of the cytoplasm*

Let us look in more detail at Stage 4 of Figure 19.4E. Once the new nuclei have formed, the cytoplasm begins to divide. Mitochondria and chloroplasts divide. Other cell structures are built up from materials in the cytoplasm. The new structures are distributed more or less equally between the two daughter cells.

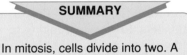

Division of the cytoplasm happens differently in animal cells and plant cells (see Figures 19.4F and G).

IT'S A FACT

When cells are grown on dishes in a solution of all the substances they need to live, the cells divide. They spread out until they form a complete layer over the bottom of the dish. At this point, the cells are touching neighbouring cells and, in the case of normal cells, cell division stops. This is called contact inhibition (stopping by touching). Cancer cells are different. They continue to divide even after they are all touching. In the body, masses of cancer cells are called tumours. By multiplying faster than normal cells, cancer cells destroy healthy tissue. Many cancers can be cured if they are detected early, but left untreated cancer can endanger a person's life.

Figure 19.4F ● The start of division of cytoplasm in an animal cell (in this case a frog's egg). A furrow develops. It pinches the cell membrane in. As the furrow deepens, the parent cell divides into two daughter cells

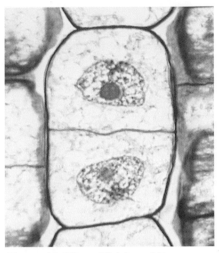

Figure 19.4G ● Division of the cytoplasm in a plant cell. A thin, slab-like structure called the cell plate develops across the middle of the spindle. As it extends outwards, the cell plate meets the sides of the cell dividing the cytoplasm into two daughter cells.

SUMMARY

In mitosis, cells divide into two. A full set of chromosomes is passed to each daughter cell. The chromosomes in each daughter cell are identical to those of the parent cell.

● *The importance of mitosis*

Mitosis divides the chromosomes of the parent cell into two identical groups. Daughter cells are therefore genetically the same as the parent cell and one another.

Why do you think that keeping the genes constant from generation to generation is so important? (Hint: Remember that mitosis is the method by which living things repair damage and also grow. For example, old skin cells are always replaced by new skin cells. As roots grow through the soil, root tip cells divide by mitosis to form new root tissue.)

CHECKPOINT

❶ (a) Why do the cells of a tissue need to undergo mitosis?
   (b) What effect does mitosis have on the chromosomes of the parent cell?
   (c) What is the relationship between the chromosomes of the parent cell and the chromosomes of the daughter cells?
   (d) What is the importance of this relationship for the health of the tissue?

❷ (a) In everyday language, what is a 'replica'?
   (b) What is formed by the replication of DNA?
   (c) Refer to Figure 19.4B, which shows the replication of DNA. Explain briefly what is happening.

❸ Refer to Figure 19.4C. Explain the relationship between
   (a) DNA and chromatin,
   (b) chromatin and a chromosome.

❹ Refer to Figure 19.4D. Explain the relationship between
   (a) a chromosome and a chromatid,
   (b) a chromatid and a centromere.

19.5 ◇ Cells, tissues and organs

All cells have certain features in common (see Topic 19.1). This section deals with the differences in shape and structure between different types of cell.

Do you remember that some cells exist as independent organisms? You can see that the organisms in Figures 3.5C and 3.5D are made of single cells. Other cells cannot survive on their own; they exist as members of multicellular organisms. The bodies of multicellular organisms are made of different types of cell. Each type of cell is specialised to perform a particular biological task.

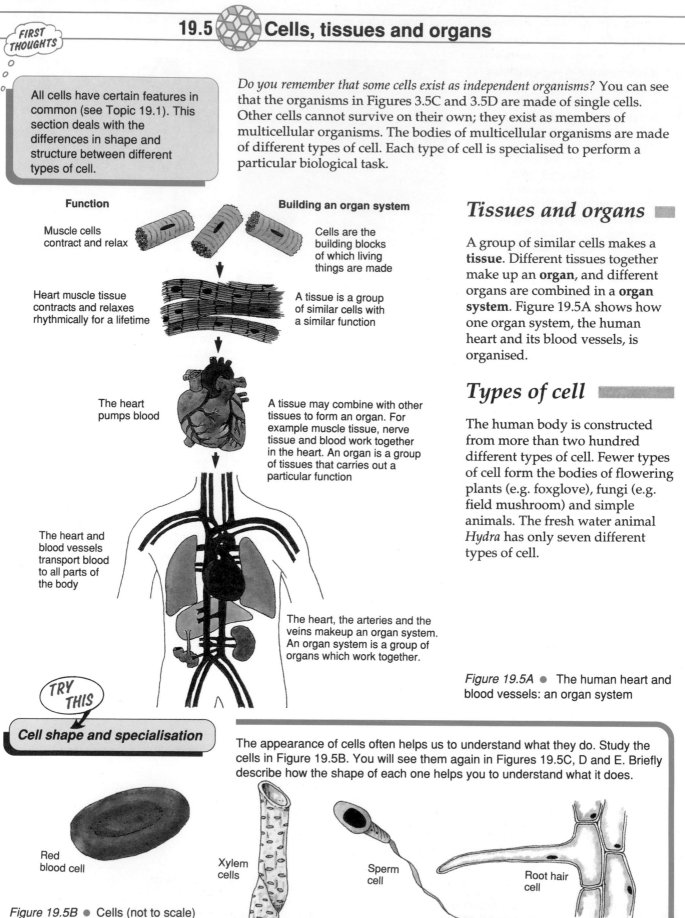

Function

Muscle cells contract and relax

Heart muscle tissue contracts and relaxes rhythmically for a lifetime

The heart pumps blood

The heart and blood vessels transport blood to all parts of the body

Building an organ system

Cells are the building blocks of which living things are made

A tissue is a group of similar cells with a similar function

A tissue may combine with other tissues to form an organ. For example muscle tissue, nerve tissue and blood work together in the heart. An organ is a group of tissues that carries out a particular function

The heart, the arteries and the veins makeup an organ system. An organ system is a group of organs which work together.

Tissues and organs

A group of similar cells makes a **tissue**. Different tissues together make up an **organ**, and different organs are combined in a **organ system**. Figure 19.5A shows how one organ system, the human heart and its blood vessels, is organised.

Types of cell

The human body is constructed from more than two hundred different types of cell. Fewer types of cell form the bodies of flowering plants (e.g. foxglove), fungi (e.g. field mushroom) and simple animals. The fresh water animal *Hydra* has only seven different types of cell.

Figure 19.5A ● The human heart and blood vessels: an organ system

TRY THIS

Cell shape and specialisation

The appearance of cells often helps us to understand what they do. Study the cells in Figure 19.5B. You will see them again in Figures 19.5C, D and E. Briefly describe how the shape of each one helps you to understand what it does.

Red blood cell

Xylem cells

Sperm cell

Root hair cell

Figure 19.5B ● Cells (not to scale)

Figures 19.5C, D and E show cell types from different kingdoms. Notice the features that all the cells have in common, such as cytoplasm, cell membranes and nuclei. Notice also how specialisation for particular biological tasks makes each type of cell different.

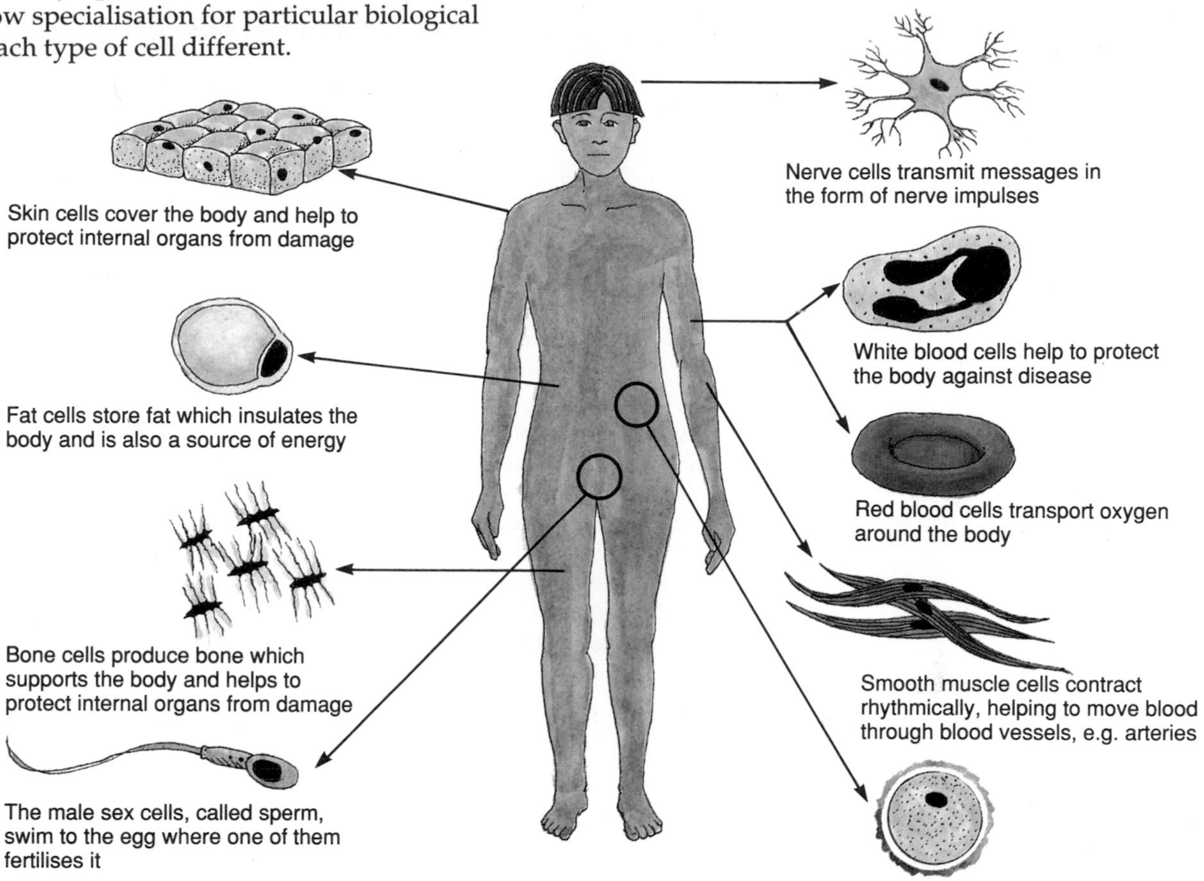

Skin cells cover the body and help to protect internal organs from damage

Fat cells store fat which insulates the body and is also a source of energy

Bone cells produce bone which supports the body and helps to protect internal organs from damage

The male sex cells, called sperm, swim to the egg where one of them fertilises it

Nerve cells transmit messages in the form of nerve impulses

White blood cells help to protect the body against disease

Red blood cells transport oxygen around the body

Smooth muscle cells contract rhythmically, helping to move blood through blood vessels, e.g. arteries

The female sex organ, called the ovum (egg) is fertilised when a sperm fuses with it

Figure 19.5C ● Animal kingdom – human

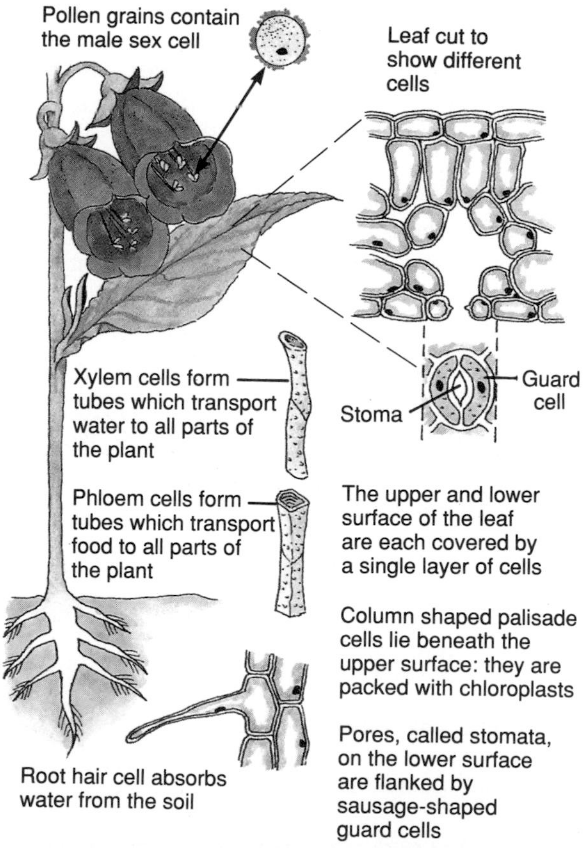

Pollen grains contain the male sex cell

Leaf cut to show different cells

Xylem cells form tubes which transport water to all parts of the plant

Phloem cells form tubes which transport food to all parts of the plant

Guard cell

Stoma

The upper and lower surface of the leaf are each covered by a single layer of cells

Column shaped palisade cells lie beneath the upper surface: they are packed with chloroplasts

Pores, called stomata, on the lower surface are flanked by sausage-shaped guard cells

Root hair cell absorbs water from the soil

Figure 19.5D ● Plant kingdom – foxglove

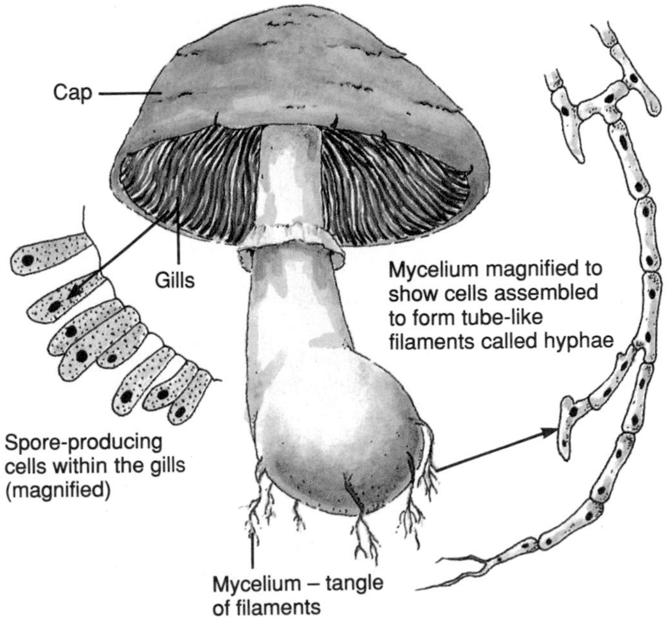

Cap

Gills

Spore-producing cells within the gills (magnified)

Mycelium magnified to show cells assembled to form tube-like filaments called hyphae

Mycelium – tangle of filaments

Figure 19.5E ● Kingdom Fungi – field mushroom

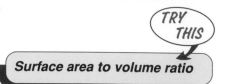

TRY THIS

Surface area to volume ratio

Cell size

Figure 19.5F shows three cubes of different sizes. A cube has six faces.

A
1 cm

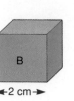

B
◄2 cm►

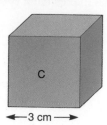

C
◄— 3 cm —►

Figure 19.5F ●

Copy and complete the table

	Cube A	Cube B	Cube C
Surface area of one face	1 cm x 1 cm = 1 cm²		
Surface area of cube	6 x 1 cm² = 6 cm²		
Volume of cube	1 cm x 1 cm x 1 cm = 1 cm³		
Ratio: surface area/ volume	6 cm²/1 cm³ = 6/cm		

Say whether the surface area/volume ratio of a cube increases or decreases as the cube increases in size.

Amoeba

Bacterium

Human cheek cell

Red blood cell

0.03 mm

Figure 19.5G ● A range of cells drawn to scale

Cells are not cube-shaped, but your calculations on cubes apply to any shape of cell. What you have found out is that when a cell grows the surface area of the cell membrane increases more slowly than the volume of the cell (because surface area increases with the square of the side, and volume increases with the cube of the side). As the cell grows, it needs to take in more food and gases. But the area of the cell membrane is not increasing at the same rate as the volume. After the cell reaches a certain size, the surface area becomes insufficient to meet the needs of the larger volume. At this point, the cell either dies or divides into daughter cells.

Cell size depends on the rate at which it uses materials. Cells with a fast turnover of materials are usually smaller than cells with a low turnover.

Figure 19.5G gives an idea of the range of size of cells. Comparing the different sizes is rather like comparing the difference in size between a mouse and a whale. The range is enormous! However, the size of most cells falls somewhere in between: invisible to the naked eye but easily seen under a light microscope.

CHECKPOINT

❶ Copy and complete the following paragraph. You may use the words in the list, once, more than once or not at all.

(a)   an organ   organs   cells   types   tissues

Living things are made of _____. Groups of similar _____ with similar functions form _____ that can work together as _____. A group of _____ working together form _____ system.

❷ (a) What effect does the division of a cell into small daughter cells have on the surface area/volume ratio?
(b) Why are cells with a high material turnover usually smaller than those with a low material turnover?

? THEME QUESTIONS

● **Topic 15**

1 (a) What sort of mixture can be separated by
(i) filtration, (ii) chromatography, (iii) centrifuging?
(b) A mixture contains two liquids, A and B. A boils at
75 °C, and B boils at 95 °C. Draw an apparatus you
could use to separate A and B. Label the drawing.

2 The police are investigating a case of poison pen letters.
The police chemist makes chromatograms from the ink
in the letters and the ink in the pens of three suspects.
The diagram below shows her results. What conclusion
can you reach?

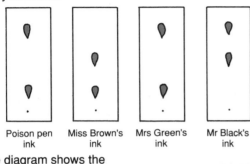

Poison pen	Miss Brown's	Mrs Green's	Mr Black's
ink	ink	ink	ink

3 The diagram shows the
structure of a fractionating
column in an oil refinery.
(a) The technique used to
separate the fractions
is called:
A   chromatography
B   distillation
C   evaporation
D   filtration

Bubble cap

Preheated
crude oil

The table gives information about the various fractions.

Fraction	Boiling point range (°C)	Number of carbon atoms in molecule
Bitumen	Above 350	More than 25
Fuel gases	Below 40	1–4
Gasoline	40–100	4–8
Heavy gas oil	300–350	20–25
Kerosene	160–250	10–16
Light gas oil	250–300	16–20
Naphtha	80–180	5–12

(b) (i) Which fraction will collect at the top of the
column and why?
(ii) Which fraction will collect at the bottom of the
column?
(c) Petrol consists mainly of compounds containing
eight carbon atoms. About 10% of petrol comes
directly from the fractions containing these
compounds. The remainder of the petrol is obtained
by cracking.
(i) Which **two** fractions in the table could be used
directly for petrol?
(ii) What is cracking and how is it done?   (LEAG)

● **Topic 16**

4 The indicator phenolphthalein is colourless in neutral
and acidic solutions and turns pink in alkaline solutions.
Of the solutions A, B and C, one is acidic, one is
alkaline, and one is neutral. Explain how, using only
phenolphthalein, you can find out which solution is
which.

5 Seven steel bars were placed in solutions of different pH
for the same time. The table shows the percentage
corrosion of the steel bars.

pH of solution	1	2	3	4	5	6	7
Percentage corrosion of steel bar	65	60	55	50	20	15	10

(a) On graph paper, plot the percentage corrosion
against the pH of the solution.
(b) Read from your graph the percentage corrosion at
pH 4.5.

6 Look at the information from the label of a bottle of
concentrated orange squash.

Concentrated orange squash
Ingredients: Sugar, Water, Citric acid,
Flavourings, Preservative E250, Artificial sweetener,
Yellow colourings E102 and E103

(a) Explain what is meant by 'concentrated'.
(b) A sample of concentrated orange squash is mixed
with water. A piece of universal indicator paper is
dipped in. What colour will the paper turn?
(c) Why does using universal indicator paper give a
better result than adding universal indicator solution
to the orange squash?
(d) Describe a simple experiment you could do to
prove that **only two** yellow substances are present
in the concentrated orange squash.

● **Topic 17**

7 Zinc sulphate crystals, $ZnSO_4.7H_2O$, can be made from
zinc and dilute sulphuric acid by the following method.
Step 1   Add an excess of zinc to dilute sulphuric acid.
Warm.
Step 2   Filter.
Step 3   Partly evaporate the solution from Step 2.
Leave it to stand.
(a) Explain why an excess of zinc is used in Step 1.
(b) How can you tell when Step 1 is complete?
(c) Name the residue and the filtrate in Step 2.
(d) Explain why the solution is partly evaporated in
Step 3.
(e) Would you dry the crystals by strong heating or by
gentle heating? Explain your answer.
(f) Write a word equation for the reaction. Write a
symbol equation.

8 What method would you use to make the insoluble salt lead(II) carbonate? Explain why you have chosen this method. Say what starting materials you would need, and say what you would do to obtain solid lead(II) carbonate. (For solubility information, see Theme D, Table 17.7.)

9 Explain the following:
(a) Tea changes colour when lemon juice is added.
(b) Sodium sulphate solution is used as an antidote to poisoning by barium compounds.
(c) Washing soda takes some of the pain out of bee-stings.
(d) Toothpastes containing aluminium hydroxide fight tooth decay.
(e) Calcium fluoride is added to some toothpastes.
(f) Scouring powders often contain sodium hydroxide and powdered stone.

10 A student receives the following instructions: 'Make a solution of copper sulphate by neutralising dilute sulphuric acid, using the base copper oxide.'
(a) Explain the meanings of the terms:
solution, neutralising, dilute, base.
(b) Draw an apparatus which the student could use for carrying out the instructions.
(c) Describe exactly how the student should carry out the instructions.

● *Topic 18*

11 Graph 1 shows how temperature affects an enzyme-controlled reaction.

Graph 1

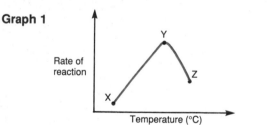

(a) Explain what is happening (i) between **X** and **Y** (ii) between **Y** and **Z**.
(b) At what temperature would you expect the reaction to be most rapid?
(c) Suggest how high temperature might affect the active site of the enzyme.
Graph 2 shows how pH affects the rate of two different enzyme-controlled reactions.

Graph 2

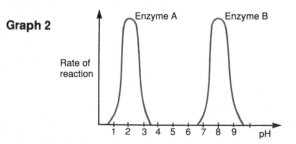

(d) Which enzyme is likely to be most active in (i) the stomach (ii) the duodenum?
(e) What does the graph tell you about the range of pH over which these enzymes are active.

12 Match the chemicals in Column A with their correct chemical composition in Column B and function in Column C.

Column A	Column B	Column C
Lipids	CHONP	Growth and repair of cells
Nucleic acids	CHO	Solvent
Carbohydrates	HO	Store of energy
Water	CHONSP	Material of heredity
Proteins	CHO	Main source of energy

13 Match the chemicals in Column A with their functions in Column B.

Column A	Column B
Chitin	Pairs with cytosine
Cellulose	Makes up the cell membrane
Glycerol	Carries genetic information
Phospholipid	Same formula as glucose
DNA	Involved in protein synthesis
Fructose	Protein present in hair
Keratin	Present in insect exoskeletons
Guanine	Forms a triglyceride with 3 fatty acids
RNA	Makes up plant cell walls

● *Topic 19*

14 Match each of the biological terms in Column A with the descriptions in Column B.

Column A	Column B
Ribosome	Contains genetic material
Cell wall	Contains cell sap
Vacuole	Site of aerobic respiration
Mitochondrion	A food reserve in animal cells
Nucleus	Site of photosynthesis
Starch grain	Site of protein synthesis
Cell membrane	Made of cellulose
Chloroplast	A food reserve in plant cells
Endoplasmic reticulum	Controls the passage of substances into and out of the cell
Glycogen	Network of channels running through the cytoplasm

15

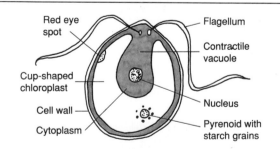

(a) Look carefully at the diagram and try to decide which kingdom it belongs to. Give reasons for your choice.
(b) Which of the structures contains the genetic information?
(c) (i) This organism lives in freshwater. Explain why it constantly has to get rid of excess water from the cell.
(ii) Which structure enables it to do this?
(iii) What would happen to this cell if it were placed in sea water?

Air and Water

A modern industrial society makes plenty of goods to keep us free from squalor and starvation. Plenty has led to pollution. The air is polluted by objectionable gases, dust and smoke from our cars and factories. Rivers and lakes are polluted by waste from our factories, fields and our own bodies. The land is polluted by our rubbish tips. Urgent measures are needed to combat pollution. If we take the necessary steps, we can avoid disaster. We can reduce the pollutants in our atmosphere; we can make our rivers and lakes clean again; by making use of much of our rubbish, we can conserve the Earth's resources.

AIR

20.1 Oxygen the life-saver

FIRST THOUGHTS

As you study this topic, think about the vital importance of air as a source of:
- oxygen – which supports the life of plants and animals
- carbon dioxide – which supports plant life
- nitrogen – the basis of natural and synthetic fertilisers
- the noble gases – filling our light bulbs

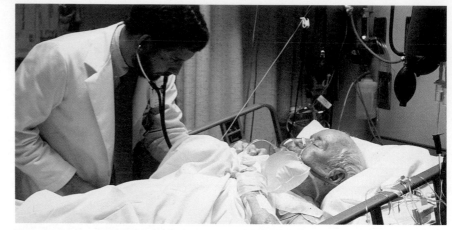

Figure 20.1A ● Oxygen in hospitals

Hospitals need oxygen for patients who have difficulty in breathing. Tiny premature babies often need oxygen. They may be put into an oxygen high pressure chamber. This chamber contains oxygen at 3–4 atmospheres pressure, which makes 15–20 times the normal concentration of oxygen dissolve in the blood. People who are recovering from heart attacks and strokes also benefit from being given oxygen. Patients who are having operations are given an anaesthetic mixed with oxygen.

In normal circumstances, we can obtain all the oxygen we need from the air. Figure 20.1B shows the percentages of oxygen, nitrogen and other gases in pure, dry air. Water vapour and pollutants may also be present in air.

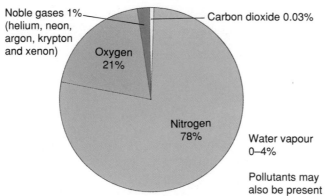

Noble gases 1% (helium, neon, argon, krypton and xenon)

Carbon dioxide 0.03%

Oxygen 21%

Nitrogen 78%

Water vapour 0–4%

Pollutants may also be present

Figure 20.1B ● Composition of clean, dry air in percentage by volume

20.2 How oxygen and nitrogen are obtained from air

The method used by industry to obtain oxygen and nitrogen from air is **fractional distillation** of liquid air. Air must be cooled to –200 °C before it liquefies. It is very difficult to get down to this temperature. However, one way of cooling a gas is to compress it and then allow it to expand suddenly. Figures 20.2A and 20.2B show how air is first liquefied and then distilled.

LOOK AT LINKS
for **fractional distillation**
See Theme D, Topic 15.8.

LOOK AT LINKS
How the industry uses the products of fractional distillation of air is discussed in Topics 20.3, 20.4 and 20.10

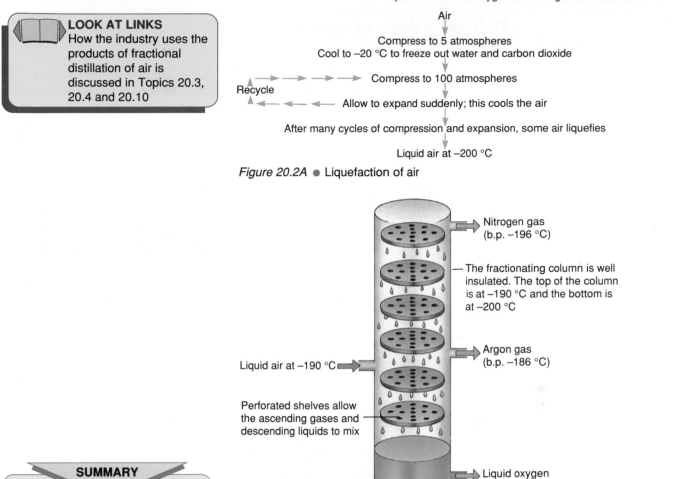

Figure 20.2A ● Liquefaction of air

Figure 20.2B ● Fractional distillation of air

SUMMARY

Air is a mixture of nitrogen, oxygen, noble gases, carbon dioxide, water vapour and pollutants. The fractional distillation of liquid air yields oxygen, nitrogen and argon.

Oxygen, nitrogen and argon are redistilled. They are stored under pressure in strong steel cylinders. Industry finds many important uses for them.

CHECKPOINT

❶ The top of the fractionating column in Figure 20.2B is at −190 °C. Explain why nitrogen is a gas at the top of the column but oxygen is a liquid.

❷ The table lists nitrogen, oxygen and the noble gases.

Gas	Boiling point (°C)
Argon	−186
Helium	−269
Krypton	−153
Neon	−246
Nitrogen	−196
Oxygen	−183
Xenon	−108

(a) Which gas has (i) the lowest boiling point and (ii) the highest boiling point?

(b) List the gases which would still be gaseous at −200 °C.

20.3 Uses of oxygen

Oxygen is a colourless, odourless gas which is slightly soluble in water. All living things need oxygen for respiration. Breathing becomes difficult at a height of 5 km above sea level, where the air pressure is only half that at sea level. Climbers who are tackling high mountains take oxygen with them. Aeroplanes which fly at high altitude carry oxygen. Astronauts must carry oxygen, and even unmanned space flights need oxygen. Deep-sea divers carry cylinders which contain a mixture of oxygen and helium.

Industry has many uses for oxygen. Figure 20.3B shows an oxy-acetylene torch being used to weld metal at a temperature of about 4000 °C. The hot flame is produced by burning the gas ethyne (formerly called acetylene) in oxygen. Substances burn faster in pure oxygen than in air.

The steel industry converts brittle cast **iron** into strong **steel**. Cast iron is brittle because it contains impurities such as carbon, sulphur and phosphorus. These impurities will burn off in a stream of oxygen. Steel plants use one tonne of oxygen for every tonne of cast iron turned into steel. Many steel plants make their own oxygen on site.

The proper treatment of sewage is important for public health. Air is used to help in the decomposition of sewage. Without this treatment, sewage would pollute many rivers and lakes. One method of treating polluted lakes and rivers to make them fit for plants and animals to live in is to pump in oxygen.

IT'S A FACT

The introduction of the oxy-acetylene flame brought about a revolution in metal working. Industry moved out of the blacksmith era into the twentieth century with gas-welding and flame-cutting techniques.

LOOK AT LINKS
for **metals**
See Theme L, Topic 50.9.

SUMMARY

Uses for pure oxygen are:
- treating patients who have breathing difficulties
- supporting high-altitude pilots, mountaineers, deep-sea divers and space flights
- in steel making and other industries
- treating polluted water

Figure 20.3A ● Astronaut using oxygen

Figure 20.3B ● Oxyacetylene welding being used on an automated production line

CHECKPOINT

❶ Explain why oxygen is used in (a) steelworks (b) metal working (c) sewage treatment (d) space flights and (e) hospitals. Say what advantage pure oxygen has over air for each purpose.

FIRST
THOUGHTS

20.4 Nitrogen

So far, oxygen seems to be the important part of the air, but nitrogen has its uses too, as you will find out in this section.

LOOK AT LINKS
Sparks produced by static electricity can ignite powders.
See Theme K, Topic 42.1.

Figure 20.4A ● Oil tanker delivering oil to a refinery. Once it is empty, the tanks will be purged with nitrogen

SUMMARY

Nitrogen is a rather unreactive gas. It is used to provide an inert (chemically unreactive) atmosphere.

Nitrogen is a colourless, odourless gas which is slightly soluble in water. It does not readily take part in chemical reactions. Many uses of nitrogen depend on its unreactive nature. Liquid nitrogen (below −196 °C) is used when an inert (chemically unreactive) refrigerant is needed. The food industry uses it for the fast freezing of foods.

Vets use the technique of artificial insemination to enable a prize bull to fertilise a large number of dairy cows. They carry the semen of the bull in a type of vacuum flask filled with liquid nitrogen.

Many foods are packed in an atmosphere of nitrogen. This prevents the oils and fats in the foods from reacting with oxygen to form rancid products. As a precaution against fire, nitrogen is used to purge oil tankers and road tankers. The silos where grain is stored are flushed out with nitrogen because dry grain is easily ignited.

Figure 20.4B ● Grain silos

20.5 The nitrogen cycle

LOOK AT LINKS
The importance of proteins as food is described in Theme F, Topic 25.3.

Nitrogen is an essential element in **proteins**. Some plants have nodules on their roots which contain nitrogen-fixing bacteria. These bacteria **fix** gaseous nitrogen, that is, convert it into nitrogen compounds. From these nitrogen compounds, the plants can synthesise proteins. Members of the legume family, such as peas, beans and clover, have nitrogen-fixing bacteria.

Plants other than legumes synthesise proteins from nitrates. *How do nitrates get into the soil?* Nitrogen and oxygen combine in the atmosphere during lightning storms and in the engines of motor vehicles during combustion. They form nitrogen oxides (compounds of nitrogen and oxygen). These gases react with water to form nitric acid. Rain showers bring nitric acid out of the atmosphere and wash it into the ground, where it reacts with minerals to form nitrates. Plants take in these nitrates

Figure 20.5A ● Nodules containing nitrogen fixing bacteria on the roots of a legume

through their roots. They use them to synthesise proteins. Animals obtain the proteins they need by eating plants or by eating the flesh of other animals.

In the excreta of animals and the decay products of animals and plants, **ammonium salts** are present. Nitrifying bacteria in the soil convert ammonium salts into nitrates. Both nitrates and ammonium salts can be removed from the soil by **denitrifying bacteria**, which convert the compounds into nitrogen. To make the soil more fertile, farmers add both nitrates and ammonium salts as fertilisers. The balance of processes which put nitrogen into the air and processes which remove nitrogen from the air is called the **nitrogen cycle** (see Figure 20.5B).

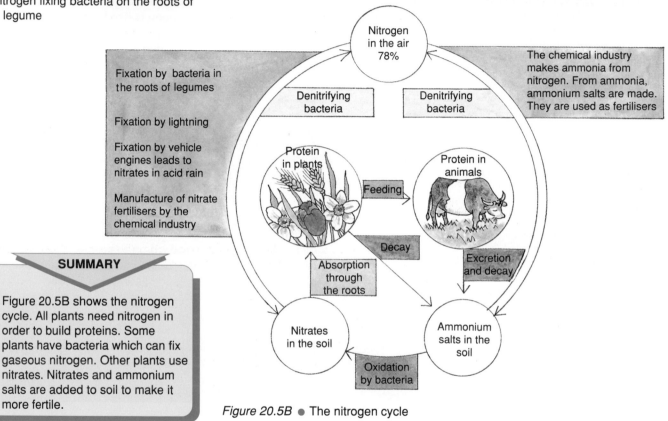

Figure 20.5B ● The nitrogen cycle

SUMMARY

Figure 20.5B shows the nitrogen cycle. All plants need nitrogen in order to build proteins. Some plants have bacteria which can fix gaseous nitrogen. Other plants use nitrates. Nitrates and ammonium salts are added to soil to make it more fertile.

CHECKPOINT

❶ *Process A* Nitrogen-fixing bacteria convert nitrogen gas into nitrates.

Process B Nitrifying bacteria use oxygen to convert ammonium compounds (from decaying plant and animal matter) into nitrates.

Process C Denitrifying bacteria turn nitrates into nitrogen.

(a) Say where *Process A* takes place.
(b) Say what effect the presence of air in the soil will have on *Process B*.
(c) Say what effect waterlogged soil which lacks air will have on *Process C*.
(d) Explain why plants grow well in well-drained, aerated soil.
(e) A farmer wants to grow a good crop of wheat without using a fertiliser. What could he plant in the field the previous year to ensure a good crop?
(f) Explain why garden manure and compost fertilise the soil.

❷ Explain why nitrogen is used in (a) food packaging (b) oil tankers (c) hospitals and (d) food storage.

20.6 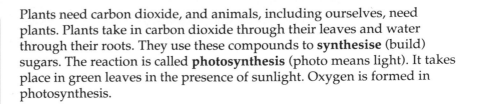 Carbon dioxide and the carbon cycle

FIRST THOUGHTS

The percentage by volume of carbon dioxide in clean, dry air is only 0.03%. Perhaps you think this makes carbon dioxide sound rather unimportant. Through studying this section, you may change your mind about the importance of carbon dioxide!

LOOK AT LINKS
For a fuller account of photosynthesis and respiration.
See Theme F, Topics 25 and 26.

LOOK AT LINKS
A reaction like photosynthesis, in which energy is taken in, is called an endothermic reaction. A reaction like respiration, in which energy is given out, is called an exothermic reaction.
See Theme L, Topic 49.1 and 49.2.

Plants need carbon dioxide, and animals, including ourselves, need plants. Plants take in carbon dioxide through their leaves and water through their roots. They use these compounds to **synthesise** (build) sugars. The reaction is called **photosynthesis** (photo means light). It takes place in green leaves in the presence of sunlight. Oxygen is formed in photosynthesis.

Photosynthesis (in plants)

catalysed by chlorophyll in green leaves

Sunlight + Carbon dioxide + Water → Glucose + Oxygen
(a sugar)

The energy of sunlight is converted into the energy of the chemical bonds in glucose.

Animals eat foods which contain starches and sugars. They inhale (breathe in) air. Inhaled air dissolves in the blood supply to the lungs. In the cells, some of the oxygen in the dissolved air oxidises sugars to carbon dioxide and water and energy is released. This process is called **respiration**. Plants also respire to obtain energy.

Respiration (in plants and animals)

Glucose + Oxygen → Carbon dioxide + Water + Energy

The processes which take carbon dioxide from the air and those which put carbon dioxide into the air are balanced so that the percentage of carbon dioxide in the air stays at 0.03%. This balance is called the **carbon cycle** (see Figure 20.6A).

SUMMARY

Figure 20.6A shows the carbon cycle. Photosynthesis is the process in which green plants use sunlight, carbon dioxide and water to make sugars and oxygen. Respiration is the process in which animals and plants oxidise carbohydrates to carbon dioxide and water with the release of energy.

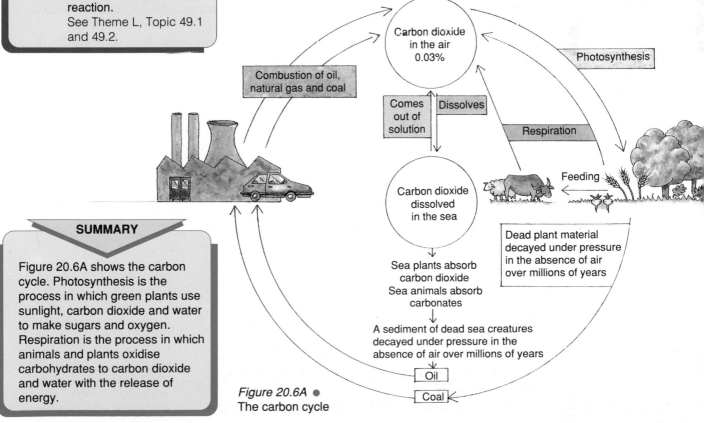

Figure 20.6A ●
The carbon cycle

20.7 The greenhouse effect

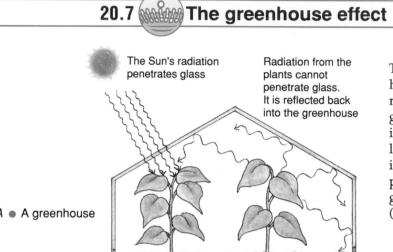

The Sun's radiation penetrates glass

Radiation from the plants cannot penetrate glass. It is reflected back into the greenhouse

Figure 20.7A ● A greenhouse

The Sun is so hot that it emits high-energy radiation. The Sun's rays can pass easily through the glass of a greenhouse. The plants in the greenhouse are at a much lower temperature. They send out infra-red radiation which cannot pass through the glass. The greenhouse therefore warms up (Figure 20.7A).

LOOK AT LINKS
Infra-red radiation and light are electromagnetic waves.
See Theme B, Topic 7.7.

LOOK AT LINKS
Other gases which contribute to the greenhouse effect are methane (see Topic 23.8), oxides of nitrogen (from vehicle exhausts; see Topic 23.7) and CFCs (from aerosols and refrigerators; see Topic 23.11).

Radiant energy from the Sun falls on the Earth and warms it. The Earth radiates heat energy back into space as infra-red radiation. Unlike sunlight, infra-red radiation cannot travel freely through the air surrounding the Earth. Both water vapour and carbon dioxide absorb some of the infra-red radiation. Since carbon dioxide and water vapour act like the glass in a greenhouse, their warming effect is called the greenhouse effect. Without carbon dioxide and water vapour, the surface of the Earth would be at -40 °C. Most of the greenhouse effect is due to

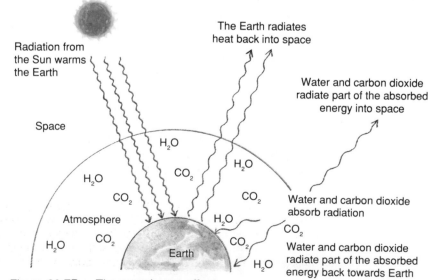

The Earth radiates heat back into space

Radiation from the Sun warms the Earth

Space

Water and carbon dioxide radiate part of the absorbed energy into space

H_2O
CO_2
H_2O
H_2O
CO_2
CO_2

Atmosphere

Water and carbon dioxide absorb radiation

H_2O
CO_2
CO_2
H_2O
CO_2

Earth

H_2O

Water and carbon dioxide radiate part of the absorbed energy back towards Earth

Figure 20.7B ● The greenhouse effect

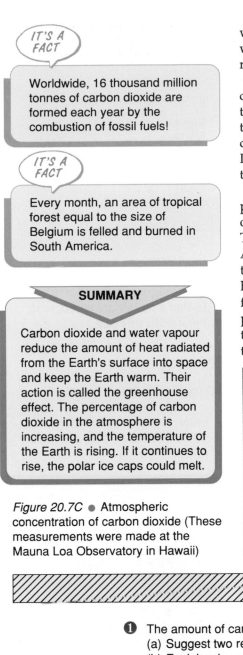

SUMMARY

Carbon dioxide and water vapour reduce the amount of heat radiated from the Earth's surface into space and keep the Earth warm. Their action is called the greenhouse effect. The percentage of carbon dioxide in the atmosphere is increasing, and the temperature of the Earth is rising. If it continues to rise, the polar ice caps could melt.

Figure 20.7C ● Atmospheric concentration of carbon dioxide (These measurements were made at the Mauna Loa Observatory in Hawaii)

water vapour. The Earth does, however, radiate some wavelengths which water vapour cannot absorb. Carbon dioxide is able to absorb some of the radiation which water vapour lets through.

The surface of the Earth has warmed up by 0.75 °C during the last century. The rate of warming up is increasing. Unless something is done to stop the temperature rising, there is a danger that the temperature of the Arctic and Antarctic regions might rise above 0 °C. Then, over the course of a century or two, polar ice would melt and flow into the oceans. If the level of the sea rose, low-lying areas of land would disappear under the sea.

One reason for the increase in the Earth's temperature is that we are putting too much carbon dioxide into the air. The combustion of coal and oil in our power stations and factories sends carbon dioxide into the air. The second reason is that we are felling too many trees. In South America, huge areas of tropical forest have been cut down to make timber and to provide land for farming. In many Asian countries, forests have been cut down for firewood. The result is that worldwide there are fewer trees to take carbon dioxide from the air by photosynthesis. The percentage of carbon dioxide is increasing, and some scientists calculate that it will double by the year 2000 (see Figure 20.7C). This would raise the Earth's temperature by 2 °C.

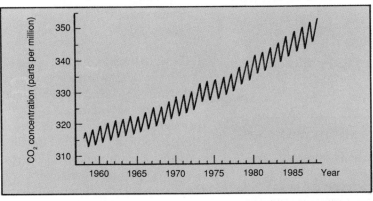

CHECKPOINT

❶ The amount of carbon dioxide in the atmosphere is slowly increasing.
(a) Suggest two reasons why this is happening.
(b) Explain why people call the effect which carbon dioxide has on the atmosphere the 'greenhouse effect'.
(c) Why are some people worried about the greenhouse effect?
(d) Suggest two things which could be done to stop the increase in the percentage of carbon dioxide in the atmosphere.

❷ *Selima* Did you hear what Miss Sande said about the greenhouse effect making the temperature of the Earth go up?
Joshe I don't know what she's worried about. We wouldn't be here at all if it weren't for the greenhouse effect.
(a) What does Joshe mean by what he says? What would the Earth be like without the greenhouse effect?
(b) Is Joshe right in thinking there is no cause for worry?

❸ The burning of fossil fuels produces 16 000 million tonnes of carbon dioxide per year. Carbon dioxide is thought to increase the average temperature of the air. It is predicted that the effect of this increase in temperature will be to melt some of the ice at the North and South Poles. Describe the effects which this could have on life for people in other parts of the world.

20.8 Carbon dioxide

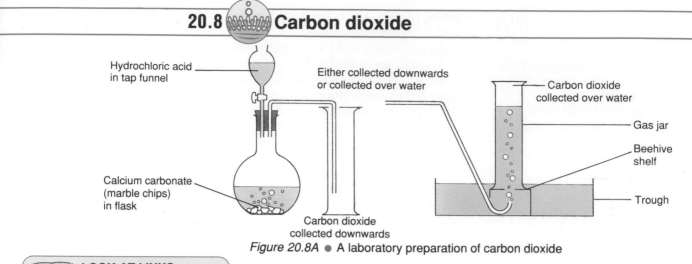

Figure 20.8A ● A laboratory preparation of carbon dioxide

LOOK AT LINKS
Why is carbon dioxide used as a fire extinguisher?
See Topic 21.8.

Carbon dioxide can be made in the laboratory. Figure 20.8A shows one method. You will remember from Topic 16 that a carbonate reacts with an acid to form carbon dioxide, a salt and water. In this case

| Calcium carbonate (marble chips) | + | Hydrochloric acid | → | Carbon dioxide | + | Calcium chloride | + | Water |

$$CaCO_3(s) + 2HCl(aq) \rightarrow CO_2(g) + CaCl_2(aq) + H_2O(l)$$

Carbon dioxide can be collected over water. (*What does this tell you about the solubility of carbon dioxide?*) It can also be collected downwards. (*What does this tell you about the density of carbon dioxide?*)

In water, carbon dioxide dissolves slightly to form the weak acid carbonic acid, H_2CO_3. Under pressure, the solubility increases. Many soft drinks are made by dissolving carbon dioxide under pressure and adding sugar and flavourings. When you open a bottle of fizzy drink, the pressure is released and bubbles of carbon dioxide come out of solution. People like the bubbles and the slightly acidic taste.

When carbon dioxide is cooled, it turns into a solid. This is known as **dry ice** and as **Dricold**. It is used as a refrigerant for icecream and meat. When it warms up, dry ice sublimes (turns into a vapour without melting first).

Figure 20.8B ● Subliming carbon dioxide being poured from a gas jar

SCIENCE AT WORK

Pop stars sometimes use Dricold on stage. As it sublimes, it cools the air on stage. Water vapour condenses from the cold air in swirling clouds.

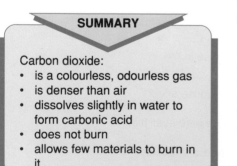

SUMMARY

Carbon dioxide:
- is a colourless, odourless gas
- is denser than air
- dissolves slightly in water to form carbonic acid
- does not burn
- allows few materials to burn in it

CHECKPOINT

❶ Why do icecream sellers prefer dry ice to ordinary ice?

❷ Why is carbon dioxide used by the soft drinks industry?

20.9 Testing for carbon dioxide and water vapour

LOOK AT LINKS
for **copper sulphate**
See Theme D, Topic 17.3.

SUMMARY

The carbon dioxide in the air turns limewater cloudy. The water vapour in the air turns anhydrous copper(II) sulphate from white to blue.

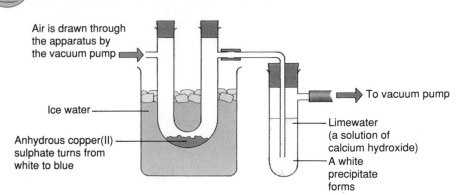

Figure 20.9A ● Testing for carbon dioxide and water vapour in air

Figure 20.9A shows how you can test for the presence of carbon dioxide and water vapour in air.

● *Test for carbon dioxide*
A white precipitate is formed when carbon dioxide reacts with a solution of calcium hydroxide, **limewater**.

Carbon dioxide	+	Calcium hydroxide (limewater)	→	Calcium carbonate (white precipitate)	+	Water
$CO_2(g)$	+	$Ca(OH)_2(aq)$	→	$CaCO_3(s)$	+	$H_2O(l)$

● *Test for water vapour*
Water turns anhydrous copper(II) sulphate from white to blue.

Copper(II) sulphate (anhydrous, a white solid)	+	Water	→	Copper(II) sulphate-5-water (blue crystals)
$CuSO_4(s)$	+	$5H_2O(l)$	→	$CuSO_4.5H_2O(s)$

CHECKPOINT

❶ Malachite is a green mineral found in many rocks. How could you prove that malachite is a carbonate?

❷ (a) How could you prove that whisky contains water?
  (b) How could you show that whisky is not pure water? (Don't say 'Taste it': tasting chemicals is often dangerous.)

20.10 The noble gases

Deep-sea divers have to take their oxygen with them (see Figure 20.10A). If they take air in their cylinders, nitrogen dissolves in their blood. Although the solubility of nitrogen is normally very low, at the high pressures which divers experience the solubility increases. When the divers surface, their blood can dissolve less nitrogen than it can at high pressure. Dissolved nitrogen leaves the blood to form tiny bubbles. These cause severe pains, which divers call 'the bends'. The solution to this problem is to breathe a mixture of oxygen and **helium**. Since helium is much less soluble than nitrogen, there is much less danger of the bends.

IT'S A FACT

Why are the noble gases so called?

They don't take part in many chemical reactions. Like the nobility of old, they don't seem to do much work.

Helium is a safe gas to use because it takes part in no chemical reactions. It is one of the **noble gases** (see Figure 20.1B).

For a long time, it seemed that the noble gases (helium, neon, argon, krypton and xenon) were unable to take part in any chemical reactions. They were called the 'inert gases'. Argon, the most abundant of them, makes up 0.09% of the air. Figure 20.2B shows how argon is obtained by the fractional distillation of liquid air.

Figure 20.10A ● A diver carries a mixture of oxygen and helium

Neon, argon, krypton and xenon are used in display lighting (see Figure 20.10B). The discharge tubes which are used as strip lights contain these gases at low pressure. When the gases conduct electricity, they glow brightly. Most electric light bulbs are filled with argon. The filament of a light bulb is so hot that it would react with other gases. Krypton and xenon are also used to fill light bulbs.

The low density of helium makes it useful. It is used to fill balloons and airships.

Figure 20.10B ● Neon lights

SUMMARY

The noble gases take part in few chemical reactions. Argon is used to fill light bulbs. Neon and other noble gases are used in illuminated signs. Helium is used to fill airships.

CHECKPOINT

❶ The first airships contained hydrogen. Modern airships use helium. The table gives some information about the two gases and air.

	Hydrogen	Helium	Air
Density (g/cm³)	8.3×10^{-5}	1.66×10^{-4}	1.2×10^{-3}
Chemical reactions with air	Forms an explosive mixture with air	No known chemical reactions	

(a) What advantage does helium have over hydrogen for filling airships?
(b) What disadvantage does hydrogen have compared with helium?
(c) Why is air not used for 'airships'?

TOPIC 21 OXYGEN

21.1 Blast-off

FIRST THOUGHTS

In this topic, you can find out about some of the elements and compounds that react with oxygen. Oxygen is a very reactive element, and many substances burn in it.

LOOK AT LINKS
for **rockets**
Why do rockets need to be so powerful? Topic 36.8 will tell you.

On 16 July 1969, ten thousand people gathered at the Kennedy Space Centre in Florida, USA. They had come to watch the spacecraft *Apollo 11* lift off on its journey to the moon. While the *Saturn* rocket stood on the launch pad, its roaring jet engines burned 450 tonnes of kerosene in 1800 tonnes of pure oxygen. The thrust from the jets shot the rocket through the lower atmosphere, trailing a jet of flame. At a height of 65 km the first stage of the rocket separated. For six minutes, the second stage burned hydrogen in pure oxygen, taking the spacecraft to a height of 185 km. Then the second stage separated. The third stage, burning hydrogen in oxygen, put *Apollo 11* into an orbit round the Earth at a speed of 28 000 km/hour. From this orbit, *Apollo 11* headed for the moon. The energy needed to lift *Apollo 11* into space came from burning fuels (kerosene and hydrogen) in pure oxygen. Fuels burns faster in oxygen than they do in air. They therefore deliver more power. We shall return to this important reaction of burning in Topic 21.7.

Figure 21.1A ● Rocket launch

21.2 Test for oxygen

Who's behind the science

A new gas was discovered by the British chemist, Joseph Priestley, on 1 August 1786. He had heated mercury in air and found that it combined with part of the air to form a solid which he called 'red calx of mercury'. When Priestley heated 'red calx of mercury', he obtained mercury and a new gas. He tried breathing the new gas and found that it produced a 'light and easy sensation in his chest'. The gas came to be called oxygen. What do you think 'red calx of mercury' is called now?

Oxygen is a colourless, odourless gas, which is only slightly soluble in water. It is neutral. Oxygen allows substances to burn in it: it is a good **supporter of combustion**. One test for oxygen is to lower a glowing wooden splint into the gas. If the splint starts to burn brightly, the gas is oxygen.

Oxygen relights a glowing splint (see Figure 21.2A).

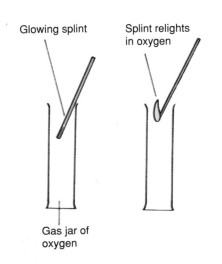

Glowing splint

Splint relights in oxygen

Gas jar of oxygen

Figure 21.2A ● Testing for oxygen

21.3  The percentage by volume of oxygen in air

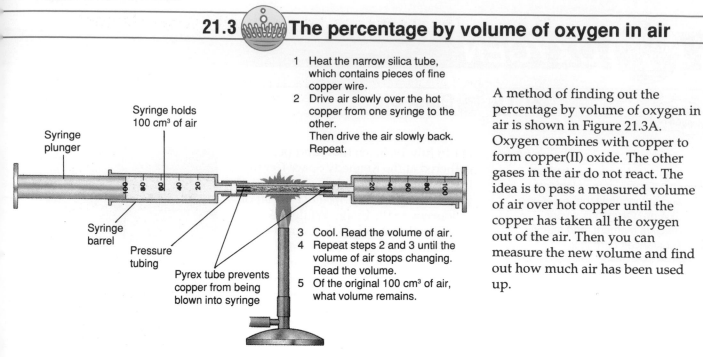

1 Heat the narrow silica tube, which contains pieces of fine copper wire.
2 Drive air slowly over the hot copper from one syringe to the other.
  Then drive the air slowly back. Repeat.

Syringe holds 100 cm³ of air

Syringe plunger

Syringe barrel

Pressure tubing

Pyrex tube prevents copper from being blown into syringe

3 Cool. Read the volume of air.
4 Repeat steps 2 and 3 until the volume of air stops changing. Read the volume.
5 Of the original 100 cm³ of air, what volume remains.

A method of finding out the percentage by volume of oxygen in air is shown in Figure 21.3A. Oxygen combines with copper to form copper(II) oxide. The other gases in the air do not react. The idea is to pass a measured volume of air over hot copper until the copper has taken all the oxygen out of the air. Then you can measure the new volume and find out how much air has been used up.

Figure 21.3A ● Finding the percentage by volume of oxygen in air

21.4  A method of preparing oxygen in the laboratory

LOOK AT LINKS
for **catalysts**
See Theme L, Topic 46.7.

Hydrogen peroxide is a colourless liquid which decomposes to give oxygen and water.

Hydrogen peroxide → Oxygen + Water
$$2H_2O_2(aq) \rightarrow O_2(g) + 2H_2O(l)$$

IT'S A FACT

The mass of oxygen in the atmosphere is 12 hundred million million tonnes!

Solutions of hydrogen peroxide are kept in stoppered brown bottles to slow down the rate of decomposition. If you want to speed up the formation of oxygen, you can add a **catalyst**. A substance which speeds up a reaction without being used in the reaction is called a catalyst. The catalyst manganese(IV) oxide, MnO_2, is often used.

RESOURCE ACTIVITY PACK

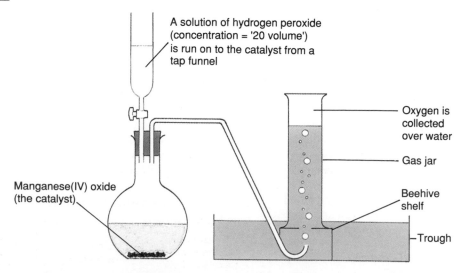

A solution of hydrogen peroxide (concentration = '20 volume') is run on to the catalyst from a tap funnel

Oxygen is collected over water

Gas jar

Beehive shelf

Trough

Manganese(IV) oxide (the catalyst)

Figure 21.4A ● A laboratory preparation of oxygen

21.5 The reactions of oxygen with some elements

FIRST
THOUGHTS

Most elements combine with oxygen; many elements burn in oxygen.

Table 21.1 shows how some elements react with oxygen. The products of the reactions are **oxides**. An oxide is a compound of oxygen with one other element.

Table 21.1 ● How some elements react with oxygen

Element	Observation	Product	Action of product on water
Calcium (metal)	Burns with a red flame	Calcium oxide, CaO (a white solid)	Dissolves to give a strongly alkaline solution
Copper (metal)	Does not burn; turns black	Copper(II) oxide, CuO (a black solid)	Insoluble
Iron (metal)	Burns with yellow sparks	Iron oxide, Fe_3O_4 (a blue-black solid)	Insoluble
Magnesium (metal)	Burns with a bright white flame	Magnesium oxide, MgO (a white solid)	Dissolves slightly to give an alkaline solution, pH = 9
Sodium (metal)	Burns with a yellow flame	Sodium oxide, Na_2O (a yellow-white solid)	Dissolves readily to form a strongly alkaline solution, pH = 10
Carbon (non-metal)	Glows red	Carbon dioxide, CO_2, (an invisible gas)	Dissolves slightly to give a weakly acidic solution, pH = 4
Phosphorus (non-metal)	Burns with a yellow flame	Phosphorus(V) oxide, P_2O_5, (a white solid)	Dissolves to give a strongly acidic solution, pH = 2
Sulphur (non-metal)	Burns with a blue flame	Sulphur dioxide, SO_2, (a fuming gas with a choking smell)	Dissolves readily to form a strongly acidic solution, pH = 2

21.6 Oxides

A pattern can be seen in the characteristics of oxides. The oxides of metallic elements are **bases**. The bases which dissolve in water are called **alkalis**. Most of the oxides of non-metallic elements are acids, but some are neutral. Acids react with bases to form **salts**.

LOOK AT LINKS
for **salts**
See Theme D, Topic 17.

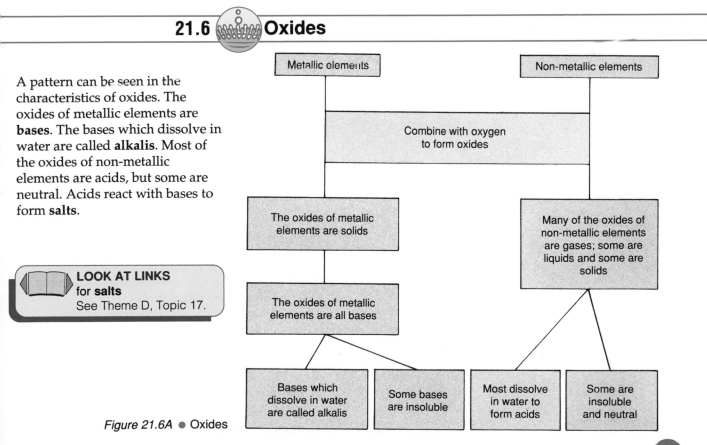

Figure 21.6A ● Oxides

When an element combines with oxygen, we say it has been **oxidised**. Oxygen **oxidises** copper to copper(II) oxide. This reaction is an **oxidation**.

Copper is oxidised

| Copper | + | Oxygen | → | Copper(II) oxide |
| 2Cu(s) | + | O_2(g) | → | 2CuO(s) |

This reaction is oxidation

The opposite of oxidation is **reduction**. When a substance loses oxygen, it is **reduced**. Copper(II) oxide can be reduced by heating it and passing hydrogen over it.

Copper(II) oxide is reduced

| Copper(II) oxide | + | Hydrogen | → | Copper | + | Water |
| CuO(s) | + | H_2(g) | → | Cu(s) | + | H_2O(l) |

Hydrogen is oxidised

You can see from the equation that oxidation and reduction occur together. Copper(II) oxide is reduced to copper while hydrogen is oxidised to water. Copper(II) oxide is called an **oxidising agent** because it gives oxygen to hydrogen. Hydrogen is called a **reducing agent** because it takes oxygen from copper(II) oxide.

RESOURCE ACTIVITY PACK

SUMMARY

Most elements combine with oxygen to form oxides. Many elements burn in oxygen. The oxides of metals are basic. The oxides of non-metallic elements are acidic or neutral. An oxidising agent gives oxygen to another substance. A reducing agent takes oxygen from another substance.

CHECKPOINT

❶ (a) Describe two differences in the physical characteristics of metallic and non-metallic elements (see Topic 9.7 also).
(b) State two differences between the chemical reactions of metallic and non-metallic elements (see Topic 16.1 also).

❷ Write word equations and balanced chemical equations for the combustion in oxygen of (a) sulphur (b) carbon (c) magnesium (d) sodium.

21.7 Combustion

LOOK AT LINKS
for the **combustion of food**
See Theme D, Topic 19.3 and Theme E, Topic 20.6.

LOOK AT LINKS
for **petroleum oil**
See Theme D, Topic 15.8.

In many oxidation reactions, energy is given out. The fireworks called 'sparklers' are coated with iron filings. When the iron is oxidised to iron oxide, you can see that energy is given out in the form of heat and light. An oxidation reaction in which energy is given out is called a combustion reaction. A combustion in which there is a flame is described as burning. Substances which undergo combustion are called fuels.

Daily, we make use of the combustion of fuels. In respiration, the **combustion of foods** provides us with energy. We use fuels to heat our homes, to cook our food, to run our cars and to generate electricity. Many of the fuels which we use are derived from petroleum oil. Petrol (used in motor vehicles), kerosene (used in aircraft and as domestic paraffin), diesel fuel (used in lorries and trains) and natural gas (used in gas cookers) are obtained from **petroleum oil**. These fuels are mixtures of **hydrocarbons**. Hydrocarbons are compounds of carbon and hydrogen

LOOK AT LINKS
for **carbon monoxide**
Carbon monoxide combines with haemoglobin, the red pigment in blood, and prevents haemoglobin from combining with oxygen.
See Theme J, Topic 38.3.
A burning cigarette also produces some carbon monoxide.
See Theme F, Topic 26.2.

only. It is important to know what products are formed when these fuels burn. Figure 21.7A shows how you can test the products of combustion of kerosene which is burned in paraffin heaters. **Do not use petrol in this apparatus**. You can burn a candle instead of kerosene. Candle wax is another hydrocarbon fuel obtained from crude oil.

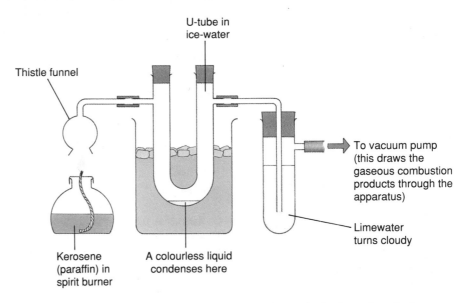

Figure 21.7A ● How to test the combustion products of a hydrocarbon fuel, e.g. kerosene or candle wax (*NOTE: do not use petrol*)

The combustion products are carbon dioxide and water. Other hydrocarbon fuels give the same products.

Hydrogen + Oxygen → Carbon dioxide + Water vapour

If you burn a candle in this apparatus, you will see a deposit of carbon (soot) in the thistle funnel. This happens when the air supply is insufficient to oxidise all the carbon in the hydrocarbon fuel to carbon dioxide, CO_2. Another product of incomplete combustion is the poisonous gas carbon monoxide, CO. Because you cannot see or smell carbon monoxide, it is doubly dangerous. Many times, people have been poisoned by carbon monoxide while running a car engine in a closed garage. The engine could not get enough oxygen for complete combustion to occur. The exhaust gases from petrol engines always contain some carbon monoxide, some unburnt hydrocarbons and some soot, in addition to the harmless products: carbon dioxide and water.

SUMMARY

The combustion of fuels is an oxidation reaction. The combustion of hydrocarbon fuels is a vital source of energy in our economy. These fuels burn to form carbon dioxide and water. If the supply of air is insufficient, the combustion products include carbon monoxide (a poisonous gas) and carbon (soot).

SUMMARY

Oxidation is the addition of oxygen to a substance. Combustion is oxidation with the release of energy. Burning is combustion accompanied by a flame. Respiration is combustion which takes place in living tissues. In respiration, food materials are oxidised in the cells with the release of energy.

CHECKPOINT

1 (a) What type of compound is present in petrol?
    (b) What products are formed in combustion (i) if there is plenty of air and (ii) if there is a limited supply of air?

2 In February 1988 newspapers carried a report of a woman who fell asleep in front of a fire and never woke up. Later, workmen removed three buckets full of birds' nesting materials from the chimney. What do you think had caused the woman's death?

3 Why should you make sure the window is open if you use a gas heater in the bathroom?

21.8 ● Fire-extinguishers

Sometimes fires get out of control and methods of extinguishing them are important.

The fire triangle in Figure 21.8A illustrates the three things which a fire needs: fuel, oxygen and heat. If one of these three is removed, the fire goes out.

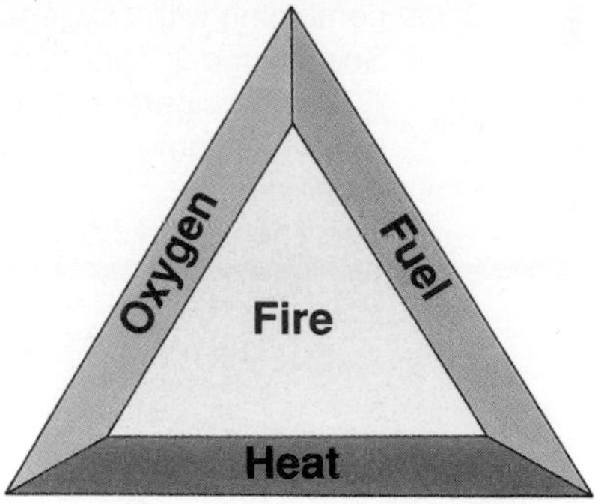

Firefighters deal with four types of fire:
- **Class A** Materials such as wood, paper, cloth and plastics
- **Class B** Flammable liquids and gases such as petrol, cooking oil and natural gas
- **Class C** Electrical equipment
- **Class D** Metals

Figure 21.8A ● The fire triangle

● Class A fires

These fires are usually tackled by removing the heat side of the fire triangle. For every fuel, there is an ignition temperature. Below this temperature the fuel will not burn. Directing water on to the burning material cools it until it is below its ignition temperature.

Figure 21.8B shows a water fire-extinguisher. It contains a small cartridge of carbon dioxide under pressure. When someone operates the lever, the cartridge is punctured, and carbon dioxide is released. The pressure of the gas forces a powerful jet of water out of the nozzle.

In the older soda–acid extinguishers, carbon dioxide is generated in the cylinder from the reaction of an acid and a carbonate. Foam extinguishers contain a foam-stabiliser as well as water. Out of the nozzle comes a foam of water and bubbles of carbon dioxide. The foam-stabiliser stops the bubbles dispersing.

When a person's clothing is on fire, the best thing to do is to wrap them in a fire blanket. A fire blanket, which is usually made from glass fibre, keeps out air. If there is no fire blanket handy, you should lie the person on the floor and wrap a carpet or rug round them.

● Class B fires

Water is not used on burning gases and liquids. Burning petrol or oil floats on water, and the water makes things worse by spreading the fire. This makes fires at sea especially dangerous. A chip pan fire is easier to deal with (see Figure 21.8C).

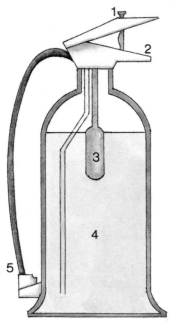

1 Remove the safety pin
2 Squeeze the lever
3 This action pierces the cartridge of pressurised carbon dioxide
4 The steel cylinder contains water
5 The pressure of carbon dioxide forces a jet of water out of the nozzle

Figure 21.8B ● A water fire-extinguisher

No! Don't use water!
Switch off the gas or electricity
Wet a towel. Wring it out
Put the damp towel over the pan
Wait. Don't remove until the fire has been out for some time

Figure 21.8C ● How to put out a chip pan fire

Figure 21.8D ● A fireman demonstrates how using the wrong kind of extinguisher can make the problem worse – in this case he is using a water extinguisher on an oil fire

Figure 21.8E ● Don't use water

SUMMARY

A fire needs fuel, oxygen and heat. Many fire-extinguishers work by cooling the fire. Others use carbon dioxide to exclude air. Metal fires are often extinguished with an inert liquid, e.g. BCD.

To extinguish burning oil or petrol, the oxygen side of the fire triangle must be removed. One way is to use a carbon dioxide extinguisher. Carbon dioxide does not support combustion. It is denser than air and a layer of carbon dioxide will form a 'blanket' over the fire and keep out oxygen. Starved of oxygen, the fire goes out.

Powder extinguishers can be used on burning liquids. They contain a powder, such as sodium hydrogencarbonate, which is decomposed by heat to release carbon dioxide. If this powder is thrown on to a fire, it generates carbon dioxide at the base of the fire, and is very effective. Workers on drilling rigs light gas flares. When they want to extinguish a flare, they tip a large quantity of dry powder extinguisher on to it.

● Class C fires

Electrical fires pose a problem. They cannot be extinguished with water extinguishers. If you direct a jet of water on to a smouldering piece of electrical equipment, a current of electricity can pass through the jet of water and give you an electric shock. You should switch off at the mains and use one of the carbon dioxide extinguishers.

● Class D fires

Burning metals are difficult fires to fight. Some metals, such as sodium and magnesium, react with cold water. When they are hot enough, iron and steel react with water. The reaction between metals and water produces the flammable gas hydrogen, which burns in air with an explosion. This is why firefighters never use water on burning metals.

On some metal fires, powder extinguishers can be used, but some metals react with carbon dioxide. There are gases other than carbon dioxide which do not support combustion and are denser than air. BCD extinguishers contain bromochlorodifluoromethane, $CBrClF_2$. On hot surfaces this liquid forms a dense vapour which excludes air. It is chemically unreactive, even at high temperatures.

CHECKPOINT

❶ How would you put out these fires?
 (a) A waste paper basket fire.
 (b) A smouldering television set.
 (c) A chip pan fire.
 (d) A person whose lab coat was on fire.
 (e) A child whose nightdress was on fire.

❷ What special difficulties do metal fires present to firefighters? How are metal fires extinguished?

❸ What special difficulties do fires in oil rigs present? How are they extinguished?

❹ A small fire in a school laboratory can often be put out with dry sand. Explain how this method works.

21.9 Rusting

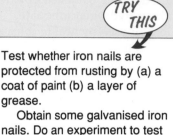

TRY THIS

Test whether iron nails are protected from rusting by (a) a coat of paint (b) a layer of grease.

Obtain some galvanised iron nails. Do an experiment to test whether they rust more slowly in brine than ordinary nails do.

LOOK AT LINKS
The important aspect of this work on rusting is to devise methods of preventing or at least slowing down the process. Methods of delaying rusting are described in Theme L, Topic 50.9.

SUMMARY

Rusting is the oxidation of iron and steel to iron(III) oxide.

TRY THIS

● **Iron and rust**

Many metals become corroded by exposure to the air. The corrosion of iron and steel is called rusting. Rust is the reddish brown solid, hydrated iron(III) oxide, $Fe_2O_3.nH_2O$ (The number of water molecules, n, varies.)

Rusting is an oxidation reaction:

$$\text{Iron} + \text{Oxygen} \rightarrow \text{Iron(III) oxide}$$
$$4Fe(s) + 3O_2(g) \rightarrow 2Fe_2O_3(s)$$

Rusting is a nuisance. Cars, ships, bridges, machines and other costly items made from iron and steel rust. To prevent rusting, or at least to slow it down, saves a lot of money. Before you can prevent rusting, you first have to know what conditions speed up rusting. Figure 21.9A shows some experiments on the rusting of iron nails.

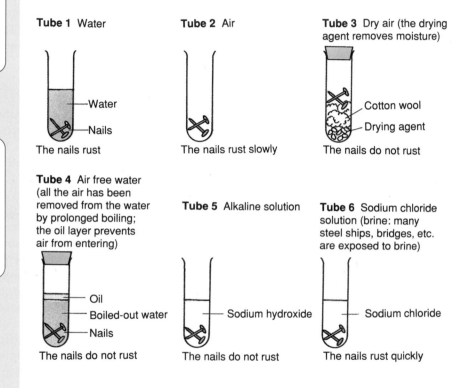

Tube 1 Water
—Water
—Nails
The nails rust

Tube 2 Air
The nails rust slowly

Tube 3 Dry air (the drying agent removes moisture)
—Cotton wool
—Drying agent
The nails do not rust

Tube 4 Air free water (all the air has been removed from the water by prolonged boiling; the oil layer prevents air from entering)
—Oil
—Boiled-out water
—Nails
The nails do not rust

Tube 5 Alkaline solution
—Sodium hydroxide
The nails do not rust

Tube 6 Sodium chloride solution (brine: many steel ships, bridges, etc. are exposed to brine)
—Sodium chloride
The nails rust quickly

Figure 21.9A ● Experiments on the rusting of iron nails

The experiments show that in order to rust, iron needs air and water and a trace of acid. The carbon dioxide in the air provides sufficient acidity. Rusting is accelerated by salt. Bridges and ships are exposed to brine, and cars are exposed to the salt that is spread on the roads in winter. It is obviously very important to find ways of rust-proofing these objects.

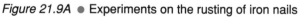

Derive experiments which you could do to answer the questions. If possible, check your ideas with your teacher, and try them out. (Be careful to use iron nails, not rust-proofed nails, and don't forget to set up control experiments.)
(a) Does iron increase in mass when it rusts?
(b) Do salts other than sodium chloride speed up rusting?
(c) Does steel wool rust more quickly or more slowly than iron nails?

WATER

22.1 The water cycle

FIRST
THOUGHTS

The first living things evolved in water. As more complex plants and animals evolved, water remained essential for life.

LOOK AT LINKS
for **transpiration**
See Theme J, Topic 38.1.

IT'S A FACT

A large tree can lose 300 litres of water vapour in an hour by transpiration.

LOOK AT LINKS
for **clouds**
See Theme G, Topic 28.4 and 28.5.

LOOK AT LINKS
for **acid rain**
See Theme E, Topic 23.5.

SUMMARY

The water cycle:
- Evaporation, transpiration and respiration send water vapour into the atmosphere.
- Condensation forms clouds which return water to the Earth as rain, hail or snow.

Where does all the rain come from? Why does the atmosphere never run out of water? Four-fifths of the world's surface is covered by water. From oceans, rivers and lakes, water evaporates into the atmosphere. Plants give out water vapour in **transpiration**. As it rises into a cooler part of the atmosphere, water vapour condenses to form clouds of tiny droplets. If the clouds are blown upward and cooled further, larger drops of water form and fall to the ground as rain (or snow). *Where does the rain go?* Rain water trickles through soil, where some is taken up by plants. The rest passes through porous rocks to become part of rivers, lakes, ground water and the sea. This chain of events is called the **water cycle** (see Figure 22.1A).

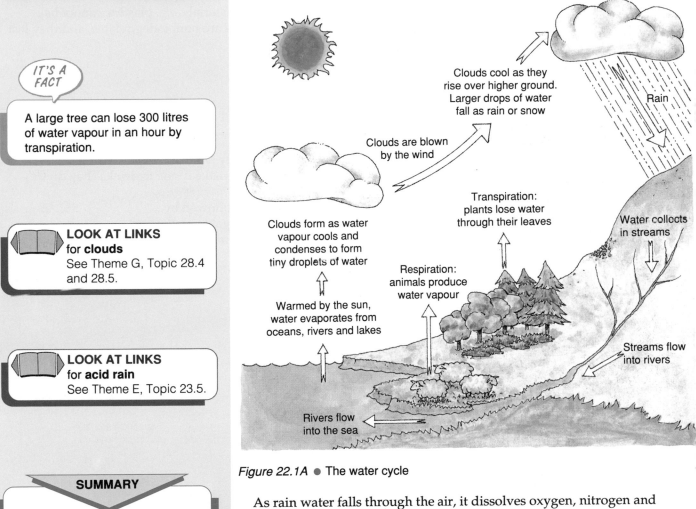

Clouds cool as they rise over higher ground. Larger drops of water fall as rain or snow

Rain

Clouds are blown by the wind

Clouds form as water vapour cools and condenses to form tiny droplets of water

Transpiration: plants lose water through their leaves

Water collects in streams

Respiration: animals produce water vapour

Warmed by the sun, water evaporates from oceans, rivers and lakes

Streams flow into rivers

Rivers flow into the sea

Figure 22.1A ● The water cycle

As rain water falls through the air, it dissolves oxygen, nitrogen and carbon dioxide. The dissolved carbon dioxide forms a solution of the weak acid, carbonic acid. Natural rain water is therefore weakly acidic. In regions where the air is polluted, rain water may dissolve sulphur dioxide and oxides of nitrogen, which make it strongly acidic; it is then called **acid rain**. As rain water trickles through porous rocks, it dissolves salts from the rocks. The dissolved salts are carried into the sea. When sea water evaporates, the salts remain behind.

22.2 Dissolved oxygen

Oxygen sensors connected to a computer are used to monitor the concentration of dissolved oxygen in commercial fish tanks. Fish farmers and breeders are warned when the concentration starts dropping and can take preventive action before any damage is done.

SUMMARY

Air dissolves in water. The dissolved oxygen in water keeps fish alive. If too much organic matter, e.g. sewage, is discharged into a river, the dissolved oxygen is used up in oxidising the organic matter, and the fish die.

The fact that oxygen dissolves in water is vitally important. The solubility is low: water can dissolve no more than 10 g oxygen per tonne of water, that is 10 p.p.m. (parts per million). This is high enough to sustain fish and other water-living animals and plants. When the level of dissolved oxygen falls below 5 p.p.m. aquatic plants and animals start to suffer.

Water is able to purify itself of many of the pollutants which we pour into it. Bacteria which are present in water feed on plant and animal debris. These bacteria are **aerobic** (they need oxygen). They use dissolved oxygen to oxidise organic material (material from plants and animals) to harmless products, such as carbon dioxide and water. This is how the bacteria obtain the energy which they need to sustain life. If a lot of untreated sewage is discharged into a river, the dissolved oxygen is used up more rapidly than it is replaced, and the aerobic bacteria die. Then **anaerobic** bacteria (which do not need oxygen) attack the organic matter. They produce unpleasant-smelling decay products.

Some synthetic (manufactured) materials, e.g. plastics, cannot be oxidised by bacteria. These materials are nonbiodegradable, and they last for a very long time in water.

22.3 Water treatment

The earliest human settlements were always beside rivers. The settlers needed water to drink and used the river to carry away their sewage and other waste. Obtaining clean water is more difficult now.

SCIENCE AT WORK

The water industry makes use of computers. Sensors detect the pH, oxygen concentration and other qualities of the water and relay the measurements to a computer. This constant monitoring enables the industry to control the quality of the water it provides.

IT

Water Treatment
(program)

This program allows you to control and maintain a town's domestic water supply.

The water that we use is taken mainly from lakes and rivers. Water treatment plants purify the water to make it safe to drink. They do this by:
- filtration to remove solid matter followed by...
- bacterial oxidation to get rid of organic matter and...
- treatment with chlorine to kill germs.

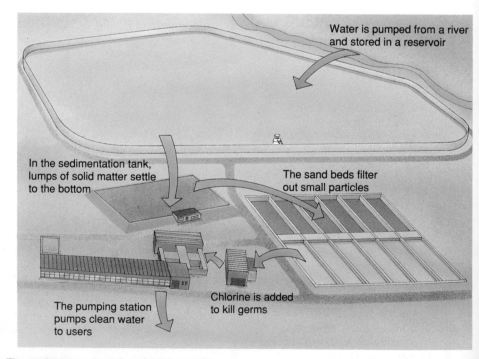

Water is pumped from a river and stored in a reservoir

In the sedimentation tank, lumps of solid matter settle to the bottom

The sand beds filter out small particles

Chlorine is added to kill germs

The pumping station pumps clean water to users

Figure 22.3A ● A water treatment works

SUMMARY

Water treatment works take water from lakes and rivers. After filtration, followed by chlorination, the water is safe to drink.

In some areas, the water supply comes from ground water (water held underground in porous layers of rock). As rain water trickles down from the surface through porous rocks, the solid matter suspended in it is filtered out. Ground water therefore does not need the complete treatment. It is pumped out of the ground and chlorinated before use.

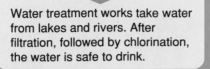

Who's behind the science

In 1854, 50 000 people died of cholera in London. Dr John Snow did some scientific detective work to find the source of the disease. He marked the deaths from cholera and the positions of the street pumps from which people obtained their water on a map of London. Dr Snow came to the conclusion that one of the pumps was supplying contaminated water. *Which was it?* He tested his theory by removing the handle of the pump. There was a sudden fall in the number of people getting cholera. The pump water had been contaminated by sewage leaking into it.

FIRST THOUGHTS

22.4 Sewage works

Rivers carry away our sewage, our industrial grime, the waste chemicals from our factories and the waste heat from our power stations. Sewage works try to ensure that rivers are not overloaded with waste.

Homes, factories, businesses and schools all discharge their used water into sewers which take it to a sewage works. There, the dirty water is purified until it is fit to be discharged into a river (see Figure 22.4A). The river dilutes the remaining pollutants and oxidises some of them. The digested sludge obtained from a sewage works can be used as a fertiliser. Raw sewage cannot be used as fertiliser because it contains harmful bacteria.

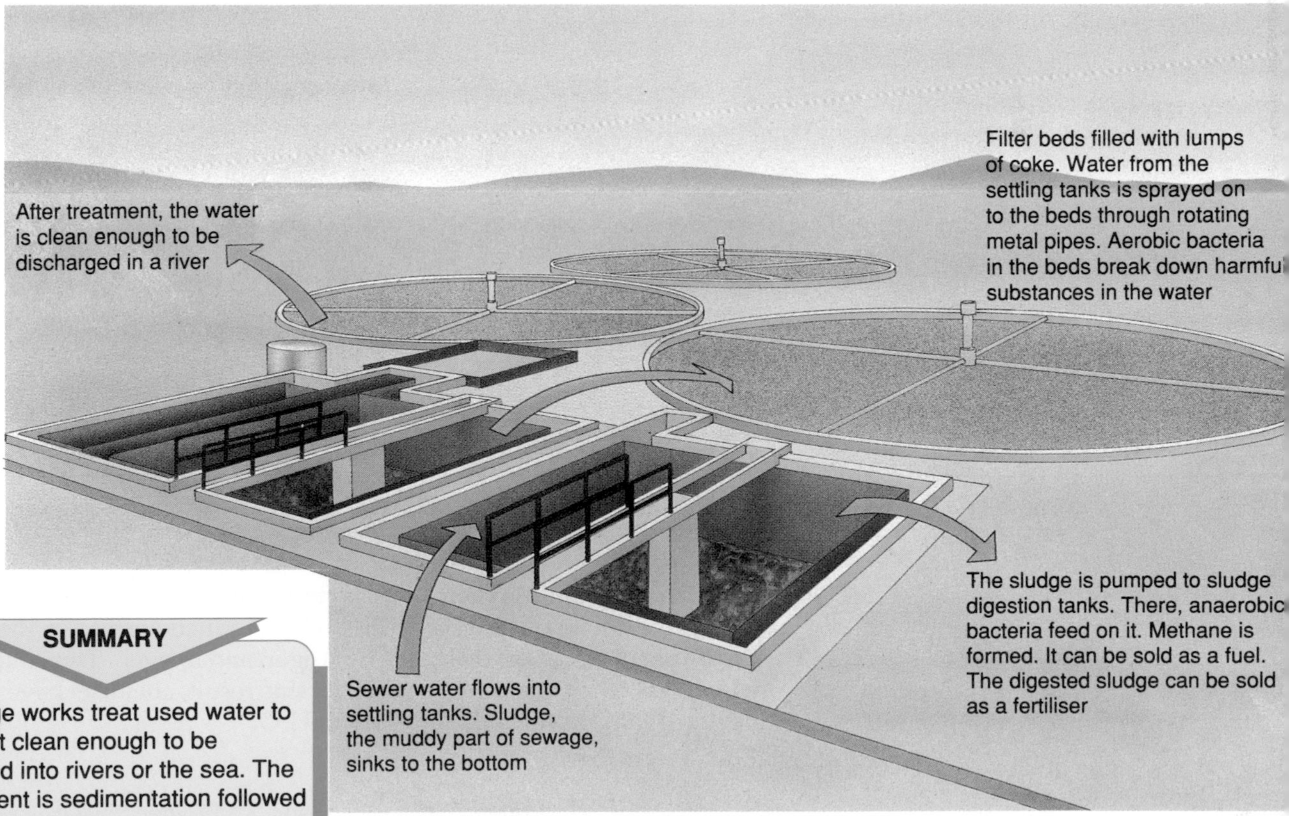

After treatment, the water is clean enough to be discharged in a river

Filter beds filled with lumps of coke. Water from the settling tanks is sprayed on to the beds through rotating metal pipes. Aerobic bacteria in the beds break down harmful substances in the water

The sludge is pumped to sludge digestion tanks. There, anaerobic bacteria feed on it. Methane is formed. It can be sold as a fuel. The digested sludge can be sold as a fertiliser

Sewer water flows into settling tanks. Sludge, the muddy part of sewage, sinks to the bottom

SUMMARY

Sewage works treat used water to make it clean enough to be emptied into rivers or the sea. The treatment is sedimentation followed by aerial oxidation.

Figure 22.4A ● A sewage works

22.5  Uses for water

| Washing and baths 50 litres | Lavatory 50 litres | Laundry 15 litres | Washing up 15 litres | Cooking 5 litres | Gardening 5 litres | Waste (dripping taps, leaking pipes) 20 litres |

Figure 22.5A ● Water: 160 litres a day

The uses shown in Figure 22.5A show only 10% of the total amount of water you use. The other 90% is used:
* to grow your food (agricultural use),
* to make your possessions (industrial use as a solvent, for cleaning and for cooling),
* to generate electricity (used as a coolant in power stations).

The total water consumption in an industrialised country amounts to around 80 000 litres (80 tonnes) a year per person. The manufacture of:
* 1 tonne of steel uses 45 tonnes of water,
* 1 tonne of paper uses 90 tonnes of water,
* 1 tonne of nylon uses 140 tonnes of water,
* 1 tonne of bread uses 4 tonnes of water,
* 1 motor car uses 450 tonnes of water,
* 1 litre of beer uses 10 litres of water.

Water used for many industrial purposes is purified and recycled.

> IT'S A FACT
>
> An industrial country uses about 80 tonnes of water per person per year.

CHECKPOINT

❶ The table shows the world consumption of water over the past 30 years.

Year	World consumption of water (millions of tonnes per day)
1960	10.0
1970	11.5
1975	13.0
1980	15.0
1985	17.0
1990	20.0

(a) On graph paper, plot the consumption (on the vertical axis) against the year (on the horizontal axis).
(b) Say what has happened to the demand for water over the past 30 years.
(c) Suggest three reasons for the change.
(d) From your graph, predict what the consumption of water will be in the year 2000.

22.6  Water: the compound

> **LOOK AT LINKS**
> for **electrolysis**
> See Theme C, Topic 13.

Water is a compound. When a direct electric current passes through it, water splits up: it is electrolysed. The only products formed in the electrolysis of water are the gases hydrogen and oxygen. The volume of hydrogen is twice that of oxygen. From this result, chemists have calculated that the formula for water is H_2O.

$$\text{Water} \xrightarrow{\text{electrolyse}} \text{Hydrogen} + \text{Oxygen}$$
$$2H_2O(l) \rightarrow 2H_2(g) + O_2(g)$$

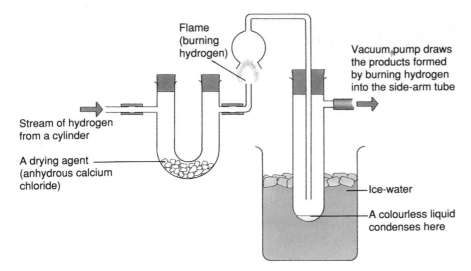

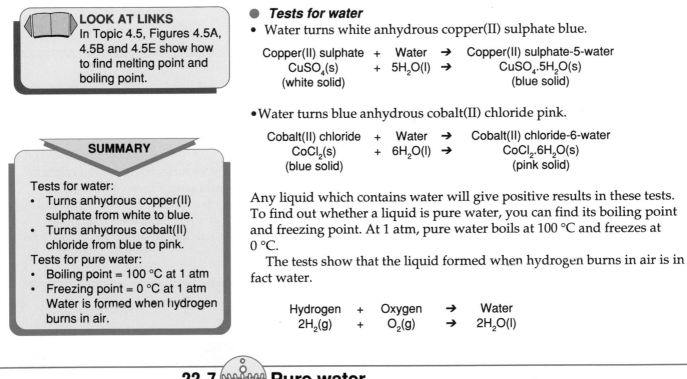

Figure 22.6A ● What is formed when hydrogen burns in air?

Water is the oxide of hydrogen. *Can it be made by the combination of hydrogen and oxygen?* Figure 22.6A shows an experiment to find out what forms when you burn hydrogen in air. The only product is a colourless liquid. You can test this liquid to see whether it is water.

> **LOOK AT LINKS**
> In Topic 4.5, Figures 4.5A, 4.5B and 4.5E show how to find melting point and boiling point.

● **Tests for water**

• Water turns white anhydrous copper(II) sulphate blue.

$$\text{Copper(II) sulphate} + \text{Water} \rightarrow \text{Copper(II) sulphate-5-water}$$
$$\text{CuSO}_4(s) + 5\text{H}_2\text{O}(l) \rightarrow \text{CuSO}_4.5\text{H}_2\text{O}(s)$$
$$\text{(white solid)} \qquad\qquad\qquad \text{(blue solid)}$$

• Water turns blue anhydrous cobalt(II) chloride pink.

$$\text{Cobalt(II) chloride} + \text{Water} \rightarrow \text{Cobalt(II) chloride-6-water}$$
$$\text{CoCl}_2(s) + 6\text{H}_2\text{O}(l) \rightarrow \text{CoCl}_2.6\text{H}_2\text{O}(s)$$
$$\text{(blue solid)} \qquad\qquad\qquad \text{(pink solid)}$$

> **SUMMARY**
>
> Tests for water:
> • Turns anhydrous copper(II) sulphate from white to blue.
> • Turns anhydrous cobalt(II) chloride from blue to pink.
> Tests for pure water:
> • Boiling point = 100 °C at 1 atm
> • Freezing point = 0 °C at 1 atm
> Water is formed when hydrogen burns in air.

Any liquid which contains water will give positive results in these tests. To find out whether a liquid is pure water, you can find its boiling point and freezing point. At 1 atm, pure water boils at 100 °C and freezes at 0 °C.

The tests show that the liquid formed when hydrogen burns in air is in fact water.

$$\text{Hydrogen} + \text{Oxygen} \rightarrow \text{Water}$$
$$2\text{H}_2(g) + \text{O}_2(g) \rightarrow 2\text{H}_2\text{O}(l)$$

22.7 Pure water

> **LOOK AT LINKS**
> for **solubility**
> See Theme B, Topic 4.6.

> **SUMMARY**
>
> Water is a good solvent. The presence of a solute raises the boiling point and lowers the freezing point. Pure water is obtained by distillation.

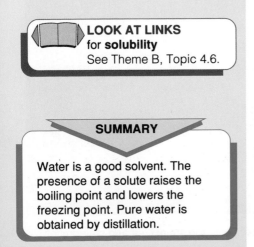

Almost all substances dissolve in water to some extent: that is, water is a good **solvent**. Since water is such a good solvent, it is difficult to obtain pure water. Distillation is one method of purifying water. In some countries, distillation is used to obtain drinking water from sea water. The technique is called desalination (desalting). Hong Kong has a large desalination plant which has never been used because the cost of importing the oil needed to run it is so high. Saudi Arabia and Bahrain operate desalination plants. *Why do you think they need the plants and can afford to run them?*

When chemists describe water as pure, they mean that the water contains no dissolved material. This is different from what a water company means by pure water: they mean that the water contains no harmful substances. Safe drinking water contains dissolved salts. Water which contains substances that are bad for health is **polluted** water.

CHECKPOINT

These questions will enable you to revise solubility curves. Use the figure opposite to help you.

❶ One kilogram of water saturated with potassium chloride is cooled from 80 °C to 20 °C. What mass of potassium chloride crystallises out?

❷ One kilogram of water saturated with sodium chloride is cooled from 80 °C to 20 °C. What mass of sodium chloride crystallises out?

❸ Dissolved in 100 g of water at 100 °C are 30 g of sodium chloride and 50 g of potassium chloride. What will happen when the solution is cooled to 20 °C?

❹ Dissolved in 100 g of water at 80 °C are 15 g of potassium sulphate and 70 g of potassium bromide. What will happen when the solution is cooled to 20 °C?

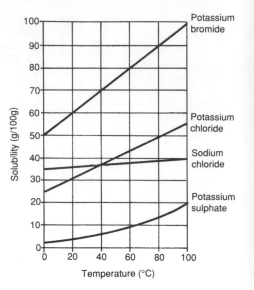

22.8 Underground caverns

LOOK AT LINKS
for **carbonates**
See Theme D, Topic 16.7.

In limestone regions, rain water trickles over rocks composed of calcium carbonate (limestone) and magnesium carbonate. These carbonates do not dissolve in pure water, but they react with acids. The carbon dioxide dissolved in rain water makes it weakly acidic. It reacts with the carbonate rocks to form the soluble salts, calcium hydrogencarbonate and magnesium hydrogencarbonate.

Calcium carbonate + Water + Carbon dioxide → Calcium hydrogencarbonate
(limestone) solution
$$CaCO_3(s) \quad + \quad H_2O(l) \quad + \quad CO_2(g) \quad \rightarrow \quad Ca(HCO_3)_2(aq)$$

LOOK AT LINKS
for **caves**
How the landscape was shaped is discussed in Theme A, Topic 2.6.

Figure 22.8A ● A cavern at Wookey Hole (note the stalactites and stalagmites)

This chemical reaction is responsible for the formation of the underground **caves** and potholes which occur in limestone regions. Over thousands of years, large masses of carbonates have been dissolved out of the rock (see Figure 22.8A).

The reverse reaction can take place. Sometimes, in an underground cavern, a drop of water becomes isolated. With air all round it, water will evaporate. The dissolved calcium hydrogencarbonate turns into a grain of solid calcium carbonate.

SUMMARY

In limestone regions, acidic rainwater reacts with calcium carbonate to form soluble calcium hydrogencarbonate. The reverse process leads to the formation of stalactites and stalagmites.

Calcium hydrogencarbonate → Calcium carbonate + Water + Carbon dioxide

$$Ca(HCO_3)_2(aq) \rightarrow CaCO_3(s) + H_2O(l) + CO_2(g)$$

Slowly, more grains of calcium carbonate are deposited. Eventually, a pillar of calcium carbonate may have built up from the floor of the cavern. This is called a **stalagmite**. The same process can lead to the formation of a **stalactite** on the roof of the cavern.

22.9 Soaps

FIRST THOUGHTS

Have you ever tried to wash greasy hands without using soap? The problem is that grease and water do not mix. You can find out how soap solves the problem in this section.

LOOK AT LINKS
for **carboxylate group**
See Theme L, Topic 51.5.

Soaps are able to form a bridge between grease and water. They are the sodium and potassium salts of organic acids. One soap is sodium hexadecanoate, $C_{15}H_{31}CO_2Na$. A model of the soap is shown in Figure 22.9A.
(Hexadecane means sixteen. Count up. *Are there 16 carbon atoms?*)
It consists of a sodium ion and a hexadecanoate ion, which we will call a *soap* ion for short. The *soap* ion has two parts (see Figure 22.9B). The head, which is attracted to water, is a —CO_2^- group (a **carboxylate** group). The tail, which is repelled by water and attracted by grease, is a long chain of —CH_2— groups. Figure 22.9C shows how *soap* ions wash grease from your hands.

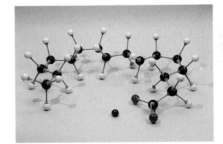

Figure 22.9A ● A model of the soap, sodium hexadecanoate

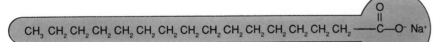

Figure 22.9B ● A *soap* ion

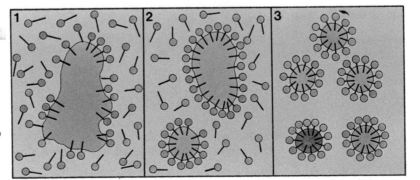

Figure 22.9C ● The cleansing action of soap

1 The tails of the *soap* ions begin to dissolve in the grease. The heads remain dissolved in the water
2 The negatively charged heads of the *soap* ions repel one another; this repulsion makes the grease

break up into small droplets, which are suspended in water. The soap has **emulsified** the grease and water (made them mix)
3 The emulsified grease is washed away by water

● Manufacture of soap

Soaps are made by boiling together animal fats or vegetable oils and a strong alkali, e.g. sodium hydroxide. The reaction is called **saponification** (soap-making).

Fat (or oil) + Sodium hydroxide → Soap + Glycerol

When sodium chloride is added to the mixture, soap solidifies. The product is purified to remove alkali from it. Perfume and colouring are added before the soap is formed into bars.

22.10 Soapless detergents

LOOK AT LINKS
Soapless detergents have some advantages over soaps.
See Theme E, Topic 22.12.

Which is better for the condition of your hair, washing with soap or mild soapless detergent (shampoo)? Think up an experiment to find out. **Do not** experiment on your own hair: obtain samples of hair from a local hairdresser. Obtain your teacher's permission before you carry out your experiment.

Soaps are one type of detergent (cleaning agent). There is another type of detergent known as **soapless detergents**. Many washing powders and household cleaning fluids are soapless detergents. Often they are referred to simply as 'detergents'. Soapless detergents are made from petroleum oil. They are the sodium salts of sulphonic acids (see Figure 22.10A).

Figure 22.10A ● A model of a soapless detergent (note the tail, a chain of —CH$_2$— groups which dissolves in grease, and the head, a sulphate group, —SO$_4^-$, which dissolves in water)

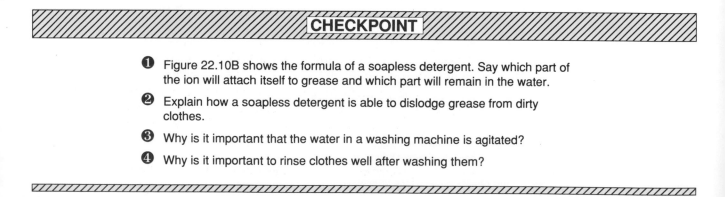
$$CH_3 \; CH_2 \; CH_2 \; CH_2 \; CH_2 \; CH_2 \; CH_2 \; CH_2 \; CH_2 \; CH_2 \; CH_2 \; CH_2 \; —O\!-\!\overset{O}{\underset{O}{S}}\!-\!O^- \; Na^+$$

Figure 22.10B ● A soapless detergent

SUMMARY

Washing powders contain soapless detergent.

Soapless detergents are very good at removing oil and grease. They are too powerful for use on the skin, and the gentler action of a soap is better. Shampoos are mild detergents.

CHECKPOINT

❶ Figure 22.10B shows the formula of a soapless detergent. Say which part of the ion will attach itself to grease and which part will remain in the water.

❷ Explain how a soapless detergent is able to dislodge grease from dirty clothes.

❸ Why is it important that the water in a washing machine is agitated?

❹ Why is it important to rinse clothes well after washing them?

22.11 Bleaches and alkaline cleaners

Bleaches

Many household bleaches contain chlorine compounds, e.g. sodium chlorate(I), NaClO. They are powerful oxidising agents, killing germs and oxidising dirt. You should not use bleaches together with other cleaning agents. An acid will react with sodium chlorate(I) to liberate the poisonous gas chlorine.

Alkaline cleaners

Many household cleaners are alkalis. They react with grease and oil to form an emulsion of glycerol and soap, which can be washed away. The reaction is saponification. Sodium hydroxide, NaOH, is used in oven-cleaners; sodium carbonate, Na_2CO_3, is used in washing powders, and ammonia is used in solution as a household cleaner. You should not use ammonia together with a bleach because they can react to form poisonous chloroamines.

SUMMARY

Household bleaches are chlorine compounds. They work by oxidising dirt and germs. It is not safe to use a bleach together with an acid. Alkaline cleaners work by saponifying grease and oil. It is not safe to use ammonia and a bleach together.

CHECKPOINT

Oven-cleaners contain sodium hydroxide. A greasy oven is wiped with a pad of oven-cleaner and left for a few minutes. The grease can then be washed off with water.

❶ Explain how sodium hydroxide makes it easier to remove grease.

❷ Explain why you should wear rubber gloves when you use this kind of oven-cleaner.

❸ What effect does it have on the cleaning job if you warm the oven first?

22.12 Hard water and soft water

In some parts of the country, the tap water is described as **hard water**. This means that it is hard to get a lather with soap. Instead of forming a lather, soap forms an insoluble scum. Water in which soap lathers easily is **soft water**. Hard water contains soluble calcium and magnesium salts. They combine with *soap* ions to form insoluble calcium and magnesium compounds. These compounds are the insoluble scum that floats on the water.

Soap ions (in solution)	+	Calcium ions (in solution)	→	Scum (insoluble solid)

If you go on adding soap, eventually all the calcium ions and magnesium ions will be precipitated as scum. After that, the soap will be able to work as a cleaning agent.

Soapless detergents are able to work in hard water because their calcium and magnesium salts are soluble. For many purposes, people prefer soapless detergents to soaps. Sales of soapless detergents are four times as high as those of soaps.

22.13 Methods of softening hard water

Temporary hardness

Figure 22.13A ● Scale on a kettle element

Hardness which can be removed by boiling is called temporary hardness. Temporarily hard water contains dissolved calcium hydrogencarbonate and magnesium hydrogencarbonate, and these compounds decompose when the water is boiled. The resulting water is soft water.

Calcium hydrogencarbonate → Calcium carbonate + Carbon dioxide + Water
$$Ca(HCO_3)_2(aq) \rightarrow CaCO_3(s) + CO_2(g) + H_2O(l)$$

A deposit of calcium carbonate and magnesium carbonate forms. This is the **scale** which is deposited in kettles and water pipes.

Permanent hardness

Hardness which cannot be removed by boiling is called permanent hardness. It is caused by dissolved chlorides and sulphates of calcium and magnesium. These compounds are not decomposed by heat.

Washing soda

Washing soda is sodium carbonate-10-water. It can soften both temporary and permanent hardness. Washing soda precipitates calcium ions and magnesium ions as insoluble carbonates.

Calcium ions + Carbonate ions → Calcium carbonate
$$Ca^{2+}(aq) + CO_3^{2-}(aq) \rightarrow CaCO_3(s)$$

Exchange resins

Ion exchange resins are substances which take ions of one kind out of aqueous solution and replace them with ions of a different kind. Permutits are manufactured ion exchange resins. They replace calcium and magnesium ions in water by sodium ions.

Calcium ions + Sodium permutit → Sodium ions + Calcium permutit

22.14  Advantages of hard water

SUMMARY

- Temporary hardness is removed by boiling.
- Permanent hardness is removed by adding sodium carbonate (washing soda) or by running water through an exchange resin.
- Hard water is better than soft water for drinking.

Hard water has some advantages over soft water for health reasons. The **calcium** compounds in hard water strengthen bones and teeth. The calcium content is also beneficial to people with a tendency to develop heart disease.

Some industries prefer hard water. The leather industry prefers to cure leather in hard water. The brewing industry likes hard water for the taste which the dissolved salts give to the beer.

CHECKPOINT

❶ Gwen washes her hair in hard water. Which kind of shampoo would you advise her to choose: a mild soapless detergent or a soap? Explain your advice.

❷ (a) Explain the difference between hard and soft water.
(b) Why is drinking hard water better for health than drinking soft water?
(c) Which solutes make water hard? Explain how the substances you mention get into tap water.
(d) Name a use for which soft water is preferred to hard water. Explain why.
(e) Describe one method of softening hard water. Explain how it works.
(f) Why are detergents preferred to soaps for use in hard water?
(g) Why is it better to use distilled water rather than tap water in a steam iron?

❸ The table gives some information on three brands of shampoo.

Brand	Price of bottle (p)	Volume (cm³)
Soffen	40	204
Sheeno	50	350
Silken	60	480

(a) Which brand is sold in the smallest bottle?
(b) Calculate what volume of shampoo (in cm³) you get for 1p if you buy (i) Soffen (ii) Sheeno and (iii) Silken. Say which shampoo is the cheapest.
(c) Suggest three things which a person might consider, other than price, when choosing a shampoo.
(d) Describe an experiment you could do to find out which of the shampoos is best at producing a lather. Mention any steps you would take to make sure the test was fair.

❹ Some washing powders contain enzymes. Zenab decides to test whether the washing powder Biolwash, which contains an enzyme, washes better than Britewash, which does not. Zenab decides to use 1 g of washing powder in 100 cm³ of warm water and to do her tests on squares of cotton fabric.
(a) Suggest some everyday substances which stain cloth and which would be interesting to experiment on.
(b) Describe how Zenab could do a fair test to compare the washing action of Biolwash and Britewash. What factors must be kept the same in the two experiments?
(c) Zenab finds that Biolwash washes better than Britewash on many stains. Another student, Ahmed, did his tests at 80 °C and found that Britewash gave a cleaner result than Biolwash. Can you explain the difference between Zenab's and Ahmed's results? (For enzymes: see Topic 18.4.)

TOPIC 23 AIR POLLUTION

23.1 Smog

As you read through this topic, think about the 15 000 or 20 000 litres of air that you breathe in each day. Obviously you hope that it is clean air. Unfortunately the air that most of us breathe is polluted. In this topic, we shall look into what can be done to reduce the pollution of air.

Four thousand people died in the great London smog of December 1952. Smog is a combination of smoke and fog. Fog consists of small water droplets. It forms when warm air containing water vapour is suddenly cooled. The cool air cannot hold as much water vapour as it held when it was warm, and water condenses. When smoke combines with fog, fog prevents smoke escaping into the upper atmosphere. Smoke stays around, and we inhale it. Smoke contains particles which irritate our lungs and make us cough. Smoke also contains the gas sulphur dioxide. This gas reacts with water and oxygen to form sulphuric acid, H_2SO_4. This strong acid irritates our lungs, and they produce a lot of mucus which we cough up.

The Government did very little about the cause of smog until 1956. Then there was another killer smog. A private bill brought by a Member of Parliament (Mr Robert Maxwell, the newspaper owner) gained such widespread support that the Government was forced to act. The Government introduced its own bill, which became the Clean Air Act of 1956. The Act allowed local authorities to declare smokeless zones. In these zones, only low-smoke and low-sulphur fuels can be burned. The Act banned dark smoke from domestic chimneys and industrial chimneys. People started using natural gas and electricity.

23.2 The problem

Hyperbook
(data base)

Use *Hyperbook* to read about:
* acid rain,
* the greenhouse effect,
* pollution generally.

With the computer, try moving from one article to another and perhaps printing out any particularly interesting documents.

All the dust and pollutants in the air pass over the sensitive tissues of our lungs. Any substance which is bad for health is called a **pollutant**. The lung diseases of cancer, bronchitis and emphysema are common illnesses in regions where air is highly polluted. From our lungs, pollutants enter our bloodstream to reach every part of our bodies. The main air pollutants are shown in Table 23.1

Table 23.1 ● The main pollutants in air (Emmissions are given in millions of tonnes per year in the UK.)

Pollutant	Emission	Source
Carbon monoxide, CO	100	Vehicle engines and industrial processes
Sulphur dioxide, SO_2	33	Combustion of fuels in power stations and factories
Hydrocarbons	32	Combustion of fuels in factories and vehicles
Dust	28	Combustion of fuels; mining; factories
Oxides of nitrogen, NO and NO_2	21	Vehicle engines and fuel combustion
Lead compounds	0.5	Vehicle engines

In this chapter, we shall look at where these pollutants come from, what harm they do and what can be done about them.

23.3 Dispersing air pollutants

LOOK AT LINKS
for **convection currents**
Why does warm air rise?
See Theme B, Topic 7.5.

The surface of the Earth absorbs energy from the Sun and warms up. The Earth warms the lower atmosphere. The air in the upper atmosphere is cooler than the air near the Earth. **Convection currents** carry warm air upwards. Cold air descends to take its place (see Figure 23.3A). In this way, the warm dirty air from factories and motor vehicles is carried upwards and spread through the vast upper atmosphere.

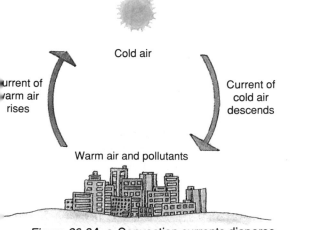

Cold air

Current of warm air rises

Current of cold air descends

Warm air and pollutants

Figure 23.3A ● Convection currents disperse pollutants

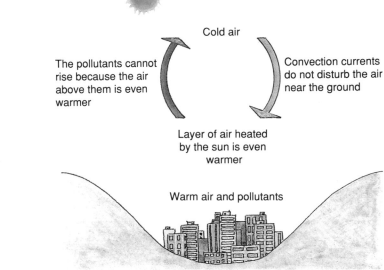

Cold air

The pollutants cannot rise because the air above them is even warmer

Convection currents do not disturb the air near the ground

Layer of air heated by the sun is even warmer

Warm air and pollutants

Figure 23.3B ● A temperature inversion traps pollutants

SUMMARY

Pollutants are carried upwards by rising currents of warm air. A temperature inversion stops the dispersal of pollutants. Temperature inversions occur in places with a hot climate and still air.

A low-lying area surrounded by higher ground tends to have still air. If an area like this has a hot climate, it is possible for the Sun to warm a layer of air in the upper atmosphere (Figure 23.3B). If the Sun is very hot, this layer of air may become warmer than that near the ground. There is a **temperature inversion**. The air near the ground is no longer carried upwards and dispersed. Pollutants accumulate in the layer of still air at ground level, and the city dwellers are forced to breathe them.

23.4 Sulphur dioxide

IT   *Pollution*

Use a word-processing system or better still a desktop publishing package to design and print a poster or news-sheet on the topic of pollution.

● *Where does sulphur dioxide come from?*
Worldwide, 150 million tonnes of sulphur dioxide a year are emitted. Almost all the sulphur dioxide in the air comes from industrial sources. The emission is growing as countries become more industrialised. Half of the output of sulphur dioxide comes from the burning of coal. Most of the coal is burned in power stations. All coal contains between 0.5 and 5 per cent sulphur.

Sulphur	+	Oxygen	→	Sulphur dioxide
(coal)		(air)		
$S(s)$	+	$O_2(g)$	→	$SO_2(g)$

Industrial smelters, which obtain metals from sulphide ores, also produce tonnes of sulphur dioxide daily.

══ SCIENCE AT WORK ══

It is possible to monitor the emission from the chimneys of factories and power stations from a distance. A van can carry equipment using infra-red radiation to detect sulphur dioxide. The readings are automatically recorded by a computer.

IT'S A FACT

In 1979, 31 European countries, including the UK, signed the Convention on Long Range Transboundary Pollution. All the nations agreed to stop exporting pollution across their borders. In 1986, the UK joined the **30 per cent club**. All the nations in the 'club' agreed to reduce their emissions of sulphur dioxide by 30 per cent.

IT'S A FACT

Together, the USA, Canada and Europe send 100 million tonnes of sulphur dioxide into the air each year. Nine tenths of this comes from burning coal and oil.

══ SCIENCE AT WORK ══

The CEGB is fitting FGD to Drax power station in Yorkshire and Fidlers' Ferry in Wales. At a cost of £40 million, the FGD plant at Drax power station will be in operation by 1993.

The acidic rain water trickles through the soil until it meets rock. Then it travels along the layer of rock to emerge in lakes and rivers. Lakes are more affected by acid rain than rivers are. They become more and more acidic, and the concentrations of metal salts increase. Fish cannot live in acidic water. Aluminium compounds, e.g. aluminium hydroxide, come out of solution and are deposited on the gills. The fish secrete mucus to try to get rid of the deposit. The gills become clogged with mucus, and the fish die. An acid lake is perfectly transparent because plants, plankton, insects and other living things have perished.

Thousands of lakes in Norway, Sweden and Canada are now 'dead' lakes. One reason why these countries suffer badly is that acidic snow piles up during the winter months. In the spring thaw, the accumulated snow melts suddenly, and a large volume of acidic water flows into the lakes. Acid rain is partially neutralised as it trickles slowly through soil and over rock. Limestone, in particular, keeps damage to a minimum by neutralising some of the acidity. There is not time for this partial neutralisation to occur when acid snow melts and tonnes of water flow rapidly down the hills and into the lakes.

The UK is affected too. In 1982, lakes and rivers in south-west Scotland had become so acidic that the water companies started treating the lakes with calcium hydroxide (lime). The aim is to neutralise the acidic water and revive stocks of fish. In Wales, the water company has for some years poured tonnes of powdered limestone into acidic lakes. A number of lakes are 'dead' and the fish in many others are threatened.

Figure 23.5D ● The effects of acid rain

● *What can be done about acid rain?*

There are three main methods of attacking the problem of acid rain. They all cost money, but then the damage done by acid rain costs money too.

❶ Low-sulphur fuels can be used. Crushing coal and washing it with a suitable solvent reduces the sulphur content by 10 to 40 per cent. The dirty solvent must be disposed of without creating pollution on land or in rivers. Oil refineries could refine the oil which they sell to power stations. The cost of the purified oil would be higher, and the price of electricity would increase.

❷ Flue gas desulphurisation, FGD, is the removal of sulphur from power station chimneys after the coal has been burnt and before the waste gases leave the chimneys. As the combustion products pass up the chimney, they are bombarded by jets of wet powdered limestone. The acid gases are neutralised to form a sludge. The method will remove 95 per cent of the acid combustion products. FGD can be fitted to existing power stations. One of the products is calcium sulphate, which can be sold to the plaster board industry and to cement manufacturers.

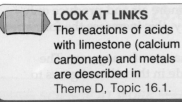

LOOK AT LINKS
The reactions of acids with limestone (calcium carbonate) and metals are described in Theme D, Topic 16.1.

❸ Pulverised fluidised bed combustion, PFBC, uses a new type of furnace. The furnace burns pulverised coal (small particles) in a bed of powdered limestone. An upward flow of air keeps the whole bed in motion. The sulphur is removed during burning. The PFBC uses much more limestone than the FGD method: one power station needs 1 million tonnes of limestone a year (4 times as much as the FGD method). The PFBC method also produces a lot more waste material, which has to be dumped.

CHECKPOINT

❶ What is the advantage of building a power station close to a densely populated area? What is the disadvantage?

❷ Why do power stations and factories have tall chimneys? Are tall chimneys a solution to the problem of pollution? Explain your answer.

❸ Why does acid rain attack (a) iron railings (b) marble statues and (c) stone buildings?

❹ (a) Why does Sweden suffer badly from acid rain?
(b) Why do lakes suffer more than rivers from the effects of acid rain?

❺ A country decides to increase the price of electricity so that the power stations can afford to use refined low-sulphur fuel oil. In what ways will the country actually *save* money by reducing the emission of sulphur dioxide?

23.6 Carbon monoxide

LOOK AT LINKS
for **hydrocarbons**
See Theme E, Topic 22.5.

LOOK AT LINKS
for **haemoglobin**
See Theme J, Topic 38.3.

● *Where does it come from?*

Worldwide, the emission of carbon monoxide is 350 million tonnes a year. Most of it comes from the exhaust gases of motor vehicles. Vehicle engines are designed to give maximum power. This is achieved by arranging for the mixture in the cylinders to have a high fuel to air ratio. This design leads to incomplete combustion. The result is the discharge of carbon monoxide, carbon and unburnt **hydrocarbons**.

● *What harm does carbon monoxide do?*

Oxygen combines with **haemoglobin**, a substance in red blood cells. Carbon monoxide is 200 times better at combining with haemoglobin than oxygen is. Carbon monoxide is therefore able to tie up haemoglobin and prevent it combining with oxygen. A shortage of oxygen causes headache and dizziness, and makes a person feel sluggish. If the level of carbon monoxide reaches 0.1% of the air, it will kill. Carbon monoxide is especially dangerous in that, being colourless and odourless, it gives no warning of its presence. Since carbon monoxide is produced by motor vehicles, it is likely to affect people when they are driving in heavy traffic. This is when people need to feel alert and to have quick reflexes.

● *What can be done?*

Soil contains organisms which can convert carbon monoxide into carbon dioxide or methane. This natural mechanism for dealing with carbon monoxide cannot cope in cities, where the concentration of carbon monoxide is high and there is little soil to remove it. People are trying out a number of solutions to the problem.

CHECKPOINT

❶ What products are formed by the combustion of hydrocarbons in petrol engines?

❷ How does the supply of air affect the course of combustion?

❸ What is the advantage of increasing the air to fuel ratio in the combustion chamber?

❹ What are the pollutants that form when the air to fuel ratio is high? What can be done about them?

❺ Copy and complete this summary.
In internal combustion engines, a high air to fuel ratio:
decreases the emission of unburnt _____ A
decreases the emission of _____ B
increases the emission of _____ C
A way of reducing the emission of C would be to run the engine at a lower temperature. A _____ would be needed to promote _____ combustion and reduce the emission of A and B.

❻ The figures opposite show approximately how the emissions of carbon monoxide, oxides of nitrogen and hydrocarbons change with the speed of a vehicle. (Note that the scale for carbon monoxide goes up to 30 g/l, while that of the other pollutants goes up to 3 g/l.)
  (a) Say what speed is best for reducing the emission of (i) carbon monoxide (ii) oxides of nitrogen (iii) hydrocarbons.
  (b) (i) What speed would you recommend as the best to reduce overall pollution? (ii) What is this speed in miles per hour (5 mile = 8 km)?

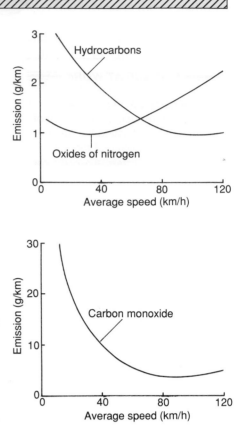

23.9 Smoke, dust and grit

LOOK AT LINKS
for **smog**
See Theme E, Topic 23.1.

LOOK AT LINKS
for **electrostatic attraction**
How do electrostatic precipitators work?
See Theme K, Topic 42.1.

SUMMARY

Particles of smoke and dust and grit are sent into the air by factories, power stations and motor vehicles. Dirt damages buildings and plants. It pollutes the air we breathe; mixed with fog, it forms smog.

Millions of tonnes of smoke, dust and grit are present in the atmosphere. Dust storms, forest fires and volcanic eruptions send matter into the air. Human activities such as mining, land-clearing and burning coal and oil add to the solid matter in the air.

● What harm do particles do?

Particles darken city air by scattering light. Smoke increases the danger of smog. Solid particles fall as grime on people, clothing, buildings and plants.

Sunlight which meets dust particles is reflected back into space and prevented from reaching the Earth. Some scientists believe that the increasing amount of dust in the atmosphere is serious. A fourfold increase in the amount of dust would make the Earth's temperature fall by about 3 °C. This would affect food production.

● How can particles be removed?

Industries use a number of methods. These include:
- using sprays of water to wash out particles from their waste gases
- passing waste gases through filters,
- electrostatic precipitators, which remove dust particles from waste gases by **electrostatic attraction**

23.10 Metals

Many heavy metals and their compounds are serious air pollutants. 'Heavy' metals are metals with a density greater than 5 g/cm^3.

Mercury

Earth-moving activities, such as mining and road-making, disturb soil and rock and allow the mercury which they contain to escape into the air. Mercury vapour is also released into the air during the smelting of many metal ores and the combustion of coal and oil. Both mercury and its compounds cause kidney damage, nerve damage and death.

Lead

● Where does it come from?

The lead compounds in the air all come from human activity. Vehicle engines, the combustion of coal and the roasting of metal ores send lead and its compounds into the air. Unlike the other pollutants in exhaust gases, lead compounds have been purposely added to the fuel. Tetraethyl lead, TEL, is added to improve the performance of the engine.

● What harm does it do?

Lead compounds settle out of the air on to plant crops, and contaminate our food. The level of lead in our environment is high: some areas still have lead plumbing; old houses may have peeling lead-based paint. City dwellers take in lead from many sources. Many people have blood levels of lead which are nearly high enough to produce the symptoms of lead poisoning. Symptoms of mild lead poisoning are headache, irritability, tiredness and depression. Higher levels of lead cause damage to the brain, liver and kidneys. Scientists have suggested that behaviour disorders such as hooliganism and vandalism may be due in part to lead poisoning.

● What can be done?

This type of pollution can be remedied. We can stop adding lead compounds to petrol. Research chemists have found other compounds which can be used to improve engine performance. Vehicles made in the UK after autumn 1990 are adjusted to run on lead-free petrol. Most petrol stations now stock lead-free petrol. The USA, Germany and Japan use lead-free petrol because the catalytic converters fitted to their cars are 'poisoned' by lead compounds.

Figure 23.10A ● City dwellers breathe exhaust gases

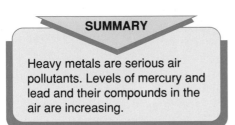

SUMMARY

Heavy metals are serious air pollutants. Levels of mercury and lead and their compounds in the air are increasing.

CHECKPOINT

❶ Name the pollutants which come from motor vehicles.

❷ Name the pollutants which can be reduced by fitting catalytic converters into vehicle exhausts. What effect will this modification have on the price of cars?

❸ Catalytic converters will only work with lead-free petrol. When TEL is no longer added to petrol, motorists will have to use high octane (4 star) fuel. What effect will this have on the cost of motoring?

④ What effect does the use of TEL have on the air, apart from its effect on catalytic converters?

⑤ In which ways will the control of pollution from vehicles cost money? In which ways will a reduction in the level of pollutants in the air save money? (Consider the effects of pollution on people and materials.) Will the expense be worthwhile?

23.11  Chlorofluorohydrocarbons

The ozone layer

There is a layer of ozone, O_3, surrounding the Earth. It is 5 km thick at a distance of 25–30 km from the Earth's surface. The ozone layer cuts out some of the ultraviolet light coming from the Sun. Ultraviolet light is bad for us and for crops. Long exposure to ultraviolet light can cause skin cancer. This complaint is common in Australia among people who spend a lot of time out of doors. If anything happens to decrease the ozone layer, the incidence of skin cancer from exposure to ultraviolet light will increase. An excess of ultraviolet light kills **phytoplankton**, the minute plant life of the oceans which are the primary food on which the life of an ocean depends.

> **LOOK AT LINKS**
> for **phytoplankton**
> See Theme M, Topic 52.

When the pressure is released, the propellant liquid vaporises and forces the polish out of the can

Mixture of propellant and useful liquid, e.g. polish or insecticide, under pressure

● *The problem*
Ozone is a very reactive element. If the upper atmosphere becomes polluted, ozone will oxidise the pollutants. Two pollutants are accumulating in the upper atmosphere. One is the **propellant** from aerosol cans (see Figure 23.11A).

Figure 23.11A ● An aerosol can

Many of the propellants are chlorofluorohydrocarbons (CFCs). They are very unreactive compounds. They spread through the atmosphere without reacting with other substances and drift into the upper atmosphere. There they meet ozone, which oxidises CFCs and in doing so is converted into oxygen.

Ozone + CFC → Oxygen + Oxidation products

Another pollutant found at this height is nitrogen monoxide, NO. It comes from the exhausts of high-altitude aircraft, such as Concorde. Ozone oxidises nitrogen monoxide to nitrogen dioxide:

Ozone	+	Nitrogen monoxide	→	Oxygen	+	Nitrogen dioxide
$O_3(g)$	+	$NO(g)$	→	$O_2(g)$	+	$NO_2(g)$

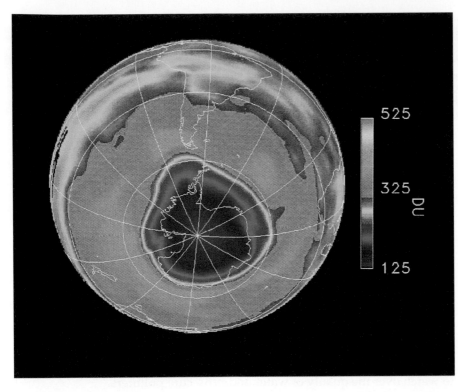

Figure 23.11B ● The ozone hole

● What should be done?

Is it happening? Is the ozone layer becoming thinner? In June 1980 the British Antarctic Expedition discovered that there was a gap in the ozone layer over Antarctica during certain months. In 1987, research workers in the US confirmed that there was a thinning of the ozone layer which was 'large, sudden and unexpected... far worse than we thought'. In 1988 a team of scientists working in the Arctic Ocean discovered that the ozone layer over Northern Europe was thinner than it had been.

Knowing that the danger had appeared over more populated regions of the globe, spurred many countries to take action. At a meeting in Montreal in 1987 many countries agreed to reduce their use of CFCs by 50% by the year 2000. Since that date, many countries have agreed to speed up their programme of phasing out CFCs. Aerosols containing CFCs have been banned in the USA since 1988. In 1988 many makers of toiletries in the UK agreed to stop using CFCs by the end of 1989. They are now using spray cans with different propellants, which they label 'ozone-friendly', or pump-action cans. There is more of a problem with the CFCs used as refrigerants, in air conditioners, in the manufacture of polyurethane foam and as solvents. Chemists are now finding stable compounds to replace CFCs. In the USA, Du Pont Chemicals have agreed to stop using CFCs after the year 2000. In the UK, ICI chemists are working hard to find substitutes to enable ICI to do the same.

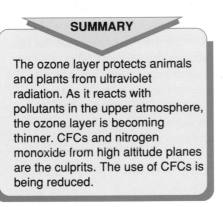

SUMMARY

The ozone layer protects animals and plants from ultraviolet radiation. As it reacts with pollutants in the upper atmosphere, the ozone layer is becoming thinner. CFCs and nitrogen monoxide from high altitude planes are the culprits. The use of CFCs is being reduced.

CHECKPOINT

❶ Look round your kitchen, bathroom and garage. How many products in aerosol cans do you buy? How convenient is it to have each of these products in an aerosol can? What inconvenience would you suffer if aerosol cans were banned? How many of the aerosol cans are labelled 'ozone-friendly'? What does this mean?

❷ Speaking on 23 February 1988, the Prince of Wales announced that he had banned aerosols from his household. He said that some members of his household had difficulty in finding a suitable alternative hairspray.
   (a) What concern led the Prince of Wales to take this step?
   (b) What properties must the propellant in the hairspray possess to work effectively and to be safe in use?
   (c) What substitute can you suggest for an aerosol hairspray?

❸ How does their lack of chemical reactivity make CFCs (a) useful and
   (b) dangerous?

WATER POLLUTION

TOPIC
24

24.1 Pollution by industry

What's the problem? We need clean drinking water – nothing could be more important. We need industry, and industry needs to dispose of waste products; in the process our water is polluted.

SUMMARY

The National Rivers Authority controls pollution of inland rivers. It does not regulate the discharge of pollutants into tidal rivers, estuaries and the sea. The estuaries in the UK are heavily polluted by industry and by sewage.

IT'S A FACT

B & N Chemicals in 1981 filled the town of Haverhill in Suffolk with chemical smells. The River Stow was so polluted that the water works was unable to draw water from the river. The company was prosecuted and convicted. The fine was a mere £325.
British Tissues was prosecuted in 1983 after discharging far more waste than it was allowed into the River Don. The fine was £750. It was obviously cheaper to pay fines than to treat the waste.

SUMMARY

Many industrial firms do not keep their discharges of wastes within the limits set by law.

Controls

You will notice that many industrial firms are on river banks. These firms can get rid of waste products by discharging them into rivers. Until 1989, the quantities of waste which industries were allowed to discharge into rivers were controlled by the water authority of each region. Under the 1974 Control of Pollution Act, the water authorities had power to control pollution in inland rivers but not in tidal rivers, estuaries and the sea (except for the discharge of radioactive waste: see Topic 12.8. In spite of the Act, more than 2800 km of Britain's largest rivers are too dirty and lacking in oxygen to keep fish alive.

In 1989 the UK Water Privatisation Bill became law. The water authorities were sold to private companies, and are now run for profit as other industries are. The Government set up a National Rivers Authority to watch over the quality of water and prosecute polluters.

● Estuaries

Many of the worst polluters discharge into coastal waters and estuaries. The oil refineries, chemical works, steel plants and paper mills on coasts and estuaries can pour all the waste they want into estuaries and the sea. In the 1930s, fishermen could make a living in the Mersey. Now, it is too foul to keep fish alive. One reason is the discharge of raw sewage into the Mersey. The other is that too many firms pour waste into the estuary. There is unemployment in Merseyside, and the Government does not want to make life difficult for industry in the area. The industries on the banks of the Mersey have been given permission to fall below the standards of the Control of Pollution Act.

Other estuaries, such as the Humber, the Tees, the Tyne and the Clyde, are also polluted by industry.

Figure 24.1A ● The Mersey

Mercury and its compounds

FIRST THOUGHTS

Why has it taken so long for industry to react to the tragedy of Minamata?

LOOK AT LINKS
for **food chains**
See Theme M, Topic 52.

A well-known case of industrial pollution is the tragedy of Minamata, a fishing village on the shore of Minamata Bay in Japan. A plastics factory started discharging waste into the bay in 1951. By 1953, a thousand people in Minamata were seriously ill. Some were crippled, some were paralysed, some went blind, some became mentally deranged, and some died. The cause of the disease was found to be the mercury compounds which the plastics factory discharged into the Bay. Although the level of mercury compounds in the Bay water was low, mercury was concentrated by a **food chain** (see Figure 24.1B). The level of mercury in the fish in the Bay was high, and fishers and their families became ill through eating the fish.

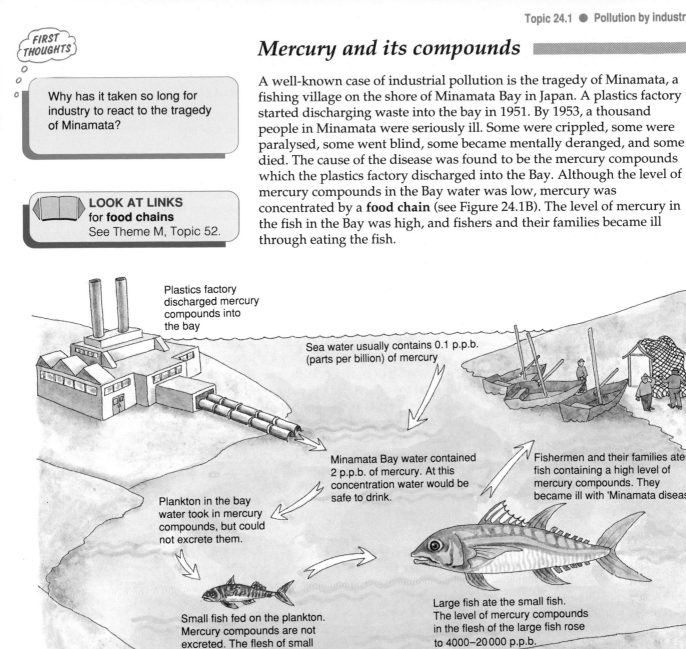

Plastics factory discharged mercury compounds into the bay

Sea water usually contains 0.1 p.p.b. (parts per billion) of mercury

Minamata Bay water contained 2 p.p.b. of mercury. At this concentration water would be safe to drink.

Plankton in the bay water took in mercury compounds, but could not excrete them.

Fishermen and their families ate fish containing a high level of mercury compounds. They became ill with 'Minamata disease'

Small fish fed on the plankton. Mercury compounds are not excreted. The flesh of small fish contained up to 200 p.p.b. of mercury

Large fish ate the small fish. The level of mercury compounds in the flesh of the large fish rose to 4000–20 000 p.p.b.

Figure 24.1B ● The food chain which led to the Minamata disease

SUMMARY

Mercury and its compounds are poisonous. If mercury gets into a lake or river, it is converted slowly into soluble compounds. These are likely to accumulate in fish and may be eaten by humans.

Other countries have experienced the results of mercury pollution. In 1967, many lakes and rivers in Sweden were found to be so contaminated by mercury that fishing had to stop. In 1970, high mercury levels were found in hundreds of lakes in Canada and the USA. As late as 1988, the ICI plant on Merseyside discharged more mercury than the permitted level. Now that the danger is known, the polluting plants have taken care to reduce spillage of mercury. The danger is still there, however. Mercury from years of pollution lies in the sediment at the bottom of lakes. Slowly it is converted by bacteria into soluble mercury compounds. These may get into a food chain.

CHECKPOINT

❶ When a car engine has an oil change, the waste oil is sometimes poured down the drain. What is wrong with doing this?

❷ Does it matter whether rivers are clean and stocked with fish or foul and devoid of life? Explain your answer.

❸ The Minamata tragedy happened when Japan was building up its industry after the war. In spite of Japan's experience, Sweden, Canada and the USA found an excess of mercury in their lakes twenty years later. Why had they not learned from Japan's mistake? (You will not find the answer in the back!)

24.2 Thermal pollution

FIRST THOUGHTS

What's wrong with warming up the water?

SUMMARY

Thermal pollution means warming rivers and lakes. It reduces the concentration of oxygen dissolved in the water.

Industries use water as a coolant. A large nuclear power station uses 4000 tonnes of water a minute for cooling. River water is circulated round the power station, where its temperature increases by 10 °C, and is returned to the river. If the temperature of the river rises by many degrees, the river is **thermally polluted**. As the temperature rises, the solubility of oxygen decreases. At the same time, the **biochemical oxygen demand** increases. Fish become more active at the higher temperature, and need more oxygen. The bacteria which feed on decaying organic matter become more active and use more oxygen.

24.3 Pollution by sewage

FIRST THOUGHTS

The population of the UK is increasing. One result is the need for more sewage works. What happens when a country does not keep up with this need?

Inside Science
(program)

Use this software to deal with an accidental pollution spillage.

Life and Death of a River
(data base)

Explore a case of river pollution and see what can be done to clean it up. Use this with either the *Key* or *Keysheet* package.

Figure 24.3A ● British beaches and the EC standard

In Topic 22.4, you read how sewage is treated before it is discharged into rivers or the sea. Unfortunately, as some water companies do not have enough plants to treat all their area's sewage, they discharge some raw sewage into rivers and estuaries. The Mersey receives raw sewage from Liverpool and other towns. In Sussex, sewage treatment works are inadequate and sewage is discharged into the sea. This creates some nasty results at several bathing beaches in the country.

SUMMARY

During the 1980s, the United Nations set a target of safe water and sanitation for all by 1990. The aim was to provide wells and pumps, kits for disinfecting water and hygienic toilets. The sum needed was £25 billion, slightly more than the world spends on its armies in one month. The target was not reached by 1990, but the work is continuing.

The quality of the water at dozens of Britain's bathing beaches fails to meet standards set by the European Community (EC). Many British beaches have more coliform bacteria and faecal bacteria in the water than the EC standard.

The Third World

Of the four billion people in the world, two billion have no toilets, and one billion have unsafe drinking water. In Third World countries (the developing countries) three out of five people have difficulty in obtaining clean water. Some Third World communities have to use a river as a source of drinking water as well as for disposal of their sewage. Bacteria are present in faeces, and they infect the water. Many diseases are spread by contaminated water. They include cholera, typhoid, river blindness, diarrhoea and schistosomiasis. Four-fifths of the diseases in the Third World are linked to dirty water and lack of sanitation. Five million people each year are killed by water-borne diseases.

Figure 24.3B ● Their water supplies

24.4 Pollution by agriculture

FIRST THOUGHTS

Farmers need to use fertilisers. What happens when a crop does not use all the fertiliser applied to it? There can be pollution, as this section explains.

Fertilisers

A lake has a natural cycle. In summer, algae grow on the surface, fed by nutrients which are washed into the lake. In autumn the algae die and sink to the bottom. Bacteria break down the algae into nutrients. Plants need the elements carbon, hydrogen, oxygen, nitrogen and phosphorus. Water always provides enough carbon, hydrogen and oxygen; plant growth is limited by the supply of nitrogen and phosphorus. Sometimes farm land surrounding a lake receives more fertiliser than the crops can absorb. Then the unabsorbed nitrates and phosphates in the fertiliser wash out of the soil into the lake water. When fertilisers wash into a lake, they upset the natural cycle. The algae multiply rapidly to produce an **algal bloom**. The lake water comes to resemble a cloudy greenish soup. When the algae die, bacteria feed on the dead material and multiply. The increased bacterial activity consumes much of the dissolved oxygen. There is little oxygen left in the water, and fish die from lack of oxygen. The lake becomes difficult for boating because masses of algae snag the propellers. The name given to this accidental fertilisation of lakes and rivers is **eutrophication**.

Many parts of the Norfolk Broads are now covered with algal bloom. The tourist industry centred on the Broads would like to see them restored to their former condition.

Use an oxygen sensor and probe to measure the percentage of oxygen in air. The same probe can be used to measure dissolved oxygen in water. You'll need to connect the sensor to a computer or a datalogger.

Lough Neagh in Northern Ireland is the UK's biggest inland lake. It supplies Belfast's water and it also supports eel-fishing. Algae now block the filters through which water flows to the water treatment plant. Eels and other fish are in danger as the level of dissolved oxygen falls. The problem is being tackled by removing phosphates from the treated sewage which enters the lough. Treatment with a solution containing aluminium ions and iron(III) ions precipitates phosphates. Each year, this stops 60 tonnes of phosphorus in the form of phosphates from entering Lough Neagh. This pollution is unnecessary. Detergents without phosphates would leave laundry only a little less sparkling white, but would not pollute our rivers and lakes.

Fertiliser which is not absorbed by crops can be carried into the ground water (the water in porous underground rock). Ground water provides one third of Britain's drinking water. The EC has set a maximum level of nitrates in drinking water at 50 mg/l (12 p.p.m. of nitrogen in the form of nitrate). Four out of the ten water companies in England and Wales have drinking water which exceeds this nitrate level. In 1989, the EC decided to prosecute the UK for falling below EC water standards.

Figure 24.4A ● Algal bloom

SUMMARY

When a crop receives more fertiliser than it can use, nitrates and phosphates wash into lakes and rivers. There, they stimulate the growth of weeds and algae. When the plants die, bacterial decay of the dead material uses oxygen. The resulting shortage of dissolved oxygen kills fish.

The level of nitrates in ground water, from which we obtain much of our drinking water, is rising.

Pollution can be reduced by reducing the application of fertilisers and by omitting phosphates from detergents.

There are two health worries over nitrates. Nitrates are converted into nitrites (salts containing the NO_2 ion). Some chemists think that nitrites are converted in the body into nitrosoamines. These compounds cause cancer. The other worry is that nitrites oxidise the iron in haemoglobin. The oxidised form of haemoglobin can no longer combine with oxygen. The extreme form of nitrite poisoning is 'blue baby' syndrome, in which the baby turns blue from lack of oxygen. Babies are more at risk than adults because babies' stomachs are less acidic and assist the conversion of nitrates into nitrites.

The level of nitrites in drinking water permitted by the EC is 0.1 mg/l. Some parts of London have nitrite levels which are higher than this. The UK Government has agreed to bring the UK into line with the rest of Europe. To install nitrate-stripping equipment would cost £200 million. *Should the Government reduce the use of fertilisers? How? Should the Government introduce a tax on fertilisers or ration fertilisers?*

Pesticides

FIRST THOUGHTS

What are the 'drins'? Why is the EC worried about the level of drins in UK water?

Other pollutants which must worry us are the pesticides dieldrin, endrin and aldrin (sometimes called the 'drins'). They cause liver cancer and affect the central nervous system. The EC sets a maximum level of 5×10^{-9} g/l for 'drins'. Half the water in the UK exceeds this level. The danger with the 'drins' is that fish take them in and do not excrete them. The level of 'drins' in fish may build up to 6000 times the level in water.

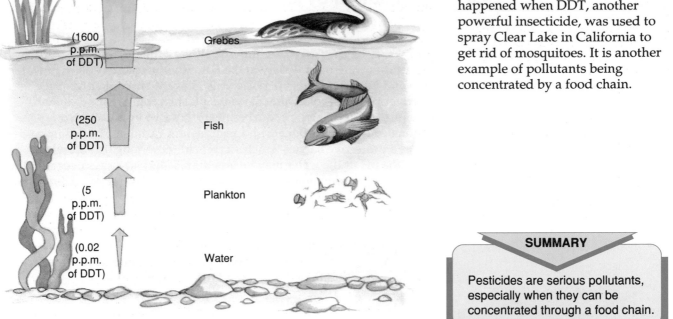

Figure 24.4B shows what happened when DDT, another powerful insecticide, was used to spray Clear Lake in California to get rid of mosquitoes. It is another example of pollutants being concentrated by a food chain.

(1600 p.p.m. of DDT)   Grebes

(250 p.p.m. of DDT)   Fish

(5 p.p.m. of DDT)   Plankton

(0.02 p.p.m. of DDT)   Water

Figure 24.4B ● A food chain in Clear Lake, California

SUMMARY

Pesticides are serious pollutants, especially when they can be concentrated through a food chain.

CHECKPOINT

❶ Groups of settlers in North America always built their villages on river banks, and discharged their sewage into the river. How did the river dispose of the sewage? Why can this method of sewage disposal not be used for larger settlements?

❷ British Tissues make toilet paper, paper towels, paper handkerchiefs, etc. They use a lot of bleach on the paper, and this bleach is one of the chemicals which the firm has to dispose of. Can you suggest how the firm could reduce the problem of bleach disposal?

❸ (a) Why do some lakes develop a thick layer of algal bloom?
   (b) Why is algal bloom less likely to occur in a river?
   (c) What harm does algal bloom do to a lake that is used as (i) a reservoir (ii) a fishing lake (iii) a boating lake?

❹ The concentration of nitrates in ground water is rising. Explain:
   (a) why this is happening,
   (b) why some people are worried about the increase.

❺ Water companies can tackle the problem of high nitrate levels by:
   • blending water from high-nitrate sources with water from low-nitrate sources
   • closing some sources of water
   • treating the water with chemicals
   • ion exchange
   • microbiological methods

   (a) Say what you think are the advantages and disadvantages of each of these methods.
   (b) Which do you think would be the most expensive treatments? How will water companies be able to pay for the treatment?
   (c) Suggest a different method of reducing the level of nitrates in ground water.
   (d) Say who would pay for the method which you mention in (c) and how they would find the money.

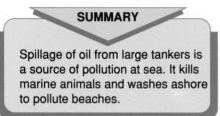

SCIENCE AT WORK

Bacteria can be used to clean out a tanker's storage compartment. The empty tank is filled with sea water, nutrient, air and bacteria. When the tanker reaches its destination, the tank contains clean water, a small amount of recoverable oil and an increased number of bacteria. The bacteria can be used as animal feed.

SUMMARY

Spillage of oil from large tankers is a source of pollution at sea. It kills marine animals and washes ashore to pollute beaches.

nations have not signed the agreements. Enforcing agreements is very difficult as it is impossible to detect everything that happens at sea.

Various methods have been tried for the removal of oil from the surface of the sea.

- **Dispersal**   Chemicals are added to emulsify the oil. The danger is that they may be toxic to marine life.

- **Sinking**   Oil may be treated with sand and other fine materials to make it sink. A danger is that the sunken oil may cover and destroy the feeding areas of marine creatures.

- **Burning**   Burning oil is dangerous as a fire can spread rapidly over the sea. Research has been done on safe methods of burning oil, but they leave 15 per cent of the oil behind as lumps of tar.

- **Absorbing**   Absorbents do not work well in the open sea. They provide the best way of cleaning a beach or preventing an oil spill from reaching the shore.

- **Skimming off**   The method of surrounding an oil spill with a line of booms to prevent it spreading and then pumping oil off the surface has been used with some success.

- **Solidifying**   Scientists at British Petroleum have discovered chemicals which will solidify oil spills. The chemicals must be sprayed on to the oil slick from the air. They convert the oil into a rubber-like solid which can be skimmed off the surface in nets.

- **Bacteria**   There are bacteria which will decompose petroleum. A mixture of bacteria (of the correct strain) and nutrients is sprinkled on to the spill from the air.

CHECKPOINT

❶ (a) What are the causes of oil spills at sea?
  (b) What damage do they do?
  (c) Who pays to clean up the mess?
  (d) Suggest what can be done to stop pollution of the sea by oil.

? THEME QUESTIONS

● *Topic 20*

1 (a) What happens to the temperature of a gas if the gas is compressed suddenly?
  (b) What happens to the temperature of a gas if the gas is allowed to expand suddenly? How is this effect used to liquefy air? Why is this method chosen for the liquefaction of air?
  (c) Boiling points are nitrogen, –196 °C; oxygen, –183 °C.
     Explain how the difference in boiling points makes it possible to separate oxygen and nitrogen from liquid air.
  (d) Give one-large scale industrial use for (i) oxygen (ii) nitrogen and (iii) another gas which is obtained from liquid air. Say why each gas is chosen for that particular use.

2 Three of the gases in air dissolve in water.
  (a) Which of them dissolves to give an acidic solution? What use is made of this solution?
  (b) Which of the three gases is a nuisance to deep-sea divers? Explain why, and say how the problem has been solved.
  (c) The life processes of plants and animals depend on the solubility of two of these gases. Explain why.

3 The table shows the composition of inhaled air and exhaled air, excluding water vapour, and a comment on the content of water vapour.

	Percentage by volume	
	Inhaled air	Exhaled air
Oxygen	21	17
Nitrogen	78	78
Carbon dioxide	0.03	4
Noble gases	1	1
Water vapour	Variable	Saturated

  (a) Describe the differences between inhaled air and exhaled air.
  (b) Briefly give the cause of each of these differences.

● *Topic 21*

4 A classroom contains 36 pupils. The doors and windows are closed for half an hour. Answer these questions about the air at the end of the half hour.
  (a) Will the air temperature be higher or lower? Explain your answer.
  (b) Will the air be more or less humid (moist)? Explain your answer.
  (c) Will the percentage of carbon dioxide in the air be higher or lower? Explain your answer. Say how the change in carbon dioxide content will affect the class.

5 You are given four gas jars. One contains oxygen, one nitrogen, one carbon dioxide and one hydrogen. Describe how you would find out which is which.

6 The diagram shows an apparatus which is being used to pass a sample of air slowly over heated copper.

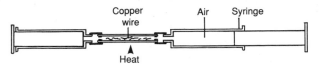

  (a) Describe how the appearance of the copper changes.
  (b) Which gas is removed from the air by copper? Name the solid product formed.
  (c) If 250 cm³ of air are treated in this way, what volume of gas will remain?
  (d) Name the chief component of the gas that remains.
  (e) Name two other gases that are present in air.

7 When petrol burns in a car engine, carbon dioxide and carbon monoxide are two of the products.
  (a) Write the formula of (i) carbon dioxide (ii) carbon monoxide.
  (b) Explain the statement 'Carbon monoxide is a product of incomplete combustion.'
  (c) Red blood cells contain haemoglobin. What vital job does haemoglobin do in the body?
  (d) If people breathe in too much carbon monoxide, it may kill them. How does carbon monoxide cause death?
  (e) Explain how people can be poisoned accidentally by carbon monoxide.
  (f) What precautions can people take to make sure that carbon monoxide is not formed in their homes?
  (g) The blood of people who smoke contains more carbon monoxide than the blood of non-smokers. Can you explain why?

● *Topic 22*

8 Ruth carried out an experiment to compare the hardness of the water from three towns. She measured 50 cm³ of each water sample into separate conical flasks. She added soap solution gradually to each flask, shaking them until a lather was formed. Her results are shown in the table.

Water sample	Volume of soap solution (cm³)
Distilled water	2.0
Johnstown water	7.5
Mansville water	10.0
Rumchester water	4.0

  (a) Say what piece of apparatus Ruth could use for measuring (i) the 50 cm³ samples of water and (ii) the volume of soap solution added.
  (b) Explain why she did a test on distilled water.
  (c) Why does distilled water require the smallest volume of soap solution to form a lather?
  (d) Which town has the hardest water? Explain your answer.

(e) When Ruth boiled a 50 cm³ of Rumchester water before testing it, she found that the volume of soap solution needed to produce a lather was 2.0 cm³. Explain why she got a different result with boiled water.

(f) Recommend two measures that the hard water towns could take to cut down on their soap consumption.

9 The diagram shows rain falling on the ground and trickling over underground rocks.

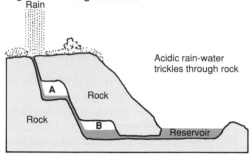

(a) Explain why natural rain water is weakly acidic.
(b) Name a type of rock which will be attacked by acidic rain water.
(c) Name the type of cavity, A, that is formed as a result of the action of rain water on the rock.
(d) Name the type of water that accumulates at B.
(e) Water flows from B into a reservoir. What treatment does the water need before it is fit to drink? Explain why this water receives a different treatment from river water.
(f) Will the water in the reservoir be hard water or soft water? Explain your answer.
(g) State one advantage and one disadvantage of hard water compared with soft water.

10 (a) What is the difference between raw sewage and digested sludge?
(b) Why can raw sewage not be used as a fertiliser?
(c) The digested sludge which sewage works produce is sold to farmers. Who benefits from this sale?
(d) Why do water treatment works treat drinking water with chlorine?
(e) How and why does the treatment of ground water differ from that of river water?

● *Topic 23*
11 (a) Name three pollutants that are produced by power stations.
(b) For one of the pollutants, describe the kind of cleaning system that can be used to stop the pollutant being discharged into the air.
(c) How will the cost of electricity be affected by (i) installing the cleaning system and (ii) stocking the chemicals consumed in running the cleaning system?

12 (a) What is the difference between oxygen and ozone?
(b) What converts oxygen into ozone?
(c) What converts ozone into oxygen?
(d) What is the ozone layer? Where is it?
(e) Why is the ozone layer becoming thinner?
(f) Why does the decrease in the ozone layer make people worry?

13 The nitrogen monoxide content of the atmosphere is 5×10^6 tonnes. One supersonic transport (SST) flies on average 2500 hours per year and emits 3 tonnes of nitrogen monoxide per hour.
(a) How much nitrogen monoxide will be emitted in one year by a fleet of 50 SSTs?
(b) Calculate the ratio

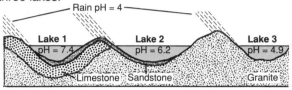

14 Cleopatra's needle has corroded more in London since 1878 than it did in 30 centuries in the Egyptian desert. Can you explain this?

15 The diagram shows acid rain falling on the shores of three lakes.

(a) Unpolluted rain water has a pH of 6.8. What gives it this weak acidity?
(b) By acid rain, we mean rain with a pH below 5.6. Name two substances that react with rain to make it strongly acidic.
(c) Explain why Lake 3 is more acidic than Lake 2.
(d) Explain why Lake 2 is more acidic than Lake 1.
(e) Lakes in Sweden become more acidic in the spring. Suggest an explanation.
(f) Acidic lakes in Sweden are treated with crushed limestone. Explain how this reduces the acidity. Give two disadvantages of this solution to the problem.

● *Topic 24*
16 Many industrial plants take water from a river and then return it at a higher temperature. What harm can this do? What name is given to this practice?

17 Bacteria in river water are able to convert many pollutants into harmless products. What, then, is the harm in dumping waste into rivers?

18 What happens when plastics are dumped in lakes and rivers?

19 It takes 60 g of oxygen per day to oxidise the sewage from one person.
Water contains 10 p.p.m. of dissolved oxygen. What mass of water is robbed of its dissolved oxygen by oxidising the sewage from a village of 400 people in one day? (1 tonne = 1000 kg)

20 Water normally contains 10 p.p.m. of oxygen. It takes 4 g of oxygen to oxidise completely 1 g of oil. A garage does an oil change on a car, and pours the 4 kg of dirty oil down the drain. What mass of water will be stripped of its dissolved oxygen by oxidising the oil from this car?

21 Why is the pollution of estuaries so common? Who gains from being able to pollute estuaries? Who loses from this pollution?

THEME F
Life Processes

What makes living things different from non-living things?

There is no easy answer to this question. The best we can hope to do is to find features shared by all living things that are absent from non-living things. These features are the characteristics of life. There are seven characteristics: nutrition, respiration, excretion, sensitivity, movement, growth and reproduction. In this theme we shall look at the first three characteristics in more detail – how we respire, feed and excrete, and how organisms from other kingdoms do the same. The remaining four characteristics of life are examined in Theme J.

NUTRITION

25.1 Green plants make food by photosynthesis

Life on Earth depends on light. Why? Because light energy is converted into the energy of the chemical bonds in food substances by photosynthesis, and all living things need food.

LOOK AT LINKS
for **energy**
For how energy can be converted from one form into another
See Theme B, Topic 6.2.

LOOK AT LINKS
for **chloroplasts** and the structure of plant cells
See Theme D, Topic 19.1.

LOOK AT LINKS
for **catalysts**
See Theme L, Topic 46.7.

RESOURCE
-ACTIVITY-
PACK

LOOK AT LINKS
for **light** and **colour**
See Theme H, Topic 33.1.

The Sun floods the Earth with light. Plant cells use light to help them to make food by **photosynthesis**. They trap the energy in sunlight and use it to convert carbon dioxide and water into sugars. A summary of the chemical reactions that take place is

catalysed by chlorophyll

Carbon dioxide + Water → Glucose + Oxygen

$$6CO_2(g) + 6H_2O(l) \rightarrow C_6H_{12}O_6(aq) + 6O_2(g)$$

How does photosynthesis get its name? 'Photo' means light (in Greek) and 'synthesis' means putting together. Photosynthesis takes place in the **chloroplasts** found in the cells of green plants. Chloroplasts contain the green pigment chlorophyll, which acts as a **catalyst** in the chemical reactions of photosynthesis.

Since the energy of the chemical bonds on the left hand side of the equation above is less than the energy of the chemical bonds on the right hand side, the reactants must take in energy before the reaction can happen. This energy is supplied by the sunlight that falls on the leaves of the plant.

Leaves, light, water and gases

Leaf cells are 'factories' which collect sunlight, water and carbon dioxide, and manufacture food. Figure 25.1A shows how leaves are adapted for photosynthesis and traces the path of water and carbon dioxide molecules from the air into a leaf, a leaf cell and a chloroplast.

Photosynthesis involves a series of chemical reactions inside chloroplasts. The reactions fall into two stages: *stage 1*, absorbing sunlight; *stage 2*, transforming the energy of sunlight (which is an unlimited supply) into the energy of chemical bonds (see Figure 25.1A). The sugars formed by photosynthesis are the source of energy for the plant. When animals eat plants, the food substances built up in the plants become available to them.

Different pigments in photosynthesis

Chlorophyll absorbs light of all colours except green. It therefore appears green. In fact there are several kinds of chlorophyll. The green **pigments**, chlorophyll A and chlorophyll B, are found in most plants. They strongly absorb red and blue light. Other pigments, called carotenoids, are also present. They are red, yellow and orange and absorb light of other colours. Together, the assortment of pigments enables a plant to absorb sunlight over a wide spectrum (Figure 25.1B).

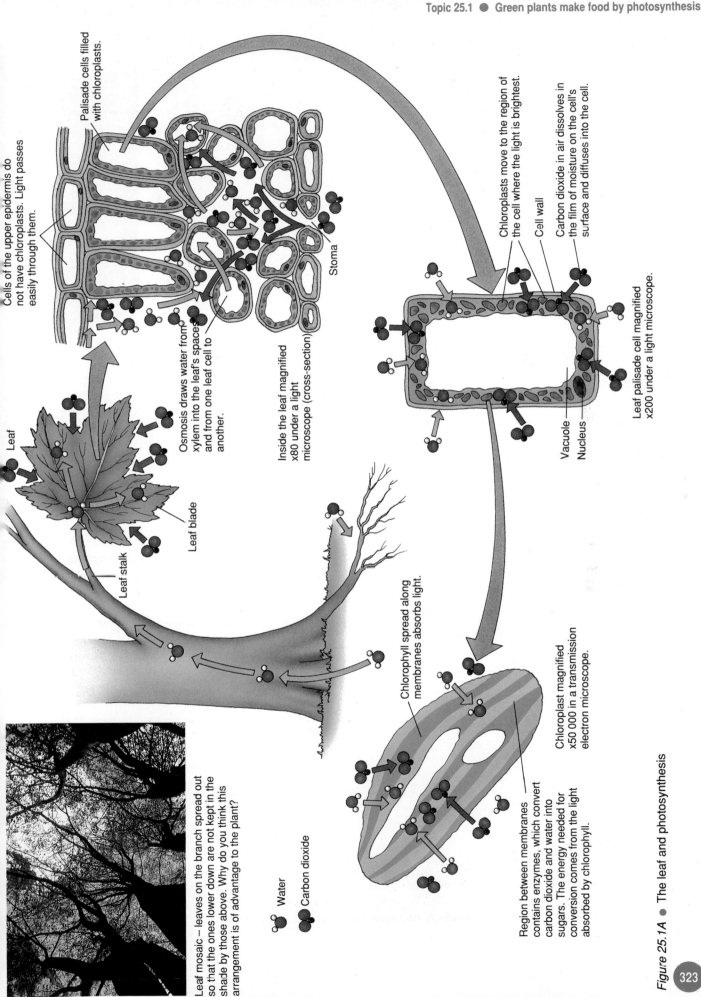

Palisade cells filled with chloroplasts.

Cells of the upper epidermis do not have chloroplasts. Light passes easily through them.

Chloroplasts move to the region of the cell where the light is brightest.

Cell wall

Carbon dioxide in air dissolves in the film of moisture on the cell's surface and diffuses into the cell.

Leaf palisade cell magnified x200 under a light microscope.

Vacuole

Nucleus

Stoma

Osmosis draws water from xylem into the leaf's spaces and from one leaf cell to another.

Inside the leaf magnified x80 under a light microscope (cross-section)

Leaf

Leaf blade

Leaf stalk

Chlorophyll spread along membranes absorbs light.

Chloroplast magnified x50 000 in a transmission electron microscope.

Region between membranes contains enzymes, which convert carbon dioxide and water into sugars. The energy needed for conversion comes from the light absorbed by chlorophyll.

Leaf mosaic – leaves on the branch spread out so that the ones lower down are not kept in the shade by those above. Why do you think this arrangement is of advantage to the plant?

Water

Carbon dioxide

Figure 25.1A ● The leaf and photosynthesis

323

LOOK AT LINKS
You can separate the pigments in plant leaves by chromatography.
See Theme D, Topic 15.9.

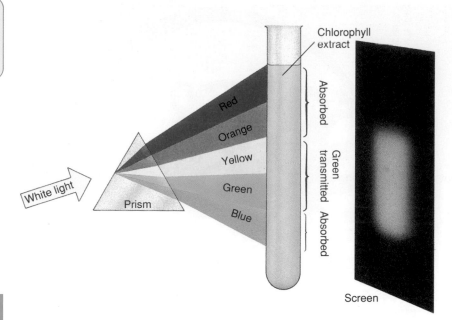

Figure 25.1B ● Spectrum of white light and chlorophyll

SUMMARY

Photosynthesis is the process by which plants make food. Carbon dioxide and water combine in the presence of the catalyst, chlorophyll, to form glucose and oxygen. The reaction takes place in sunlight. The energy of sunlight is converted into the energy of the chemical bonds in glucose.

In summer nearly all leaves are green, because the colours of the carotenoids are masked by the chlorophylls. In autumn however, when the production of chlorophylls tails off, the colours of the carotenoids blaze through. Tomatoes, carrots and ripe fruits of different kinds get their colours from carotenoids.

What conditions are best for photosynthesis?

Light intensity, temperature and supplies of carbon dioxide and water together affect the rate at which plants make sugars by photosynthesis. They are called **limiting factors** because if any one of them falls to a low level, photosynthesis slows down or stops.

Why do plants usually grow better in a greenhouse? Look at the greenhouse in Figure 25.1C and notice the bright lights, the water sprinklers and the machine for releasing carbon dioxide into the atmosphere. The farmer can control these conditions so that photosynthesis occurs at maximum efficiency, and the plants grow quickly. With the sunlight streaming through the windows, no wonder the plants are growing well! All the conditions they need for photosynthesis are just right.

Figure 25.1C ● The maximum efficiency greenhouse

Buttercups in the sun

Dog's mercury in the shade

● Light

Look at Figure 25.1D, showing plants growing in different light conditions. The graph shows that in both cases the rate of photosynthesis increases as the light intensity increases. However, once a particular light intensity is reached (the compensation point) the rate of photosynthesis stays constant even if the light intensity increases further.

Notice that the compensation points for dog's mercury and the buttercup are not the same. *How has dog's mercury adapted to shady conditions?*

Light on a sunny summer's day is about 10 times brighter than the compensation point for most plants. Light, therefore, is not usually a limiting factor, except for plants growing in shady places.

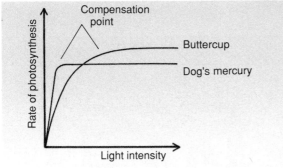

Figure 25.1D ● Light intensity as a limiting factor

● Carbon dioxide

Figure 25.1E shows two crops of lettuces grown in a glasshouse. One crop has had carbon dioxide added to the atmosphere; the other has not. *What is the percentage increase in yield of lettuces grown in a carbon dioxide enriched atmosphere?*

Increasing the amount of atmospheric carbon dioxide is only practical in a glasshouse. Outdoors, the level of carbon dioxide in the air is about 0.03%. The graph shows how the rate of photosynthesis increases with increasing carbon dioxide concentration.

The rate of photosynthesis stays constant after a certain concentration of carbon dioxide is reached. In the short term this limit point is about 0.5%, but over long periods the best level is about 0.1%. Above this level the amount of light often limits the plant's ability to use the extra carbon dioxide.

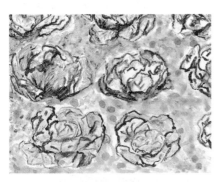

With added carbon dioxide
Mass of 10 lettuces = 1.1 kg

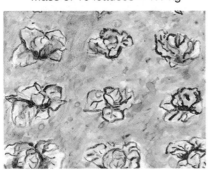

Without added carbon dioxide
Mass of 10 lettuces = 0.9 kg

Glasshouse crops like lettuces and tomatoes are commonly grown in an atmosphere of 0.1% carbon dioxide. The extra cost to the grower is more than offset by the increased crop yield.

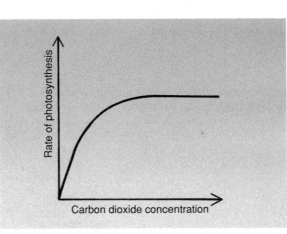

Figure 25.1E ● Carbon dioxide concentration as a limiting factor

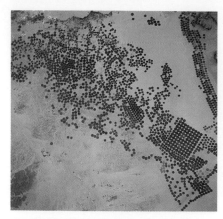

Figure 25.1F ● Turning the desert green

● Warmth

Most plants grow best in warm conditions. The higher the temperature, the faster the chemical reactions of photosynthesis – within limits! **Enzymes** are proteins that control chemical reactions (including photosynthesis) in living things. Temperatures below 0 °C and above 40 °C destroy proteins and reduce enzyme activity.

Plants which grow well at 20–25 °C grow in the UK; plants which thrive at 35–40 °C are found in tropical regions.

● Water

Water is one of the raw materials for photosynthesis. However, lack of water affects so many cell processes that it is impossible to single out its direct effect on photosynthesis. Figure 25.1F highlights the importance of water for plant growth. It makes farming possible – even in the desert!

CHECKPOINT

1 The diagram opposite shows a leaf and a small portion of it cut through lengthways.

(a) How does the structure of the leaf enable it to collect light?

(b) Name the parts labelled A, B, C and D.

(c) Where in the leaf is most of the plant's food made by photosynthesis?

(d) Where do gases pass into and out of the leaf?

(e) How does C help the circulation of gases and water vapour?

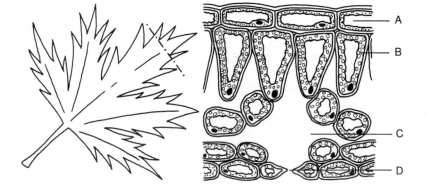

2 The diagram opposite represents the inside of a chloroplast.

(a) What happens at A during photosynthesis?

(b) How does the structure of A enable it to play a part in photosynthesis?

(c) What happens at B during photosynthesis?

(d) Briefly explain the relationship between what happens at A and what happens at B during photosynthesis.

(e) Which gas is released into the environment during photosynthesis?

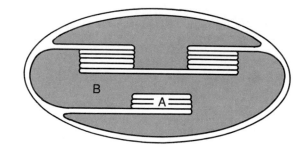

3 The table shows the number of bubbles of gas given off in one minute by water weed illuminated with light of different colours.

Colour of light	Number of bubbles given off in one minute
Blue	85
Green	10
Red	68

What relationship between colour of light and rate of photosynthesis do the results indicate? Suggest how results like this might help a gardener to grow bigger plants in a shorter time in a greenhouse.

❹ The diagram below shows an experiment that was carried out to measure the rate of photosynthesis in water weed at 20 °C.

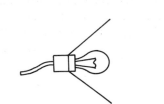 

The rate of photosynthesis was assessed at different light intensities by counting the number of bubbles of gas given off by the plant in a given time. The results are shown in the table.

Number of bubbles per minute	6	15	21	25	27	28	28
Light intensity (arbitrary units)	1	2	3	4	5	6	7

(a) Plot the results on a graph, putting 'Light intensity' on the horizontal axis and 'Number of bubbles' on the vertical axis.

Now answer the following questions, using the diagram and your graph to help you.

(b) At what light intensity did the plant produce 25 bubbles per minute?
(c) Suggest a better way of measuring the rate of photosynthesis than counting the bubbles.
(d) If the experiment was done at the following temperatures, what would be the effect on the rate of photosynthesis?
    (i)   2 °C
    (ii) 33 °C
    (iii) 65 °C
(e) What other factors affect the rate of photosynthesis?

25.2   Food – why do we need it?

FIRST THOUGHTS

We all have favourite foods. This section tells you why we need food and how our bodies use it.

Cars need good maintenance and fuel to keep them going. Without petrol they wouldn't get very far! Have you ever thought how we keep going? Food is the fuel that our bodies need if we are to keep active. But food is more than just a fuel. It also provides the raw materials that we need to build up our bodies and to keep them working properly. It is vital for:
- **Energy** – it is the fuel that keeps us going.
- **Growth** and repair of cells and tissue.
- **Metabolism** – all the complex chemical reactions that take place in the cells of our bodies.

Food contains water, and food from plants contains fibre. However, water and fibre are not usually thought of as nutrients, although fibre is an important part of our food and water is essential for life. Adults can survive for many weeks without nutrients but only for a few days without water.

As well as nutrients, water and fibre, food also has flavour, colour and texture. Small quantities of a range of substances give food these qualities. Cooks and food technologists aim to enhance them to make food more attractive.

IT'S A FACT

Water makes up about two-thirds of your body weight.

327

Energy nutrients

All the processes of life need **energy**. Every time you move, think, speak, read or blink, you use energy. Your body needs energy to grow, to resist disease, and to heal itself, and for all the other processes that make it work.

Energy for living comes from the **carbohydrates**, **fats** and **proteins** in food. It is stored in the chemical bonds of their molecules, and released in the oxidation reactions of cellular respiration. Carbohydrates, fats and proteins are known as the 'energy nutrients' and give foods their energy content.

The energy value of food is measured in the laboratory with an instrument called a bomb calorimeter (Figure 25.2A). Food is burnt and releases food energy as heat. The heat given off by the burning food is transferred to the surrounding water through the heat exchange coil. The change in water temperature is measured with the thermometer and used to work out the energy value of the food. *How is the heat transferred from the heated wire to the water?*

LOOK AT LINKS
for **carbohydrates**, **fats**, and **cellular respiration**
See Theme D, Topic 18 and Theme F, Topic 26.

TRY THIS

Looking at labels – Energy values

Food labels usually carry information on the energy content of the food. Look at the 'Nutrition information' or 'Nutrition – typical values' on a selection of food labels. The food's energy content is often called its **energy value**, and is usually given in kilojoules (kJ) per 100 g of food.

List your selection of foods and write down the energy value for each one.

• Which food on your list has the highest energy value and which the lowest?

• What nutrients would you find in the high energy food?

• Why are energy values given per 100 g of food?

• Work out the total amount of energy available from a container of one of the foods (the weight will be printed on the container).

IT'S A FACT

If a small slice of full fat cheese is burned, it releases enough heat to make four cups of cool water too hot to touch.

LOOK AT LINKS
How to measure and work out how much energy is needed to heat 100 g of water by 1 °C is explained in Theme B, Topic 7.3.

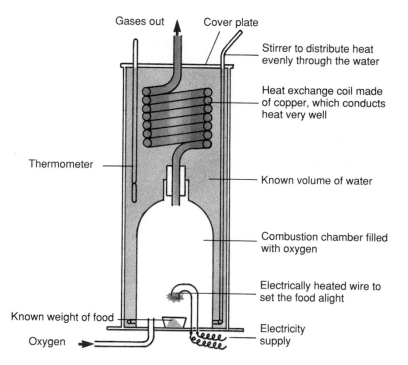

Figure 25.2A ● A bomb calorimeter

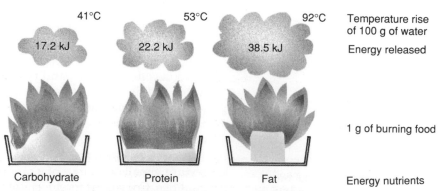

Figure 25.2B ● Energy released from different foods

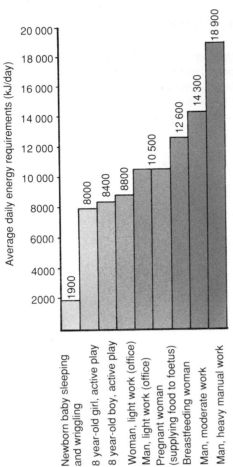

Figure 25.2C ● Average daily energy requirement of different people undertaking different activities

Our energy needs

The rate at which the body uses energy is called the **metabolic rate**. It is lowest (called the **basal metabolic rate**) when the body is at rest (sleeping). Breathing, the heartbeat, maintenance of body temperature, repair and replacement of cells and growth are some of the body activities that contribute to the basal metabolic rate. Any kind of activity increases the metabolic rate. Figure 25.2C shows the energy needed each day by people doing different things.

Measuring energy needs

The man in Figure 25.2D is running on a treadmill. The scientists are measuring the amount of energy he is using. The runner has not eaten and has rested for at least 12 hours before this test. *Why has he taken these precautions?* The amount of energy he uses in running is found by measuring how much oxygen he consumes. His nose is plugged so he breathes through the tubes in his mouth.

Figure 25.2E shows the balance between energy used and food energy needed. We are in 'energy balance' when the amount of energy we get from food equals the amount of energy our bodies use. Measure the height of each block on the right hand side of the see-saw. The total height represents the total amount of energy the man in Figure 25.2D used. *How much energy did he use for running? What is the answer as a fraction of the total energy he used?*

What will happen to the runner's weight if the energy see-saw drops to the left? The right?

Figure 25.2D ● Using energy

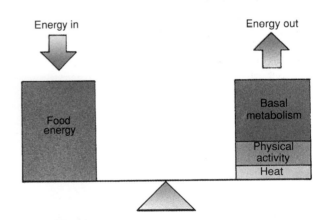

Figure 25.2E ● The energy balance

CHECKPOINT

❶ Look at Figure 25.2D. The runner uses 5 litres of oxygen to provide 84 joules of energy. In running 1 km in 6 minutes, he uses 25 litres of oxygen. How much energy does he use?

❷ Look at Figure 25.2E. Measure the height (in mm) of each part of the right hand block. Let the total height (in mm) represent your answer (in joules) to question 1. What height (in mm) represents the athlete's running?
How much energy (J) is represented by the height of this block?

329

❸ What fraction is the energy used in running (answer to 2) of the total energy used by the athlete (answer to 1)?

❹ The basal metabolic rate varies with weight, age and sex. Women are generally lighter than men because muscle forms a lower proportion of their body weight, and they usually have a higher proportion of fat. Muscle as a proportion of body weight decreases with age. Think about the following statements:
- The heavier you are, the more energy you need.
- Young people need more energy than adults.
- Women need less energy than men.

Briefly explain each statement in the light of what you have read in this section and the background information given. Why do you think young people need more energy than adults? In what circumstances do you think the energy needs of a woman would increase sharply?

IT'S A FACT

Astronauts need more energy in the weightless conditions of space than when on Earth. They take in 12 600 kJ of food energy daily, yet still lose weight on space flights lasting more than two weeks. To help to prevent this, space-travellers are provided with high-energy foods. A typical meal prepared by NASA for astronauts aboard the space shuttle is cream of mushroom soup, mixed vegetables, smoked turkey and strawberries.

Nutrients for growth, repair and the control of metabolism

● Protein

Although protein is an 'energy nutrient' this is not its primary role in the body. Its most important use is for growth and repair. Muscle, blood and other body tissues are made of protein.

Amino acids are the 'building blocks' of protein.

Of the 20 naturally occurring amino acids, nine cannot be made by the body and must be supplied in food. They are called **essential amino acids**. The other eleven can be made by the body and are called **non-essential amino acids**.

Some proteins in food contain all of the essential amino acids the body needs for growth and repair. Other proteins lack one or two essential amino acids. Figure 25.2F shows the percentage and type of protein in different foods.

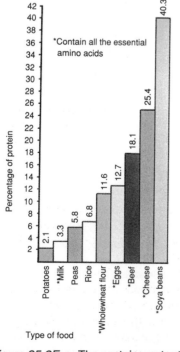

*Contain all the essential amino acids

Percentage of protein

Potatoes	2.1
*Milk	3.3
Peas	5.8
Rice	6.8
*Wholewheat flour	11.6
*Eggs	12.7
*Beef	18.1
*Cheese	25.4
*Soya beans	40.3

Type of food

● Minerals

Some minerals are also important for growth and repair of the body. Others control metabolism. We need small amounts of them in our food for good health.

Minerals such as calcium sulphate and sodium chloride are present in the blood and tissue fluids.

Calcium is needed for making strong bones and teeth and for clotting blood. An adult needs about 1.1 g of calcium each day. Calcium deficiency can cause rickets (Figure 25.2G).

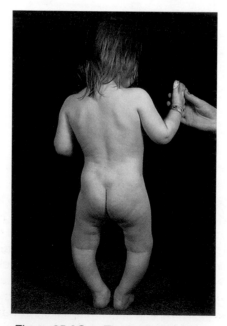

Figure 25.2F ● The protein content of different foods

Figure 25.2G ● The badly bowed legs of a child with rickets

Iron is needed to make the blood protein **haemoglobin**. Insufficient iron in the diet causes anaemia. An adult needs about 16 mg of iron each day. Since only a small amount of iron is needed compared with calcium, iron is called a **trace element**. Minerals that are needed in larger amounts are called **major elements**. Diseases caused by mineral deficiency are called **deficiency diseases**. Table 25.1 summarises the information on the minerals we need for good health.

Table 25.1 ● Summary of minerals needed by humans – find out about beri-beri and goitre.

Mineral	Some sources	Importance in body	Deficiency disease
Major elements			
Calcium	Milk, cheese and other dairy products, bread	Making bones and teeth Blood clotting	Rickets (soft bones)
Sodium and Chlorine	Table salt, cheese, green vegetables	Keeping level and make-up of body fluids correct Transmission of nerve impulses	Cramp
Phosphorus	Most foods	Making bones and teeth Important in nucleic acids and energy release in cells	Rarely deficient
Sulphur	Dairy products, beans and peas	Part of vitamin B_1	Beri-beri
Potassium	Meat, potatoes, most fruit and green vegetables	Keeping level and make-up of body fluids correct Transmission of nerve impulses	Rarely deficient
Magnesium	Cheese, green vegetables, oats, nuts	Energy metabolism Calcium metabolism	Rarely deficient
Trace elements			
Iron	Liver, egg, meat, cocoa	Making haemoglobin	Anaemia
Fluorine	Water, tea, sea-food	Helps tooth enamel to resist decay	
Iodine	Fish, iodised table salt, water	Making the hormone thyroxin (which controls growth) in the thyroid gland	Goitre
Zinc	Meat, peas and beans	Protein metabolism Enzymes	Poor healing, skin complaints
Copper	Liver, peas and beans	Making haemoglobin Energy release	Rarely deficient
Cobalt	Meat, yeast, comfrey (a herb)	Part of vitamin B_{12}	Pernicious anaemia (failure to produce haemoglobin)

IT'S A FACT

Before iron tablets became available, people used to stick iron nails into oranges to make a tonic for the treatment of anaemia. The iron in the nails reacted with the ascorbic acid (vitamin C) in the orange, which was then squeezed and the iron-rich juice drunk as an iron tonic.

● **Vitamins**

We also need small amounts of vitamins for good health. A few vitamins are made in the body. The rest come from food or are made by the bacteria that live in our intestines. They are organic substances, which play an important role in the control of metabolism.

As different vitamins were discovered they were labelled alphabetically (A, B, C, etc.). However, in some cases a substance which was first thought to be a single vitamin later turned out to be several related substances, and numbers were added to the letter label (B_1, B_2, etc.). Table 25.2 lists the sources and functions of some of the vitamins needed by humans. Notice that some vitamins are soluble in fat and some in water. *Which vitamins are more likely to be stored in the body?*

Table 25.2 ● Summary of vitamins needed by humans. (The B vitamins help to release energy from food and to prevent anaemia. They promote healthy skin and muscle.)

Vitamin	Some sources	Importance in body	Deficiency disease
Fat soluble			
A	Liver, fish-liver oil, milk, dairy produce, green vegetables, carrots	Gives resistance to disease Protects eyes Helps you to see in the dark	Infections Poor vision in dim light
D	Fish-liver oil, milk, butter, eggs Made by the body in sunlight	Helps the body to absorb calcium from food	Rickets in children Brittle bones in adults
E	Milk, egg yolk, wheatgerm, green vegetables	Antioxidant, protects vitamins A, C, D, K and polyunsaturated fatty acids	Poorly understood in humans Causes sterility in rats
K	Green vegetables, pig's liver, egg yolk Produced by bacteria in gut	Helps to make blood clot	Spontaneous bleeding Long clotting time
Water soluble			
B_1	Whole cereals, wheatgerm, yeast, milk, meat	Helps body to oxidise food to release energy	Beri-beri Nervous disorders
B_2	Fish, eggs, milk, liver, meat, yeast, green vegetables	Helps body to oxidise food to release energy	Dry skin, mouth sores, poor growth
B_6	Eggs, meat, potatoes, cabbage	Helps to digest protein	Anaemia
B_{12}	Meat, milk, yeast, comfrey (herb)	Helps in the formation of red blood cells	Pernicious anaemia
C	Oranges, lemons and other citrus fruits, green vegetables, potatoes, tomatoes	Helps to bond cells together Helps in the use of calcium by bones and teeth	Scurvy (bleeding gums, and internal organs)

Deficiency diseases occur when the body lacks particular vitamins. They are easily cured by supplying the missing vitamins. Many sailors died of scurvy, a deficiency disease, on long sea voyages in the sixteenth and seventeenth centuries (see below). It causes bleeding in various parts of the body, particularly the gums (Figure 25.2H).

Who's behind the science

● ***Scurvy***

In 1747 the naval doctor James Lind made the following report.

'On the 20th May I took twelve patients in the scurvy, on board the *Salisbury* at sea …. They all in general had putrid gums …. Two had each two oranges and one lemon given them every day …. The consequence was, that the most sudden and visible good effects were perceived from the use of the oranges and the lemons; one of those who had taken them being at the end of six days fit for duty.'

(From James Lind's account of how he treated scurvy aboard the HMS Salisbury.)

The other ten sailors received different treatments and did not recover.

By the early 1780s a daily ration of lemon juice was a compulsory part of a sailor's rations and scurvy was no longer a problem on board ship. Look at Table 25.2 to find out which vitamin is responsible for preventing scurvy. *Why do you think sailors on long sea voyages were particularly prone to scurvy?*

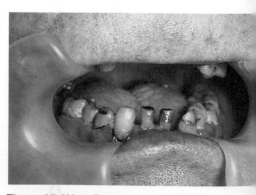

Figure 25.2H ● Scurvy

IT'S A FACT

Some desert animals such as the oryx take in all the water they need from their food and never drink.

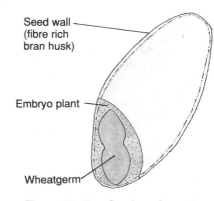

IT'S A FACT

Fog rolling in from the coast of south-west Africa is virtually the only source of water in the Namib desert. When it is foggy the 'head standing beetle' creeps to the top of a sand dune and stretches its back legs, tilting its body forward, head down. The beetle drinks as fog condenses onto its body and runs down to its mouth.

LOOK AT LINKS
for **plant cells**
See Theme D, Topic 19.

Vitamin D promotes absorption of calcium by the small intestine and incorporation of calcium into bones. A severe shortage of vitamin D reduces the calcium availability and may cause rickets in children (Figure 25.2G). Bones fail to grow properly and become soft, so when children with rickets start walking the bones bend with the weight of the body. Eating vitamin D-rich foods like fish-liver oil, butter, eggs and milk, prevents rickets. Bright sunlight also changes a chemical in the skin into vitamin D. In hot countries, where there is a lot of sunshine, people make most of the vitamin D they need in this way. If they move to cooler, cloudier climates, they need extra vitamin D in their food to prevent rickets. Children under five years old need about 0.1 mg of vitamin D daily; over fives need about 0.0025 mg daily. In adults the bones have stopped growing and lack of vitamin D causes a disease called osteomalacia. The bones lose calcium, become brittle and snap.

Water

Water makes up about two-thirds of your body weight. It is taken in either directly by drinking or indirectly as part of food.

Chemical reactions in the body also produce water. For example, the oxidation of carbohydrates and fats to release energy produces water.

Water is used in the body:
- as a solvent in which chemical reactions take place,
- as a solvent for waste matter which passes out of the body in solution,
- for transporting substances round the body (water is a major part of **blood** and **lymph**,
- as a means of keeping cool.

An adult needs about 2500 cm³ of water each day. The body loses and gains water through its different activities. Losses and gains roughly balance as Table 25.3 shows.

Table 25.3 ● Daily water balance sheet for an adult

Daily gains (cm³/day)		Daily losses (cm³/day)	
Drinks	1400	Urine	1500
Food	800	Faeces	100
Cellular respiration	300	Evaporation from lungs	350
		Sweat	550
Total	2500	Total	2500

Dietary fibre

Dietary fibre comes from plant foods. There are two types:
- Soluble fibre from fruit pulp, vegetables, oat bran and dried beans.
- Insoluble fibre from the cellulose of plant cell walls and the bran husk that covers wheat, rice and other cereal grains (Figure 25.2I). Wholemeal bread contains much more fibre than white bread because it is made from wholemeal flour – flour

Seed wall (fibre rich bran husk)

Embryo plant

Wheatgerm

Figure 25.2I ● Section of a grain of wheat

Try to dissolve pectin and cellulose in water. Compare your results. *Which is the soluble fibre and which is the insoluble one?*

LOOK AT LINKS
for more about the relationship between **cholesterol** and heart disease
See Theme J, Topic 38.4.

made from the whole grain. In white flour the outer husks of the grain have been removed. The wheatgerm and the bran also contain most of the vitamins.

Soluble fibre dissolves in water to produce a gel. Insoluble fibre does not dissolve, but it 'holds' water and swells up if mixed with water.

The two types of dietary fibre have different effects. Insoluble fibre adds bulk to food. The muscles of the intestine can work against it and help food to pass through quickly. As a result, disease-causing substances produced by bacteria in the intestine and in the food do not remain in the intestine for very long.

Soluble fibre has the opposite effect. It slows down the passage of food through the intestine. It also seems to decrease the absorption of some minerals, and of glucose and **cholesterol**, into the body. Many people want to lower their cholesterol level. Perhaps this is why porridge is becoming more popular. With its high content of soluble fibre, porridge may reduce the absorption of cholesterol.

CHECKPOINT

❶ Why do we need water?

❷ Look at the amount of water needed daily by an adult (Table 25.3). What percentage of it is produced by 'cellular respiration'?

❸ (a) What is meant by 'fat-soluble vitamin' and 'water-soluble vitamin'?
(b) Which type is difficult to store in the body?

❹ What are the sources and functions of (a) vitamin C and (b) vitamin D?

❺ What can happen when we do not have enough (a) vitamin C and (b) vitamin D?

❻ Which foods are sources of calcium and iron?

❼ What can happen when a person does not have (a) enough calcium and (b) enough iron in his/her diet?

❽ Why is fibre important in the diet?

❾ Susan and Mary want to find out the energy values of sugar and butter. Their apparatus is shown in the diagram.

Susan set the sugar and butter alight and measured the rise in temperature of the water in each beaker after three minutes. All the sugar had burnt away but the butter was still alight.

Her results were: Rise in water temperature in beaker 1 = 3 °C
Rise in water temperature in beaker 2 = 5 °C

Mary also set alight the sugar and butter but she let all the food burn away before measuring the rise in temperature of the water in each beaker.

Her results were: Rise in water temperature in beaker 1 = 6 °C
Rise in water temperature in beaker 2 = 10 °C

(a) Susan and Mary both believe that butter contains more energy than sugar. Why do you think that Mary's experimental evidence is better than Susan's? You should find four reasons.
(b) What could Mary do to improve her accuracy?
(c) Since butter is mainly fat, Susan's and Mary's results might give them the idea that all fats contain more energy than sugar. Briefly explain how they could test this idea.

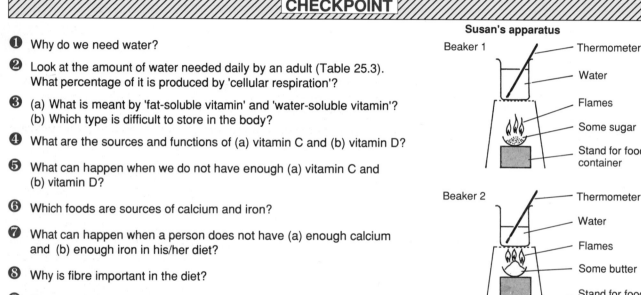

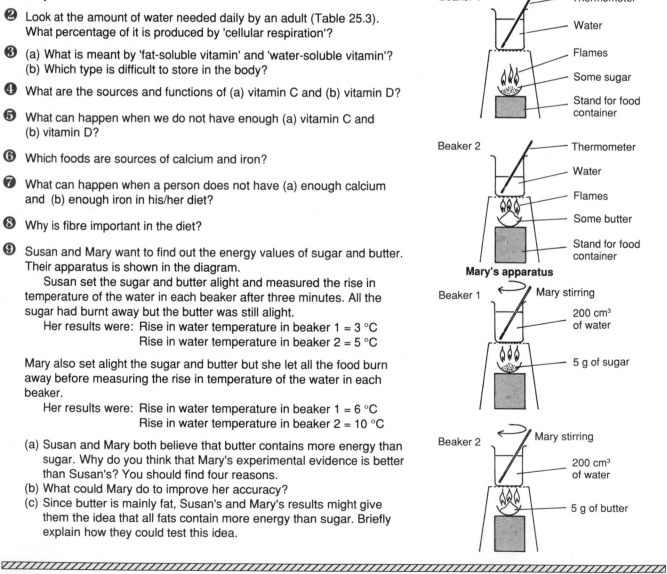

25.3  Diet and food

FIRST THOUGHTS

What is your diet? Is it healthy? This section will help you assess the food you eat and understand what makes a healthy diet.

RESOURCE ACTIVITY PACK

IT'S A FACT

Babies rely on milk to meet all their nutritional needs. Nutrients which are low in milk, such as iron, are already stored in large amounts in the baby's liver. However, older children and adults do not store enough of these nutrients, so milk alone does not provide a balanced diet for them.

Your diet is the food you eat and drink. It should contain nutrients, water and fibre in the correct amounts and proportions for good health. If it does, then your diet is said to be balanced or complete.

A healthy diet

By the time you are 70 years old you will have eaten about 30 tonnes of food. Advice about what you eat is big business. 'Experts' tell you that some foods are healthy and others are not. *Who is right? Who should you believe?*

If a diet consists of a single food then the food will be 'unhealthy' no matter what the food is, because no single food contains all the nutrients in the proportions we need for healthy living. For example, both beef and wholemeal bread lack vitamins A, C and D and are low in calcium. Beef also lacks dietary fibre, which wheat provides. Wheat lacks vitamin B_{12}, which beef provides. Together beef and bread provide more nutrients than either on its own, but between them vitamins A, C and D and calcium are still missing. If salad, fruit and vegetables are added, then vitamins A and C are brought into the diet. Milk and cheese add the missing calcium and vitamin D.

A healthy diet, therefore, is a mixture of foods which together provide sufficient nutrients. Notice that each of the foods above lacks some nutrient which the other foods make up between them. They each represent one of the group of foods shown in Figure 25.3A.

Nutritionists have developed the idea of the 'basic four' food groups to help us choose a balanced diet. *Do you eat at least one helping of food from each group daily?*

You should also aim for variety. Daily helpings of the same food from each group may contribute to a balanced diet but not necessarily a healthy one. For example, the vitamin C content of fruits may range from next-to-nothing in raw pears to 150 mg per 100 g in stewed blackcurrants. Also, eating the same foods all the time is not only boring but may provide too much fat, sugar and salt. In excess these foods, together with too much alcohol, probably cause more disease in developed countries than any other single factor.

Eat a variety of foods from each group every day

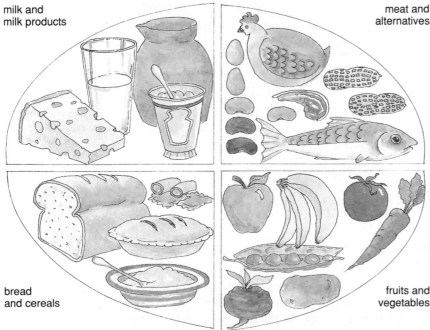

milk and milk products

meat and alternatives

bread and cereals

fruits and vegetables

Figure 25.3A ● The four basic food groups

The table compares the amount of energy and some nutrients that an adult human needs each day with the energy/nutrients in milk.

Energy/ foodstuff	Daily needs of adult	Content of 100 g of cow's milk
Energy	12 000 kJ	272 kJ
Protein	72 g	3.2 g
Calcium	0.5 g	0.10 g
Vitamin A	0.75 mg	0.06 mg
Vitamin C	30 mg	1.5 mg

Study the table and answer the following questions:

❶ On a diet of milk only, how much would an adult have to drink to satisfy daily energy needs?

❷ Milk is a 'balanced diet' for a baby. What is meant by a 'balanced diet'?

❸ Give one reason why milk is particularly important for the development of bones and teeth in babies.

❹ How much milk would an adult need to satisfy his/her daily need for calcium?

Alcohol

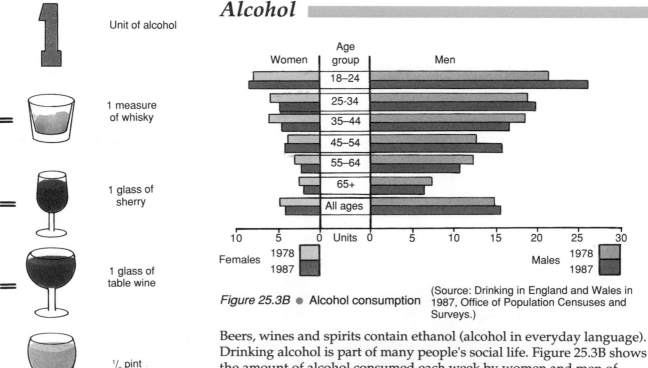

Unit of alcohol

1 = 1 measure of whisky

1 = 1 glass of sherry

1 = 1 glass of table wine

1 = ½ pint of beer

Figure 25.3C ● Units of alcohol

Figure 25.3B ● Alcohol consumption

(Source: Drinking in England and Wales in 1987, Office of Population Censuses and Surveys.)

Beers, wines and spirits contain ethanol (alcohol in everyday language). Drinking alcohol is part of many people's social life. Figure 25.3B shows the amount of alcohol consumed each week by women and men of different ages. It also shows how drinking habits have changed. *Which age group drinks the most alcohol each week? How do drinking habits change with increasing age?* Units of alcohol are shown in Figure 25.3C.

Drinking too much alcohol is one cause of diseases such as cirrhosis of the liver, heart disease and damage to the nervous system. The liver metabolises alcohol, and the link between heavy drinking and cirrhosis is

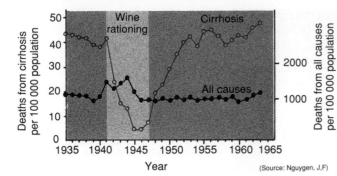

Figure 25.3D ● Deaths from all causes and deaths from cirrhosis in Paris, 1935–65

(Source: Nguygen, J,F)

well-established. Figure 25.3D shows the number of deaths from all causes and the number of deaths from cirrhosis in Paris between 1935 and 1965. Notice that deaths from cirrhosis fell by 80% when wine was rationed during World War II. The number of cirrhosis-related deaths rose rapidly to pre-war levels when wine rationing stopped. More recent figures from France suggest wine consumption has fallen. Estimates predict that a 50% decrease would cut cirrhosis by about 58%.

How much alcohol is too much? This depends on a person's sex, age, size and metabolic rate. For example, the 'safe' level of alcohol for a woman is only about two-thirds as much as for a man of the same weight. Also, different drinks contain different concentrations of alcohol (Figure 25.3C). Look at Figure 25.3B and compare the drinking habits of men and women.

It is difficult to give 'safe' limits for drinking alcohol because the level varies so much from person to person. The Royal College of Physicians suggests that a man should not drink more than the equivalent of four pints of beer a day. Other experts think this is too much and suggest two pints of beer a day is enough. All agree that drinking alcohol affects your behaviour and heavy drinking harms your health (Figure 25.3E). One of the first things to be affected by drinking alcohol is your driving ability. The message is clear – **DO NOT DRINK AND DRIVE**.

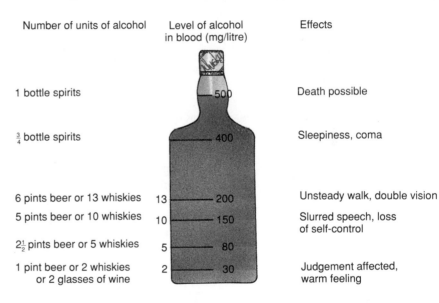

Figure 25.3E ● The effects of alcohol

LOOK AT LINKS
The link between sugar and dental caries is discussed in Theme F, Topic 25.4.

LOOK AT LINKS
for **atheroma** as a cause of heart attack
See Theme J, Topic 38.4.

Sugar and fat

The amounts of sugar and fat we eat also affect our risk of heart disease. If people eat too much sugar and fat they tend to put on weight. Overweight people have a higher risk of heart disease (Figure 25.3F).

Too much of the wrong sort of fatty food also increases the level of a substance called cholesterol in the blood. Cholesterol is found in nearly all body tissues. Large amounts of cholesterol are found in **atheroma** deposits, which block arteries and restrict the flow of blood through them. The more cholesterol there is in the blood, the greater the risk of heart attack (Figure 25.3G).

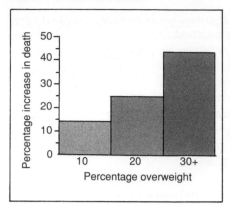

Figure 25.3F ● Increase in deaths from heart disease due to overweight

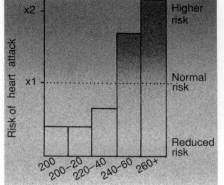

Level of cholesterol in blood (mg/100 cm³)

Figure 25.3G ● Cholestrol and the risk of heart disease

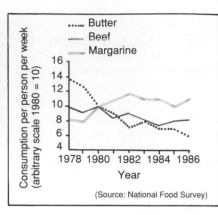

(Source: National Food Survey)

Figure 25.3H ● Consumption of saturated and unsaturated fat

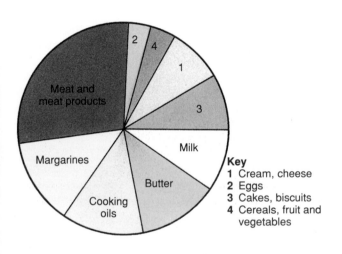

Key
1 Cream, cheese
2 Eggs
3 Cakes, biscuits
4 Cereals, fruit and vegetables

Figure 25.3I ● Sources of fat in the average UK diet

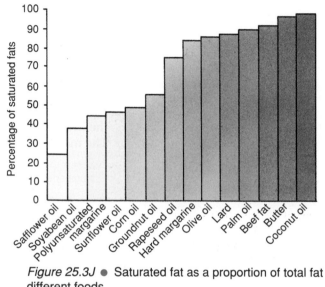

Figure 25.3J ● Saturated fat as a proportion of total fat in different foods

Eating food containing a lot of **saturated fats** seems to raise the level of cholesterol in the blood and therefore increase the risk of heart attack.

Look at Figures 25.3H, and 25.3I and 25.3J. We need some fat in our diet for good health. It comes from different foods. Different fats contain different proportions of saturated and unsaturated fatty acids. *Which foods are high in saturated fats?* You should eat less of these. *Which foods can be substituted because they contain more unsaturated fats? What are the trends in consumption of saturated and unsaturated fats?*

The P/S ratio, which is the ratio of polyunsaturated fats to saturated fats in the diet, helps us calculate what proportion of saturated and unsaturated fats to eat. It can be worked out as follows

$$\frac{P}{S} = \frac{\text{Mass of polyunsaturated fat in diet}}{\text{Mass of saturated fat in diet}}$$

In 1985 the national average for P/S was 0.25. In 1984 a government report suggested a P/S value of 0.45 would reduce the risk of heart disease. That is, if 0.45 g of every gram of fat we ate was polyunsaturated.

So far the evidence seems straightforward: the higher your cholesterol level the greater your risk of developing heart disease. In fact the story is more complicated than this and more research is needed. However, it is much better that you act now to improve your diet than do nothing while waiting for more information.

LOOK AT LINKS
for **saturated fats**
See Theme D, Topic 18.

LOOK AT LINKS
Fats are a store of energy and an important component of cell membranes
See Theme D, Topic 18 and 19.

LOOK AT LINKS
for **sodium chloride**
See Theme D, Topic 17.1.

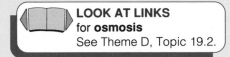
LOOK AT LINKS
for **osmosis**
See Theme D, Topic 19.2.

LOOK AT LINKS
for **blood pressure**
See Theme J, Topic 38.2.

IT'S A FACT

Your body loses salt when you sweat, which is why sweat tastes salty. People who work in hot places sweat a lot and may suffer from muscle cramps because of the salt they lose. Taking salt tablets helps replace the salt lost.

Salt

When we talk about salt in food we mean **sodium chloride**.

The muscles, nervous system and kidneys need salt to work properly. Salt also helps to maintain the correct **osmotic** balance between blood and tissues.

Too much salt in the diet can raise **blood pressure** and a person with blood pressure higher than normal is more likely to suffer from heart disease.

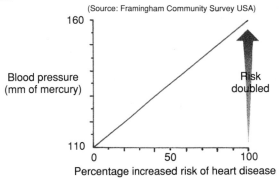

Figure 25.3K ● Blood pressure and the risk of heart disease

High blood pressure can also damage the kidneys and eyes, and increase the risk of an artery tearing open. When an artery tears which supplies blood to the brain it is called a cerebral haemorrhage or 'stroke'.

Very few young people have high blood pressure, but after the age of 35 it becomes more common. The reason is not clear, but different studies show that lifestyle can have an important effect. Eating less salt helps to keep blood pressure within normal levels.

Food additives

Food additives are substances that manufacturers put into food to make it tastier, improve its texture, make it look more attractive and prevent it from spoiling. Table 25.4 summarises the main types of food additive and what they do.

Figure 25.4 ● Types of food additive and what they do

Types of food additive	What they do
Preservatives	Stop micro-organisms such as bacteria and fungi from spoiling food
Antioxidants	Prevent oxygen in the atmosphere oxidising fats and oils, turning them rancid
Emulsifiers	Keep oil and water in sauces mixed together
Drying agents	Prevent foods like flour from caking
Thickeners	Make foods like soups less 'runny'
Supplements	Nutrients added to help prevent deficiency diseases, e.g. vitamins A and D added to margarine
Colourings	Enhance natural colours to make foods look more attractive
Flavourings	Make foods tastier by bringing out their flavours
Moisteners (humectants)	Prevent food from drying out

When you look at the labels on food containers for information about energy values, you may notice the letter E printed with a number after it. This is an 'E Number', given to additives that are recognised as safe for use in food by the European Community. Each additive has its own E Number. Some examples are given in Table 25.5.

Table 25.5 ● The identity of some common E numbers

E Number	Additive	E Number	Additive
	Antioxidants		**Emulsifiers**
E300	l-Ascorbic acid	E400	Alginic acid
E320	Butylated hydroxyanisole (BHA)	E406	Agar
	Colours		**Preservatives**
E102	Tartrazine	E210	Benzoic acid
E110	Sunset yellow FCF	E220	Sulphur dioxide
E120	Cochineal		**Sweeteners**
E162	Beetroot red (betanin)	E421	Mannitol
		E420	Sorbitol

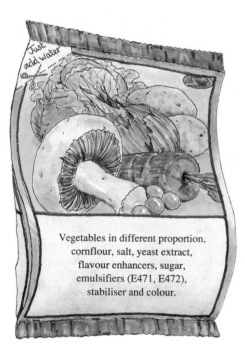

Vegetables in different proportion, cornflour, salt, yeast extract, flavour enhancers, sugar, emulsifiers (E471, E472), stabiliser and colour.

Figure 25.3L ● The ingredients of a vegetable soup mix. How many have side-effects?

Food additives are carefully tested to make sure they are safe to eat before they are given an E Number. However some approved additives can make some people ill. For example, some people are sensitive to the yellow colouring tartrazine (E102). If they eat food containing E102 they may have an asthmatic attack or develop a skin rash. More examples of the side-effects of some additives are listed in Table 25.6.

Doubts about the long-term effects of additives have led to some of them being withdrawn from use, even though they have been declared 'safe'. You must remember that additives help to stop food from spoiling and make it more convenient to use. However, public worries have led food manufacturers to cut down on their use, which in turn may create new problems. For example, bacteria and fungi multiply much more quickly in food without preservatives (in everyday language, the food goes 'bad'). Eating 'bad' food causes food poisoning.

Table 25.6 ● Additives with side effects

E Number		Effects on some people
E102	Tartrazine	Skin rashes, blurred vision, breathing problems, hyperactivity in children
E122	Carmoisine or Azorubine	Skin rashes, swellings
E150	Caramel	None proven although suspect for many years
E220	Sulphur dioxide	Irritation of gut
E320*	Butylated hydroxyanisole	Raises lipid and cholesterol levels in blood
E321*	Butylated hydroxytoluene	Skin rashes, behavioural effects, blood cell changes
E331	Sodium citrate	None known
E481	Sodium stearoyl 2-lactylate	None known

* Not allowed in baby foods

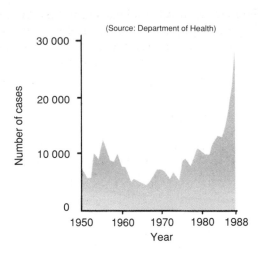

Figure 25.3M ● The rise in reported cases of food poisoning

Look at Figure 25.3M. The rapid increase in the number of cases of food poisoning since 1980 coincides with the growing public pressure to cut down additives in food. *Do you think the two are linked?* (Scientists call this 'cause and effect'.) *Can you interpret the data in a different way?* For example, there has been an increase in the consumption of ready-made meals and takeaways. Also people go out for meals more often than they used to. *Do you think these factors influence the data in the graph?* Briefly summarise your opinion on food additives in the light of the evidence.

CHECKPOINT

❶ What is meant by the word 'preservative'?

❷ Why is a diet rich in plant fat probably more healthy than one rich in animal fat?

❸ Why do people who work in very hot countries sometimes take salt tablets?

❹ List some diseases caused by drinking too much alcohol.

❺ How many glasses of table wine contain the same amount of alcohol as $1\frac{1}{2}$ pints of beer?

❻ List some good effects and some bad effects of food additives.

Vegetarianism – fad or healthy alternative? ▪

Vegetarians do not eat meat: some because they think it cruel to kill animals for food; others for religious and cultural reasons. A growing number of people in Britain claim to be vegetarian, but what does it mean to be one? Table 25.7 compares the different types of vegetarian diet and the diets of carnivores and omnivores.

Table 25.7 ● Different types of diet. Lacto refers to milk; ovo to eggs.

Type of diet	Foods eaten				
	Beef and other 'red' meats	Pork, poultry, fish, seafood	Eggs	Milk, cheese and other milk products	Vegetables, fruits, grains, and grain products, legumes, nuts, seeds, oils, sugars
Omnivore	✓	✓	✓	✓	✓
Semivegetarian		✓*	✓	✓	✓
Lacto-ovovegetarian			✓	✓	✓
Lactovegetarian				✓	✓
Vegan					✓
Carnivore	✓	✓			

* May not include all types of food in this group

Many semivegetarians say that they 'feel better' for not eating 'red' meat, so practical reasons govern their choice of diet. Vegans choose their diet because of a principle, believing it not only cruel to kill animals for food but also to use them to produce dairy products.

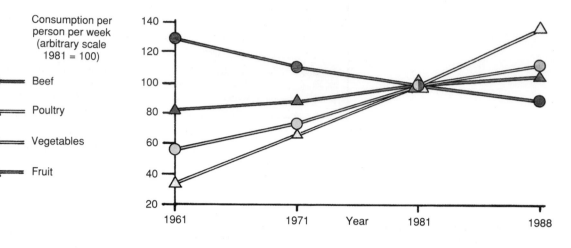

Figure 25.3N ● Changes in food consumption on England and Wales

Look at Figure 25.3N and notice how consumption of red meat has declined and consumption of white meat, vegetables and fruit has increased. People are more aware that food affects health and are changing their diets accordingly. *Do you think these changes are for the better?* Give reasons for your answer.

If foods are selected carefully then it is possible to obtain a complete range of nutrients from a vegetarian diet, especially if eggs, milk and cheese are included. In fact, properly balanced vegetarian diets have advantages over some non-vegetarian diets. They contain:
● more dietary fibre,
● less saturated fat and cholesterol,
● less high-energy food.

Vegetarians are less likely to be overweight than people who regularly eat meat. They are also less likely to develop heart disease, diabetes and some types of cancer. *Why should this be so?*

IT'S A FACT

The soya bean has overtaken wheat and maize as the most important cash crop in the USA. It contains a higher percentage of protein than beef does (see Figure 25.2F). Food manufacturers turn soya beans into 'meat' products or grind them into flour as a basis for savoury snacks.

CHECKPOINT

❶ Which nutrient found in meat could be in short supply in a vegetarian diet?

❷ How do eggs, milk and cheese help vegetarians to obtain a complete range of nutrients?

❸ Why do vegans have more difficulty than other groups in obtaining all the nutrients they need?

Thin or fat – what are the facts?

Magazines, newspapers, television and advertisements bombard us with body images. The message is: thin is beautiful, fat is ugly. This has not always been the case. In the late sixteenth century a much plumper body image was fashionable. Comparison between the past and the present shows how fashion trends shape our image of thinness and fatness.

Life insurance companies have calculated healthy weights for people of different heights (Figure 25.3O). Overweight people are more likely to be ill (Figure 25.3F) and are therefore a greater risk to insure.

Notice that Figure 25.3O shows a range of weights for each height. The range allows for differences in the size of the skeleton which forms the body frame. A small-framed person will tend to weigh in at the lower limit of the weight range for his/her particular height; a large-framed person of the same height will tend to be at the upper limit of the weight range.

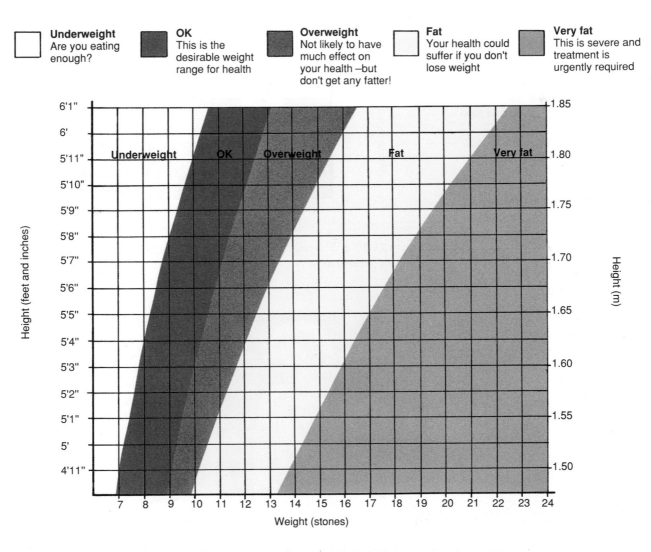

Figure 25.3O ● Healthy weights

LOOK AT LINKS
Growth is discussed in more detail in Theme J, Topic 39.5.

TRY THIS

Assessing food advertisements. Next time you watch television, count how many advertisements you see in a given time and how many are for food.
- What percentage of advertisements are for food?
- What types of foods are being advertised?
- Use Tables 25.1 and 25.2 to help you to check the nutrients each advertised food contains.
- Which of the advertised foods would tend to make you put on weight? Give reasons for your answer.

Sports people and others with a muscular physique may weigh in as overweight for their height. Muscle is more dense than fat, so although the graph seems to be saying that they are overweight, they probably have less body fat than people of the same weight who do not take regular exercise.

Weight-for-height figures for children are more difficult to calculate than for adults. As you grow up the proportions of water, muscle and fat in your body alter as much as the lengths of your arms, legs and trunk. However, childhood obesity is a growing problem in the UK and other developed countries. As well as the increased risk to health, obese children may become targets for other children's teasing and ridicule. Although some obesity has medical causes, lack of exercise seems to be a major factor. In the USA there is a decline in levels of physical activity among children and obese children tend to be much less physically active than children of normal weight. Watching too much television could be part of the problem (Figure 25.3P).

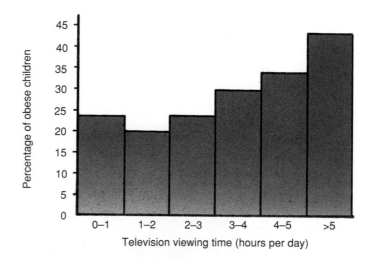

Figure 25.3P ● The relationship between obesity in children and the time spent watching television

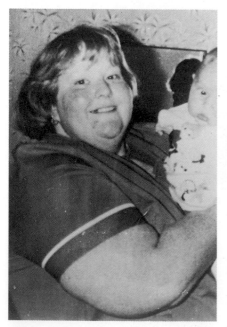

Figure 25.3Q ● Slimming (before and after)

Slimming

Congratulations Jackie Hendry for slimming from 184 kg to 64 kg in less than a year – a loss of 120 kg (Figure 25.3Q). How did you do it?

If a person eats more food than is necessary for his or her energy needs, then the excess is turned into fat and stored in fat cells under the skin and he or she puts on weight.

The only way to lose weight and slim is to make sure that the energy input (food) is less than the energy output (metabolism and physical activity). The options are:
- take more exercise, which increases energy output,
- eat less high-energy food, which decreases energy input.

IT'S A FACT

A weight loss of 1.00 kg per week requires a reduction in food energy intake of 32 300 J over that time (4600 J/day).

The first option is not very effective on its own. For example, a man trying to lose weight uses about 420 kJ/hour more taking a brisk walk than sitting down. If the walk makes him thirsty and he drinks a pint of beer at the end of it, he will take in more energy than he used up. The result: his weight increases.

Fortunately the second option is effective if carried out properly. The sensible approach to slimming includes:

* eating smaller amounts of food,
* eating fewer high-energy foods (Figure 25.3R),
* more physical activity.

A programme for slimming designed with these points in mind not only results in weight loss but also helps to maintain it. The aim is to alter gradually a person's exercise and eating habits. It is much easier to adjust to modest changes – smaller amounts of food, using stairs instead of lifts, for example – than to make sudden drastic changes. Weight is reduced quickly at the start of a weight control diet. Most of the popular diets promoted by the multi-million pound 'slimming' industry owe their success to sudden weight loss. However, few people stick to a diet that demands major upheavals in their eating habits and the weight soon goes back on.

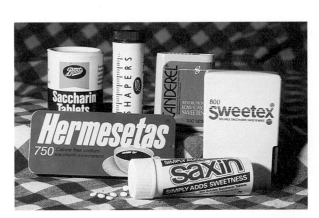

Figure 25.3R ● Many low-energy foods have a high fibre content so eating lots of bread, fruit and vegetables can help you slim. Substituting artificial sweetners for sugar in tea and coffee and low-fat cottage cheese for full-fat cheese could also help you lose weight.

Anorexia

Some people take slimming too far, by following a strict low-energy diet to lose weight. They lose their appetite, eat little food and become dangerously thin. This disease is called anorexia nervosa. It is most common in teenage girls and young women from middle- to high-income families.

The effects of anorexia nervosa:

* Muscle tissue is used as a source of energy once the body's fat reserves are exhausted.
* Body temperature, metabolism and heart rate decrease.
* Depression sets in.
* Growth and sexual development in teenagers stop.
* Thoughts become dominated by food and eating.

IT'S A FACT

Rapid weight loss at the start of a weight control diet is mainly due to losses in body water. After the first week further weight loss is from the body's fat stores.

People with anorexia nervosa do not recognise that they are in effect starving themselves (see Figure 25.3S). They often have a low opinion of themselves. Treatment focuses on building up their self-image. If these problems are overcome, then normal eating patterns and weight gain often follow. Many people recover from anorexia nervosa, and the earlier it is discovered, the more likely it is that treatment will be successful.

Figure 25.3S ● The devastating effects of anorexia nervosa

CHECKPOINT

❶ The table shows the percentage of British people in different age groups who are overweight.

Age group	Percentage overweight	
	Men	Women
20–24	22	23
25–29	29	20
30–39	40	25
40–49	52	38
50–59	49	47
60–65	54	50

(from: Report of Royal College of Physicians, 1983)

(a) Draw two bar charts to show the percentage of men and women overweight on the vertical axis and age group on the horizontal axis.
(b) How many times more overweight are the men in the 60–65 age group than the men in the 25–29 age group? Suggest reasons for the increase in weight.
(c) Why do you think that more men than women in all age groups except the first are overweight?
(d) Plan two menus – one that could lead to people becoming overweight, and one that overweight people could use to reach normal weight. Describe briefly the differences between the menus which bring out the gain and loss in weight. Do both of your menus give a balanced diet?
(e) 'Overweight people are more likely to suffer from ill health than normal weight people.' Briefly give reasons why you think this statement is true or false.

❷ 'You are what you eat.' Discuss the meaning of this popular saying by comparing a meal of hamburgers, egg and chips and steamed jam pudding with a meal of fish, salad and fruit.

25.4 🌐 Teeth

FIRST THOUGHTS

Teeth – what is their structure and how are they adapted for different types of feeding? This section will tell you!

When animals take in (ingest) food we say they are feeding. Different animals have different structures for feeding. Teeth are the feeding structures in most vertebrates (except birds).

Tooth structure

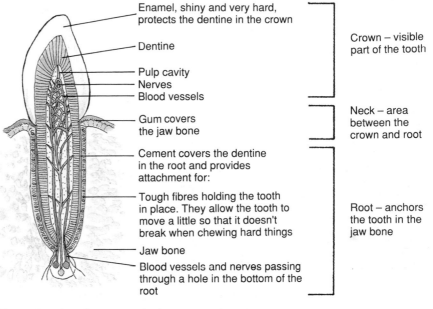

Figure 25.4A ● Structure of a human tooth

LOOK AT LINKS

You will find more about different feeding structures in Theme A, Topic 3.5.

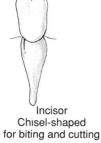

IT'S A FACT

Tooth enamel is the hardest substance in the body. It is made of crystals of calcium hydroxide phosphate, bound together by the protein **keratin**.

LOOK AT LINKS

What do teeth have in common with hair, nails, claws and feathers? They all contain **keratin**.
See Theme D, Topic 18.4.

Figure 25.4A shows the internal structure of a human tooth. Notice that blood vessels and nerves enter the tooth through a hole at the bottom of the root. In carnivores and omnivores this hole becomes smaller when the tooth is fully grown, reducing the supply of blood. The tooth is then said to have a **closed root**; dentine is no longer produced, and the tooth stops growing. The roots of herbivores' teeth stay open, so dentine production continues and their teeth keep growing throughout life. These animals feed on rough material like grass. Continuous growth of the teeth makes sure that the abrasive food does not wear them away.

Types of teeth

The teeth of fish, amphibia and reptiles are usually cone-shaped. The teeth of mammals are different shapes and sizes (Figure 25.4B).

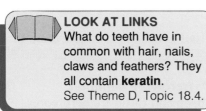

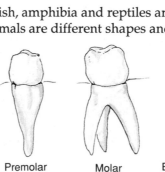

Incisor
Chisel-shaped for biting and cutting

Canine
Pointed for piercing, slashing and tearing

Premolar   Molar

Broad surface made uneven by 'bumps' called cusps. For crushing and grinding. A molar has three 'prongs' to its root; some premolars have two

Figure 25.4B ● The four basic types of human teeth

Figure 25.4C ● The arrangement of teeth in an adult human jaw. There are 32 teeth in total; eight on each side of the upper and lower jaw.

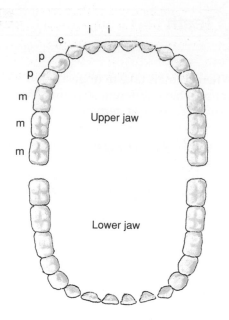

Key

i = incisor
c = canine
p = premolar
m = molar

The different types of teeth are positioned in the mouth according to their functions. Figure 25.4C shows the arrangement of teeth in an adult human jaw.

Humans have two sets of teeth. The first set of 'milk' (or deciduous) teeth form in the jaw before birth and begin to appear (or erupt) about three to six months after birth. There are 24 teeth in the first set, 20 of which are gradually replaced by the permanent teeth between the ages of six and twelve. The third molars (the 'wisdom' teeth) do not appear until the age of about 18 years, if at all.

The word **dentition** is used to describe the number and arrangement of teeth in an animal. Humans and other omnivores have all four basic types of teeth to deal with a mixed diet of plants and meat. The dentition of adult humans is described in a dental formula using the key letters in Figure 25.4C.

Number and kind of teeth on each side of upper jaw

$$i\frac{2}{2} \ c\frac{1}{1} \ p\frac{2}{2} \ m\frac{3}{3}$$

Number and kind of teeth on each side of lower jaw

Herbivores and carnivores have different dentition, to enable them to deal with their particular diets.

● **Herbivore dentition**

Sheep and cattle are herbivores. They eat tough plants and grasses. Instead of having incisors in the front of the upper jaw, sheep and cattle have a tough, horny pad which the incisors of the lower jaw bite against. There are no canines in the upper jaw and the canines in the lower jaw look like incisors. There is a space in both jaws in front of the premolars. This space is called the diastema (Figure 25.4D). The animal can push its long, muscular tongue through the diastema to sweep grasses into its mouth, where they are cut off by the action of the lower incisors against the pad in the upper jaw (Figure 25.4E).

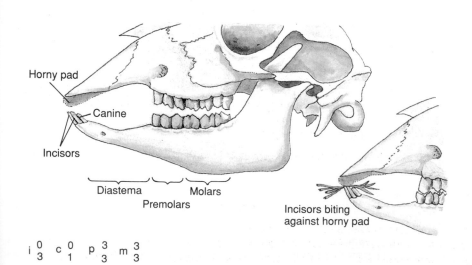

$$i\frac{0}{3} \ c\frac{0}{1} \ p\frac{3}{3} \ m\frac{3}{3}$$

Figure 25.4D ● The dentition of a sheep and its dental formula

Figure 25.4E ● Herbivore feeding

The premolars and molars have layers of cement, enamel and dentine which wear away at different rates. This causes ridges of enamel to form, which make a good surface for grinding the food (Figure 25.4F). The joint of the jaw and skull can move from side to side as well as up and down, which also makes grinding food easier.

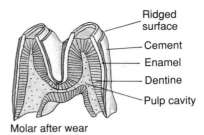

Molar when first formed   Molar after wear

Figure 25.4F ● The crown of a sheep's tooth showing how a herbivores teeth wear into ridges

● *Carnivore dentition*

Carnivores' teeth are adapted for catching struggling prey and cutting through soft flesh and hard bones (Figure 25.4G).

Dogs and cats are carnivores. Their canines are long and well-developed for grasping and tearing, and they have powerful jaw muscles. Their incisors, premolars and molars are used for cutting. The last premolar on each side of the upper jaw and the first molar on each side of the lower jaw are very large and are called the carnassial teeth. They are especially suitable for cutting through flesh and bone (Figure 25.4H). The jaw joint only allows up and down movements.

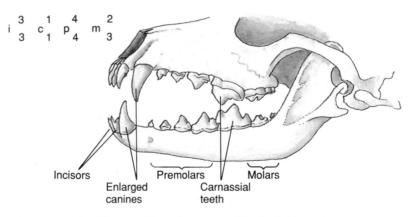

$$i\frac{3}{3} \quad c\frac{1}{1} \quad p\frac{4}{4} \quad m\frac{2}{3}$$

Incisors   Premolars   Molars

Enlarged   Carnassial
canines   teeth

Figure 25.4G ● Carnivore feeding

Figure 25.4H ● The dentition of a dog and its dental formula

CHECKPOINT

❶ Explain the words carnivore, herbivore and omnivore.

❷ Look at Figure 25.4A. Name the innermost part of the tooth? What does it contain?

❸ (a) Name the four basic types of teeth.
   (b) Describe the functions of two of the basic types of teeth in humans.

❹ (a) How are the teeth of a sheep adapted for grinding food?
   (a) How are the teeth of a dog adapted for grasping and cutting food?
   (b) Compare Figures 25.4D and 25.4H and list the differences between sheep's teeth (herbivore) and dogs' teeth (carnivore).

Even after you have cleaned your teeth, bacteria soon collect on them and multiply. They form plaque on the rough surfaces of teeth, in the areas next to the gums and in between teeth. Plaque is almost invisible. It accumulates and hardens, forming tartar.

Looking after your teeth

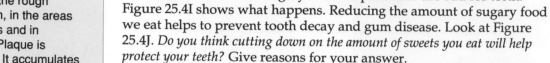

With proper care, a set of human teeth can last a lifetime. However, it is a sad fact that in the UK a child of twelve years has on average eight decayed teeth. What can we do to improve this?

Evidence shows that sugary foods in particular are bad for teeth. Figure 25.4I shows what happens. Reducing the amount of sugary food we eat helps to prevent tooth decay and gum disease. Look at Figure 25.4J. *Do you think cutting down on the amount of sweets you eat will help protect your teeth?* Give reasons for your answer.

Cleaning your teeth properly and regularly – at least after breakfast and last thing at night – is also very important. A disclosing tablet contains a dye, which colours plaque and shows you where extra cleaning is needed (Figure 25.4K).

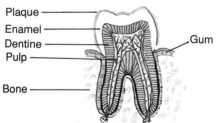

Plaque ——
Enamel ——
Dentine ——
Pulp ——

—— Gum

Bone ——

Bacteria in plaque break down sugar in the mouth, forming acids. NO PAIN

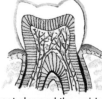

If teeth are not cleaned the acids attack and soften the enamel, which begins to decay (dental caries). The plaque thickens and irritates the gums. NO PAIN

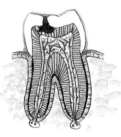

If untreated the decay eats through the dentine layer. SEVERE PAIN

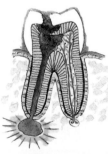

The decay eventually reaches the pulp cavity. If bacteria reaches the bone of the tooth an abscess forms. AGONY!

Figure 25.4I ● Tooth decay in progress

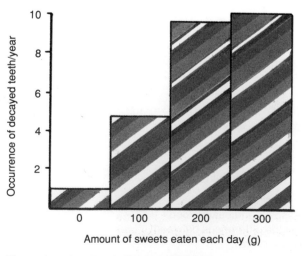

Figure 25.4J ● Tooth decay in children

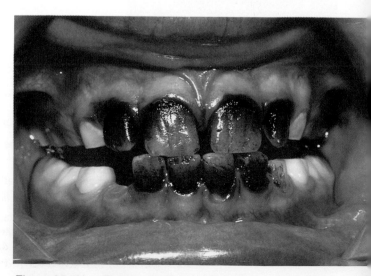

Figure 25.4K ● Dental plaque revealed using a disclosing tablet which stains plaque red

You need a good toothbrush. It should have a fairly small head, dense bristles and a firm handle. You also need to use it correctly (see Figure 25.4L). Your dentist can give you more advice on cleaning your teeth. You will need a new toothbrush about every three months. After brushing, you can use a soft thread called dental floss to clean between your teeth where the brush cannot reach (Figure 25.4M).

Having your teeth checked every six months by a dentist helps to make sure that your teeth and gums stay healthy. Dentists like to concentrate on preventing tooth decay and gum disease.

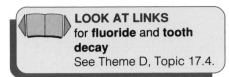

LOOK AT LINKS
for **fluoride** and **tooth decay**
See Theme D, Topic 17.4.

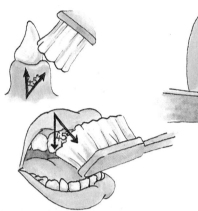
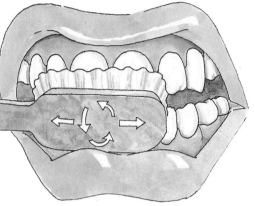

The angle between the bristles of the tooth-brush and the neck of the tooth should be about 45°.

Pressing gently, but firmly, move the brush with short strokes from side to side and also with an up–down circular movement to help clean in the spaces.

Work round the mouth on only a few teeth at a time, brushing all the front, back and biting surfaces.

Figure 25.4L ● One way of cleaning teeth properly with a toothbrush

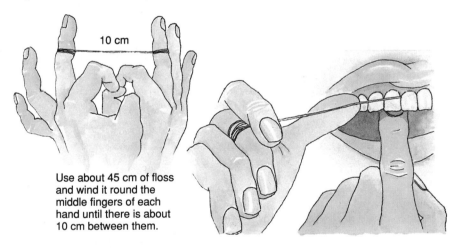

10 cm

Use about 45 cm of floss and wind it round the middle fingers of each hand until there is about 10 cm between them.

Starting with the upper teeth, use your fingers to guide the floss gently between two teeth until it reaches the gum line. Slowly slide it up and down the sides of both teeth. Repeat between all teeth, unwinding the floss from one hand to the other occasionally, for a fresh length.

Figure 25.4M ● How to clean your teeth with dental floss

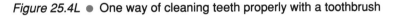

CHECKPOINT

❶ (a) Make a list of sugary foods. Tick the four that you eat most often.
(b) How does eating sugary foods cause tooth decay and gum disease?

❷ (a) How often should you visit the dentist?
(b) What is dental floss?

❸ Chlorine is added to drinking water to kill bacteria that would otherwise cause diseases like cholera and typhoid. Are you in favour of treating drinking water with chlorine? Give reasons for your answer.

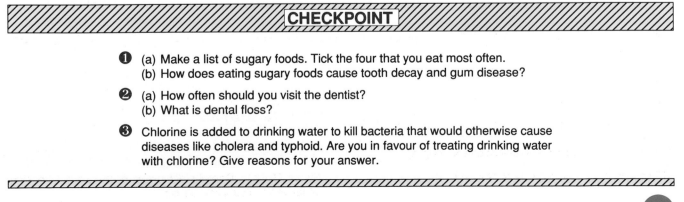

25.5 Digestion and absorption

How are nutrients in the food you eat converted into substances your body can absorb and use? The answer is – by digestion. This section tells you all about it.

LOOK AT LINKS
for **carbohydrates** see Theme D, Topic 18.2: for **lipids** see Topic 18.3: for **proteins** see Topic 18.4.

LOOK AT LINKS
for **enzymes**
See Theme D, Topic 18.4.

Carbohydrates, **lipids** and **proteins** are the main nutrients in our food. They are complex molecules which the body cannot absorb directly. To be useful they must be broken down into their basic constituents, substances which the body can absorb.

Nutrient		Absorbed as…
Carbohydrate	→	Simple sugars
Protein	→	Amino acids
Fat	→	Fatty acids and glycerol

The chemical and mechanical processes of digestion convert these foods into absorbable substances in the intestine (gut). Vitamins and minerals in food are absorbed unchanged during digestion.

Digestive enzymes

The chemical processes of digestion depend on nearly one hundred different **enzymes**. Enzymes are catalysts that speed up the chemical reactions. Without them the nutrients in the food you eat would be broken down so slowly that you would starve to death.

The absence of even one enzyme can cause illness. For example, people who do not produce the enzyme lactase cannot digest the sugar lactose ('milk' sugar). They develop cramps and diarrhoea if they consume lactose in milk and milk products, because the sugar builds up in the gut.

Enzymes are grouped according to the reactions they catalyse (Table 25.8). The rate at which they work is influenced by various factors, especially pH and temperature. Figure 25.5A illustrates the effects of these factors. *What is meant by 'optimum pH' and 'optimum temperature'? Which nutrients do pepsin and amylase digest?* Look at Figure 25.5C to find out where pepsin and amylase are made in the gut.

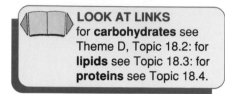
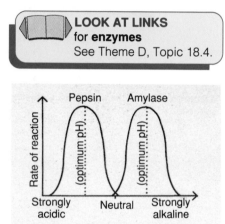

(a) The effect of pH on enzyme activity. Activity is greatest at the optimum pH for that particular enzyme. Strong acid/alkali denatures most enzymes

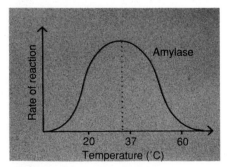

(b) The effect of temperature on enzyme activity. The activity of most enzymes at first increases with temperature reaching a maximum and then decreases. A high temperature denatures most enzymes

Figure 25.5A ● The effects of pH and temperature on the activity of the enzymes pepsin and amylase

Table 25.8 ● Enzymes that digest carbohydrates, proteins and lipids

Enzyme group	Example	Nutrient digested
Carbohydrases (catalyse the digestion of carbohydrates)	Amylase Lactase Sucrase Maltase	Starch Lactose Sucrose Maltose
Proteases (catalyse the digestion of proteins)	Pepsin Trypsin Chymotrypsin	Proteins Proteins Polypeptides
Lipases (catalyse the digestion of lipids)	Intestinal lipase	Fats

The gut and how it works

Figure 25.5B shows the human gut and its position in the body. It is a tube. At one end food is put into the mouth (**ingested**). At the other end the undigested remains of a meal are removed through the anus (egested). In between mouth and anus the mechanical and chemical processes of **digestion** break down food into substances suitable for **absorption**. These processes are explained in Figure 25.5C. *Why do you think the action of renin is particularly important in babies? How do the actions of teeth and bile make it easier for enzymes to digest food?*

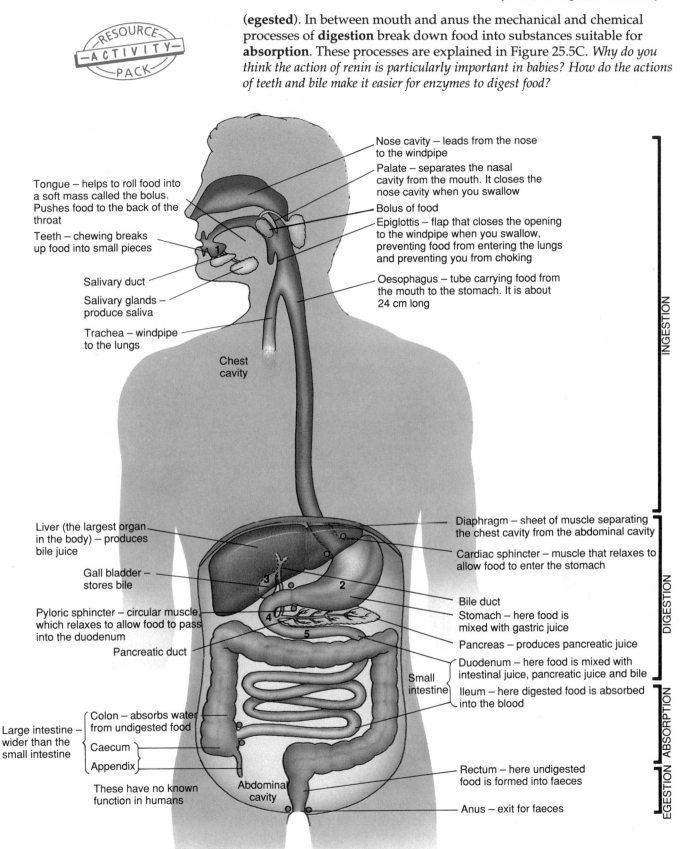

Figure 25.5B ● The human gut (The functions are explained in Figure 25.5C; the numbers ❶ to ❺ refer to the sections of Figure 25.5C)

● *Chemical processes*

What happens

❶ **Saliva** moistens the food. It contains the enzyme amylase, which begins the digestion of starch in the mouth.

❷ Pits in the stomach wall produce **gastric juice**, which contains hydrochloric acid and the enzymes pepsin and renin.
Hydrochloric acid:
• lowers the pH of the stomach contents
• kills bacteria on the food
• stops the action of the enzyme amylase in the saliva
Pepsin:
• starts the digestion of protein
Renin:
• clots milk so it stays long enough in the gut to be digested

❸ **Bile** is a green alkaline liquid produced by the liver and stored in the gall bladder. It neutralises acid from the stomach and breaks fats into small droplets which are easier for the enzymes to digest.

❹ **Pancreatic juice** contains four different enzymes which digest carbohydrate, fat and protein. It also contains sodium carbonate which helps to neutralise stomach acid.

❺ Glands in the wall of the duodenum produce **intestinal juice** which contains enzymes that complete the digestion of carbohydrates and fats.

Where it happens

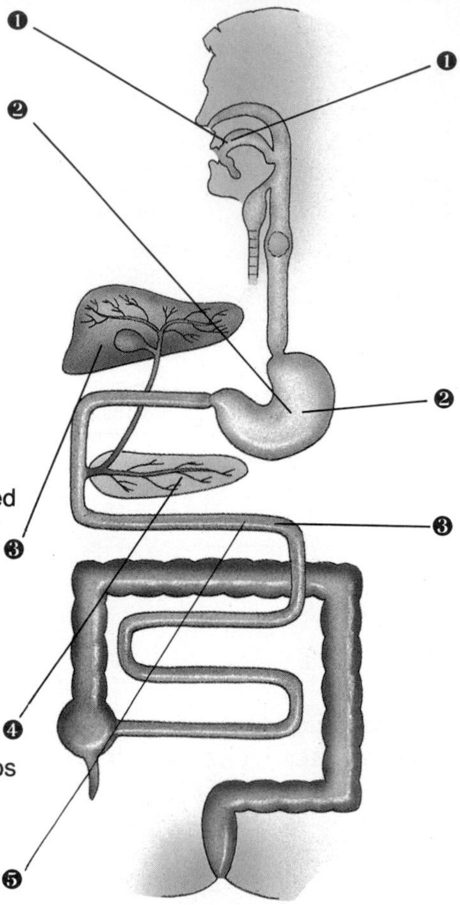

● *Mechanical processes*

What happens

❶ Chewing breaks the food up into small pieces which are easier to digest. Mucus, produced by membranes lining the mouth, and saliva make food slippery for easy swallowing.

❷ Muscles of the stomach wall rhythmically contract and relax, mixing food with the gastric juices into a liquid paste called chyme.

❸ Rhythmic contractions of the muscles in the small intestine mix chyme with bile, pancreatic juice and intestinal juice.

Figure 25.5C ● How we digest food

Different parts of the gut perform different tasks in processing food as it passes through. The human gut is 7–9 m long. The longest part of it is composed of the small intestine and the large intestine. These lie folded and packed in the space of the abdominal cavity. The **liver** and **pancreas** are connected by ducts to the gut and play an important part in the digestion of food. They also have a major role in the metabolism of food substances once these have been absorbed into the body.

● *Absorption of digested food*

Figure 25.5D summarises what has happened to the food so far. *Which nutrients are not digested? Is fat digested in the stomach?*

The next stage – absorption – takes place mostly in the ileum, although alcohol and small amounts of simple sugars and water are absorbed by the lining of the stomach. Water is also absorbed by the colon.

Figure 25.5B shows that folding and coiling packs as much gut as possible into the restricted space of the abdominal cavity. The extra length means that food not only travels greater distances through the gut so that enzymes have more time to digest the food, but also that the surface area for absorption is increased. Closely packed finger-like projections called **villi** line the small intestine and increase its surface area further (Figure 25.5E).

In 1822 Alexis St Martin, a Canadian fur trapper, was wounded in his left side by a shotgun blast. He was nursed back to health by an army surgeon, Dr William Beaumont. When his wound healed a small hole remained between the stomach and the outside. Beaumont took samples of food from his stomach through this hole. He looked after St Martin for more than two years and carried out experiments on the role of gastric juice in digestion. His work greatly increased our understanding of how the stomach works.

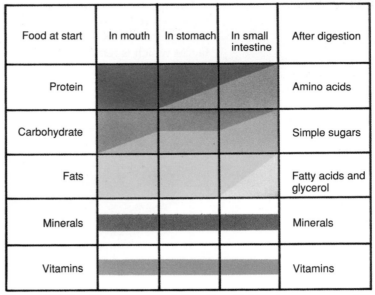

Food at start	In mouth	In stomach	In small intestine	After digestion
Protein				Amino acids
Carbohydrate				Simple sugars
Fats				Fatty acids and glycerol
Minerals				Minerals
Vitamins				Vitamins

Figure 25.5D ● The progress of digestion. Solid colours represent the nutrients in food before digestion

LOOK AT LINKS
Absorption involves **diffusion** and **active transport**. See Theme D, Topic 19. Transport by the lymph system and by blood vessels is discussed in Theme J, Topic 38.3.

Figure 25.5F shows inside a villus. Absorption occurs when nutrients pass through its cells and into the blood and lymph vessels. Most fatty acids and fat-soluble vitamins (see Table 25.2) pass into the lymph vessels. Water, glucose, glycerol, amino acids and other substances pass into the network of capillary blood vessels and are transported to the liver. Mucus helps to protect the gut wall from its own digestive enzymes. Microvilli project from the surface of each cell lining the villus. They increase the surface area for absorption about 20 times more compared with the villi alone! *Altogether, how large a surface area do villi and microvilli make for absorption?* (See Figure 25.5E.)

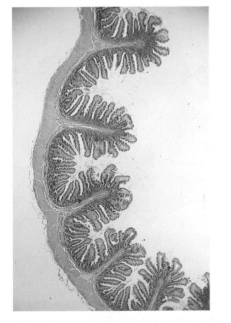

Figure 25.5E ● Section of the small intestine. Five million villi, each about 1 mm long, cover the inside of the small intestine. They provide approximately 10 m² of surface for absorption in your gut!

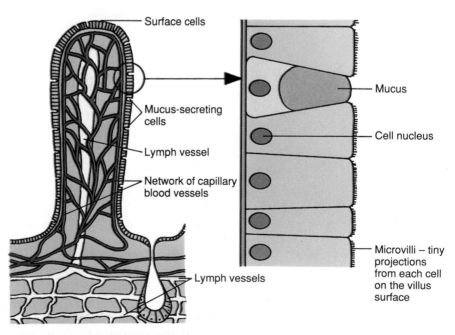

Surface cells

Mucus-secreting cells

Lymph vessel

Network of capillary blood vessels

Lymph vessels

Mucus

Cell nucleus

Microvilli – tiny projections from each cell on the villus surface

Figure 25.5F ● Inside a villus (part of its surface is shown at high magnification)

Undigested food passes out of the small intestine into the colon. Here, water poured onto the food during digestion is absorbed back into the body (Figure 25.5G). The food remnants dry out into a compact mass of faeces which is removed from the body through the anus – a process called **defaecation**.

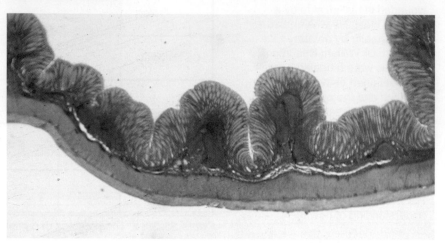

Figure 25.5G ● Section of large intestine. Compare with the section of small intestine shown in Figure 25.5E. *What differences can you see?*

Moving food through the gut

Repeated contraction and relaxation of **muscle** layers in the gut wall move food through the gut. This muscular action is called **peristalsis** (Figure 25.5H).

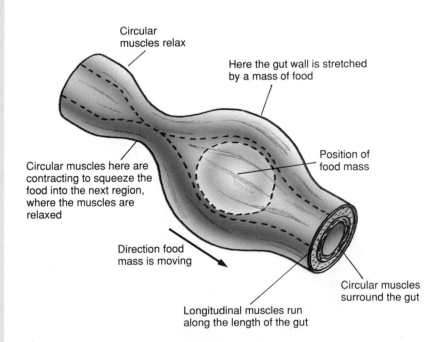

Figure 25.5H ● Peristalsis – the gut narrows when the circular muscles contract and shortens when the longitudinal muscles contract

Another type of gut movement happens when the circular muscles alone contract. This muscular action is called **segmentation** (Figure 25.5I). Together peristalsis and segmentation move a meal through the gut in about 24 hours.

LOOK AT LINKS
You can find out more about **muscles** and how they work in
Theme J, Topic 41.2.

LOOK AT LINKS
for how an **X-ray**
photograph is taken see
Theme H, Topic 33.2.
For barium meals
See Theme D, Topic 17.4.

Imitating circular muscle
You need a lump of plasticine.
Roll it into a cylinder about 2 cm
in diameter. Lightly grip it in
your hand – the diagram shows
you how. Now gently squeeze
the cylinder and notice what
happens.
- How does your hand imitate
  the action of circular muscle?
- Briefly describe what
  happens to the plasticine
  when you squeeze it. What
  does this tell you about the
  movement of food through
  the gut?

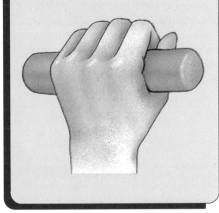

LOOK AT LINKS
for more about **omnivores**,
herbivores and
carnivores
See Topic 25.3.

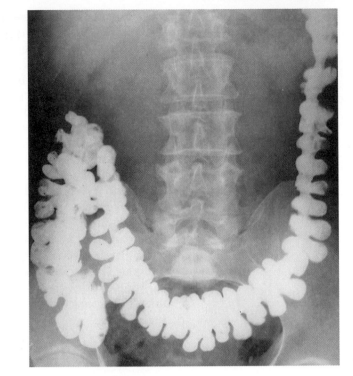

Figure 25.5I ● Segmentation. The X-ray picture shows that contraction of the circular muscle temporarily divides the gut into a series of segments

The gut suits the diet

Different guts are adapted to deal with different types of diet. Most humans, for example, are omnivores and the human gut is adapted to deal with a mixture of plant and animal foods. Rabbits and cows are herbivores, with guts adapted for plant foods, and cats are carnivores, with guts adapted for meat. Figure 25.5J compares them. List the differences between them. *How is each gut adapted to deal with a particular diet?*

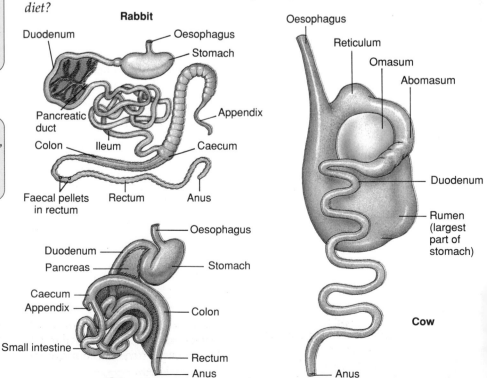

Figure 25.5J ● The guts of the cow, rabbit and cat

Most animals do not possess enzymes to digest the cellulose in the walls of plant cells. However, some species of **bacteria** and **protozoa** do. These micro-organisms live in different parts of the gut of an animal and digest the cellulose in food. In rabbits, for example, the caecum and appendix are the home of these micro-organisms. In cows they live in the stomach, which consists of four parts. The rumen and reticulum receive the food first of all. The cellulose-digesting micro-organisms live in the rumen. Here the food forms into balls of cud before returning to the mouth where it is thoroughly re-chewed (animals that chew cud are called ruminants). Swallowing takes the cud to the remaining two parts of the stomach, where protein digestion takes place.

Rabbits do not chew cud. Instead they eat the pellets of faeces produced from the food's first journey through the gut. The pellets are soft and contain a lot of undigested food which the cellulose-digesting micro-organisms have another chance of dealing with as they pass through the gut a second time. Faecal pellets produced after the food's second journey through the gut are hard.

Cats do not chew their food – they swallow it whole or in large chunks. The stomach is large so that it can store the meal while it is digested.

CHECKPOINT

❶ Mechanical digestion breaks up food, and chemical digestion converts its insoluble nutrients into soluble substances which the gut can absorb.

   (a) Rewrite the following list under two headings – mechanical digestion and chemical digestion – placing each in the correct column.

action of teeth	action of bile
action of amylase	action of saliva
action of peristalsis	

   (b) Why do you think that mechanical digestion usually occurs before chemical digestion?

❷ Experiments to investigate the effects of temperature and pH on the activity of the protein-digesting enzyme pepsin produced the following results.

Temperature (°C)	Time taken for digestion to be completed (s)	
	pH5.8	pH8.5
20	275	
25	221	
30	169	
35	114	Digestion not completed during the experiment
40	137	
50	196	
60	Digestion not completed during the experiment	

Plot the results on graph paper and then comment on the results.

❸ Relative to the size of the rest of the body, frog tadpoles have a long, coiled gut and adult frogs have a short one. Briefly explain why you suspect frog tadpoles are herbivores and adult frogs are carnivores.

RESPIRATION

26.1 What is respiration?

FIRST THOUGHTS

Cells use the oxygen in air to release energy from sugars. The process produces carbon dioxide, which living things pass to the environment.

Figure 26.1A ● Breathing hard

Figure 26.1A shows a man and his best friend doing something that we all do – breathing: in their case, breathing hard!

Breathing describes inhaling (taking in) and exhaling (giving out) air. Look at Table 26.1. It shows that the proportions of gases in inhaled and exhaled air are different. Oxygen is used by the body and carbon dioxide is produced. Oxygen and carbon dioxide are exchanged between the inhaled air and the blood across the inner surface of the lungs. *What is oxygen used for in the body?*

Table 26.1 ● Differences between inhaled and exhaled air.

Gas	Inhaled air (%)	Exhaled air (%)
Nitrogen	78	78
Oxygen	21	16
Noble gases	1	1
Carbon dioxide	0.03	4
Water vapour	0	1

Cellular respiration

Digested food substances are **oxidised** in cells to release energy. These oxidation reactions are called **cellular respiration**.

Look at Table 26.1. *Why is there less oxygen in exhaled air than in inhaled air?* The reason is that some of the oxygen inhaled is used by the cells to oxidise food. Cellular respiration that uses oxygen is called **aerobic respiration**.

The aerobic respiration is **exothermic** – it gives out energy.

$$\text{Glucose} \quad + \quad \text{Oxygen} \quad \rightarrow \quad \text{Carbon dioxide} \quad + \quad \text{Water}$$
$$C_6H_{12}O_6(aq) \quad + \quad 6O_2(g) \quad \rightarrow \quad 6CO_2(g) \quad + \quad 6H_2O(l)$$

Energy released = 16.1 kJ/g glucose

In Figure 26.1A aerobic respiration in the cells of the man's leg muscles gives him a flying start. Soon, however, in spite of rapid breathing and strenuous pumping by the heart, oxygen cannot reach the muscles fast

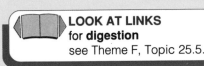

LOOK AT LINKS
for **digestion**
see Theme F, Topic 25.5.

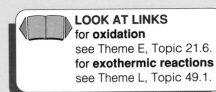

LOOK AT LINKS
for **oxidation**
see Theme E, Topic 21.6.
for **exothermic reactions**
see Theme L, Topic 49.1.

LOOK AT LINKS
for the transport of oxygen in the blood
see Theme J, Topic 38.3.

enough to supply their needs. The muscles then switch from aerobic respiration to **anaerobic respiration**, which does not use oxygen. Lactic acid is produced and collects in the muscles. The reactions are

$$\text{Glucose} \rightarrow \text{Lactic acid}$$
$$C_6H_{12}O_6(aq) \rightarrow 2CH_3CHOHCO_2H(aq)$$

Energy released = 0.83 kJ/g glucose

The energy released is less than in aerobic respiration. An 'oxygen debt' builds up. After the muscles have respired anaerobically for a few minutes, the lactic acid they have built up stops them from working. The dog's leg muscles will also have been respiring anaerobically. Both the man and the dog will be unable to run further until the lactic acid is removed from the muscles. During the recovery period, which lasts several minutes, man and dog pant vigorously (Figure 26.1B). The rush of oxygen to the muscles promotes aerobic respiration. Some lactic acid is oxidised to carbon dioxide and water; the rest is converted into glucose. In this way the 'oxygen debt' is repaid.

Figure 26.1B ● Recovery period

Bacteria, yeasts and root cells of plants can also change from aerobic respiration to anaerobic respiration if they are short of oxygen. Certain bacteria live permanently without oxygen: in fact oxygen is poisonous to some of them.

Yeast cells use anaerobic respiration to convert glucose into ethanol and carbon dioxide, with the release of energy. The reaction, called **fermentation**, is used commercially for the production of ethanol (alcohol) by yeast.

$$\text{Glucose} \rightarrow \text{Ethanol} + \text{Carbon dioxide}$$
$$C_6H_{12}O_6(aq) \rightarrow 2C_2H_5OH(aq) + 2CO_2(g)$$

Energy released = 1.17 kJ/g glucose

LOOK AT LINKS
for **fermentation**
See Theme L, Topic 51.5.

The energy released is less than in aerobic respiration. Other differences between aerobic and anaerobic respiration are summarised in Table 26.2.

Why is there a difference in energy output? Aerobic respiration completely oxidises glucose to carbon dioxide and water and releases all the available energy from each glucose molecule. Anaerobic respiration converts glucose into ethanol or lactic acid. More energy can be obtained by oxidising lactic acid aerobically.

Cellular respiration is sometimes compared with the combustion of petrol in vehicle engines, but there is a vital difference. When fuel is burnt in an engine, energy is released suddenly in an explosive reaction. If cells were to release energy from food suddenly, the sharp rise in temperature would kill them. Cellular respiration is not a one-step chemical change, but a series of chemical changes that release energy from food gradually.

Table 26.2 ● A comparison of aerobic and anaerobic respiration

Process	Oxygen used or not used	Products of process	Energy released (kJ/g glucose)
Aerobic respiration	Used	Carbon dioxide and water	16.1
Anaerobic respiration in yeast	Not used	Ethanol and carbon dioxide	1.17
Anaerobic respiration in muscle cells	Not used	Lactic acid	0.83

Stages of cellular respiration

LOOK AT LINKS
for **mitochondria**
See Theme D, Topic 19.1.

IT'S A FACT

Cells do not use the energy from the oxidation of food as soon as it is released. It is converted into the energy of the chemical bonds in a substance called adenosine triphosphate (ATP). ATP is found in the cells of nearly all living things, and is the link between the cell's energy-releasing activities and energy-using activities.

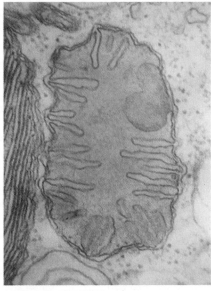

The first stage in both aerobic and anaerobic respiration is the conversion of glucose into pyruvic acid. This happens in the cell's cytoplasm. Then, if oxygen is present, pyruvic acid is oxidised in the **mitochondria** to carbon dioxide and water (Figure 26.1C).

Figure 26.1C ● Mitochondria (x 40 000)

If no oxygen is present, anaerobic respiration takes place and lactic acid is formed.

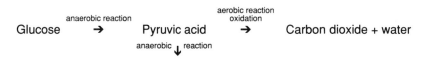

Glucose → Pyruvic acid → Carbon dioxide + water

Lactic acid

Cellular respiration and photosynthesis

Cellular respiration and photosynthesis form a cycle. The products of one are the starting materials of the other (Figure 26.1D).

During the day photosynthesis produces more oxygen than is used in aerobic respiration. The surplus oxygen diffuses through the stomata out of the leaf. At night photosynthesis stops but plant cells still need oxygen for aerobic respiration. Oxygen therefore diffuses through the stomata into the leaf.

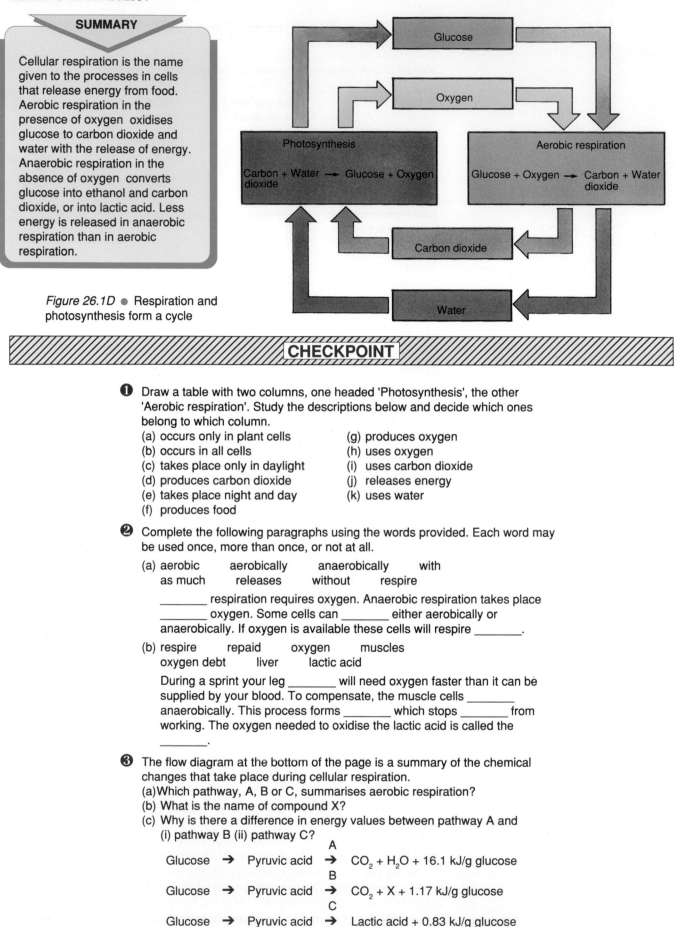

Figure 26.1D ● Respiration and photosynthesis form a cycle

CHECKPOINT

❶ Draw a table with two columns, one headed 'Photosynthesis', the other 'Aerobic respiration'. Study the descriptions below and decide which ones belong to which column.

(a) occurs only in plant cells
(b) occurs in all cells
(c) takes place only in daylight
(d) produces carbon dioxide
(e) takes place night and day
(f) produces food

(g) produces oxygen
(h) uses oxygen
(i) uses carbon dioxide
(j) releases energy
(k) uses water

❷ Complete the following paragraphs using the words provided. Each word may be used once, more than once, or not at all.

(a) aerobic   aerobically   anaerobically   with
     as much   releases   without   respire

_____ respiration requires oxygen. Anaerobic respiration takes place _____ oxygen. Some cells can _____ either aerobically or anaerobically. If oxygen is available these cells will respire _____.

(b) respire   repaid   oxygen   muscles
     oxygen debt   liver   lactic acid

During a sprint your leg _____ will need oxygen faster than it can be supplied by your blood. To compensate, the muscle cells _____ anaerobically. This process forms _____ which stops _____ from working. The oxygen needed to oxidise the lactic acid is called the _____.

❸ The flow diagram at the bottom of the page is a summary of the chemical changes that take place during cellular respiration.
(a)Which pathway, A, B or C, summarises aerobic respiration?
(b) What is the name of compound X?
(c) Why is there a difference in energy values between pathway A and
    (i) pathway B (ii) pathway C?

                                A

Glucose → Pyruvic acid → CO_2 + H_2O + 16.1 kJ/g glucose

                                B

Glucose → Pyruvic acid → CO_2 + X + 1.17 kJ/g glucose

                                C

Glucose → Pyruvic acid → Lactic acid + 0.83 kJ/g glucose

26.2 Surfaces for exchanging gases

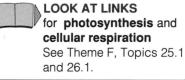

FIRST THOUGHTS

One of the processes vital to living things is the exchange of gases across a surface. Read on to find out why this is so important.

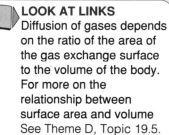

LOOK AT LINKS
for **photosynthesis** and **cellular respiration**
See Theme F, Topics 25.1 and 26.1.

LOOK AT LINKS
Diffusion of gases depends on the ratio of the area of the gas exchange surface to the volume of the body. For more on the relationship between surface area and volume
See Theme D, Topic 19.5.

RESOURCE –ACTIVITY– PACK

LOOK AT LINKS
for *Hydra* and *Planaria*
See Theme A, Topic 3.5.

Figure 26.2A shows some different organisms that live in water. The organisms are taking in and giving out air. In the tissues there is an exchange of gases because of:

- **photosynthesis** (in plants only)
- **cellular respiration** (in nearly all organisms)

These exchanges take place across the membranes of gas exchange surfaces. Notice the gills of the newt tadpole and the dragonfly nymph and the flat, thin leaves of the water weed. *Which gas (oxygen or carbon dioxide) does each process (a) use and (b) produce?*

Figure 26.2A ● (a) Newt tadpole   (b) Dragonfly nymph

In small animals like *Hydra* and *Planaria* gas exchange occurs across the body wall. Their surface areas are large enough to supply sufficient oxygen to the inside of the body and let carbon dioxide pass out. The body of the flatworm *Planaria* is flattened to a leaf-like shape which allows gases to diffuse easily through it. (Figure 26.2B).

Only small organisms can obtain enough oxygen by diffusion through the body wall. Larger animals have special organs for supplying oxygen to tissues in the deepest parts of the body and removing carbon dioxide from them.

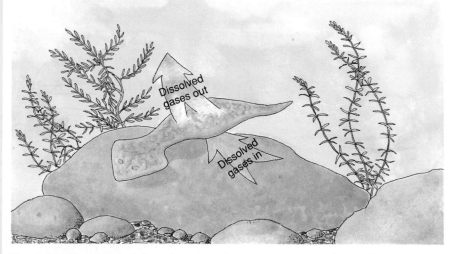

Figure 26.2B ● *Planaria* lives in water where gases are in solution. The gases diffuse into and out of the animal across its body wall

LOOK AT LINKS
for more about gas exchange in leaves see Topic 25.1.

Leaves are also flat. Figure 26.2C shows the small holes called stomata that pierce the undersurface. Oxygen and carbon dioxide diffuse into and out of the leaf through the stomata.

The cells on either side of the stomata are called guard cells. Each one is sausage-shaped and has many chloroplasts. Guard cells control the size of the stomata and therefore control the rate of diffusion.

Figure 26.2C ● Underside of a leaf. The oval holes are stomata. Guard cells on either side of a stoma are packed with chloroplasts, unlike the surrounding cells of the epidermis

Lungs

The fish in Figure 26.2D breathes air! It has simple sac-like structures, called lungs, through which it exchanges oxygen and carbon dioxide in air. It also has gills through which it exchanges oxygen and carbon dioxide in water. Breathing air is a safety device for this animal. It enables it to survive periods of drought when the swamps and rivers it lives in dry out temporarily.

IT'S A FACT

The ancestors of lungfish were among the first land-living vertebrates 300 million years ago. Breathing air through lungs allowed them to survive times of drought.

Figure 26.2D ● A South American lungfish

The human lungs and upper respiratory tract

Our lungs are large and honeycombed with passages. Gases are exchanged across the surfaces in the lungs. Figure 26.2E shows the position of the lungs in the human body. They lie inside the **thoracic cavity**. The **upper respiratory tract** is a tube from the nostrils and mouth to the lungs.

There are mechanisms to prevent food from entering the larynx from the pharynx. The act of swallowing closes the glottis and lifts up the whole larynx so that it is blocked by the base of the tongue. At the same time, the flap-like epiglottis moves backward and protects the opening of the glottis. If food does lodge in the larynx, it triggers off violent coughing, which usually clears the obstruction.

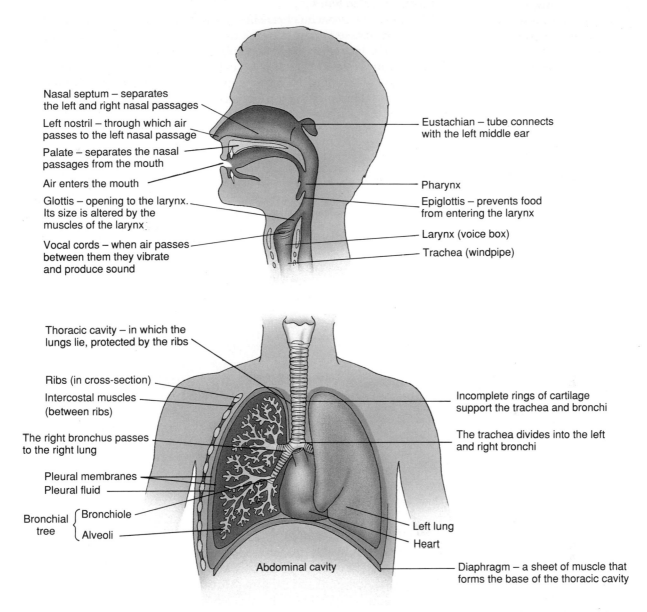

Nasal septum – separates the left and right nasal passages

Left nostril – through which air passes to the left nasal passage

Palate – separates the nasal passages from the mouth

Air enters the mouth

Glottis – opening to the larynx. Its size is altered by the muscles of the larynx

Vocal cords – when air passes between them they vibrate and produce sound

Eustachian – tube connects with the left middle ear

Pharynx

Epiglottis – prevents food from entering the larynx

Larynx (voice box)

Trachea (windpipe)

Thoracic cavity – in which the lungs lie, protected by the ribs

Ribs (in cross-section)

Intercostal muscles (between ribs)

The right bronchus passes to the right lung

Pleural membranes
Pleural fluid

Bronchial tree { Bronchiole
Alveoli

Incomplete rings of cartilage support the trachea and bronchi

The trachea divides into the left and right bronchi

Left lung

Heart

Abdominal cavity

Diaphragm – a sheet of muscle that forms the base of the thoracic cavity

Figure 26.2E ● The lungs (viewed from the front) and the upper respiratory tract (viewed from the left hand side) in the human body

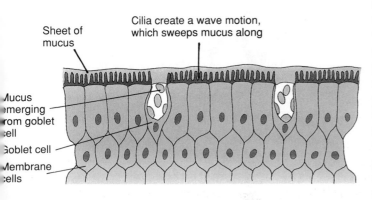

Sheet of mucus

Cilia create a wave motion, which sweeps mucus along

Mucus emerging from goblet cell

Goblet cell

Membrane cells

Figure 26.2F ● The membrane lining of the upper respiratory tract

● *The upper respiratory tract at work*

The upper respiratory tract is an air-conditioning system. It warms and filters inhaled air. The membrane which lines the upper respiratory tract is well supplied with blood, which warms the air to body temperature. Hairs in the nasal passage filter out large particles of dust. A sheet of mucus lines the upper respiratory tract and traps bacteria, viruses and dust particles (Figure 26.2F). The mucus comes from cells in the membrane lining called goblet cells. Cilia, rows of fine hairs, sway to and fro and sweep the mucus, and with it trapped bacteria, viruses and dust, into the pharynx. It is either swallowed, sneezed out or coughed up. The air which then passes to the lungs is cleaned and freed from germs. What happens when the body fails to remove all germs is described later in this topic.

LOOK AT LINKS
You can find out more about the transport of gases by the blood in Theme J, Topic 38.2.

IT'S A FACT

There are millions of alveoli in a pair of human lungs. Together they give a surface area of approximately 90 m²!

● The alveoli at work

In the lung, each bronchus branches many times into small tubes called **bronchioles**. These form a network called the **bronchial tree** (see Figure 26.2E). The bronchioles divide and sub-divide into even smaller tubes which end in clusters of small sacks called **alveoli** (singular: alveolus).

The walls of the alveoli are very thin and surrounded by capillary blood vessels. Figure 26.2G shows gas exchange between the walls of the alveoli and the capillary blood vessels.

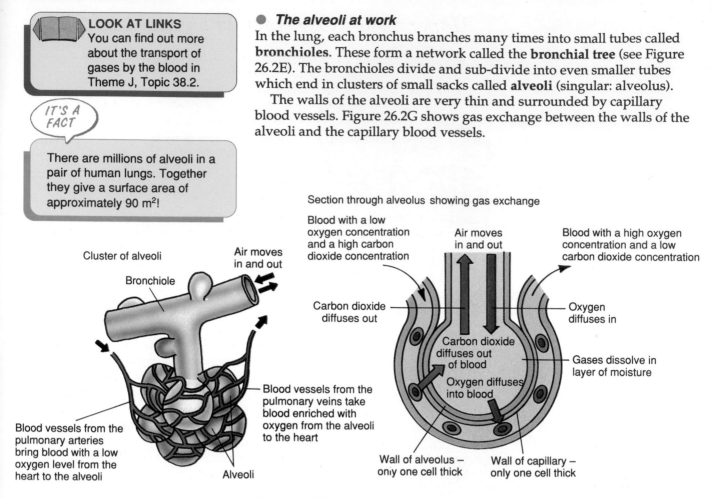

Cluster of alveoli

Bronchiole

Air moves in and out

Blood vessels from the pulmonary arteries bring blood with a low oxygen level from the heart to the alveoli

Blood vessels from the pulmonary veins take blood enriched with oxygen from the alveoli to the heart

Alveoli

Section through alveolus showing gas exchange

Blood with a low oxygen concentration and a high carbon dioxide concentration

Air moves in and out

Blood with a high oxygen concentration and a low carbon dioxide concentration

Carbon dioxide diffuses out

Oxygen diffuses in

Carbon dioxide diffuses out of blood

Oxygen diffuses into blood

Gases dissolve in layer of moisture

Wall of alveolus – only one cell thick

Wall of capillary – only one cell thick

Figure 26.2G ● The alveoli at work (notice that oxygen and carbon dioxide diffuse in solution between alveolus and capillary blood vessel

● Breathing movements

The cage formed by the ribs and diaphragm is elastic. As it moves the pressure in the lungs changes. It is the change in pressure that causes inhaling (breathing in) and exhaling (breathing out) (Figure 26.2H).

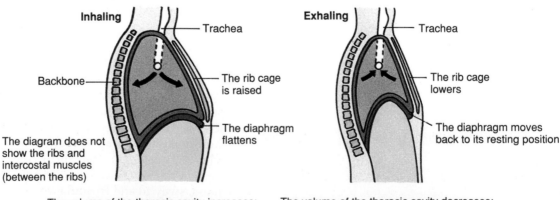

Inhaling

Trachea

Backbone

The rib cage is raised

The diaphragm flattens

The diagram does not show the ribs and intercostal muscles (between the ribs)

Exhaling

Trachea

The rib cage lowers

The diaphragm moves back to its resting position

The volume of the thoracic cavity increases: therefore the pressure of the air inside it decreases. It becomes less than atmospheric pressure, and air is drawn into the lungs

The volume of the thoracic cavity decreases: therefore the pressure of the air inside it increases. It becomes greater than atmospheric pressure and forces air out of the lungs into the trachea

Figure 26.2H ● Inhaling and exhaling

Upper respiratory tract and lung diseases

The mechanism for sweeping dust, bacteria and viruses out of the upper respiratory tract and lungs has been described in Figure 26.2F. Coughing and sneezing remove the mucus with its load of dust and micro-organisms. Even so, any part of the upper respiratory tract and lungs can become infected by disease-causing micro-organisms.

Infection of the:

- throat (pharynx) is called **pharyngitis**,
- voice-box (larynx) is called **laryngitis**,
- windpipe (trachea) is called **tracheitis**,
- bronchus and bronchioles is called **bronchitis**.

Infection of the lungs by a particular type of bacterium causes pneumonia. The patient becomes breathless because fluid collects in the alveoli, reducing the surface area available for the absorption of oxygen. Pneumonia is treated with antibiotic drugs such as penicillin.

The **pleural membranes** line the rib cage and cover the surface of the lung (Figure 26.2E). Between them the **pleural fluid** stops the lungs sticking to the chest wall. Sometimes bacteria infect the pleural membranes, making them rough and causing pain when they rub together. The infection is called pleurisy and it is treated with antibiotics.

Other common lung diseases like lung cancer and asthma are not caused by bacteria or viruses. Lung cancer can be caused by many different things such as smoking or can just occur naturally. Tumours form in the lung and if they are not discovered quickly the cancer can spread to other parts of the body. Asthma is often caused by allergies. If you have asthma sometimes it is difficult to breathe, you wheeze and your chest feels tight. The occurence of both lung cancer and asthma can be linked to the quality of the air that we breathe.

● The air we breathe

Motor vehicle exhaust fumes, smoke and dust from industry, cigarette smoke and all the other substances that human activities put into the air are part of our environment . Breathing this mixture affects our lungs.

Figure 26.2I shows the effect of fine coal dust on a coalminer's lungs. People who work in a dusty atmosphere can be affected in a similar way.

FIRST THOUGHTS

What is in the air we breathe? How does it affect our lungs? This section tells you.

LOOK AT LINKS
for **air pollution**
See Theme E, Topic 23.

SUMMARY

Gases are exchanged in solution by diffusion across gas exchange surfaces. These surfaces are thin and have a large surface area: adaptations for efficient diffusion.

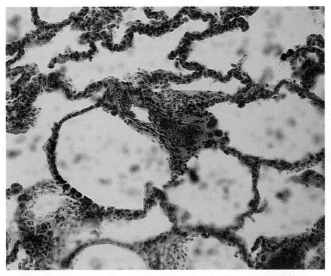

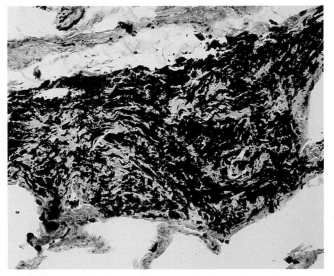

Figure 26.2I ● (a) Section of lung taken from a healthy person

(b) Section of lung taken from a coal miner with a lung disease called pneumoconiosis. Notice the deposits of coal dust in the lung tissue

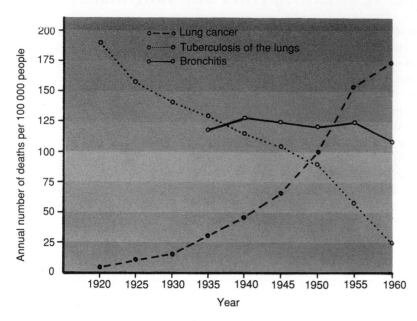

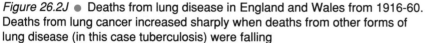

Figure 26.2J ● Deaths from lung disease in England and Wales from 1916-60. Deaths from lung cancer increased sharply when deaths from other forms of lung disease (in this case tuberculosis) were falling

Smoking is harmful: the evidence and attitudes

Research into the links between smoking and disease was prompted by the sort of data shown in Figure 26.2 J.

Scientists soon suspected a correlation (relationship) between smoking cigarettes and **lung cancer** but could not prove the link completely. However, new data strengthened the case against cigarettes.

- When doctors saw the early evidence many of them gave up smoking cigarettes. Deaths from lung cancer among doctors went down compared with the population as a whole.

- Studies clearly established the relationship between the risk of dying from lung cancer and number of cigarettes smoked – the more cigarettes smoked, the greater the risk (Figure 26.2L).

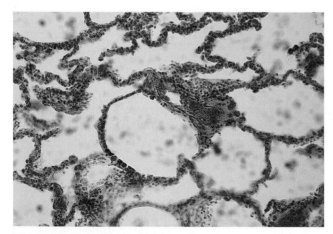

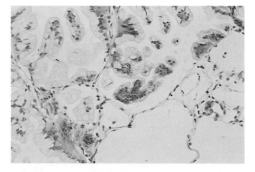

Figure 26.2K ● (a) Healthy lung tissue   (b) Cancerous lung tissue

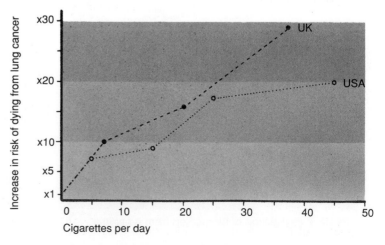

Figure 26.2L ● Death rates from lung cancer in men who smoke

● *Why are cigarettes dangerous?*

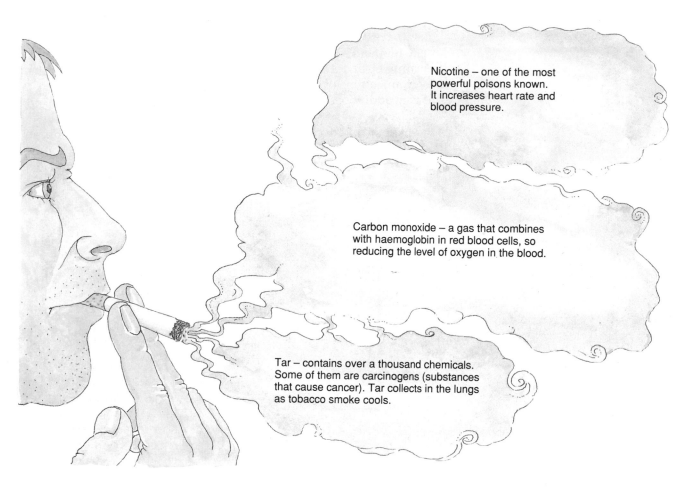

Nicotine – one of the most powerful poisons known. It increases heart rate and blood pressure.

Carbon monoxide – a gas that combines with haemoglobin in red blood cells, so reducing the level of oxygen in the blood.

Tar – contains over a thousand chemicals. Some of them are carcinogens (substances that cause cancer). Tar collects in the lungs as tobacco smoke cools.

Figure 26.2M ● Dangers to health from the chemicals in cigarette smoke

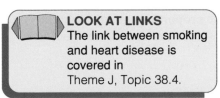

LOOK AT LINKS
The link between smoking and heart disease is covered in Theme J, Topic 38.4.

A lighted cigarette produces a number of substances. Many of them are harmful (Figure 26.2M). Some irritate the membrane lining the upper respiratory tract. Others stop the cilia from beating (Figure 26.2F). Extra mucus (phlegm) forms in the trachea and bronchi, causing 'smoker's cough'; it is the only way to get rid of the build up of phlegm. Smoking also weakens the walls of the alveoli and repeated coughing can destroy some of them. This breakdown of the alveoli is called **emphysema** (Figure 26.2N). *Why does a person with emphysema become breathless and exhausted easily?*

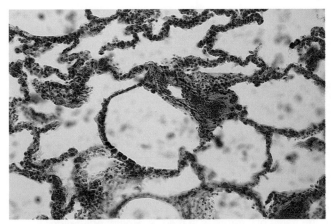

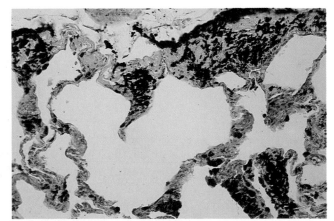

Figure 26.2N ● (a) Healthy alveoli

(b) Alveoli destroyed by emphysema

LOOK AT LINKS
for for development of the
baby in the uterus
See Theme J, Topic 39.4.

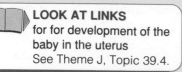

Pregnant women are always advised not to smoke. The chemicals in cigarette smoke enter the mother's bloodstream and reach the developing baby across the placenta.

Babies born to mothers who smoke are generally lighter than babies born to mothers who do not smoke and there is an increased risk of premature birth. It seems that chemicals in cigarette smoke prevent the baby from getting all the nourishment she or he needs from the mother. This is in addition to the other dangers listed in Figure 26.2M.

Children see parents, older brothers and sisters, pop stars and film stars smoking and decide that smoking is the 'grown up' thing to do, so they copy them. Other children copy them, and so on (Figure 26.2O). This is the way smoking usually starts and once 'hooked' it is difficult to give up because the nicotine in tobacco is habit-forming.

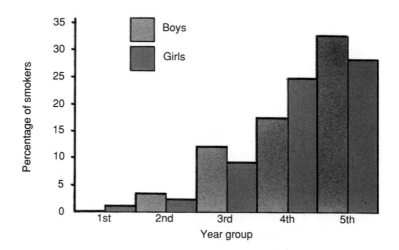

Figure 26.2O ● The smoking behaviour of girls and boys at secondary school. *Can you explain why girls who smoke outnumber boys who smoke in the fourth year?*

● *Living sensibly*

In 1971 The Royal College of Physicians said:

'Premature death and disabling illnesses caused by cigarette smoking have now reached epidemic proportions and present the most challenging of all opportunities for preventive medicine ...'

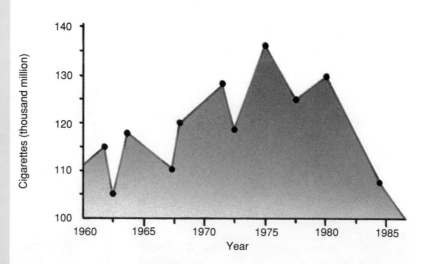

Figure 26.2P ● Drop in the sales of cigarettes in the UK. Health education and heavy taxes on tobacco have persuaded people to give up smoking

SUMMARY

Smoking cigarettes is a major cause of lung disease, especially lung cancer. It has taken scientists many years to establish the link. Fewer people smoke today than previously but many people continue to damage their health by smoking cigarettes.

Since then the campaign against cigarette smoking has been fought hard. Cigarette sales have gone up and down, but the overall trend is downwards (Figure 26.2P). Smoking is now banned in some public places, because non-smokers also suffer increased risks of ill health when they breathe in smoke from other people's cigarettes. This is called 'passive smoking'.

Between 1972 and 1984 cigarette smoking in Britain dropped by almost a third. In 1982, for the first time, there were fewer smokers than non-smokers. However, among women deaths from lung cancer continue to increase. Cigarette manufacturers are now putting their efforts into exports to the Third World! Cigarette smoking in these countries is increasing, and so too are deaths from lung cancer. Think about this and look at the evidence once again. The message is clear: **DO NOT START SMOKING**.

CHECKPOINT

❶ What is a gas exchange surface?

❷ Write a brief statement against each of the following items to show how efficient alveoli are as gas exchange surfaces:
a) large surface area
b) short diffusion distance
c) good blood supply
d) moist
e) in contact with air

❸ Complete the following paragraph using the words given. Each word may be used more than once or not at all.

| uptake | respire | inhalation | oxygen | alveoli |
| energy | exchange | moist | exhalation | |

The _____ of oxygen and removal of carbon dioxide occur in the _____ of the lungs. These provide a large surface area (about 90 m²) for efficient gas _____. They are thin-walled, have an excellent blood supply, are _____ and kept well supplied with air by breathing. Air is taken into the lungs by _____ and removed by _____.

❹ Why do you think people should not smoke in the presence of a pregnant woman?

TOPIC 27 EXCRETION

27.1 Getting rid of wastes

Metabolism produces waste substances, which must be removed from the body. How is it done? This section will tell you.

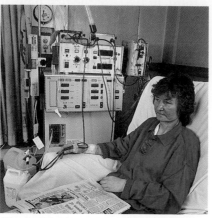

The person in Figure 27.1A is attached to a machine that has taken over the work of her kidneys. This is one way of treating people whose kidneys are not working (kidney failure).

The kidney machine removes waste substances from the patient's blood. Figure 27.1B explains how it works.

LOOK AT LINKS
Transplant rejection is an example of the immune reaction at work.
See Theme J, Topic 38.3.

Figure 27.1A ● The patient must use the kidney machine two or three times a week. Each treatment takes about ten hours

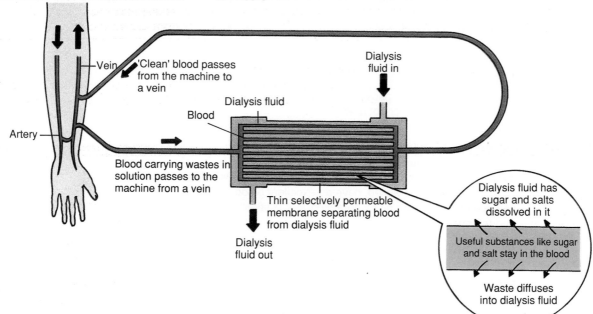

Vein — 'Clean' blood passes from the machine to a vein

Dialysis fluid in

Dialysis fluid

Blood

Artery —

Blood carrying wastes in solution passes to the machine from a vein

Thin selectively permeable membrane separating blood from dialysis fluid

Dialysis fluid out

Dialysis fluid has sugar and salts dissolved in it

Useful substances like sugar and salt stay in the blood

Waste diffuses into dialysis fluid

Figure 27.1B ● A kidney machine at work. A thin semi-permeable membrane separates the patients blood from the dialysis fluid. Wastes from the blood diffuse into the dialysis fluid. The process is called dialysis. *Explain why wastes diffuse out of the blood but sugars and salts do not?*

Figure 27.1C ● Donor card

A person with kidney failure may have a kidney transplant. A healthy kidney is taken from a person (the donor) who has just died (Figure 27.1C), or from someone living who wants to help the patient. Live donors are very often close relatives of the patient because their body tissues are similar, which reduces the chances of the patient's body rejecting the transplant. We have two kidneys, but it is possible to live a healthy life with only one.

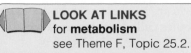
LOOK AT LINKS
for **metabolism**
see Theme F, Topic 25.2.

Where do wastes come from?

Thousands of chemical reactions take place inside a living cell. These reactions are called **metabolism**.

Compounds are broken down and new ones are made. The waste products formed could be harmful to the body if they were allowed to accumulate (Table 27.1). Removal of these waste substances is part of the process of excretion.

Table 27.1 ● Waste substances produced by metabolism

Waste substances	How waste is made	Where waste is made	Where waste is excreted
Carbon dioxide	Cellular respiration	All cells	From lungs or other gas exchange surfaces
Urea and other compounds containing nitrogen	Deamination of amino acids	Liver cells	From the kidney
Bile pigments	Breakdown of haemoglobin	Liver cells	In bile which passes into the duodenum
Oxygen	Photosynthesis	Inside the chloroplasts of plant cells	From leaf cells through the stomata

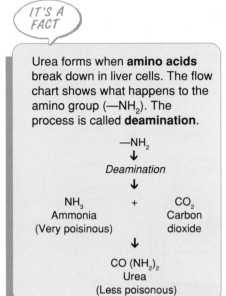

IT'S A FACT

Urea forms when **amino acids** break down in liver cells. The flow chart shows what happens to the amino group ($-NH_2$). The process is called **deamination**.

$$-NH_2$$
$$\downarrow$$
Deamination
$$\downarrow$$
$$NH_3 \quad + \quad CO_2$$
Ammonia   Carbon
(Very poisinous)   dioxide
$$\downarrow$$
$$CO(NH_2)_2$$
Urea
(Less poisonous)

Water and mineral salts are needed for cells to work properly. However, water and salts in excess of the body's needs must be excreted. In humans and other mammals the kidney is the main excretory organ.

LOOK AT LINKS
for **amino acids**
See Theme D, Topic 18.

LOOK AT LINKS
for the role of water and mineral salts see Topic 25.

The kidneys at work

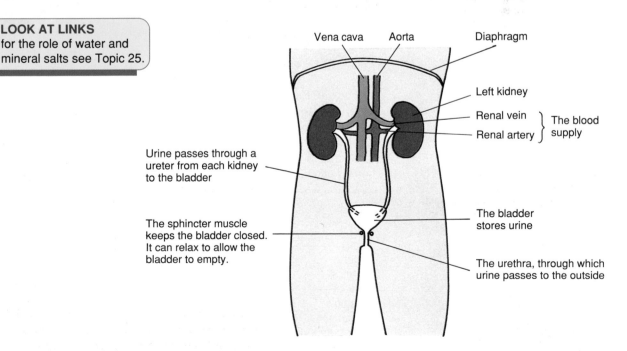

Figure 27.1D ● The position of the kidneys in the human body

Vena cava   Aorta   Diaphragm

Left kidney

Renal vein
Renal artery
} The blood supply

Urine passes through a ureter from each kidney to the bladder

The sphincter muscle keeps the bladder closed. It can relax to allow the bladder to empty.

The bladder stores urine

The urethra, through which urine passes to the outside

373

LOOK AT LINKS
Other excretory organs:
the **lungs** remove carbon
dioxide and water vapour –
see Topics 26.1 and 26.2.

Figure 27.1D shows you where the kidneys are in the human body. Each one consists of about one million tiny tubules called **nephrons**. The nephron is the working unit of the kidney (Figure 27.1E). Blood is brought to the kidneys by the renal arteries. It contains wastes (mostly urea) which the nephrons remove from the blood along with glucose, salts and other substances in solution. Some of these are useful and the nephron reabsorbs them into the blood. In this way the composition of blood is kept constant (**homeostasis**).

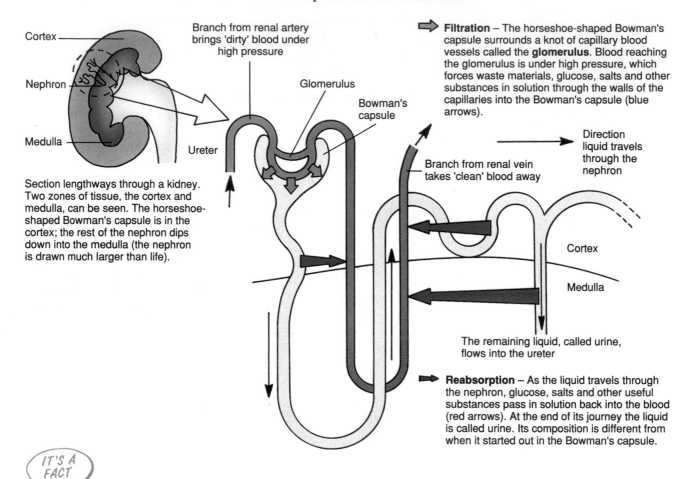

Section lengthways through a kidney. Two zones of tissue, the cortex and medulla, can be seen. The horseshoe-shaped Bowman's capsule is in the cortex; the rest of the nephron dips down into the medulla (the nephron is drawn much larger than life).

Filtration – The horseshoe-shaped Bowman's capsule surrounds a knot of capillary blood vessels called the **glomerulus**. Blood reaching the glomerulus is under high pressure, which forces waste materials, glucose, salts and other substances in solution through the walls of the capillaries into the Bowman's capsule (blue arrows).

The remaining liquid, called urine, flows into the ureter

Reabsorption – As the liquid travels through the nephron, glucose, salts and other useful substances pass in solution back into the blood (red arrows). At the end of its journey the liquid is called urine. Its composition is different from when it started out in the Bowman's capsule.

Figure 27.1E ● A kidney nephron

Look at Table 27.2. Notice the composition of blood in the glomerulus, before treatment by the nephron, and the composition of the liquid (called urine) at the end of its journey through the nephron.

Table 27.2 ● Composition of the blood in the glomerulus and the urine of a healthy adult

	Blood in the glomerulus	Urine
	(percentage by mass)	
Water	91.7	96.5
Proteins	7.5	0
Urea	0.03	2
Ammonia	trace	0.05
Sodium ions (NA⁺)	0.3	0.6
Potassium ions (K⁺)	0.02	0.15
Chloride ions (Cl⁻)	0.36	0.6
Glucose	0.1	0

IT'S A FACT

The organs of excretion in insects are called malpighian tubules. They are slender tubes bathed in the blood which fills the inside of the insect's body. Each tube is closed at one end and opens at the other into the intestine. Wastes in the blood are removed by the malpighian tubes and converted into uric acid, which is excreted through the anus.

LOOK AT LINKS
for **homeostasis**
see Theme J, Topic 40.3.

CHECKPOINT

These questions refer to Table 27.2.

❶ What is the mass of water in 100 cm³ of urine?

❷ Why do you think there are no proteins in urine?

❸ What percentage of glucose does the nephron reabsorb into the blood?

❹ Name the main waste product formed from the deamination of amino acids.

IT'S A FACT

In tropical rainforests where humidity is high, some plants have special structures round the edges of their leaves to get rid of excess water. Why is excess water not removed from rainforest plants by evaporation?

Excretion in plants

Plants do not have specialised structures like nephrons for the excretion of waste. Oxygen, which is a waste product of photosynthesis, and carbon dioxide, which is a waste product of respiration, diffuse out through the leaves. In land plants excess water which is a waste product of respiration is removed by evaporation. If more water is taken up by the roots than can be removed by evaporation, then the excess oozes from the leaves.

Plants dispose of wastes by combining them with inorganic salts to form insoluble crystals. The wastes are stored in this state in different parts of the plant (Figure 27.1F).

SUMMARY

The kidney is the chief organ of excretion in humans and other mammals. It is made up of many tubules called nephrons. Each nephron removes wastes produced by metabolism and substances in excess of the body's needs. Plants excrete wastes by storing them in harmless forms in different parts of the plant body. Wastes stored in leaves are lost when the leaves fall in autumn.

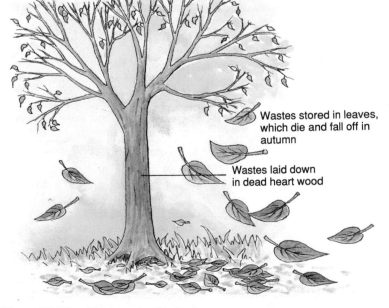

Wastes stored in leaves, which die and fall off in autumn

Wastes laid down in dead heart wood

Figure 27.1F ● Plant waste disposal

CHECKPOINT

❶ The diagram shows the position of the kidneys in the body and their connections with blood vessels and the bladder.
(a) Name the parts labelled A – G.
(b) Briefly explain why the concentration of urea in A is much less than in B.
(c) What is the role of E?
(d) Where is urine stored before it is released to the outside?

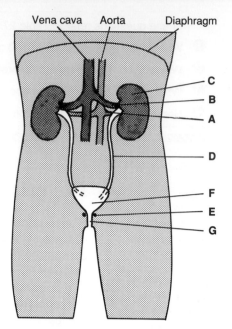

❷ Copy the table below. It lists parts of the kidney and its connections to blood vessels and the bladder. Tick each substance present in the part listed in the left hand column (assume the person is healthy).

	Protein	Glucose	Urea	Water	Salt
Blood in the renal artery					
Blood in glomerulus					
Fluid that passes into the Bowman's capsule					
Urine in the bladder					
Blood in the renal vein					

❸ State three ways in which blood leaving the kidney is different from blood entering the kidney.

❹ Match the lettered statements with the appropriate numbered parts.

A takes urine from the kidney to the bladder   1 sphincter
B prevents urine leaving the bladder   2 renal artery
C removes urea from the blood   3 renal vein
D carries urine out of the body   4 kidney
E carries blood to the kidney   5 urethra
F stores urine   6 ureter
G carries blood away from the kidney   7 bladder

❺ Complete the following paragraph about the kidney, using the words provided. Each word may be used once, more than once, or not at all.

Bowman's capsule   ureter   cortex   one million   medulla
renal vein   bladder   glomerulus

A kidney cut lengthways has two regions, an outer _____ and an inner _____. Under a microscope many tiny nephrons are visible: there are about _____ in each kidney. Each nephron has a cup-shaped capsule called the _____ at one end. This surrounds a small bunch of capillaries called the _____. Leading away from each capsule is a narrow tubule which twists and turns and eventually joins the _____, which takes urine from the kidney to the _____.

❻ What is dialysis and why do some people need it?

? THEME QUESTIONS

● *Topic 25*

1 The table below gives the approximate amounts of energy required by different people.

Energy (kJ/day)		Energy (kJ/day)	
Newborn baby	1890	Office worker	11 327
Child 1 year	3347	Factory worker	12 575
Child 3 years	5852	Coal miner	15 075
Child 5 years	7621	Pregnant woman	10 065
Girl 12–15 years	9705	Breast-feeding	11 325
Boy 12–15 years	11 753		

(a) Explain the increase in energy requirement from a newborn baby to a 12–15 year old.
(b) Why do the following require more energy than an office worker:
(i) a 12–15 year old boy (ii) a coal miner?
(c) Why does a breast-feeding woman require more energy than a pregnant woman?

2 In order to demonstrate that a green leaf has carried out photosynthesis (and so made starch) you have to carry out the stages described below. In each case say why you think that the action is taken.
The leaf is:
(a) dipped into boiling water,
(b) boiled in ethanol,
(c) washed in cold water,
(d) covered with dilute iodine solution.

3

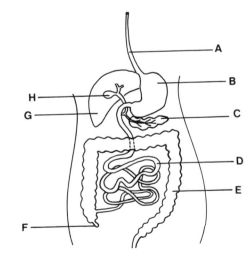

(a) Copy and label the parts of the diagram of the human alimentary canal.
(b) Which organs in the diagram (i) produce bile (ii) store bile (iii) have acidic conditions (iv) reabsorb a lot of water from food?
(c) What are the two major functions of the gland C?
(d) The organ D is very long. How does this help it to carry out its function?
(e) How would organ F be different in the alimentary canal of a rabbit? How is this connected with the rabbit's diet?

4 A scientist carried out an experiment growing cereal plants in a field. He took a sample of the plants every four hours and measured how much sugar had been made in their leaves. The sugar concentrations, expressed as a percentage of the dry mass of the leaves, are given below.

Time of day	Sugar concentration
4.00 a.m.	0.45
8.00 a.m.	0.60
12 noon	1.75
4.00 p.m.	2.00
8.00 p.m.	1.45
12 midnight	0
4.00 a.m.	0.45

(a) Plot the data on graph paper, with time of day on the horizontal axis.
(b) From the graph, suggest the likely sugar concentration at (i) 10 a.m. and (ii) 2 a.m.
(c) At what time of day is the sugar concentration likely to be at a maximum?
(d) Look at the graph and try to explain the variations that occur in the sugar concentration over 24 hours.

5 The two test tubes were set up as shown in the diagram and placed in a water bath at 40 °C for 20 minutes. The contents of each tube were then tested for the presence of starch (using iodine solution) and for glucose (by boiling with Benedict's solution).

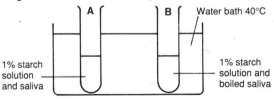

(a) Copy and complete the table with the results that you would expect.

Test tube	Colour after adding iodine solution	Colour after boiling with Benedict's
A		
B		

(b) Explain the results in test tube A.
(c) Explain the results in test tube B.
(d) Why would digestion not take place if the saliva in this experiment was replaced with gastric juice?

● *Topic 26*

6 Look carefully at the diagram of the alveoli and blood capillary in a lung on the next page.
(a) Which arrow represents (i) deoxygenated blood (ii) carbon dioxide?
(b) (i) By what process is oxygen able to pass from the air in the alveoli into the red blood cells in the capillary?

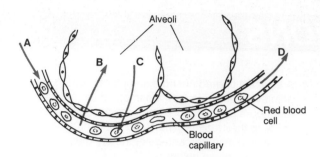

Alveoli

A

B   C

D

Red blood cell

Blood capillary

(ii) Through how many layers of cells does the oxygen have to pass?
(c) Give two features of the alveoli that help this passage of gas.
(d) Which structures allow gas exchange to take place in (i) a leaf (ii) a fish?

7 The respirator was set up as shown in the diagram and after a short interval of time the coloured liquid rose in arm X of the capillary tubing.

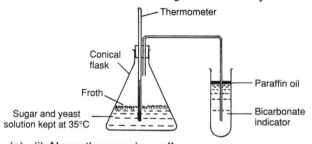

Rubber bung

Boiling tube

Maggots

Zinc gauze

Capillary tubing

Roll of filter paper soaked in a chemical

Coloured liquid

(a) (i) Name the chemical in the boiling tube.
    (ii) Which gas does it absorb?
    (iii) What is the function of the roll of filter paper?
(b) Explain why the coloured liquid rose up arm X.
(c) Suggest two possible sources of error in this experiment.
(d) If germinating green peas are used instead of maggots, the boiling tube has to be blacked out. Why is this so?

8 The apparatus was set up as shown and the flask kept in a water bath at 35 °C. After about 20 minutes the bicarbonate indicator had changed from red to yellow.

Thermometer

Conical flask

Froth

Paraffin oil

Sugar and yeast solution kept at 35°C

Bicarbonate indicator

(a) (i) Name the gas given off.
    (ii) What process had caused the gas to be produced?
(b) Why was the flask kept at a constant 35 °C?
(c) What was the purpose of the paraffin oil layer?
(d) The experiment could have been improved by using sugar solution that had been boiled and cooled before adding the yeast. Why is this so?
(e) Suggest a control for this experiment.

● *Topic 27*

9 The diagram shows a kidney dialysis machine in simplified form. The patient's blood flows on one side of a selectively permeable membrane (like visking tubing). The dialysing fluid, which has a composition similar to that of human plasma, flows on the other side of the membrane.

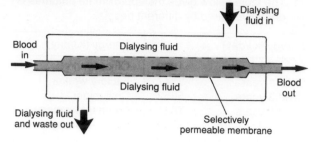

Dialysing fluid in

Blood in

Dialysing fluid

Dialysing fluid

Blood out

Dialysing fluid and waste out

Selectively permeable membrane

(a) By what processes does (i) excess water and (ii) excretory products pass from the blood into the dialysing fluid?
(b) (i) Name the excretory products that would pass out of the blood.
    (ii) Why should protein not pass out of the blood?
(c) (i) What structures in the kidney would act like the selectively permeable membrane?
    (ii) Suggest why the presence of protein in the urine could be an indication of kidney damage.
(d) In the cases of permanent kidney failure it is more convenient and more economical for a patient to be given a kidney transplant rather than treatment with an artificial kidney machine. Explain why this is so.

10 The diagram shows a kidney tubule and blood supply.

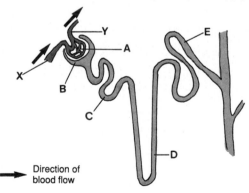

Y

E

A

X

B

C

D

Direction of blood flow

(a) Label structures **A–E**.
(b) Explain the significance of the difference in the diameters of blood vessels **X** and **Y**.
(c) Study the table below.

Substance	Concentration in blood plasma (g/1000 cm³)	Concentration in urine (g/1000 cm³)
Protein	78	0
Glucose	1	0
Urea	0.3	20
Salt	9	12

Explain the differences in the concentration of
(i) protein (ii) glucose (iii) urea and salt in the blood plasma and in the urine.

THEME G
The Physical Environment

Often, the weather is a harmless topic of conversation. Sometimes, it can be a very different matter. With its snow storms, heat waves, hurricanes, monsoon rains and floods, weather can become a matter of life and death importance. With reliable forecasts of the weather which is coming their way, people have a chance to take action to minimise damage and loss of life. This is why meteorology, the study of weather conditions, is so important. You will learn something about weather forecasting in the topic *Weather*.

Land is the environment of millions of kinds of plants and animals, including humans. We use part of the land for agriculture, to grow crops and to raise livestock. Modern methods of agriculture are intensive: they are highly mechanised and require extensive use of fertilisers and pesticides. Conflicts arise between utilising the land for the maximum benefit of humans and allowing plants and animals to flourish in their natural habitats. In the topic *Land*, you will be able to weigh up some of the pros and cons of different farming methods.

TOPIC 28 · THE WEATHER

28.1 · **The weather: a matter of life and death**

FIRST THOUGHTS

As you read these accounts, think of the importance of weather in our lives. Think about how disasters due to bad weather can be minimised if we know what weather to expect.

Figure 28.1A ● The weather forecast

King Philip II of Spain sent three armadas to England. The first was defeated by the English navy in 1588. The second was driven back by storms off the south coast of England in 1596. The third, in May 1597, was another disaster for Spain. Out of 130 ships, only one was sunk in battle, but fifty were wrecked in storms 'worse than any they had seen at this time of year'.

Four centuries later, we are still at the mercy of the weather. On the night of 15–16 October, 1987, a storm hit south-east England. By morning, 15 million trees had been destroyed, houses and cars had been damaged by falling trees, the whole of south-east England was without power, and London was blacked out for the first time since the Second World War. Warning messages from the Meteorological Office had been completely inadequate. It was fortunate that the storm struck during the night when few people were using the roads.

IT

Weather and Climate
(data base)

This data base contains the data from 80 weather stations around the world. You will be able to use the information to analyse world weather patterns.

Figure 28.1B ● Storm damage in October 1987

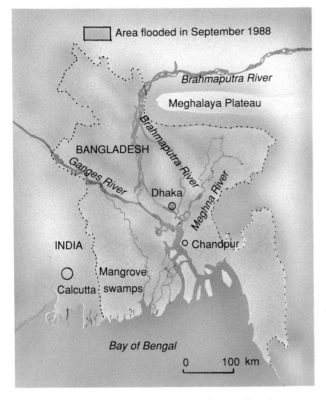

Figure 28.1C ● Bangladesh is at risk from flooding

In September, 1988, catastrophic flooding occurred in Bangladesh. The monsoon rain ran off the hills more rapidly than in previous years because so many trees have been chopped down in the Himalayas. The rivers, swollen by monsoon rain, overflowed their banks. The flood left 800 people dead and half a million homes destroyed.

On 12 September, 1988, Hurricane Gilbert arrived on the coast of Jamaica. After a 9 hour rampage the length of the island, the devastation was unbelievable. One-quarter of the buildings in the country were unusable; one hundred people were dead and 50 000 people were homeless. The wind speed in the core of the hurricane had been 200 km/hour. Although the Jamaicans knew that a tropical storm was heading their way, the speed with which the storm developed into a hurricane took weather forecasters by surprise.

Figure 28.1D ● Satellite image of Hurrican Gilbert

SUMMARY

Meteorologists use powerful computers to process all the information they receive from their weather stations. These computers can perform in minutes calculations which would take weeks to do without a computer. An accurate weather forecast would not be much use if it arrived too late to warn of change in the weather!

These incidents show how the weather can be a matter of life and death importance. If people have reliable forecasts of the weather coming their way, they have a chance to minimise the loss of life and the damage. An early warning system can reduce casualties by avoiding crowds on roads and public transport. People who study the weather are called meteorologists. The UK Meteorological Office employs 2300 people. They process information from 4000 weather stations on land, 1200 weather ships and 1400 aircraft as well as upper atmosphere balloons, radar stations and satellites. Using computers, meteorologists convert all the information into weather maps.

381

28.2 ● How the Earth is heated by the Sun

On a global scale

Earth is heated by the Sun's radiation. As the radiation travels through the upper atmosphere, certain wavelengths are absorbed by the gases in the air. By the time the radiation reaches the lower atmosphere no further absorption of the Sun's radiation can take place, and the lower atmosphere is therefore not warmed by the Sun. When the radiation reaches Earth, it is absorbed by the land and by the sea. The air is warmed by contact with the land and the sea.

LOOK AT LINKS
for **convection**
See Theme B, Topic 7.5.

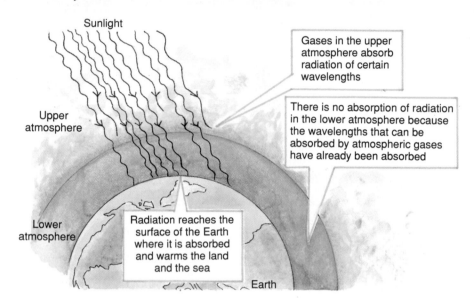

Sunlight

Gases in the upper atmosphere absorb radiation of certain wavelengths

There is no absorption of radiation in the lower atmosphere because the wavelengths that can be absorbed by atmospheric gases have already been absorbed

Upper atmosphere

Lower atmosphere

Radiation reaches the surface of the Earth where it is absorbed and warms the land and the sea

Earth

Figure 28.2A ● The Sun warms the Earth

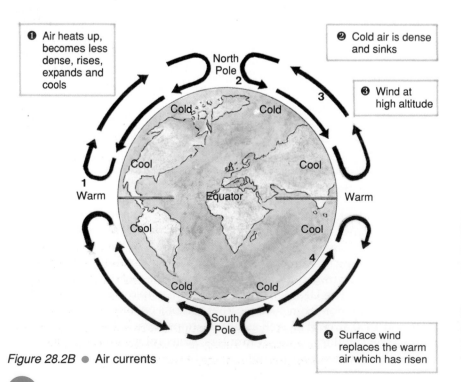

❶ Air heats up, becomes less dense, rises, expands and cools

❷ Cold air is dense and sinks

❸ Wind at high altitude

North Pole

Cold   Cold

Cool   Cool

Warm   Equator   Warm

Cool   Cool

Cold   Cold

South Pole

❹ Surface wind replaces the warm air which has risen

Figure 28.2B ● Air currents

In equatorial regions, the sun is more directly overhead than in polar regions. Equatorial regions therefore receive more heat from the sun than polar regions do. In the absence of winds, this would lead to equatorial regions becoming warmer and warmer. **Convection currents** prevent this happening. As air is heated up, it becomes less dense than cold air and rises. As a result, air currents are set up, and transfer heat from warm regions to colder regions.

Ocean currents also redistribute the sun's heat. Warm currents carry heat from equatorial to polar regions. Other currents carry cold water from the poles to the tropics.

On a local scale

● **Land and sea breezes**

Land and sea breezes are felt in coastal areas. The Sun's energy falls equally on land and sea. Land heats up more easily than sea; this means that the temperature of land rises more than the temperature of sea when they receive the same amount of solar radiation. On a sunny day, the air in contact with the land becomes warm and rises. Cooler air from over the sea moves in to take its place. If you are on the coast, you can feel this air as a **sea breeze**.

After the sun sets, the land cools more quickly than the sea. The air in contact with the land becomes colder and denser than the air over the sea. As a result, a breeze blows from land to sea: a **land breeze**.

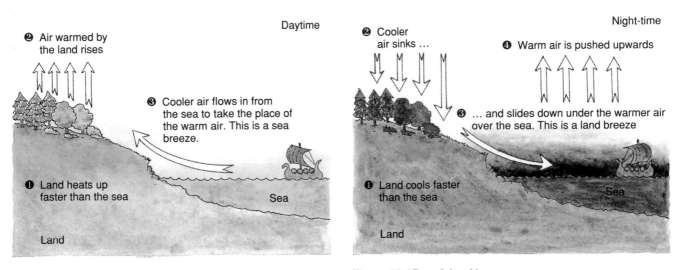

Daytime

❷ Air warmed by the land rises

❸ Cooler air flows in from the sea to take the place of the warm air. This is a sea breeze.

❶ Land heats up faster than the sea

Sea

Land

Night-time

❷ Cooler air sinks …

❹ Warm air is pushed upwards

❸ … and slides down under the warmer air over the sea. This is a land breeze

❶ Land cools faster than the sea

Sea

Land

Figure 28.2C ● A sea breeze

Figure 28.2D ● A land breeze

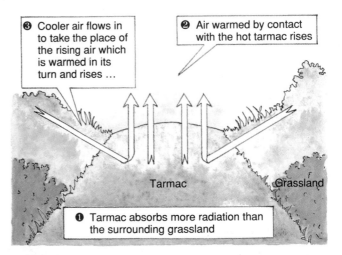

❸ Cooler air flows in to take the place of the rising air which is warmed in its turn and rises …

❷ Air warmed by contact with the hot tarmac rises

Tarmac

Grassland

❶ Tarmac absorbs more radiation than the surrounding grassland

Figure 28.2E ● A thermal

LOOK AT LINKS
Satellites equipped with heat-sensitive cameras are used to investigate heat radiation from the Earth's surface.
See Theme B, Topic 7.7.

● **Thermals**

Some types of land absorb heat better than others do. A rough, dark-coloured surface absorbs **radiation** better than a smooth, light-coloured surface. As a result, some areas of land become warmer than others. When air is warmed by contact with warm land, it becomes less dense than the surrounding air and rises. The column of rising air is called a **thermal**. Glider pilots take advantage of thermals.

28.3 Weather maps

The atmosphere exerts a pressure on everything within it. The experiment shown in Figure 28.3A shows this dramatically.

To vacuum pump — Bung

(a) The vacuum pump removes air from the can

(b) The can collapses

Figure 28.3A ● Air pressure

LOOK AT LINKS
Atmospheric pressure is measured by barometers. See Theme I, Topic 35.4.

IT *The Weather Report*

Use the Weather Report system to make a record of wind speed and direction, temperature, hours of sunshine and daylight, and rainfall.

Why does the can collapse? The force of atmospheric pressure squeezes it from outside, and there is no air inside to oppose this force. At sea level, the atmosphere exerts a pressure of 101 000 Pa (pascals) on average. This is called **standard atmospheric pressure**. (1 Pa = 1 N/m^2; one pascal = one newton per square metre).

Meteorologists use the millibar (mb) as the unit of pressure

1000 mb = Standard atmospheric pressure = 101 000 Pa
So   1 mb = 101 Pa

In the UK, atmospheric pressure varies from 975 mb (low pressure) to 1030 mb (high pressure).

Figure 28.3B is a **weather map**. The lines on the map join places which have the same atmospheric pressure. They are called **isobars**.

Air moves, that is the wind blows, from regions of high pressure to regions of low pressure. When isobars are close together, atmospheric pressure changes rapidly over a short distance: there are strong winds. When isobars are widely spaced, the wind is light and variable.

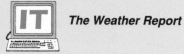

| The lines join places which have the same atmospheric pressure. They are called isobars. | A region of high pressure enclosed by isobars. This is called an anticyclone. | A region of low pressure enclosed by isobars. This is called a depression. |

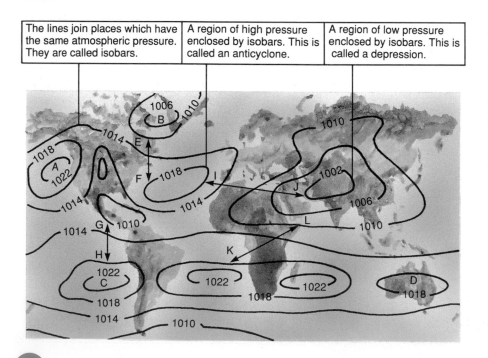

Figure 28.3B ● Isobars

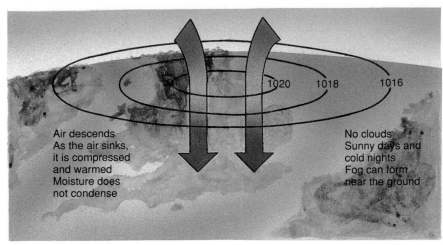

Figure 28.3C ● Anticyclone weather

High pressure

An anticyclone is often referred to simply as a 'high'. Anticyclones may be warm or cold. The air in an anticyclone flows in from above (see Figure 28.3C). As it descends, the air, becoming warmer, can hold more water vapour and therefore disperses clouds. At night, when the ground cools, water vapour may condense to form fog near the ground.

Large warm anticyclones form over warm regions. The Azores anticyclone sometimes extends to Britain, bringing good weather. Cold anticyclones form in the cold interiors of continents, e.g. central North America. Anticyclones usually last for two days to three weeks. In the UK, the longest 'highs' are in September, and the fewest high pressure days come in July and August. Figure 28.3D shows what is meant by a **ridge** of high pressure.

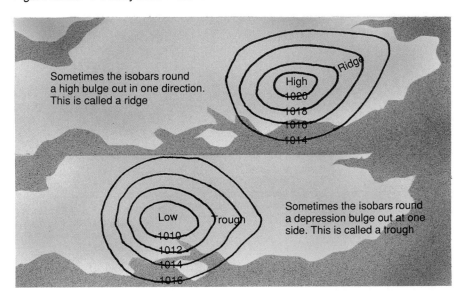

Figure 28.3D ● *Above:* a ridge of high pressure. *Below:* a trough of low pressure

Low pressure

A depression is often referred to as a 'low'. Air flows in from below and rises to flow out at a higher level. The flow is in the opposite direction to that in an anticyclone. As the air moves upward, it cools. It can therefore hold less water vapour. As water vapour condenses, clouds form, and there may be rain or snow. Most depressions give rise to strong winds. A depression may take two or three days to pass over the UK. Figure 28.3D shows what is meant by a **trough** of low pressure.

Anticyclones occur less frequently than depressions over the UK. The isobars of anticyclones are more widely spaced than those in depressions, and winds are light and variable. Since winds are moving away from a high pressure area, clouds tend to disperse, leaving clear blue skies.

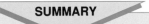

SUMMARY

Isobars are lines on maps which join points of equal atmospheric pressure. A region of high pressure enclosed by isobars is termed an anticyclone or a high, and a region of low pressure enclosed by isobars is termed a depression or a low.

CHECKPOINT

Refer to Figure 28.3B.

❶ Say whether each of the following is an anticyclone or a depression: A, B, C, D.

❷ State the wind direction along (a) EF (b) GH (c) IJ (d) KL.

28.4 How clouds form

LOOK AT LINKS
for **weather fronts**
See Topic 28.6.

Atmospheric pressure decreases with increasing height. When air rises, it moves to regions of lower pressure and therefore expands. The energy which it needs to expand comes from the air itself, and its temperature drops. The rate of decrease of temperature is about 1 °C per 100 m. A number of causes may make air rise.

❶ Air may be forced upwards because it meets hills or mountains.

❷ Convection currents carry air upwards.

❸ When warm and cold **fronts** meet, air is forced upwards.

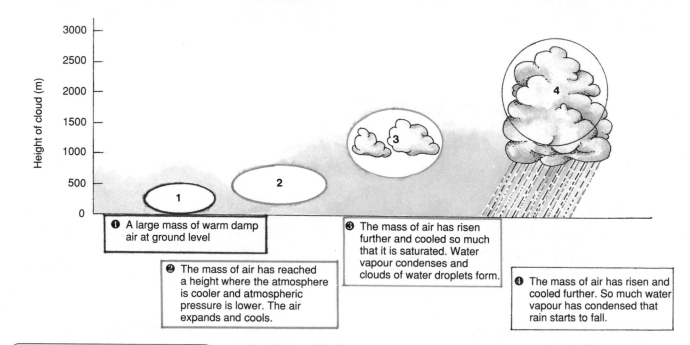

❶ A large mass of warm damp air at ground level

❷ The mass of air has reached a height where the atmosphere is cooler and atmospheric pressure is lower. The air expands and cools.

❸ The mass of air has risen further and cooled so much that it is saturated. Water vapour condenses and clouds of water droplets form.

❹ The mass of air has risen and cooled further. So much water vapour has condensed that rain starts to fall.

Figure 28.4A ● How clouds form

The mass of water vapour that air can hold depends on the temperature. Warm air can hold more water vapour than cold air can. If humid (damp) air is cooled, it reaches a temperature at which it is saturated: it can hold no more water vapour. If the temperature falls further, water vapour will condense as tiny droplets of water, and clouds or fog will be formed.

IT

Do you have access to data from weather satellites? If you have, talk to your teacher about using satellite images to monitor cloud movement. How would this help you to explain weather patterns.

SUMMARY

Clouds form when warm air rises over hills, when convection currents carry warm air to higher levels and by the actions of fronts.

CHECKPOINT

❶ Look at the diagram below. Explain (a) why clouds form at B and (b) why there are none at C.

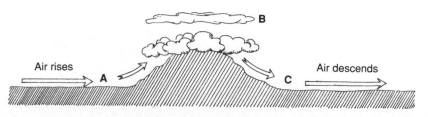

Air rises   A   C   Air descends

❷ Explain how a fine summer morning can develop into a very wet afternoon.

28.5 Clouds

Figure 28.5A ● Clouds

(a) Cirrus clouds

Clouds can de divided into three main groups according to their shape: cirrus clouds, stratus clouds and cumulus clouds.

● Cirrus clouds

Cirrus clouds are delicate white wispy clouds, sometimes called 'mares tails', which form at high level (above 6000 m). They can extend to form a thin veil of whitish cloud, often with a halo, called **cirrostratus** cloud. They do not produce rain.

● Stratus clouds

Stratus clouds are uniform layers of cloud, like fog, formed at low level. At medium height (2500 m – 6000 m), they are called **altostratus** clouds. They can develop into anvil-shaped **nimbostratus** clouds.

● Cumulus clouds

Cumulus clouds are 'piles' of thick, lumpy cloud, dome-shaped or cauliflower shaped with flat bases, which form at low level (below 2500 m). At greater heights, they are called **altocumulus** clouds. They can grow and become flat-topped **cumulonimbus** clouds which are shaped like a blacksmith's anvil. Light cumulus clouds may give a little rain but often produce none at all. Large cumulus clouds produce light showers, and cumulonimbus clouds give heavier showers and thunderstorms.

(b) Stratus clouds

(c) Cumulus clouds

SUMMARY

The three main types of cloud are cirrus, cumulus and stratus. Large cumulus clouds and anvil-shaped cumulonimbus clouds produce rain.

28.6 ● Winter weather

Rain is not the only form in which water reaches the ground.

● Freezing rain

When rain falls on a ground surface which is below 0 °C, it freezes immediately. The layer of ice formed is often called 'black ice'. It makes road conditions very dangerous. When an aeroplane flies from very cold air into a rain storm, ice can form on the plane. Aeroplanes must be fitted with de-icers to prevent this happening.

● Snow

When the temperature is low, snow falls instead of rain. Snow consists of ice crystals. The crystals form in clouds below freezing point, when water vapour turns directly into ice.

Figure 28.6A ● A snowflake

● Hailstones

The top of a cumulonimbus cloud is composed of ice crystals. When the ice crystals fall, they become coated with more water. Currents of air may carry them up again to be refrozen. This may happen several times before they fall as hailstones. Cutting through a hailstone shows the layers made by the upward and downward journeys.

● Dew

On a still night, as the Earth cools, water vapour condenses from the air to form dew.

● Hoar frost

If the temperature of the ground is below freezing point, instead of forming dew, water vapour changes directly into ice crystals. These are called hoar frost.

● Fog and mist

If there is only a slight movement of air, the water vapour that condenses from the air will appear as fog or mist. A breeze prevents fog by moving air away from the cold ground.

IT'S A FACT

When Captain Cook, the discoverer of Australia, landed in the Hawaiian Islands, the inhabitants hailed him as a god. Later, the damage caused by an unexpected storm infuriated the islanders. They murdered Captain Cook for failing to use his powers as a god to prevent the storm.

28.7  Fronts

A front is a boundary between two masses of air which have different temperatures and humidities.

● Warm fronts

As a warm front moves, it pushes cold air in front of it.

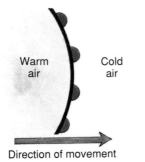

Figure 28.7A ● Weather map symbol for a warm front moving from left to right

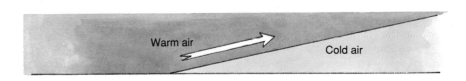

Figure 28.7B ● A cross-section of a warm front

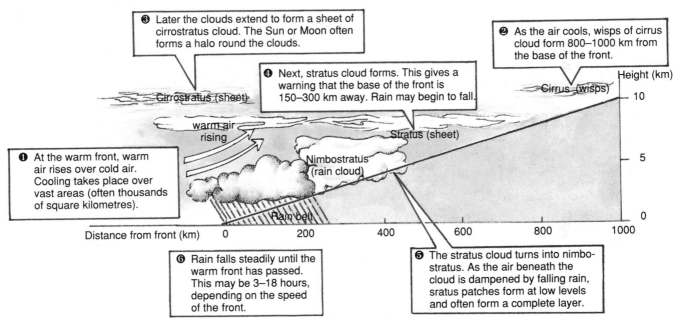

❸ Later the clouds extend to form a sheet of cirrostratus cloud. The Sun or Moon often forms a halo round the clouds.

❷ As the air cools, wisps of cirrus cloud form 800–1000 km from the base of the front.

❹ Next, stratus cloud forms. This gives a warning that the base of the front is 150–300 km away. Rain may begin to fall.

❶ At the warm front, warm air rises over cold air. Cooling takes place over vast areas (often thousands of square kilometres).

❻ Rain falls steadily until the warm front has passed. This may be 3–18 hours, depending on the speed of the front.

❺ The stratus cloud turns into nimbo-stratus. As the air beneath the cloud is dampened by falling rain, sratus patches form at low levels and often form a complete layer.

Figure 28.7C ● Rain from a warm front

● Cold fronts

As a cold front moves, it pushes warm air upwards.

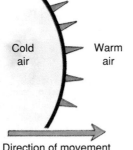

Figure 28.7D ● Weather map symbol for a cold front moving from left to right

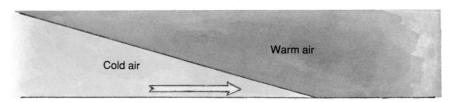

Figure 28.7E ● Cross section of a cold front

On days when the air rises very quickly, the clouds build up differently. Instead of layered clouds, big cumulonimbus clouds develop. They produce heavy rain and sometimes thunderstorms. Cold fronts travel fast, and the rain lasts 1–4 hours. Rain stops when the front arrives.

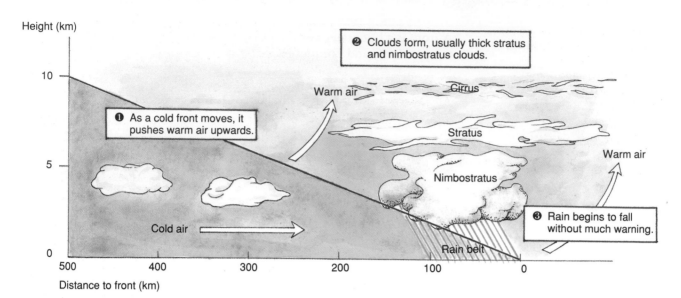

Height (km)

❷ Clouds form, usually thick stratus
and nimbostratus clouds.

❶ As a cold front moves, it
pushes warm air upwards.

Warm air

Cirrus

Stratus

Warm air

Nimbostratus

❸ Rain begins to fall
without much warning.

Cold air

Rain belt

Distance to front (km)

Figure 28.7F ● Rain from a cold front

During the Second World War,
aeroplanes coming back from a
bombing mission could not land
if the runway was covered in
dense fog. The solution to this
problem was to employ a line of
petrol burners alongside the
runway to raise the temperature
and vaporise the fog. Although
a very costly practice, it was
justified in wartime.

● *Occlusions*

Cold fronts usually travel faster
than warm fronts. When a cold
front catches up with a warm
front, warm air is pushed
upwards, and an occlusion
develops. The weather that results
from an occlusion is similar to that
produced by a warm front.

Figure 28.7G ● Weather map
symbol for an occlusion

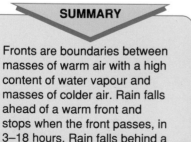

SUMMARY

Fronts are boundaries between
masses of warm air with a high
content of water vapour and
masses of colder air. Rain falls
ahead of a warm front and
stops when the front passes, in
3–18 hours. Rain falls behind a
cold front and starts when the front
arrives, in 1–4 hours. An occlusion
behaves like a warm front

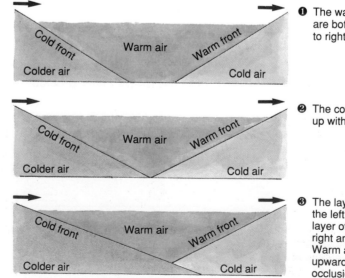

❶ The warm and cold fronts
are both moving from left
to right. They are still apart.

Cold front
Warm air
Warm front
Colder air
Cold air

❷ The cold front has caught
up with the warm front.

Cold front
Warm air
Warm front
Colder air
Cold air

❸ The layer of cold air on
the left is colder than the
layer of cold air on the
right and sinks below it.
Warm air is pushed
upwards to form an
occlusion.

Cold front
Warm air
Warm front
Colder air
Cold air

Figure 28.7H ● An occlusion

CHECKPOINT

❶ Why would the following people want to have accurate information about the weather?
   (a) An airline choosing a site for a new airport.
   (b) A regional water company.
   (c) A shipping company.
   (d) A forestry company.

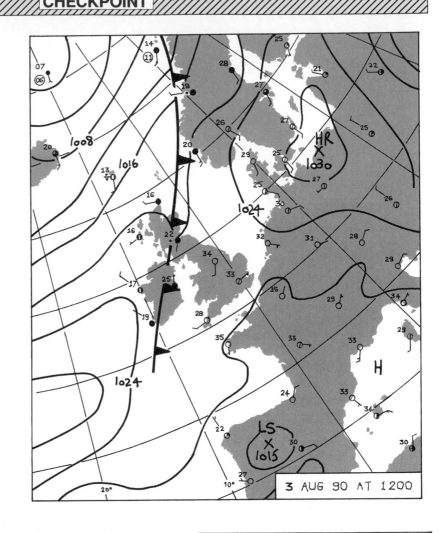

❷ The figure shows a Meteorological Office weather map.
Use the weather map and the key to work out the weather for the places shown in the table.

Place	Temperature (°C)	Wind speed	Wind direction	Cloud cover	Rain	Pressure (mb)
London						
Barcelona						
Plymouth						
Faeroe Islands						
Warsaw						

❸ Explain how the following weather conditions can be dangerous.
   (a) A very high rainfall.
   (b) Many months of dry weather.
   (c) Strong winds.
   (d) Freezing rain.

❹ Refer to the figure opposite. Imagine you travel from A to B. What sort of weather would you meet at C, at D, at E, at F and at G?

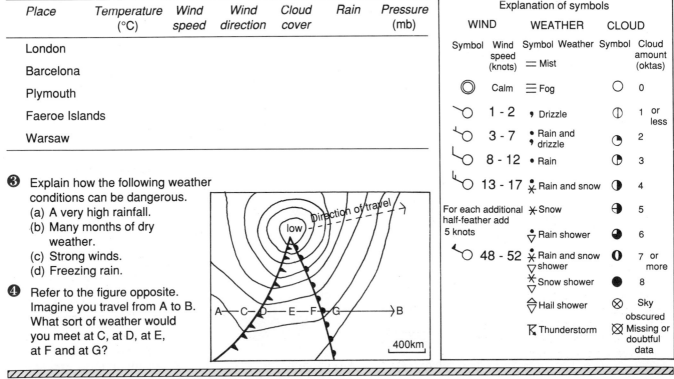

Explanation of symbols		
WIND	WEATHER	CLOUD

Symbol	Wind speed (knots)	Symbol	Weather	Symbol	Cloud amount (oktas)
		=	Mist		
◎	Calm	☰	Fog	○	0
	1 - 2	❜	Drizzle	◑	1 or less
	3 - 7	•❜	Rain and drizzle	◕	2
	8 - 12	•	Rain	◔	3
	13 - 17	✻	Rain and snow	◐	4
For each additional half-feather add 5 knots		✻	Snow	◑	5
		⋮▽	Rain shower	◕	6
	48 - 52	✻▽	Rain and snow shower	◖	7 or more
		✻▽	Snow shower	●	8
		▽	Hail shower	⊗	Sky obscured
		⚡	Thunderstorm	⊠	Missing or doubtful data

TOPIC 29 ● LAND

29.1 ● Soil

Rocks are acted upon by rain, snow and frost. They break up into small particles. The process is called **weathering**. The small particles become part of the soil. Soil also contains **organic** matter: matter that was once part of plants or animals. This is the part of the soil called **humus** (see Figure 29.1C). Water is another ingredient of soil. Soils differ in the size of the particles, in the humus content, the water content, the pH and the chemicals which are present.

The difference in particle size means that different soils have different properties (see Figure 29.1B and Table 29.1).

LOOK AT LINKS
for **weathering**
See Theme A, Topic 2.8.

Figure 29.1A ● Clay and sandy soils

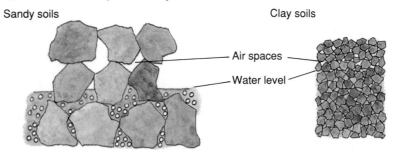

Sandy soils

Clay soils

Air spaces

Water level

Table 29.1 ● The properties of sandy soils and clay soils

	Sandy soils	*Clay soils*
Particle size	Large, > 0.2 mm	Small, < 0.002 mm
Air spaces	Large	Small
Drainage	Rapid, leaving a dry soil	Slow, leaving a wet soil
Temperature	Fluctuates, tending to be higher	More consistent, tending to be lower
Cultivation	Easy to dig and plough because they are dry and loose	Difficult to dig and plough because they are wet and sticky
For plant growth ...	Plants may suffer from lack of water. Minerals may be leached (washed) from the soil by rain	Plant roots may lack oxygen if the soil becomes waterlogged. The mineral content is high since minerals tend to stick to clay particles.

Soil crumbs form when sand and clay particles stick together
A film of water binds to the soil crumbs
Excess water drains out of the air spaces so that the soil does not become waterlogged
Air spaces provide oxygen for the growth of roots and for useful microbes
Air spaces make the loam less dense and easier to cultivate

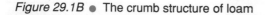

Most soils are a mixture of particles of different sizes. They therefore combine the properties listed in Table 29.1, and the advantages and disadvantages are balanced. Such a mixture is called **loam** and is ideal for growing plants.

The 'feel' of a soil depends on the proportion of large and small

Figure 29.1B ● The crumb structure of loam

particles in it. This 'feel' is called **texture**. The texture of a soil decides the amount of air in the soil and the speed at which water drains from the soil. These factors affect the plants which grow in the soil and also the animals and micro-organisms which keep the soil in good condition.

Humus

Part of the soil is called **humus**. It has been formed from the decayed remains of dead organisms. A variety of organisms take part in the formation of humus. Figure 29.1C shows some of them at work in the dead wood of a fallen tree.

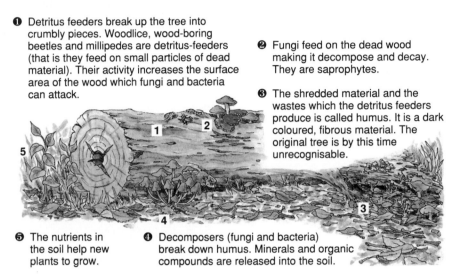

❶ Detritus feeders break up the tree into crumbly pieces. Woodlice, wood-boring beetles and millipedes are detritus-feeders (that is they feed on small particles of dead material). Their activity increases the surface area of the wood which fungi and bacteria can attack.

❷ Fungi feed on the dead wood making it decompose and decay. They are saprophytes.

❸ The shredded material and the wastes which the detritus feeders produce is called humus. It is a dark coloured, fibrous material. The original tree is by this time unrecognisable.

❺ The nutrients in the soil help new plants to grow.

❹ Decomposers (fungi and bacteria) break down humus. Minerals and organic compounds are released into the soil.

Figure 29.1C ● The formation of humus

Humus improves soils by the following means:
* It improves the texture of clay soils by helping the particles to stick together to form crumbs.
* It improves the texture of sandy soils by increasing the soil's ability to hold water.
* Humus reduces the leaching of minerals.
* By absorbing water, humus makes soil more fertile. This is especially important in sandy soils.
* Humus provides food for detritus feeders, e.g. woodlice and earthworms, which in turn fertilise the soil.
* Its high water content enables humus to absorb heat and warm the soil.

Water table

The roots of a plant anchor it in the ground and extract nutrients from the soil. Many plants have enough room for their roots in a layer of soil 15 cm deep: some plants need a layer of soil 4 m deep.

The natural level of water is called the **water table**. Plants need to have their roots above this, so that they can draw water from the water table without becoming wet. Roots should not be immersed in water the whole time. By means of a good drainage system, it is possible to lower the water table. Farmers are careful to ensure good drainage in their fields. Sometimes, they install underground pipes. Good drainage helps air to enter the soil; it helps seeds to start growing, and it helps to control plant diseases.

SUMMARY

Sandy soil: easy to cultivate; contains air, which assists growth of plant roots; needs frequent rain; may lack minerals as minerals are leached from the soil.
Clay soil: sticky and difficult to cultivate in wet weather; can sustain crop growth in dry periods; may become waterlogged and lack air; rich in minerals.
Loam: a mixture of sandy soil and clay soil; easily worked; contains air; holds water without becoming waterlogged.
Humus: improves all soils; binds sand particles together; increases water retention.

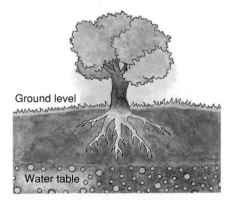

Ground level

Water table

Figure 29.1D ● The water table

Soil as a habitat for animals

Soil is teeming with living organisms. One hectare (10 000 m²) of soil contains a million earthworms and millions of mites, springtails, millipedes, centipedes, woodlice, fly larvae, beetles, ants and micro-organisms. Some soil organisms are pests, for example wireworms burrow into root crops such as potatoes and ruin them. Others play a vital part in maintaining the fertility of the soil. Some bacteria feed on the dead remains of plants and animals to make humus. Other bacteria **fix** nitrogen; that is, convert nitrogen in the air into nitrogen compounds, on which plants can feed. Earthworms improve the texture of the soil. Moving through it, they open channels for roots to spread through. As well as mixing the soil, they help air to enter and help water to drain from the soil.

Water

Plants obtain water from the soil. Plants lose water constantly as water vapour passes out through openings in the leaves of plants into the atmosphere. This process is called **transpiration**. Plants take in water through their roots to replace that lost by transpiration. Dissolved in the water are many nutrients the plants need. During a dry spell, plants need to be watered.

Figure 29.1E ● Many plants need to be watered during dry spells

Air

Soil must be aerated (contain air) so that plant roots can obtain air. Many of the micro-organisms in the soil also need air. If soil is packed down by tramping feet as hikers walk across the land, or by heavy vehicles, such as tractors, it will contain little air.

Nutrients

Plants need certain chemical elements. In photosynthesis, plants obtain carbon and oxygen from air, and hydrogen and oxygen from water. Land plants obtain the rest of the elements which they need from the soil. Aquatic plants obtain their nutrients from water. Table 29.2 shows the elements which plants obtain from soil. The major elements are needed in large amounts (on a kilogram per hectare scale), and the trace elements are needed in small amounts (on a gram per hectare scale).

LOOK AT LINKS
for **nitrogen fixation**
See Theme E, Topic 20.1.

LOOK AT LINKS
for **plant nutrition**
See Theme F, Topic 25.

LOOK AT LINKS
for **transpiration**
See Theme J, Topic 38.1.

Table 29.2 ● Elements obtained by plants from soil

Major elements	Importance	Trace elements
Nitrogen	Needed for protein synthesis	Manganese
Phosphorus	Needed for development of roots, energy-transfer reactions, nucleic acids	Copper Iron Zinc
Potassium	Needed in photosynthesis	Chlorine
Magnesium	Present in chlorophyll	Boron
Sulphur	Needed for synthesis of some proteins	Molybdenum
Calcium	Needed for transport	

Soil Analysis
(program)

Have you experimented with soil in a laboratory? You can try some computer experiments as well using this software.

The natural cycle is for plants to die and decay, returning chemicals to the soil. When crops are harvested, the chemicals they contain are not returned to the soil. Fertilisers are needed to replenish the soil with the nutrients which the crops have taken out of it.

pH

A soil may be acidic or alkaline or neutral. For each type of plant, there is a range of soil pH over which the plant can be grown successfully.

Table 29.3 ● Crop growth and pH

Crop	Potatoes	Swedes	Oats	Wheat	Sugar beet	Kale	Barley
pH	2	4.7–5.6	4.8–6.3	6.0–7.5	7.0–7.5	9–11	12

Farmers have a choice. They can measure the pH of their soil and then choose a crop which will grow well on it. Alternatively, they can alter the pH of the soil to suit the crop which they want to grow. Often soils are too acidic. Rainwater, being weakly acidic, neutralises bases which are present in topsoil. When soils are too acidic, farmers add lime (calcium oxide). This neutralises the excess of acid. Occasionally, soils are too alkaline. Then iron(II) sulphate is added. This salt is weakly acidic in solution and neutralises the excess of alkali in the soil.

LOOK AT LINKS
for **pH** and **neutralisation**
See Theme D, Topic 15.

Erosion

The top few centimetres of soil contain the most nutrients. This **topsoil** can be **eroded**: that is, washed away by high rainfall or blown away by strong winds. When farmers convert grassland into arable fields, erosion may follow. A field of winter wheat can lose 2.4 kg/m^2 of soil or more to erosion by wind and rain each year. Loss of soil leads to weaker plants which are more likely to become diseased.

There are many methods of preventing soil erosion.

- Grass prevents erosion: its roots keep the soil in place.
- Hedges reduce erosion by reducing the speed of the wind.
- Forests reduce erosion as the roots of the trees hold soil in place.
- Farmers plough land so that furrows lie across the natural slope of the land; rainwater will then not run down the furrows and cause erosion.
- A terraced hillside is less likely to be eroded than a natural hillside. By slowing down the flow of rain down a hillside, terraces give the water time to soak in and nourish the crop (see Figure 29.1G).

The flooding which Pakistan experienced in 1988 was made much worse by deforestation. The acute shortage of fuel had made people cut down trees for burning. As a result, when the rains came, the flood waters were not held back by the forests which had previously helped to avoid a disaster.

Figure 29.1F ● Terracing to prevent soil erosion

Figure 29.1G ● Soil erosion

SUMMARY

Soil contains small particles of weathered rock and humus – decayed organic matter. Plants need enough soil for their roots to grow in. They also need water, air and certain chemical elements as nutrients. The soil must have a suitable pH. Topsoil can be eroded by rain and by wind. Soil needs to be cultivated if it is to grow crops.

Cultivation

Soil needs to be cultivated, that is, broken up. A gardener digging the garden and a farmer ploughing the land are both cultivating the soil. The benefits of cultivation are:

* uprooting weeds,
* mixing fertilisers and decaying plants with the soil,
* introducing air into the soil,
* giving plants enough depth for their roots to grow.

CHECKPOINT

❶ Christine measured 50.0 cm³ of soil in a large measuring cylinder. She added 50.0 cm³ of water from a second measuring cylinder. After she had stirred the soil to dislodge all the air bubbles, the final volume was 90 cm³.
  (a) Why did Christine take care to tap the soil down in the measuring cylinder?
  (b) What volume of air was driven out of the soil?
  (c) What is the percentage by volume of air in this sample of soil?

❷ Christopher weighed 20.0 g of soil and put it into an oven at 100 °C. After an hour, he took the sample from the oven, let it cool and reweighed it. The mass was 15.0 g.

(a) What is the mass of the water lost on heating?
(b) What is the percentage by mass of water in the soil?
(c) What should Christopher have done to make sure that *all* the water has been driven out of the soil sample?

❸ Caroline took 10.0 g of the dry soil from Christopher's experiment. She heated it strongly in a crucible for 20 minutes. The humus burnt away to form carbon dioxide and water. The mass of the soil was 9.0 g.
(a) What mass of humus was present in the soil sample?
(b) What is the percentage by mass of humus in this soil sample (that is, Caroline's dry soil)?
(percentage by mass of humus = (mass of humus/total mass of soil) x 100)
(c) Why did Caroline not use a fresh sample of soil for her experiment?
(d) What should she have done to make sure that all the humus had been burnt away?

❹ A friend of yours is given an indoor potted plant. She asks your advice about looking after it. What advice do you give her about:
(a) watering (how often),
(b) the size of pot (what to do when the plant grows),
(c) forking the soil in the pot occasionally?

❺ A propagator is a heated tray covered with a plastic lid. It contains potting compost. Its purpose is to help seeds to propagate. Why do seeds sown in a propagator have a better chance than seeds sown in a field?

❻ Miss Sue N Dunn decides that there ought to be an easier way of gardening. She does not like digging so she pulls out the weeds and rakes over the topsoil. Then she plants her seeds. What are the disadvantages of Sue's method?

❼ Give two reasons in each case why the following are important features of soil: good drainage, cultivation, micro-organisms, the level of the water table.

❽ A load of topsoil is delivered to a new housing development, Newstate. Overnight, half the load disappears. Round the corner, in Old Road, there is a garden covered with a layer of new topsoil. Where has it come from? The police chemist takes samples of soil from Newstate and Old Road. He takes two crucibles, puts 100 g of Newstate soil into one crucible and 100 g of Old Road soil into the other, and heats the crucibles gently. Both soil samples lose water. He weighs each crucible at intervals. His results are shown in the table.

Time (minutes)	Mass of Newstate sample (g)	Mass of Old Road sample (g)
0	100	100
5	88	86
10	80	76
15	73	68
20	69	61
30	68	57
40	68	55
50	68	55

(a) On graph paper, plot the mass of each sample (on the vertical axis) against the time (on the horizontal axis).
(b) How long did it take to dry (i) the Newstate sample (ii) the Old Road sample?
(c) What is the percentage of water in (i) the Newstate sample (ii) the Old Road sample?
(d) Has the Old Road gardener carted off soil from Newstate?

29.2 Farming

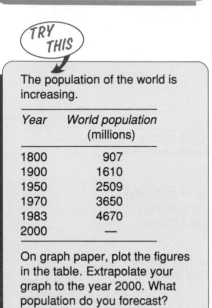

FIRST THOUGHTS

In 1990 there were twice as many people in the world as there were in 1950. Farmers have to supply more food to meet the needs of the growing world population.

TRY THIS

The population of the world is increasing.

Year	World population (millions)
1800	907
1900	1610
1950	2509
1970	3650
1983	4670
2000	—

On graph paper, plot the figures in the table. Extrapolate your graph to the year 2000. What population do you forecast?

When the human population began to rise sharply in the nineteenth century, the need for food increased. Farming methods had to become more **intensive**, that is, to produce as much food as possible from the land available for raising crops (arable farming) and animals (livestock farming).

Figure 29.2A ● Intensive cereal production

The field of wheat in Figure 29.2A has been grown by intensive methods. Chemical fertilisers have been applied to produce stronger, larger plants in a shorter time. Chemical pesticides have been used: insecticides have been sprayed to kill insect pests and herbicides have been applied to kill weeds. The use of all these chemicals costs the farmer money. The farmer has to balance this expense against the increased yield of wheat grain. Most of our bread is made from cereals which have been grown by intensive methods.

Most of the beef and pork we eat is produced by intensive methods. Cattle and pigs will find their own food if free to graze. The pigs shown in Figure 29.2B have been kept in pens and given fodder which has been bought in, not produced on the farm. As a result of the lack of exercise, cattle and pigs gain weight more quickly and so are ready for slaughter earlier. The farmer has to balance the cost of feed against the shorter time for which he has to feed the cattle.

Scientists and engineers have developed new technologies to help farmers to produce food in great quantities. In the following sections we shall look at the various factors that contribute to intensive farming. Sometimes the new methods have an unwanted effect on the environment. We have to balance the advantages of the new methods against the impact which they have on the environment.

Figure 29.2B ● Intensive pork production

LOOK AT LINKS
The invention of the refrigerator in the nineteenth century allowed meat to be transported to the UK from overseas in refrigerated ships. Plentiful supplies of meat helped to get rid of hunger and starvation.
See Theme B, Topic 4.6. for the refrigerator

CHECKPOINT

❶ (a) Why are cereals so important for the diet of the human population? (See Topic 25.)

(b) Use the bar chart opposite to work out the ratio:
Cereal production in 1985/
Cereal production in 1965.

(c) What changes in farming methods have made the increase possible?

(d) Which block shows the greatest percentage increase over the preceding figure?

Cereal production (million tonnes) — axis values: 220, 200, 180, 160, 140, 120, 100; years: 1965 1970 1975 1980 1985 1990 (Estimate)

29.3 Irrigation

FIRST THOUGHTS

One major solution to the problem of infertile land is irrigation: bringing water to parched land.

IT'S A FACT

By the year 2000, the area of irrigated land in different countries will total three million square kilometres.

Lake Nasser in Egypt is 500 km long. From it flows the River Nile. When there is heavy rainfall, the level of water in Lake Nasser rises. The Aswan High Dam prevents Lake Nasser overflowing into the Nile. Instead, the lake serves as a reservoir of water in dry years. In 1985 when other African countries, such as Ethiopia, suffered from drought, Egypt had the water from Lake Nasser. There have, however, been some drawbacks.

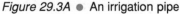

Figure 29.3A ● An irrigation pipe

SCIENCE AT WORK

● The Aswan High Dam, Lake Nasser and the Nile

Lake Nasser in Egypt is 500 km long. From it flows the River Nile. When there is heavy rainfall, the level of water in Lake Nasser rises. The Aswan High Dam was built to prevent Lake Nasser overflowing into the Nile. Instead, the lake serves as a reservoir of water in dry years. In 1985 when other African countries, such as Ethiopia, suffered from drought, Egypt had the water from Lake Nasser. There have, however, been some drawbacks.

• Before the dam was built, the Nile used to flood. The silt which it carried to vast areas on its banks was rich in minerals. Now that the Nile no longer carries this fertiliser to the farms on its banks, farmers must buy synthetic fertilisers.

- The sodium chloride content of the banks of the river has increased because it is no longer washed out by flood waters. Many crops do not grow well in soil with a high salt content.
- Irrigation canals carry water from the Nile to the farmlands on its banks. They also carry snails from Lake Nasser. Some of the snails act as hosts to a tiny worm called the **bilharzia fluke**. These worms can infect anyone wading in the canal. When they do, they cause bilharzia, which is a serious disease, attacking the liver, lungs and heart. There has been a big increase in bilharzia since the dam was built because the slow-flowing water in the irrigation canals is ideal for the snails.
- Fishermen used to make good catches in the Nile Delta (see Figure 29.3B). Now that the Nile silt no longer reaches the delta, natural food chains are broken. There is little plankton for fish to live on, and catches are poor.

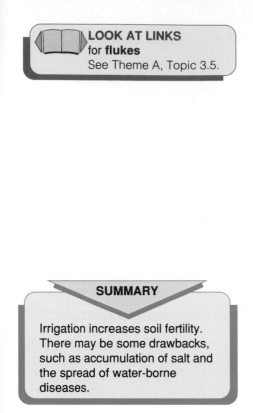

LOOK AT LINKS
for **flukes**
See Theme A, Topic 3.5.

SUMMARY

Irrigation increases soil fertility. There may be some drawbacks, such as accumulation of salt and the spread of water-borne diseases.

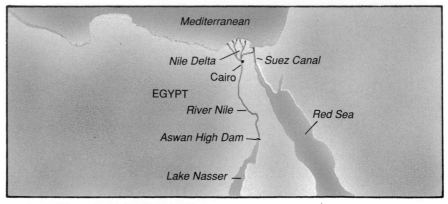

Figure 29.3B ● Egypt and the Nile

CHECKPOINT

❶ (a) Name a benefit which the Aswan Dam has brought to Egypt.
(b) What drawbacks have there been to damming Lake Nasser?
(c) On balance, do you think the Aswan Dam has been a good investment for Egypt? Give reasons for your answer.

FIRST THOUGHTS

29.4 Mechanisation and its effect on wildlife

Since 1945, 200 000 km of hedges have been removed in England and Wales.

The change from traditional farming practices to intensive farming methods happened in the UK after 1945. An important part of the change was the invention of large machines for cultivation and harvesting. These modern machines work best in large fields where they do not have to stop for hedges and fences. Small fields were joined to form large fields by chopping down copses and uprooting hedges. The animals and plants which lived in the woods and hedgerows lost their habitats. Table 29.4 shows how some wildlife habitats have decreased. Table 29.5 shows how some animals have been affected.

Table 29.4 ● Losses in some habitats between 1945 and 1990

Habitat	Percentage lost
Unimproved grassland, including hay meadows rich in flowers	95
Lowland heaths	40
Lowland woods	40
Upland heaths	30

Figure 29.4A ● Large machinery means large fields

Table 29.5 ● Numbers of species in traditional and modernised farms

Group	Number of species of each group in the two habitats	
	Traditional farm habitat	Corresponding habitat in modernised farm
	(Hedges and natural grass verges)	(Wire fences and sown grass)
Mammals	20	5
Birds	37	6
Butterflies	17	0
	(Permanent ponds and ditches)	(Temporary ditches and piped water)
Amphibians	5	2
Fish	9	0
Dragonflies	11	0
Snails	25	3

Large fields mean that large machinery can be used more effectively. Crops can be harvested more quickly, with a resulting decrease in labour costs. Land drainage can be improved and boundary hedges can be dispensed with. However, the creation of large fields has some bad effects on the environment.

- Hedges and pockets of woodland provide habitats for our native wildlife. These habitats are lost when large fields are created.
- Heavy machinery can compact the land, which may then become waterlogged.
- Large machines use a lot of fuel.
- Hedges are natural windbreaks. When they are removed, the wind can cause more erosion of topsoil and more loss of water from the soil by evaporation.

SUMMARY

Combining small fields to form large fields makes agriculture more efficient. However, plants and animals lose their habitats when woods and hedges are destroyed, and soil erosion is increased.

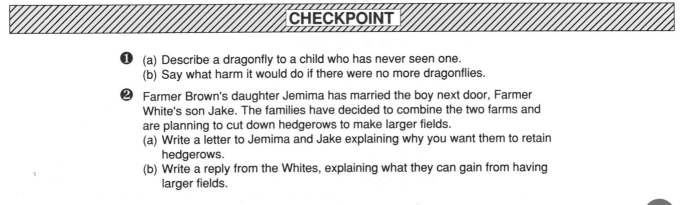

CHECKPOINT

❶ (a) Describe a dragonfly to a child who has never seen one.
   (b) Say what harm it would do if there were no more dragonflies.

❷ Farmer Brown's daughter Jemima has married the boy next door, Farmer White's son Jake. The families have decided to combine the two farms and are planning to cut down hedgerows to make larger fields.
   (a) Write a letter to Jemima and Jake explaining why you want them to retain hedgerows.
   (b) Write a reply from the Whites, explaining what they can gain from having larger fields.

❸ (a) Plot the following figures as a bar graph.

Year	1947	1969	1980	1985
Length of hedgerows (x1000 km)	750	650	610	590

(b) Who benefits from the removal of hedgerows? Give two benefits which the destruction of hedgerows makes possible.
(c) Who loses by the removal of hedgerows? Give two disadvantages of destroying hedgerows.

29.5 Monoculture

Intensive arable farms specialise in growing a small number of cash crops. Growing only one crop over a large area is called **monoculture**. It enables a farmer to obtain high yields which he can sell in bulk for a better price. Monoculture makes efficient use of expensive machinery and also reduces labour costs.

Monoculture also has drawbacks.

• It encourages an organism that feeds on the crop to increase to such large numbers that it becomes a pest. The farmer then has to pay the cost of treatment with pesticide.
• Growing a single crop exhausts the soil of the nutrients on which the crop depends. The farmer has to buy fertilisers to replace these nutrients.

Figure 29.5A ● Monoculture

29.6 Natural fertilisers: manure and slurry

A substance which adds nutrients to the soil is called a **fertiliser**. In a mixed arable and livestock farm, the dung of farm animals is collected, left for a few months to decay and then used as **manure**, a natural fertiliser. When a herd of animals is reared indoors on an intensive farm, the dung has to be disposed of. Most intensive farms specialise, and a livestock farm may have no arable land to spread manure on. Figure 29.6A shows how the dung is collected.

LOOK AT LINKS
for **dissolved oxygen** and **ground water**
See Theme E, Topics 22.2 and 22.3

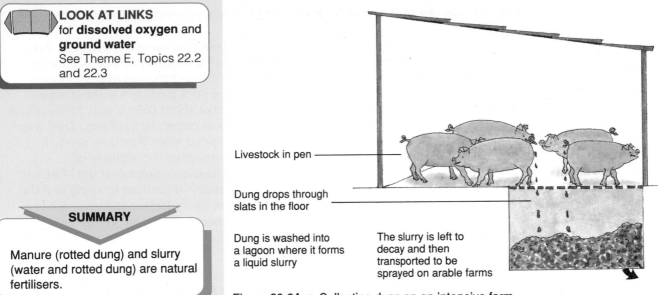

Livestock in pen

Dung drops through slats in the floor

Dung is washed into a lagoon where it forms a liquid slurry

The slurry is left to decay and then transported to be sprayed on arable farms

Figure 29.6A ● Collecting dung on an intensive farm

SUMMARY

Manure (rotted dung) and slurry (water and rotted dung) are natural fertilisers.

A serious hazard to the environment arises if slurry leaks from the lagoon. Then slurry may seep into rivers and lakes, where it will be broken down by bacteria. As the bacteria multiply, they use up dissolved oxygen in the water. The result is that fish and other forms of aquatic life die. The slurry may even find its way into ground water and contaminate drinking water.

29.7 Synthetic fertilisers

FIRST THOUGHTS

Most modern farms do not produce enough manure for their needs and use synthetic (man-made) fertilisers.

In the present century, we have seen the dramatic effects of synthetic fertilisers in the **green revolution**. This is the way fertilisers have turned barren areas in many parts of the world into green, fertile agricultural land. In India, the rice yield has increased by 50%; in Indonesia, the maize crop has doubled.

Figure 29.7A ● Compare the fertilised plot and the control plot

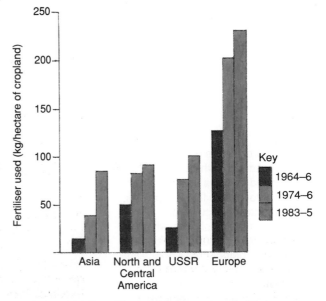

Key
■ 1964–6
■ 1974–6
■ 1983–5

Fertiliser used (kg/hectare of cropland)

Asia | North and Central America | USSR | Europe

Figure 29.7B ● The worldwide use of fertilisers

How much fertiliser?

Most fertilisers concentrate on supplying the necessary nitrogen (N), phosphorus (P) and potassium (K). **NPK fertilisers** are consumed in huge quantities: in 1990, the world consumption was over 20 million tonnes. In the UK, the consumption of NPK fertilisers is about seven million tonnes a year. The fertilisers cost about £60 a tonne. Farmers and market gardeners need to invest a lot of money in fertilisers. They want good crops, but they do not want to spend more than they need on fertilisers. They can obtain expert advice from the Ministry of Agriculture, Fisheries and Food. Agricultural chemists at the Ministry will advise them on the type and quantity of fertiliser to apply and the best season of the year for applying it. Every farmer and grower has a different problem. The agricultural chemists must weigh up the type of crop and the type of soil before they can recommend the most suitable treatment.

Drawbacks of using fertilisers

Using too much fertiliser is a waste of money. There is also another drawback. Rain leaches (washes out) soluble substances from the soil. The application of too much fertiliser results in the leaching of nitrates and phosphates into rivers, lakes and ground water. Phosphates and nitrates have caused **eutrophication** of lakes and rivers. Nitrates in the ground water find their way into the drinking water. Many people think this is a health hazard.

What can be done about the problem of leaching? There is less leaching from grassland because grass covers the topsoil all the year round. From arable land, about one third of the fertiliser applied is leached out. Matching the supply of fertiliser to the crop's ability to use it helps to reduce leaching. Winter crops, such as winter barley and winter wheat, reduce the leaching of fertiliser by winter rains.

Obviously, farmers cannot maintain their very high productivity without fertilisers. They are so efficient that the EC produces far more food than it needs. The excess of food is kept in vast stores. We pay the cost of storing all this food; it amounts to £150 per person per year in the UK. There is an argument for cutting back on production. To persuade farmers to use less fertiliser, the Government could either ration fertiliser or put a tax on it so that the farmers who use the most fertiliser and gain the biggest harvests would have the most fertiliser tax to pay.

LOOK AT LINKS
for **NPK fertilisers**
Their manufacture is described in Theme L, Topic 51.3.

IT'S A FACT

With 2–3 million tonnes of nitrogen (in the form of nitrates) going on to the soil of the UK each year, 600 000 tonnes of nitrate ion leach out every year.

LOOK AT LINKS
for the **eutrophication** (unintentional enrichment with nutrients) of lakes and rivers and the pollution of ground water by fertilisers. See Theme E, Topic 24.4.

Fertiliser
(program)

Investigate the chemistry of hydrogen, nitrogen and ammonium nitrate. You can also develop and operate a production system which is commercially viable.

IT'S A FACT

There are islands off the coast of South America which are inhabited by large flocks of sea birds. Mounds of their droppings, called guano, accumulate. Since sea birds eat a fish diet, which is high in protein, guano is rich in nitrogen compounds. For a century, European farmers imported guano from South America to use as a fertiliser.

Figure 29.7C ● Applying synthetic fertiliser to winter wheat

Advantages of synthetic fertilisers

- Synthetic fertilisers are easy for the farmer to store and to apply.
- The application of fertiliser can be adjusted to the needs of the soil. Both the type and the amount of nutrient can be controlled.
- They replace bulky manure which cannot be applied evenly and is difficult to store. The farmer does not have to keep animals to produce manure.
- Land does not need a rest period between crops. The efficiency of a farm can be increased by growing one or two crops a year.

Disadvantages

- Synthetic fertilisers do not add humus to the soil. The structure of the soil deteriorates. Soil erosion may occur.
- Fertilisers which are not absorbed by the crop may be leached into rivers and lakes. The resulting eutrophication encourages the growth of algae.
- The manufacture of synthetic fertilisers uses a lot of fuel. This eats into the Earth's fuel reserves.

SUMMARY

Synthetic fertilisers enable farmers to obtain large yields per hectare. NPK fertilisers contain nitrogen (for protein synthesis), phosphorus (for healthy roots), potassium (to help photosynthesis) and some calcium and magnesium. There are some disadvantages to the use of synthetic fertilisers.

CHECKPOINT

❶ The figure below shows how the yields of winter wheat and grass increase as more nitrogenous fertiliser is used. After studying the graphs, say what mass of nitrogen you would apply to a 100 hectare field to avoid waste and to give a maximum yield of (a) winter wheat and (b) grass.

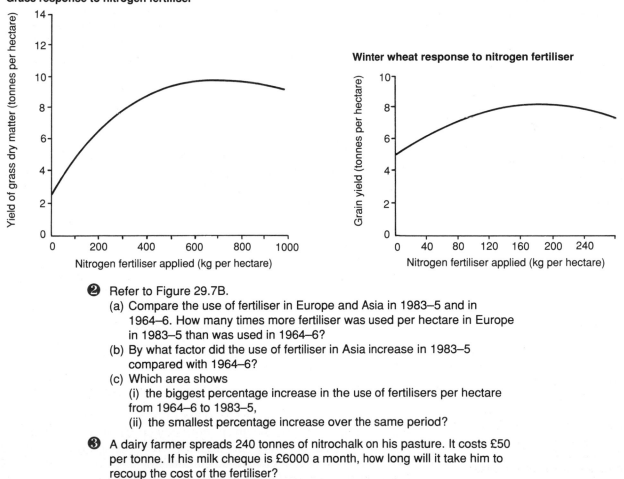

❷ Refer to Figure 29.7B.
  (a) Compare the use of fertiliser in Europe and Asia in 1983–5 and in 1964–6. How many times more fertiliser was used per hectare in Europe in 1983–5 than was used in 1964–6?
  (b) By what factor did the use of fertiliser in Asia increase in 1983–5 compared with 1964–6?
  (c) Which area shows
      (i) the biggest percentage increase in the use of fertilisers per hectare from 1964–6 to 1983–5,
      (ii) the smallest percentage increase over the same period?

❸ A dairy farmer spreads 240 tonnes of nitrochalk on his pasture. It costs £50 per tonne. If his milk cheque is £6000 a month, how long will it take him to recoup the cost of the fertiliser?

❹ Fertilisers are organic (made from plant or animal material) and slow-acting or inorganic (man-made) and quick-acting. The table lists some common fertilisers.

Fertiliser	N	P	K
Compound fertiliser	✓	✓	✓
Ammonium sulphate	✓		
Nitrochalk (ammonium nitrate + calcium carbonate)	✓		
Superphosphate		✓	
Potassium sulphate			✓
Farmyard manure	✓	✓	✓
Dried blood	✓		
Bone meal	✓	✓	
Garden compost	✓	✓	✓

(a) What do N, P and K stand for?

(b) List (i) the organic fertilisers in the table and (ii) the inorganic fertilisers.

(c) What are (i) the advantages (ii) the disadvantages of using organic fertilisers?

(d) Some people choose to buy 'organically grown' vegetables although they are usually dearer than other vegetables. What are organically grown vegetables? What reasons might these people have for their choice?

❺ (a) The table below shows the mass of nitrogen, phosphorus and potassium (in kg/hectare) removed from the soil when different crops are grown. Name the crops which take out a large quantity of potassium. How do these crops differ from the rest?

Crop	Mass (kg/hectare)		
	N	P	K
Wheat grain	115	22	26
Oat grain	72	13	18
Sugar beet root	86	14	302
Potatoes	109	14	133
Pasture grass	128	14	100

(b) The table below shows the composition of three NPK fertilisers that a farmer uses. Which fertiliser should she use (i) on her pasture (ii) on her wheat and (iii) on her sugar beet? Explain your choices.

Fertiliser	Composition (percentage mass)		
	N	P	K
Fertiliser A	62	13	25
Fertiliser B	22	27	51
Fertiliser C	44	19	37

FIRST THOUGHTS

29.8  Straw burning

In the UK before 1992, 8 million tonnes of straw were burnt each year.

Traditionally, straw was used as food or bedding for livestock. Dung mixed with straw was used as manure. The modern arable farm does not have livestock to use straw. Burning the straw was a means of getting rid of it. The Government gave these guidelines:

● No straw should be burnt at night or at weekends.

LOOK AT LINKS
for **greenhouse effect**
See Theme E, Topic 20.7.

SUMMARY

Before 1992 burning straw was one way of getting rid of it, but it destroyed insects and was a nuisance to the public.

- Two people should be in charge.
- A fire break should be ploughed. (This is a clear margin of land to prevent fire spreading.)

Advantages of straw burning

- It was a cheap way of disposing of straw; it saved the cost of ploughing it in.
- Burning destroyed weed seeds and soil pests.
- Minerals in the ash were added to the soil.
- The soil structure was not disturbed by ploughing.

Disadvantages

- Uncontrolled fires caused damage, for example, to hedges. Fire brigades were called out at public expense.
- Other species in addition to soil pests were killed. Many may help the farmer by preying on harmful species.
- Smoke could be a nuisance to the public.
- The carbon dioxide and water vapour produced contributed to the **greenhouse effect**.

In 1992, a law was passed which stopped farmers from getting rid of straw by burning it. *Do you think the law is a good one? Give reasons for your answer.*

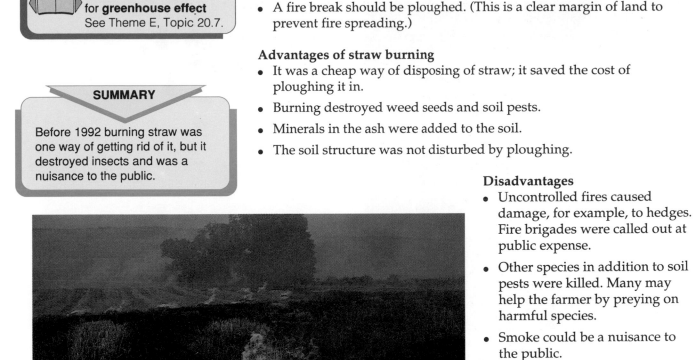

Figure 29.8A ● Straw burning

29.9 Herbicides

FIRST THOUGHTS

Farmers and gardeners have to cope with pests. These include weeds which compete with crops for nutrients, animals which eat crops, and disease-causing organisms like harmful fungi which attack plants and livestock. Substances which are used to kill pests are pesticides. There are three main types: herbicides, which kill plants, insecticides, which kill insects (Topic 29.10) and fungicides, which kill fungi (Topic 29.11).

Fertile soil is a good growing ground for weeds as well as for the crops that farmers sow. Weeds are plants that compete with crops for space, light and nutrients. At one time, farmers employed many farmhands, and one of the jobs they did was pulling out weeds by hand. Now, farmers employ fewer people and save labour by using chemical weedkillers – herbicides. By using a **selective herbicide**, they can kill weeds and leave the crop untouched. The most common selective herbicides are 2,4-D and 2,4,5-T. They kill broad-leaved plants, (dandelions, thistles and nettles).

Figure 29.9A ● A crop treated with herbicide and a control

Figure 29.9B ● Broad-leaved and narrow-leaved plants

Figure 29.9C ● Models of 2,4-D and 2,4,5-T molecules

They do not harm plants with narrow leaves (grasses and cereals). These selective herbicides are organic compounds which contain chlorine. Other weedkillers, such as paraquat and sodium chlorate(V), are **non-selective**: they kill all plants.

Chemical weedkillers are of great benefit to us. It is difficult to see how scientific farming could continue without them. There have also been some tragic results of using herbicides.

Agent Orange

From 1961–71, there was a war in Vietnam between the USA and the communist Vietcong forces. The US planes found it difficult to carry out bomb attacks on the Vietcong because the Vietcong positions were hidden by dense jungle vegetation. US planes dropped a herbicide called Agent Orange, which killed all the trees and other vegetation where it landed. It destroyed the forests which sheltered Vietcong fighters and their bases and killed their crops. Agent Orange contained 2,4,5-T and an impurity, **dioxin**. At the time, no-one knew that dioxin has teratogenic effects (effects on unborn babies). Terribly deformed babies were born to Vietnamese mothers. Dioxin also has genetic effects. When US servicemen returned home and started families, some of them found to their dismay that they had become the fathers of deformed babies. Agent Orange had affected the fathers' genes. As a result of these tragedies, 2,4,5-T has been banned in many countries. The method of manufacture always produces some dioxin as impurity.

IT'S A FACT

Vietnam received 72 million litres of herbicides during the war. About half of this was Agent Orange. An arsenic compound called Agent Blue was also used.

SUMMARY

Selective weedkillers are of enormous benefit to agriculture. Nevertheless, one of them, 2,4,5-T, is now banned because it contains an impurity called dioxin, which has teratogenic effects and genetic effects.

CHECKPOINT

❶ Explain what is meant by (a) herbicide and (b) selective herbicide.

❷ What are the advantages of selective herbicides over non-selective herbicides?

29.10  Insecticides

The previous section dealt with weeds – plant pests. Insects are the major animal pests, although many insects are beneficial. The pesticides which are used to kill insects are called insecticides.

IT'S A FACT

A family in the USA became very ill after eating a pig which they had raised. One of the children suffered permanent brain damage. The cause of the illness was the grain which the family had fed to the pig. It was in a bag labelled 'Seed grain. Not for consumption. Contains mercury salts as fungicide.' The tragedy was that they could not read. Mercury salts had been used to treat the seed grain before storage so that it would not be attacked by fungi before the time came to plant it the following spring.

SUMMARY

Insecticides are used to protect crops against being eaten by insects. Insecticides have played a big part in increasing food supplies worldwide.

LOOK AT LINKS
for **petrochemicals**
See Theme L, Topic 48.

Insects, weeds and plant diseases destroy about one third of the world's crops. Aphids attack the flowers of many fruits and vegetables. Cutworms chew off plants at soil level. Wireworms bore into potatoes and other root vegetables. Grain weevils eat stored grain. Unchecked, insects would consume most of the food we grow, and humans would starve. On the other hand, many insects are helpful. Some pollinate flowers, and some eat harmful insects.

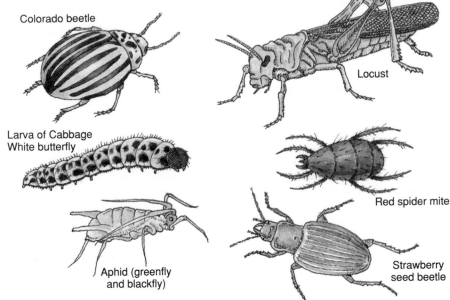

Figure 29.10A ● pests

The first chemicals which were used as insecticides were general poisons, such as compounds of arsenic, lead and mercury. These compounds are poisonous to all animals which swallow them. Children and family pets were sometimes accidentally poisoned. These poisons are stable: they remain in the soil for many years.

The DDT story

In 1939, a scientist called Paul Mueller discovered that a substance called DDT was very poisonous to houseflies. His experiments soon showed that DDT was a very useful substance indeed, killing many insects such as lice and mosquitoes and agricultural pests such as potato-blight and grape-blight. The exciting aspect of DDT was that it left species other than insects unharmed. It is a **broad spectrum insecticide**. That is, it kills many types of insect. DDT is a **petrochemical**. Together with similar compounds, it is often referred to as an 'organochlorine'.

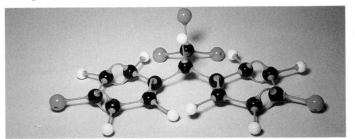

Figure 29.10B ● A model of a DDT molecule (Dichlorodiphenyltrichloroethane)

IT'S A FACT

Ten million tonnes of DDT have been applied to the Earth in the last 25 years.

DDT has saved more lives than any other single substance. It has saved million of lives and prevented billions of illnesses by killing insects which carry disease. It has saved people from hunger and starvation by killing insects which eat crops. Thanks to the use of DDT, 550 million people in tropical countries now no longer live in constant fear of malaria. The World Health Organisation says that DDT has saved five million lives. Cholera is another disease which is carried by insects and which can now be fought with DDT.

Figure 29.10C ● Crop spraying today. In countries where DDT is banned, safer, often biodegradable chemicals are used.

DDT has also contributed to agriculture. It was used successfully to control tea parasites in Sri Lanka and cotton pests in the USA. In the desert regions of North Africa, crops are often consumed by swarms of locusts. The result is famine, and a whole population will face starvation. DDT has reduced the harm done by locusts.

People predicted that DDT would exterminate all insect pests. In 1948, Paul Mueller was awarded the Nobel Prize for his discovery. No sooner had he received the prize than people began to discover some worrying effects of DDT. In 1962 Rachel Carson wrote a book called *Silent Spring*. She suggested that killing insects would deprive birds of their natural food, and birds would die out, giving a spring without birdsong. Many of her fears have been borne out. Since DDT does not break down easily, an application of DDT will remain in the soil and in water for many years.

In Topic 24, Figure 24.4D shows what happened when Clear Lake in California was sprayed with DDT to combat mosquitoes. People were surprised when aquatic birds, such as grebes, died. The concentration of DDT in the lake water was only 0.02 p.p.m. However, DDT is soluble in fat and therefore difficult to excrete. Along the food chain, the level of DDT built up: micro-organisms 5 p.p.m., fish 250 p.p.m. and at the top of the food chain, grebes 1600 p.p.m., a lethal dose.

SUMMARY

Insecticides fight disease by killing disease-carrying insects, e.g. lice and mosquitoes. The insecticide DDT has saved thousands of human lives. Worry over the build up of DDT in animals has led to strict limits on its use.

IT'S A FACT

Central Florida is the fruit basket of the USA. Without insecticides to kill mosquitoes, the area would be uninhabitable. To combat fruit fly, boxes of oranges and lemons are sprayed with an insecticide before they are sold. In 1984, scientists discovered that the insecticide used, EDB (1, 2-dibromoethane), is a carcinogen. Fruit-growers now use a different insecticide. Fruit which is to be juiced or canned is not sprayed. Alternatives to spraying are refrigeration and irradiation (see Topic 12.3). Both of these cost twelve times as much as spraying.

SUMMARY

It would benefit the environment if we could find ways of cutting down on the use of insecticides. Research is being carried out on the use of predator insects, sterilisation and trapping.

DDT has been carried through food chains to the remotest parts of Earth, far from the places where it was used. Figure 29.10D shows how DDT can build up along a food chain on land. A problem is that many insects are becoming immune to DDT. As a result, higher concentrations must be used in spraying.

❶ An elm tree is treated with 2,4,5,-T to stop Dutch elm disease

❷ A worm eats dead leaves which contain the pesticide.

❸ A robin eats the worm.

❹ After the robin flies away, it is eaten by a bird of prey.

Figure 29.10D ● The robins' place in a food chain

DDT does not react with air or water. Since it is such a stable compound, the amount of DDT in the world is steadily increasing. We know that it kills insects and that, in sufficiently large amounts, it kills fish and birds. A human being may eat fish and birds contaminated with DDT over a long period of time. We do not know what the results of the buildup of DDT will be. There is no direct evidence that DDT causes illness in humans. It has been found, however, that cancer victims in the USA have twice as much DDT in their fatty tissues as the rest of the population.

In the USA and Europe, DDT is now banned. DDT is still used for essential jobs, for example., fighting malaria. Safer insecticides are used for agricultural purposes. One choice is organic compounds of phosphorus, which are broken down in time to safe compounds.

Other methods of controlling insects

Scientists are looking for other ways of controlling insects. Some methods are described as **biological control**. One such method is to breed **predator insects**. These are insects which kill the insects that are eating the crops. Of course, the predator insects must not eat the crops! Another idea is to use radioactivity to sterilise male insects so that they cannot breed. Insects give out aromatic chemicals called **pheromones** when they want to attract a mate. Research workers have worked out a method of extracting pheromones from insects and using the extract to bait a trap. The insects which are lured into the trap are then killed.

Great Spruce Bark beetles lay their eggs under the bark of spruce trees. When the larvae hatch, they feed on the tree's nutrients, thus killing the tree. Belgian beetles are predators of Great Spruce Bark beetles. Belgian beetles also lay their eggs under the bark of spruce trees. When the larvae of the Belgian beetles hatch, they eat the larvae of Great Spruce Bark beetles, but they do not harm the tree.

CHECKPOINT

❶ In the spring of 1988, North Africa was threatened by the worst plague of locusts for 30 years. The locust control programme financed by the United Nations uses short-lived insecticides such as fenitrothion. These do not last long enough to lie in wait for advancing swarms of locusts. An area sprayed with fenitrothion is safe for locusts after only three days. With long-lasting insecticides, such as dieldrin, strips of desert can be sprayed to prevent the advance of locusts. Experts say that dieldrin would do no harm to a desert environment. However, dieldrin has been shown to cause genetic damage (see Topic 29.6). Which would you use – fenitrothion or dieldrin – if you were in charge of the locust control programme? Explain your views.

❷ The Mediterranean fruit fly is an insect pest. Large numbers of male flies were irradiated by a colbalt-60 source (see Topic 12.3) and then released. They mated but they produced no offspring.
(a) Why were fruit farmers pleased with the use of radioactivity?
(b) What is the advantage of this technique over the use of chemical pesticides?

29.11 Fungicides and molluscicides

LOOK AT LINKS
for **bilharzia**
See Theme G, Topic 29.3.

IT'S A FACT

The pesticide picture
In 1985 nearly 10 000 tonnes of pesticide were applied to farmland in the UK. More than 800 000 tonnes were used worldwide, at a cost of about £28 billion. The use of pesticide will continue to grow at a rate of 2–4% a year in developing countries and 7–8% a year in developed countries.

SUMMARY

Fungicides and molluscicides are used to kill harmful fungi and molluscs.

Fungi cause the expensive diseases of mildew and potato-blight. To prevent these diseases, crops are sprayed with fungicides. Many copper salts are fungicides, e.g. copper(II) sulphate.

Molluscs, including slugs and snails, eat crops and spread diseases. Molluscicides are being used to fight them. Bilharzia is a disease which affects people in tropical countries. It is spread by water snails.

Advantages of using pesticides
• They kill pests quickly.
• Pesticides increase food production.
• They are easy to store and use.
• There is such a large variety of chemicals available that most pests can be eliminated.

Disadvantages
• Pests can develop resistance to a particular pesticide.
• The spray can be carried by the wind and so affect wildlife.
• Pesticides can seep into the soil and drain into rivers and lakes, where they will harm wildlife.
• Pesticides can enter food chains and build up from one feeding level to the next. They can reach a toxic level at the top of a food chain.

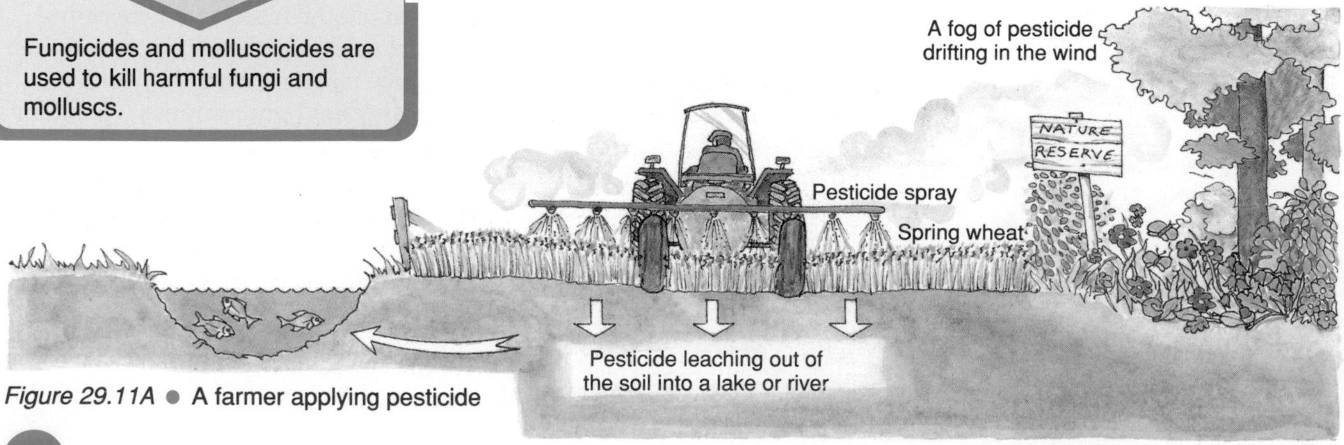

A fog of pesticide drifting in the wind

NATURE RESERVE

Pesticide spray

Spring wheat

Pesticide leaching out of the soil into a lake or river

Figure 29.11A ● A farmer applying pesticide

CHECKPOINT

❶ (a) How do chemical insecticides help farmers?
  (b) What did farmers use as insecticides before DDT?
  (c) In what way is DDT better than the insecticides which were used previously?
  (d) Why has the use of DDT on farms been banned?
  (e) For what purpose is DDT still used? Why is it in such demand?

❷ Why did Rachel Carson's book get people worried?

❸ Do you think we should give up using chemical insecticides?

❹ DDT was found in the flesh of eagles. They are birds of prey: they do not eat insects. How did the insecticide get into the eagles' flesh?

❺
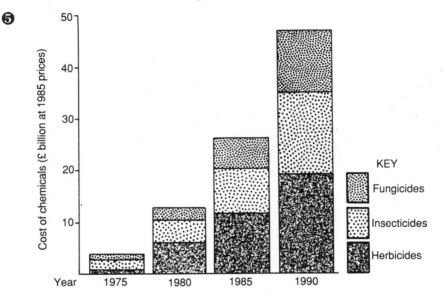

Refer to the figure above.
  (a) Give approximate figures for the money spent on (i) fungicides, (ii) insecticides and (iii) herbicides in 1975 and in 1990.
  (b) Give the ratio:
      Cost of pesticides used in 1990/Cost of pesticides used in 1980
  (c) Name crops on which a farmer might use (i) a fungicide (ii) an insecticide and (iii) a herbicide.

29.12 🏞 Energy

An ecosystem consists of a community of organisms living in a particular part of the physical (non-living) environment. Ecosystems are more or less self-supporting. The animals, plants, soil, water, etc. which make up a farm are an ecosystem.

Farms are ecosystems which are managed so as to produce as much food as possible. The amount of food produced can be assessed in terms of the energy content of the food produced. For example, the energy content of beef is 1050 kJ/100 g; the energy content of oatmeal is 170 kJ/100 g. The amount of food produced depends on the amount of energy which enters the farm ecosystem and also on the efficiency with which the energy is converted into the energy content of plant and animal tissue. The energy which enters the system is the **input**, and the energy content of the food produced is the **output**.

Input (GJ)

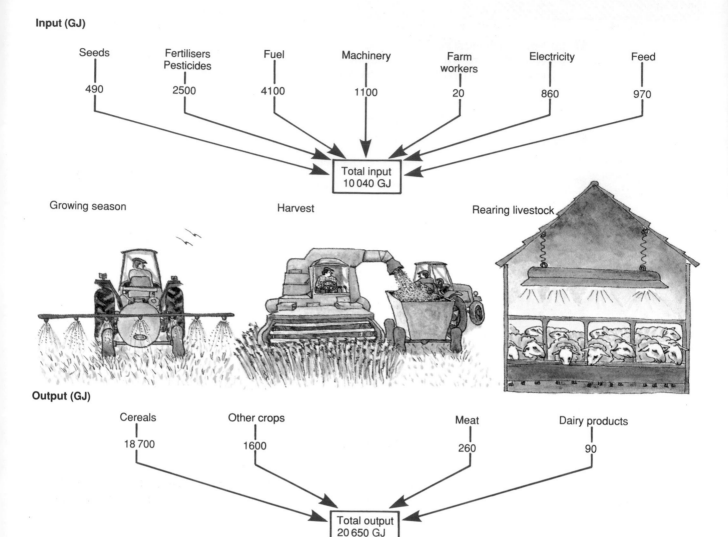

Figure 29.12A ● Energy input and output on a 640 hectare farm in the 1980s. Note that fuel is used to power machinery, in the generation of electricity and in the manufacture of fertilisers, pesticides, etc. In total, fuel accounts for nearly 99% of energy input. Manual work accounts for less than 0.2% of energy input.

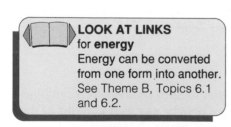

LOOK AT LINKS
for **energy**
Energy can be converted from one form into another.
See Theme B, Topics 6.1 and 6.2.

LOOK AT LINKS
Photosynthesis converts the energy of sunlight into the energy of chemical bonds in sugars
See Theme F, Topic 25.0.

Figure 29.12A shows the input and output of a typical intensive farm of 640 hectares in southern England. The farm is chiefly arable but raises some livestock. Figure 29.12B shows the output and input on a farm of the same size and type in the 1820s. The figures have been worked out from historical records. The unit is the gigajoule, GJ (1 GJ = 10^9 J).

The values in Figures 29.12A and B do not include the energy of sunlight as input. It is assumed to be the same today as it was in the 1820s. The values in the two figures are summarised in Table 29.6.

Table 29.6 ● A comparison of intensive and traditional farms. (Energy values are in GJ.)

Energy	Intensive farm	Traditional farm	Ratio: Intensive farm / Traditional farm
Input	10 000	245	41
Output	20 700	3440	6
Ratio: Output/Input	2	14	

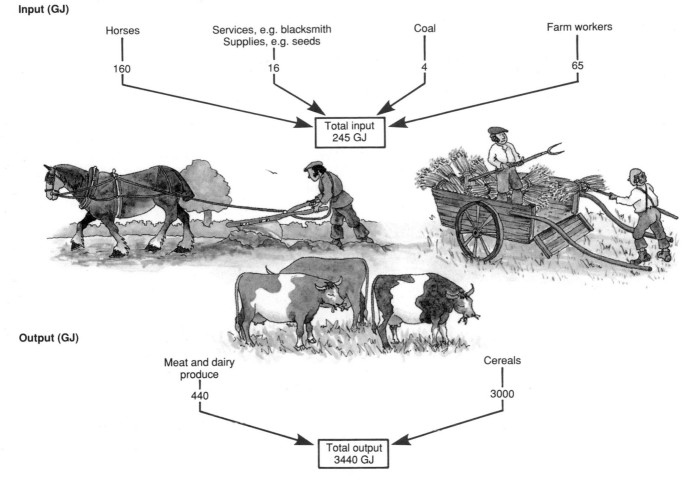

Input (GJ)

Horses	Services, e.g. blacksmith Supplies, e.g. seeds	Coal	Farm workers
160	16	4	65

Total input
245 GJ

Output (GJ)

Meat and dairy produce	Cereals
440	3000

Total output
3440 GJ

Figure 29.12B ● Energy input and output on a 640 hectare farm in the 1820s. Note that a horse uses 8 MJ/hour at work, while a farm worker uses 0.8 MJ/hour (MJ = megajoule, 1 MJ = 10^6 J). More than 98% of the work is done by horses and people.

The increase in productivity (output per hectare) from the 1820s to the 1980s was achieved with a decreasing number of farm workers per hectare. Today's farm worker produces 60 times more food than a farm worker in the 1820s. As you see from Table 29.6, the sixfold increase in output per hectare is achieved by means of a 40-fold increase in the input of energy. This energy comes almost entirely from oil. Each year a farm worker uses the energy from over 11 tonnes of oil to enable him or her to produce so much food per worker. This brackets the energy demands of agriculture with those of the steel industry and the ship building industry. When the world's supplies of oil dwindle, the **energy crisis** will affect intensive farming.

LOOK AT LINKS
for the **energy crisis**
See Theme B, Topic 8.2.

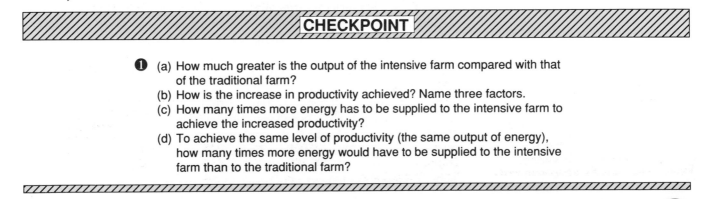

CHECKPOINT

❶ (a) How much greater is the output of the intensive farm compared with that of the traditional farm?
(b) How is the increase in productivity achieved? Name three factors.
(c) How many times more energy has to be supplied to the intensive farm to achieve the increased productivity?
(d) To achieve the same level of productivity (the same output of energy), how many times more energy would have to be supplied to the intensive farm than to the traditional farm?

29.13 Hunger

Much of the food which intensive farming methods produce in the UK is in excess of what the country needs. The reason why farmers continue to grow more and more is that the Government guarantees to pay farmers high prices for their produce. Crops, meat and dairy produce which are not eaten have to be stored. They form the very expensive grain, beef and butter 'mountains' which are stored by the European Community (EC). Food production in Western Europe as a whole has steadily increased since 1950. The population has remained almost constant. With so much food available, we eat more than we need, yet in poorer countries millions of people do not have enough food. Figure 29.13A compares Western Europe with Africa, where the population is increasing at a fast rate.

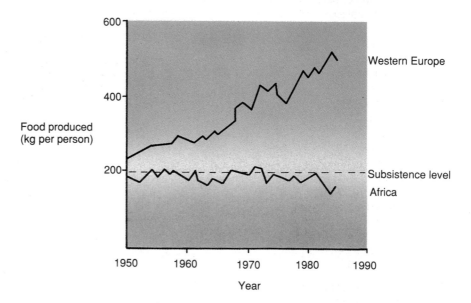

Figure 29.13A ● Food production in Western Europe and in Africa. (Source: US Department of Agriculture) Note the subsistence level, the minimum food needed to stay healthy. Millions of people in Africa are below this level. Note the gap in food production between Western Europe and Africa. Why has it increased since 1950?

What is the solution to the problem of countries which cannot feed themselves adequately? Should we ship over supplies of food from Europe? Shipping over massive food supplies is of course necessary in times of famine. It is, however, not a satisfactory way of life for a country or a region to be completely dependent on food supplies from outside.

Should we help such countries to develop intensive farming? The dependence on oil makes intensive farming an unwise choice for poorer countries. High-technology machinery is expensive to buy and expensive to run. If spare parts are not available or if local people are not trained in repair work, the machinery may lie idle. On the other hand, infertile lands in many parts of the world have been improved by the application of traditional, non-intensive systems. Sinking wells and digging irrigation channels have been very successful in increasing food crops. Planting trees and shrubs to prevent erosion has helped to save deforested areas. The **cross-breeding** of plants has resulted in new varieties of crops. Planting new varieties of crops which can survive a lack of rainfall has helped to increase yields in infertile areas.

LOOK AT LINKS
for **cross-breeding**
See Theme N, Topic 54.

? THEME QUESTIONS

● **Topic 29**

1 The table shows the average prices paid to UK farmers for some products. All prices are shown in 1980 money values. (From *CAS Report 9*, 1985)

Crop	1900	1920	1940	1960	1980
Wheat (£/tonne)	155	161	179	136	99
Barley (£/tonne)	172	241	284	141	93
Potatoes (£/tonne)	123	105	78	66	51
Milk (p/litre)	—	23	23	17	13

(a) On graph paper, plot the price of each product (on the vertical axis) against the year (on the horizontal axis).

(b) In which year was barley (i) most expensive (ii) cheapest?

(c) In which year were potatoes (i) most expensive (ii) cheapest?

(d) By what percentage did the price of wheat decrease between (i) 1900 and 1980 (ii) 1940 and 1980?

(e) By what percentage did the price of potatoes drop between 1940 and 1980?

(f) What was the percentage fall in the price of milk between 1940 and 1980?

(g) Explain why farm produce is cheaper now than it was in 1940.

(h) Name other people, besides the general public, who have benefited from the changes in agriculture since 1940.

2 (a) What type of plants can use atmospheric nitrogen as a nutrient?

(b) Why can't most plants use atmospheric nitrogen in this way?

(c) Name the nitrogen-containing compounds that are built by plants.

(d) Name one natural process that produces nitrogen compounds that enter the soil and are used by plants.

(e) Explain why there is not enough nitrogen from natural sources to support the growth of crop after crop on the same land.

3 (a) Explain why ammonium salts are used as fertilisers even though plants cannot absorb them (see Topic 20.5).

(b) Describe how you could make ammonium sulphate crystals (see Topic 17.5).

4 (a) Explain what is meant by the **nitrogen cycle**.

(b) Are we likely to run out of nitrogen?

(c) Say how the human race alters the natural nitrogen cycle (i) by taking nitrogen out of the cycle and (ii) by adding nitrogen.

(d) Explain how fertilisers have created a problem concerning nitrogen compounds.

(e) Suggest two ways in which this problem could be attacked.

5 Farmer Short had a field in which his crops did not grow well. One year, he added fertiliser to the soil and his crops grew better. However, a pond near the field became stagnant and full of algae, and the fish in the pond died. When the pond was tested, it was found to contain fertiliser.

Farmer Long did not use fertiliser. She rotated her crops between fields so that every few years each field grew peas, beans or clover.

(a) Explain how fertiliser got into the pond.

(b) Why did the algae in the pond increase?

(c) Why did the fish die?

(d) How do crops of peas, beans and clover make up for the lack of fertiliser?

(e) Give one advantage and one disadvantage of Farmer Long's system compared with Farmer Short's.

6 Equal amounts of four soil samples, taken from different locations, were shaken up with water in graduated cylinders and left to settle. The results are shown below.

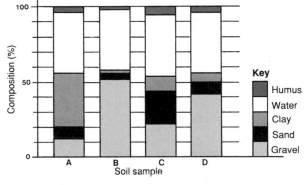

(a) Which soil had (i) the highest humus content (ii) the lowest gravel content?

(b) What was the percentage of clay in (i) sample A (ii) sample B? (iii) Explain how the addition of sand and humus would improve the texture and properties of sample A.

(c) What was the percentage of sand in (i) sample C (ii) sample D? (iii) Which of these two samples was taken from a good vegetable garden? Give your reasons.

(d) (i) Soil B contained the smallest number of earthworms. Try to explain this.
(ii) Soil B was also unsuitable for the growth of root crops such as carrots and turnips. Suggest an explanation for this.

7 Complete the table below to highlight the differences between a clay soil and a sandy soil.

Property	Clay soil	Sandy soil
Particle size		
Crumb structure		
Aeration and drainage		
Mineral content		
How can it be improved?		

8 (a) Name five other constituents of soil apart from rock particles.
  (b) What is a loam?
  (c) (i) What is humus and how is it formed?
  (ii) Describe two ways in which humus can be renewed in the soil.
  (d) Irrigation can vastly increase food production in hot regions of the world, but what are the drawbacks it can bring?
  (e) Outline the advantages and disadvantages of each of the following agricultural practices
  (i) monoculture (ii) the use of large fields (iii) straw burning.

9 A student carried out the following experiment in order to estimate the percentages of water and humus in a sample of soil. She weighed an evaporating dish and then re-weighed it containing some of the soil sample. She then placed the dish in an oven at 100 °C for 24 hours to dry the soil. After this time the dish was removed from the oven, cooled and re-weighed. Here are her results:

Weight of evaporating dish = 35.00 g
Weight of dish + fresh soil = 60.00 g
Weight of dish + dried soil = 55.00 g

  (a) Work out the percentage of water in the soil sample.

The student then placed the soil sample into a hotter oven and left it at 600 °C for 30 minutes to burn all the humus.

Weight of dish + burnt soil = 52.00 g

  (b) Work out the percentage of humus in the original soil sample.

10 Explain each of the following statements:
  (a) Prolonged use of artificial fertilisers is bad for the soil.
  (b) Extensive use of fertilisers on arable land can lead to the pollution of waterways.
  (c) Growing clover improves the fertility of the soil.

11 The experiment was set up as shown in the diagram. A sample of unsterilised soil was suspended in flask A and sterilised soil in flask B. Both flasks contained potassium hydroxide solution. At the start of the experiment, the levels of the coloured liquid were equal in both arms of the U-tube.

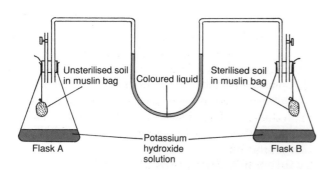

Flask A — Unsterilised soil in muslin bag — Coloured liquid — Sterilised soil in muslin bag — **Flask B** — Potassium hydroxide solution

  (a) What change is likely to have taken place in the levels of the coloured liquid after 48 hours?
  (b) Explain fully your answer.

12 The diagram shows the nitrogen cycle. The labelled arrows represent different processes.

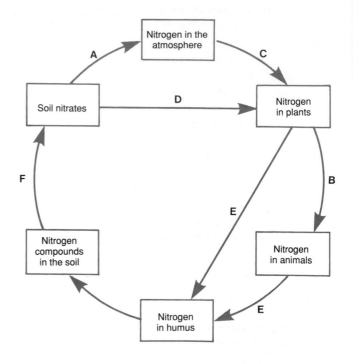

  (a) Name the processes A–F, e.g. A = denitrification.
  (b) (i) Why is process C useful to plants?
  (ii) Process C takes place in clover but not in grass. Why is this so?
  (c) What organisms are responsible for process E?
  (d) In what form is nitrogen passed in process B?

13 Many pesticides are potentially harmful because they are not biodegradable and can build up two lethal limits in animals. The food chain shows the build up of a particular pesticide.

Aphid → Lacewing larva → Blue tit → Buzzard
  5   500   5000   2500

(Pesticide levels shown in relative amounts)

  (a) How did the pesticide enter the food chain in the first place?
  (b) Which animal in the food chain is likely to receive a lethal amount first?
  (c) The most widespread insecticide use in Britain used to be DDT. Why do you think that its use has been banned?
  (d) One of the sub-lethal effects of DDT was that it affected the shell-producing gland in many birds of prey such as the peregrine falcon. It resulted in eggs being laid with thinner than normal shells. How did this lead to the death of many young?
  (e) An alternative method of keeping down pest numbers is biological control. Explain how it works.

Teachers' Notes

Selection of IT activities

There is an extensive range of software and hardware now available for science teaching, although its quality may be variable. In selecting IT items for the book we have drawn on our own experience and judgement and on the views of other science educators working with IT. We have attempted to give suggestions of what we feel are valuable resources for teaching different topics in science. It is not suggested that the items featured are perfect and they may even conflict with some teachers' ideas of how IT should be used. In some cases, for example, straight tutorial type software has been included either to revise or reinforce a topic. Increasingly, the move is toward open ended or content free software – however, we feel that some traditional CAL can still be useful.

Hardware requirements

The requirements are given after each entry. We appreciate that not all schools will have the resources required for every activity at the present time. In some cases there may be an opportunity to share or to borrow equipment, e.g. videodisc, which can be taken up by a school when the right moment arises.

Software requirements

Again, we appreciate that not every school will have every item of software suggested, and borrowing is not always possible for legal and other reasons. Software has been chosen which comes largely from the well known suppliers and which to our knowledge is most commonly found in schools. Most of the software featured is relatively inexpensive. Where it has been possible to list alternative, equivalent software we have attempted to do so.

Keeping up to date

High quality software, particularly if fairly general in scope (such as database applications) can remain valuable teaching resources for many years. Likewise, hardware built for extension and development can have a long working life in schools. Inevitably, software and hardware will become obsolete. We feel that this need neither daunt nor depress teachers. Through the type of IT activities suggested in the book, teachers can develop a 'feel' for IT in science which, in our experience, can be transferred to the next generation of hardware and software.

J Scaife
J J Wellington

Activities

● Theme A

The Earth in Space The package includes two discs. One is a *Teletype* simulation, which simulates information and beliefs related to the solar system, e.g. Galileo's views compared with those of the Church. The other disc stores a data base (DIY base) of facts on the solar system. The package contains a large number of activities and teachers' notes related to the two discs. It covers the following areas: historical ideas; the night sky; planetary motion; the Sun and the planets; the universe. The package provides excellent support for a large part of Theme A.
Hardware: BBC micro
Supplier: BBC Enterprises

Motion in Space This program simulates space walking and space missions in which a *female* astronaut can be moved around by firing four gas jets. As the astronaut moves, the horizontal and vertical speeds are given allowing the components of motion to be studied in some detail. The fuel used and oxygen supply remaining are given on the screen. Having learnt to space walk, an interesting experience in itself, the user can then try a space mission. Three of the missions involve space rescues, two involve rebuilding a damaged satellite. Motion can be studied in the idealised world of frictionless movement and perfectly elastic collisions. It is enjoyable and if used carefully by the teacher, educational.
Hardware: BBC B or Master
Supplier: Cambridge Micro Software

Volcanoes The Earth's structure is one of the themes in the interactive videodisc (IV) Volcanoes. This disc, which contains a large volume of film, pictures, text and programs, also covers the movement of the Earth's crust, the way eruptions occur and other related issues. The videodisc could be used as a demonstration or in group work.
Hardware: BBC
Supplier: BBC Enterprises, OUP 1988
Alternatives: *Domesday* IV system, BBC Enterprises. The IV system and discs are available for loan in some LEA's.

Theme B

Molecules This simulation program allows pupils to experiment with particles inside a vessel. The simulation is based on the kinetic energy model of matter and allows a number of variables to be altered, e.g. pressure, volume, temperature, (though not all at once!). Students should be told that this is a computer simulation, based on a model.
Hardware: BBC Micro
Supplier: Cambridge Micro Software

Housewarming The program is designed to allow pupils to discover how 'heating energy' can be conserved in the home, to save both fuel and money. The user is given a choice of fuels and heating systems; gas, electricity, oil and solid fuel. With each system a clearly displayed range of energy-saving methods can be employed to save fuel and money. These range from shutting doors (free option) to buying loft insulation to buying a cow to produce methane! After running through a simulated year (from spring to winter in four three-monthly periods) the user is shown a picture of the house and where the 'heating energy' is escaping from (wall, windows, roof, etc.) in percentage terms. A bill is presented after each quarter and at the end of the year, the user is given a score related to their success in conservation through the year.
Hardware: BBC Micro
Supplier: Resources for Learning Ltd., Bradford, for the Solid Fuel Advisory Service

Domestic Heating This program is clear and easy to use with ample supporting documentation, including two important appendices on the U-values involved and most importantly the computer model itself underlying the simulation. Users can construct a house or flat virtually from scratch. The nature of the walls, floor, glazing and roof can all be decided and U-values are given. Pupils soon realise that the 'U-value' is, roughly speaking, a measure of how rapidly a given area of construction 'loses heat': refinement can be introduced later. The location of the property, its altitude, its ventilation, its dimensions and the people inside it can all be varied. Given all the variables, the program then gives a figure for the total energy, in megajoules, needed to heat the home for a year. People inside it can live between the rather high temperatures of 19 °C to 23 °C – this provides another important discussion point and shows how critical living temperature is in determining heating bills.
Hardware: BBC micro
Supplier: Longman Software
Alternatives: *Watts in Your Home* and *Home Heating*

BP Energy File A database of world energy use. It is updated regularly using data from readily available sources.

Hardware: BBC, Nimbus, IBM PC
Supplier: BP Educational Resources, London, W1

Power Plan This program has been produced for schools and colleges on behalf of British Nuclear Fuels plc. The program begins by showing the names and location of the nuclear power stations around Britain's coast. The simulations of Magnox and AGR reactors which follow are useful, though some of the information (in the form of labelling) is given too quickly. A third part of the program involves a so called 'challenging game' which involves combining nuclear power, coal, gas and oil to keep Britain's electricity supply going over a period of time. Graphs are displayed on the screen showing supply and demand while the user has to press three pairs of keys (one for up, one for down) to control gas, coal and oil supplies.
Hardware: BBC micros, B, B+ and Master
Supplier: Resources for Learning Ltd., Bradford

Theme C

Chemdata and **Periodic Properties** Both programs allow students to 'discover' the relationships between the properties of the chemical elements. Both can display data in a table or in graphical form. Data files are provided on melting point, boiling point, density and many other properties.
Hardware: BBC
Supplier: *Chemdata* from Longman Software, *Periodic Properties* from Hodder and Stoughton

Analysis This program contains three challenges for pupils to sharpen their analytical skills:
• *Basic Analysis* – pupils race against time to identify a random selection of five compounds.
• *Advanced Analysis* – results of analysis are given in the form of pictures showing the changes in test-tubes.
• *Element Identification* – pupils use a series of clues to identify unknown elements.
Hardware: BBC micros, IBM, Nimbus
Supplier: AVP, Gwent

Balancing Equations This is a revision and practice program in which students have the opportunity to supply correct formulas for compounds in a chemical equation and to balance the equation. It is possible to balance equations for which correct formulas have already been supplied.
Hardware: BBC, Nimbus
Supplier: Longman Micro Software

Atomic Theory This is a suite of seven games to complement other work on atomic theory. Topics covered include electron orbits, an atomic fruit machine game, the nucleus, elements, symbols and radicals, ionic bonding and naming compounds.
Hardware: BBC, Archimedes, Nimbus
Supplier: AVP, Gwent

Key A data handling package which is ideal for pupils at Key Stage 4. It contains the following datafiles which can all be used with this book: Acid Drops, Birds of Britain, Mammals, Materials, Minibeasts, Periodic Table, Weather and Climate, World Population.
Hardware: *Key* runs on BBC, *Key Plus* runs on Archimedes and Nimbus
Supplier: Anglia Television

Investigating Radioactive Sources This is a collection of programs which simulate the investigation and identification of an unknown source, and is accompanied by data sheets and pupil worksheets. When the program is run, a source is randomly selected and a choice of three experiments is available for its investigation. Results from these experiments are recorded by pupils, who must then make deductions about either the type of particles emitted or the half-life. At the end of each experiment, pupil deductions are checked and help is given as necessary.
Hardware: BBC B, Archimedes, Nimbus
Supplier: AVP, Gwent

Ionic and Molar Chemistry Six programs; each includes a test to be attempted when the user is familiar with the relevant theory. *Chemical Formulae* explains a method of working out formulas and allows the user to enter the names of many simple compounds to show how their formulas are deduced. *Chemical Equations* shows how to construct balanced equations. *Ionic Bonding* explain how and when ions form. *Covalent Bonding* explains how and when covalent bonds form. *Titrations* gives some of the main points of the theory and practice of acid–alkali titrations. *Electrolysis* explains the theory of electrolysis.
Hardware: Archimedes, BBC, Nimbus
Supplier: AVP, Gwent

Electrolysis A program showing animated diagrams of several examples of electrolysis. The animated diagrams show the migration of ions, the movement of charge and where appropriate, the re-arrangement of molecules prior to liberation. Animation may be frozen by using the space bar. The following examples are available: molten sodium chloride, molten lead bromide, saturated sodium chloride solution, copper sulphate solution with carbon electrodes. Half-equations are given at the end of each animated sequence and an attempt is made to show how the charge released at the anode appears at the cathode.
Hardware: BBC, Nimbus
Supplier: AVP, Gwent

Chemical Structures This program uses computer graphics to depict various metallic, ionic, covalent and molecular structures. For the molecular and ionic lattices, in each case the unit cell is built up on screen atom by atom or ion by ion. Different parts of the lattice are coloured accordingly, enabling the structure to be more fully understood. For the other structures, covalent bonds are represented by overlapping spheres and the whole structure is loaded directly onto screen.
Hardware: BBC, Archimedes, Nimbus
Supplier: AVP, Gwent

● **Theme D**
Make a Million This is an educational game involving the industrial production of a variety of substances and electricity from basic raw materials. The process involved are blasting, electrolysis, fractionating, generating electricity and making and adding acid. Users choose their pathways to financial success with coloured graphics and sound throughout. A set of worksheets containing information about the processes covered in the package is provided.
Hardware: BBC, Nimbus
Supplier: AVP, Gwent

Industrial Chemistry Pack This package consists of two programs, the second of which would be more appropriately included in the material covering Theme L, Book 2.
• *The Manufacture of Sulphuric Acid* – an investigation into aspects of a chemical industrial process. The conflicting demands of high daily production, best equilibrium yield and profitable manufacture are all investigated.
• *Siting an Aluminium Plant* – students are able to consider some of the factors which must be considered when planning the siting and production targets of an aluminium plant.
Hardware: BBC, Nimbus
Supplier: Longman Software

Salts – Properties, Preparation and Solubility
This collection of programs is designed to revise the structure and formation of salts, test the methods of preparation, and produce the raw results obtained when determining the solubility of a salt at different temperatures. One of six common salts can be selected for experimentation and, because some experiments are very time-consuming, there is an option to produce a set of results in a short time so that a pupil may concentrate on calculations and graph plotting.
Hardware: BBC, Nimbus
Supplier: Garland Software

● **Theme E**
Water Treatment This program allows the user to regulate the domestic water supply of a town in a variety of circumstances.

Hardware: BBC, Nimbus
Supplier: Longman Logotron

Inside Science
This program allows the user to choose between a variety of methods to deal with accidental pollution spillages.
Hardware: BBC, Nimbus
Supplier: Longman Logotron

Hyperbook This is a program which stores text on a range of science and technology issues (around 100 000 words a disk). Of particular value will be:
• *The Pollution File* – a collection of articles and documents on environmental issues
• *Science and Technology* – a selection of newspaper articles on current issues. Look out for 'the green disk'!
Hardware: BBC
Supplier: AVP, Gwent

Life and Death of a River This is a *Key/Keysheet* datafile
Hardware: BBC, Nimbus, Archimedes
Supplier: Anglia Television

Oxygen probes can be useful tools for investigating air, water and their contents. Those from the main science suppliers can be connected to computers and dataloggers. Software can be obtained with the probes and techniques are similar for a wide range of probes. Some manufacturers sell purpose-built body monitors such as Griffin's Bodysense System and educational Electronics range of sensors.
Vision Software (Disney Ltd.) produce a chemistry package which contains assessment materials appropriate to Theme E.

● **Theme F**
Fit to Eat This is a *Key/Keysheet* datafile.
Hardware: BBC, Nimbus, Archimedes
Supplier: Anglia Television

Food
Hardware: BBC
Supplier: Stanley Thornes Software

Microdiet
Hardware: BBC
Supplier: Longman Logotron

Diets
Hardware: BBC
Supplier: AVP, Gwent

Your Diet
Hardware: BBC
Supplier: Cambridge Micro Software

Respiration
Hardware: BBC and Archimedes
Supplier: AVP, Gwent

Excretion
Hardware: BBC and Archimedes
Supplier: AVP, Gwent

The British Gas Laboratory Gas Meter is a stand-alone device which measures the volume of a gas flow. It can also be used with a computer. British Gas sell software which is designed to widen the teaching applications.
Vision Software (Disney Ltd.) produce a Biology package which contains assessment materials appropriate to Theme F.

● **Theme G**
The Weather Report This weather station monitors continuously and operates with several computers.
Hardware: BBC, Nimbus, Archimedes
Supplier: The Advisory Unit for Microtechnology in Education, Hatfield

Soil Analysis This program is intended as an extension to standard school laboratory soil experiments.
Hardware: BBC
Supplier: Longman Logotron

Weather and Climate This is a *Key/Keysheet* datafile.
Hardware: BBC, Archimedes, Nimbus
Supplier: Anglia Television

Fertiliser The production system demonstrated in this program is based on the ICI plant at Billingham. An associated programme is *Chemistry in Action – Out of the Air*.
Hardware: BBC
Supplier: ITV Schools Software

The main science suppliers provide satellite tracking equipment. Additionally, a Nimbus-Linking system is available from Dartcom. Some LEA's or HE institutes may have tracking equipment to which schools can gain access.

Numerical Answers

CHECKPOINT 1.2
❸ (a) 12°   (b) 86°

CHECKPOINT 1.3
❸ (a) 0.52, 2.52   (b) 0.28, 1.28
❺ (a) 4.2 x Distance from Earth to the Sun

CHECKPOINT 1.4
❷ 2062

CHECKPOINT 1.5
❶ (a) 1°   (b) 7°

CHECKPOINT 1.6
❶ (a) 1957   (b) 1969

CHECKPOINT 2.2
❷ 2 mm

CHECKPOINT 2.4
❶ (a) Philippine or Caribbean   (b) Andes
(c) Basaltic   (d) Sliding
❷ (a) A = Continental plate, B = Oceanic trench,
C = Subduction zone   (b) Sedimentary
(c) (i) W to E   (ii) E to W   (iii) W to E
(d) Mantle, sufficiently fluid to transport plates
(e) Sea-floor spreading
❸ (a) 4 m   (b) 1.5 m–1.9 m   (c) a > 2b
❻ (a) (i) 44 million years   (ii) 7 million years
(iii) 1 million years

CHECKPOINT 2.8
❶ (a) D   (b) C (c)   F

THEME A QUESTIONS
3 (a) 10.24 p.m.   (b) 11.41 p.m.

CHECKPOINT 4.3
❶ 2.7 g/cm³
❷ 7500 g (7.5 kg)
❸ 2720 g (2.72 kg)
❹ A 0.86 g/cm³: floats,   B 4.3 g/cm³: sinks

CHECKPOINT 4.6
❽ (a) (i) 55 g   (ii) 100 g   (b) 45 g crystallise
(c) 200 g   (d) 300 g   (e) (i) 3 g   (ii) 25 g

CHECKPOINT 5.4
❸ (a) E   (b) C   (c) D   (d) A, B

CHECKPOINT 6.3
❶ (a) 3600 J   (b) 1.08 MJ   (c) 900 kJ   (d) 216 kJ
❷ (b) 400 kJ   (c) 1.6 kW

CHECKPOINT 6.4
❸ (a) 14 976 J   (b) 50 W

CHECKPOINT 7.1
❶ (a) 32 °C   (b) 39.7 °C   (c) 60 °C
❷ (b) 3.75 mV
❸ (b) 75 °C   (c) 31 °C

CHECKPOINT 7.2
❸ (a) 150 mm   (b) 10 mm
❹ (a) 4.0 m³   (b) 300 K   (c) 267 kPa   (d) 267 K
(e) 3.0 m³

CHECKPOINT 7.3
❷ (a) 54 kJ   (b) 84 MJ   (c) 510 kJ   (d) 520 kJ
❹ (a) 900 kJ, 672 kJ   (b) 33.6 kJ, 56 J/s

CHECKPOINT 7.4
❷ (b) 0.044 kg   (c) 15 000 J   (d) 341 kJ/kg
❺ (a) 90 kJ   (b) 0.039 kg

CHECKPOINT 7.6
❸ (a) 69.1 MJ   (b) £1.04   (c) 77 days

CHECKPOINT 7.8
❹ (a) 25.6 J/s   (b) 1352 J/s   (c) 1.65p/hr

CHECKPOINT 8.2
❸ (a) 15

CHECKPOINT 8.3
❶ (b) 3500 MJ/m²/year   (c) 57.1 m²

THEME B QUESTIONS
7 (b) 48 g/100 g   (c) 50 °C
(d) 55 g KNO_3 crystallise
9 (a) 300 N   (b) 360 J
11 (c) 40%

CHECKPOINT 11.2
❷ 9p, 9e, 10n
❸ (a) 17, 35   (b) 27, 59   (c) 50, 119

CHECKPOINT 11.4
❸ N 7, 7, 7;   Na 11, 11, 12;
K 19, 20 19;   U 92, 143, 92

CHECKPOINT 12.1
❷ (a) 29.5 c.p.m.   (b) 355.7 c.p.m.   (c) β-radiation
❸ (a) 92p, 146n   (b) 91p, 143n   (c) 89p, 138n
❹ (a) $^{234}_{90}$Th; $^{238}_{92}$U → $^{4}_{2}$He + $^{234}_{90}$Th
(b) $^{234}_{92}$U; $^{234}_{91}$Pa → $^{0}_{-1}$e   + $^{234}_{92}$U

CHECKPOINT 12.2
❶ (a) 4.0 mg (b) 2.0 mg (c) 0.031 mg
❷ (a) 5 years (b) 25 years
❸ 19.5 hours
❹ 1.55 hours

CHECKPOINT 12.3
❶ (b) 4000 years
❷ β, strontium
❸ Sodium-24
❹ Use cobalt-60

CHECKPOINT 12.9
❶ (a) 1860 units (b) 521 units (c) medical
(d) 2381 units (i) 0.125% (ii) 0.420%

THEME C QUESTIONS
13 11p, 12n
14 82p, 124n, No
17 (a) 375 c.p.m. (b) 6 c.p.m.
18 Sodium-24, γ-emitter with suitable half life
20 (c) 12 minutes

CHECKPOINT 17.3
❸ (a) 4 (b) 9 (c) 3 (d) 11 (e) 18
❹ (a) C (b) A (c) B

THEME D QUESTIONS
❺ (b) 45%

CHECKPOINT 22.7
❶ 200 g KCl crystallises
❷ 20 g NaCl crystallises
❸ 12 g KCl crystallises
❹ 10 g K_2SO_4 + 10 g KBr crystallise

CHECKPOINT 23.8
❻ (a) (i) 80–100 km/h (ii) 30 km/h
(iii) 100 km/h
(b) (i) 80–100 km/h (ii) 50–60 mph

THEME E QUESTIONS
13 (a) 3.75×10^5 tonnes (b) 0.075
19 2400 tonne
20 1600 tonne

CHECKPOINT 28.7
❹ C cold, raining; D rain stopping, warmer;
E fine, warm; F fine warm; G cold, raining

CHECKPOINT 29.1
❶ (b) 10 cm³ (c) 20%
❷ (a) 5 g (b) 25%
❸ (a) 1.0 g (b) 10%
❽ (b) (i) 25 min (ii) 35 min
(c) (i) 32% (ii) 45% (d) No

CHECKPOINT 29.7
❶ (a) 17 tonne (b) 70 tonne
❷ (a) 1.8 times (b) 5.5 times (c) (i) Asia
(ii) Europe
❸ 2 months
❺ (a) Sugar beet, potatoes; root crops
(b) (i) C (ii) A (iii) B

THEME G QUESTIONS
9 (a) 20% (b) 12%

Index

A

α, β and γ radiations 171–2 *see* radioactivity
absorption, digested food 354–6
acid rain 300–3
acids 220–2
  and bases 223–5
  indicators and pH 228
  reactions 226–7
additives, food 339–41
aerobic respiration 359–61
Agent Orange 408 *see* herbicides
agriculture, pollution by 313–15 *see* farming
air
  carbon dioxide 273, 276, 277
  nitrogen 268–9, 271
  noble gases 277–8
  oxygen 268–9, 270
  pollution 267, 270, 298–309
  weather effects 382–90
alcohol 336–7 *see* diet
algal bloom 313–14 *see* pollution
allotropes 148, 150–1, 207
alloys 146, 147, 149
alternative energy 136–8 *see* energy resources
alveoli 366
amino acids 246
animals 51
  hydra 62–3
  insects 68–9
  molluscs 66–7
  vertebrates 70–1
  worms 64–5
  see kingdoms
anorexia 345–6
astronomy 11–12 *see* stars
atoms 89, 161
  atomic mass 161
  and ions 191–2, 200–1
  and isotopes 168
  and nuclear energy 180–4
  and radioactivity 160
  particle arrangement 161, 162–3
  Periodic Table 164–7
  see elements; particles; radioactivity

B

bacteria 51, 52–3, 288
  centrifuging 213–4
  irradiation 177–8
  see kingdoms
bases 223–5
  and acids 220–2, 227

indicators and pH 228
  reactions of 226–7
Becquerel's key 160 *see* radioactivity
Big Bang 18
binomial system 47 *see* life
biological keys 44–6 *see* life
boiling point, liquid 79–82
boundaries, plate 25
breathing 359, 366 *see* respiration
Brownian motion 92–3

C

calcium fluoride 234 *see* teeth
carbohydrates 240–2, 328 *see* organic compounds
carbon 147–8 *see* elements
carbon-14 dating 175–6 *see* radioactivity
carbon cycle 273
carbon dioxide 273, 276, 277
  and photosynthesis 325
  see air
carbon monoxide 303–4
  see pollution
catalyst 280
cells 251–2, 262–3
  division 258–61
  movement 254–6
  nucleus 256–7
  protein manufacture in 257–8, 330
  size 264
  structure 253
cellular respiration 361–2, 363–4
cellulose 241 *see* carbohydrates
Celsius scale 105
centrifugation 213–4 *see* bacteria
CFCs (chlorofluorohydrocarbons) 308–9 *see* pollution
changes, energy 98–100
chemical bond
  covalent bond 205–8
  ionic bond 200–4, 208
chemical energy 96, 98
chemical equations 158–9 *see* compounds; elements
chemical reaction 152–3
chlorine 149, 295 *see* elements
cholesterol 337–8 *see* diet
CHP (Combined Heat and Power Stations) 137
chromatography 218–9
circumpolar stars 14
classification, life 48–50
cleavage, rock 35
clouds 386–7
coal 129, 130–1 *see* fuel reserves
combustion 279, 282–3

comets 9–10
composite materials 84
compounds 88–9, 152–3
  as air pollutants 307
  covalent bond and 205–7, 208
  formulas of 155–6, 158–9
  ionic 201–2, 203–4, 208
  mixtures and 154
  organic 239, 240–8
  see elements; particles
compressive strength 84–5
conduction, electricity 190
conduction, heat 121–2
constellations 6–8
continental drift 26–8
controls, pollution 300, 301, 302–3, 304, 305, 306, 307, 309, 310, 314
convection, heat 120–1
conveyor belt, plate movement 26
copper 146, 149 *see* elements
covalent bond 205–6, 208 *see* chemical bond
crystallisation 213
  water 231
crystals 91–2
cycle
  carbon 273
  nitrogen 271–2
  rock 34
  water 38–9, 129, 134, 287

D

dating
  carbon-14 175–6
  relative 40–1
DDT (dichlorodiphenyltrichoroethane) 409–11
decay, radioactive 170, 173–4
deformation, rocks 35–7
density 77 *see* matter
diamonds 147–8, 149 *see* elements
diet 335
  and alcohol 336–7
  and cholesterol 337–8
  vegetarianism 341–2
  see food
diffusion
  gas 92
  in solutions 254
digestion 352
  and absorption 354–6
  human gut 352–4, 356–8
distillation 214–15
  fractional 216–17, 268–9
DNA (deoxyribonucleic acid) 247–50, 257–8
  replication 258–9

E

Earth
    life on 42
    structure of 19–22
    Sun's radiation and 382–3
earthquakes 20–2, 23, 24, 36
eclipses 4–6
ecosystems, man-made 413–5
elastic limit 85
electrical energy 96, 98, 103, 104 *see*
    energy
electrodes 190–4
electrolysis 190–6
electromagnetic waves 123–5
electrons 161, 163–4, 191–3, 196
electroplating 197–8
electrostatic attraction 200–1
elements 88–9, 149–50, 239
    and alloys 146, 147, 149
    metallic 145–7
    non-metallic 142–4, 147–9
    structure of 150–1
    symbols for 155, 158–9
    valency of 157
    see atoms; compounds; particles
energy 95–7
    changes 98–100
    human 96, 104, 327, 328–9
    input and output 413–15
    measuring 101–2, 104
    transporting 103
    see heat
energy resources
    alternative 136–8
    fuel reserves 130–3
    needs 128–9
    renewable 129, 134–5
enzymes 246–7
    digestive 220, 352, 354, 358
erosion
    by sea 33, 41
    soil 395–6
evaporation 93–4
excretion *see* waste
expansion, gas 110–13

F

farming 398, 400–1, 402, 406
    energy input and output 413–15
    see soil
fats 243–4, 337–8 *see* diet
faults, rock 35–6
fertilisers 402–4
    pollution by 313–14
    see soil
fibre, dietary 327, 333–4
filtration 213
fire-extinguishers 284–5
flexibility, material 85
folding, rock 35

food 327
    additives 339–41
    dietary fibre 333–4
    for energy 328, 329
    for growth and repair 330–3
    see diet
formulas, compound 155–6, 158–9
    ionic 203–4
fossil fuels 129, 130–1
fronts, weather 388–90
fuel reserves 129, 130–1, 136
    nuclear 132–3, 136
fungi 51, 56–7 *see* kingdoms
fungicides 412

G

gas
    expansion 110–13
    laws 111–13
    see heat
geological column 40–1
glaciers 39 *see* landscape forces
gold 145, 149 *see* elements
gravity 2,3
greenhouse effect 274–5
gut
    animal 357–8
    human 352–4
    movement 356–7
    see digestion

H

hard water 295–7
hardness, material 83–4
heat 126–7
    conduction 121–2
    convection 120–1
    insulators 122
    latent 117–19
    photosynthesis and 326
    radiation 121, 123–5
    specific capacity 114–16
    theories of 115–16
    see temperature
helium 277–8
herbicides 407–8 *see* soil
high pressure 385 *see* weather
human
    energy 96, 104, 327, 328–9
    gut 352–4, 356–7
    kidneys 372, 373–4
    lungs 364–5, 366, 367–71
    organ system 262–3
    waste 372, 373–4
    weight 343–6
humus 392, 393 *see* soil
hunger 416
hydra 62–3 *see* animals
hydrates 231

hydrocarbons 305
hydrogen bomb 184 *see* nuclear
    energy

I

igneous rocks 31–2
indicators 228, 395
insects 68–9, 394
    control 411
    see animals
insecticides 409–11
insoluble salts 237–8
ionic bond 200–1 *see* chemical bond
ionic compounds 201–2, 203–4, 208
ions 191–4, 196
    and Periodic Table 202
irrigation 399–400
isotopes 168
    radioisotopes 170, 173–4, 175–7 *see*
    radioactivity
insulators, heat 122
iron 147, 149 *see* elements

J

joints, rock 35–6
joules 101–2, 104

K

kidneys, human 372, 373–4
kinetic energy 96
kinetic theory 88, 90–4 *see* matter
kingdoms 50–2
    animal 62–71
    bacteria 52–3
    cell types and 262–3
    fungi 56–7
    plant 58–61
    protists 54–5
    see life

L

landscape forces 37
    glaciers 39
    weathering by water 33, 37–9, 392
    wind 40
latent heat 117–19
laws, gas 111–13
lead, pollution by 316
life 42–43
    biological keys 44–6
    classification 48–50
    kingdoms 50–2
    naming species 43, 46–7, 48
    see kingdoms

light energy 96–7, 98
lipids 242–4 *see* organic compounds
liquids, separating 214–17
lithosphere 24
living things *see* life
low pressure 385 *see* weather
lungs, human 364–5, 366
  diseases of 367–71

M

maps, weather 384–5
matter 76–7
  boiling points 81–2, 117–18
  change of state 78–9
  density 77
  kinetic theory 90–4
  melting points 79–81
  properties 83–6
  thermal expansion 108–13
  see particles
mechanisation, wildlife and 400–1
melting point 79–81
mercury, pollution by 311
metabolism 327, 329, 330, 331, 373
metallic elements 145–7
metals, pollution by 307
metamorphic rocks 33,34
meteors 10
  meteorites 22
microscopes 251–2
minerals 330–1
mitosis 259–261
mixtures 154
  separating 212–19
  compounds and 154
molecules 88–90, 150, 205–7, 241
molluscs 66–7 *see* animals
monoculture 402 *see* farming
Moon 3–6

N

natural gas 103, 129, 131–2 *see* fuel
  reserves
neutralisation 227
neutrons 161, 164 *see* atoms
nitrogen 268–9, 271
  cycle 271–2
  oxides 304–5
noble gases 277–8
non-metallic elements 142–4, 147–9
nuclear
  bomb 180–2
  change 170
  energy 180–4
  fuels 132–3, 136
  waste 185–6
  see radioactivity
nucleic acids 247–8
  DNA story 249–50

see organic compounds
nucleus
  atom 162–4
  cell 256–7
nutrients 327
  for energy 328–9
  for growth and repair 330–3
  from soil 394–5
  from fertilisers 402–6

O

occlusions 390
oil 129, 130, 131–2, 316–18 *see* fuel
  reserves
organ system, human 262–3
organic compounds 239
  carbohydrates 240–2
  lipids 242–4
  nucleic acids 247–8
  proteins 245–7
osmosis 254–5
oxides 281–3, 299–300, 303–4, 304–5
  see oxygen; pollution
oxygen 268–9, 270, 279–80
  dissolved 288
  fire and 284–5
  oxides and 281–3, 299–300, 303–4
  see air
ozone layer 308–9

P

particles 88–9
  kinetic theory and 90–4
  subatomic 161, 162, 163–4
  see atoms; matter
Periodic Table 164–7, 202 *see* atoms
pesticides 130
  pollution by 314–5 *see* soil
petrochemicals industry 130
pH 228, 395
phases, Moon 3–4
photosynthesis 97, 273, 322–6
  cellular respiration and 361–2,
    363–4
planets 6–9, 15–16, 18
plants 51
  excretion in 375
  nutrients for 393, 394–5
  seed-producing 60–1
  spore-producing 58–9
plate tectonics 24–6
  theory of 26–30
Pole Star 11
pollution
  air 267, 270, 298–309
  water 310–18
polysaccharides 241 *see* organic
  compounds
potential energy 96

precipitation 237–8
primary waves 21–2
properties, material 79–82
proteins 245–7, 257–8, 271, 330 *see*
  organic compounds
protists 51, 54–55 *see* kingdoms
protons 161, 164 *see* atoms
pure atoms 89–90 *see* particles

R

radiation
  heat 121, 123–5
  Sun's 382–3
radioactivity 160, 170–1, 187
  α, β and γ radiations 171–2
  dangers of 179–80
  nuclear energy 180–4
  radioisotopes 170, 173–4, 175–7
  waste disposal 185–6, 187–9
  see atoms
radioisotopes 170, 173–4, 175–7
rain 37, 287, 289, 292–3
  acid 300–3
  see water
raw materials 212
  separation methods 212–19
relative atomic mass 161
renewable energy 129, 134–5
respiration 359
  cellular 359–62, 363–4
  upper respiratory tract 364–7
Richter scale 21
RNA (ribonucleic acid) 247–8
rock
  cycle 34
  dating 40–1
  deformation 35–7
  geothermal energy and 135
  types 31–4
rust 286

S

salt *see* sodium chloride
salts
  making 231, 236–8
  sodium chloride 200–1, 230, 339
  uses 232–5
saturated fats 243–4, 337–8 *see* diet
scurvy 332
sea-floor spreading 25, 28–30
secondary waves 21–2
sedimentary rocks 33, 34
seed-producing plants 60–1
seismology 20–2 *see* earthquakes
separation methods 212–9
sewage 289
  pollution by 312–13
  see water
silicon 142–4, 149 *see* elements

slimming 344–6
smog 298, 306 *see* pollution
smoking 368–71
soaps 293–4
   household cleaners 295
   soapless detergents 294
   see water
sodium chloride 200–1, 230, 339 *see* salts
soil 392–6
   fertilisers 402–4
   herbicides 407–8
   irrigation 399–400
   see farming
solar system 2–12
   and beyond 15–18
solubility 86
soluble salts 236–7
sound energy 97
space missions 15–16
species, naming 43, 46–7, 48 *see* life
specific heat capacity 114–16
specific latent heat 118–19
spore-producing plants 58–9
starch 241 *see* carbohydrates
stars 11–12, 14, 17–18
strength, material 84–5
sugar 240, 357 *see* carbohydrates
sulphur dioxide 299–300 *see* pollution
summer solstice 13
Sun 2, 5, 6, 9, 42, 135
   photosynthesis and 322–6
   radiation from 382–3
   timekeeping and 13–14
symbols, element 155, 158–9

T

teeth 234, 337, 347–51
temperature 105
   freeze-drying 118–19
   thermal expansion 108–13
   thermometers 106–7
   see heat
tensile strength 85
thermal
   expansion 108–13
   pollution 312
   see temperature
thermometers 106–7 *see* temperature

U

U-values 126 *see* heat
unsaturated fats 243–4, 337–8 *see* diet

V

valency 157 *see* elements; compounds
vapour 78–9
   vaporisation 117–18
vegetarianism 341–2
vertebrates 45–6, 48, 70–1 *see* animals
vitamins 331–3, 335 *see* food
volcanoes 22, 23, 31–2

W

waste
   human 372, 373–4
   nuclear 185–6
   plants 375
water
   cycle 38–9, 129, 134, 287
   daily intake 327, 333
   hard 295–7
   oxygen and 288
   photosynthesis and 326
   pollution 310–18
   pure 291
   rain 37, 287, 289, 292–3
   table 393
   tests for 290–1
   treatment 288–9
   uses 290
   weathering by 33, 37–9, 392
weather 380–1
   clouds 386–7
   fronts 388–90
   maps 384–5
   Sun 382–3
   winter 388
weathering 33, 37–40, 392
weight, human 343–6
wildlife, mechanisation effects 400–1
wind, weathering by 40
winter weather 388
worms 64, 65 *see* animals

X

X-ray diffraction, DNA and 249